USING

Financial Accounting Information

A DECISION CASE APPROACH

Sally L. Adams, MBA, CPA
California State University, Chico

LeRoy J. Pryor, DBA, CPA
California State University, Chico

Donald E. Keller, DBA, CPA, CMA
California State University, Chico

South-Western College Publishing
an International Thomson Publishing company I(T)P®

Cincinnati · Albany · Boston · Detroit · Johannesburg · London · Madrid · Melbourne · Mexico City
New York · Pacific Grove · San Francisco · Scottsdale · Singapore · Tokyo · Toronto

Team Director: Richard K. Lindgren
Aquisitions Editor: Sharon Oblinger
Developmental Editor: Sara Wilson
Marketing Manager: Matt Filimonov
Production Editor: Marci Dechter

Excel and Power Point are registered trademarks® of the Microsoft Corporation.
The Excel program and screen formats are copyrighted by the Microsoft Corporation.

ISBN: 0-324-00387-0

 2 3 4 5 6 7 8 9 WST 6 5 4 3 2 1 0

Printed in the United States of America

I(T)P®
International Thomson Publishing
South-Western is an ITP Company. The ITP trademark is used under license.

USING FINANCIAL ACCOUNTING INFORMATION:
A DECISION CASE APPROACH

MODULE 3 - USING ACCOUNTING INFORMATION IN BUSINESS EXPANSION

MODULE 4 - USING ACCOUNTING INFORMATION TO EVALUATE BUSINESSES

APPENDICES, GLOSSARY AND INDEX

PREFACE

Many authoritative groups have called for different and expanded learning objectives in the first accounting course. In this preface we present the overall objectives of this text, which focus on decision-making, accounting information, and business knowledge, as well as problem solving, interpersonal and computer skills. We present the rationale of why and how we designed this introductory text. Because team skills are increasingly viewed by employers as a necessary attribute of new hires, we review what students must do to participate effectively in group assignments.

COURSE AND LEARNING OBJECTIVES

Individuals in today's society inevitably become members of many different organizations, including businesses, governmental units, social clubs, charities, and other. All such organizations share a common problem: *limited resources available for pursuing organizational goals.* Consequently, individuals are continually confronted with the need to use resources wisely. Accounting information plays a vital role in doing that. Hence, individuals need to know how to use accounting information effectively in making wise economic decisions. In short, individuals in today's society need to become "accounting literate."

This text will provide students with exposure to a broad range of economic decision problems that arise in a variety of organizational situations and with various types of accounting and other information that are relevant in addressing those problems. Specific objectives to be met regarding decision-making, accounting, and business are as follows:

Economic Decision-Making - Introduce students to a broad range of decision- making problems that arise in various organizational settings and to approaches for dealing with such problems, including their ethical considerations;

Accounting Literacy - Introduce students to the role of accounting in a global market economy and to fundamental accounting concepts that underlie the development and communication of information that supports economic decision-making; and

Business/Organization Literacy - Assist students in gaining a basic understanding of the business/organizational situation in which economic decision-making takes place.

To become effective economic decision makers in today's society, individuals not only need to meet the three "knowledge acquisition" objectives presented above, but also must develop skills in the following three key areas related to decision-making:

Problem Solving - Assist students in enhancing their analytical/problem solving skills by involving them in a variety of real world, unstructured problems that require problem definition and clarification, data collection, interpretation, and analysis, and defense of proposed solutions;

Interpersonal - Assist students in improving their abilities to communicate and to work together with others by assigning writing exercises, oral presentations, and group activities; and

Computer - Assist students in becoming more adept in the use of computers by involving them in frequent computer applications in business, accounting, and economic decision-making activities.

The relevance of these skills to decision-making is clear and immediate. First, the possession of creative problem-solving skills is obviously desirable. In business, economic decision problems neither present themselves in nicely structured, clearly defined terms, nor do they typically lead to well-defined solutions with a single, correct answer. Instead, real problems are ill-structured and "messy" with solutions that involve several defensible positions. Students need to recognize these complexities and gain practice in dealing with them.

Secondly, most (if not all) significant economic decision-making activities involve interpersonal relationships. In real settings, problems are mostly addressed by teams rather than individuals. Problem analyses generally have to be communicated to others, both orally and in writing. Proposed courses of action may need to be vigorously defended in open debate or in position papers. Thus, it is clear that such interpersonal skills play a critical role in economic decision-making. *Using Financial Accounting Information* includes several extensions of cases which require a group solution.

Finally, it should also be clear that computers, particularly personal computers, will play an ever-increasing role in economic decision-making activities. *Using Financial Accounting Information* is designed to enhance skills in using a computer for analysis and decision making.

Course Modules

Using Financial Accounting Information is divided into the following four modules:

Using Accounting Information for Economic Decisions;
Using Accounting Information in Small Businesses;
Using Accounting Information in Business Expansion;
Using Accounting Information to Evaluate Businesses.

Each module focuses on "decision scenarios" that students must address as the module progresses. These decision problems provide the context and rationale for studying related accounting and business subjects. The authors extend a warm welcome to you with the hope that you have a successful academic experience.

SUPPLEMENTS

Faculty Supplements

Instructor's manual This manual is a combination of an instructor's resource manual and a solutions manual. It is an excellent resource to help the instructor plan and teach the course. The manual includes a suggested syllabus and course schedule, an overview of each case, teaching notes for each case reading and case, and PowerPoint transparency masters. Suggested solutions to all cases and case reading exercises and problems are also a part of this package.

Test bank This resource book contains a wide variety of questions and question formats. There are multiple choice questions, structured problems, unstructured problems and written response problems. Many of the test-bank questions are formatted similar to the materials in the text. There are quizzes for the end of each case reading and sample tests for each module. An electronic version of the test bank will also be available.

Web site The web site for this book is an excellent resource for both faculty and students. The web site contains considerable information that is useful in teaching this course. Faculty will be able to visit the site to secure solutions to exercises and problems (in addition to the solutions in the instructor's manual). PowerPoint slides for each case reading are also included in the web site.

Student Supplement

Web site Students find the web site to be a very important resource for this book. The wide variety of items contained in the site include helpful hints for completing the case assignments, templates for selected problems and cases, accounting careers information, links to corporation data, downloadable spreadsheet templates, review problems, and module exam review sheets. Students should visit this site at least once a week to see what new materials may have been added.

Acknowledgements

The original concept of this material was derived from a Fund for the Improvement of Post Secondary Education (FIPSE) grant from the U.S. Department of Education to the accounting faculty at California State University, Chico. We thank the U.S. Department of Education for their confidence in us and our research concept and also to the following CSU, Chico faculty who were originally involved in developing much of this material: Steven J. Adams, Curtis L. DeBerg, Wesley E. Harder, Paul Krause, Richard B. Lea, Brock Murdoch, and Leslie B. Thengvall.

We gratefully acknowledge the contributions of the following reviewers for their suggestions and support: Sharon Lightner, San Diego State University; Alastair Murdoch, University of Manitoba; Ann O'Brien, University of Iowa; Ted D. Skekel, University of Texas-San Antonio; and Robert Walsh, Marist College.

We also gratefully acknowledge the contributions of the following persons who have shared ideas and comments on various parts of the materials:

Sherri Anderson	Sonoma State University
Scottie Barty	Northern Kentucky University
Susan R. Blackman	Fort Lewis College
Angele Brill	Castleton State College
Janet Cassagio	Nassau Community College
Joe Colgan	Fort Lewis College
Y Datta	Northern Kentucky University
Jack Flanagan	Australian Catholic University
Karen J. Frey	Gettysburg College
Glenn W. Goodale	Castleton State College
Bob Harrington	Fort Lewis College
Norma C. Holter	Towson University

Lynn Mazzola	Nassau Community College
Kevin H. McBeth	Weber State University
Herbert Olivera	Towson University
Patrick Reihing	Nassau Community College
Randy Serrett	Fort Lewis College
Alan Taylor	Australian Catholic University
Charles Walton	Gettysburg College

The following persons have developed or otherwise contributed to the development of the materials indicated. We thank them for their extensive comments and contributions.

Case Reading 1-3	Richard B. Lea
Case Reading 1-3	Wesley E. Harder
Case Reading 2-8	Steven J. Adams
Case Reading 4-3	Brock Murdoch
Case Reading 4-5	Angele Brill
Case Reading 4-7	Wesley E. Harder
Case Reading 4-7	Leslie B. Thengvall
Case Reading 4-8	Steven J. Adams
Case Reading 4-9	Dianna R. Coker
Case 4-9	Mary E. Harston
Group Assignment 4-9	Mary E. Harston

We are indebted to the following persons for their help in putting this manuscript together: Geri Drivon, Matt Edwards, Sandy Jensen, Glori Mardesich, Gary McMahon, Lorenzo Pope, Beverly Reading, Amber Serna, and Josie Smith. We also thank the Accounting and Tax Team of South-Western College Publishing for their hard work and dedication. And, finally we thank our families for their encouragement, patience and support in this labor of love.

Sally Adams
Lee Pryor
Don Keller

AUTHORS' MESSAGE TO INTRODUCTORY ACCOUNTING STUDENTS

THE FIRST ACCOUNTING COURSE

For many of you, studying how accounting is used to support management decisions will be a new and different college learning experience. As a result, it may take you a couple of weeks to begin to feel comfortable with the learning environment your instructor has developed. The authors believe strongly that you will find the experience more rewarding if you have an understanding of why this text is designed to parallel real-life business situations.

Change in Accounting Education

As a student, you are lucky to be attending college at a time of revolutionary change in higher education. Nowhere is that change more pervasive than in business education in general and accounting education in particular. Most of the elite business schools (including Harvard and Chicago) are in the process of radically changing the curriculum and the way business courses are taught. Hundreds of other schools also are involved in reengineering their business programs. Reengineering is a common business term that means redesigning a process without constraints or limitations.

The Accounting Education Change Commission

The major push for accounting education change came from the formation of the Accounting Education Change Commission (AECC). The AECC was funded in the amount of $4 million by several large certified public accounting (CPA) firms. The AECC's charge is to stimulate radical change in accounting education. The reason the CPA firms were willing to put up so much of their own money was that they were unhappy with the educational background of the students they were hiring. The AECC has issued a statement describing what the first year accounting course should be like. *Using Financial Accounting Information* closely follows the AECC's recommendations.

Employers of Business School Graduates

CPA firms are not the only employers concerned about the educational background of business graduates. Throughout the nation employers are demanding that business schools change the curriculum and the way courses are taught.

A *Business Week* article stated that, to perform adequately in the new work environment, employees must:[1]

- Become self-directed and be able to work without management direction;
- Be able to use newly available information on their jobs by developing new math, technical [computer], and analytical skills;

---

[1] Breaking the Chains of Command," *Business Week*, Special Information Revolution Issue, 1994, page 113.

- Learn group interaction skills in order to resolve disputes within their work group and how to work with other functions across the company; and
- Become financially literate so they can understand the business implications of what they do and changes they suggest.

Alumni Surveys

Alumni surveys of business school graduates who have worked two to five years in professional jobs also indicate a need to change business education. When asked what should have been covered more extensively in college, alumni frequently cite:

- More writing integrated into the curriculum;
- More practical applications and examples;
- More exposure to information technology found in practice; and
- More unstructured, "real world" type of problems.

U.S. Department of Education

Because major changes in the introductory accounting courses are felt to be a critical step in improving business education, the U.S. Department of Education (DOE) awarded a $200,000 grant that helped support development of the text you are now using. The grant was made through DOE's Fund for the Improvement of Post-Secondary Education (FIPSE) program.

Text Design

Real-life cases form the core learning experience in this course. The cases provide the business decision context in which accounting information is used. The cases have been carefully designed to promote active learning, emphasize decision uses of accounting information, stimulate collaborative learning, improve problem solving skills, and integrate the use of computer software.

Active Learning

The philosophy behind active learning stems from the old, but true, adage:

> Tell me .... and I will forget,
> Show me .... and I will remember,
> Involve me ..... and I will understand.

Research shows (and common sense validates) that we all retain information much better if we learn it for ourselves, rather than passively receiving the information from an instructor. Although active learning places more of the responsibility on students, we are convinced that you will retain the information much better and enjoy the sense of accomplishment of completing a challenging learning project. Better retention will help you in your future courses and in the business world. Please remember that the substantial work required to create an active learning environment (the traditional lecture/problem mode is much easier for faculty) was not done to create anxiety or frustration, but to improve your education. In addition, note the first *Business Week* "must" focuses on employee initiative and independence. Development of these critical "learning how to learn" skills is another key benefit of active learning.

Decision Uses of Accounting Information

The readings and cases in this text are built around important, "real world" business decisions. Accounting concepts are presented as you need them to address a specific decision. By learning accounting in a relevant decision context normally found in business firms, accounting will make more sense and should be more interesting and meaningful.

The authors have experimented with many different approaches to introductory accounting. The design of the readings, cases, web page, and other supplementary materials is based upon successful results from seven years of in-class testing. We found that typical college students gain a better mastery of introductory accounting concepts if they understand the relevant business context.

To illustrate the importance of context, consider the 2-point conversion strategy in football. Most coaches would agree that the 1-point conversion (kicking the ball through the goal posts) has a higher probability of success than the 2-point conversion (running or passing the ball into the end zone). Yet there are times when the coach will call for the 2-point conversion. To the observer who does not know the game of football, the 2-point strategy may not make sense due to a lack of context

Suppose you were to describe to your friend, a football neophyte, a situation where Team A has just scored a touchdown and is one point ahead of Team B. There are two minutes left to play in the game and Team B has an excellent field goal kicker. Team A's coach must decide whether to go for the 1-point or 2-point conversion. You explain to your friend that if Team A makes the 1-point conversion followed by Team B making a field goal (three points) in the closing seconds of the game, Team A will lose by one point. Instead, if Team A makes the 2-point conversion followed by Team B's field goal, the score would be tied, giving Team A a chance to win in overtime. By providing the context, your friend is in a position to understand the rationale of the coach's decision to take the riskier 2-point strategy. Your friend would have a better understanding of the game of football than if you just taught him the rules, independent of context.

Collaborative Learning

Research shows by participating extensively in "study groups" people enjoy their college experience more and earn better grades. In addition, employers and alumni both believe that students should develop effective group interaction skills during college. *Using Financial Accounting Information* does, therefore, include group activities. Remember that groups are most effective when *every* member comes to every meeting prepared. Group members who don't pull their weight soon create undesirable tension within the group.

Problem Solving Skills

Solving unstructured, "real world" problems is one of the most sought after skills in business. It is also a skill that both employers and recent alumni believe is insufficiently developed in college. As a result, many of the cases in this course are somewhat unstructured and have no single "correct" answer. The football illustration is an example of an unstructured problem. With different assumptions, the 1-point strategy could be deemed the "correct" decision.

Use of Computer Software

The cases in *Using Financial Accounting Information* require that you use word processing and spreadsheet software. If you are not yet minimally proficient with these two types of software, you

How to Succeed in This Course

Understanding the uses of accounting for decision making will require that you:

- Carefully read case readings;
- Complete all course assignments on time;
- Work diligently with members of you group;
- Take extensive notes of in-class discussion of lectures and case discussions;
- Ask questions when you do not understand a concept; and
- Make frequent visits to this book's web site.

How Will You Benefit From the Changes?

If we are successful in developing this text and you are diligent in completing the assignments, you should:

- Retain the material better;
- Have a more realistic and positive view of what accountants do;
- Develop important job-market skills; and
- Find the course more interesting and relevant.

GROUP ACTIVITIES

The ability to work effectively in groups has become one of the key skills employers are looking for when they recruit college graduates. The guidelines for effective participation in groups are presented as Exhibit A-1, at the end of this section. Before reviewing this exhibit, you should refer back to "The First Accounting Course" section of this authors' message. Note that:

The Accounting Education Change Commission specifically indicated that the ability to work in groups is a skill that should be emphasized in the first accounting courses;

Surveys of business school graduates and employers consistently rank the ability to work effectively in groups as a critical skill that students should acquire in college. A survey reported in the *Wall Street Journal* found that two-thirds of 1,811 employers nationwide are using formal teams to conduct work;[2] and a *Business Week* article on the information revolution highlights the importance of learning group skills.[3]

Second, the "delayering" or flattening of the management structure that has swept the private sector in the U.S. has pushed much of the decision making traditionally done by individual managers down to groups of employees actually doing the work. Finally, the increased complexity of the business world has resulted in a situation where no single employee has the breath of knowledge necessary to make many decisions. Therefore, a team with a diverse set of skills relevant to the problem at hand usually will arrive at better decisions than individual managers.

You may have noticed the use of the terms "groups" and "teams" used in the above discussion, and wondered how they differ. A commonly used distinction is that a group is a number of people

---

[2]*Wall Street Journal*, November 28, 1995, page 1.

[3]"Breaking the Chains of Command," *Business Week*, Special Information Revolution Issue, 1994, page 113.

assigned to a particular task. A team is a group that has learned to work effectively together. It is not easy for a group to become an effective team, and many groups never really develop into a team.

In this course you will be assigned to groups. Your instructor may ask you to complete the student information sheet shown as Exhibit A-2. The information collected on this form will help your instructor create diverse groups. The diversity of background should allow you to learn from your group members, as well as from your instructor and the assigned materials. The amount you learn from your group depends on how well your group functions and whether it becomes at true team.

An important outcome of this course is for you to learn how to build an effective team. The key to creating an effective team is to follow the guidelines for group participation presented in Exhibit A-1. As soon as possible after your group has been created, your group should meet and discuss each of the points in this exhibit in detail. If your group is having difficulty working together, the group should ask your instructor for assistance *immediately*. Group conflicts can escalate quickly and destroy your group.

Exhibit A-1

Group Assignments
Guidelines for Participation

1. Everyone must contribute to the group's consensus solutions of assigned problems. No sandbaggers (free riders) or dominators allowed.

    *   To participate effectively in a group, each group member is individually responsible for doing the assigned "advance preparation."

    *   Each group member is responsible for making sure that everyone contributes.

    *   Peer evaluation sheets will be completed by each group member to monitor individual contributions.

2. Each group member is responsible for all other team members' learning. Help each other to understand your group's solution.

    *   Each group member is responsible for making sure that everyone understands the group's consensus solution.

    *   The instructor will frequently call on group members at random to explain the group's solution.

    *   The objective of each group assignment is not to finish first, but to have all group members master the materials.

3. You can criticize ideas, but not the person presenting the ideas. Keep disagreements at a professional level. Work hard to resolve conflicts in a "team spirit."

4. Each member brings unique knowledge and skills to group tasks, e.g., computer skills. Look for ways to create sharing opportunities through monitoring relationships, both before and during in-class group activities.

    *   The group's computer consultant is "officially" responsible for assisting other group members on computer assignments.

5. You can't participate unless you attend class.

    *   Bonus points will be given for good attendance in group activities, both in class and outside of class

    *   The group's "recorder" is responsible for recording attendance on each group assignment form before it is turned in to the instructor.

Exhibit A-2

Using Financial Accounting Information **Student Information Sheet**	Class Section

All requested information other than name is optional	
Name	Phone

Year (Freshman, Sophomore, Junior, Senior, Graduate)	Gender M ❑ F ❑

Other colleges attended:	From	To

Proposed concentration/option (e.g., English, math, marketing, finance, etc.):	Cumulative GPA

Is English your first language?   Yes ❑   No ❑

Do you know how to use a computer spreadsheet (e.g., Excel, etc.)?   Yes ❑   No ❑

If you have an e-mail address, list it here:

Prior bookkeeping or accounting course(s) taken	Date Taken	Where Taken	Instructor	Grade

Is your commute to campus more than 10 miles?   Yes ❑   No ❑   If yes, please indicate city or town from which you commute:

Briefly describe any prior business-related work experience that you have acquired (clerical, sales, warehousing, bookkeeping, etc.):

Briefly indicate any career plans that you intend to pursue or are thinking about pursuing:

Do you have a seating preference in the classroom?

ABOUT THE AUTHORS

Sally L. Adams

Sally L. Adams is a lecturer of accounting at California State University, Chico. Her primary teaching interests include the introductory accounting course and auditing. She has played a lead role in a project funded by U.S. Department of Education's Fund for the Improvement of Post-Secondary Education (FIPSE) to disseminate changes in the first year introductory courses.

Sally is a Certified Public Accountant (CPA) and holds an MBA from the University of Cincinnati. Prior to teaching, she was a member of the audit staff in the Cincinnati office of Arthur Andersen and Co. Sally has co-authored an article in *Issues in Accounting Education* which explored factors important to accounting majors in selecting the accounting option and investigated ways to recruit and retain high aptitude students to the accounting major. She has also given numerous presentations at regional conferences regarding innovations in the introductory accounting course.

Sally lives with her husband, Steve, and their two children, Jennifer and Kristen. She is a life master duplicate bridge player and enjoys computers, spending time with her family and traveling.

LeRoy J. Pryor

LeRoy J. Pryor is professor of accounting and management information systems at California State University, Chico. He teaches courses in accounting information systems, financial accounting, and managerial accounting. He has served as chair of the Department of Accounting and Management Information Systems and is a member of the Accounting Education Advisory Committee and the Corporate Accounting Policy Committee of the American Accounting Association. In 1998, he served as Director of Continuing Professional Education for the American Accounting Association.

Lee is a Certified Public Accountant and holds a Doctorate in Business Administration from the University of Southern California and an MBA with distinction from DePaul University. His undergraduate degree was awarded by the University of Illinois. Prior to entering academe, he worked in public accounting as an auditor for an international firm. He has consulted in many types of businesses, principally in the design of their accounting systems. Dr. Pryor has published articles in the *Journal of Accountancy*, *Management Accounting*, *Issues in Accounting Education*, and in several other journals. Dr. Pryor received the joint American Accounting Association/Institute of Management Accountants 1997 James Bulloch Award for Innovations in Management Accounting Education. The Bulloch Award was for a unique pedagogical approach called the California Car Company case. He has received his college's Outstanding Faculty Member Award.

Lee is married to Cathy Sweet. He has a son, Steven, daughter, Ashlee, and three grandchildren, Cooper, Berlyn, and Perris. His hobby is competitive sailing.

Donald E. Keller

Donald E. Keller is a professor and past chair of the Department of Accounting and Management Information Systems at California State University, Chico. Before joining CSU, Chico, he was professor and chairman, Department of Accounting and Finance at Seton Hall University, South Orange, New Jersey. From 1974 to 1982, he was Director of Technical Services for the National Association of Accountants (now the Institute of Management Accounts) in New York City. His prior experience includes position with the American Institute of CPAs, California State University, Northridge, University of Arizona, University of Southern California, San Diego State University, and an international public accounting firm.

Don teaches managerial and financial accounting courses at both the graduate and undergraduate levels. He has published in *Management Accounting* and has been author or editor of nine accounting books.

Don's education includes a B.S. degree from the University of Arizona, an M.S. degree from San Diego State University, and a D.B.A. from the University of Southern California. Dr. Keller is a CPA and a CMA and past president of the Chico Area Chapter of the Institute of Management Accountants, National Director of the Institute of Management Accountants, and is an active member of the American Institute of CPA's, American Accounting Association and the California Society of CPA's.

Don lives with his wife, Merlene in San Marcos, California. The Keller's have three children and three grandchildren. His favorite pastime is playing golf.

MODULE ONE

USING

Accounting Information

FOR ECONOMIC DECISIONS

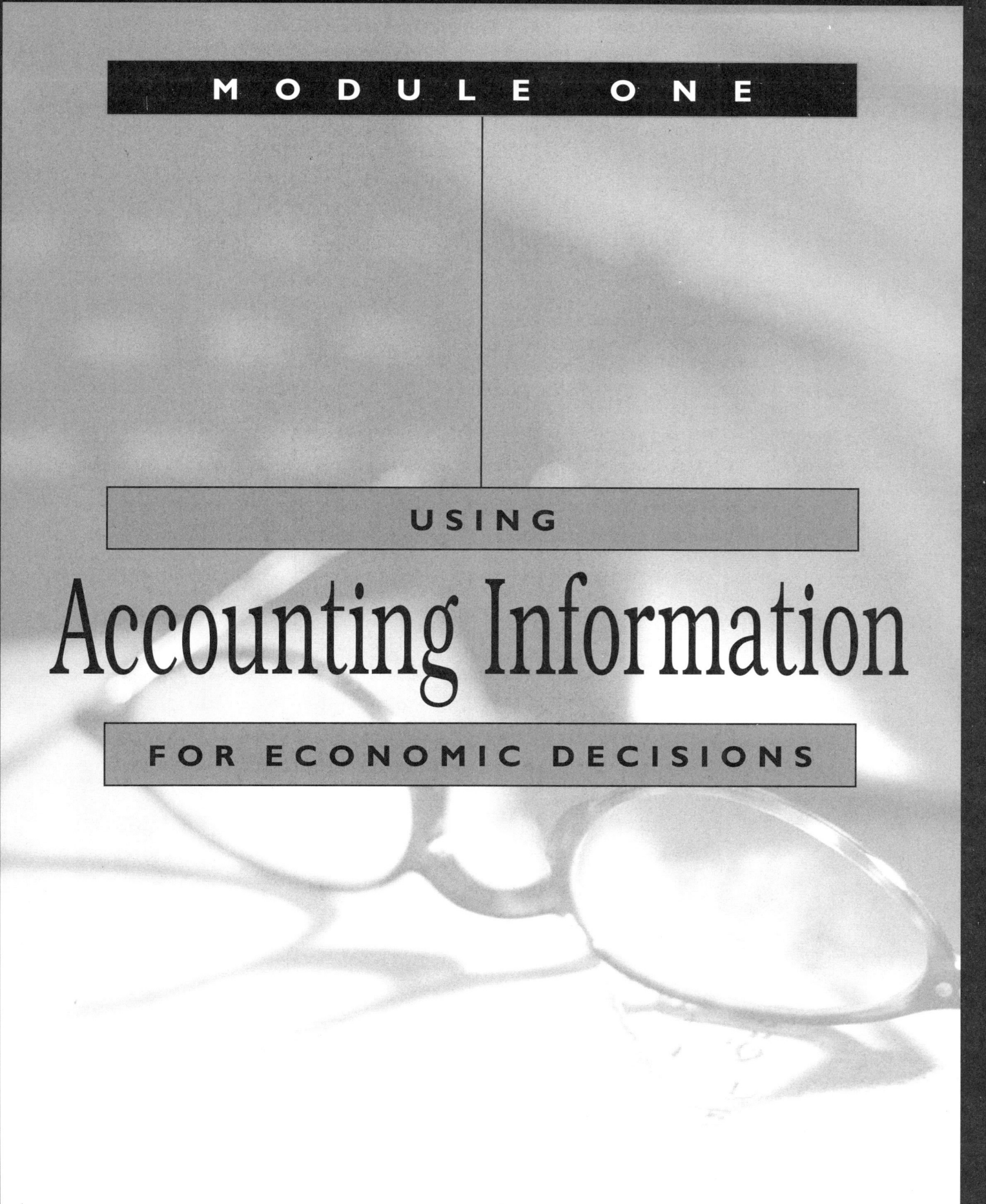

Module 1 Introduction

USING ACCOUNTING INFORMATION
FOR ECONOMIC DECISIONS

MODULE OVERVIEW

Module 1 demonstrates how accounting information and financial statements are used in making investment decisions. The module also discusses the role that accounting plays in society, and the career paths that are available for accounting graduates. It provides an introduction to some foundation concepts, including elements of decision-making processes and ethical considerations in decision making. The decision context in which these concepts are examined involves a student, John Miller, who is faced with a major question: Should I (John) start a summer painting business? This is your first encounter with John Miller, who will be the subject of many cases and discussion.

Learning Objectives

1. Understand the role of accounting information in society.

    - Case Reading 1-1   Introduction to Uses of Accounting Information
    - Case Reading 1-2   Accounting Information and Society
    - Case 1-2   The Role of Accounting in Society
    - Exercises and Problems   Exercises and Problems at the end of Case Readings 1-1 and 1-2

2. Become aware of accounting career opportunities and the skills desired by employers in the accounting field.

    - Case Reading 1-2   Accounting Information and Society
    - Case 1-2   The Role of Accounting in Society
    - Exercises and Problems   Exercises and Problems at the end of Case Reading 1-2

3. Understand the basic steps involved in making decisions and apply those steps to simple personal and business decision problems, including those with ethical considerations.

    - Case Reading 1-3   Decision Making
    - Case 1-3   John's Decision
    - Group Assignment 1-3   Holly's Hurdle
    - Exercises and Problems   Exercises and Problems at the end of Case Reading 1-3

4. Understand how financial statements can be used to help make sound investment decisions.

    - Case Reading 1-4   Using Accounting Information to Understand Personal Investments
    - Case 1-4   Using Accounting Information for Investment Decisions
    - Exercises and Problems   Exercises and Problems at the end of Case Reading 1-4

5. Become familiar with and be able to use the web site for the course.

    -Case 1-1   A "Site" to Behold

Case Reading 1-1

INTRODUCTION TO USES OF ACCOUNTING INFORMATION

INTRODUCTION

People invest in business to earn a return on their investment and thereby increase their wealth. Investing requires that decisions be made. Wise decisions require accurate information. In Module 1 you will learn how accounting helps people make business decisions. The readings and cases are designed to introduce you to the world of business by studying how owners of small businesses and large corporations make decisions and are ultimately rewarded for those decisions.

HOW ACCOUNTING INFORMATION IS USED IN BUSINESS DECISIONS

To start, let's use an example that most of you know something about: sports. A baseball manager or football coach must pay close attention to the performance of individual players on the team. This can be a daunting task since most sports teams have many players. Also, the performance of a certain player in a particular game may not be typical of the player's skill on the field. On a given day, any athlete may perform significantly better or worse than his or her normal effectiveness on the field. Faced with decisions such as adding a new player or cutting an existing one, using a pinch hitter, or selecting one of several strategies, managers and coaches need a lot of information on each player. Such data is compiled into statistics that measure the performance of athletes on the team. The summarized data is valuable information that can be used in making decisions that are aligned with team goals, such as winning. No doubt you are familiar with some of the more common statistics: batting averages and pass completion percentages. There are countless occasions when a manager or a coach will base a game's strategic decision on the information the averages contain. Think of a situation in which a baseball manager or a football head coach will deviate from the normal strategy because statistical information says the athletes have a very high batting average or a very high pass completion percentage.

Business is similar to sports. Business managers and investors must pay close attention to the performance of the enterprise. Business managers, like baseball managers, must make a variety of decisions to keep business performance, such as profits, in line with the expectations of its owners and **creditors**—those people or institutions which have loaned money to the enterprise. Deciding whether to raise prices to recover an increase in wage costs when your competitor has not raised prices is an example of a tough decision that must be made. Whatever decision is made, it is essential for the manager to be aware of the consequences of that decision.

Accounting is a system that collects and processes financial and nonfinancial information about economic activities and creates summarized reports for decision makers of an entity. Accounting plays a vital role in the success of any business by providing information that (1) helps owners and managers anticipate the effect of a decision and (2) discloses to them in numerical terms the actual outcome of a decision. Accounting measures the final score in business. In other words, **accounting information** guides decision makers to attain economic goals.

> *The purpose of accounting is to provide accurate financial information to decision makers to enable them to achieve their personal and organizational economic goals.*

An Example

To illustrate the purpose of accounting, we will examine the business situation of Peggy Glenville. Peg is a computer engineer four years out of college. She supervises a team of software analysts and is responsible for the development of new products for a large multinational company. Peg has always dreamed of being in business for herself. In her spare time she has developed a computer game that includes unique features. Peg has asked her younger cousins and the teenage children of her closest friends to test the game. She needs to know if the game appeals to this group since it is the teenage market that typically buys computer games. Fortunately, the computer game was a hit with the sample of prospective buyers.

Peg's goals are twofold. She wants to be in business for herself, but she also wants to earn an income approximately equal to the $75,000 salary she now earns. No one can predict the future, but Peg can use an accounting tool to assess whether she can meet her financial goal. The accounting tool that Peg can utilize to forecast how much profit her new game will bring is the **income statement**.

> *The income statement measures revenues earned and expenses incurred in a specific time period for the purpose of calculating the profit or loss of an enterprise.*

The income statement is used in two ways: first, to forecast the future level of revenues and expenses and second, to report the measurements of past revenues and expenses. Peg hasn't started her business yet so she must forecast the amount of revenues and expenses of the computer game business. The first thing that Peg must do to use the income statement tool is to estimate the quantity of games that she will sell in the first year of business. She recalls from her college economics classes that typically a lower price will increase the quantity demanded. Conversely, one can reasonably predict that a high price will reduce the quantity demanded. Peg is aware of this axiom and accordingly sets the suggested retail price at $50, at the low end of game products currently on the market.

Next Peg must estimate the quantity of games she will sell. She is negotiating with a distributor of computer accessories to promote her new game. Currently the distributor sells 100,000 game units of various types to retail stores and mail-order catalog outfits. The distributor estimates that because of the uniqueness of Peg's new game and its modest price, 10 percent of his volume of sales will shift to her new product. This means that Peg can reasonably forecast sales of 10,000 units in her first year of business. The distributor and retailer markups are $5 and $20, respectively. Therefore, Peg will net $25 per unit. Peg did not realize that 50 percent of the suggested retail price would be needed to channel her product to end users. In researching the topic of retail distribution costs she concluded that this proportion is normal. If her business is to generate sufficient profit in relation to the risk she would take, namely giving up her $75,000 salary and investing her savings account, she will need to cover expenses and her profit goal with the $25 per unit. Peg now has the information to estimate **revenue.**

Revenue is the total money or value received in exchange for providing customers with goods or services.

Considering the advice of the distributor, Peg estimates revenues from the sale of games in the first year as follows:

10,000 units @ $25 each = $250,000

Next Peg must estimate the expenses of producing and delivering 10,000 units. To do this she will need to design an **operating plan** that can meet the above quantity goal.

An operating plan specifies how a business will employ humans, machines, knowledge, and other resources to create value for customers.

Let's assume that Peg's operating plan specifies that she enter into an agreement with another business that will supply a packaged product complete with the game CD, instructions, and additional promotional literature. An operating plan is usually very detailed, laying out how the product will be produced and marketed. A well-conceived operating plan enables Peg to estimate the **expenses** of her new venture.

Expenses are the cost of economic resources consumed in the process of earning revenue.

Peg's estimated expenses to deliver 10,000 game units to the distributor in the next year are shown in Exhibit 1-1.1 below.

Exhibit 1-1.1
Peg's Estimated Expenses

Packaged game ($10 per unit)	$100,000
Wages (one full-time person)	25,000
Advertising	20,000
Utilities, telephone, fax	12,000
Office rent	6,000
Insurance	5,000
Total expenses	$168,000

These estimated expenses reflect the specific nature of Peg's operating plan. By hiring another business entity to produce the game package, Peg and her employee can focus on the marketing and development of new computer games.

The income statement is the algebraic sum of revenues minus expenses. If revenues and expenses are measured in accordance with accepted methods, the resulting difference, profit or loss, tells the owner and investor how the business has performed during the period covered by the income statement. It is possible, and even desirable, to prepare an income statement for a relatively short time period such as a month or even a week. Sophisticated accounting systems found in larger companies can track revenues and expenses on a real-time basis. **Real-time** is a term referring to the instantaneous capture of relevant data in an enterprise's computer information system. Once data of the business's revenue and expenses are contained within the system, various reports such as the weekly income statement can be requested by managers.

Let's combine Peg's estimate of revenues and expenses to predict if it is likely that the business venture will meet her financial goals. The typical format of an income statement is shown in Exhibit 1-1.2.

Exhibit 1-1.2
Projected Income Statement

Peg's Computer Game Enterprise Projected Income Statement Year Ended December 31, 2002		
Revenue		
Sales of Computer Games		$250,000
Expenses		
Cost of Goods Sold		100,000
Gross Profit		150,000
Operating Expenses		
Wages	$25,000	
Advertising	20,000	
Utilities, telephone, fax	12,000	
Office rent	6,000	
Insurance	5,000	
Total Operating Expenses		68,000
Net Income (Loss)		$ 82,000

The income statement presented above is Peg's estimate of the profit her business will earn in its first year, 2002. More common are income statements that cover a past time period. For example, IBM Corporation makes a public announcement of the recent history of its income every three months: March 31, June 30, September 30, and December 31. For internal management, a more frequent reading of a company's income performance is desirable. Accordingly, many companies have sophisticated accounting and database systems. These systems enable managers to assess whether the company is achieving its financial goals by providing reports that cover monthly and even weekly time periods. Such reports often compare estimates with actual data to tell managers where the trouble spots may be in the company's operating plan.

If we move forward in time and assume that Peg has gone into business for herself, we would find that the income statement for the year ended December 31, 2002 is of great interest to Peg. The income statement is no longer an estimate but rather the actual income measured in accordance with generally accepted accounting rules and regulations. (These rules and regulations will be discussed in Case Reading 1-2.) Peg will be able to evaluate whether the new venture is as successful as she planned.

Suppose Peg has completed her first year in business and that the historical income statement shows $60,000 as net income. **Net income** is the earnings from operations for an entity for a period of time. This amount cannot be compared to the salary Peg was receiving from her employer. The reason for this is that her salary was paid in the form of cash. After deductions for taxes, insurance, and other withholdings, Peg was free to spend the net cash amount from her salary in any way she wished. The net income of the business generally is *not* the same as cash. As you will learn in later modules, the income that has been earned during a specific time period may have been reinvested in new equipment or increased inventory or used to pay off debts outstanding at the beginning of the time period. If transactions like these occur, the owner may not be able to withdraw cash from the business in an amount equal to the net income.

What would Peg decide about the new venture? It is clearly a tough decision and should be based on many other factors rather than simply a one-year forecast of business income. By following a systematic process to gather accounting information in order to project the future performance of her business, Peg has gained greater insight into the risks and rewards that could come from the decision to go into business for herself. This insight will enable Peg to make a better economic decision and avoid mistakes that would reduce her wealth rather than increase it.

Forms of Business Organizations

Our example took the point of view of an owner who would also be the manager of a startup business. This form of business is referred to as a **sole proprietorship.** In a sole proprietorship the owner is the key decision maker. The funds to start a business are usually those of the proprietor. In some cases, the personal savings of the proprietor are transferred to the business's checking account. It is also possible that relatives and friends of the proprietor might lend money to him/her, or, perhaps a bank loan could be obtained. Generally, this requires the pledging of personal or business assets as collateral.

An important concept in accounting requires that the business unit be accounted for separately from its owners. This is called the **entity concept.** For accounting information to be useful to the various interested decision makers, it is vital that the recording of business activities not be mixed up with the personal financial transactions of owners. Suppose Peg had interest income from government bonds she inherited from her grandmother. To include this income in her computer game business would overstate the true income of her new venture, rendering the income statement useless for business decisions she needs to make. Whenever the entity concept is ignored, the resulting accounting information is certain to be flawed. Decisions made with erroneous information are likely to place the business or owner/investor in an undesirable economic state.

Another form of business is the **partnership.** The partnership is formed when two or more individuals join to create a new business. In this form of business, decisions generally require the collaboration of all of the partners. All states have laws that govern the formation, operation, and dissolution of partnership businesses. One universal aspect of a general partnership is the unlimited liability of each of the partners. Any partner can act as an **agent** of the business. An agent has the legal authority to enter into contracts on behalf of others, thereby binding them to the responsibilities stated in the contract. It is possible, therefore, to have a partner obligate the business by entering into an extremely disadvantageous contract. If the other partner(s) knew of the prospective contract, they might vehemently oppose the transaction. The agent status of all partners makes it possible to lock in the obligations without the knowledge of other partners. A serious financial mistake by one partner will impact on the other partner(s) because they are jointly and severally responsible for each others' actions. A partnership business which fails can result in the personal bankruptcies of one or more of the partners.

Because of these disadvantages of the partnership form of business, most states have enacted a hybrid form of partnership called the **limited liability partnership.** Limited liability partnerships are governed by state law. The objective of this relatively recent form of business organization is to facilitate the partnership concept but without the unlimited liability characteristics of general partnerships. Many professional service businesses, such as medical, financial consulting, legal, and engineering firms are organized in this way.

A third form of business organization is the **corporation**. The corporate form of business has a very different legal standing from the sole proprietorship or the partnership. In a corporation, the owners are the shareholders, and there are usually many of them. Most shareholders of a corporation are not involved in the management of the enterprise.

Sole proprietors and partners are exposed to losses of not only their business investment but also their personal assets. For example, if a business becomes bankrupt, the proprietor or partner may be called upon to satisfy the demands of creditors by using personal assets, such as a home, car, savings, or investments. In contrast, shareholders of a corporation risk only the amount they paid into the corporation to purchase shares. The personal assets of shareholders are protected from losses sustained by the corporation.

The corporation concept made possible the industrialization of capitalist economies because it gave new business ventures sources of investment capital to fund the building of mass-production factories. People were drawn to invest in corporations because the expected rewards appeared to be worth the risk, in part because their potential risk of loss was limited to the amount invested. Also, shareholders in a corporation do not need to be involved in the day-to-day affairs of the business. Instead, the shareholders elect a board of directors who are responsible for overseeing the professional managers and evaluating their performance in meeting the goals of the corporation. It is not uncommon to read in the business press of a board of directors ousting members of top management because the company's financial goals are not being attained. Recently, Apple Computer hired Gilberto Amelio as its chief executive officer. This is the highest management level, and Mr. Amelio had the responsibility to reverse the downward trend in sales and profits of Apple. But after less than two years the board of directors fired him, apparently for not being able to turn the company around.

All three forms of organizations can be found in today's business world. There are many similarities in the accounting information used in each form of organization. These will become apparent as you proceed through this book. In the continuing case which begins later in this module, we demonstrate how a business can grow from a sole proprietorship to a partnership and then to a corporation. As a business expands, both the number of decision makers and the complexities of the decisions increase. We separate the users of accounting information into two groups: internal decision makers and external decision makers.

Internal Decision Makers

Managers within a company are usually the primary **internal decision makers**. They are interested in financial information so that they can properly plan, control, evaluate performance, and make pricing and profitability decisions. For example, a manager might need to make a decision about whether to increase or decrease the selling price of a particular product. A good accounting system would be able to generate information concerning the sales volume, current price, sales and cost data for that particular product. The manager could then estimate future sales and income. Over time, these projections can be compared with the actual results, and the accounting information gathered will help the manager to evaluate the product's performance and perhaps even provide feedback for possible improvements.

External Decision Makers

The **external decision makers** consist of investors, creditors, the general public, and the government. These groups are primarily interested in the external financial statements that are published by the company. External users analyze the past and present performance of the company because it is an important predictor of future performance.

Exhibit 1-1.3 depicts the many business professionals who make decisions that are affected by accounting information. Those listed inside the box are internal decision makers. They are primarily interested in accounting information that helps them manage the company. Those listed outside the box must make decisions that are at least partially affected by the accounting information generated by the company. For example, investment advisors are constantly reviewing the financial reports of many companies in order to find the best investment opportunity for their clients.

Exhibit 1-1.3

Internal and External Decision Makers

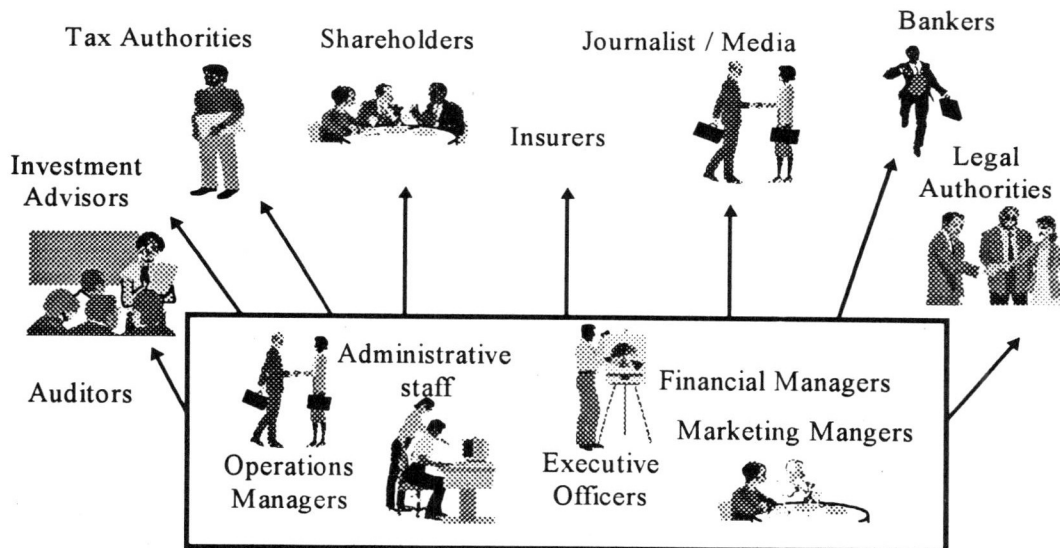

Tax Authorities   Shareholders   Journalist / Media   Bankers

Insurers

Investment
Advisors   Legal
Authorities

Auditors

Administrative
staff

Operations
Managers   Financial Managers

Marketing Mangers

Executive
Officers

Investors

Investors are primarily interested in financial information that allows them to make the decision whether or not to invest in a company. Having invested, they may need financial information to help them vote on corporate issues. They also evaluate management's performance as well as estimate future profitability of this investment versus other competing uses of their monetary resources.

Creditors

Creditors want to know if they should lend money to the company. They use information provided in the company's financial statements as well as loan application information and credit history data to make numerous business decisions such as:

- Should we lend this company money? If so, how much?

- What collateral should we demand?

- What interest rate and repayment period should we demand?

- How can we monitor the loan?

- Should we require the company to maintain certain financial ratios during the loan period?

Careful analysis of the risk involved is mandatory and requires review of the financial statements provided by the company.

General Public

Other users consist of a variety of groups including current and potential future employees of the company, general consumers, unions, and voters. Because of the wide diversity of these groups, their use of the financial information varies widely as well. Current employees want to make sure their jobs are secure and that the company will be able to pay their salary and benefits both now and in the future. Prospective employees have similar needs and may be evaluating different job packages before making a commitment to a potential employer. The general consumer wants to know that the company is financially stable before he or she purchases its goods and services. What good is a company warranty if the company has gone bankrupt? What will happen if the purchased product breaks down and parts are not available because the company has shut down? When labor contracts are being negotiated, unions use financial information to evaluate whether or not the salary package offered to the employees is reasonable compared to those of similar companies. Voters use financial information to evaluate different uses for their tax dollars. For instance, a voter may dislike the government spending money on space exploration. If the member of Congress representing that voter is an advocate of space exploration, the voter may support the opposing candidate at the next election.

Government

Many government agencies use accounting information. The Internal Revenue Service (IRS) uses accounting information to compute the amount of taxes owed by business owners. In addition, corporate taxes are computed based on accounting data, as are sales and payroll taxes. The Securities and Exchange Commission (SEC) uses accounting information to determine if specific companies should be allowed to trade their securities on the stock and bond exchanges. All publicly traded companies are required to file financial statements with the SEC. Lastly, other government agencies such as the Environmental Protection Agency may collect financial information from companies as necessary.

The accounting information that is most widely used by external decision makers is the information contained in annual financial statements.

THREE IMPORTANT FINANCIAL STATEMENTS

The three key **financial statements** issued periodically by an entity are the

- Income statement
- Balance sheet (statement of financial position)
- Statement of cash flows

Income Statement

As previously presented, income can be determined by a simple equation:

$$Revenues - Expenses = Net\ Income$$

The format of the income statement for "Peg's Computer Game Enterprise" was shown in Exhibit 1-1.2 and was discussed previously in this case reading.

Balance Sheet (also called Statement of Financial Position)

The balance sheet is also known as the statement of financial position. It can be stated as a simple equation:

$$Assets = Liabilities + Owners'\ (Shareholders')\ Equity$$

The **balance sheet** is a snapshot of the business showing the recorded amounts for these three elements of the accounting equation. Therefore, the balance sheet is stated at a *discrete point in time*. Typically this is at the end of a month, quarter, or fiscal year. It is important to note the date in the heading of the balance sheet because one can compare the company's financial position at one date with its financial position at a previous date to gain insight into whether there was economic progress. The format of the balance sheet (Exhibit 1-1.4) is based on Peg's new business venture. Note that the date of the balance sheet is at the end of Peg's first year of business.

Assets

Assets are economic resources that are owned or controlled by the business and that can reasonably be expected to benefit the business striving to earn net income. Examples of assets are cash, receivables from customers, inventory, buildings, land. equipment, patents, and copyrights. All businesses need economic resources to sustain an existence. The responsibility of managers is to acquire and utilize economic resources to maximize the benefit such resources provide in earning a profit.

Exhibit 1-1.4
Peg's Balance Sheet

Peg's Computer Game Enterprise Balance Sheet December 31, 2002				
Assets		**Liabilities and Owner's Equity**		
Cash in Bank	$ 4,000	Accounts Payable		$ 10,000
Accounts Receivable	10,000	Notes Payable		10,000
Inventory of Games	50,000	Total Liabilities		20,000
Office Furniture	10,000	Owner's Equity:		
Leasehold Improvements	6,000	Contributed Capital	$ 50,000	
Computer Equipment	50,000	Retained Earnings	60,000	
		Total Owner's Equity		110,000
		Total Liabilities and		
Total Assets	$130,000	Owner's Equity		$130,000

Assets enter the balance sheet at the actual cost incurred to acquire them. At a later date the balance sheet will report the unexpired cost of assets. The expiration of assets occurs through the using up of the assets in order to earn revenues and income. In Modules 2, 3 and 4 we will study processes such as depreciation and cost of goods sold that record using up assets.

Liabilities

Liabilities are debts of the business. Liabilities are common and arise from transactions with others who have extended credit to the business. A typical transaction that creates a liability is the purchase of supplies inventory. If the vendor does not require cash to be paid upon delivery of the supplies, a liability called **accounts payable** is created on the balance sheet. This is referred to as a purchase on credit. The vendor is thus contributing to the total assets in this transaction. Another example is when a business needs cash to carry out its operating plan. The transaction is a bank extending credit to the business by providing it with cash in return for a legal promise to repay the loan called a **promissory note payable.** Similar to the above example, the bank loaning money to a business is also contributing to the assets. There are many other types of transactions which create a business liability, and we will study these in Module 2.

Before leaving the discussion of liabilities, recall the balance sheet equation:

Assets = Liabilities + Owners' (Shareholders') Equity

Using a basic algebraic operation we bring the liability term to the left side of the equal sign and obtain:

Assets – Liabilities = Owners' (Shareholders') Equity

This variation of the balance sheet equation illustrates the concept that liabilities are a claim against the assets of the business. When a promissory note comes due, the business must use its cash asset to satisfy the lender's demand for repayment. Similarly, a vendor who sells manufacturing supplies on credit will expect payment in 30–45 days; otherwise the vendor may not make further shipments until the account is paid off.

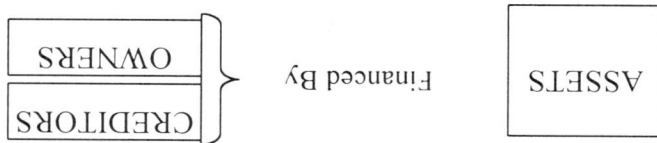

```
  ┌──────────┐            ┌──────────────┐
  │  ASSETS  │ Financed By │  CREDITORS   │
  └──────────┘            ├──────────────┤
                          │    OWNERS    │
                          └──────────────┘
```

Owners' (Shareholders') Equity

Owners' equity is calculated by subtracting liabilities from assets. At any point in time the amount of equity measures the contribution the owners have made to total assets. The assumption that a business will continue indefinitely makes it possible to report the original cost of assets less expirations of such cost in the process of earning revenue. An example of an expiration of cost is found in Peg's Computer Game Enterprise. As she sells games the balance sheet is impacted in several ways. First, the revenue generated by the sale of the games increases an asset (assume cash) and increases owner's equity. Second, the inventory of games is decreased by the cost of the games sold. The effect of the second impact is to decrease the asset and decrease owner's equity. Note that owner's equity is both increased and decreased in this process. The objective of the owners is naturally to have the increase be larger than the decrease, which is the way profit is reflected in owners' equity.

Statement of Cash Flows

The statement of cash flows shows the cash receipts and the cash withdrawals of the company. A simple statement of cash flows for Peg's computer store is shown in Exhibit 1-1.5.

Exhibit 1-1.5
Peg's Statement of Cash Flows

Peg's Computer Game Enterprise		
Statement of Cash Flows		
Year Ended December 31, 2002		
Cash Receipts		
Cash collected from customers	$ 240,000	
Cash received from owner	50,000	
Total Cash Receipts		290,000
Cash Disbursements		
Cash paid to suppliers of games	$(140,000)	
Cash paid for wages	(25,000)	
Cash paid for advertising	(20,000)	
Cash paid for utilities	(12,000)	
Cash paid for rent	(6,000)	
Cash paid for insurance	(5,000)	
Cash paid for computer equipment	(40,000)	
Cash paid for furniture	(10,000)	
Cash paid for leasehold improvements	(6,000)	
Cash withdrawn by owner	(22,000)	
Total Cash Disbursements		(286,000)
Net Increase in Cash During the Year		4,000
Add Cash Balance, January 1, 2002		-
Cash Balance, December 31, 2002		$ 4,000

Cash in the bank is a critical asset because it is needed to satisfy debt obligations when they come due and to pay for operating expenses. Recall that the balance sheet is a snapshot of the assets and claims against those assets at a point in time. The statement of cash flows tells Peg *why* the cash balance rose to $4,000. We will study the statement of cash flows in more detail in Module 2. For now, however, note that Peg withdrew $22,000. This decision, together with other disbursements of cash, brought the cash balance to a relatively low level as of December 31, 2002. Suppose in the weeks following the close of Peg's first year in business she realizes that the cash balance is too low to sustain an orderly payment of expenses and liabilities. She will either transfer money from her personal funds into the business or borrow money from a bank or other sources. A possible strategy is to find a partner who can contribute the necessary capital. This strategy would require the formal establishment of a partnership, requiring contractual agreements to be drawn up defining the ownership percentages and a formula for distributing profits and losses.

As we saw in the projected income statement, Peg gained greater insight into the risks and potential rewards of entering into a new business venture. In the same way, a projected statement of cash flows (for example the year 2003) can help Peg plan the cash receipts and disbursements. The plan imbedded in the statement of cash flows will give Peg an early warning of cash shortages that could arise. She can then be prepared to take action to raise the necessary cash to sustain growth of the business and thus avoid the plight of so many new businesses: lack of sufficient cash.

The balance sheet, income statement, and statement of cash flows are the primary components of accounting information. As historical reports of the financial affairs of the business, they assist external decision makers in evaluating whether their particular goal in the business is being attained. As projected reports, they help the internal decision maker guide the path of the business to maximize the probability that it will succeed. However, accounting information provided in the financial statements has not always been useful in decision making. In fact, in the past, financial statement information was often purposely misleading. The history behind the regulation of accounting information is described in the next section.

SUMMARY

The principle elements of accounting information are the balance sheet, the income statement, and the statement of cash flows. The balance sheet gives details on the status of assets, liabilities, and owners' equity (or shareholders' equity in the case of a corporation) at a particular point in time. The income statement reports the revenues and expenses of the business for a period of time. This can be a month, quarter of the year, or a 12-month period which is usually referred to as the fiscal year. Generally accepted accounting principles specify how the recognition of revenues and expenses in a particular time period should be accomplished

The statement of cash flows reports the details of why the cash asset of the company increased or decreased. It gives the owner or manager a different perspective on the business. For example, it can explain to the reader how a company can earn a good income and be short of cash.

EXERCISES

Exercise 1 Purpose.   What is the purpose of accounting?

Exercise 2 Revenues and Expenses.   Define the two main categories comprising the income statement.

Exercise 3 Operating Plan.   How does an operating plan help a business owner or manager forecast income?

Exercise 4 Forms of Business Organization.   Compare and contrast the three forms of business.

Exercise 5 Equation.   Define the three elements of the balance sheet equation.

Exercise 6 Analysis of Owner's Equity.   What caused Peg's owner's equity to increase from $50,000 to $110,000?

Case 1-1

A "SITE" TO BEHOLD

Case Objective

To become familiar with the web site for this course.

Requirements

1. Visit the web site for this course. Spend about ten minutes investigating the site.

2. Write a one page paper (typed, double-spaced, and carefully edited) that includes the following:

   - One paragraph that gives a brief overview of the contents of the web site.

   - One to two paragraphs briefly identifying the items at the web site you feel will be the most helpful to you during the semester.

   - One to two paragraphs that briefly identify questions you may have about the web site or additional information you would like to see at the site.

3. Print out the hints for Case 1-3. Attach the printout to the one page paper you prepared for Requirement 2.

Case Reading 1-2

ACCOUNTING INFORMATION
AND SOCIETY

INTRODUCTION

The fact that over one million people in the United States are employed in accounting-related jobs is evidence of the important role accounting information plays in society. So many people work at accounting jobs because of the recognized importance for businesses and individuals to constantly measure economic performance. Case Reading 1-1 discussed how income is measured. We didn't dwell on examples of a company that reports losses year after year. That would not be as interesting. But think about the money-losing company for a moment. If you were an investor who still had a chance to get some of your money out of a losing venture, you might consider the decision whether to cut your losses and put the recovered money to work in a more profitable investment. If you did not have the appropriate financial statements, you would not have a basis for reallocating your resources. Without financial statements you might not be informed of the losses until it was too late to divest your interest in the money-losing venture. Reliability and quality of financial statements are of critical importance in a free market economy. This case reading concludes with a presentation on the many and varied opportunities for careers in accounting.

Feedback

Society deems accounting information to be important because of the concept of feedback. **Feedback** is information about the performance of the system that is needed to control the system. An example of feedback is the temperature warning light on a car's dashboard. If the engine's coolant rises above a predetermined safe level, the red warning light is feedback about the system. You, the user of the system, must use this information to exercise control to correct the problem. The human body has many feedback loops that automatically exercise control over the biologic system. For example, as exertion from strenuous physical activity raises the temperature of the body, automatic control systems set off triggers to cool the body by perspiration. Another example is where the body sends blood to an injured area to begin healing the wound. In your home there are many feedback loops that help control your environment and comfort. See if you can think of some.

Accounting information is feedback vital to all economic organizations. Company managers must get feedback on revenues, expenses, cash flow, and many other items in order to keep control of the company. Frequently, the failed business is one where the owner or manager did not have appropriate financial feedback or didn't know how to use the information.

Accounting Information in an Economy

Access to accounting information contributes to the efficiency of an economy. The economic system in the United States is based upon free competition, so it is called a free market economy. A free **market economy**, also called **capitalism**, is one characterized by free-floating prices for goods and services. The equilibrium price of a specific item results from unrestricted supply and demand. In a market economy, business owners and investors use accounting information to maximize profits, and they allocate land and capital to ventures they believe will beat out the competition. The market economy is efficient because investment capital is not wasted on the production of goods or services nobody wants. Pure capitalism is an economic system in which the government does not intervene. The free market system in the U.S. today is subject to many government regulations, but our economy is still defined as a free market economy because the means of production are privately owned and prices are determined by supply and demand.

Even in communist countries, accounting information is needed, because managers of state-owned enterprises must also control expenses. However, a major difference between a free market economy and a communist system is that in the latter situation the means of production are owned by the government and prices are set by the government, rather than by free market forces. Since the dissolution of the U.S.S.R., the economies of the Soviet Bloc countries have collapsed completely. While there are now fewer government controls on economic forces, there is also an absence of free competition and private enterprise. The old communist system did not operate on a profit incentive, so there was no motivation to create high-quality products consumers would want to buy. Other factors have contributed to inefficiencies in the allocation of capital—for example, since government-run companies did not make a profit, workers were paid very low wages or often were not paid at all. Thus these workers had no money to purchase consumable items. Now the standard of living is declining at a rapid rate, and the former Soviet Bloc countries are struggling to realign their economic system to facilitate the development of a free market economy. State-owned enterprises are being sold to private entrepreneurs, and, as this changeover occurs, owners, managers, and investors will need accounting information as a feedback loop to help allocate resources in a more efficient manner.

Attributes of Accounting Information

For many years the accounting profession has tried to improve the usefulness of accounting information. The Financial Accounting Standards Board (FASB) has provided the accounting profession with a set of guidelines to use when evaluating the usefulness of accounting information. According to these guidelines, accounting information must have:

- **Relevance** – The information must be timely and provide either a good basis for predicting return on investment or for assessing the progress of past investments.
- **Reliability** – The information must be verifiable, must correctly measure economic inflows and outflows, and must be free of any bias in those measurements.
- **Comparability** – The comparison of financial information of two companies must be logically made and inferences drawn from them can be trusted to be correct. The rules of measurement must be essentially the same.
- **Consistency** – The comparison of two years of financial information of the same company can be made and inferences drawn from them can be trusted to be correct. The rules of measurement must be the same from one year to the next.

Accounting and the Environment

There continues to be concern about the impact our way of life has on the environment, especially with respect to our dependence on fossil fuels for electric power, transportation, and the production of polymer products. To reverse the deterioration of the earth's atmosphere and water resources, many regulations and laws have been enacted. For example, a paint manufacturer using volatile substances must now install sophisticated equipment to prevent chemical vapors from entering the atmosphere. When a company is required to buy such equipment, accountants analyze the new costs and their effect on profits.

In some European countries, manufacturers are required to take back their products when they become worn out and no longer usable. Tire, auto, and appliance manufacturers there have developed complex schemes to dismantle and recycle their returned products in a way that is environmentally friendly. This can represent a huge cost that occurs long after the sale has been made. Accountants again are needed to analyze such deferred costs and to advise the management of the future financial implications of the environmental costs.

EVOLUTION OF ACCOUNTING REGULATIONS

The 19th Century

Public ownership of corporations in the United States became more prevalent in the mid-nineteenth century. During the Industrial Revolution, unscrupulous promoters often swindled the unsuspecting public out of vast sums of money. No governmental regulations existed to prevent such financial fraud. Investment decisions were very difficult to make because the type of accounting information available today did not exist. To make matters worse, the financial information contrived to entice prospective investors frequently contained flagrant misrepresentations of the true economic status of corporations. There were no certified public accountants (CPAs) to perform audits.

The rapid growth of railroads and of the corporations that owned them attracted the public's attention, because investing in this new technology promised enormous profits. One type of fraud that victimized many investors was the issuance of "watered stock." The promoter would give financial information that exaggerated the value of the assets, and the issue price of the stock was based upon this inflated value. Later the truth would surface and the stock would become worthless. In another type of "scam," corporations would pay big dividends to shareholders to attract more investors. But the money to pay the dividends did not come from company profits; it came from new investors. Eventually the company would go bankrupt as this "borrowing from Peter to pay Paul," also known as a "ponzi," scheme failed.

The 20th Century

The **Sixteenth Amendment to the Constitution**, passed in 1913, was a pivotal event. This amendment granted authority to the U.S. government to levy taxes on the income of individuals and corporations. Even though the purpose of the amendment was to raise revenue for the government, the tax code that evolved as a result of the amendment began a process of standardizing the way business income is measured.

The **Stock Market Crash of 1929** focused attention on the dismal state of affairs in the U.S. capital markets and banking system. Some have argued that inadequate accounting and financial information fueled rampant speculation by investors, and this set the stage for the financial collapse.

Congress passed the **Securities Act of 1933** to reform the U.S. financial investment system. This act requires companies issuing securities to the public to first file a registration statement (Form S-1). This registration statement contains information about the company, including financial statements for the previous three years. Before any securities can be sold to the public, investors must be given a prospectus that includes the most significant information from the registration statement.

The **Securities Exchange Act of 1934** established the Securities and Exchange Commission (SEC) as the governmental body responsible for ensuring that companies prepare and file registration statements and annual stockholder reports, which must include audited financial statements. The purpose of this act was to ensure that the public has access to current information concerning publicly traded companies. The Securities Act also established margin requirements for trading stocks, which means that a percentage of the stock purchase must be paid in cash. In recent years the margin requirement has been 50 percent. Before the Crash of 1929 the margin requirement was only 10 percent.

While the SEC has the power to set accounting and financial reporting standards, it has for the most part delegated the task to the accounting profession. The **Financial Accounting Standards Board (FASB)** is recognized by both the Securities and Exchange Commission and the business community as the chief standard-setting organization. The body of opinions, standards, interpretations and memoranda produced by the FASB constitute **generally accepted accounting principles (GAAP)**. GAAP have become a matter of public policy, and these guidelines are universally accepted in the United States as the standard for all publicly traded companies. GAAP give investors confidence that the financial statements published by corporations are reliable. A summary of these principles is provided in Exhibit 1-2.1.

Before discussing these principles, it is important to remember that the objective of financial reporting is to provide users of financial statements with information so that they can make informed decisions. The users of financial statements want the information they receive for a specific entity to be:

- inclusive of information for only that business entity
- relevant to the decisions they need to make
- timely, so that they receive the information in time to use it to make decisions
- presented in a format that is easy to understand and interpret
- objective, so that the user knows any bias has been eliminated
- presented in a way that is comparable to previous years' information
- presented in a way that is comparable to other companies information
- reliable and an accurate representation of what has actually happened

Generally accepted accounting principles are only required for external financial reporting of companies that are publicly traded on a stock exchange. Many smaller, privately owned companies choose not to follow these suggested guidelines. Unpublished internal accounting reports used by companies are never required to adhere to these standards. Managers of companies are free to develop accounting reports in a manner they deem appropriate for their particular needs, which may be at variance from that of external parties.

There are certain fundamental concepts that form the basis of accounting information. These concepts require that financial statements be prepared using the accrual basis of accounting.

Exhibit 1.2-1
Generally Accepted Accounting Principles (GAAP)

Principle	Description
Revenue Recognition	Revenue should be recorded when the earnings process has been completed and an exchange has taken place.
Matching	Requires all costs incurred in generating revenue to be recognized as an expense in the same period as the related revenue.
Entity	Accounting information is accumulated and reported for a clearly defined economic entity regardless of its legal status.
Going Concern	For financial statement reporting purposes it is assumed that the business will continue operating for the foreseeable future.
Historical Cost	Assets should be recorded in the accounting records and reported in the financial statements at their historical (original) cost.
Stable Dollar	Amounts in the financial statements should be stated in terms of dollars with the implication that the dollar is a stable unit of measure.
Objectivity	Measurements should be made as objectively as possible.
Conservatism	If two possible outcomes are equally as likely to occur, accounting information must be presented in the least optimistic way.
Materiality	Only material items need be reflected in financial statements.
Comparability	Financial statements must be comparable not only from year to year within the same company, but also between one company and another.
Time Period	The periodicity assumption states that financial statements are to be broken up into various time periods.

Accrual Basis of Accounting

The accrual basis of accounting states that revenues should be recorded in the period earned and expenses in the period incurred, regardless of whether the cash has been received or paid. The concept of accrual accounting can be further explained by two accounting principles: the revenue recognition principle and the matching principle.

> The **revenue recognition principle** requires that revenue should be recorded when the earnings process has been substantially completed and an exchange has taken place.

To apply this principle, let's suppose that you purchase a bike from your neighborhood bike store. You pick up the bike today but you purchase the bike on credit and will not be paying the bill until next week. Accrual basis accounting and the revenue recognition principle require that since the earnings process is complete, the bike store should record the sale on the day that the bike changes hands and thus legal title to the bike was conveyed to the purchaser, even though the cash has not been received on that date.

The **matching principle** requires all costs incurred in generating revenue be recognized in the same period as the related revenue.

For example, let's suppose that employees work for a company during September but they will not be paid for that work until October. Accrual basis accounting and the matching principle require that the expense must be recorded in the month when the work is performed (September), regardless of whether or not the expense has been paid in cash. We assume that the productivity of employees enhanced the revenue earned in September. By recording the expense in September, expenses for that month are properly matched with the revenues for the month.

Some additional accounting principles are defined in the following pages.

The **entity concept** states that accounting information is accumulated and reported for a clearly defined economic entity regardless of its legal status.

For example, accounting for the business transactions of a sole proprietorship would be separate from the accounting of the owner's personal transactions. This means that the assets of a business must be viewed separately from the personal assets of its owners. Whether the owner is a sole proprietor, a partner, or a shareholder of a corporation, the owner's personal assets must never be commingled with the business assets on the balance sheet. For example, a savings account of an owner of a veterinary hospital cannot appear as an asset on the business's balance sheet. Similarly, the business owner's home, car, other investments, and interests in other business ventures should not be included in the veterinary hospital balance sheet.

The **going concern concept** states that, for financial statement reporting purposes, it is assumed that the business will continue operating for the foreseeable future.

Since the business is considered to be continuous, the company must periodically report on its earnings. It is further assumed that the assets of the business will be used in operations rather than be liquidated.

The **historical cost principle** states that assets should be recorded in the accounting records and reported in the financial statements at their historical (original) cost.

Because companies are considered to be going concerns, the assets will not be sold but rather will be used in operations. For this reason, assets are not shown at market or liquidation values, but rather at cost.

The **stable dollar concept** states that amounts in the financial statements should be stated in terms of dollars with the implication that the dollar is a stable unit of measure.

Financial statements are prepared using historical costs that have not been adjusted for changes in the general price level.

The **objectivity principle** states that measurements should be made as objectively as possible.

This is another reason that assets are reported at cost in the financial statements. Cost is considered to be more objective in that it does not favor any one user. In addition, cost can be easily verified by examining documents (such as the purchase invoice).

The **conservatism principle** requires that accounting information be presented in the least optimistic way.

In other words, if two possible outcomes are equally as likely to occur, the financial information should be presented in the more unfavorable way. By doing this, the assets of the business will have a tendency to be understated versus overstated, while liabilities will have a tendency to be overstated.

The **materiality principle** requires that only material items be reflected in the financial statements.

An item is considered to be material if that item, when omitted from or reported erroneously in the financial statements, would have changed the user's opinion or judgment about the financial statements. What is material for one company may not be material for another company. For example, omitting a $1,000 sale for a company with annual sales of $20,000 would be material, but for a company with annual sales of $1 million the $1,000 sale is immaterial.

The **comparability principle** requires that the financial statements must be comparable not only from year to year within the same company but also between one company and another company.

Even though the financial information must be comparable, the company still has certain alternative methods from which to choose in recording specific types of transactions.

The **time period assumption,** or periodicity, states that financial statements are broken up into various time periods.

For example, since the going concern concept assumes that the company will continue to operate in the foreseeable future, the time period assumption breaks this continuous existence into individual financial reporting periods. The most common reporting period is one year. Many companies use a calendar year for a reporting period while others use a fiscal year. A **fiscal year** is a year that does not end on December 31. Companies that use fiscal years usually plan for their year end to occur when inventory is at its lowest level.

By using these guidelines, users of accounting information can better understand the financial information that is provided to them as an aid in making business decisions. These accounting concepts underlay all of accounting, including the materials presented in the rest of this course.

CAREERS IN ACCOUNTING[1]

Accountants have been termed "business physicians" because they are often asked to diagnose business problems and prescribe remedies to these problems. An **accountant** is a professional who manages the collection of financial and nonfinancial data and is responsible for the analysis, interpretation and reporting of information to decision makers. **Bookkeepers** and accounting clerks, in contrast, are responsible for collecting and entering data into the accounting system.

---

[1] The authors thank Steven J. Adams from California State University, Chico for his major contribution to this Case Reading.

The most common student misconception about accounting is that the job requires hours upon hours of solitary number crunching and little or no human interaction. On the contrary, accounting is people-oriented and requires excellent communication and teamwork skills. The misconception arises because the jobs of bookkeepers and accounting clerks (often called accountants in many organizations) tend to be solitary, number-crunching positions, but professionals with degrees in accounting do not perform these tasks. Accountants also perform a wide variety of services to organizations, so it is possible to find positions that fit your interests and personality.

ACCOUNTING EMPLOYMENT OUTLOOK

Employment prospects for accountants are excellent. The U.S. Bureau of Labor Statistics predicts that accounting and financial management will have one of the largest increases in employment of any profession between 1996 and 2006, as shown in Exhibit 1-2.2. Most accounting graduates are offered an accounting or related job either before or shortly after they graduate. Many non-accounting graduates, including those in some business options, have great difficulty finding jobs after graduation, and those who do get offers often end up working outside their area of academic training.

In addition, many accountants, particularly those with some computer training, are employed as systems analysts. As Exhibit 1-2.2 indicates, system analysis is projected to be the fastest growing of all professions. Accountants often are employed as systems analysts because the largest system in most companies is the accounting system. Although the Bureau of Labor Statistics does not make a projection, college placement officers confirm that a combination of accounting and computer information course work results in some of the "hottest" recruiting efforts and highest paying job offers.

TYPES OF ACCOUNTING POSITIONS

Every organization in every country requires the services of accountants. The variety of services used includes the management of a firm's financial systems, auditing, managerial accounting, consulting, tax accounting and environmental accounting. Many of these areas of opportunity are described in the following section. If some of these areas sound like an attractive career path, you should talk to your instructor and search the library and World Wide Web for additional information. There are several good accounting career web sites, many of which can be accessed through the web site for this course.

External Auditing

Certified public accountants (CPAs) perform audits of an organization's financial statements and render an opinion as to whether the statements present fairly the financial position and the results of operations of the organization. Auditors spend much of their time at their clients' premises and have the opportunity to work with a number of different organizations. Auditors also frequently serve as business consultants, particularly to smaller clients.

Auditing is a demanding profession. Firms are looking for graduates with the following traits:

- Good oral and written communication skills
- Excellent analytical abilities (ability to analyze complex, unstructured problems)
- Ability to learn independently (have learned how to learn)
- Broad business knowledge

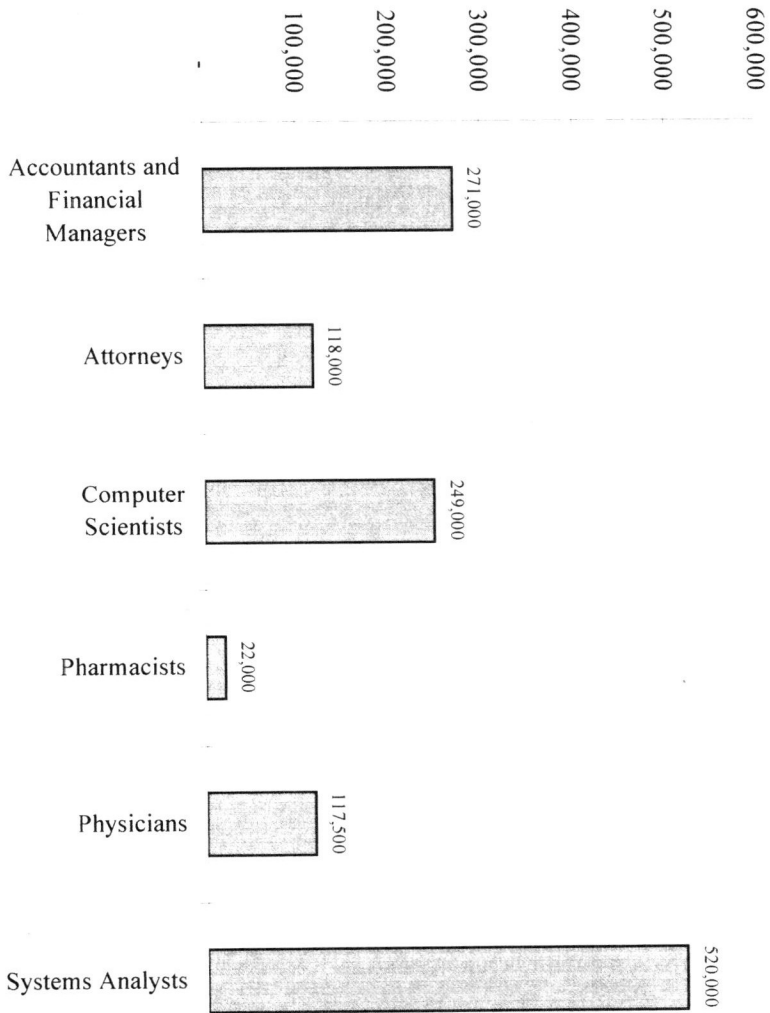

Exhibit 1-2.2
Growth in Selected Professions

Growth in Selected Professions 1996-2006
Bureau of Labor Statistics

Many CPA firms specialize in certain industries or areas such as real estate, small business, high technology, or international trade. For example, one CPA firm has offices in Los Angeles, Palm Springs, New York, and Nashville. Their specialty is providing accounting services for musical performers ranging from Barbara Streisand to rap groups.

Since organizations in all industries and throughout the world require accounting services, auditing (as well as corporate accounting) provides students with the opportunity to combine an interest in accounting with another outside interest. Accounting graduates can enhance their marketability greatly by combining an accounting degree with other coursework in areas such as MIS, real estate, small business, or a foreign language.

Salary range:
| Entry level: | $25,000 to $35,000 |
| Senior partner at a large firm: | $250,000 and up. |

Corporate Accounting

The majority of degreed accountants work for corporations. Corporate accountants perform a variety of specialized tasks, as described below.

- Managerial accounting is the preparation of information that helps management operate a company more effectively. Introduction to Accounting II focuses on this area of corporate accounting. Additional coursework in operations management and MIS will enhance your career opportunities.

- Internal auditing is similar to the work done by external auditors. One major difference is the increased emphasis on operational or management audits.

- Accounting systems involves the design and operation of a company's computerized accounting information systems.

- Financial and tax accounting involves the management of the accounting data collection process and the preparation of financial statements and tax reports.

Salary range:
| Entry level: | $20,000 to $40,000 |
| Vice-President, Finance at a sizable company: | $200,000 and up |

Some typical advertisements for corporate accounting positions are presented in Exhibit 1-2.3 on the following page.

Tax Accounting

Tax accountants are responsible for the preparation of federal, state, and local tax returns. More importantly, they work with management and individuals to structure business decisions in a way that minimizes tax liabilities. This type of work is called tax planning.

As noted in the corporate accounting section, some tax accountants work in corporate tax departments. Others work in the tax areas of larger CPA firms and government agencies, including the Internal Revenue Service (IRS) and state tax agencies. In addition, most CPAs who have their own practice have a heavy focus on tax accounting.

Exhibit 1-2.3
Sample Corporate Accounting Position Announcements

Electronics manufacturing company seeks a CMA with 10 plus years' related experience and a strong understanding of various costing systems. Other responsibilities include strategic planning and risk analysis of product lines. Salary to $80,000 plus an excellent benefits package.[1]

International manufacturing company seeks a CMA to oversee a staff of four. Candidate will be responsible for all areas of the accounting operation. Excellent opportunity with a growing organization. Excellent benefits, including salary to $60,000.[1]

Manufacturing firm seeks a "shirt-sleeve" Controller. Ideal candidate will have ten years plus experience analyzing financial information, with extensive knowledge of financial reporting. Food industry and computer system design capability is a plus. Salary to $90,000 with excellent benefits.[2]

Fast growing international company seeks a Vice President of Finance. A CPA is preferred for this challenging and exciting position. The ideal candidate will have a minimum of 15 years of experience. International and treasury experience preferred, knowledge of re-engineering processes is a plus. Compensation package includes a salary to $135,000.[2]

Sources: [1] *Management Accounting*, August, 1998. [2] *Controller Magazine*, August, 1997

Management

Accounting has traditionally been an excellent path to middle and upper management positions. Numerous chief executive officers (CEOs) and chief operating officers (COOs) of major companies are accountants by training. One study showed that accounting was the second most common undergraduate background of CEOs at large U.S. companies (engineering was the most common undergraduate degree), although most CEOs in the study also had an MBA degree. One example is the first woman president of an operating division at a major oil company, who is an accountant by training. Another example is the president of the huge international advertising company, Saatchi & Saatchi, who is an accountant.

Why is accounting good training for management positions? Obviously, accounting develops strong analytical skills and excellent data analysis abilities, which are invaluable to managers. Less obvious to students is the broad exposure to all areas of an organization many accountants receive early in their careers. Accountants routinely work with marketing people to help solve marketing problems, production people to help solve production problems, human resources people to help solve human resources problems, etc. It is this unique opportunity to learn how the different areas of a company operate and the extensive professional contacts developed in the process that give accountants an edge when management positions become available.

Governmental Accounting

Federal, state, and local governments, as well as not-for-profit organizations, hire an enormous number of accountants for a wide variety of positions. All organizations have a need for financial and systems accountants. The General Accounting Office (GAO) estimates that about 15 percent of all federal expenditures (over $200 billion) are unaccounted for. Naturally there is a big push to hire accountants and increase governmental accountability. Government agencies at all levels also hire tax accountants.

Several especially interesting government agencies also hire accountants. The GAO prepares, at the request of Congress, reports evaluating the costs and effectiveness of federal programs. The Federal Bureau of Investigation (FBI), which primarily recruits accountants and lawyers, aggressively pursues accounting majors. The reason for the FBI's interest in accountants is the investigation of white-collar crime (remember that the FBI nailed Al Capone on income tax evasion charges!).

Specialty Areas

There are a number of more specialized areas of accounting that are growing quickly and provide exciting career opportunities. One is **environmental accounting**. This rapidly growing area involves computing the costs and benefits of environmental protection programs and estimating companies' potential environmental legal liabilities.

A second specialty area is **forensic accounting**. This involves the investigation of financial fraud and abuse and the presentation of results in a court of law. This is a booming area that has been fueled by fraudulent real estate, securities, and savings and loan cases.

A third rapidly growing specialty area is quality auditing. The International Standards Organization (ISO) has a rigorous quality certification program known as ISO 9000. Most European and many Japanese and American companies are requiring that all products purchased be from an ISO 9000 certified vendor. As a result, virtually all major U.S. companies plan to become ISO 9000 certified in the near future. A key requirement of certification is an ongoing quality audit of all major processes within a firm. Accountants with extensive training in quality management have the ideal background to become quality auditors.

SUMMARY

This case reading emphasizes the concept of feedback and the importance of accounting information in a market economy. Several different attributes of accounting information are discussed; specifically relevance, reliability, comparability, and consistency. The case reading also contained materials on the impact of accounting information on the environment.

The accrual method of accounting states that revenues and expenses should be recognized when they are earned and incurred, respectively, rather than when cash flows in or out of the business entity. The accrual method has been accepted as a more accurate measurement approach than its alternative, the cash basis.

The use of generally accepted accounting principles (GAAP) is critical to users of accounting information in placing trust in the truthfulness of the financial statements. Statements lacking the adherence to sound standards such as those promulgated by the Financial Accounting Standards Board cannot be compared to other company reports. At times in the history of the U.S. financial markets such recklessly prepared financial statements were used to defraud investors out of vast amounts of money. Today, the rapid pace of electronic dissemination of information has been the impetus for the Securities and Exchange Commission and the FASB to redouble their efforts to monitor the reports of publicly held companies.

Accounting is a people-oriented profession that requires excellent communication and team skills. An accounting degree, particularly when combined with supporting coursework. provides an enormous variety of career opportunities. You are encouraged to schedule an appointment with your instructor to discuss accounting career opportunities further. More information about accounting careers can be found at the web site for this book.

EXERCISES

Exercises

Exercise 1 Feedback. Define the systems concept of feedback.

Exercise 2 Feedback in education. Give an example of feedback in an educational system.

Exercise 3 Feedback in mechanical systems. Give an example of feedback in a mechanical system.

Exercise 4 Feedback in the economy. Give an example of feedback in the U.S. economic system.

Exercise 5 Feedback in an enterprise. Give an example of feedback in the operation of an enterprise.

Exercise 6 Compare economic systems. What is the distinguishing characteristic between a free market economy and a government-controlled economy?

Exercise 7 Relevance of financial statements. As an investor, give an example of how financial statements meet the criterion of relevance.

Exercise 8 Reliability of financial statements. As a government official working for the Securities and Exchange Commission, give an example of how you would judge financial statements to meet the criterion of reliability.

Exercise 9 Comparability of financial statements. As a loan officer for a bank, why would it be important for you to trust that financial statements presented to you by prospective borrowers meet the test of comparability?

Exercise 10 Consistency of financial statements. As an investment advisor, why is it important for you to trust that financial statements of a certain company meet the test of consistency?

Exercise 11 GAAP. What is the importance of GAAP?

Exercise 12 Accrual Accounting. Define the accrual basis of accounting.

Exercise 13 When to Recognize Revenue. If Adac Corporation ships $100,000 of goods to its customers in the month of December, but is not paid until January, in which month should the income or loss from the sale be reported?

Exercise 14 When to Recognize an Expense. Perris Incorporated wrote a check in 2002 for $500,000 to pay (in advance) rent on its corporate offices for the year 2003. In which year will net income be affected by this payment?

Exercise 15 Answer the following questions.

    a. Why have accountants been called "business physicians"?

    b. How are employment prospects for accountants?

    c. How do these prospects compare with the job prospects for bookkeepers?

    d. What is the difference between the jobs performed by accountants versus the jobs of bookkeepers?

Exercise 16 Jobs of CPAs and management accountants. Compare and contrast the jobs of external auditors with that of corporate accountants, including a discussion of entry level salaries and the type of work each accountant can expect to perform.

Exercise 17 Abbreviations. What do the following abbreviations mean?

    a. CPA

    b. CEO

    c. COO

    d. IRS

    e. GAO

Exercise 18 How does the FBI use its accountants? The FBI is a large employer of accountants. Why would this governmental agency want accounting expertise? Another form of investigative work is performed by forensic accountants. What type of crime do forensic accountants usually investigate?

Exercise 19 See the web site for this book. Go to the web site for this course to the section on Accounting Careers. Visit at least one web site listed on this page. Print the web page(s) and summarize the information contained at that web site in a short paragraph.

Case 1-2

THE ROLE OF ACCOUNTING
IN SOCIETY

Case Objective

To become familiar with some aspect of the role of accounting in society.

Requirements

1. Go to the library and search the accounting periodicals listed at the end of this case to find a recent (1994 or later) feature-length article (i.e., an article at least four pages in length) that deals with some aspect of the use, preparation, or audit of accounting information or the development of rules for the preparation or audit of accounting information.

2. Write a one- or two-page paper, (typed, double-spaced, and carefully edited) that includes the following:

    *   One paragraph that summarizes the major thesis of the article.

    *   One to two paragraphs that briefly identify the most important things you learned from the article about users, uses of accounting information, preparers, auditors, rules, and/or rule-making bodies involved with accounting information.

    *   One to two paragraphs that briefly identify the most important questions about accounting that you would like to have answered as a result of reading your selected article.

    *   Attach a copy of the article to the paper when it is turned in.

This paper is due at the beginning of the class period that is indicated on the course schedule. No late papers will be accepted. Papers will be graded according to the following criteria:

*   Appropriateness of the selected article.

*   Conformance of paper to the paragraph requirements set forth above.

*   Quality of editing and writing style (e.g., clear, coherent, and free of spelling errors, typos, and incomplete sentences).

List of Appropriate Accounting Periodicals

New Accountant
Journal of Accountancy
CPA Journal
Government Accountants' Journal

Management Accounting
Journal of Cost Management
Internal Auditor

Case Reading 1-3

DECISION MAKING

INTRODUCTION

All forms of organizations engage in economic transactions resulting from decisions made within these organizations. We as individuals also make many decisions each day, both economic and noneconomic in nature. Each of us made the decision today as to when to get up, what to wear, what activities to do, and to read this text. Each of these activities required a decision on your part.

We are especially concerned about decision making for economic transactions in this course because of its effect on recording accounting transactions. Accounting is transaction-based, and transactions are based on economic decisions. As you progress through this course it will become increasingly evident that accounting is based on economic decision making.

This case reading addresses decision making with emphasis on both economic and ethical considerations. All decisions contain ethical dimensions whether the decision maker is aware or unaware of the ethical implications of his/her actions. The need for ethical behavior in society is explained, and an eight-step process to make ethical decisions is suggested.

DECISION MAKING[1]

Economic decision making is the process of making decisions that have economic consequences and is a normal and constant activity in most organizations. An economic decision-making process may be divided into the steps shown in Exhibit 1-3.1 and described below.

Define the Problem

The formal economic decision-making process begins with a statement of the problem being addressed. What is the problem? For example, sales have declined, but why? Are prices too high? Has quality deteriorated? Is advertising effective? Asking the right questions at this step clarifies the problem and removes some of the surrounding ambiguities.

Specify the Goal(s)

Goals (objectives) are statements of what an organization wants to achieve. Is the goal to maximize profit, minimize cost, or attain a particular product quality level? If two or more goals are specified, the decision maker must determine which goals act as constraints (for example, to maximize profit subject to a specified impact on the environment).

---

[1] The authors thank Richard B. Lea from California State University, Chico for his major contributions to this Case Reading.

Exhibit 1-3.1

	Economic Decision-Making	
1	Define the problem	
2	Specify the goal(s)	
3	Identify feasible alternatives (mutually exclusive and exhaustive set)	
4	Predict possible outcomes (mutually exclusive and exhaustive set for each alternative)	
5	Collect additional relevant quantitative data	
6	Identify relevant qualitative considerations	
7	Make the decision	

Identify Feasible Alternatives

A decision involves the choice among a set of two or more mutually exclusive, **feasible alternative** courses of action–for example, different possible prices, different levels of advertising. etc. (A set of alternatives is mutually exclusive if the selection of one of the alternatives precludes the selection of any of the other alternatives.)   An infeasible alternative would be advertising that exceeds the company's current level of available resources.

Predict Possible Outcomes

For each alternative course of action, the decision maker must identify/predict a set of mutually exclusive and exhaustive outcomes that may occur and the nature of the costs and benefits associated with those outcomes. Because the future is uncertain, a particular alternative may lead to two or more different outcomes.   For example, the effect of increasing advertising for a particular product may or may not lead to competitors' retaliation, which in turn may or may not lead to a reduction in sales volume.

Collect Additional Quantitative Data

Quantitative estimates (predictions) of costs and benefits are needed. **Quantitative information** is information that can be measured in numerical terms. In general, more effort should be devoted to obtaining reliable (accurate) estimates of those costs or benefits that are most relevant (critical) to the decision. **Relevant information** has the capacity to make a difference in decisions. **Reliable information** accurately portrays the phenomenon it is meant to represent and is free from error and bias.

Identify Relevant Qualitative Considerations

Important economic decisions rarely depend solely on quantitative analysis. **Qualitative factors** cannot be measured in numerical terms (for example, the effect of a decision on the morale of company employees).

Make the Decision

The alternative is selected that appears to "best" satisfy the decision maker's specified goal(s), taking into account both quantitative and qualitative considerations. The effect of the decision should be to maximize the net benefit to the organization from the feasible alternatives available.

AUTO LOAN EXAMPLE

The economic-decision making process can be illustrated by considering a decision problem involving a personal car loan. Exhibit 1-3.2 presents an analysis of this problem from the perspectives of two different decision makers–the auto loan officer in a bank and the individual car buyer.

Exhibit 1-3.2

Steps in Decision Making

Decision Elements/Steps	Loan Officer	Borrower
The Problem	• Borrower approaches bank for an auto loan	• Needs a car and related bank financing
The Goals	• Profit • Growth • Responsiveness to community funding needs	• Minimize cost of the auto purchase
The Alternatives	• Whether to lend • If money is lent: --Interest rate --Repayment period --Default provisions	• Bank A vs. Bank B
Possible Outcomes	• If money is not lent: --no profit, etc. • If money is lent: --Timely repayment --Default/repossession --Gain --Loss	• Repay loan • Default: --Future credit --Lose car
Relevant Data	• Borrower's financial condition • Competitor's loan offerings • Bank funds available for lending	• Financial condition • Bank A vs. Bank B deal
Qualitative Considerations	• Is the borrower a special case (e.g., granddaughter of the bank President)?	• How "good" a car is needed?
Decision	• Lend?	• Borrow? If so, from which bank?

COLLEGE LIVING EXAMPLE

Decision-making concepts are further illustrated by the following example involving a college student.

Susan Jones is about to enter her second year of college. She intends to major in finance. During her freshman year, Susan lived in a residence hall where she shared a two-person-occupancy apartment and subscribed to the 15-meals-per-week food service. Room and board for her freshman academic year amounted to $3,600. Her experience at the dorm was mixed: "Although I liked my roommate, things got a little crazy at times. Also, it's very hard to study in the dorm," she explained.

Susan is considering whether to (1) continue to live in a residence hall, (2) enter the thematic living program, or (3) find an off-campus apartment. If she enters the thematic living program, she will share a living unit with 14 other students who are majoring in one of the business options (finance, accounting, etc.). Under this program, room and board would cost approximately $4,000 for the academic year. In thinking about this option, Susan observed, "I think it would be great to live with students who are all pursuing a common academic program, but I worry about a lack of privacy in a unit shared by 14 students."

Susan estimates that an off-campus, two-person apartment would cost each occupant from $165 to $325 per month, plus utilities. Susan would have to seek a roommate because none of her friends want to rent an apartment. She also anticipates the need to subscribe to the college's 15-meals-per-week food plan since she hates to cook. However, this could change if her roommate turned out to be a good cook.

A step-by-step analysis of Susan's economic decision problem would proceed as follows:

1.   The decision problem:

> Susan must decide upon appropriate room and board arrangements for her sophomore year.

2.   Goals:

> In selecting her living arrangements, Susan's goals are likely to include:
> - Keeping costs within some specified budget (or cost minimization)
> - Availability of "quiet" study time
> - Compatible room/unit mates
> - Avoidance of food preparation

3 and 4. Alternatives and possible outcomes:

A.   Live in a residence hall:
1. Costs as expected, quiet, likable roommate, good food
2. Costs higher than expected, noisy, terrible roommate, bad food

B.   Enter the thematic living program:
1. Costs as expected, quiet, compatible group within unit, good food
2. Other permutations of elements of B1

C. Find an off-campus apartment:
  1. Costs as expected, quiet, likable roommate, good food
  2. Other permutations of elements of C1

5. Additional relevant quantitative data:

Susan should collect the following additional financial information:

- Estimate of her resources available for room and board–what is her budget?
- Estimate of next year's room and board for a residence hall (the $3,600 is last year's cost)
- More precise estimate for the cost of an apartment
- Cost of utilities for an apartment
- Cost of food if the apartment roommate does the cooking
- Cost of the 15-meals-per-week food plan

6. Qualitative considerations:

- Importance of quiet time, compatible roommates, associating with other business majors, quality of food, and experience of living off campus.

7. The decision:

- What would you do in Susan's position?

ETHICAL DECISION MAKING[2]

Ethics can be defined as the moral principles that determine the "rightness" or "wrongness" of human behavior. Even though thoughtful, caring individuals may disagree about the details of ethical behavior, everyone seems to recognize **ethical failure** when it appears in the media as current events or humor. There are many different approaches to resolving ethical dilemmas. Ultimately each individual must decide and is responsible for what is right or just.

Even though there may be disagreements about peripheral issues, there is a core set of ethical principles that transcend time, religion, and culture. Most individuals agree on the nature of these ethical principles regardless of religious or cultural background. An example of these fundamental ethical principles developed by the Josephson Institute of Ethics is provided in Exhibit 1-3.3. The Josephson Institute is a not-for-profit organization that promotes and encourages ethical behavior in business, professions, and personal activities.

According to Michael Josephson of the Josephson Institute, surveys of politicians, journalists, lawyers, accountants, and others reveal that our society suffers from a lack of **ethical behavior**. Most individuals believe that ethical problems stem from other groups (not their own). If their own profession has had problems, it is due to "a few bad apples." Generally, people believe that their own organization is more ethical than others in their profession. Additionally, these individuals feel that they personally are more ethical than others in their organizations. It is impossible for everyone to be more ethical than everyone else. The reason

[2] The authors thank Wesley E. Harder of California State University, Chico for his major contributions to this Case Reading.

for these apparent contradictory perceptions is that we judge our own ethical behavior based on our best moment, while others judge our ethical behavior based on our worst moment.

This list of **ethical principles** incorporates the characteristics and values that most people associate with ethical behavior.

Exhibit 1-3.3
List of Ethical Principles[3]
Developed by the Josephson Institute of Ethics

Honesty Be truthful, sincere, forthright, straightforward, frank, candid; do not cheat, steal, lie, deceive, or act deviously.

Integrity Be principled, honorable, upright, courageous, and act on convictions; do not be two-faced or unscrupulous, or adopt an end-justifies-the-means philosophy that ignores principle.

Promise Keeping Be worthy of trust; keep promises; fulfill commitments; abide by the spirit as well as the letter of an agreement; do not interpret agreements in an unreasonably technical or legalistic manner in order to rationalize non-compliance or create excuses and justifications for breaking commitments.

Loyalty (Fidelity) Be faithful and loyal to family, friends, employers, clients, and country; do not use or disclose information learned in confidence; in a professional context, safeguard the ability to make independent professional judgments by scrupulously avoiding undue influences and conflicts of interest.

Fairness Be fair and open-minded; be willing to admit error and, where appropriate, change positions and beliefs; demonstrate a commitment to justice, the equal treatment of individuals, and tolerance for and acceptance of diversity; do not overreach or take undue advantage of another's mistakes or adversities.

Caring for Others Be caring, kind, and compassionate; share; be giving; be of service to others; help those in need and avoid harming others.

Respect for Others Demonstrate respect for human dignity, privacy and the right to self-determination of all people; be courteous, prompt, and decent; provide others with the information they need to make informed decisions about their own lives; do not patronize, embarrass, or demean.

Responsible Citizenship Obey just laws; if a law is unjust, openly protest it; exercise all democratic rights and privileges responsibly by participation (voting and expressing informed views); openly respect and honor democratic processes of decision making; avoid unnecessary secrecy or concealment of information, and assure that others have all the information they need to make intelligent choices and exercise their rights.

Pursuit of Excellence Pursue excellence in all matters; in meeting your personal and professional responsibilities, be diligent, reliable, industrious, and committed; perform all tasks to the best of your ability; develop and maintain a high degree of competence; be well informed and well prepared; do not be content with mediocrity; do not "win at any cost."

Accountability Be accountable, accept responsibility for decisions, for the foreseeable consequences of actions and inactions, and for setting an example for others. Parents, teachers, employers, many professionals and public officials have a special obligation to lead by example, to safeguard and advance the integrity and reputation of their families, companies, professions, and the government itself; an ethically sensitive individual avoids even the appearance of impropriety, and takes whatever actions are necessary to correct or prevent inappropriate conduct of others.

---

[3] Reprinted with the permission of the Josephson Institute.

The Cost of Ethics

The cost of behaving ethically is often overestimated. For example, you may feel that being ethical in a given situation might be an unpopular choice. Peer pressure might suggest that you should make an unethical decision. At the time, the cost of behaving ethically may seem very high, but over the long run the benefits of ethical behavior should outweigh the costs.

These benefits (self-esteem, personal integrity, respect, clear conscience, etc.) are often underestimated in the short run, but become more evident over a longer time span. For every ethical decision that is made, you should ask yourself if you feel comfortable about the decision. Could you tell others about it? Your parents? Your spiritual advisor? Your supervisors? The judge?

Ethical Principles vs. Nonethical Principles

Often times ethical issues involve a conflict of ethical and nonethical principles. For example, a person might cheat on a test to obtain prestige for receiving one of the highest grades in the class. In this case the conflict could be stated as honesty vs. prestige. Examples of ethical principles were given in Exhibit 1-3.3. Nonethical principles include the following:

- wealth
- safety
- security
- prestige
- status
- self-esteem
- fame

Nonethical principles are ethically neutral. That is, they are neither ethical nor unethical.

Ethical Theory

Over the years many different approaches to solving ethical dilemmas have been suggested. One of the most famous is the Utilitarian approach. This approach suggests that the final solution to an ethical dilemma should be the solution that provides the greatest amount of good for the greatest number of people. Another well-known approach suggests that each alternative should be evaluated based on its fairness to all stakeholders. The "Golden Rule" is an example of another common ethics framework. Even though there are many different ideas on how to approach ethical situations, all of them recognize the fact that, in the end, it is each individual who must evaluate the alternatives and make the decision.

Steps in the Ethical Decision-Making Process

The ethical decision-making process can be summarized in the steps shown below. This exhibit is the same as Exhibit 1-3.1 except a new step, number 3, has been added so there are eight steps in the ethical decision making process instead of seven as illustrated for economic decision making.

Exhibit 1-3.4

	Ethical Decision Making	
1	Define the problem
2	Specify the goal(s)
3	Define the ethical issues and identify stakeholders
4	Identify feasible alternatives
5	Predict possible outcomes (mutually exclusive)
6	Collect additional relevant quantitative data
7	Identify relevant qualitative considerations
8	Make the decision

1. Define the problem

   The ethical decision-making process begins with a careful statement of the problem being addressed. What is the problem and what are the relevant facts in the problem faced by the decision maker? Try to avoid thinking about alternative courses of action until Step 4. It is very important that the problem is carefully defined before continuing with the rest of the ethical decision-making process.

2. Specify the goal(s)

   Goals are statements of what a person or an organization wants to achieve. Is the goal to maximize profit, minimize cost, attain a particular quality level, or have a superior reputation? If two or more goals are specified, the decision maker must determine which goals are subject to constraints. For example, a goal to maximize profit may be subject to a specified impact on the environment.

3. Define ethical issues and identify stakeholders

   State the major ethical issues from the decision maker's point of view. Ethical dilemmas arise in situations involving a choice between two (or more) alternatives that have significant–often adverse–impacts on others. State the issues as conflicts between some combination of ethical and/or nonethical principles. Examples include fairness vs. wealth or honesty vs. prestige. There are often several such dilemmas in any decision situation.

   Stakeholders are all of the parties that may be affected by the alternative courses of action under consideration by the decision maker. Try to think broadly about all parties that may be affected by the possible courses of action. Determine who is affected by the outcome of the decision and how each person or group is affected.

4. Identify feasible alternatives

   A decision involves making a choice among a set of two or more mutually exclusive, feasible alternative courses of action available to the person who must resolve the dilemma. (A set of alternatives is mutually exclusive if the selection of one alternative precludes the selection of any of the other alternatives.) Try to think broadly and creatively about all alternative courses of action available to the decision maker. Problems are rarely of the either/or variety. For example, a narrow view of a problem may suggest that the decision maker must either comply with his supervisor or quit. More broadly, however, other alternatives might be to refuse to comply and point out to the supervisor your reservations about her request; go around the supervisor and gain necessary support from others; "blow the whistle" (i.e., go outside the organization and report your supervisor's questionable request).

5. Predict possible outcomes (include consequences)

For each particular alternative course of action, the decision maker must identify/predict a set of mutually exclusive and collectively exhaustive outcomes that may occur and the nature of the costs and benefits associated with those outcomes. *Each outcome should address the goals of the decision maker.* Ethical consequences should also be considered in the cost and benefits associated with the outcomes. Consequences should include consideration of economic cost and benefits; basic human "rights"; and matters of justice, fairness, and equity. When identifying the likely consequences of each alternative, it is essential to evaluate both the short- and long-term effects to the stakeholders.

6. Collect additional relevant quantitative data

Quantitative estimates of the costs and benefits related to each feasible alternative are needed to provide the decision maker with information on the consequences associated with each alternative. Reliable (accurate) estimates of the costs or benefits that are most relevant (critical) to the decision should be collected and presented. Relevant information has the capacity to make a difference in decisions. Reliable information accurately portrays the phenomenon it is meant to represent and is free from error and bias.

7. Identify relevant qualitative considerations

Important decisions rarely depend solely on quantitative analysis. Important qualitative considerations, which cannot be measured in terms of numbers, are also important. For example, what is the relative importance of the separate goals identified in Step 2?

8. Make the decision

The "best" alternative satisfies the decision maker's specified goal(s), taking into account ethical issues, alternatives, consequences, and the quantitative and qualitative considerations. Whenever an ethical principle is in conflict with a nonethical principle the alternative that includes the ethical principle should be selected. If two ethical principles are in conflict, either alternative is acceptable. Keep in mind that the ethical quality of each decision made will be used by others to assess the decision maker's character.

Application of the Ethical Decision-Making Steps

George Jones works as a staff accountant for a large public accounting firm. His job entails frequent overnight visits to out-of-town clients. George is reimbursed for his out-of-pocket travel expenses on the basis of travel expense reports that he prepares on a weekly basis. These expenses, in turn, are charged to the appropriate out-of-town clients.

A good friend, Sid Smith, lives in the same town as one of George's major clients. George has been trying to make a decision as to where he will stay while working at this out-of- town client's location. George wants to be able to spend time with his friend during the audit engagement. Sid has been pressuring George to eat and sleep at his house. Sid currently works for a large hotel in town and has access to the hotel's blank lodging and restaurant invoice forms. Sid has suggested that George fill out these forms to show that he stayed at the hotel and ate meals there. When George gets reimbursed for the fictitious expenses, the two of them can split the proceeds. Sid reasons, and George agrees, that the firm (and eventually the client) should pay for lodging and meals when he's out of town. Sid persists and argues that it should be up to George where he wants to sleep and eat.

George realizes that he could stay and eat at the hotel and submit the actual expense receipts. George figures that the hotel room averages about $80 per day and meals another $50 per day. George would be reimbursed for his actual expenditures and the client would then be billed. By staying and eating in the hotel, George would have more interaction with other members of the audit staff and get to know them better. The CPA firm likes the staff to spend social time to get to know each other on out-of-town engagements and George likes his job and the people he works with. He thinks that he has a very bright future with this firm and, above all, he wants to keep his job.

Alternatively, he could stay at Sid's place and eat at the hotel. By eating at the hotel, he could still interact with the other auditors and be able to visit with Sid and Sid's wife for the remaining part of the night. George figures that it wouldn't "cost" Sid any money if he just slept there and didn't eat. Sid just grumbles. Why should the client benefit when George sleeps at his house? The client will never know and, after all, he (Sid) could sure use the extra cash. George doesn't want to lie to his firm but he doesn't want to make Sid unhappy either. He could possibly give all the money to Sid and not feel as guilty about violating company policy.

Step 1. Define the problem

The problem is to determine where George should eat and sleep when he is out of town and how the expenses (if any) should be reported. The facts are:

- Company policy about out of town expenditures
- Availability of blank hotel receipts and restaurant receipts
- Sid's desire for George to lie about receipts and split proceeds
- CPA firm's desire for staff members to socialize in off hours

Step 2. Specify the goal(s)

- George wants to keep his job with the firm first and foremost
- George wants to visit his friend.
- George wants to keep his friend happy

Step 3. Define ethical issues and identify stakeholders

Ethical issues are:

> Honesty vs. Wealth - Should George correctly report his expenses and therefore receive reduced compensation (honesty) or should he report fictitious expenses and split the proceeds with Sid (wealth)? Notice that an ethical principle is in conflict with a nonethical principle.

> Loyalty vs. Loyalty - Should George comply with the firm's travel policy (loyalty to the firm) or do as his friend requests and submit fake receipts (loyalty to Sid)? Here it appears there is an ethical principle on both sides of the dilemma. However, loyalty to Sid must be discounted since Sid is asking George to be dishonest.

Stakeholders are:

- George and his family
- Sid and his family
- CPA firm
- Client
- Hotel and restaurants
- Other staff accountants
- Accounting profession
- IRS and other tax jurisdictions

Step 4. Identify feasible alternatives

- George could sleep and eat at the hotel and report actual expenses.
- George could prepare fictitious invoices and stay with Sid and,
- Split proceeds with Sid, or
- Give all proceeds to Sid.
- George could eat and sleep at Sid's and report no travel expenses.
- George could eat at hotel and sleep at Sid's.
- George could discuss his situation with the firm's administrative partner to see if they would be able to adjust the policy to his situation.

Step 5. Predict possible outcomes

In this step, each alternative would be addressed and a list of outcomes, including consequences, for each stakeholder would be identified (we have only included outcomes for a few stakeholders here). The solution here lists a possible solution for Alternative A and a partial solution for Alternative B. (Note below how each outcome addresses all three of the decision maker's goals.)

Goals: Keep his job, visit Sid, keep Sid happy

Alternative A: George could sleep and eat at the hotel and report actual expenses.

Outcome 1 George would keep his job, be able to visit Sid, convince Sid that lying on the travel forms is wrong, and therefore keep his friend happy.

The positive consequences of this action are:

1. George could still mingle with his audit staff members.
2. George would still feel good that he had acted ethically and therefore had upheld the ethical standards of the CPA firm and the accounting profession.
3. Sid and the hotel would not be involved in fraudulent paperwork.
4. The client would be reimbursing for actual expenses according to the CPA firm policy.

The negative consequences are:

1. Sid and George would not receive any extra money over what was actually spent for travel.
2. George might not get to visit as much with Sid as he would like.

Outcome 2   George would keep his job, be able to visit Sid, but Sid might continue to be unhappy with George. (Note how changing just one of the items in the outcome set creates a new mutually exclusive outcome.)

The positive consequences of this action are:

1. George could still mingle with his audit staff members.
2. George would feel good that he had acted ethically and therefore had upheld the ethical standards of the CPA firm and the accounting profession.
3. Sid and the hotel would not be involved in fraudulent paperwork.
4. The client would be reimbursing for actual expenses according to the CPA firm policy.

The negative consequences are:

1. Sid and George would not receive any extra money over what was actually spent for travel.
2. Sid could be angry with George's decision, which might strain their friendship.

Outcome 3, etc. Other permutations of the three goals.

Alternative B: George could prepare fictitious invoices and stay with Sid.

Outcome 1   George eventually loses his job because of his dishonesty, he gets to visit Sid, and Sid is happy.

The positive consequences of this action are:

1. Sid and George receive extra money from the travel reimbursement.
2. George might enjoy Sid's company more than that of his audit staff members.
3. The other audit staff members are more aware of the firm's ethical standards.
4. The hotel might learn to keep better control over its blank food and lodging receipts.

The negative consequences are:

1. George, Sid, and the hotel are involved in fraudulent paperwork which is eventually discovered.

2. George feels guilty that he has not acted ethically and therefore has not upheld the ethical standards of the CPA firm and the accounting profession.
3. The client would be reimbursing for fictitious expenses.
4. After George is fired, the remaining audit staff have increased workloads.

Outcome 2, etc. Other permutations of the three goals.

Step 6. Collect additional relevant quantitative data

George might want to contact the hotel and calculate a more accurate estimate of the travel expenditures. He might ask the audit manager how many days they expect to be out of town so that he could estimate just how many nights and meals there are. He also might want to calculate how far Sid's house is from the client and ask Sid if he could take him to work each day or if he would have to rent a car. Who would pay for the food if he stayed at Sid's?

Step 7. Identify relevant qualitative considerations

George might want to ask Sid where he would sleep if at Sid's house. A hotel room is certainly more comfortable than a sofa bed. Other considerations would be if Sid and/or his wife are good cooks. How much time does George really want to spend with Sid? George might also consider how he would feel if he allowed Sid to falsify hotel records and consequently Sid was caught and lost his job, etc. How would the quality of George's own life change if he were dismissed for unethical behavior?

Step 8. Make the decision

In making the decision, George must consider the ethical/nonethical issues, the alternatives available to him, the possible outcomes, and the consequences (both positive and negative) to the various stakeholders for any decision he makes. Ultimately, the decision made will reflect George's personal integrity, principles, and values.

SUMMARY

Decision making is a normal part of life. In any decision-making process, you need to address your goals of the decision maker, the alternatives that are available, the possible outcomes within each alternative, and the costs and benefits of each outcome. The decisions that we make, both ethical and unethical, affect those around us. As business professionals, we should have a positive influence on society as a whole. Our success, however, should not be attained regardless of cost. The end does not always justify the means. Even though wealth and other nonethical principles are considered to be important goals, decisions made to attain those goals should contain ethical considerations and do have ethical implications.

EXERCISES AND PROBLEMS

Exercises

Exercise 1 Define the problem. Explain why the first step in the decision-making process is so important.

Exercise 2 Goals in decision making. How do organizational or personal goals fit into the economic decision-making process? How important are goals in making decisions?·

Exercise 3 Relevance definition and example. Define *relevance* as it relates to the decision-making process. Give an example of relevance to a decision you recently made.

Exercise 4 Reliable definition and example. Define *reliable* as it relates to the decision-making process. Give an example of reliable information to a decision you recently made.

Exercise 5 Considering qualitative factors. Why are qualitative factors included in decision making? Give an example of a qualitative factor that may be more important than any quantitative factor in a decision.

Exercise 6 Ethics. Define the term *ethics*. Explain what is ethical decision making.

Exercise 7 Relating to Josephson ethical principles. Select one of the principles from Exhibit 1-3.3 and explain why it is important to you in your personal life.

Exercise 8 Relating "pursuit of excellence" to accounting. One of the principles in Exhibit 1-3.3 is the "pursuit of excellence." Explain how the pursuit of excellence relates to accountants in the process of accounting in a business.

Exercise 9 Stakeholders in the ethical decision-making process. Define stakeholders as they relate to the decision making process. How do they affect the decision-making process?

Problems

Problem 1 Seven-step decision-making process to attend college. Use the seven-step decision-making process outlined in this case reading to illustrate how you made the decision to attend this college/university. Your solution should follow the form of the Susan Jones example.

Problem 2 Recent decision put into seven steps. Use the seven-step decision-making process outlined in this case reading to illustrate how you made a recent economic decision. Your solution should follow the form of the Susan Jones example.

Problem 3 Step 5, predicting possible outcomes. Refer to the George Jones illustration in the case reading. Step 5 predicts possible outcomes. Outcomes for alternatives A and B are illustrated in the case reading. Prepare two alternative outcomes for alternative C given in the case illustration. Alternative C states "George could eat and sleep at Sid's and report no travel expenses."

Problem 4 Personal ethical decision. Use the eight-step ethical decision-making process outlined in this case reading to illustrate how you made a recent ethical decision. Your solution should follow the form of the George Jones example in this case reading.

Case 1-3

JOHN'S DECISION

Case Objective

To identify the major components and steps involved in a specific personal business decision problem.

Decision: How should John spend the upcoming summer?

Near the end of his freshman year at college, John Miller is faced with the decision of whether to get a summer job, attend summer school, or start a summer painting business. John has had some experience painting houses with his father and uncle and believes it might be the most lucrative of his summer alternatives. It is now mid-April 2000 and John is contemplating the factors involved in his decision.

In early April, John was offered a job in a dry cleaning plant a few blocks from his home. He would receive a monthly salary of $800 and work from June through August. The bright side of this option is that he would know what he would earn each month (most of which he could save while living at home) and he would have a break from school. Also, he wouldn't have the risks associated with running his own business.

The school option involves taking nine units during the summer quarter at a total cost of about $3,200. Summer courses are more expensive than those taken during the regular year, but if he attends summer school three years in a row, he will graduate almost a year ahead of schedule. This would put him in his career job market (tentatively a marketing major in business) a year earlier, but he isn't sure he wants to go to school year round. He thinks he might get "burned out."

The option of starting a summer painting business is a bit scary for John because of the highly uncertain outcomes associated with such a venture. John has looked through the Yellow Pages and determined that there are over forty paint contractors operating in the vicinity. Although John has several leads and two firm commitments for house painting contracts from friends of the family, he is unsure of the total number of contracts needed during the summer to make his business a success. Also, John is uncertain about the nature and amounts of expenses that he might incur in carrying out this business.

Requirements

In brief outline format, identify and record the following components of John's decision problem (see Case Reading 1-3):

- A one-sentence statement of the problem
- Possible goals that John should consider
- Specific alternative courses of action that are under consideration

- For each alternative, two or more mutually exclusive outcomes that might occur if that alternative is selected

- For each possible outcome, a list of costs and benefits (i.e., various unfavorable or favorable impacts on John--both quantitative and qualitative) that might arise if that outcome takes place

- Additional information John needs and should collect before making a decision

- Relevant qualitative considerations John should reflect upon

Group Assignment 1-3

HOLLY'S HURDLE

Objective

To gain practice in applying a step-by-step analysis of a decision problem involving ethical considerations.

Holly Hurdle has recently been hired as a loan officer for home equity loans at Fidelity Bank. She is paid a salary of $3,000 per month and a quarterly bonus computed as follows:

Actual Loan Volume/Quarter	Budgeted Loan Volume/Quarter	Bonus
$490,000 and below	$500,000	-0-
$490,000 - $510,000		$1,000
$510,001 - $530,000		$2,000
$530,000 and above		$6,000

Top management is very aggressive in meeting its yearly profit goals and puts tremendous pressure on loan officers to generate a high volume of loans. Holly knows that a few of the loan officers (but not all), in response to this pressure, carefully review the status of their own cumulative quarterly loan volume three weeks before the end of each quarter. If they are either well below $490,000 or have reached $530,001, they purposely "drag their feet" on all loan applications in process in order to ensure that those loans do not close until the next quarter. On the other hand, if they are near the $490,000 volume level, they aggressively pursue additional loan closings to bring their total volume up to $530,001.

Additionally, Holly recently learned that a few of these same loan officers increase their loan volume significantly by paying (from their own pockets) their outside appraisers an extra $200 per appraisal. This cash payment encourages appraisers not only to speed up the appraisal process by as much as two to three weeks, but it also leads to rendering relatively higher (inflated) appraisal values.

Holly is aware that the actions of the loan officers are unethical, but she also realizes that these loan officers are the ones who are being rewarded with large bonuses. The extra cash would be especially useful to Holly as she has just learned that her daughter needs braces.

Requirements

1. What are the key facts in this decision problem?

_____

_____

_____

2. What are the ethical issues faced by Holly? Do the appraisers also face an ethical issue? Explain.

_____

_____

_____

3. What alternatives are available to Holly in addressing her problem?

_____

_____

_____

4. Who are the stakeholders in this problem (name at least five stakeholders)?

_____

_____

5. Select one of your specified alternatives from Requirement 3 and identify consequences (both positive and negative) to three of the stakeholders you identified in Requirement 4.

_____

_____

_____

_____

Case Reading 1-4

USING ACCOUNTING INFORMATION TO UNDERSTAND PERSONAL INVESTMENTS

INTRODUCTION

This case reading discusses how accounting information is used to help people make personal investing decisions. Several scenarios are examined and the concept of return on equity (ROE) is explained in each investment choice. The element of risk is also mentioned, including its correlation to the ROE of the specific investment.

WHY INVEST?

The need for accounting information is the result of people's desire to invest. **Investing** is the exchange of cash resources for other assets that promise income. For example, banks typically do not pay interest on checking accounts. Someone with cash in a checking account or safety deposit box foregoes the chance to earn income by not investing that cash balance. If the cash was placed in an interest bearing savings account in the bank it would earn interest at the current rate, perhaps 4 percent. This introduces the concept of opportunity cost. An **opportunity cost** is the benefit that could have been obtained by following an alternative course of action. Thus, the opportunity cost of having cash in a checking account is the lost interest of not having the cash in an interest bearing savings account.

The motivation to invest is to increase income. Our example in Case Reading 1-1 illustrated that Peg Glenville transferred $50,000 of her personal savings into the business venture she called Peg's Computer Game Enterprise. In doing this Peg made an investment. Her motivation was twofold. She wanted to be in business for herself and she wanted to increase her income by more than the interest earned on her savings account.

The concept of **return on equity (ROE)** is fundamental to business formation and growth. The word *return* means the profit or income generated by the investment that accrues to owners. *Equity* refers to the amount invested by owners, those assuming the risks. The cost of an investment often requires more money than the owner can commit. In those instances, the owner borrows the needed amounts to acquire the investment.

The return on equity concept is also important for personal investment decisions. From a personal perspective, investors can evaluate the performance of their investment by comparing their return to other possible investments. From a business perspective, managers can use ROE to judge the effectiveness of their past decisions in deploying the resources entrusted to them by the owners of the business. The measurement of the return on investment is derived from accounting information:

Return on Equity = $\dfrac{\text{Income (Loss) Accruing To Investment Owners}}{\text{Owners' Investment Equity}}$

A savings account can be used to illustrate the concept of ROE. Suppose you take a $1,000 cash gift and open a savings account at a bank. Your equity in the investment is $1,000. If after one year the account balance is $1,035, the ROE of this investment would be determined as follows:

$$ROE = \$35 \div \$1,000 = .035 \text{ or } 3.5\%$$

As an investor, you will compare the ROE of your savings account with that of other potential investments. You may find other investments that yield a higher ROE but may quickly conclude that they are not as safe as your bank savings account. How safe or unsafe is an investment? One must assess the risk.

Risk is the chance that the ROE will be negative or less than normal for that category of asset. There is a probability of losing some or all of the value of many types of investments. The probability can be quite low, as in the case of short-term government bonds, or it can be high, as in the case of bonds of an oil exploration company. While this undesirable outcome is not possible in a guaranteed (insured) savings account, other forms of investment can produce a negative ROE.

Note that the numerator of the ROE formula is "income (loss) accruing to investment owners." Suppose you decided to invest your $1,000 gift in baseball cards because you believed that they would be worth 20 percent more in one year. If your prediction was proved true by the sale of your collection for $1,200 a year later, the increase in the value of your asset would be $200 and you would have enjoyed a 20 percent ROE:

$$\$200 \div \$1,000 = .20 \text{ or } 20\%$$

On the other hand, suppose you place your baseball card collection up for auction. To your disappointment, the auction brings only $900 for your collection. In this case your ROE is negative:

$$-\$100 \div \$1,000 = -.10 \text{ or } -10\%$$

Given this scenario, you would quickly conclude that there is relatively more risk associated with baseball card investments than bank accounts or short-term government bonds. ROE of conservative investments tends to be relatively low, but the probability of a negative return is also low. Conversely, large profits on baseball cards are known to have occurred but there is a relatively high probability that an investor could experience a negative return. In sum, high risk should be correlated by high expected ROE and low risk should be correlated with low ROE.

Our objective in this case reading is to introduce the characteristics of several typical investments and how accounting information can help the decision maker. Space does not allow an exhaustive study of the vast array of investment choices. Instead, we will examine a few of the more common investment vehicles. We divide the review of investments between personal investments and business investments. By **personal investment** we mean the transfer of personal savings into assets which individuals purchase in order to increase their wealth. By **business investment** we mean the decision of managers to transfer cash assets into operating assets (for example, equipment and buildings) for the purpose of increasing income and stockholders' equity. Business investments will be discussed in detail in Modules 3 and 4.

PERSONAL INVESTMENTS

Let's examine three possible personal investments. Investment experts are quick to point out that the selection of investments to consider must relate to the investor's station in life. A person nearing retirement would be ill-advised to make risky investments because the accumulated equity in investments are usually needed to support the retirement years when job income has ceased. A loss of some or all of the equity could seriously jeopardize the retired investor's financial plan. Conversely, a person with 20 or 30 years before retirement may prudently make risky investments if the expected return is commensurately high. Investing inevitably brings the chance of loss but good research and common sense will help reduce or prevent losses. A loss sustained by a younger person is not as potentially devastating because time can help the investor recover from an unexpected investment loss.

To illustrate how accounting information can help investors evaluate the merits of different kinds of investment we will use the following three examples:

- Certificate of deposit
- Government bond
- Small business investment

Certificate of Deposit

A **certificate of deposit** is an account at a bank, savings and loan, or credit union where a person has placed money for a specified period of time in order to earn interest on the money. For example, a person could place $20,000 in a one-year, 5.5 percent certificate of deposit (CD) in a bank. This would be a low risk investment because savings and CDs are insured by the Federal Deposit Insurance Corporation (a federal agency) for up to $100,000 for each person. This one-year CD will earn $1,100 interest, which is the 5.5 percent agreed interest rate on the $20,000 given to the bank. The return on equity is computed as follows:

$$\text{Income for the year} = 5.5\% \times \$20,000 = \$1,100$$

$$\text{ROE} = \$1,100 \div \$20,000 = 5.5\%$$

In this simple illustration it is easy to see that the 5.5 percent CD interest rate results in a 5.5 percent return on equity (the amount invested in the CD). This is a very low risk investment and a relatively low yield on an investment.

Government Bond

A **bond** is a legal contract between an investor (bond holder) and a government or corporation needing money (bond issuer). The contract specifies when the borrowed money is to be repaid and when and how much interest is to be paid to the investor. The U.S Treasury regularly sells bonds to the pubic to raise funds to run the government. Corporations also issue bonds to raise money to expand their business or to pay off other debt. Investors are willing to purchase the bonds because they yield income and have a relatively high probability of recovery of the investment. A bond issued by the U.S. Treasury is usually considered to have less risk than a bond issued by a corporation. Further, bonds issued by a large corporation such as IBM are considered to have less risk than bonds issued by a small company with less resources. However, at various times in history, investors in all three type of bond issues have sustained losses.

There are three key attributes of a bond: coupon interest rate, face value, and maturity date. **Coupon interest rate** is the fixed rate of interest paid annually to the bondholder. Multiplying the coupon percentage rate times the face value gives the dollar amount of interest to be paid the bondholder. The **face value** is the denomination of the bond and is also the amount to be paid back to the bondholder at the maturity date. The **maturity date** is the date on which the issuer must repay the face value to the bondholder.

To illustrate the above definitions, suppose the U.S. Treasury issues bonds in March of 2001. Investor G purchases bonds having a face value of $10,000, a coupon rate of 5.75 percent per year and a maturity date 30 years from the date of issue. The calculation of ROE is as follows:

Income for the year = coupon interest rate × face value = .0575 × $10,000 = $575

ROE = $575 ÷ $10,000 = .0575 or 5.75%

Note that the ROE is equal to the coupon rate. The above illustration is designed to show how accounting information can be applied to evaluating the performance of an investment in a government bond. Next we study the situation of a small business investment.

Small Business Investment

Established businesses are often put up for sale. The owner may want to retire or move on to another line of work. Whatever the reason, a prospective buyer must carefully review the financial statements of the business to assess the profit that can be expected in relation to the price being asked for the business. Said another way, the investor wants to know the expected ROE of the business before entering into a contract to purchase it.

To illustrate this investment scenario, we assume that EMAILMAX, an Internet service provider, is a small company which its founder wants to sell. The company provides Internet connections to individuals for $25 per month. During 2001, EMAILMAX had an average of 1,000 subscribers of its service. Investor B is interested in this business based upon Exhibit 1-4.1, the income statement for the previous year:

Exhibit 1-4.1
Income Statement -2001

EMAILMAX Income Statement Year Ended December 31, 2001		
Fees Revenue		$ 300,000
Expenses		
Telephone line expense	$ 100,000	
Software maintenance	50,000	
Depreciation of equipment	50,000	
Insurance, legal, and accounting	50,000	
Total expenses		250,000
Net income		$ 50,000

The price asked for this going business is $400,000. Investor B has $100,000 of savings available. B has a commitment from a local bank to lend the remaining $300,000 at 10 percent. The loan is due in two years. B realizes that interest expense on the borrowed funds will be in the future income statements. However, B believes that accounting costs can be reduced by $8,000 and software costs can be reduced by $22,000 because he will do the work himself. Offsetting some of these savings is the increase in depreciation expense by $10,000 due to the installation of new computer equipment. Competition is strong and B is of the belief that he will need to decrease his fee rates by 5 percent in 2002. Exhibit 1-4.2 contains the projected income statement for 2002 prepared by B:

Exhibit 1-4.2
Income Statement -2002

EMAILMAX Projected Income Statement Year Ended December 31, 2002		
Fees Revenue		$285,000
Expenses		
Telephone line expense	$100,000	
Software maintenance	28,000	
Depreciation of equipment	60,000	
Insurance, legal, and accounting	42,000	
Interest expense	30,000	
Total expenses		260,000
Net income		$ 25,000

B is now in a position to compute the ROE of this investment opportunity:

$$ROE = \$25,000 \div \$100,000 = .25 \text{ or } 25\%$$

The relatively high ROE is attractive but could mask a high level of risk. For example, an unforeseen small increase in expenses of only 4 percent could reduce income by a whopping 40 percent! If expenses increased by $10,000, income would be $15,000; 40 percent below the original projection. Conversely, an increase in revenues and/or a decrease in expenses could cause net income and ROE to rise sharply. To illustrate, suppose B finds that he does not need to reduce his fee rates by 5 percent. Revenues would then remain at $300,000 and total expenses would be $260,000. Income then would be $40,000, a $15,000 increase in income. The ROE calculation is

$$ROE = \$40,000 \div \$100,000 = .40 \text{ or } 40\%$$

SUMMARY

The objective of this case reading and Case 1-4 which follows is to provide you with an understanding of the use of accounting information in making investment decisions. Return on equity (ROE) is a useful ratio for comparing investment alternatives. In general, the ROE of an investment is correlated with risk. The higher the ROE, the greater the risk; the lower the ROE, the lower the risk. However, the difficult aspect of investment decision making is evaluating risk. Our approach to risk assessment is the variability of net income (the numerator of ROE). The income statement format is a useful vehicle for testing the "what if" of an investment. No one can predict the future level of revenues and expenses with precision.

However, estimates based upon reasoned assumptions can provide insight into the variability of line items appearing in an income statement. A prudent approach to investment decision making requires the effective use of accounting information.

In Case 1-4, we present three scenarios and ask you to evaluate the ROE of each and to rank them on the basis of risk.

EXERCISES

Exercises

Exercise 1 Why people invest. What is the primary reason that people invest?

Exercise 2 U.S Treasury bill ROE. If you purchase a six-month Treasury bill today, what is your expected ROE of that investment? (Hint: Look at a recent Wall Street Journal to determine Treasury bill interest rates.)

Exercise 3 How a negative investment can occur. Create a scenario that produces a negative ROE.

Exercise 4 Source of investment capital. What is the usual source of funds used for personal investments?

Exercise 5 Opportunity cost. Define opportunity cost.

Exercise 6 Determining opportunity cost. Suppose you are offered an investment which will require cash of $100,000 and promises a return of $10,000. How would you estimate the opportunity cost of this investment?

Exercise 7 A student needs to determine the opportunity cost of an internship. Suppose you are offered a glamorous six-month internship with a high-tech company. This will delay your graduation by one semester. How will you determine the opportunity cost of accepting the internship?

Exercise 8 Investment risk. Define risk in the context of personal investing.

Exercise 9 Create a projected income statement for an investment. Create a scenario in which an investor in a $500,000 small business who has $50,000 invested will enjoy an ROE of 50 percent.

Case 1-4

USING ACCOUNTING INFORMATION FOR INVESTMENT DECISIONS

Case Objectives

1. Learn how accounting information is helpful in making investment decisions.
2. Learn about the concept of return on equity.
3. Use return on equity to rank alternative investments.

Decision: Using return on equity as a criterion, determine which of three investment alternatives is best.

You have $100,000 to invest. You are trying to decide which of the following three investments should be selected:

1. Government bond
2. Rental property
3. Fitness/exercise business

The financial characteristics of the three alternative investments are presented below.

Government Bond

- The cost (equal to the face value) of the bond is $100,000.
- The bond will mature in five years.
- The government will pay 5 percent interest (coupon rate) at the end of each year.

Rental Property

- The cost of the rental property is $200,000.
- The seller loans you $100,000 to finance the difference between the purchase price and your equity contribution.
- The loan is to be repaid five years from the date of purchase.
- You must pay interest at 10 percent on the loan at the end of each year.
- Rental income is $2,000 per month.
- Taxes, insurance, and maintenance expenses total $6,000 per year.

Fitness/Exercise Business

- This is a going business which is for sale at a firm price of $300,000.
- The most recent income statement for 2002 is as follows:

Exhibit C1-4.1
Income Statement

Fitness/Exercise Business Income Statement Year Ended December 31, 2002		
Revenue from membership fees		$ 250,000
Operating expenses:		
Manager's salary	$ 50,000	
Trainers' salaries	75,000	
Rent	75,000	
Utilities and other	20,000	
Total expenses		220,000
Net income		$ 30,000

- You can obtain a bank loan for $200,000 for the difference between your equity contribution and the purchase price.
- The bank will require payment of 10 percent interest at the end of each year and require repayment of the $200,000 at the end of five years.

Requirements

1. Use the spreadsheet template shown on the following page as Exhibit C1-4.2 to calculate the return on equity of each investment.

2. From the accounting information you developed in Requirement 1, rank the three investments from highest to lowest return on equity.

3. Rank the three investments in terms of risk, highest risk to lowest risk.

4. Comment on the rankings in Requirements 2 and 3.

5. Based only on the information in this case, what is the opportunity cost in each of the investment alternatives?

Exhibit C1-4.2
Template for Requirement 1

	Government Bonds	Rental Property	Fitness Business
Investment Gross Income			
Interest Expense	0		
All Other Expenses	0		
Estimated Earnings (A)			
Cost of Investment			
Less Amount Borrowed	0		
Equity in Investment (B)			
Return on Equity (A ÷ B)			

MODULE TWO

USING

Accounting Information

IN SMALL BUSINESSES

Module 2 Introduction

USING ACCOUNTING INFORMATION
IN SMALL BUSINESSES

MODULE OVERVIEW

Module 2 begins the study of a simple business and the role of accounting information in starting and operating a small service business.

The decision context in which these concepts are examined continues with the student, John Miller. In Module 1, John was faced with the decision as to whether or not he should start a summer painting business. In this module, John starts the business and is faced with the following decision context:

> Having launched the business, how well did I do?

The module focuses on the following learning objectives (relevant readings and cases are listed after each objective):

Learning Objectives

1. Understand the nature of assets, liabilities, and owners' equity of an economic entity; understand various value measurements (e.g., historical cost, current value) that may be associated with those items; construct a balance sheet that reflects those items; and be able to interpret the information given.

- Case Reading 2-1	Recording Accounting Information
- Case Reading 2-2	Making Decisions Using Balance Sheet Information
- Case Reading 2-7	Identifying Assets and Liabilities
- Case 2-1	Laura's Law Practice
- Case 2-2	John's Painting Business
- Case 2-7	Upside-Down Ski School
- Group Assignment 2-1	Sara's Shopping Service
- Group Assignment 2-2	Was John's Business Successful?
- Group Assignment 2-7	Should Right-Side-Up Get a Loan?
- Exercises and Problems	Exercises and Problems at the end of Case Readings 2-1, 2-2, and 2-7

2. Understand the nature of accounting transactions and how transactions affect the accounting equation; translate economic events into accounting transactions that identify increases and decreases in assets, liabilities, and owners' equity; and prepare an accounting worksheet (computer spreadsheet) that records those transactions.

- Case Reading 2-1	Recording Accounting Information
- Case Reading 2-3	Making Decisions Using Income Statement Information
- Case Reading 2-7	Identifying Assets and Liabilities
- Case 2-1	Laura's Law Practice

- Case 2-3	Juan Rodriguez, M.D.
- Case 2-7	Upside-Down Ski School
- Group Assignment 2-1	Sara's Shopping Service
- Group Assignment 2-7	Should Right-Side-Up Get a Loan
- Exercises and Problems	Exercises and Problems at the end of Case Readings 2-1, 2-3, and 2-7

3. Understand the nature of net income (profit) and its two major components, revenue and expenses; understand how the accrual basis of accounting recognizes revenues and expenses and matches those items in measuring net income and construct an income statement that reflects those items; understand the uses and limitations of income statements; understand transactions that involve owners' equity transactions; and understand the concept of opportunity cost.

- Case Reading 2-3	Making Decisions Using Income Statement Information
- Case Reading 2-4	Making Decisions Using Cash Flow Information
- Case Reading 2-6	Interpreting Financial Statement Information
- Case Reading 2-7	Identifying Assets and Liabilities
- Case 2-3	Juan Rodriguez, M.D.
- Case 2-4	Compute The Difference—Part I
- Case 2-6	John's Profitability or Not?
- Case 2-7	Upside-Down Ski School
- Group Assignment 2-6	How Did John's Business Perform?
- Group Assignment 2-7	Should Right-Side-Up Get a Loan?
- Exercises and Problems	Exercises and Problems at the end of Case Readings 2-3, 2-4, 2-6, and 2-7

4. Understand the nature of cash inflows and outflows; understand the differences between those cash items compared to revenues and expenses; construct a statement of cash flows that reflects cash inflows and outflows that have occurred during a period; and understand the uses and limitations of the statement of cash flows.

- Case Reading 2-4	Making Decisions Using Cash Flow Information
- Case Reading 2-5	Understanding the Indirect Method
- Case Reading 2-6	Interpreting Financial Statement Information
- Case 2-4	Compute The Difference—Part I
- Case 2-5	Compute The Difference—Part II
- Case 2-6	John's Profitability or Not?
- Group Assignment 2-6	How Did John's Business Perform?
- Exercises and Problems	Exercises and Problems at the end of Case Readings 2-4, 2-5, and 2-6

5. Become familiar with the content of an annual report.

- Case Reading 2-8A	Using Published Financial Statements
- Case Reading 2-8B	The Gap, Inc. Financial Statements
- Case 2-8	Using Financial Statements of Publicly Held Companies
- Group Assignment 2-8	Bridging "The Gap"
- Exercises and Problems	Exercises and Problems at the end of Case Reading 2-8

Case Reading 2-1

RECORDING
ACCOUNTING INFORMATION

INTRODUCTION

This case reading introduces an accounting transaction worksheet which will be used to record the day to day economic activities of a company called the Corliss Accounting Firm. This worksheet will then be used to summarize the transactions and ultimately prepare a balance sheet and a statement of owner's equity. Accounts which are generally present on a balance sheet will be introduced and explained in detail.

BALANCE SHEET ACCOUNTS

One of the financial statements prepared by a company is called a balance sheet. As mentioned in Case Reading 1-1, the balance sheet contains information about the assets, liabilities and owner's equity accounts of the company. A more detailed description of these accounts is given below.

Assets

Assets are probable future economic benefits owned or controlled by the company that result from past transactions or events. Some examples of assets include cash, accounts receivable, short-term investments, prepaid expenses, supplies, inventory, equipment, land, machinery, building, and furniture. Assets may be further categorized as current or long term. **Current assets** are assets the company expects to convert into cash or use up within the next year. Assets the company expects to use for more than a year are called **long-term** or **fixed assets**. A more in-depth description of some of the various asset accounts follows.

Cash includes money or other instruments that a bank will accept for deposit to an account. (e.g., checks, money orders, or currency).

Accounts receivable represents amounts owed to the company as a result of credit sales transactions. The company usually expects to collect the accounts receivable within 30 to 60 days.

Short-term investments include stocks and bonds that represent investments in other companies that the company intends to sell within the next year.

Prepaid expenses, such as prepaid rent or prepaid insurance, represent amounts paid in advance by the company for future services. For example, if the company pays a six-month insurance premium on December 31 for the following six months, the company has exchanged an asset, cash, for the benefit of receiving future insurance coverage for the six-month period.

Supplies are items the company consumes during the course of business. For example, office supplies consist of paper, business forms, pencils, staplers, etc. When a company purchases supplies, the amount purchased increases the supplies on hand. This asset is reduced at the end of the period for the amount of the supplies used.

Inventory includes tangible property that is held for sale. For example, the inventory of a car dealer is automobiles. Inventory can also be used in the production of goods or services for sale. Raw Materials and Work in Process are typical names given to manufacturing-related inventories.

Long-term investments include stocks and bonds that represent investments in other companies that the company intends to keep for more than one year.

Equipment represents fixed assets the company will use for longer than one year. For example, store equipment might include tables, chairs, light fixtures, computers, cash registers, etc. These items are purchased because they are needed to conduct the long-term operations of the business.

Liabilities

Liabilities are obligations or debts of the business which must be paid off at a future date. Liability accounts often include the word *payable*. Liabilities may be further categorized as current or long-term, depending on when the debts become due. Liabilities due within one year from the balance sheet date are usually classified as **current liabilities**. Liabilities maturing after one year from the balance sheet date are normally considered **long-term liabilities**. Examples of current liabilities include notes payable, salaries payable, accounts payable, interest payable, unearned revenue, and taxes payable. Examples of long-term liabilities are mortgages payable and bonds payable. Some of these accounts are described below.

Accounts payable are amounts owed to suppliers for goods and services purchased on credit. The company generally pays the debt within sixty days, but the actual due date is based on agreements with individual suppliers. Interest is not charged by creditors for accounts payable balances. However, discounts are sometimes offered for quick payments such as ten days or less.

A note payable is a formal written promise to pay which bears interest. The note payable designation refers specifically to the principal amount borrowed. The interest on a note is recorded in a separate account called interest payable. The interest is based on the borrowed amount, the interest rate, and the length of time the note is outstanding. A note payable will be classified as either a short-term note (due within one year) or a long-term note (due after one year).

Unearned revenue represents amounts received before shipping the goods or providing the service. It is the opposite of a prepaid expense. We record a prepaid expense when we pay in advance; we record an unearned revenue when we receive an amount in advance. The company usually satisfies this type of liability by providing a service. A good example is magazine subscriptions. When the magazine company receives a check for a six-month subscription, it records an obligation or a liability called Unearned Magazine Revenue or Magazine Revenue Received in Advance. The company reduces its debt by sending the magazines.

Bonds payable are similar to notes in that they also have interest. The debt, however, is recorded on a bond certificate instead of a note. Bonds are generally issued by companies that need to borrow large amounts of money. By issuing bonds, the company increases both total assets and total liabilities by the amount of the proceeds from the sale of bonds to the public.

Mortgage payable is used when the written promise to pay is secured by pledging assets, usually real estate, as **collateral**. If a company defaults on its loan, the creditor has a right to force the company to repay the loan by selling or forfeiting the collateral.

Owners' Equity

Owners' equity includes the contributed capital and the retained earnings accounts of the company. **Contributed capital** represents money or other assets transferred from personal ownership to the business entity. In many cases the owner will contribute personal assets, such as land, buildings, or equipment, to the business. **Retained earnings** are the profits (losses) the company has earned since it began that have not been distributed to the owners and therefore have been retained in the business.[1]

Before preparing a balance sheet, the company must record the information in the accounting records. **Accounting records** are the books or computer files in which all transaction data and other information are recorded for the purpose of preparing financial statements and other reports. (Appendix D discusses the various accounting records which are used by the company such as the **general journal** and the **general ledger**.) To understand how accountants record information we will be using an accounting transaction worksheet which is described below.

THE ACCOUNTING TRANSACTION WORKSHEET

Accounting involves collecting, processing, analyzing, and reporting financial information of a business. Part of the collecting and processing functions entails the day-to-day analysis and recording of the monetary transactions of the company. **Transactions** are events that affect or change the amount or makeup of assets, liabilities, and/or equity of an entity. Most businesses use accounting software to accomplish these tasks. Learning accounting software can be complex and is beyond the scope of this course. In this course, transactions will be recorded and summarized by using an **accounting transaction worksheet**. This worksheet shows the effect of each monetary transaction on the various accounts contained in the balance sheet. The accounting worksheet illustration (Exhibit 2-1.1) will show how various transactions affect the three major categories of the balance sheet.

The major features of this worksheet[2] are as follows:

➜   Separate columns are included for each asset, liability, and owners' equity account. (Note: A list of all accounts used by a business is referred to as a **chart of accounts**. A sample chart of accounts can be found in Appendix D.)

➜   For each account, the worksheet starts with the beginning balance and adds/deducts all transactions that caused increases/decreases in the account to arrive at the ending balance for the account. The ending balance in the account is called the **account balance**.

---

[1] Contributed capital and retained earnings are not used in sole proprietorships and partnerships. By initially using these two accounts for all forms of business, one can better differentiate between capital contributions and earnings. The correct terminology for all forms of business will be covered in Module 3.

[2] Note: All of the accounting transaction worksheets that are illustrated in this course have been prepared using Microsoft Excel spreadsheet software.

Exhibit 2-1.1
The Accounting Transaction Worksheet

	A		=	L	+	OE	
	Assets			**Liabilities**		**Owner's Equity**	
	Cash	Accounts Receivable	Etc.	Accounts Payable	Etc.	Contributed Capital	Retained Earnings
Beginning Balance	$XXXX	$XXX	$XXX	$XXX	$XX	$XXXX	$XX
Date	(XXX)			(XXX)			
List Transactions: Analyze and record events that increase/decrease the accounts							
Ending Balance	$XX	$XXX	$XXX	$X	$XX	$XXXX	$XX

Statement of Cash Flows
(Direct Method)
(increases/ decreases in Cash column)

Income Statement and
Statement of Retained Earnings
(increases/ decreases in Retained Earnings column)

Balance Sheet
(Ending Balances in A, L, and OE)

Note: the entry in the "date" row is an example of how the transaction to pay off a liability is handled; decreasing cash and decreasing accounts payable

➜   The worksheet contains all of the information necessary to prepare a set of financial statements.

⇒   The Cash column contains the information used to prepare the statement of cash flows under the direct method.

⇒   The Retained Earnings column contains the information used to prepare the income statement and the statement of retained earnings.

⇒   The Ending Balance row contains the information used to prepare the balance sheet.

The accounting transaction worksheet analyzes the effect that transactions have on the balance sheet equation. The **balance sheet equation** is:

Assets = Liabilities + Owner's Equity

A   =   L   +   OE

The asset side of the equation shows the economic resources of the company. The liability and owner's equity side shows who provided those resources. If the increase to an asset account causes a corresponding increase in a liability account, then the resources were provided by creditors who lent the resources to the company and expect to be repaid at a future date. If an increase to owner's equity, the resources were provided by the owner.

CORLISS ACCOUNTING FIRM EXAMPLE

To illustrate how an accounting transaction worksheet is used, consider Corliss Accounting Firm, which was organized on May 25, 2000. During May, the company had the following four transactions.

May 25   Received a capital contribution of $50,000 cash from Devenie Corliss, the owner.

     25   Purchased supplies for $1,000 from Leslie Co., amount to be paid in 30 days.

     29   Paid $700 of the amount due to Leslie Company.

     31   Purchased land for $30,000 and a building for $100,000, making a cash down payment of $20,000 and giving a 30-year mortgage payable at 8 percent interest for the remainder. Monthly principal and interest payments are $806.

An accounting transaction worksheet for the company has been set up as Exhibit 2-1.2. Notice that the account titles are in row 2 of the spreadsheet. The dates of each transaction shown above are listed in column A. Beginning balances in the accounts as of May 1 have been recorded in row 3. These amounts are all zeros as this is the first month of operations and the company is just beginning. Although zeros were actually entered in each cell because the row was formatted for currency (see Excel instructions in Appendix C) the zeros are displayed as dashes. This type of display is quite common. The computer will still store the zero value in each cell.

Exhibit 2-1.2
Corliss Accounting Firm
Accounting Transaction Worksheet
May 2000

	A	B	C	D	E	F	G	H	I
1		ASSETS				LIABILITIES + OWNER'S EQUITY			
2	Date	Cash	Supplies	Land	Building	Accounts Payable	Mortgage Payable	Contributed Capital	Retained Earnings
3	Beg. Bal. 5/25/00	$ -	$ -	$ -	$ -	$ -	$ -	$ -	$ -
4	5/25/00	50,000						50,000	
5	5/25/00								
6	5/29/00								
7	5/31/00								
8	End. Bal. 5/31/00								

Before analyzing each individual transaction, you need to identify at least two accounts that are affected. This is called **double entry** accounting and means that each transaction is viewed as an exchange: something is given up and something of equal value is received. Let's look at the first transaction again.

May 25   Received a capital contribution of $50,000 cash from Devenie Corliss, the
           owner.

This transaction is recorded as an increase to cash and an increase to contributed capital of
$50,000. Cash for the Corliss Accounting Firm goes up because the owner is contributing
$50,000 cash to the business.

To enter that amount in the worksheet on a computer just key in the number. (Do not use any
commas. See Appendix C for additional help in using spreadsheet software to enter
transactions.) As mentioned previously, each transaction affects two or more accounts. The
increase to cash shows that the assets or economic resources of the company increased. The
other part of that entry explains who provided that resource. In this case, the resource was
provided by the owner and is therefore contributed capital. The entry causes an increase in
assets and an increase in owner's equity of $50,000. Liabilities or debts are not changed as a
result of this transaction.

Go back to Exhibit 2-1.2 and see if you can enter the remaining three transactions in the
worksheet by using this same analysis process. Keep in mind that *each* transaction must
maintain the balance sheet equation (Assets = Liabilities + Owners' Equity) and that each
transaction must affect two or more accounts.

Exhibit 2-1.3 below shows the completed accounting transaction worksheet for May. A discussion follows describing the remaining entries on each row of the worksheet.

Exhibit 2-1.3
Corliss Accounting Firm
Completed Accounting Transaction Worksheet
May 2000

	A	B	C	D	E	F	G	H	I
1		ASSETS				LIABILITIES + OWNER'S EQUITY			
2	Date	Cash	Supplies	Land	Building	Accounts Payable	Mortgage Payable	Contributed Capital	Retained Earnings
3	Beg. Bal. 5/25/00	$ -	$ -	$ -	$ -	$ -	$ -	$ -	$ -
4	5/25/00	50,000						50,000	
5	5/25/00		1,000			1,000			
6	5/29/00	(700)				(700)			
7	5/31/00	(20,000)		30,000	100,000		110,000		
8	End. Bal. 5/31/00	$ 29,300	$ 1,000	$ 30,000	$ 100,000	$ 300	$ 110,000	$ 50,000	$ -

$$\text{Assets} = \text{Liabilities} + \text{Owner's Equity}$$
$$\$160,300 = \$110,300 + \$50,000$$

The second transaction occurring on May 25 states that the company purchased supplies but did not pay in cash on that date.

May 25   Purchased supplies for $1,000 from Leslie Co., amount to be paid in 30 days.

The asset account supplies increases by $1,000. In this transaction, the resources were provided by a creditor, the Leslie Company, instead of the owner. Corliss will record this in accounts payable, a liability, because it intends to pay off the balance in a short period of time (thirty days). The liability account increases (vs. decreases) because the company owes more after this economic event. If there was a written promise to pay and interest charged, the liability account increased would have been notes payable. To summarize this transaction, assets and liabilities both increased by $1,000.

The third transaction occurred on May 29 and states that Corliss paid off $700 of the amount owed to the Leslie Company.

May 29   Paid $700 of the amount due to Leslie Company.

The transaction narrative does not specifically state that the liability was paid off with cash, but unless the transaction states otherwise, the best inference is that cash, rather than some other asset, was paid. Both accounts payable, a liability account, and cash, an asset, are reduced by $700 as a result of this transaction.

The last transaction for the month is the most complex. This entry on the spreadsheet is called a **compound entry** as it involves three or more accounts.

> May 31   Purchased land for $30,000 and a building for $100,000, making a cash down payment of $20,000 and giving a 30-year mortgage payable at 8 percent interest for the remainder. Monthly principal and interest payments are $806.

In this case Corliss purchased land for $30,000 and a building for $100,000, paid $20,000 cash and took a mortgage for the rest. On the asset side, Corliss received economic resources in the forms of land for $30,000 and building for $100,000 so the land and building asset accounts will increase by those amounts. The company also gave up an economic resource of cash to acquire those assets. Cash will therefore decrease. Corliss owes $110,000 (computed by adding land of $30,000 and building of $100,000 and subtracting cash of $20,000) to the seller for the unpaid portion of the purchase price. The transaction states that Corliss took out a mortgage to finance the purchase. The liability account mortgage payable will go up by $110,000 as a result of this increased amount of debt. (Although not specifically stated in the transaction, because it is a mortgage, the land and building are collateral for the debt.)

The transaction description gives you an interest rate and a monthly payment as well. This information is not relevant at this point in time. Because the mortgage began on that date, no interest is due until the date of the first payment. Interest is a charge for using someone else's money over a period of time. Since no time has passed since borrowing the money, there is no interest to record. As a result of this transaction, assets increased by $110,000 and liabilities increased by the same amount. The net resources gained by Corliss were provided by a creditor.

After the above transactions were recorded on the worksheet shown in Exhibit 2-1.3, the ending balances shown in row 8 were computed by summing the amounts entered in each column.

The ending balance for the cash column was computed by summing the amounts in cells B3 through B7. A similar computation was made for each column to compute the ending account balance. Once computed, the ending balances are then used to prepare a balance sheet as of May 31, 2000. This process is explained further in the next section.

Balance Sheet

A **balance sheet** is a formal financial statement that lists the balances of assets, liabilities, and owners' equity of a company at a particular point in time. Exhibit 2-1.4 shows the classified balance sheet for Corliss. The amounts shown are taken directly from the ending balances of the accounting transaction worksheet. A balance sheet (also called a statement of financial position) is prepared at the end of an accounting period, which may be at the end of a month, a quarter, or a year.

Exhibit 2-1.4
Balance Sheet

	A	B	C	D	E	F	G	H
1				Corliss Accounting Firm				
2				Balance Sheet				
3				May 31, 2000				
4								
5			Assets				Liabilities and Owner's Equity	
6								
7	Current Assets						Current Liabilities	
8		Cash		$ 29,300			Accounts Payable	$ 300
9		Supplies		1,000				
10	Total Current Assets			30,300				
11							Long Term Liabilities	
12	Fixed Assets						Mortgage Payable	110,000
13		Land	$ 30,000					
14		Building	100,000				Total Liabilities	110,300
15	Total Fixed Assets			130,000				
16							Owner's Equity	
17							Contributed Capital	50,000
18								
19	Total Assets			$ 160,300			Owner's Equity	$ 160,300
20								

The first line of the balance sheet heading is critical because it tells the reader the name of the entity for which the financial statements are being prepared. The balance sheet of Corliss Accounting Firm, therefore, contains only assets, liabilities, and equities of the *business*. The owner's personal items are not included on the financial statements of the business.

Major Balance Sheet Classifications

The balance sheet consists of asset, liability, and owner's equity accounts. Most companies prepare a **classified balance sheet** which contains further subcategories as stated below. This facilitates deeper analyses into the financial strengths and weaknesses of the company.

Current Assets. Current assets are assets that the company expects to convert to cash or use up within the next year. Corliss considers cash, accounts receivable, supplies, and prepaid insurance to be current.

Fixed Assets. The fixed asset category is used for long-term assets that will be used over more than one year. Fixed assets generally include land, buildings, equipment, furniture, autos, etc. Generally accepted accounting principles require that these assets must be recorded at **historical cost** which means their invoice cost plus any additional costs that the company must incur to get the asset ready to use.

Over time, fixed assets (except land) are reduced by the estimated amount of the asset that has been used up during the period. The amount estimated to be used up in one accounting period is called **depreciation** expense. The fixed asset account will be reduced directly by the amount of the estimated depreciation. (In actual practice, the company maintains a separate account called accumulated depreciation that keeps track of the cumulative depreciation over time. We will use this account later in Module 4).

Total Assets. You will note that the assets section of the balance sheet ends with a figure called total assets. This calculation is merely the sum of all the asset account balances. You should also notice that total assets do equal total liabilities and owner's equity, thus maintaining the balance sheet equation; Assets of $160,300 equal liabilities of $110,300 plus owner's equity of $50,000.

Current Liabilities. Current liabilities are debts or other obligations that will be paid in cash or satisfied with other assets or services within one year. In this case the company considers accounts payable to be its only debt due within the next year.

Long-Term Liabilities. Long-term liabilities are liabilities the company expects to pay off in a period of time greater than one year. Corliss Accounting Firm considers mortgage payable to be their only long-term liability.

Owner's Equity. The **equity** section of the balance sheet reports the owner's interest in the business. The heading of this section differs according to whether the business is a sole proprietorship (Owner's Equity), a partnership (Owners' Equity) or a corporation (Stockholders' Equity.) The heading of "owner's equity" for Corliss shows that it is a sole proprietorship.

Accounting Transaction Worksheet for June

To continue the illustration, assume that the Corliss Accounting Firm had the following ten transactions for the month of June 2000.

June 1   Purchased a two-year insurance policy for $960 cash.

4   Paid remaining $300 liability due to Leslie Company.

15   Corliss Accounting Firm performed accounting services, billing its clients $3,000 for the first half of the month. A total of $2,000 was received in cash and the remainder will be received within 30 days (accounts receivable).

16   The owner, Corliss, withdrew $1,000 cash for personal use.

30   Services were performed for clients for the last half of the month. Clients were billed $2,200, of which half has been received in cash. The remaining were performed on credit.

30   Paid employees' wages of $1,600 for the month.

30   Recorded depreciation on the building for the month of June. The building has a 40-year life and a salvage value of $4,000.

30   Recorded the expiration of insurance for the month of June.

30   An inventory of supplies showed the supplies still on hand cost $250.

30   Paid the first monthly principal and interest payment of $806 on the 8 percent mortgage loan.

A worksheet showing how these June transactions affected assets, liabilities, and owner's equity is shown in Exhibit 2-1.5, which includes additional columns for Accounts Receivable and Prepaid Insurance. Study the worksheet carefully, noting how each transaction affects two or more accounts and how the balance sheet equation is always in balance.

Exhibit 2-1.5
Corliss Accounting Firm
Completed Accounting Transaction Worksheet
June 2000

	A	B	C	D	E	F	G	H	I	J	K	L
					ASSETS				**LIABILITIES + OWNER'S EQUITY**			
1	Date	Cash	Accounts Receivable	Supplies	Prepaid Insurance	Land	Building	Accounts Payable	Mortgage Payable	Contributed Capital	Retained Earnings	Equality Check
2	Beg Bal 6/1/00	29,300	-	1,000	-	30,000	100,000	300	110,000	50,000	-	0
3	6/1/00	(960)			960							0
4	6/1/00											0
5	6/4/00	(300)						(300)				0
6	6/15/00	2,000	1,000								3,000	0
7	6/16/00	(1,000)									(1,000)	0
8	6/30/00	1,100	1,100								2,200	0
9	6/30/00	(1,600)									(1,600)	0
10	6/30/00						(200)				(200)	0
11	6/30/00				(40)						(40)	0
12	6/30/00			(750)							(750)	0
13	6/30/00	(806)							(73)		(733)	0
14	EndBal 6/30/00	$ 27,734	$ 2,100	$ 250	$ 920	$ 30,000	$ 99,800	$ -	$ 109,927	$ 50,000	$ 877	0

The accounting transaction worksheet for June begins with recording the beginning balances for June in row 3. These balances are the same as the ending balances for the month of May and come from the worksheet prepared in Exhibit 2-1.3.

The June 1 transaction is recorded in row 3 of the worksheet and is repeated below.

    June 1   Purchased a two-year insurance policy for $960 cash.

The worksheet entry made consists of an increase to the asset account prepaid insurance (insurance paid for in advance) and a decrease to the asset account cash. On June 1, none of the insurance has expired yet so the entire amount is still an asset because the insurance coverage will benefit the company in the future.

The transaction on June 4 shown in row 5 of Exhibit 2-1.5 states:

    June 4   Paid remaining $300 liability due to Leslie Company.

This is recorded as a reduction of accounts payable and a reduction of cash. The $300 was the remaining liability shown in the accounting transaction worksheet for May. (See row 8 of the May transaction worksheet shown in Exhibit 2-1.3).

On June 15, the Corliss Accounting Firm recorded the increase in earnings that resulted from performing accounting work for clients. This is recorded in row 6 of Exhibit 2-1.5.

    June 15   Corliss Accounting Firm performed accounting services, billing its clients $3,000 for the first half of the month. A total of $2,000 was received in cash and the remainder will be received within 30 days (accounts receivable).

This amount that Corliss recorded for providing accounting services is revenue and is recorded as an increase to retained earnings. **Revenues** are increases in the (net) resources of an entity from the sale of goods or services. Revenues increase retained earnings because revenues increase earnings or profits.

The $2,000 received on the service date will be recorded as an increase to cash. The remaining $1,000 is recorded as the asset accounts receivable. The company will receive the resources at a later date. Accounts receivable is an asset because the company should collect the cash in the future without providing any additional services.

On June 16, the owner withdrew some of the earnings in the business in cash. This is recorded in row 7 of Exhibit 2-1.5.

    June 16   The owner, Corliss, withdrew $1,000 cash for personal use.

An **owner withdrawal** represents a withdrawal of company assets by the owner for personal use. This withdrawal is recorded by a decrease to cash and a decrease to retained earnings. Retained earnings decreases because the owner is withdrawing the profits of the business.

Row 8 of Exhibit 2-1.5 shows the recording of revenue for the last half of the month.

    30   Services were performed for clients for the last half of the month. Clients were billed $2,200, of which half has been received in cash. The remaining were performed on credit.

Notice that cash went up by the amount of cash received, accounts receivable of $1,100 was recorded for services performed on credit, and $2,200 was recorded for the total amount of revenue generated from the fees. When services are performed on **credit**, this means that the company providing the service has granted the buyer an extended period of time to pay for the service. Until payment is made, the company performing the service will record this as accounts receivable, an asset account. Note that retained earnings increases by the total amount of revenue even though cash has not been received to date for the full amount.

On June 30, the company paid employees for their work during June. Row 9 of the worksheet shows this transaction.

June 30   Paid employees' wages of $1,600 for the month.

Cash goes down by the amount paid and retained earnings goes down as well. Wages are a cost or expense of a business which is incurred so that the company can generate revenue. The cost of goods or services consumed in the process of generating revenue is called an **expense.** Expenses are recorded as decreases to retained earnings because they cause a reduction in profit or earnings.

On June 30 the company also recognized the cost of using the building for the month to conduct business called depreciation. This transaction is recorded in row 10 of the worksheet.

June 30   Recorded depreciation on the building for the month of June. The building
has a 40-year life and a salvage value of $4,000.

Depreciation is recorded by spreading the cost of the asset less its salvage value over its useful life. Salvage value is the amount the company expects to get for the asset when it is used up. Another name for salvage value is scrap value.

$$\frac{\text{Cost} - \text{Salvage value}}{\text{Useful Life}} = \text{Depreciation expense for one year}$$

$$\frac{\$100,000 - \$4,000}{40 \text{ years}} = \$2,400 \text{ per year or } \$200 \text{ a month}$$

The expense incurred of $200 for June for using the building is a reduction of retained earnings and at the same time a reduction of the building account as the economic resource diminishes.

On June 30, the company recorded in row 11 that one month's insurance had been used up.

June 30   Recorded the expiration of insurance for the month of June.

This entry relates back to the two-year insurance policy which was purchased on June 1. The amount used up in June would be 1/24 of the two-year premium cost, or $40.

Notice that this entry decreases the asset prepaid insurance and at the same time recognizes a reduction of retained earnings of the same amount. One way to determine if retained earnings is involved is to ask yourself if the item in question (in this case insurance) is a cost that the company incurred and used up this period in order to conduct the company's business of providing accounting services for clients. If the answer is yes, it is an expense and a reduction of retained earnings.

The transaction recorded in row 12 of the worksheet shows that part of the $1,000 of supplies on hand at the beginning of June has been used up. A description of the June transaction is repeated below.

> June 30   An inventory of supplies showed the supplies still on hand cost $250.

Generally supplies purchased are recorded as additions to the supplies account. At the end of the period, a count is made of the supplies. If the supplies are not on hand, the assumption is that they were used and therefore would be recorded as an expense which would reduce retained earnings. If $250 of supplies are on hand at the end of June, $750 must have been used during the month.

The final June 30 transaction is recorded in row 13 of the worksheet. This transaction is the first monthly payment on the mortgage.

> June 30   Paid the first monthly principal and interest payment of $806 on the 8 percent
>   mortgage loan.

As is typically the case, each monthly payment contains both principal and interest. The easiest way to determine the amount of the principal is to calculate the interest first. The interest is calculated by using the following equation:

$$\text{Interest} = \text{Principal} \times \text{Rate} \times \text{Time}$$

The principal is the mortgage payable balance of $110,000, the interest rate is 8% per year and the time is one month or 1/12 of a year. The **interest rate** is the percentage rate that is multiplied by the principal amount of the loan to compute the amount of interest

$$\text{Interest} = \$110,000 \times 8\% \times 1/12 = \$733$$

The transaction states that the entire payment is $806. If $733 of this payment is interest, then the remaining $73 must be principal. The interest of $733 is recorded as an expense, which is a reduction of retained earnings, the $73 principal payment reduces mortgage payable, and cash is reduced for the total cash payment of $806. (Note: Next month's interest calculation will be $109,927 [$110,000 – $73 principal payment] × 8% × 1/12 = $732.85).

Equality Check

To help insure the equality of each transaction entered in a row of the worksheet, it is helpful to add a column for an **equality check**. This column, column L in Exhibit 2-1.5, is used to insure that for each row, total assets do in fact equal total liabilities and owner's equity. This is done by entering the following equation for the equality check.

For row 3 of the worksheet the equation entered in cell L3 would be as follows:

$$=\text{sum}(b3{:}g3){-}\text{sum}(h3{:}k3)$$

Note that this equation is mathematically equivalent to the balance sheet equation.

$$\text{assets} - (\text{liabilities} + \text{owner's equity}) = 0$$

After entering the formula, the number zero should appear on the worksheet in cell L3. If the amount is not zero but the equation entered is correct, that means that the assets do not equal the sum of the liabilities and owner's equity. Once an equality check formula has been entered for row 3, the equation can be copied and pasted to the remaining rows of column L. (See Appendix C for Microsoft Excel instructions on copying and pasting.)

Statement of Retained Earnings

Financial statement users are very interested in the changes in retained earnings because this account records what happened to the earnings (net income) of the company during the period. Potentially the earnings can either be kept in the business or withdrawn by the owner. For this reason, companies prepare a financial statement describing these changes called the **statement of retained earnings**.

As mentioned previously, retained earnings increases by the amount of revenues earned during the period and decreases by the amount of expenses and owner withdrawals. The statement of retained earnings usually combines revenues and expenses into one total called **net income**. Exhibit 2-1.6 shows a statement of retained earnings for Corliss. The beginning retained earnings amount comes from cell K3 of the worksheet and the ending retained earnings amount comes from cell K14. The owner withdrawal amount can be found in cell K7. If the beginning and ending amounts of retained earnings as well as the owner's withdrawal are known, the net income amount for Corliss can be mathematically calculated. Later, in Case Reading 2-3, we will give a more detailed description of the revenue and expense amounts that make up net income.

Exhibit 2-1.6

	A	B
1	**Corliss Accounting Firm**	
2	**Statement of Retained Earnings**	
3	**Month Ended June 30, 2000**	
4		
5	Retained Earnings, June 1, 2000	$ -
6	Add Net Income	1,877
7	Subtotal	1,877
8	Less Withdrawals by Owner	(1,000)
9	Retained Earnings, June 30, 2000	$ 877
10		

Note that the owner's withdrawal of $1,000 is not included in net income. That is because a withdrawal is *not* an expense; that is, it is not a sacrifice of resources for the purpose of generating revenue.

Statement of Owner's Equity

Some companies prefer to prepare a **statement of owner's equity** instead of a statement of retained earnings. This statement is very similar to the statement of retained earnings except that it also contains changes in other owner's equity accounts, mainly contributed capital. Because contributed capital increases when the owner puts more capital in the business, this statement includes owner capital contributions. Note the similarity between this statement shown in Exhibit 2-1.7 and the retained earnings statement in Exhibit 2-1.6.

Exhibit 2-1.7

	A	B	C	D	E
1	**Corliss Accounting Firm**				
2	**Statement of Owner's Equity**				
3	**Month Ended June 30, 2000**				
4					
5	Owner's Equity, June 1, 2000				$ 50,000
6	Add:				
7	Investments by Owner				-
8	Net Income				1,877
9	Subtotal				51,877
10	Less Withdrawals by Owner				(1,000)
11	Owner's Equity, June 30, 2000				$ 50,877
12					

After recording all the June transactions in the accounting transaction worksheet, Corliss Accounting Firm will want to prepare a balance sheet at the end of June. The balance sheet amounts will come from row 14, the ending balance row of the accounting transaction worksheet shown in Exhibit 2-1.5, which is recreated below.

	A	B	C	D	E	F	G	H	I	J	K
1		ASSETS						LIABILITIES + OWNER'S EQUITY			
2	Date	Cash	Accounts Receivable	Supplies	Prepaid Insurance	Land	Building	Accounts Payable	Mortgage Payable	Contributed Capital	Retained Earnings
14	End. Bal. 6/30/00	$ 27,734	$ 2,100	$ 250	$ 920	$ 30,000	$ 99,800	$ -	$ 109,927	$ 50,000	$ 877

A classified balance sheet for June is shown in Exhibit 2-1.8. Note how total assets equal total liabilities and owner's equity. Also notice how there are captions for current assets. fixed assets, current liabilities and long-term liabilties.

Exhibit 2-1.8

	B	C	D	E F	G	H	I
1			Corliss Accounting Firm				
2			Balance Sheet				
3			June 30, 2000				
4							
5	Assets				Liabilities and Owner's Equity		
6							
7	Current Assets				Current Liabilities		
8	Cash		$ 27,734		Accounts Payable		$ -
9	Accounts Receivable		2,100				
10	Supplies		250		Long Term Liabilities		
11	Prepaid Insurance		920		Mortgage Payable		109,927
12	Total Current Assets		31,004				
13					Total Liabilities		109,927
14	Fixed Assets						
15	Land	$ 30,000			Owner's Equity		
16	Building	99,800			Contributed Capital	$ 50,000	
17	Total Fixed Assets		129,800		Retained Earnings	877	
18					Total Owner's Equity		50,877
19							
20	Total Assets		$ 160,804		Total Liabilities and Owner's Equity		$ 160,804
21							

Two additional financial statements will be discussed in future case readings. One is the income statement and is shown in Exhibit 2-3.2 of Case Reading 2-3. The last financial statement presented in this course is the statement of cash flows and this will be covered in Case Readings 2-4 and 2-5.

SUMMARY

This case reading reviews the balance sheet equation and provides an overview of the various balance sheet classifications. In addition, the case reading demonstrates the concepts underlying transaction analysis by recording transactions in an accounting transaction worksheet. A balance sheet and statement of retained earnings is then prepared from the worksheet. A more thorough discussion of the balance sheet and its uses can be found in Case Reading 2-2.

EXERCISES AND PROBLEMS

Exercises

Exercise 1   Balance Sheet Equation. Which of the following balance sheet equations is not correct? Explain your answer briefly.

1. $A = L + OE$
2. $A - L = OE$
3. $L + OE = A$
4. $A + OE = L$
5. $L = A - OE$

Exercise 2 Identifying Assets, Liabilities, and Owners' Equity. Identify each of the following balance sheet accounts of El Paseo Company as either an asset, liability, or owners' equity account.

1.   Accounts payable
2.   Accounts receivable
3.   Building
4.   Cash
5.   Contributed capital
6.   Delivery truck
7.   Interest payable on mortgage
8   Retained earnings

9.   Land
10. Mortgage payable (due in 2005)
11. Notes receivable
12. Notes payable
13. Office furniture
14. Office supplies (on hand)
15. Prepaid rent
16. Unearned revenue

Exercise 3 Classifying Assets, Liabilities, and Owners' Equity. Identify each of the following as a current asset, fixed asset, current liability, long-term liability or owners' equity.

1.   Accounts payable
2.   Accounts receivable
3.   Building
4.   Cash
5.   Computer (used in office)
6.   Contributed capital
7.   Land

8.   Mortgage payable (due in 2005)
9.   Note receivable (due in 180 days)
10. Office supplies on hand
11. Prepaid insurance
12. Retained earnings
13. Salaries payable
14. Taxes payable (on real property)

Exercise 4 Balance Sheet Preparation. Reproduced below is the ending balance row from Rosebud Company's accounting transaction worksheet for the month ended October 31, 2000. Use this information to prepare a classified balance sheet in good form for Rosebud Company at October 31, 2000.

Date	Cash	Accounts Receivable	Supplies	Prepaid Insurance	Computer	Office Furniture	Accounts Payable	Mortgage Payable	Contributed Capital	Retained Earnings
End. Bal. 10/31/00	$9,700	$ 20,000	$1,100	$ 800	$ 8,400	$ 4,000	$ 2,500	$ 9,500	$ 30,000	$ 2,000

Exercise 5 Prepare a Statement of Retained Earnings. Prepare a statement of retained earnings for December 2000 for Yorkshire Company based on the following information taken from the Retained Earnings column of its accounting transaction worksheet. Net income can be computed by summing the revenues and the expenses in the retained earnings column.

Date	Retained Earnings	Explanation
12/1/00	$ -	Beginning balance
12/5/00	2,400	Revenues earned
12/16/00	(500)	Wages expense
12/20/00	(600)	Owner withdrawal
12/31/00	(400)	Rent expense
12/31/00	(300)	Utilities expense
12/31/00	(500)	Wages expense
12/31/00	$ 100	Ending balance

Problems

Problem 1 Recording Transactions in the Accounting Transaction Worksheet. Record the following transactions for Rodeo Company in an accounting transaction worksheet for February 2000. Be sure to complete the worksheet by summing each account column.

Feb. 1 Robert Rodeo used $33,000 of his personal funds to open a bank account in the name of Rodeo Company.

2 Purchased a two-year insurance policy for $2,400 cash.

4 Three computers were purchased for $6,000 with a $2,000 cash payment and the balance to be paid in two years as evidenced by a note payable.

8 Purchased $800 of office supplies on credit.

14 Hired an employee to begin work the next day. Salary is to be $1,400 per month.

20 The owner withdrew $500 cash for personal use.

25 Paid $400 of the amount due for the office supplies purchased on February 8.

28 Received $1,500 cash for fees revenue earned.

29 Paid employee for one-half month's work.

29 Recorded $100 for insurance expired for month of February.

29 Depreciation expense for the computers was computed to be $150.

29 Interest payable on the note was computed to be $30.

Suggested format for your accounting transaction worksheet is as follows:

Date	Cash	Office Supplies	Prepaid Insurance	Computer	Interest Payable	Accounts Payable	Note Payable	Contributed Capital	Retained Earnings	Explanation of Retained Earnings
Beg. Bal 2/1/00	$ 33,000	$ -	$ -	$ -	$ -	$ -	$ -	$ 33,000	$ -	

Problem 2 Preparing a Balance Sheet (using the accounting transaction worksheet prepared in Problem 1). After recording the information in Problem 1 in an accounting transaction worksheet, prepare a balance sheet for Rodeo Company at February 29, 2000. Be sure to classify the assets and liabilities as current or long term.

Problem 3 Prepare a Balance Sheet from Information in an Accounting Transaction Worksheet. Use the information given in the accounting transaction worksheet for Budlong Company to prepare a balance sheet at February 29, 2000.

Budlong Company
February 2000

Date	Cash	Office Supplies	Prepaid Insurance	Computer	Interest Payable	Accounts Payable	Note Payable	Contributed Capital	Retained Earnings	Explanation of Retained Earnings
Beg. Bal 2/1/00	$ 33,000	$ -	$ -	$ -	$ -	$ -	$ -	$ 33,000	$ -	
2/2/00	(2,400)		2,400							
2/4/00	(2,000)			6,000			4,000			
2/8/00		800				800				
2/14/00					No entry needed					
2/20/00	(500)								(500)	Withdrawal by owner
2/25/00	(400)					(400)				
2/28/00	1,500								1,500	Fees revenue
2/29/00	(700)								(700)	Salary expense
2/29/00			(100)						(100)	Insurance expense
2/29/00				(150)					(150)	Depreciation expense
2/29/00					30				(30)	Interest expense
End. Bal. 2/29/00	$ 28,500	$ 800	$ 2,300	$ 5,850	$ 30	$ 400	$ 4,000	$ 33,000	$ 20	

Problem 4   Describing Accounting Worksheet Transactions. For each row in the accounting transaction worksheet given in Problem 3, describe the events that took place on each given date in February.

Problem 5   Prepare a Statement of Retained Earnings and a Statement of Owner's Equity.

1. Using the information in the accounting transaction worksheet in Problem 3, prepare a statement of retained earnings for Budlong Company for the month ended February 29, 2000.

2. Using the information in the accounting transaction worksheet in Problem 3, prepare a statement of owner's equity for Budlong Company for the month ended February 29, 2000.

Problem 6   Correcting a Balance Sheet. The balance sheet for Hawthorne Company is presented below. The balance sheet was prepared in a hurry by the owner because the accountant was ill. You are to look over the balance sheet and make any corrections needed before the owner, Happy Hawthorne, takes it to his bank to apply for a loan.

Hawthorne Company
Balance Sheet
March 31, 2000

Current Items		Long-Term Items	
Accounts receivable	$3,000	Mortgage payable	$50,000
Accounts payable	2,500	Land	20,000
Cash	1,000	Building	40,000
Retained earnings	7,500	Contributed capital	27,000
Salaries payable	4,000	Office furniture	5,000
Supplies on hand	2,000		
Total	$20,000	Total	$142,000

Case 2-1

LAURA'S LAW PRACTICE

Case Objectives

1. To understand how to record the impact of economic events on assets, liabilities, and owners' equity.
2. To gain practice in using a computer spreadsheet by performing a worksheet analysis of accounting transactions.
3. To learn how to prepare a balance sheet from information contained in a worksheet of accounting transactions.
4. To understand how to interpret and use information contained in a balance sheet.

Decision: Should Laura's loan request be granted?

Laura Jordan decided to start her own law practice after several years as a partner with Woodward and Sneesby, a statewide legal firm. She had considered organizing her practice as a professional corporation, but finally decided to operate as a sole proprietorship. The events that follow occurred during April 2000, the month Laura organized her law practice.

April 1		Laura opened a business bank account by depositing $73,000 she had saved during her years with Woodward and Sneesby.
	1	The law firm purchased a small office building for $210,000 and land for $95,000. A down payment of $39,000 was made, and a 30-year, 12 percent mortgage loan requiring monthly principal and interest payments of $2,736 was signed for the balance.
	4	The firm purchased two personal computers for $5.500 cash.
	7	Laura wrote a business check for $21,000 for office furniture.
	13	The firm purchased office supplies on account for $4,700, agreeing to pay for them within the next thirty days.
	16	Laura discovered that a desk purchased on April 7 and costing $1,500 had been damaged in shipping. She returned the desk to the supplier for a full cash refund.
	18	The firm paid $3,900 of the amount owed to the supplier from the supplies purchased on April 13.
	24	Since Laura and her husband owned two cars, Laura transferred ownership of their 1989 Mercedes to her law practice. They had purchased the car for $45,000, but it had a current retail blue book value of $24,000.
	28	After Laura finished setting up her office, she provided legal services for a walk-in client. The client paid the firm $4,700 cash.
	30	Laura paid the April utility bill, $275.

April 30	Laura wrote a check to pay the first mortgage payment. (Hint: the mortgage payment should be broken down into interest and repayment of principal components. Calculate the interest first, then determine the principal component. Round the interest computed to the nearest dollar before computing the principal.)
30	Laura hired a receptionist/secretary for the firm, agreeing to pay her $1,800 per month. She would start work on the following Monday.
30	Laura paid the phone bill for her personal home with a check from the business bank account. The amount of dollars she paid is equal to the last two digits of your student ID number (show your ID# at the top of your spreadsheet–if the last two digits are 00 use $25).

Requirements

1. Using the computer, prepare an accounting transaction worksheet. One possible format for the worksheet is given on the following page in Exhibit C2-1.1. Since this is Laura's first month of operations, all the accounts will have zero balances to start. Include a row for the beginning balances. Next, record April's transactions. Compute the ending balances in the accounts by summing each column.

2. Perform an equality check on each row of your worksheet as shown in column L of Exhibit 2-1.5 in Case Reading 2-1.

3. Using the worksheet information, prepare a classified balance sheet at April 30, 2000. A sample balance sheet is provided as Exhibit 2-1.8 in Case Reading 2-1.

4. Laura notes from her April 30 balance sheet that she has owner's equity of about $97,000. She needs to acquire a good law library and some additional business assets. so she takes her balance sheet to First National Bank, the bank that holds her mortgage, and requests a 60-day, $15,000 loan. Assume that you are the loan officer who receives Laura's loan request. Write an analysis of whether First National Bank should approve Laura's loan request. Your analysis should include the benefits and risks of granting the loan as well as your decision. Be sure to include references to the financial data given in the case.

Exhibit C2-1.1
Laura's Law Practice
Accounting Transaction Worksheet
April, 2000

	A	B	C	D	E	F	G	H	I	J	K	L	M
1	Date	Cash	Office Supplies	Land	Computer	Furniture	Auto	Building	Accounts Payable	Mortgage Payable	Contributed Capital	Retained Earnings	Equality Check
2	Beg. Bal. 4/1/00												
3	4/1/00												
4	4/1/00												
5	4/4/00												
6	4/7/00												
7	4/13/00												
8	4/16/00												
9	4/18/00												
10	4/24/00												
11	4/28/00												
12	4/30/00												
13	4/30/00												
14	4/30/00												
15	4/30/00												
16	End. Bal. 4/30/00												

Group Assignment 2-1

SARA'S SHOPPING SERVICE

Group Number _____ Group members present and participating:

_____

_____

Objectives

1. To learn how to use formulas in spreadsheets, including the sum command and an equality check.
2. To learn the meaning of icons on a toolbar.
3. To learn how to prepare a classified balance sheet based on information contained in an accounting transaction worksheet.

Requirements

1. An accounting transaction worksheet labeled Exhibit G2-1.1 has been provided for you for Sara's Shopping Service at the end of this group assignment. After reviewing this worksheet, provide the following information.

   a. What is the formula for cell L13 (the equality check)?

   b. What is the formula for cell B13 (the cash ending balance)?

2. Complete the following tasks relating to the toolbar shown in Exhibit G2-1.1.

   a. Circle the icon on the toolbar of the worksheet that allows you to copy what is highlighted.

   b. Put a box around the icon on the toolbar that represents the sum command.

   c. Choose one other icon on the toolbar and explain its purpose. Be sure to designate which icon you are choosing.

3. Complete the balance sheet below based on the information given in the accounting transaction worksheet shown in Exhibit G2-1.1.

```
┌──────────────────────────────────────────────────────────────────────────┐
│                           Sara's Shopping Service                          │
│                               Balance Sheet                                │
│                               June 30, 2003                                │
│                                                                            │
│              Assets                     Liabilities and Owner's Equity      │
│                                                                            │
│  Current Assets                         Current Liabilities                │
│                                                                            │
│                                                                            │
│  Total Current Assets                   Long-term Liabilities              │
│                                                                            │
│  Fixed Assets                                                              │
│                                         Total Liabilities                  │
│                                                                            │
│                                         Owner's Equity                     │
│  Total Fixed Assets                                                        │
│                                                                            │
│                                                                            │
│                                         Total Liabilities and              │
│  Total Assets                           Owner's Equity                     │
└──────────────────────────────────────────────────────────────────────────┘
```

4. Describe the transactions for Sara's Shopping Service that are shown in rows 4, 6 and 11 of the worksheet in G2-1.1.

   Row 4:

   Row 6:

   Row 11:

Exhibit G2-1.1
The Accounting Transaction Worksheet

	A3		6/1/2003									

	Date	Cash	Office Supplies	Land	Equipment	Auto	Accounts Payable	Mortgage Payable	Contributed Capital	Retained Earnings	Explanation of Retained Earnings	Equality Check
1												
2	Beg. Bal. 6/1/03	0	0		0	0	0	0	0	0		
3	6/1/03	$30,000							$30,000			0
4	6/1/03	($12,000)		$35,000	$8,000			$31,000				0
5	6/6/03	($7,000)			$7,000							0
6	6/13/03		$3,200				$3,200					0
7	6/18/03	($1,700)					($1,700)					0
8	6/25/03					$28,000			$28,000			0
9	6/28/03	$1,400								$1,400	Fees revenue	0
10	6/30/03	($450)								($450)	Utility expense	0
11	6/30/03	($2,073)						($1,742)		($331)	Interest expense	0
12	6/30/03	($320)								($320)	Withdrawal	0
13	End. Bal. 6/30/03	$7,857	$3,200	$35,000	$15,000	$28,000	$1,500	$29,258	$58,000	$299		0

Ready   Sum=6/1/03   NUM

Case Reading 2-2

MAKING DECISIONS USING BALANCE SHEET INFORMATION

INTRODUCTION

In Case Reading 2-1 you learned how to prepare an accounting transaction worksheet. This worksheet was used to record the monetary transactions of the company and then to prepare a balance sheet. In this case reading, you will learn how to interpret the information on a balance sheet without knowing the day-to-day activities of the company.

WHAT DOES THE BALANCE SHEET TELL YOU?

As a user of financial statements, you usually will not have any knowledge of the day-to-day activities of the company. Instead, you will be given a complete set of financial statements and will be expected to make your decisions based on this limited knowledge. If the financial statements have been prepared in accordance with generally accepted accounting principles (GAAP), the reader of the financial statements can make certain assumptions about the information without having all the minute details of every specific transaction.

Exhibit 2-2.1 shows the classified balance sheet of Bouncing Bungies Company. Even though a balance sheet can be prepared at any time, this specific balance sheet represents a snapshot of the assets, liabilities, and owner's equity of the company after its first month of operations. The heading of the balance sheet states that the company name is Bouncing Bungies Company and that the statement date is December 31, 2000. Because of the entity concept, the balance sheet of Bouncing Bungies contains only assets, liabilities, and equities of the business. The owner's personal items are not included in the financial statements of the business.

Assets

By listing accounts as assets, the company is representing that these items are probable future benefits owned or controlled by the company that have resulted from past transactions or events.

Current Assets

The balance sheet (statement of financial position) for Bouncing Bungies includes a heading for current assets. As mentioned previously, current assets are assets that the company expects to convert to cash or use up within the next year. In this case, Bouncing Bungies considers cash, accounts receivable, supplies, and prepaid insurance to be current assets.

Cash. The cash balance of $8,141 shows the reader the amount of cash that the company had recorded in its books as of December 31, 2000, which was available for use at the end of that day. This amount may differ from the amount that the bank shows as the ending balance per the bank statement due to outstanding checks, deposits in transit, and other items. Many times students have complained that they went to the 24-hour teller machine, asked their account

Exhibit 2-2.1

Bouncing Bungies Company					
Balance Sheet					
December 31, 2000					

Assets			Liabilities and Owner's Equity		
Current Assets			**Current Liabilities**		
Cash	$ 8,141		Accounts Payable	$ 2,000	
Accounts Receivable	1,000		Gift Certificates	25	
Supplies	500		Wages Payable	2,400	
Prepaid Insurance	4,400		Total Current Liabilities		$ 4,425
Total Current Assets		$ 14,041			
			Long Term Liabilities		
Fixed Assets			Note Payable		5,290
Bungies, net		7,900			
			Owner's Equity		
			Contributed Capital	10,000	
			Retained Earnings	2,226	
			Total Owner's Equity		12,226
			Total Liabilities and		
Total Assets		$ 21,941	Owner's Equity		$ 21,941

balance, and decided to withdraw that exact balance only to get a call the following day from the bank that their account was overdrawn! How can this happen?

It usually happens because previously written checks have not yet been presented to the bank for payment; therefore the bank has not deducted them from the account. Checks are "outstanding" until they clear the bank. Similarly, "deposits in transit" are deposits that have been recorded in the checkbook, but not by the bank. Besides outstanding checks and deposits in transit, there may be other reconciling items or differences between the checkbook balance and the balance per the bank records. These usually consist of various service charges, interest earned on the account balance, and errors. A company should reconcile its bank balance to the book balance at least once a month. The following is an example of a bank reconciliation.

Balance per Bank Statement	$10,552
Less Outstanding Checks	– 3,513
Add Deposits in Transit	+ 1,102
Adjusted Balance per Bank	$8,141
Balance per Books	$8,156
Less Service Charges	– 15
Adjusted Balance per Books	$ 8,141

Once again, it is the $8,141, the adjusted balance, that is shown on the balance sheet because this amount correctly reflects all of the company's most recent activities.

The cash amount shown on the balance sheet may also represent a summary dollar amount. In other words, the totals of many different cash accounts are combined into one summarized figure. This is true for most of the items on the balance sheet. The company may actually have

10 cash accounts or 100 accounts receivable accounts but on the balance sheet they are summarized into one account called cash (for the cash accounts) or accounts receivable (for the accounts receivable accounts). Having one condensed figure makes the statements far easier for the reader to use and all necessary information can usually be gathered from the summarized figures.

Accounts Receivable. The accounts receivable balance shows that the company extends credit to customers who buy tickets for bungy jumping. Some customers have outstanding balances and $1,000 is still owed at December 31, 2000. Since this is a current asset, we know that Bouncing Bungies expects to collect this amount within the next year. Credit terms offered by most businesses provide for the collection of accounts receivable within 30 to 60 days. (Note that uncollectible accounts are ignored here. They will be discussed in Module 4).

Supplies. The supplies balance on the balance sheet shows $500 of supplies still on hand at year end. The fact that supplies are listed as a current asset assures us that management expects the supplies to be used up within the next year.

Prepaid Insurance. The company's balance sheet shows prepaid insurance of $4,400. This means that the company still has that amount of unused insurance or future coverage.

Fixed Assets

The fixed asset category tells us that Bouncing Bungies has one long-term asset, bungies.

Bungies, net. The word *net* shows that the original cost of the bungies was reduced by the amount of cumulative depreciation. The $7,900 represents the amount not yet depreciated (also called the undepreciated cost or the book value). Depreciation is the allocation of a portion of the cost of the equipment to expense each accounting period over the useful life of the equipment.

Total Assets

This calculation is merely the sum of all the asset account balances. You should notice that total assets equal total liabilities and owner's equity, thus maintaining the balance sheet equation.

Liabilities

Liabilities are debts or obligations to transfer cash or other assets to other entities. They are listed after assets on the balance sheet and before owner's equity.

Current Liabilities

You may remember that current liabilities are debts or other obligations that will be paid in cash or satisfied with other assets or services within one year. This section of the balance sheet tells us that the company considers accounts payable, gift certificates, and wages payable to be current liabilities, meaning that these obligations should be satisfied within one year.

Accounts Payable. As mentioned previously, accounts payable are amounts owed to suppliers for items purchased that the company intends to use during the normal course of business operations. Most accounts payable are due within 30 days, but the actual due date is based on agreements with the individual suppliers. The accounts payable amount shown, like most other items on the balance sheet, is a combination of the balances from many suppliers.

Gift Certificates. The gift certificates amount represents the obligation (debt) the company recognizes for bungy jumps that have been paid for in advance. In this company's case, it receives the cash and gives the customer a gift certificate entitling the bearer to a future bungy jump. Assuming that a bungy jump costs $25, the balance sheet reflects an obligation of one bungy jump to the bearer of the gift certificate.

Wages Payable. Wages payable refers to wages earned by employees who have worked but have not yet been paid. The balance of $2,400 in wages payable means that $2,400 worth of work was performed and is unpaid as of the balance sheet date. Wages payable will always be a current liability as very few employees are willing to wait for more than a year to get paid!

<u>Long-Term Liabilities</u>

Because the classified balance sheet has a section called long-term liabilities, we can conclude that there are liabilities the company expects to pay in a period of time greater than one year.

Note Payable. Note payable can either be a short-term (current) liability or a long-term liability. Since this note payable is shown under the long-term caption, we can assume that the note is not due within a year from the balance sheet date. Notes payable can include notes to banks, individuals, or other businesses. Notes payable differ from accounts payable because there is a written promise to pay and a due date. Interest is also involved.

Owner's Equity

The owner's equity section of the balance sheet reports the owner's interest in the business. Because the heading says owner's equity (instead of owners' equity or stockholders' equity) we can conclude that Bouncing Bungies is a sole proprietorship.

Contributed Capital. From this balance sheet we can tell that the owner invested a total of $10,000 since the start of the business. No details are provided as to whether the amount the owner invested was cash or another type of asset. Any investment the owner makes in the business will result in an increase to contributed capital.

Retained Earnings. The retained earnings amount on the balance sheet represents the earnings the company has kept or retained in the business since its inception. The reconciliation of the retained earnings account is illustrated on the statement of retained earnings for Bouncing Bungies shown in Exhibit 2-2.2.

Exhibit 2-2.2

Bouncing Bungies Company Statement of Retained Earnings Month Ended December 31, 2000	
Retained Earnings, December 1, 2000	$ -
Add Net Income	2,269
Subtotal	2,269
Less Withdrawals by Owner	(43)
Retained Earnings, December 31, 2000	$ 2,226

You will note that it is the statement of retained earnings that ties the income statement information to the balance sheet information. Retained earnings is increased by the amount of net income (or decreased if there is a net loss) and decreased by the amount of an owner's withdrawal.

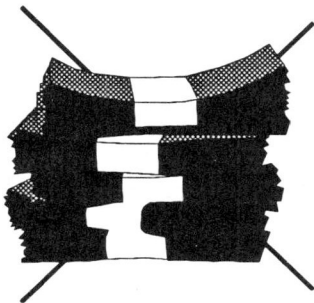

A common misconception is that retained earnings is cash. This is not the case. The company can have a large amount of retained earnings but very little or no cash. Several possible ways this can happen include selling on credit, purchasing fixed assets with cash, and paying off existing liabilities with cash. Retained earnings is a part of owner's equity and represents the cumulative income earned and *not* withdrawn by owners. In most cases, publicly held corporations pay out about one-third of income as dividends and reinvest the remainder in acquiring new assets or paying off debt.

OTHER POSSIBLE CONCLUSIONS AND ASSUMPTIONS

The accounts that are listed on the balance sheet give us very specific information. After reading the balance sheet, we can come to some additional conclusions. For example, we can conclude that the company did not have any additional material[1] amounts of assets such as long-term investments, inventory, other prepaid expenses, equipment, building, etc. If the company had any additional material assets, they would be shown on the balance sheet in the assets section. A similar conclusion can be reached about liabilities. That is, the company must not have any material unpaid salaries or unpaid taxes that they owe at year end because there is no liability shown for those items at the balance sheet date. The company likewise does not have any material interest outstanding at month end, or interest payable would be listed as a liability. Remember that the interest owed is shown in a separate account from the principal owed, so the note payable account shown on the balance sheet would not reflect any interest that might be unpaid. If, however, the company has small immaterial amounts of several of the items mentioned, these immaterial items would probably be included with similar accounts. For example, if Bouncing Bungies owed only a small immaterial amount of salaries, it might have included the salaries with the wages payable. Small amounts of interest owed might be included with the note payable or with the accounts payable.

In this discussion it has been assumed that the financial statements were accurately prepared and that they were prepared in accordance with GAAP. Before accepting any financial information from a company, however, you need to determine whether or not the financial statements were audited by an independent public accountant. Most small business do not have their financial statements audited so the user needs to be cautious. For this reason, creditors may require loan applicants to submit audited statements before considering their application. Usually audited financial statements contain a statement at the bottom of every financial statement telling the reader that additional information about that statement could be found in the footnotes of the financial statements. The footnotes provide additional narrative to help in the decision-making process.

---

[1] Any financial statement item is considered to be material when knowledge of that item would cause a financial statement user to change a decision.

HOW DO WE USE THIS INFORMATION?

Once the balance sheet has been reviewed, the reader may want to perform certain mathematical calculations. The balance sheet is one of the financial statements used for assessing liquidity.

Liquidity

Each financial statement user has a unique perspective in how to use the information that the balance sheet provides. Although profit is always important, a creditor is much more interested in repayment of the debt when it comes due. A creditor will want to look at the potential sources of future cash and the probable uses of that future cash to make sure that the liability will be repaid in a timely manner.

Some profitable companies have gone bankrupt because they were not able to pay their debts on time.

Liquidity refers to how quickly a company can convert its assets to cash and the length of time until its liabilities mature. One popular measure of liquidity is the current ratio.

<u>Current Ratio</u> - The **current ratio** is computed by dividing current assets by current liabilities.

$$\text{Current Ratio} = \frac{\text{Current Assets}}{\text{Current Liabilities}}$$

As you might already have noticed, all accounts on the balance sheet are listed in order of liquidity. In other words, cash is listed first as it is considered to be the most liquid asset. The company wants to have a current ratio which indicates that the current assets are sufficient to cover the current liabilities when they come due. This would suggest that the current ratio must be at least 1:1. Most companies like to maintain a higher current ratio, usually between 1.5:1 or 2:1 because, in some cases, certain current assets such as inventory might not be converted to cash very easily. Many banks require businesses who have borrowed money to maintain a minimum specified current ratio.

The current ratio for the Bouncing Bungies Company is calculated as follows:

$$\frac{\text{Current assets} = \$14,041}{\text{Current liabilities} = \$4,425} = 3.17$$

A 3.17 current ratio suggests that the company has sufficient current assets to repay the current liabilities as they become due. A closer examination might look at the type of current asset to determine how liquid (easily converted to cash) it is. Having computed the current ratio, the ratio should then be compared with other similar companies in the same industry. Such comparison gives the balance sheet reader a better idea of how this company's balance sheet compares with other companies in the same industry. If it is much higher than the norm, perhaps the company should try to reduce the amount of current assets and invest in longer-term assets that might possibly provide a higher return.

A Note on Opportunity Costs

As mentioned previously, the change in the retained earnings account provides us with information concerning the profit of the company during the accounting period. Besides computing profit during the period to assess operating performance, it is also helpful to look at the opportunity costs. Opportunity costs are the benefits lost or forfeited as a result of selecting one alternative course of action over another. An example of an opportunity cost is the salary that is foregone by choosing to attend a university instead of working full time during the college years. While accountants do not subtract opportunity costs from revenues in computing net income, economists do recognize opportunity costs in their measurement of profit.

Decision making is selecting the best alternative among two or more courses of action in regard to some item under consideration. Thus, opportunity costs are present in all decision-making situations we encounter, whether we consciously recognize it or not. A typical example of opportunity cost follows.

Assume that Joseph Risktaker quits his job as a successful corporate attorney to start his own law practice. Before quitting, Joe was earning $75,000 annually working in the legal department of a large corporation. He had accumulated personal financial assets that earned him an 8 percent return prior to leaving the firm.

On January 1, 2000, Joe liquidated $100,000 of his personal financial assets and opened a bank account for his law practice. During 2000, Joe worked at his law practice, generating revenues of $200,000 and incurring expenses (not including opportunity costs) of $130,000. The difference between how accountants and economists handle opportunity costs in measuring net income/profit is demonstrated below.

	Accountant's computation of net income	Economist's computation of profit
Revenues	$200,000	$200,000
Expenses	(130,000)	(130,000)
Annual salary foregone (opportunity cost)		(75,000)
Annual earnings of financial assets foregone $100,000 × .08 (opportunity cost)		(8,000)
Net income/profit (loss)	$ 70,000	($ 13,000)

As you can see, the economist's computation of profit takes into consideration the other "opportunity" that Joe had, including his former salary as well as the interest that he could have earned from a bank on the $100,000 he invested in the business. From an accounting standpoint Joe would show profit of $70,000, but the economist calculates that Joe is actually worse off by $13,000 in choosing this alternative.

The economist would also consider non-financial opportunity costs. Did Joe spend more or less time in his own practice? Was there more or less pressure running his own practice (and how did this impact his family/significant others)? Did he have a greater/lesser sense of accomplishment?

SUMMARY

This case reading discusses the interpretation of information contained in a classified balance sheet. The concepts of materiality and liquidity are introduced. The case reading demonstrates the calculation of the current ratio and gives an example of how the ratio might be used in financial decision making. The topic of opportunity costs and how the viewpoints of an accountant and an economist might differ is also analyzed.

EXERCISES AND PROBLEMS

Exercises

Exercise 1 Bank Reconciliation Items. Indicate how each of the following items will affect your company's bank reconciliation where the bank statement balance and book balance are reconciled to the same "adjusted balance" as shown in this case reading. Indicate if each item will be (a) added to the book balance, (b) deducted from the book balance, (c) added to the bank statement balance, or (d) deducted from the bank statement balance.

1. Outstanding checks
2. Bank service charge
3. Deposit in transit
4. Interest earned on average cash balance in bank account
5. Bank erroneously charged another company's check to your account
6. A check received from a customer was returned with your bank statement stating that the customer had insufficient funds
7. A $36 check was erroneously recorded as $63 by your company

Exercise 2 Determine Purchases of Supplies. Determine the cost of supplies purchased during May for Plummer Company if it had $700 of supplies on hand on May 1, $1,000 on hand at May 31, and used supplies of $2,350 for the month of May.

Exercise 3 Determine Cost of Building. If Safford Company had a building listed in its June 30 balance sheet as "Building net, $66,500" and had recorded accumulated depreciation of $10,700 on the building, what was the original cost of the building? Explain briefly.

Exercise 4 Prepare the Current Liabilities Section of a Balance Sheet. Prepare the current liabilities section of a balance sheet for Nino Company from the following list of accounts and balances. Not all accounts listed are current liabilities.

Accounts Payable	$ 2,200	Salaries Payable	$ 1,700
Mortgage Payable	80,000	Retained Earnings	12,000
Taxes Payable	1,000	Fees Received in Advance	700
Prepaid Rent	2,700	Interest Payable	630

Exercise 5 Determine Cash Payments to Employees. What amount of cash was paid to employees in July if there were $880 of salaries payable at July 31, $200 of salaries payable at July 1, and salaries expense for July was $7,000? Explain briefly.

Exercise 6 Determine Current Ratio. Based on the following data, determine the current ratio for Kelley Company. If the average current ratio for the industry is 1.9, is Kelley Company doing better or worse than the average? Explain briefly.

Current assets	$36,000	Current liabilities	20,000
Fixed assets	120,000	Long-term liabilities	80,000

Problems

Problem 1 Prepare a Bank Reconciliation. Prepare a bank reconciliation at April 30, 2000 for the Luana Company based on the following information.

Balance per books, April 30	$10,800
Balance per bank statement, April 30	10,220
Outstanding checks	1,300
Deposit in transit	786
Bank charge for check printing	34
Interest earned on average cash balance	40
Bank error—recorded a $1,100 Luana deposit in another company's account	

Problem 2 Prepare Statement of Retained Earnings. The following information was taken from the accounting records for Eldredge Company. All items relate to the equity accounts of Eldredge for August 2000. Net income for August was $8,600; owner's withdrawal was $2,800; additional investment by Thomas Eldredge, owner, was $20,000; at August 1 the Retained Earnings account had a balance of $74,200 and the Contributed Capital account balance was $94,000.

a. Based on the above data, prepare a statement of retained earnings for August 2000.
b. How does this differ from a statement of owner's equity?
c. Compute ending owner's equity.

Problem 3 Current Ratio Error. Slippery Company has current assets of $180,000 and current liabilities of $90,000 listed on its balance sheet at October 31. Erroneously, $30,000 of current assets and $30,000 of current liabilities were omitted from the balance sheet. Joe Slippery states that the omitted amounts have no effect on the current ratio because both the current assets and current liabilities are understated by the same amount. Is Joe correct? Show computations and explain briefly.

Problem 4 Preparation of a Classified Balance Sheet. Prepare a classified balance sheet for Knapp Company at August 31, 2000, based on the following account balances. Note that no account balance is given for Retained Earnings—you are to determine what amount should be included in the balance sheet for retained earnings at August 31, 2000.

Accounts Payable	$18,000	Land	44,000
Accounts Receivable	30,000	Office Equipment, net	12,000
Building, net	66,000	Mortgage Payable	90,000
Cash	7,000	Prepaid Insurance	4,800
Contributed Capital	55,000	Retained Earnings	??
Current portion of		Salaries Payable	2,000
long-term debt	3,000	Supplies	2,500
Delivery Truck, net	20,000	Taxes Payable	4,000
Fees Received in Advance	3,300		

Case 2-2

JOHN'S PAINTING BUSINESS

Case Objectives

1. To understand how to construct a balance sheet using the balance sheet equation (assets = liabilities + owner's equity) and information about assets and liabilities and transactions affecting those items (i.e., accounts).
2. To understand how an analysis of the changes in owner's equity that have occurred during a period may be used to evaluate the success of a business during that same period.

Decision: Was John's business financially successful?

After considering the pros and cons of the three alternatives described in Case 2-1 (i.e., get a summer job, go to summer school, or start a summer painting business) John, at the end of April 1999, decided to start the summer painting business. Accordingly, during May he began making arrangements to commence operations.

John located a compressor and other painting equipment and supplies that cost $3,300. His uncle agreed to loan him $3,300 at 9 percent annual interest for the summer. The agreement was for John, at the end of the summer, to pay all of the interest accrued during the summer. At that point John and his uncle would decide whether the loan would be paid off or continued (with annual interest at 9 percent) in order to finance the following summer's business.

John planned to use his three-year-old Toyota pickup truck, which has a $9,200 blue book value, to carry his paint and supplies to and from job sites. Since John planned to use this truck exclusively for business during the next few summers, he paid $1,500 cash from his personal bank account for a used motorcycle. He planned to use the motorcycle for all of his personal (non-business) transportation needs.

John's business officially started on June 1, 1999, at which point he transferred $1,400 of his $2,600 savings account balance to a business checking account so that he would have some working capital. On the same date, he deposited his uncle's $3,300 loan in this same account and immediately wrote checks totaling $3,300 ($2,400 for the compressor, $600 for two ladders, and $300 for the paint for his first job). John began painting on June 2. Apart from an additional $1,000 he contributed in cash in mid-July and $1,200 he withdrew from the business in early August to help his parents pay his Fall semester college expenses, all activity in the business checking account involved business receipts or expenditures.

It is now September 10, 1999. John has just written a check to pay his uncle the interest owed through August 31. He now is attempting to evaluate the financial success of his summer business in order to decide whether he should continue the business next summer. John has identified the following (partial) list of business assets and liabilities as of August 31, 1999.

Balance at 8/31/99

Cash in bank account..	$6,660
Amount owed to John by customers	1,300
Cost of unused supplies	95
Unused paint	0
Compressor (at cost)...	2,400
Ladders (at cost)...	600
Loan payable to uncle..	3,300
Unpaid bill for paint	300
Unpaid bill for advertising	275
Other assets..	?
Other liabilities..	?
Owner's equity	?

The compressor and ladders are still in good condition, despite their heavy use during the summer. John believes that, if he decides to continue in business the next two summers, both the compressor and the ladders could be used again and he could sell them at the end of the third summer at approximately 12 percent of their original cost. John's pickup has also seen heavy use over the last three months, with almost the entire 10,500 miles driven during this time related to business use. He thinks that if he uses it for two more summers, he can probably sell it for about $2,500. John plans to continue to use his motorcycle for personal transportation needs.

Requirements

1. Prepare a balance sheet for John's painting company as of August 31, 1999. A good format to use for the balance sheet can be found in Exhibit 3-2.1 *Do not attempt to use the "worksheet" approach for this problem.* It will not work because all transactions are not given. Instead, think about how you can use the balance sheet equation to prepare a balance sheet. Some hints are given below.

     a. Which of the items listed represent assets to John's company? Are there any assets not listed? Also, having used various assets during the summer, should the balance sheet show those assets at their original (historical) cost?

     b. Which of the items listed represent liabilities to John's company? Are there any liabilities not listed? For example, how much interest does John owe his uncle at August 31?

     c. How could we compute owner's equity from the information given? What accounts make up owner's equity?

2. Prepare a brief explanation of how you might evaluate the financial success of John's business. Defend your answer with supporting computations. (Hint: On June 1, before John opens his business checking account and officially starts his business, owner's equity is $0. At the end of August, owner's equity is what amount? How do you account for the change in owner's equity that has occurred during this three-month period, that is, what causes owner's equity to increase or decrease?).

Group Assignment 2-2

WAS JOHN'S BUSINESS SUCCESSFUL?

Group Number _____ Group members present and participating:

_____

_____

Objectives

1. To understand how to construct a balance sheet using the balance sheet equation (assets = liabilities + owner's equity) and information about assets and liabilities and transactions affecting those items i.e., accounts.
2. To understand how an analysis of the changes in owner's equity that have occurred during a period may be used to evaluate the success of a business during that same period.

Requirements

After discussing your individual answers to the questions raised at the end of Case 2-2 (John's Painting Business), record your group's consensus responses to the following questions.

1. What is the financial position of John's Painting Business at August 31, 1999? Complete the balance sheet shown on the next page. Some account names have already been entered but others have been omitted. Be sure to complete the balance sheet before answering any other questions.

2. Was John's business a financial success? Refer to specific numbers from the balance sheet to support your answer.

3. Would an economist's definition of profit differ from the accountant's definition? Explain the difference as it relates to this case.

4. Does it appear that John made the right decision to start his own business rather than to work as an employee of the dry cleaning plant or to go to summer school? Explain.

John's Painting Business

Balance Sheet

August 31, 1999

Assets	Liabilities and Owner's Equity
Current Assets	Current Liabilities
Cash	Accounts Payable
Accounts Receivable	
Supplies	
	Total Current Liabilities
Total Current Assets	
	Long-term Liabilities
Fixed Assets	
Compressors	Owner's Equity
Ladders	Contributed Capital
	Retained Earnings
Total Fixed Assets	Total Owners Equity
Total Assets	Total Liabilities and Owner's Equity

Note: All account names may not be listed in the balance sheet above. You may need to add additional accounts.

Case Reading 2-3

MAKING DECISIONS USING INCOME STATEMENT INFORMATION

INTRODUCTION

This case reading introduces the income statement and the concept of profitability. The accounting transaction worksheet from Case Reading 2-1 is reviewed and the preparation of an income statement and a statement of Retained Earnings from the information given in the retained earnings column of the worksheet is demonstrated. Revenues and expenses are defined and the concept of accrual accounting is presented.

THE INCOME STATEMENT

The **income statement** is a financial statement that shows the company's profit or net income for an accounting period. The format for the income statement expressed in equation form is

Revenues – Expenses = Net Income

- Increases in retained earnings are caused by a company earning revenue from selling a product or a service.
- Decreases in retained earnings are caused by expenses and owners' withdrawals. Expenses represent resources consumed in order to generate revenues. Owner withdrawals are a distribution of earnings to the owner(s). Note carefully that expenses, but *not* withdrawals, are deducted from revenues in computing net income.

The statement summarizes the revenues and expenses of the firm. Corliss Accounting Firm earned revenues when they provided accounting services to their clients. The rules for the recognition of revenue are described below.

Revenue

Revenue is the increase in the resources of an entity from the sale of goods or services and is generally recorded at the time the sale or service is provided. If the revenue was received in cash, both cash and retained earnings (Fees Revenue) would be increased. If the service was provided on credit, the accounts receivable account and the retained earnings account (Fees Revenue) would be increased. If the company is selling a product instead of a service, the revenue is recorded at the time the title of the product transfers to the buyer. The timing of the recording of revenue is described in the revenue recognition principle.

The revenue recognition principle requires that revenue should be recorded when the earning process has substantially been completed and an exchange has taken place.

Note that the recording of revenue does not depend on the receipt of cash.

Expenses

Expenses are the cost of goods or services used up in the process of generating revenue. In the case of Corliss Accounting Firm, the company borrowed cash and therefore incurred an interest cost, incurred insurance costs, used fixed assets to operate and therefore had depreciation costs, had employees who worked during the period, and also had supplies that were used during the period. Notice that the identification of these costs as expenses does not depend on whether the cost was paid. The fact that it was recorded as an expense merely means that it was a cost that was incurred for the purpose of generating revenue. The recording of expenses follows the matching principle.

> The *matching principle* requires that all costs incurred in generating revenue be recognized in the same period as the related revenue.

The rules for recording revenues and expenses follow the accrual basis of accounting.

> The *accrual basis of accounting* states that revenues and expenses are recognized in the period when earned or incurred regardless of when the cash is received or paid.

The time period in which a transaction is recorded is critical to accountants. For example, if an employee works in September, the expense must be recognized as salaries expense in September regardless of whether the employee has been paid. In fact, the payment policy is totally irrelevant to the timing of the recording of the expense. Regardless of whether the item is paid for in advance or not paid for until later, the expense will be recorded in the period in which the cost was incurred and the period in which that cost can be matched with the related revenue.

The worksheet shown in Exhibit 2-3.1 is almost identical to the worksheet for June which was shown in Exhibit 2-1.5 in Case Reading 2-1. This worksheet, however, adds a column to give a more detailed explanation of the changes in retained earnings. This column indicates the nature of each revenue, expense, or withdrawal transaction affecting retained earnings. It is useful to Corliss to have this detailed information so that they can make better decisions. For example, if the company noted that salaries expense seemed high, the manager would take different actions to correct that problem than would be taken if interest expense seemed too high. By identifying the type of expense the company is incurring, the manager is one step closer to controlling that cost.

In Case Reading 2-1, you learned how the information in the retained earnings columns is used to prepare the statement of retained earnings. These same columns (dollar amounts and explanations) are also used to prepare the income statement. The retained earnings and explanation of retained earnings columns from the accounting transaction worksheet are recreated as Exhibit 2-3.2.

Exhibit 2-3.1
Corliss Accounting Firm
Accounting Transaction Worksheet
June 2000

	A	B	C	D	E	F	G	H	I	J	K	L	M
				ASSETS				LIABILITIES + OWNER'S EQUITY					
1													
2	Date	Cash	Accounts Receivable	Supplies	Prepaid Insurance	Land	Building	Accounts Payable	Mortgage Payable	Contributed Capital	Retained Earnings	Explanation of Retained Earnings	Equality Ck.
3	Beg.Bal. 6/1/00	$ 29,300	$ -	$ 1,000	$ -	$ 30,000	$ 100,000	$ 300	$ 110,000	$ 50,000	$ -		0
4	6/1/00	(960)			960								0
5	6/4/00	(300)						(300)					0
6	6/15/00	2,000	1,000								3,000	Fees Revenue	0
7	6/16/00	(1,000)									(1,000)	Owner Withdrawal	0
8	6/30/00	1,100	1,100								2,200	Fees Revenue	0
9	6/30/00	(1,600)									(1,600)	Wage Expense	0
10	6/30/00						(200)				(200)	Depreciation Expense	0
11	6/30/00				(40)						(40)	Insurance Expense	0
12	6/30/00			(750)							(750)	Supplies Expense	0
13	6/30/00	(806)							(73)		(733)	Interest Expense	0
14	End.Bal. 6/30/00	$ 27,734	$ 2,100	$ 250	$ 920	$ 30,000	$ 99,800	$ -	$ 109,927	$ 50,000	$ 877		0

Exhibit 2-3.2
Selected Columns from an Accounting Transaction Worksheet

	A	K	L	M
2	Date	Retained Earnings	R E D	Explanation of Retained Earnings
3	Beg.Bal. 6/1/00	$ -		
4	6/1/00			
5	6/4/00			
6	6/15/00	3,000	R	Fees Revenue
7	6/16/00	(1,000)	D	Owner Withdrawal
8	6/30/00	2,200	R	Fees Revenue
9	6/30/00	(1,600)	E	Wage Expense
10	6/30/00	(200)	E	Depreciation Expense
11	6/30/00	(40)	E	Insurance Expense
12	6/30/00	(750)	E	Supplies Expense
13	6/30/00	(733)	E	Interest Expense
14	End.Bal. 6/30/00	$ 877		

Notice that we have added a column (called RED) to identify each retained earnings transaction during the period as either a revenue, expense, or owner withdrawal by labeling them with a R, E, or D respectively. All activity recorded in the retained earnings column during the period with the exception of owner's withdrawal (D) is included in the calculation of net income. The owner's withdrawal represents earnings that are withdrawn by the owner and are therefore not retained in the business.

The income statement is shown in Exhibit 2-3.3. (Cell formulas used to create this exhibit can be found in Appendix B at the end of this book.) The heading shows that the statement is for the Corliss Accounting Firm and that the statement covers an accounting period of one month, the month of June. In general, the **accounting period** for a company is the time period covered by the income statement. For most organizations, the primary accounting period is one year. Many organizations have secondary accounting periods of one month or one quarter.

Exhibit 2-3.3

	A	B	C	D
1		Corliss Accounting Firm		
2		Income Statement		
3		Month Ended June 30, 2000		
4	Revenues			
5		Fees Revenue		$ 5,200
6				
7	Expenses			
8		Wage Expense	$ 1,600	
9		Supplies Expense	750	
10		Interest Expense	733	
11		Depreciation Expense	200	
12		Insurance Expense	40	
13	Total Expenses			3,323
14	Net Income			$1,877
15				

Some businesses prepare a combined **statement of income and retained earnings** instead of two separate statements (remember, you saw a statement of retained earnings in Exhibit 2-1.6). This allows the financial statement reader to clearly see how income affected the retained earnings account. This type of analysis ties in nicely to our accounting transaction worksheet. You will notice that the Retained Earnings column is column K of the worksheet shown in Exhibit 2-3.1. The figures in this column agree with the combined statement of income and retained earnings shown in Exhibit 2-3.4.

Exhibit 2-3.4

	A	B	C	D	E
1	Corliss Accounting Firm				
2	Statement of Income and Retained Earnings				
3	Month Ended June 30, 2000				
4	Revenue				
5		Fees Revenue		$ 5,200	
6					
7	Expenses				
8		Wage Expense	$ 1,600		
9		Supplies Expense	750		
10		Interest Expense	733		
11		Depreciation Expense	200		
12		Insurance Expense	40		
13	Total Expenses			3,323	
14	Net Income			1,877	
15	Less Withdrawals by Owner			(1,000)	
16	Increase in Retained Earnings in June			877	
17	Add Retained Earnings, June 1, 2000			-	
18	Retained Earnings June 30, 2000			877	
19					

Notice how the income statement information is presented first, followed by information typically included in the statement of retained earnings. Whether a company uses a separate income statement and separate statement of retained earnings or a combined statement of the two is a matter of personal preference.

Profitability

Profitability is the increase in owner's equity created by successfully operating the business. The relevance of this accounting information to the various user groups will depend on their informational needs. The importance of profitability to two user groups, investors and managers, is described below.

- Investors are very interested in the operating performance of the company because high profits will probably cause the stock price to go up. Potentially the stock could be sold and a profit earned on the sale. Alternatively, a large profit may encourage the company to distribute some of that income to the owners. (If the company is a corporation, that distribution is called a **dividend**).

- Managers within the company use the financial information provided by financial statements on a daily basis. They need to have an accurate idea of the company's day-to-day revenues and expenses so that they can monitor the profitability of the company and adjust the operating plan accordingly. The income statement is particularly important for this type of information.

Overall, the income statement is the most valuable financial statement to review in order to evaluate the operating performance and the profitability of the company.

SUMMARY

This case reading continues the discussion of the accounting transaction worksheet and demonstrates how the information from the retained earnings column can be used to prepare the income statement. The accounting terms revenues and expenses are explained as well as the concept of accrual basis accounting. An overview of the importance of the income statement in making business decisions is also given.

EXERCISES AND PROBLEMS

Exercises

Exercise 1   Income Statement Equation. The income statement contains information concerning revenues, expenses, and net income. The determination of net income can be stated in the following equation format:

$$\text{Revenues} - \text{Expenses} = \text{Net income}$$

Based on the above equation, which of the following income statement equations is **not** correct? Explain briefly.

1. Net income = Revenues – Expenses
2. Expenses = Net income – Revenues
3. Revenues = Net income + Expenses
4. Expenses = Revenues – Net income

Exercise 2 Effect of Revenues on Retained Earnings. The earning of revenues has a direct effect on retained earnings. Do revenues increase or decrease retained earnings? Explain why revenues have the effect you indicated.

Exercise 3   Effect of Expenses on Retained Earnings. The incurring of expenses has a direct effect on retained earnings. Do expenses increase or decrease retained earnings? Explain why expenses have the effect you indicated.

Exercise 4   Define Matching Principle. Define the term *matching principle* as used in accounting. Give an example of its application.

Exercise 5 Define Accrual Accounting. Define the term *accrual basis of accounting*. Give an example of its application.

Problems

Problem 1   Prepare Income Statement and Statement of Retained Earnings. Kenilworth Company began operations on September 1, 2000. Following is the Retained Earnings and Explanation columns taken from the accounting transaction worksheet for the month of

September. Based on this information, prepare an income statement and a separate statement of retained earnings for September 2000.

Retained Earnings	Explanation
5,000	Fees earned
(1,500)	Salary expense
(700)	Supplies expense
3,200	Fees earned
(1,800)	Depreciation expense
(800)	Insurance expense
(1,000)	Owner withdrawal
(1,500)	Salary expense
(660)	Utilities expense
240	Balance September 30, 2000

Problem 2 Prepare a Combined Statement of Income and Retained Earnings. Using the information in Problem 1, prepare a combined statement of income and retained earnings for September 2000 for Kenilworth Company.

Problem 3   Recognition of Revenue. Explain when revenue was earned in each of the following independent situations.

1. On February 28, a farmer went to a local seed supply store and ordered 600 pounds of seed. On March 2, the farmer was informed that the seed had arrived. That same day the farmer went to the seed supply store, paid for the seed, and took it home with him. When should the seed supply store recognize revenue from the sale of the seed?

2. On June 20, 2000, a student sent a $200 deposit to the University of Northern Lights (UNL) to ensure him a place in the Fall 2000 freshman class. The UNL has a fiscal year ending on June 30. The student enrolled at UNL on August 15, 2000. When should UNL recognize the $200 as revenue received from the student?

Problem 4 Prepare Income Statement and Evaluate Earnings. Ridgewood Company has been in operation for over 10 years. Following is selected data taken from the accounts of Ridgewood Company. Use this data to prepare an income statement for the year ended August 31, 2000. Evaluate how well the owner is doing if he could earn a salary of $40,000 by working for another local business. Explain briefly.

Sales	$260,000	Retained Earnings	$ 20,000
Contributed Capital	40,000	Salaries Expense	100,000
Depreciation Expense	22,000	Supplies Used	15,000
Insurance Expense	10,000	Taxes Expense	8,000
Interest Expense	18,000	Utilities Expense	40,000
Other Expenses	6,000		

Problem 5 Cumulative Summary Problem. Beverly Road Company had the following transactions for October 2000. Record the transactions in an accounting transaction worksheet and then prepare (1) a combined statement of income and retained earnings and (2) a balance sheet.

Transactions for October 2000:

Oct. 1	Prepaid one-year insurance premium, $2,400.
5	Paid salaries for last half of September (in salaries payable), $3,700.
7	Earned cash fees for the first week of October, $6,200.
12	Purchased supplies on account, $1,100.
14	Earned cash fees for second week of October, $4,100.
15	Purchased new office computer for cash, $4,400.
20	Paid salaries for first half of October, $3,500.
25	Owner withdrew cash, $2,000.
28	Paid accounts payable, $1,300.
31	Earned cash fees for last half of October, $10,200.
31	Recorded insurance expired for month.
31	Supplies used in October amounted to $1,760.
31	Depreciation expense on computer was $50 and on building was $700.
31	Recorded salaries earned but not paid for second half of month, $3,600.

Account balances at October 1, 2000 were as follows:

Cash	$32,000	Accounts Payable	$ 2,000
Supplies	1,200	Salaries Payable	3,700
Prepaid Insurance	-0-	Contributed Capital	140,000
Building	182,000	Retained Earnings	69,500
Computer	-0-		

Case 2-3

JUAN RODRIGUEZ, M.D.

Case Objectives

1. To gain further understanding of how to translate economic events into accounting transactions.
2. To learn how to reflect transactions in a worksheet (computer spreadsheet).
3. To understand how to prepare a set of monthly financial statements (balance sheet, income statement, and statement of retained earnings) drawing upon information contained in a monthly worksheet of accounting transactions.

Decision: Should Dr. Rodriguez sell his medical practice to an HMO[1]?

Juan Rodriguez, M.D. has the following account balances on September 1, 2000. Cash $9,500, Accounts Receivable $4,300, Medical Supplies $1,900, Prepaid Rent $1,200, Diagnostic Equipment $22,000, Office Equipment $13,000, Salaries Payable $1,500, Contributed Capital $35,000, Retained Earnings $15,400.

Sept. 1	Juan received an inheritance from his Uncle Julio's estate in the amount of $50,000. Juan deposited 65 percent of this money into his business account.
1	Juan wrote a check for September's rent in the amount of $1,200.
2	Juan purchased new X-ray equipment for $35,000. A down payment of $15,000 was made and a 10-year note with 9 percent annual interest was signed for the balance. The note requires monthly principal and interest payments of $253 on the last day of each month.
5	Juan purchased a computer for his kids with a business check. The computer package cost $4,000 and included a free printer.
5	Juan paid his nurse $1,500 for work performed the last half of August (last month).
7	Juan purchased a new desk for his reception area for $900.
9	Juan signed a contract to provide emergency services for Pretty Quick Medical Clinic due to its shortage of physicians during September. Juan received a $1,000 check for agreeing to provide emergency services as needed. This amount represents payment in full, regardless of the number of emergency patients he sees during this period.
12	Checks in the amount of $2,000 were received for services already recorded.
15	Juan paid Simple Simon, R.N., his salary of $1,500 for the first half of September.

---

[1] HMO stands for Health Maintenance Organization. These types of corporations provide numerous health care services to enrolled participants.

Sept. 15   Fees earned for medical services provided for the first half of September amounted to $8,200, of which $3,700 was in cash and the remainder was recorded on account (i.e., accounts receivable).

15   Juan's order for medical supplies was delivered by Acute Medical Supply Company. The invoice total came to $2,800 and was to be paid by the October 15.

19   Juan was called into Pretty Quick Medical Clinic during the night and stayed for seven hours. During this time Juan treated ten patients. If Juan had treated the patients in his office he would have billed them a total of $1,000.

23   Juan withdrew $1,300 from the business account for a trip to Mexico that he was planning for a long weekend with his family.

29   Juan received September's utility bill for $360. This bill was immediately paid.

29   Juan wrote a check to Acute Medical Supply Company in the amount of $2,800.

30   Fees earned for medical services provided in the second half of September amounted to $9,900, of which $7,800 was in cash and the remainder was on account.

30   Checks in the amount of $3,100 and cash in the amount of $1,400 was received from patients who had previously been billed.

30   Juan made the first $253 payment on the note. The payment includes both principal and interest at 9 percent.

Additional information available on September 30, 2000 (which may require worksheet entries):

♦ Dr. Rodriguez estimated the useful life of the medical diagnostic equipment at 6–8 years, the X-ray equipment at 10–15 years and the office furniture at 12–16 years. All equipment and furniture is expected to have a 5 percent salvage value at the end of its useful life. The diagnostic equipment and office equipment on hand at the beginning of the month was purchased on August 31 and therefore has not been depreciated to date. Make all adjustments for depreciation on the same row of the spreadsheet.

♦ A physical count of the medical supplies on hand indicated that 55 percent had been used during September.

♦ Simple Simon, R.N., will be paid his salary of $1,500 on October 5 for work performed in September.

Requirements

1. Format a worksheet for the month of September for Dr. Rodriguez. <u>A sample format is provided for you on the last page of the case.</u> Note that the format contains a date column, an explanation of retained earnings column, and an equality check column.

2. Enter the beginning balances for all accounts.

3. Record September transactions in the appropriate accounts. Be sure to do an equality check for each row.

4. After entering all transactions, sum each column to compute the September 30 balances.

5. In the same workbook file, prepare a formal balance sheet at September 30, 2000. (You can use a new worksheet in the workbook file. See Appendix C for a discussion of workbooks and worksheets.)

6. In the same workbook file, prepare a combined statement of income and retained earnings for September 2000 as shown in Exhibit 2-3.4.

7. Which statement provides the better measure of operating performance, the balance sheet or the income statement? Why?

8. WEPAYALL Health Maintenance Organization has offered Dr. Rodriguez $100,000 for his medical practice. In addition, WEPAYALL is offering Dr. Rodriguez an employment contract as Director of Medical Practice Policies. The contract is for five years and specifies a salary of $10,000 per month and is indexed to the inflation rate. (Assume September, 2000 is representative of business during other times of the year). Should Dr. Rodriguez sell his practice? Why or why not? Reference specific financial statement information in your response.

Juan Rodriguez, M.D.
Accounting Transaction Worksheet Format
September, 2000

	A	B	C	D	E	F	G	H	I	J	K	L	M	N	O
	Date	Cash	Accounts Receivable	Medical Supplies	Prepaid Rent	X-Ray Equipment	Diagnostic Equipment	Office Equipment	Accounts Payable	Salaries Payable	Notes Payable	Contributed Capital	Retained Earnings	Explanation of Retained Earnings	Equality check
1															
2	Beg. Bal. 9/1/00														
3	9/1/00														
4	9/1/00														
5	9/2/00														
6	9/5/00														
7	9/5/00														
8	9/7/00														
9	9/9/00														
10	9/12/00														
11	9/15/00														
12	9/15/00														
13	9/15/00														
14	9/19/00														
15	9/23/00														
16	9/29/00														
17	9/29/00														
18	9/30/00														
19	9/30/00														
20	9/30/00														
21	9/30/00														
22	9/30/00														
23	9/30/00														
24	End. Bal. 9/30/00														

Case Reading 2-4

MAKING DECISIONS USING CASH FLOW INFORMATION

INTRODUCTION

This case reading focuses on the statement of cash flows. The concepts of operating, investing, and financing activities will be explained in depth. Although the indirect method of the statement of cash flows is mentioned briefly, that statement is more thoroughly discussed in Case Reading 2-5. The preparation of the direct method of the statement of cash flows from an accounting transaction worksheet will be demonstrated as well as how this statement is used to evaluate liquidity and solvency.

OVERVIEW OF THE STATEMENT OF CASH FLOWS

The statement of cash flows is one of the three primary financial reports issued by companies (the income statement and the balance sheet are the others). Some users, including many banks and financial analysts, consider the statement of cash flows to be the most important. Three major uses of the cash flow statement are to

- Explain what happened to a company's cash during the year. The company's **cash flows** include all increases and decreases to cash during the accounting period. The statement of cash flows reports where a company's cash came from and how it was spent. This information helps users assess whether the company is using its cash wisely.

- Estimate future cash flows from operations. Bankers and other creditors interested in a company's solvency use the statement to estimate future cash flows and, hence, the risk of insolvency. There have been several instances in which cash flow for companies that eventually became insolvent declined significantly several years prior to a reduction in net income. Also, shareholders are interested in cash flows to forecast future dividends.

- Determine the **quality of earnings.** All reported net income is not of equal quality. For example, if a company selects a long useful life for its assets and uses straight-line depreciation, it will report a higher net income (due to a lower depreciation expense) than if it selects a shorter useful life. The higher reported net income resulting from lower depreciation expense is said to be of lower quality. Analysts compare the amount of cash flow from operations to net income to evaluate the quality of earnings.

The statement of cash flows can be presented in two different formats. One of these formats is called the direct method; the other is called the indirect method. Both methods are used in practice but the indirect method is used over 85 percent of the time in published annual reports. The indirect method is more complex and is explained in Case Reading 2-5. The purpose of the statement of cash flows, regardless of the method used, is to show the changes in the cash account for the accounting period and what caused these changes.

The changes are described as cash inflows and outflows and are divided into three categories (operating, investing, and financing) according to a given set of criteria.

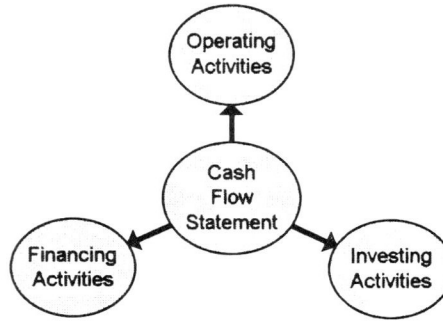

Operating activities include all cash flows that are not defined as investing or financing cash flows. Usually these are the cash flows from the daily operations of the company.

Investing activities include cash transactions which involve (1) the purchase and sale of securities, property, plant, equipment, and other assets not generally held for resale; and (2) the making and collecting of loans, for example, notes receivable.

Financing activities include cash transactions in which resources are obtained from or paid to owners (equity financing) and creditors (debt financing).

THE STATEMENT OF CASH FLOWS–DIRECT METHOD

The statement of cash flows–direct method is the form of the statement of cash flows in which the operating activities are described as cash inflows and cash outflows. This form of the statement of cash flows can be prepared from the cash column of the accounting transaction worksheet.

Sorting Activities in the Cash Column of the Transaction Worksheet

This transaction worksheet for Corliss Accounting Firm was presented to you in Exhibit 2-1.5. Exhibit 2-4.1 renames column B of that worksheet as column C. In the new column B each cash transaction is identified as either an operating (O), investing (I), or financing (F) activity. This column is called the OIF column. Column D is used temporarily in this exhibit to give a further explanation of the cash transaction. Only dollar amounts that appear in the Cash column will be shown in the statement of cash flows using the direct method.

Exhibit 2-4.1
Accounting Transaction Worksheet with OIF Column

	A	B	C	D
2	Date	OIF	Cash	Explanation of Cash
3	Beg.Bal. 6/1/00		$ 29,300	
4	6/1/00	O	(960)	Cash paid for insurance
5	6/4/00	O	(300)	Cash paid for supplies
6	6/15/00	O	2,000	Fees collected
7	6/16/00	F	(1,000)	Cash withdrawn by owner
8	6/30/00	O	1,100	Fees collected
9	6/30/00	O	(1,600)	Cash paid for wages
10	6/30/00			
11	6/30/00			
12	6/30/00			
13	6/30/00	O=(733) F=(73)	(806)	Cash paid for interest Cash paid for principal
14	End.Bal. 6/30/00		$27,734	

The statement of cash flows for Corliss Accounting Firm is shown as Exhibit 2-4.2.

Exhibit 2-4.2

	A	B	C	D
1		Corliss Accounting Firm		
2		Statement of Cash Flows–Direct Method		
3		Month Ended June 30, 2000		
4		Operating Activities		
5		Cash Inflows		
6		Fees collected		$ 3,100
7		Cash Outflows		
8		Cash paid for wages	$(1,600)	
9		Cash paid for interest	(733)	
10		Cash paid for insurance	(960)	
11		Cash paid for supplies	(300)	
12		Total Cash Outflows		(3,593)
13		Net Cash Flow from Operations		(493)
14		Investing Activities		-
15		Financing Activities		
16		Cash paid for principal on loan	(73)	
17		Cash withdrawn by owner	(1,000)	
18		Net Cash Flow from Financing Activities		(1,073)
19		Net Decrease in Cash During June		(1,566)
20		Add Cash Balance, June 1, 2000		29,300
21		Cash Balance, June 30, 2000		$27,734
22				

Notice that Corliss had a net decrease in cash during June of $1,566, even though the company had a net income of $1,877 (see Exhibit 2-3.3). Often differences arise between net income and net cash flow because companies recognize revenues when earned and expenses when incurred, regardless of whether the cash has been received or paid. This income measurement approach is called the accrual basis of accounting. This is in contrast to the cash basis of accounting, which recognizes revenues and expenses only when cash is received or paid. Generally accepted accounting principles (GAAP) require accrual basis of accounting for companies that are publicly traded.

Look at the statement of cash flows shown in Exhibit 2-4.2 more closely. The heading of the statement of cash flows indicates that this is the direct method and is for the month ended June 30, 2000. Note that the income statement and the statement of cash flows cover the same period of time. The statement of cash flows is broken down into several sections.

Operating Activities

The operating activities section shows the cash inflows and outflows from the day-to-day operations of the company, typically the items that go into determining net income.

Fees Collected. This item includes cash revenues for services rendered, as well as cash collected from accounts receivable.

Cash Paid for Wages. This item includes any cash payments for wages regardless of when the service was provided. For example, if the employee worked in May but was paid in June, the item would appear in the June statement of cash flows because this is the month the employee was paid in cash.

Cash Paid for Interest. The account Notes Payable is used when there is a written promise to pay which results in the borrower being charged with interest. Any of the charged interest that is paid during the period will be included in this caption. Cash payments of principal amounts are shown as financing activities.

Cash Paid for Insurance. This item includes cash payments to purchase insurance. Keep in mind that this statement shows the *cash* outlay only. The amount of insurance *used* during the period is shown on the income statement.

Cash Paid for Supplies. This analysis is similar to the previous one. The statement of cash flows indicates the supplies that were paid for during the period.

Net Cash Flow from Operations. This is the cash inflows less the cash outflows for the operating section.

Investing Activities

This includes all cash transactions that involve changes in nonoperating assets such as

- the purchase and sale of investment securities
- the purchase and sale of fixed assets
- the making and collecting of loans, for example, notes receivable

The fact that no investing transactions are listed means that such transactions did not occur during this accounting period. If there were cash investing activities, cash outflows would be shown in parentheses, designating a decrease in cash.

Financing Activities

This category is used for cash transactions where the resources are obtained from or paid to owners (equity financing) or creditors (debt financing). In this category, each inflow and outflow (shown in parentheses) is listed and a subtotal of all cash flows from financing activities is then computed.

Cash Paid for Principal on Loan. This item indicates the amount of cash that was paid during this accounting period to reduce the principal amount of the loan. Interest payments are not shown in this category. Cash paid for interest is considered to be an operating cash flow.

Cash Withdrawn by Owner. This is the amount of cash that the owner withdrew. In sole proprietorships and partnerships, owners do not recognize any salary expense for their work. For this reason, they will usually withdraw some of the profits to cover their personal expenses.

Other items often listed as financing activities are cash contributions by the owner or cash received as a result of borrowing.

Increase (Decrease) in Cash during June. This is the sum of the net cash flow from operations, the net cash flow from investing activities, and the net cash flow from financing activities. For Corliss, cash decreased $1,566 for the accounting period.

Add Cash Balance, June 1, 2000. This is the cash on hand at the beginning of the accounting period. This amount must agree with the beginning balance for cash on the accounting transaction worksheet.

Cash Balance, June 30, 2000. This is the cash on hand after adding the net increase (or subtracting the net decrease) for the period to the cash balance at the beginning of the period. The ending cash must agree with the cash on the balance sheet and the ending cash per the accounting transaction worksheet.

Exhibit 2-4.3 illustrates the June accounting transaction worksheet for the Corliss Accounting Firm including RED and OIF columns.

WHY IS CASH FLOW SO IMPORTANT TO FINANCIAL STATEMENT USERS?

Most users of financial statements are particularly interested in the statement of cash flows. Although the statement of cash flows deals with current cash flow information, this data is especially helpful in predicting future cash flows of the company. Managers are involved daily in cash budgeting and must be constantly aware of the cash requirements of the business and how to meet those commitments. Creditors and owners or stockholders read the statement of cash flows very carefully. The primary concern for creditors is getting paid in a timely manner and the main concern for owners is profitability and the ability of the company to generate cash which they can then withdraw. The price or value of the company's stock is basically determined by the "market's" estimation of the future cash which will be distributed by the company to the stockholders, reduced by an interest or discount factor (which is compensation for waiting to receive the cash.) The operating section of the statement of cash flows emphasizes the fact that revenues are not the same as cash received, and expenses are not the same as cash paid due to timing differences caused by accrual basis accounting.

Having a net income for the period does not necessarily mean that there will be an increase in cash.

Besides cash flow generated by operations, cash changes can also be the result of the purchase or sale of fixed assets, the borrowing or repayment of debt, or the contributions or withdrawals of cash by the owner.

Exhibit 2-4.3

Accounting Transaction Worksheet

	A	B	C	D	E	F	G	H	I	J	K	L	M	N
1		O I F					ASSETS			LIABILITIES + OWNER'S EQUITY			R E D	
2	Date		Cash	Accounts Receivable	Supplies	Prepaid Insurance	Land	Building	Accounts Payable	Mortgage Payable	Contributed Capital	Retained Earnings		Explanation of Retained Earnings
3	Beg.Bal. 6/1/00		$ 29,300	$ -	$ 1,000	$ -	$ 30,000	$ 100,000	$ 300	$ 110,000	$ 50,000	$ -		
4	6/1/00	O	(960)			960								
5	6/4/00	O	(300)						(300)					
6	6/15/00	O	2,000	1,000								3,000	R	Fees Revenue
7	6/16/00	F	(1,000)									(1,000)	D	Owner Withdrawal
8	6/30/00	O	1,100	1,100								2,200	R	Fees Revenue
9	6/30/00	O	(1,600)									(1,600)	E	Wage Expense
10	6/30/00		-					(200)				(200)	E	Depreciation Expense
11	6/30/00		-			(40)						(40)	E	Insurance Expense
12	6/30/00		-		(750)							(750)	E	Supplies Expense
13	6/30/00	O = (733) F = (73)	(806)							(73)		(733)	E	Interest Expense
14	End.Bal. 6/30/00		$ 27,734	$ 2,100	$ 250	$ 920	$ 30,000	$ 99,800	$ -	$ 109,927	$ 50,000	$ 877		

Solvency and Liquidity

Owners and managers of business enterprises must maintain the liquidity and solvency of their companies. As mentioned previously, liquidity refers to the how quickly assets can be converted into cash. **Solvency** is the ability of a company to pay its debts when they come due. Later in Module 4 various approaches that measure liquidity and solvency will be introduced. For the present, you should recognize the role the statement of cash flows plays in helping owners and managers evaluate liquidity and solvency.

Cash flow from operations is of critical importance to the decision maker. A company that is unable to sustain positive cash flow from its ongoing business is destined to fail. Chronic negative cash flow from operations means that the company will eventually need to sell revenue-generating assets to raise cash to pay for ongoing expenses such as salaries, interest, rent, utilities, etc. The consequence of selling assets is that revenues can decline, which may aggravate an already serious solvency problem. It is difficult to reverse insolvency. Drastic measures are often needed, such as protection under federal bankruptcy laws. To prevent this "late diagnosis" of a solvency weakness, company management can use the statement of cash flows model to plan the future. This planning can focus management on potential problems before they can do irreversible damage to the enterprise. An example is the plan to purchase a new facility with a short-term bank loan of three years. Here we have a long-term asset financed by a short-term loan. The question which you would naturally want to investigate is whether the company will have sufficient cash in three years to pay off the loan *and* pay for ongoing expenses. This is not to suggest that the company should not pursue a strategic expansion, but it does indicate that the financial component of the strategy has not been fully developed to get the business past the possible cash shortage.

SUMMARY

This case reading provides an overview of the statement of cash flows. Operating, investing, and financing activities are defined. The primary focus of the case reading, however, is on the preparation of the direct method of the statement of cash flows from an accounting transaction worksheet. It is then explained how this statement is used for decision making with a focus on liquidity and solvency.

EXERCISES AND PROBLEMS

Exercises

Exercise 1   Basics of the Statement of Cash Flows. What is the primary purpose of the statement of cash flows? What are the three major categories of cash flows listed in a statement of cash flows?

Exercise 2   Understanding Quality Earnings. Determining the quality of earnings is one of the three major uses of the statement of cash flows. What is meant by quality of earnings? Give an example of what causes a difference in the quality of earnings.

Exercise 3   Understanding Investing Activities. Define investing activities as it is used in relation to the statement of cash flows. Give two examples of investing activities.

Exercise 4   Understanding Financing Activities. Define financing activities as it is used in relation to the statement of cash flows. Give two examples of financing activities.

Exercise 5   Using the OIF Column in a Worksheet. Explain the purpose of the OIF column in the accounting transaction worksheet. Why doesn't every row in the worksheet contain an O, I, or F notation?

Problems

Problem 1   Determining Cash Flows. Determine the cash flow for each of the three situations given below.

a.   Accounts receivable at January 1 were $40,600 and on January 31 were $31,000. If fees earned during January were $100,000, all on open account, how much cash was collected from customers during January?

b.   Supplies on hand at February 1 were $1,200 and on February 28 were $1,900. If supplies used during February were $2,200, what amount of cash was paid for supplies purchased during February (assume all supply purchases are for cash)?

c.   Accounts payable were $41,000 on March 31 and $36,000 on March 1. If $92,000 of items were purchased on open account during March, how much cash was paid to creditors during March?

Problem 2   Identifying Types of Cash Flows. Identify each of the following transactions as (1) operating activities, (2) investing activities, or (3) financing activities (4) none of these.

a.   Collected a $1,000 account receivable.
b.   Purchased $700 of supplies on open account.
c.   Purchased office furniture for $2,200 for cash.
d.   Paid $1,500 of accounts payable.
e.   The owner withdrew $660 for personal use.
f.   Billed customers $7,600 for fees earned.
g.   Borrowed $10,000 from the bank on a 90-day note.
h.   Paid premium on a one-year insurance policy for $3,000 cash.
i.   Sold old delivery truck for $2,100 cash.

Problem 3   Prepare a Statement of Cash Flows Using the Direct Method. On the next page is a partial accounting transaction worksheet for Centennial Company for May 2000. Using the information in this worksheet, prepare a cash flow statement, direct method, for May 2000.

Date	Cash	Explanation
5/1/00	$ 16,500	Beginning balance
5/5/00	3,000	Collected account receivable
5/6/00	(1,000)	Owner withdrawal
5/8/00	2,000	Fees revenue earned
5/10/00	(1,200)	Paid accounts payable - supplies
5/15/00	(1,700)	Paid employees wages
5/16/00	4,100	Collected account receivable
5/20/00	(1,800)	Paid insurance premium
5/21/00	(600)	Purchased supplies
5/25/00	40,000	Bank funds, note payable
5/25/00	(50,000)	Bought land for parking lot
5/28/00	500	Sold old computer for book value
5/31/00	(1,900)	Paid employees wages
5/31/00	$ 7,900	Ending balance

Problem 4 Prepare a Statement of Cash Flows Using the Direct Method. The accounting transaction worksheet for October 2000 for Beverly Road follows on the next page. From the information in the worksheet, prepare a cash flow statement-direct method for October 2000.

Beverly Road Company
Accounting Transaction Worksheet

	A	B Cash	C Supplies	D Prepaid Insurance	E Building	F Computer	G Accounts Payable	H Salaries Payable	I Contributed Capital	J Retained Earnings	K Explanation
1											
2	Beg. Bal 10/1	$32,000	$1,200	$ -	$182,000	$ -	$2,000	$3,700	$140,000	$69,500	
3	10/1	(2,400)		2,400							
4	10/5	(3,700)						(3,700)			
5	10/7	6,200								6,200	Fees revenue
6	10/12		1,100				1,100				
7	10/14	4,100								4,100	Fees revenue
8	10/15	(4,400)				4,400					
9	10/20	(3,500)								(3,500)	Salaries expense
10	10/25	(2,000)								(2,000)	Owner Withdrawal
11	10/28	(1,300)					(1,300)				
12	10/31	10,200								10,200	Fees revenue
13	10/31			(200)						(200)	Insurance expense
14	10/31		(1,760)							(1,760)	Supplies expense
15	10/31				(700)	(50)				(750)	Depreciation exp.
16	10/31							3,600		(3,600)	Salaries expense
17	End. Bal. 10/31	$35,200	$540	$2,200	$181,300	$4,350	$1,800	$3,600	$140,000	$78,190	

Case 2-4

COMPUTE THE DIFFERENCE–PART I

Case Objectives

1. To understand how to prepare an income statement and statement of cash flows drawing upon information contained in a monthly worksheet of accounting transactions.
2. To understand relationships among revenue and expenses in an income statement versus receipts and disbursements in a statement of cash flows.
3. To understand transactions involving owner's equity accounts.

Decision: Which financial statement should Carrie use to evaluate her operating performance, the income statement or the statement of cash flows?

Compute the Difference has just completed its second month of business. The owner, Carrie Clotter, started the business last year with a $20,000 contribution which represented almost all of the money she had won in the state lottery. Carrie's business provides on-the-job training for companies who have recently purchased or upgraded software and need to train employees on its use. She was very happy with the results from the first month's business activity, and she recently received an accounting transaction worksheet for the second month of business which was prepared by her accountant. Knowing that you are taking an accounting class in college, she asks you for your help in evaluating the second month of operations. Glancing at the transaction worksheet, you immediately notice that retained earnings and contributed capital transactions have both been entered into one column called owner's equity. You ask Carrie some additional questions to help determine what is included in the beginning owner's equity balance on the worksheet. Carrie says that she didn't make any additional capital contributions during the first month (other than the $20,000 previously mentioned) and that she withdrew $200 from the business for personal use the previous month.

Carrie has asked you to prepare a statement of income and retained earnings and a statement of cash flows using the direct method for the second month of operations. Carrie is also interested in comparing this month's operating performance to last month's but is unsure of which of the two financial statements will provide her with the best measurement of operating performance.

Requirements

1. The completed accounting transaction worksheet for the second month of operations (illustrated at the end of the case) shows a beginning balance of $21,840 in owner's equity. How much of this beginning amount represents contributed capital and how much is retained earnings? What was the business's profit for the first month?

2. Prepare a combined statement of income and retained earnings like the one shown in Exhibit 2-3.4 of Case Reading 2-3 for the second month (May) based on the information provided in the accounting transaction worksheet.

3. Prepare a statement of cash flows using the direct method for May based on the information provided in the accounting transaction worksheet. Assume that the accounts payable amount paid off on 5/29/00 was for supplies previously purchased on 5/3/00.

4. Which financial statement should Carrie use to evaluate her operating performance, the income statement or the statement of cash flows? Explain.

5. Assume that the prepaid insurance on the accounting transaction worksheet refers to an insurance policy that the company purchased when the business began on April 1. How many months of insurance did the company purchase on that date and what was the original cost of the insurance policy?

Compute the Difference
Accounting Transaction Worksheet
May 2000

	A	B	C	D	E	F	G	H	I	J	K
		Cash	Accounts Receivable	Supplies	Prepaid Insurance	Equipment	Accounts Payable	Wages Payable	Note Payable	Owner's Equity	Explanation of Retained Earnings
1	Beg. Bal.										
2	5/01/00	$ 9,320	$ 4,000	$ 320	$ 800	$ 12,000	$ -	$ 1,600	$ 3,000	$ 21,840	
3	5/1/00	(6,000)				6,000					
4	5/1/00	1,500								1,500	Owner Contribution
5	5/1/00	(1,600)						(1,600)			
6	5/1/00	3,600	(3,600)								
7	5/3/00			80			80				
8	5/15/00	3,000	1,000							4,000	Consulting Revenue
9	5/15/00	(1,600)								(1,600)	Wage Expense
10	5/21/00	900	(900)								
11	5/22/00	(625)								(625)	Advertising Expense
12	5/29/00	(50)					(50)				
13	5/30/00	(350)								(350)	Owner Withdrawal
14	5/31/00	(360)								(360)	Utilities Expense
15	5/31/00	1.500	800							2.300	Consulting Revenue
16	5/31/00	(138)							(113)	(25)	Interest Expense
17	5/31/00				(200)					(200)	Insurance Expense
18	5/31/00					(150)				(150)	Depreciation Expense
19	5/31/00							1,600		(1,600)	Wage Expense
20	5/31/00			(190)						(190)	Supplies Expense
21	End. Bal. 5/31/00	$ 9,097	$ 1,300	$ 210	$ 600	$ 17,850	$ 30	$ 1,600	$ 2,887	$ 24,540	

Case Reading 2-5

UNDERSTANDING THE
INDIRECT METHOD

INTRODUCTION

This case reading expands the discussion of the statement of cash flows to include the indirect method. As mentioned previously, the indirect method of cash flow is used by over 85 percent of the companies that are publicly traded. Therefore, even though this method may be more complex, it is important that you understand it so that you, as a user of financial statements, can intelligently analyze a company's liquidity.

OVERVIEW OF THE INDIRECT METHOD

The indirect method of cash flow is identical to the direct method for all investing and financing activities, so an analysis of those types of activities will be limited in this section. Both methods also calculate the change in cash in the same way. Although the cash flow provided by operating activities is identical in amount under both methods, the way the amount is derived is different and will be our focus in this section.

Computing Cash Flow From Operating Activities

The key to the indirect approach is to understand the difference between accrual and cash basis accounting for items that impact depreciation, current liabilities, and most current assets. The object of the operating section in the **statement of cash flows–indirect method** is to reconcile the accrual basis net income to the actual cash flow from operations. A description of the four adjustments that are normally most important for a service company are those resulting from

1. the difference between the amount of revenues recorded and cash collections from customers (these differences are reflected by the change in the accounts receivable balance)

2. the difference between the supplies used as shown on the income statement and the amount of supplies actually purchased (these differences are reflected by the change in the supplies account balance)

3. the difference between the amount of goods and services purchased and those actually paid for (reflected by the change in the accounts payable balance)

4. depreciation (depreciation is an adjustment because it is an expense on the income statement, but it does not involve any cash outflows)

Other adjustments to net income may include

- prepaid expenses used during the period and included on the income statement and the cash paid for these prepaid items (reflected by the change in the prepaid account, which is a current asset)

- revenue received in advance (also called unearned revenue, a current liability) and the revenue shown on the income statement

- the expense shown on the income statement for other expenses and the actual cash outflow for these items (reflected by the change in related payable accounts)

In Module 4 you will be introduced to a retail company (a company which purchases goods for resale). For retail companies, there will also be an adjustment arising from the difference between the cost of the goods sold and the amount of goods actually purchased (reflected by the change in the inventory balance, a current asset).

In order to understand the direction of the adjustment to net income in determining cash flow from operations, you must determine whether the adjustment item causes accrual income to be greater than, or less than, cash flow. If accrual income is less than cash flow, a positive adjustment must be made to bring net income up to the higher cash flow number. For example, if wages expense on the income statement is greater than wages actually paid in cash to employees (that is, the wages payable account increased), then a positive adjustment in the amount of the change in the wages payable account must be made to net income to reflect the actual cash paid to employees. As another example, if the amount of sales revenue shown on the income statement is less than the amount of cash collected from sales (that is, the accounts receivable balance decreased), then a positive adjustment to net income must be made to reflect the actual amount of cash collected from customers.

In summary, the indirect method requires the following adjustments to net income (the adjustment will be zero if a company doesn't have transactions that affect the accounts listed).

Type of Account	Change in Account	Direction of Adjustment To Net Income
Current Asset	Increase	Subtracted
Current Asset	Decrease	Added
Current Liability	Increase	Added
Current Liability	Decrease	Subtracted
Depreciation Expense	NA	Added

Note that all increases in current asset accounts result in negative adjustments to net income and all increases in current liabilities result in positive adjustments. The reverse is true for decreases. Decreases in current asset accounts result in positive adjustments, while decreases in current liabilities result in negative adjustments.

The Indirect Method for Corliss

Exhibit 2-5.1 shows the operating section of the indirect method for Corliss Accounting Firm.

Exhibit 2-5.1

Corliss Accounting Firm Partial Cash Flow Statement Month Ended June 30, 2000		
Operating Activities		
Net Income		$ 1,877
Add (deduct) adjustment to cash basis:		
Depreciation expense	$ 200	
Increase in accounts receivable	(2,100)	
Increase in prepaid insurance	(920)	
Decrease in supplies	750	
Decrease in accounts payable	(300)	(2,370)
Net Cash Flow from Operations		$ (493)

Operating Activities

The purpose of this section is to calculate the amount of cash flow that is provided by the day-to-day operations of the company. This section starts with the net income figure from the income statement ($1,877 for Corliss). The objective of the operating section is to take the net income (i.e., the revenues less the expenses) and adjust it to cash flow from operations. You should remember that revenues are the sales of the goods and services provided during the period regardless of whether we received cash for them. Likewise, expenses are the costs incurred in generating revenue during the period regardless of whether the costs have been paid in cash. When there is a difference between revenue and cash collected from customers, it will be shown as a reconciling item in this section. Likewise, if there is a difference between expenses and the cash paid for those costs, it will also be described as a reconciling item. You should notice that most of these differences arise because of a change in current assets and current liabilities.

Before discussing the individual line item differences for Corliss, look at the information in Exhibit 2-5.2 which have already gathered from the income statement and from the operating section of the direct method of the statement of cash flows. If you remember correctly, the indirect method starts with net income and adjusts it by certain amounts (see the Adjustment column) to arrive at cash flow from operations.

Column A lists the various types of line items appearing on the income statement and/or the direct method of the statement of cash flows. Column B lists the amounts for items on the income statement and column D lists the amounts for those in the operating section of the direct method of the cash flow statement. It might be helpful for you to look back at Exhibit 2-3.3 for the income statement and Exhibit 2-4.2 for the direct method of the statement of cash flows. The Adjustment column was calculated by subtracting column B from column D. The last column, column E, shows how that adjustment is described in the operating section of the indirect method of the statement of cash flows.

Exhibit 2-5.2
Adjusting Information

	A	B	C	D	E
1		Income Statement	Adjustment	Statement of Cash Flows- Direct Method	Adjustment described as:
2	Fees	$ 5,200	$ (2,100)	$ 3,100	Increase in Accounts Receivable
3	Wages	(1,600)	-	(1,600)	No adjustment necessary
4	Supplies	(750)	450	(300)	Decrease in Supplies 750 and Decrease in Accts. Payable (300)
5	Interest	(733)	-	(733)	No adjustment necessary
6	Depreciation	(200)	200	-	Always add back to net income
7	Insurance	(40)	(920)	(960)	Increase in Prepaid Insurance
8	Total	$ 1,877	$ (2,370)	$ (493)	
9		Net Income	Required Adjustments	Net Cash Flow from Operations	

Notice in row 8 of the exhibit how the Income Statement column sums to net income, and how the Statement Of Cash Flows - Direct Method column sums to the net cash flow from operations for that financial statement.

A number line can be used to help illustrate the computation of these differences. For each item, if you start with the amount of the related revenue or expense on the income statement and adjust it by the amount of the reconciling item from the Adjustment column, it will provide the amount of cash flow that was generated by operations. If adjusting an expense, remember that expenses are negative amounts because they reduce income (as well as retained earnings). The process will be started with the Net Income column because the indirect method starts with net income as well.

Increase in Accounts Receivable. This reconciling item shows that the revenue per the income statement was greater than the cash collected from customers by $2,100. For Corliss, this was due to fees on credit that were still uncollected as of month end.

$3,100	($2,100)	$5,200 Revenue
Cash Flow from Operations	Adjustment	Income Statement

To compute the reconciling item using the number line, you need to ask, "How do you get from a positive $5,200 on the income statement to positive $3,100 in cash flow from operations?" The reply is that you subtract $2,100.

Decrease in Supplies/Decrease in Accounts Payable. These two reconciling items need to be reviewed together since the purchased supplies were bought on credit. The net effect of these two items is a reconciling item of $450.

Decrease in supplies	$ 750
Decrease in accounts payable	(300)
Net effect	$ 450

When considering these two line items together, the meaning of the net effect is that the expense for supplies ($750) per the income statement is less than the cash expenditure of $300 ($300 cash has been paid to date— all in reducing accounts payable).

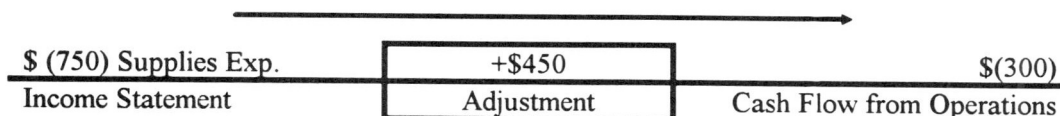

$ (750) Supplies Exp.	+$450	$(300)
Income Statement	Adjustment	Cash Flow from Operations

How do you get from a negative $750 on the income statement to a negative $300? Add a reconciling item of $450!

Depreciation Expense. Depreciation is usually the first reconciling item listed in a statement of cash flows using the indirect method. As mentioned previously, depreciation will never result in a cash flow. Since depreciation is a deduction in the initial computation of net income (it is an expense), it needs to be added back to net income to eliminate the effect of this non-cash item.

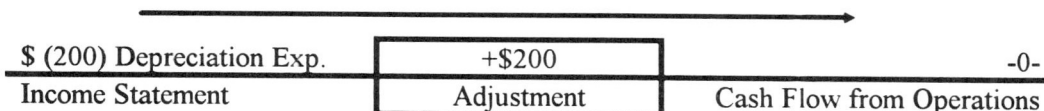

$ (200) Depreciation Exp.	+$200	-0-
Income Statement	Adjustment	Cash Flow from Operations

To further explain the use of the number line, ask yourself, "How do you get from a negative $200 on the income statement to a zero for cash flow from operations?" (It's not shown on the direct method of the statement of cash flows.) The answer is that you add $200.

Increase in Prepaid Insurance. This line item shows that prepaid insurance increased by $920, which resulted in cash flow decreasing by $920. This amount is paid insurance premiums for coverage beyond the date of the accounting period.

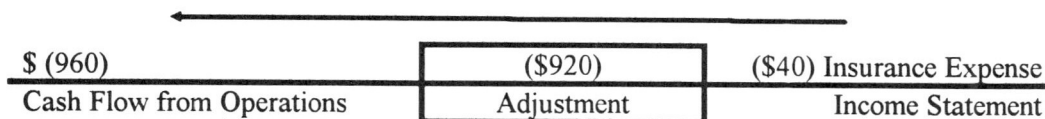

$ (960)	($920)	($40) Insurance Expense
Cash Flow from Operations	Adjustment	Income Statement

Once again, to go from a negative $40 on the income statement to a negative $960 in the direct method, $920 needs to be subtracted.

Other Information. Two expenses on the income statement do not result in any reconciling dollar amounts. They are wage expense and interest expense. These items have no reconciling amounts because there is no difference between the income statement amount shown for these items and the cash that was paid.

Reconciling items to the statement of cash flows–indirect method arise because there *is* a difference between the revenue or expense amount on the income statement and the cash received or paid for these operating activities.

The amount of this difference is generally reflected as a change in a current asset or a current liability account during the period (depreciation is the most common exception to this statement).

One more item to note is that the net cash flow from operations is identical under the direct and the indirect approach. It is only the way in which the operating section is presented that makes each method unique.

Computing Cash Flow from Investing and Financing Activities

The computation of investing and financing activities is identical in the indirect method and the direct method. Once you have prepared a statement of cash flows using the direct approach, you merely have to copy and paste the investing and financing sections into a statement of cash flows using the indirect method.

On the next page, Exhibit 2-5.3 shows a comparison of the direct and indirect methods of the statement of cash flows for Corliss.

Why is the Indirect Method so Popular?

The indirect method is popular because it directly ties the net income amount per the income statement to the cash provided by operations. Users of financial statements can easily see how much of the net income results in changes in operating cash flow and it allows analysts to access the quality of earnings. This will help users predict future cash flow requirements. In addition, companies with thousands of cash transactions in a given period would find it tedious to classify and summarize all of them for the direct statement.

Exhibit 2-5.4 shows the operating section of the statement of cash flows for Wal-Mart Stores for the three years ending January 31, 1997. The amounts shown are in millions, which is very common for annual reports.

Exhibit 2-5.4

Wal-Mart Stores, Inc. Consolidated Statements of Cash Flows (Amounts in millions)			
Fiscal years ended January 31,	1997	1996	1995
Cash flows from operating activities:			
Net income	$3,056	$ 2,740	$ 2,681
Adjustments to reconcile net income to net cash provided by operating activities:			
Depreciation and amortization	1,463	1,304	1,070
Increase in accounts receivable	(58)	(61)	(84)
Decrease/(increase) in inventories	99	(1,850)	(3,053)
Increase in accounts payable	1,208	448	1,914
Increase in accrued liabilities	430	29	496
Deferred income taxes	(180)	76	9
Other	(88)	(303)	(127)
Net cash provided by operating activities	$5,930	$2,383	$2,906

Exhibit 2-5.3

Comparison of Direct and Indirect Methods of the Statement of Cash Flows

	A	B	C	D
1		Corliss Accounting Firm		
2		Statement of Cash Flows—Direct Method		
3		Month Ended June 30, 2000		
4	Operating Activities			
5	Cash Inflows			
6	Fees collected			$ 3,100
7	Cash Outflows			
8	Cash paid for wages		$ (1,600)	
9	Cash paid for interest		(733)	
10	Cash paid for insurance		(960)	
11	Cash paid for supplies		(300)	
12	Total Cash Outflows			(3,593)
13	Net Cash Flow from Operations			(493)
14	Investing Activities			-
15	Financing Activities			
16	Cash paid for principal on loan		(73)	
17	Cash withdrawn by owner		(1,000)	
18	Net Cash Flow from Financing Activities			(1,073)
19	Net Decrease in Cash During June			(1,566)
20	Add Cash Balance, June 1, 2000			29,300
21	Cash Balance, June 30, 2000			$ 27,734
22				

	A	B	C	D
1		Corliss Accounting Firm		
2		Statement of Cash Flows—Indirect Method		
3		Month Ended June 30, 2000		
4	Operating Activities			
5	Net Income			$ 1,877
6	Add (deduct) adjustment to cash basis:			
7	Depreciation expense		$ 200	
8	Increase in accounts receivable		(2,100)	
9	Increase in prepaid insurance		(920)	
10	Decrease in supplies		750	
11	Decrease in accounts payable		(300)	(2,370)
12				
13	Net Cash Flow from Operations			(493)
14	Investing Activities			-
15	Financing Activities			
16	Cash paid for principal on loan		(73)	
17	Cash withdrawn by owner		(1,000)	
18	Net Cash Flow from Financing Activities			(1,073)
19	Net Decrease in Cash During June			(1,566)
20	Add Cash Balance, June 1, 2000			29,300
21	Cash Balance, June 30, 2000			$ 27,734
22				

You will notice that the statement starts with net income and that the first adjustment is for depreciation and amortization. The process of **amortization,** the expensing of intangible asset cost, is very similar to depreciation and it is treated in a similar fashion on the statement of cash flows. Depreciation is added because it is an expense on the income statement that will never result in an operating cash flow.

The statement also shows that accounts receivable increased, which means that revenues must have been greater than cash collections from customers, so the amount of the increase must be deducted to get to the operating cash flow. The next line item for 1997 is a decrease in inventories. This decrease is shown as a positive adjustment to net income because the expense of the inventory sold was greater than the cash paid for purchasing the inventory.

The increase in accounts payable results in a positive adjustment because there were more inventory items purchased on credit than were paid off during the period. Accrued liabilities is a name used as a summary line item for most of the other current liability accounts. The increase in accrued liabilities results in a positive adjustment because there were more items expensed than there were paid for with cash.

The last line item is for **deferred taxes.** This is a common reconciling item in a statement of cash flows using the indirect method because the company (corporations only) records tax expense based on the year's income. Due to the various tax laws, the taxes often are not paid in the same accounting period but are postponed to a future date. In this case the adjustment was negative, which means that the taxes expensed were less than the cash paid for taxes in the current period.

Sometimes, the statements of cash flows in annual reports may seem more complex than the ones you will study in this course. The important thing to remember in looking at any operating section using the indirect method is that the adjustments to net income are made because there *is* a difference between the revenues or expenses shown on the income statement and the cash received or paid during the year. Even if you don't understand the specific line item adjustment, a basic understanding of why this adjustment is necessary will help you in evaluating the company in order to make better decisions.

SUMMARY

This case reading explains the preparation of the indirect method of the statement of cash flows and also shows how this statement is used for decision making. Several techniques are given to help facilitate the preparation of this statement. The statement of cash flows of Wal-Mart is also analyzed on an item-by-item basis.

EXERCISES AND PROBLEMS

Exercise

Exercise 1 Operating Activities. The following items are included in the operating section of an indirect statement of cash flows for Lillard Company. State whether each item would be added to (A) or subtracted from (S) net income to arrive at cash flow from operations.

Increase in Accounts Receivable   Depreciation Expense
Decrease in Prepaid Insurance   Decrease in Supplies
Decrease in Accounts Payable   Increase in Wages Payable

Problems

Problem 1 Cash Provided by Operations Using Indirect Method. For the month of April 2000, Pointe Company had the following asset, liability, and owner's equity account balances on March 31 and April 30:

	April 30	March 31
Cash	$ 18,000	$ 20,000
Accounts Receivable	39,000	44,000
Supplies	2,500	2,000
Land	40,000	40,000
Buildings (net)	71,500	72,500
Total Assets	$171,000	$178,500
Accounts Payable	$ 15,000	$ 16,000
Accrued Liabilities	6,000	6,500
Taxes Payable	6,000	20,000
Contributed Capital	70,000	70,000
Retained Earnings	74,000	66,000
Total Liabilities & Owners' Equity	$171,000	$178,500

Additional Information:

Pointe Company reported net income of $8,000 for April; depreciation expense of $4,000 was included in determining net income.

Using the indirect method, determine the net cash provided by operations for Pointe Company for April 2000.

Problem 2 Statement of Cash Flows Using the Indirect Method. Comparative balance sheet information for San Pablo, Inc. for 1999 and 2000 is given below.

	December 31 2000	1999
Cash	$ 6	$ 8
Accounts Receivable	52	40
Prepaid Insurance	10	15
Office Equipment, net	70	60
Office Furniture and Fixtures, net	27	28
Total Assets	$165	$151
Accounts Payable	$ 25	$ 36
Contributed Capital	100	80
Retained Earnings	40	35
Total Liabilities and Equity	$165	$151

San Pablo, Inc. had the following net income for 2000.

Revenue	$100
Expenses	90
Net Income	$ 10

Depreciation of $4 was included in expenses in the income statement. No office furniture and fixtures were purchased or sold during the year but some office equipment was purchased. Owner withdrawals of $5 were made during the year.

Use the indirect method to prepare a statement of cash flows for San Pablo, Inc., for the year 2000.

Problem 3 Cash Provided by Operations Using Indirect Method. A worksheet similar to Exhibit 2-5.2 is presented below for Plummer Company for June 2000. Use the information in the worksheet to prepare the operating activities section of a statement of cash flows using the indirect method.

	Income Statement	Adjustments	Statement of Cash Flows - Direct Method	Adjustment described as:
Revenues	$ 10,000	$ 1,000	$ 11,000	Decrease in accounts receivable
Rent	(1,000)	-	(1,000)	No adjustment needed
Utilities	(700)	100	(600)	Increase in accounts payable
Wages	(3,000)	(200)	(3,200)	Decrease in wages payable
Interest	(260)	-	(260)	No adjustment needed
Insurance	(940)	940	-	Decrease in prepaid insurance
Depreciation	(1,200)	1,200	-	Always added back to net income
Total	$ 2,900	$ 3,040	$ 5,940	
	Net Income	Required Adjustments	Net Cash Flow from Operations	

Problem 4   Fill in the Missing Information – Cash Provided by Operations Using Indirect Method. A worksheet similar to Exhibit 2-5.2 is presented below for Longfellow Company for July 2000. Complete this worksheet by completing columns C and E with the appropriate amounts and explanations.

	A	B	C	D	E
1		Income Statement	Adjustments	Statement of Cash Flows - Direct Method	Adjustment described as:
2	Fees	$ 20,000		$ 17,500	
3	Wages	(8,000)		(7,600)	
4	Rent	(2,000)		(2,000)	
5	Utilities	(1,200)		(1,500)	
6	Interest	(2,500)		(2,000)	
7	Insurance	(200)		(2,400)	
8	Depreciation	(1900)		-0-	
9	Total	$ 4,200	$ (2,200)	$ 2,000	
10		Net Income	Required Adjustments	Net Cash Flow from Operations	

Problem 5 Prepare a Statement Of Cash Flows Using the Indirect Method. Beverly Road Company has the following accounting transaction worksheet for October 2000. From the information in the worksheet, prepare a statement of cash flows- indirect method for October 2000.

Beverly Road Company
Accounting Transaction Worksheet

	Cash	Supplies	Prepaid Insurance	Building	Computer	Accounts Payable	Salaries Payable	Contributed Capital	Retained Earnings	Explanation
Beg. Bal 10/1	$ 32,000	$ 1,200	$ -	$ 182,000	$ -	$ 2,000	$ 3,700	$ 140,000	$ 69,500	
10/1	(2,400)		2,400							
10/5	(3,700)						(3,700)			
10/7	6,200								6,200	Fees revenue
10/12		1,100				1,100				
10/14	4,100								4,100	Fees revenue
10/15	(4,400)				4,400					
10/20	(3,500)								(3,500)	Salaries expense
10/25	(2,000)								(2,000)	Owner Withdrawal
10/28	(1,300)					(1,300)				
10/31	10,200								10,200	Fees revenue
10/31			(200)						(200)	Insurance expense
10/31		(1,760)							(1,760)	Supplies expense
10/31				(700)	(50)				(750)	Depreciation exp.
10/31							3,600		(3,600)	Salaries expense
End. Bal. 10/31	$ 35,200	$ 540	$ 2,200	$ 181,300	$ 4,350	$ 1,800	$ 3,600	$ 140,000	$ 78,190	

Case 2-5

COMPUTE THE DIFFERENCE–PART II

Case Objectives

1. To understand how to prepare a statement of cash flows using the indirect method.
2. To understand relationships among revenue and expenses in an income statement versus receipts and disbursements in a statement of cash flows.

Decision: Should Carrie Clotter commit to a $1,000 monthly mortgage payment for a new house?

Compute the Difference has just completed its May transactions. The owner, Carrie Clotter, reminds you that the transactions for her business were shown on the accounting transaction worksheet provided in Case 2-4. Carrie is thinking about buying a new house that would require a $1,000 monthly mortgage payment. The cash for the proposed mortgage would need to come from additional owner withdrawals from the business. Before making that decision, Carrie has asked for your help in preparing a statement of cash flows using the indirect method.

Requirements

1. Complete the schedule below as a preliminary step to preparing the operating activities section of the statement of cash flows for May using the indirect method.

	Income Statement	Adjustment	Statement of Cash Flows — Direct Method	Adjustment Described As:
Fees				
Wages				
Supplies				
Advertising				
Insurance				
Utilities				
Depreciation				
Interest				
Totals				
	Net Income	Required Adjustments	Cash Flow From Operations	

2. Prepare a statement of cash flows for May using the indirect method.

3. Should Carrie Clotter commit to a $1,000 monthly mortgage payment for a new house? (Assume that May is representative of normal monthly activity.)

4. Assume that the $12,000 beginning equipment balance on the accounting transaction worksheet given in Case 2-4 was purchased late in April and therefore was not depreciated that month. Additionally, all equipment as of the end of May has no salvage value and has the same expected life. What is the estimated useful life of the equipment in years?

Group Assignment 2-5

THE INDIRECT JUMP

Group Number _____ Group members present and participating:

_____

_____

Objectives

1. To understand how to prepare a statement of cash flows using the indirect method.
2. To understand relationships among revenue and expenses in an income statement versus receipts and disbursements in a statement of cash flows.

Bouncing Bungies Company opened in December 2000. The company was located in a small metropolitan area and, with the spread of the bungy jumping craze, the start-up company became quite successful. The financial statements for the company are shown in Exhibit 2-6.1 and 2-6.2 of Case Reading 2-6.

Requirements

1. Complete the schedule below as a preliminary step to preparing the operating activities section of the statement of cash flows for December using the indirect method.

	Income Statement	Adjustments	Statement of Cash Flows- Direct Method	Adjustment Described As:
Tickets				
Wages				
Supplies				
Advertising				
Insurance				
Utilities				
Depreciation				
Interest				
Service Charge				
Totals				
	Net Income	Required Adjustments	Net Cash Flow from Operations	

2. Prepare the operating section of the statement of cash flows for December using the indirect method using the format below.

Bouncing Bungies Company
Partial Statement of Cash Flows- Indirect Method
Month Ended December 31, 2000

Operating Activities
Net Income
    Add (deduct) adjustment to cash basis:

Net Cash Flow from Operations

Case Reading 2-6

INTERPRETING FINANCIAL
STATEMENT INFORMATION

INTRODUCTION

This case reading will provide some basic tools to help you understand the interaction of financial statement information. The financial statements of Bouncing Bungies Company will be presented and discussed so that you have a clearer understanding of the specific information each financial statement provides. Earlier case readings presented an accounting transaction worksheet first and demonstrated how the statements were prepared from this worksheet. This case reading begins with the statements and the information that can be gathered from the statements without knowledge of the underlying information of specific day-to-day transaction activity. After this discussion, an accounting transaction worksheet for Bouncing Bungies Company will be presented to reinforce the relationship between the statements and the worksheet.

WHAT DO THE FINANCIAL STATEMENTS TELL YOU?

In previous case readings, you learned how to record economic events such as transactions in an accounting transaction worksheet, and how that worksheet was used to prepare the balance sheet, income statement, and statement of cash flows. Publicly traded companies are usually required to prepare a balance sheet, an income statement, and a statement of cash flows. Most companies also voluntarily include a fourth statement, either the statement of retained earnings or the statement of stockholders' equity, in their published financial statement package. You should recall that the balance sheet is the financial statement that shows the assets, liabilities, and owner's equity of a company at a particular point in time. It is a snapshot of the financial position of the company as of the date listed in the statement heading. The income statement, on the other hand, shows the revenues and expenses of the company during a period of time. The income statement shows the results of operations from one balance sheet date to the next and is the best measurement of operating performance. The statement of cash flows reports the company's cash inflows and outflows by categorizing them as operating, investing, or financing activities. Exhibit 2-6.1 shows the balance sheet, income statement, and statement of retained earnings for Bouncing Bungies Company after its first month of operations. Exhibit 2-6.2 shows the statement of cash flows using the direct method. Let's look at these completed statements and interpret the information that is given.

How the Statements Tie Together

You will notice that the income statement computes the profit of the company, called net income. The net income amount is then transferred as an addition to retained earnings (a balance sheet account) on the statement of retained earnings. Retained earnings are then decreased by any withdrawals by the owners (called dividends if the company is a corporation). Notice how the ending retained earnings balance from the statement of retained earnings agrees with the amount of retained earnings shown in the owner's equity section of the balance sheet. The statement of cash flows shows the changes in cash during the period.

Exhibit 2-6.1
Selected Financial Statements

Bouncing Bungies Company
Income Statement
Month Ended December 31, 2000

Revenues
  Ticket Revenue $8,525

Expenses
  Wage Expense $2,400
  Supplies Expense   1,500
  Advertising Expense   1,500
  Insurance Expense   400
  Utilities Expense   300
  Depreciation Expense   100
  Interest Expense   41
  Service Charge   15
Total Expenses   6,256

Net Income $2,269

Bouncing Bungies Company
Statement of Retained Earnings
Month Ended December 31, 2000

Retained Earnings, December 1, 2000	$ -
Add Net Income	2,269
Subtotal	2,269
Less Withdrawals by Owner	(43)
Retained Earnings, December 31, 2000	$ 2,226

Bouncing Bungies Company
Balance Sheet
December 31, 2000

Assets			Liabilities and Owner's Equity		
Current Assets			Current Liabilities		
Cash	$ 8,141		Accounts Payable	$ 2,000	
Accounts Receivable	1,000		Gift Certificates	25	
Supplies	500		Wages Payable	2,400	
Prepaid Insurance	4,400		Total Current Liabilities		$ 4,425
Total Current Assets		$ 14,041			
			Long Term Liabilities		
Fixed Assets			Note Payable		5,290
Bungies, net		7,900			
			Owner's Equity		
			Contributed Capital	10,000	
			Retained Earnings	2,226	
			Total Owner's Equity		12,226
			Total Liabilities and		
Total Assets		$ 21,941	Owner's Equity		$ 21,941

Exhibit 2-6.2 shows Bouncing Bungies company's statement of cash flows using the direct method.

Exhibit 2-6.2

Bouncing Bungies Company		
Statement of Cash Flows–Direct Method		
Month Ended December 31, 2000		
Operating Activities		
Cash Inflows		
Cash collected from customers		$ 7,550
Cash Outflows		
Cash paid for insurance	$ (4,800)	
Cash paid for advertising	(1,500)	
Cash paid for utilities	(300)	
Cash paid for interest	(41)	
Cash paid for service charge	(15)	
Total Cash Outflows		(6,656)
Net Cash Flow from Operations		894
Investing Activities		
Cash paid for bungies		(8,000)
Financing Activities		
Cash borrowed from bank	5,500	
Cash paid for principal on note	(210)	
Cash invested by owner	10,000	
Cash withdrawn by owner	(43)	
Net Cash Flow from Financing Activities		15,247
Net Increase in Cash during December		8,141
Add Cash Balance, December 1, 2000		-0-
Cash Balance, December 31, 2000		$ 8,141

You will notice that the ending cash balance on the statement of cash flows agrees with the cash balance on the balance sheet. In accounting terms, we say that these four financial statements *articulate* with each other.

The next section involves a discussion of the balance sheet, income statement, and the statement of cash flows. You will find it helpful to refer the two preceding exhibits as the statement information is discussed. Case Reading 2-2 discussed the meaning of the balance sheet accounts in detail, so in this case reading the focus will be on the information on the income statement and the statement of cash flows, as well as the interaction of the statements.

Revenues, Receivables, and Cash Collections from Customers

In general, the income statement is the financial statement that tells how much revenue is earned during the period. As previously mentioned, revenue earned is not the same as cash received from customers because the company will record revenue as soon as the service is provided, regardless of whether cash has been received (according to the accrual basis of accounting). If revenue has been earned but not collected, the company will record an accounts receivable for the difference between the earned amount and the cash collected for the service. In addition, the company may have collected some cash from customers as advance deposits for future services. These amounts are included in cash collected from customers but are not shown on the income statement as revenue until the service has been performed and the revenue earned. In cases such as this, the company records a liability for the future obligation of providing these services. This liability may have many different names such as unearned revenue, revenue received in advance, advance deposits, etc.

Expenses, Payables, Prepaids, and Cash Outflows for Expenses

The accrual basis of accounting states that expenses should be recognized in the period benefited regardless of whether the expense has been paid. The income statement therefore shows the expenses that the company incurs during the accounting period. If you want to determine if the expense has been paid, you need to look at the balance sheet accounts, specifically the related payable account and/or the related prepaid account. For example, if the income statement shows interest expense is $400, to determine if the interest was in fact paid you need to look at interest payable. If there is no interest payable account (assuming they didn't prepay the interest), you can conclude that the interest was paid during the period. If there is an interest payable account, that account balance reflects the amount of interest that has not been paid in cash.

For a prepaid example, let's look at prepaid insurance and assume that a company prepays $600 for an insurance policy. That $600 is shown as a cash outflow for insurance on the statement of cash flows but is not be recorded as an expense until the company has actually used up the insurance. For example, if it is a sixth-month policy, the company will record $100 for one month's insurance expense each accounting period.

Long-Term Assets, Depreciation, and Cash Received/Paid for Investing Activities

The types of long-term assets that we will be studying in this course are primarily fixed assets such as buildings, equipment, etc. Expenses for these long-term costs are recognized through a process called depreciation. The depreciation expense for the accounting period is management's estimate of the portion of the fixed asset cost (less salvage value) that was used up during the period. The fixed asset account on the balance sheet will be shown at the historical cost of the asset, less the accumulated depreciation. The accumulated depreciation is merely the sum of all depreciation expenses recorded for the asset since its purchase. In actual practice the company maintains a separate account called accumulated depreciation that keeps track of this accumulated depreciation over time. We will use this account later in Module 4, but for now the fixed asset account will be reduced directly by the amount of the estimated depreciation. The statement of cash flows reports cash received or paid for fixed assets as an investing activity. If a company purchases a building for $120,000 cash, the building account on the balance sheet will show $120,000, and the cash flow from investing activities will show cash paid for building of $120,000. The income statement will report the portion of that building's cost less salvage value that has been allocated to depreciation expense for the period.

Long-Term Liabilities, Owner's Equity Transactions, And Cash Received/Paid For Financing Activities

Long-term liabilities are reported on the balance sheet at their principal amounts. During the accounting period, if the company borrows more cash the liability will increase. This type of transaction is reported on the statement of cash flows as a financing activity described as cash received from note. Principal repayments will reduce the liability accounts and will be shown in the financing section of the statement of cash flows as a decrease in cash due to a loan repayment. Expenses on the income statement relating to notes are identified as interest expense. Paid interest expense is reported as cash paid for interest, an operating activity.

Owner's equity amounts include transactions affecting contributed capital and retained earnings. Contributed capital increases through investments by the owner. An investment made in cash is shown as a cash inflow from financing activities on the statement of cash flows. As mentioned earlier, retained earnings increases by the amount of profit during the period and decreases by the amount of owner withdrawals. A withdrawal of cash by the owner is shown as a cash outflow from a financing activity on the statement of cash flows.

Bouncing Bungies Company Financial Statements

Tickets. By looking at the income statement, we can determine that ticket revenue is the only source of revenue and that the company provided bungy jumps in the amount of $8,525. The accounts receivable account shows that the company extends credit to customers who buy bungy jumping tickets and that $1,000 is still owed by these customers at the statement date. Since this is a current asset, we know that Bouncing Bungies expects to collect this amount within the next year. (Note that uncollectible accounts are ignored here but they will be addressed in Module 4.)

The statement of cash flows shows cash collected from customers of $7,550. This item will usually include cash sales and cash collected from accounts receivable. In this particular case this amount also includes the $25 cash for a gift certificate issued for a future bungy jump. The unused gift certificate is shown as a liability on the balance sheet under the caption *Gift certificates*. The relationship between ticket revenue and cash collected from customers can be more clearly seen by looking at the following analysis.

Ticket revenue per the income statement	$8,525
Still uncollected and in accounts receivable	1,000
Ticket revenue collected in cash	$7,525
Cash received for unused gift certificate	25
Cash collections from customers	$7,550

Supplies. The supplies balance on the balance sheet shows $500 of supplies still on hand at year end. The fact that supplies are listed as a current asset assures us that management expects to use the supplies within the next year. The income statement shows that the amount of supplies used in December was $1,500.

Is there a way to calculate the amount of supplies the company purchased during the year, keeping in mind that since this is the first year of operations, the beginning balance in supplies must have been zero?

Yes, if supplies on hand at year end were $500, and $1,500 of supplies were used during the year, then the supplies available for use must have been the same as the amount purchased during the year, or $2,000.

Beginning supplies	$ 0
Supplies purchased	2,000
Supplies available for use	$2,000
Supplies used	1,500
Ending supplies	$ 500

Did the company pay cash or does it still owe for the supplies? On this particular balance sheet it is easy to see that the company has an accounts payable balance of $2,000. That accounts payable balance could be a total or summary of many small balances and it might relate to more than one supplier. In looking at the statement of cash flows, however, note that there is no line item listing for cash paid for supplies. This shows that the supplies were in fact purchased on credit, and the amount is still outstanding at the balance sheet date and is shown in accounts payable.

Insurance. The $400 amount shown on the income statement for insurance expense represents the amount of insurance expired (used up) during December. To determine the amount of cash paid for insurance during the month, look at the statement of cash flows. This statement reports a cash expenditure of $4,800 for insurance. If $4,800 of insurance was paid for but only $400 was used per the income statement, there must have been $4,400 of unused or prepaid insurance. This unused amount is shown as a current asset on our balance sheet. There is no way to determine from the statements if the $400 represents a full month of coverage or not. For argument's sake, let's make that assumption. Could the expiration date of the insurance policy be computed?

The answer is yes, it can. If the monthly insurance cost is $400 and there is $4,400 prepaid (unexpired) at December 31, that represents 11 months left until the expiration date. The policy must have been for one year and it should expire on November 30, 2001.

> $ 400   for December insurance (assumed full month of insurance)
> 4,400   unused at December 31 (11 months)
> $4,800   original cost of policy (12 months)

Wages. The income statement shows wage expense of $2,400. This amount represents the wages earned by the employees this month regardless of whether they have been paid or not. It is an expense because the employees have worked for the company during December 2000. How can the total amount of paid and unpaid wages at December 31 be determined?

Because the income statement amount of $2,400 is also equal to the total amount in wages payable, one can conclude that the employees have not received a paycheck for December wages (that's why the wages are payable), even though they have provided $2,400 of work (wage expense) during the month. If you look at the statement of cash flows, you will notice that it does not show any cash paid for wages in December. Let's look at a different example.

If the wages payable balance was $1,800 and wage expense was still $2,400, could you determine how much the employees had already been paid?

Yes, the employees earned $2,400 pay for their work, and $1,800 of this amount was still unpaid and in wages payable. Therefore, $600 must have been paid in cash during the month. This would be shown as cash paid for wages in the operating section of the direct method statement of cash flows.

Advertising. The amount shown on the income statement represents a $1,500 expenditure for advertising that the company incurred during the period. Because the statement of cash flows shows $1,500 in cash paid for advertising and none of these payments was advance payments (no prepaid advertising on the balance sheet), we can conclude that the advertising was paid in cash and is not owed at December 31. This is supported by the fact that there is no liability for advertising on the balance sheet. The entire $2,000 in accounts payable has already been identified as the amount still owed for supplies.

Utilities. The utilities expense shown on the income statement of $300 represents the cost of utilities used during the period. The $300 utilities bill must have been paid with cash or it would be shown as a liability on the balance sheet. This is also clearly shown on the statement of cash flows which lists cash paid for utilities of $300.

Interest. The interest expense of $41 shown on the income statement represents the cost or expense that the company incurs when it borrows money from a creditor. It is calculated by taking the outstanding principal balance times the interest rate times the period of time for which the money is borrowed. For example, if $3,000 principal was borrowed for one month at a 9 percent annual interest rate, the monthly interest would be

$$\text{Principal} \times \text{Rate} \times \text{Time} = \text{Interest, or } P \times R \times T = I$$

Principal = $3,000   Annual interest rate = 9%   Time = 1/12 year or 1 month

$$\$3,000 \times .09 \times 1/12 = \$22.50$$

To determine how much of the interest was paid in cash, you need to go to the statement of cash flows. The operating section shows that $41 of interest was paid during the month. We can tell that there is no interest unpaid, because there is no interest payable account on the balance sheet.

Service Charge. The income statement shows service charge expense of $15. This expense is the result of writing checks and maintaining a bank account and is usually deducted from your account by the bank. Usually there is no payable for this account because it is always paid or deducted from your bank account balance in the month incurred. You will notice that the statement of cash flows shows cash paid for service charges of $15.

Bungies, Net. The balance sheet for Bouncing Bungies shows that it does not have any company-owned fixed assets except for bungies. The word *net* after *bungies* shows that the original cost of the bungies was reduced by the amount of accumulated depreciation. The income statement shows that depreciation expense for December was $100. Since this was the first month of operations, $100 was the total accumulated depreciation for the bungies as well; the original cost of the bungies must have been $8,000 calculated as follows:

Bungies, net	$7,900
Accumulated depreciation	100
Original cost of bungies	$8,000

The $7,900 represents the amount not yet depreciated (also called the undepreciated cost or book value).

How did the company calculate the $100 amount for depreciation expense for the first full month? There is no easy way to tell from the balance sheet and income statement without more information. The straight-line method of depreciation is widely used by companies. It uses the following equation.

$$\frac{\text{Cost} - \text{Salvage value}}{\text{Estimated useful life in years}} = \text{Depreciation expense for one year}$$

Suppose that additional information was available from the owner that the original cost of the bungies was $8,000 and that the bungies have an estimated six-year life and an $800 salvage value. Depreciation would be $100 for the first month, calculated as follows:

$$\frac{\$8,000 - \$800}{6\ \text{years}} = \begin{array}{c}\text{Depreciation expense for one year} \\ \$1,200\ \text{or }\$100\ \text{a month}\end{array}$$

The statement of cash flows shows the investing activity, cash paid for bungies, of $8,000. Where is cash paid for depreciation reported on the statement of cash flows?

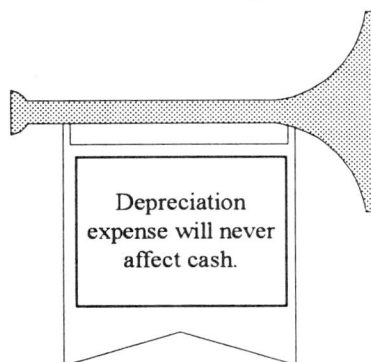

Depreciation
expense will never
affect cash.

Only the purchase or the sale of bungies (or any other fixed asset) will have a cash effect, NOT the use or depreciation of the bungies (or other fixed assets).

Companies which are publicly traded and publish financial statements include, as part of the annual report, notes to the financial statements. These notes, especially the first one entitled "Summary Of Significant Accounting Policies," provide a wealth of information and should be reviewed carefully by every financial statement reader. In the case of this company, the notes (called footnotes) would probably tell us that the company used the straight-line method of depreciation and that the company used a six-year life for its bungies.

The information that each statement provides is unique and specific. By understanding the meaning of the different statements, we can become better economic decision makers when the use of financial statement information is critical.

Recording the Daily Economic Events for Bouncing Bungies

The financial statements of Bouncing Bungies Company were presented to you in this case reading. In order to produce those financial statements, the company needed to analyze its day-to-day economic events. Exhibit 2-6.3 shows a completed accounting transaction worksheet showing how each transaction was recorded.

In looking at the worksheet, you should note that the account balances on the balance sheet were taken from row 25 of the worksheet. The income statement information comes from the Retained Earnings column (column L) and the Explanation Of Retained Earnings column (column M). The information for the direct method of the statement of cash flows comes from the cash column (column B).

In this example, all of the amounts that result in the change in retained earnings of $2,226 are amounts that are on the income statement, with the exception of the $43 owner's withdrawal. The withdrawal is *never* an income statement item.

Bouncing Bungies Company (BB) opened in December 2000. The company was located in a small metropolitan area and, with the spread of the bungy jumping craze, the start-up company became quite successful. The following events took place in December 2000, during the company's first month of operation.

Dec. 1   The owner invested $10,000 cash in the business.

1   BB borrowed $5,500 from the bank for two years. The note requires monthly payments of $251 which include principal and interest at 9 percent. Payments are due at month end (see Note 1 below).

1   BB paid $8,000 cash for bungies.

1   BB purchased a one-year insurance policy for $4,800; policy is effective immediately.

3   Advertising expenditures were $1,500. BB paid $700 cash and the remainder was on account.

7   BB hired three employees to begin work in one week; they will be paid $800 each on the 1st and the 15th of the month for work completed in the previous one-half month period.

11   BB purchased $2,000 of supplies on account.

15   Cash sales for the first half of December were $3,000; credit sales were $1,000.

21   BB received $900 cash from previous credit sales.

22   BB collected $50 from the sale of two gift certificates; the certificates are for future bungy jumps and will be recorded as ticket revenue when the certificates are used.

29   BB paid the remaining $800 owed for the advertising expenditure.

30   Wesley Harper, the owner, wrote a company check for $43 to buy groceries for his family.

31   BB paid utilities $300 for the month of December.

31   BB recorded $4,500 in sales for the last half of the month; 80 percent of these were for cash.

31   BB made the first $251 payment on the note payable. Remember that this payment includes both principal and interest. (see note 1)

31   BB noted that one full month of insurance has expired.

31   The bungies have been used for one month now. Management estimates that the bungies will have a six-year life and an $800 salvage value.

31   The employees will receive their first paychecks tomorrow for the work performed during the last two weeks. Total for all three employees is $2,400.

Dec. 31   Management noted that one $25 gift certificate was unused at year end.

31   Reconciled the bank account noting the bank charge of $15 was deducted from the account.

31   BB noted that there were $500 of supplies on hand at month end.

Note 1: The amount of the principal of the note payable which will be repaid in the next year should be classified as the current portion of long-term debt and will be a current liability. However, to keep this example simple, the entire liability will be treated as long-term debt on the balance sheet.

Exhibit 2-6.3
Bouncing Bungies Company
Accounting Transaction Worksheet

			ASSETS					LIABILITIES + OWNER'S EQUITY				
	Cash	Accounts Receivable	Supplies	Prepaid Insurance	Bungies	Accounts Payable	Gift Certificates	Wages Payable	Note Payable	Contributed Capital	Retained Earnings	Explanation of Retained Earnings
Beg. Bal. 12/1/00	$ -	$ -	$ -	$ -	$ -	$ -	$ -	$ -	$ -	$ -	$ -	
12/1/00	10,000									10,000		
12/1/00	5,500								5,500			
12/1/00	(8,000)				8,000							
12/1/00	(4,800)			4,800								
12/3/00	(700)					800					(1,500)	Advertising Expense
12/7/00						No entry required						
12/11/00			2,000			2,000						
12/15/00	3,000	1,000									4,000	Ticket Revenue
12/21/00	900	(900)										
12/22/00	50						50					
12/29/00	(800)					(800)						
12/30/00	(43)										(43)	Owner Withdrawal
12/31/00	(300)										(300)	Utilities Expense
12/31/00	3,600	900									4,500	Ticket Revenue
12/31/00	(251)								(210)		(41)	Interest Expense
12/31/00				(400)							(400)	Insurance Expense
12/31/00					(100)						(100)	Depreciation Expense
12/31/00								2,400			(2,400)	Wage Expense
12/31/00							(25)				25	Ticket Revenue
12/31/00	(15)										(15)	Service Charge
12/31/00			(1,500)								(1,500)	Supplies Expense
End Bal. 12/31/00	$ 8,141	$ 1,000	$ 500	$ 4,400	$ 7,900	$ 2,000	$ 25	$ 2,400	$ 5,290	$ 10,000	$ 2,226	

EXERCISES AND PROBLEMS

Exercises

Exercise 1 Identifying Financial Statements. Publicly traded companies generally are required to prepare three financial statements at the end of the annual accounting period. What are the three financial statements required to be published? Most companies actually publish four financial statements. What is the nature of the fourth financial statement usually included with the three required statements?

Exercise 2 Relationship of Income Statement to Statement of Retained Earnings. Financial statements articulate with each other, that is, they are tied together by a common string in some way. What major item ties together the income statement and the statement of retained earnings? Explain briefly.

Exercise 3 Relationship of the Statement of Retained Earnings and the Balance Sheet. The statement of retained earnings and the balance sheet are closely related by one item. What major item ties together the statement of retained earnings and the balance sheet? Explain briefly.

Exercise 4 Order of Preparing Financial Statements. There is a logical order to preparing financial statements for an organization at the end of the accounting period. Select the correct sequence from the following and explain why it is best to use in the preparation of a company's financial statements.

1. Balance sheet, statement of cash flows, income statement, statement of retained earnings
2. Statement of cash flows, income statement, statement of retained earnings, balance sheet
3. Income statement, statement of retained earnings, balance sheet, statement of cash flows
4. Balance sheet, income statement, statement of retained earnings, statement of cash flows
5. Income statement, balance sheet, statement of cash flows, statement of retained earnings

Exercise 5 Revenue Recognition and Cash Flows. Earning revenues and controlling cash are two of the more important aspects of running a business. Why is it that revenues earned as listed in the income statement do not equal the amount of cash received from customers for the accounting period?

Problems

Problem 1 Computing Asset Depreciation and Disclosure in the Balance Sheet. Assume the following facts for the Warner Company: Office furniture was purchased at a cost of $6,700, with an expected salvage value of $500 and a useful life of ten years. What is the amount of depreciation expense each year if Warner Company uses the straight-line depreciation method? What would be the book value of the office furniture as listed in the balance sheet at the end of the fifth year of use? Show supporting computations.

Problem 2 Interest Computation and Disclosure in Financial Statements. Frances Company borrowed $30,000 from the First Willard National Bank on October 16, 2000. The loan interest was stated at 10 percent per year and is to be paid when the note matures on November 30, 2000. What accounts will be included in the October 31, 2000, financial statements of Frances Company regarding the interest and note? Show computations and explain.

Problem 3   Notes to Financial Statements. One sentence in the reading stated that "Companies which are publicly traded and publish financial statements include, as part of the annual report, notes to the financial statements." What is the primary purpose of notes to the financial statements? Why do companies include these notes in the annual report?

Problem 4   Effect of Error on Financial Statements. At the end of this case reading was an extended illustration of Bouncing Bungies Company. At December 31 there was $2,400 of wage expense recorded for wages earned in December that will not be paid until January 2001. Assume that the wages earned were $3,200 (for four employees, not three) and that the $3,200 should have been recorded instead of the $2,400. See Exhibit 2-6.3 for the accounting transaction worksheet details and Exhibit 2-6.1 for financial statement details. Assuming that there was an error in recording the wage expense as outlined above, explain what amounts are incorrect in the (1) income statement, (2) statement of retained earnings, and (3) the balance sheet and whether the amounts reported were too small or too large. Explain any assumptions you make in answering this question.

Case 2-6

JOHN'S PROFITABILITY OR NOT?

Case Objectives

1. To gain a better understanding of the relationships between revenue versus cash receipts and expenses versus cash disbursements.
2. To gain practice in preparing an income statement and a statement of cash flows.
3. To gain understanding of the uses and limitations of income statements and statement of cash flows.

Decision: Does John's Painting Business meet the operating performance and current ratio loan criteria?

It was a cold and stormy night when John walked into the office of his uncle's CPAs in late March 2000. Robert Axel of Axel, Rose, and Hammer, Certified Public Accountants, greeted him at the door of his office. "I'm sorry to keep you waiting, John, but this time of the year I'm extremely busy. We're burning the midnight oil around here," he said.

"That's OK, Mr. Axel," replied John. "I don't have any classes tomorrow and I want to get these reports done so that I can concentrate on school."

"Exactly what is it that you want me to do for you, John?" asked Axel.

"Well, I know my uncle has spoken to you about the painting business I started last summer." John went on to explain that his uncle was considering investing in his business the following summer, but wanted some additional information on which to base his investment decision. "I've shown him my list of business assets and obligations as of the end of the summer, but he wants income and cash flow statements for the three months ended August 31, 1999. I'm not quite sure what the difference is, but I've brought along my checkbook and the list I gave Uncle Ernie. Maybe you can use them to prepare the reports he wants to see." John handed Axel the checkbook and list of assets and liabilities.

Assets and Liabilities at August 31, 1999:

	Balance at 8/31/99
Cash in bank account	$6,660
Amount owed to John by customers	1,300
Cost of unused supplies	95
Unused paint	0
Compressor (cost, $2,400; accum. depreciation, $704)	1,696
Ladders (cost, $600; accum. depreciation, $176)	424
Truck (cost [blue book], $9,200; accum. depreciation, $2,233)	6,967
Note payable to uncle	3,300
Unpaid bills	575
Interest payable	74

John also informed Axel that (1) the compressor and ladders were still in good condition and could, if necessary, be sold after the next two summers at 12 percent of their original cost, whereas the truck can probably be sold for $2,500 at the end of the third summer; (2) in early September, he paid his uncle the $74 interest owed at August 31; (3) in September and October he collected the $1,300 customer receivables, paid the $575 in liabilities, and decided to keep the supplies to use next summer.

After reviewing John's records for a minute or two, Axel asked what made up the $575 unpaid bills at August 31. John replied that $300 was for paint (all used prior to August 31) and $275 was for advertising.

"OK, John, I think I've got enough information to prepare income and cash flow statements for the three months ended August 31," said Axel. "I'll call you if I need any more information. I'll mail the reports and we can discuss them if you have any questions."

"Thank you, Mr. Axel," John said as he left. "I'll look forward to hearing from you."

A couple of days later, Axel sat down with John's list of assets and obligations and with the summary of John's checkbook that the bookkeeper had prepared. The summary follows.

Cash Receipts and Cash Disbursements (June 1 - August 31, 1999):

Beginning cash balance June 1, 1999	$ 0
John's initial cash contribution	1,400
Loan received from Uncle Ernie	3,300
Payment for compressor and ladders	(3,000)
Additional cash contribution by John in mid-July	1,000
Collected from customers	10,500
Payments for paint	(3,550)
Payments for supplies	(525)
Payments for advertising	(715)
Payments for insurance	(550)
Withdrawal of cash for John's school fees	(1,200)
Ending cash balance August 31, 1999	$ 6,660

Drawing on information contained in the preceding two lists, Robert Axel did the following:

• Adjusted various cash receipts and cash disbursements to appropriate revenues and expense amounts.

• Prepared an income statement for the three-month period ended August 31, 1999.

• Prepared a statement of cash flows for the three-month period ended August 31, 1999.

Requirements

1. Assume you are Robert Axel of Axel, Rose, and Hammer. Using a computer spreadsheet, prepare the following statements for John's Painting Business for the three months ended August 31, 1999 (you do not have to prepare an accounting transaction worksheet):

    a. Income Statement

    b. Statement of Cash Flows - Direct Method

     c.   Statement of Cash Flows - Indirect Method

2.   After receiving the financial statements, John looks them over very carefully. Because John is thinking about borrowing money from the bank in the future, he is trying to determine whether or not he meets the bank's loan requirements. The bank requires the business to be financially successful and requires a current ratio of 2 or better to ensure that the loan would be paid back on time. Would John's Painting Business meet the loan criteria?

Group Assignment 2-6

HOW DID JOHN'S
BUSINESS PERFORM?

Group Number _____ Group members present and participating:

_____

_____

Objectives

1. To gain a better understanding of the relationships between revenue versus cash receipts and expenses versus cash disbursements.
2. To gain practice in preparing an income statement and statement of cash flows.
3. To gain understanding of the uses and limitations of income statements and statement of cash flows.

Requirements

After discussing your individual solutions to Case 2-6, provide group consensus responses to the following.

1. Determine the amounts for the following items for John's Painting Business. Be sure to show net cash outflows in parentheses.

   Fees Revenue   _____

   Paint Expense   _____

   Supplies Expense   _____

   Net Cash Flow from Operations   _____

   Net Cash Flow from Investing Activities _____

   Net Cash Flow from Financing Activities _____

2. Which do you think more realistically measures operating performance, net income or cash flow? Explain.

3. Which measure of performance is more objective (i.e., requires less judgment to arrive at), net income or cash flow? Explain.

4. What is meant by accrual accounting?

Case Reading 2-7

IDENTIFYING ASSETS AND
LIABILITIES

INTRODUCTION

The proper reporting of assets and liabilities is necessary to produce not only a balance sheet on which one can rely, but also an income statement. These two primary financial statements work in tandem. As assets and liabilities are measured and accrued on the balance sheet, there is a direct effect on the measurement of revenues and expenses. This case reading introduces several criteria as a guide to the measurement and reporting of assets and liabilities.

ASSETS

Recording assets in the accounting records generally is a straightforward process. However, questions often arise as to when an asset should be recognized, at what amount it should be recorded, and how it should be accounted for in future accounting periods. The question of the amount at which an asset should be recorded is easily answered. An asset should be recorded at its cost. For accounting and business purposes, cost is defined as the fair market value of the consideration given or the fair market value of the item(s) received, whichever is more readily determinable. You already have experience at recording assets at cost in completing previous case assignments. Generally, once an asset is recorded in the accounting records it will remain at its historical cost less a portion of that amount which is deemed to be depreciation expense of the accounting period. For example, a Boeing 777 passenger jet costs over $100 million and would be recorded at the airline's purchase price. If the useful life of the aircraft is set at 20 years, each year a proportionate amount of the historical cost is classified as depreciation expense in the income statement. The balance sheet would then report the original cost less the accumulated depreciation.

When an asset should be reported on the balance sheet is determined by GAAP. We will use as a guide a pronouncement of the Financial Accounting Standards Board (FASB), Statement of Financial Accounting Concepts No. 6, Elements of Financial Statements, which defines assets as "(i) probable future economic benefits (ii) obtained or controlled by a particular entity (iii) as a result of past transactions or events." (Paragraph 25) Applying these criteria at times requires judgment and interpretation. For example, an upscale department store may have in inventory a boldly innovative line of women's fashion clothing recorded at the historical cost of that inventory. However, the store finds that the designs did not catch the fancy of their customers and drastic markdowns below cost are necessary. There is another question: at what value should an asset be recorded? In this example there are special rules called "lower of cost or market" which guide the valuation of inventory. These rules stem from the accounting profession's tradition of conservatism in the drafting of financial statements. **Conservatism** states that when there is doubt as to the value of an asset a lower alternative value should be reported. Similarly, when estimates are required for such uncertain measurements as useful life, uncollectible accounts receivable, or percentage of obsolete inventory, the application of conservatism understates assets, overstates liabilities, defers gains until realized, and recognizes losses earlier rather than later.

The concept of conservatism can be applied to gain contingencies. A **gain contingency** means that a reasonable probability exists that an economic benefit in the form of enhanced profit will occur if certain events also occur. An example of a gain contingency, which is often found in the footnotes to published financial statements, is the litigation related to patent infringement. The patent holder files a lawsuit claiming infringement and requests the court to award damages to compensate it for lost profits. For the gain to be a reality by the patent holder, several events must occur: (1) the patent rights are validated, (2) the court agrees to hear the case, (3) the court finds in favor of the patent holder or the defendant settles out of court, (4) the defendant has the ability to pay the court-ordered judgment, and (5) the defendant decides not to appeal to a higher court. In many cases such as this, years go by before a final realization of the gain occurs. Accounting practice is to wait for the contingent events to become an indisputable occurrence before the gain is reported in financial statements. To do otherwise would introduce an unacceptable degree of subjective opinion about the outcome of lawsuits and other matters that are potential gains. Conservatism creates what many consider to be a favorable bias preventing income and assets from being reported at unrealistically inflated amounts.

Probable Future Economic Benefits

The FASB's first criterion, "probable future economic benefits," means that to qualify as an asset there must be a reasonable likelihood that future positive cashflows will be generated by the asset. Such cashflows could be increased revenues, reduced operating expenses, or proceeds from sale or liquidation of the asset.

Here is an example of a situation that seems to be an asset but fails the criterion of future benefit. Suppose a company holds a parcel of land currently on its balance sheet at its historical cost of $100,000. At the time of purchase the company planned to locate a new factory on the premises. As soil tests were made, the company discovered that toxic chemicals dumped there forty years ago still contaminate the soil. It would cost more than $100,000 to repair the site, and it would be much cheaper for the company to buy another parcel. Also, the law requires that the seller disclose defects to a prospective buyer, which was not done. Now the asset is worthless. Therefore, proper accounting procedures would not allow the land to be reported on the company's balance sheet, because there will be no future benefit to the company. A loss would be recorded in the income statement in the year the contamination problem was discovered.

Another example might be advertising. Is the amount paid for advertising an asset or an expense of the period in which the advertising was done? The expectation when one enters into a contract to run advertising is that revenues will increase as a result of the ads. The phrase "future economic benefit" refers to benefits beyond the current fiscal year. Economic benefit must be reasonably predictable and quantifiable. Quantifiable means that the event or item is capable of being objectively measured. In the case of advertising, the ability to predict that certain ads will create economic benefit into and beyond the next fiscal year is suspect. Thus, while advertising may seem to qualify as an asset because of improved sales revenue which follows the ad, there are too many uncertainties to classify the money paid for advertising as an asset. It must be reported as an expense of the period in which the advertising appeared.

Owned And Controlled By A Particular Entity

The second criterion, "owned and controlled by a particular entity," refers to the fact that the business must have uncontested legal rights to the assets. A trucking company may lease a fleet of trucks on a month-to-month basis. The outward appearance of the company's operation is that it has a large fleet of trucks. But because the company is simply a lessee of the fleet, it has legal rights for use of the trucks for only the next month. It cannot legally sell or rent out the trucks to anyone else. The leased trucks cannot be shown as an asset on the trucking company's balance sheet. However, if we change the lease to a five-year term which is noncancelable, we have what is called a capital lease. A capital lease is a long-term lease obligating the lessee to make payments for the full term of the lease, which is generally equivalent to the useful life of the asset. Over the term of the capital lease, the lessor recovers its investment plus a profit. The capital lease is effectively a financing tool for companies to acquire the use of assets they need to operate their businesses without large cash outflows.

There are specific rules of the FASB regarding capital leases. Reporting capital leases on balance sheets requires the asset to be recorded at the same amount as if it were purchased for cash. In addition, the liability for the purchase price must be shown on the balance sheet at that same amount. For instance, if the trucking company entered into a capital lease for a new truck which had a cash price of $50,000, the balance sheet at the time of the transaction would show an asset of $50,000 and also a liability of $50,000. In subsequent years, the company's income statement would report depreciation expense of the leased truck. The balance sheet would show the undepreciated cost of the truck and the remaining liability owed on the lease. Details surrounding capital leases are covered in Module 4.

As A Result Of Past Transactions Or Events

The third criterion, "as a result of past transactions or events," refers to a necessary condition that an arm's-length exchange (an exchange between two independent parties) has occurred. It is not possible to report an asset that is expected to be owned in the future. To qualify as an asset the item meeting the other two requirements must be the outcome of a contract or other legally enforceable transaction that conveys title or other irrevocable legal rights to unrestricted use of the asset. This standard prevents subjective judgment regarding the existence of assets. It requires that an external person or entity, seeking their best interests, has entered into a transaction to sell or exchange an asset.

For example, suppose a city government is willing to donate a land parcel in return for a company locating its operations on that site. The proposed agreement may also call for employment of a certain number of people by the company. A letter to the company offering the land is not sufficient to place the land parcel on the balance sheet. A completely executed contract and conveyance of title to the land must occur before the asset can be reported on the balance sheet. Once these matters are accomplished, the land is reported at the fair market value. Establishing fair market value is usually based upon the opinion of an independent real estate appraiser who has no financial interest in the company.

Assets Which Do Not Appear On Balance Sheets

One area frequently discussed in the accounting literature is the status of human resources in financial reports. Are employees an asset of the business entity which employs them? When top management addresses the corporation shareholders in annual reports, they often note the "extraordinary contributions of our most important asset—our employees." Yet when one looks to the balance sheet of the company, there is not a recorded asset called "Employees" or "Human Resources." So how are the chief executive officer or the chairman of the board using the term asset? They are using asset to describe one of many resources which are available to them as professional managers. One can imagine a CEO correctly saying "the Internet has become one of our most important assets in the research and development of new products." Yet the company has surely not purchased the Internet and most societies do not permit the ownership of people. Employees are usually free to change employers just as employers are free to make justified changes of employees. Even though companies often make huge investments to train employees, their inability to predict the length of employee service to the company and to quantify the future economic benefit of the training investments make the amounts paid out expenses, not assets which at a later date can be sold or exchanged.

LIABILITIES

Liabilities are debts owed by the business entity. The form of the business—proprietorship, partnership, or corporation—may make a difference to the creditor who must resort to litigation to collect amounts due. But whatever the form of legal organization, from an accounting viewpoint the business entity is separate and distinct from it owners, and a liability is simply a claim on the assets of the business. For financial statements to be reliable and accurate, the balance sheet must disclose all liabilities. Furthermore, the related income statement must show the expenses incurred at the time the liabilities are recognized. A practical difficulty arises shortly after a year end. The owner or manager may wish to apply for additional financing from its bank, but the bills from the previous fiscal year are still caught up in the Christmas mail crunch. Both the balance sheet and the income statement will be inaccurate until all liabilities are recorded.

Accrual Basis of Accounting

The situation presented above is remedied by the accrual basis of accounting. Recall that this means that expenses must be reported in the period in which they were incurred. In addition, revenues must be reported in the period in which they were earned. For example, suppose a business received a telephone bill for $1,550 on January 10, 2000, covering the month of December 1999. Even though the company did not have precise knowledge of the bill as of the balance sheet date, December 31, 1999, it nevertheless must record the liability and expense before issuing the financial statements for calendar year 1999. Companies take as much as 90 days after the fiscal year end to publish their annual reports containing financial statements because of information that can be acquired only after the year is over.

The alternate timing for the recognition of expense is called the **cash basis of accounting**. The cash basis ignores the fact that liabilities have been created in the normal course of conducting business transactions. The cash basis never recognizes the liability and its associated expense when created. Instead, the expense is recorded at the time the cash is disbursed. This can occur in a different accounting period and thus distort both the income statement and the balance sheet. Moreover, since the timing of cash disbursements is a prerogative of the owners or managers, the financial statements prepared on a cash basis can be manipulated. Cash basis is generally not accepted for financial reporting of business enterprises. However, the Internal Revenue Service accepts the approach for individuals, because the cash basis reduces the number of estimates, thereby making enforcement of the Tax Code a somewhat easier task.

Loss Contingencies

One area that poses great difficulty is how to include the effect of litigation in the financial statements. For decision makers to have complete accounting information, it is necessary that they be fully informed of pending lawsuits and other matters that are not final judgments against the business. The FASB in Statement No. 5 has provided guidance on what is to be included in the financial statements and what is to be disclosed in a footnote to the financial statements. This is referred to as a **loss contingency**. The loss contingency guidelines are as follows:

If a loss is:

Loss Probability	Financial Statement Disclosure
Remote	No disclosure is required
Reasonably possible	Disclose in a footnote
Probable	Record liability if amount is determinable

The following statement is taken from the footnote to financial statements in a prospectus of an initial public offering of shares in a California corporation.

> In October 1997, the Company was served with a complaint that had been filed in the Superior Court of California seeking an unspecified amount of damages for personal injuries and property damage incurred by residents of a single location alleged to have resulted from the Company's and others' negligent and/or intentional handling of toxic chemicals. While the company believes it has meritorious defenses against the claims asserted in this lawsuit and intends to vigorously defend itself in this case the amount of loss, if any, that may result upon resolution of this complaint is not currently estimable nor have any amounts been accrued in the financial statements. Accordingly, there can be no assurance that the complaint can be resolved without adverse impact to the company's financial position or results of operations.

If the company and its attorneys in the above case determined that it was negligent in handling toxic chemicals and estimated that it could settle with the plaintiffs for $1,000,000, the 1997 income statement would show the expense of settlement and the December 31, 1997 balance sheet would show the liability for $1,000,000. Then in 1998 when the expected out-of-court settlement actually occurred, the company would pay out cash of $1,000,000 and extinguish the liability. Two effects of this lawsuit are that 1997 income before taxes is reduced by $1,000,000, and, assuming the loss is a deductible expense and the tax rate is 35 percent, shareholders' equity is reduced by $650,000 as of December 31, 1997.

Analysis of Litigation Loss:

Loss from lawsuit settlement	$1,000,000
Reduction of income taxes due to loss	350,000
Net reduction of shareholders' equity from loss	$ 650,000

Accruing Liabilities—An Example

To illustrate the impact of unrecorded liabilities, we will use the following three examples.

1. Ajax Corporation is required by its lending agreement with International Trust Co. to pay interest for the previous year by January 10, 2001. The loan for $1,000,000 has a five-year term and carries an interest rate of two percentage points above the prime rate, which averaged 6 percent during 2000.

2. Ajax gives its customers a 12-month warranty for all parts and labor if the product should fail due to a manufacturing defect. The company's database of serial numbers and date of purchase indicates that $500,000 of sales are still

under warranty as of December 31, 2000. Its warranty statistics also indicate that the cost of servicing warranty claims will be 1 percent of sales.

3. On December 30, 2000, Ajax received a deposit check of $100,000 as advance payment on a purchase order from one of its customers; the items ordered will be delivered in March 2001. The person handling incoming checks increased cash and increased revenues.

The worksheet below shows how the accrual of these liabilities are entered.

				Ajax's Worksheet Showing Accrual of Liabilities			
Effect	Assets	Interest Payable	Warranty Liability	Unearned Revenue	Other Liabilities	Contributed Capital	Retained Earnings
Before Accrual	XXX				XXX	XXX	XXX
Example 1		80,000					(80,000)
Example 2			5,000				(5,000)
Example 3				100,000			(100,000)
After Accrual	XXX	$ 80,000	$ 5,000	$ 100,000	XXX	XXX	$(185,000)

The first two items will add to expenses, namely interest expense, $80,000, and warranty expense, $5,000. The third item for $100,000 was improperly included in revenue for 2000. It must be reported in 2001 when the goods are delivered to the customer. The negative adjustment in retained earnings indicates a reduction in 2000 revenue from whatever amount was recorded before this accrual was made.

SUMMARY

For an asset to be included in the balance sheet of an entity, it must meet several specific criteria. It can require interpretation of the standards set by the Financial Accounting Standards Board. Liabilities too must be carefully monitored to ensure that none are omitted from the balance sheet. The accrual basis of accounting is designed to include all liabilities which have been created through business transactions. The accrual basis also ensures that revenue and expenses are correctly stated in the income statement.

Case 2-7 presents a businessperson who is applying for a loan. The financial statements he presents to the bank's loan officer are incorrect. Your task is to make a judgment on the propriety of the Upside-Down Ski School's financial statements.

EXERCISES AND PROBLEMS

Exercises

Exercise 1 Identify and Explain Asset Characteristics. What are the three characteristics of assets as defined by the Financial Accounting Standards Board? Briefly explain what each of the three characteristics means.

Exercise 2 Asset Valuation Accounts. Many assets lose value over time or because of some economic event. The costs of these assets must be adjusted, usually by reducing the carrying cost of the asset. Identify three assets that tend to lose their value over time. How does conservatism affect the value, or reduction in value, of these assets?

Problems

Problem 1 Valuing Assets in Noncash Exchanges. It is well understood in accounting and business that assets are recorded at cost. Determining cost in some situations is difficult. What is the cost of the land in the following situation?

Pablo San Marcos purchased 1,000 shares of Algeo Tech stock ten years ago for $22,000. The stock is selling in 100-unit lots in the over-the-counter market at $66 per share. Pablo wants to exchange the stock for a piece of land to use in a small business he is starting. The land cost its current owner $10,000 when purchased 30 years ago. The land has an assessed value of $25,000 by Catalina County, where the land is located. The owner of the land believes that he could sell the land for $70,000 to $75,000. Pablo and the land owner agree to swap the stock for the land with no other consideration given by either party to the deal. What value (cost) does Pablo record for the land in his accounting records? Explain how you arrived at the amount you suggested.

Problem 2 When Is a Liability a Liability? During the last thirty years there has been much concern, discussion, and some legislation concerning the use of tobacco and smoking. The discussion often centers on the harmful long-term effects of tobacco users and smoking (and smoke from smokers).

For more than thirty years, tobacco companies stated that tobacco usage was not addictive and denied any liability for its usage. In more recent years there has been increasing evidence that many of the tobacco companies made studies on how to make their products more appealing/addictive to users. At the present time there are many different court cases at the state and federal level concerning the liabilities of tobacco companies for tobacco usage. Most tobacco product companies now admit that there is liability for their products. Without getting into the specifics of health issues and events, how should/would a tobacco company account for its potential liability from the processing and selling of tobacco products? At what point should a tobacco company record a liability in the balance sheet regarding its tobacco products?

Case 2-7

UPSIDE-DOWN SKI SCHOOL

Case Objectives

1. Understand the nature of assets, liabilities, and owner's equity of an economic entity; understand various value measurements (e.g., historical cost, current value) that may be associated with those items; and construct a balance sheet that reflects those items.
2. Understand the nature of net income (profit) and its two major components, revenue and expenses; and understand how the accrual basis of accounting recognizes revenues and expenses and matches those items in measuring net income.

Decision: After adjusting the statements for the given transactions, should the loan officer grant the loan based on the given criteria?

Mr. Often Glib opened the Upside-Down Ski School in early February 2000. He wants to buy a patent from its inventor and needs $70,000 to cover the cost of the patent. His plan is to make a visit to Metropolis Commercial Bank, where his company has its account. He is confident that he can convince the Metropolis' loan officer, Jacqueline Cash, that his company is worthy of the proposed one-year loan based upon its strong balance sheet. Moreover, he projects that his company will make "millions" from the patent, thus providing more than adequate cash flow to repay the loan. The patent would allow the ski school to provide year-round training by means of a virtual reality ski simulation.

At a meeting held on January 4, 2001, Ms. Cash informed Mr. Glib that the bank's policy is to consider loans only to businesses with solid balance sheets. Specifically, balance sheets must show total liabilities to be less than 50 percent of total assets before the loan. A further test of loan eligibility is that liabilities must be less than 65 percent of the assets after the loan. In response, Mr. Glib presents the company's most recent balance sheet dated December 31, 2000.

Upside-Down Ski School
Balance Sheet (Unaudited)
December 31, 2000

Assets			Liabilities and Owner's Equity		
Current Assets			Current Liabilities		
Cash		$ 30,000	Accounts Payable		$ 40,000
Accounts Receivable		70,000	Bank Loan Payable		100,000
Advertising		50,000			
Total Current Assets		$ 150,000	Total Current Liabilities		140,000
Fixed Assets			Owner's Equity		
Land	$ 150,000		Contributed Capital	$ 150,000	
Equipment	150,000		Retained Earnings	160,000	
Total Fixed Assets		$ 300,000	Total Owner's Equity		310,000
Total Assets		$ 450,000	Total Liabilities and Owner's Equity		$ 450,000

Jacqueline noted that although Upside-Down appears to meet the first criterion (liabilities less than 50 percent of assets before the loan is made) the balance sheet is unaudited. Without the opinion of a certified public accountant as to the fairness of the balance sheet and any other financial statements that she may need, it is necessary to inquire further into the completeness and accuracy of the balance sheet. In such cases, the bank's policy is to require the gathering of additional information by interviewing the loan applicant's accountant.

On January 5, 2001, Ms. Cash conducted a lengthy interview with Glib and Upside-Down's accountant, Frank Franklin, who was new at the job, having just graduated from Ucandoit College. Both Glib and Franklin were forthright in answering her questions. The interview explored the accounting principles employed by Upside-Down. Based on the interview, Cash was unsure whether certain assets and liabilities on Upside-Down's balance sheet were stated in accordance with generally accepted accounting principles. She informed Mr. Glib that she would consult with the bank's CPA, Becka Countess, to ascertain whether Upside-Down's balance sheet was reasonably accurate so that the bank could prudently apply its loan criteria to the accounting information contained therein.

Based upon her notes, Jacqueline prepared a memo listing items of concern to give to Becka. Excerpts of the memo follow.

Items I am concerned about:

1. Accounts Receivable - When I asked Franklin about any problem accounts in the list of receivables he informed me that no estimate of bad debts is ever made. He revealed that just yesterday Upside-Down received notice of a bankruptcy hearing of one of its customers whose balance is $4,000.

2. Insurance - I was told that the company did maintain fire and damage insurance on their fixed assets. In fact, Mr. Glib said his company had written a check for $3,000 in early December to renew its insurance policy for the six-month policy period covering February 1 through July 31, 2001, and it is included in insurance expense.

3. Advertising - The $50,000 amount is the amount paid in 2000 for advertising that appeared in summer issues of various ski magazines. The company expects sales to increase in the future as a result of this advertising.

4. Equipment - Franklin stated that all equipment was installed new when the company opened on February 1, 2000. He said that the company estimates that the equipment has a five-year useful life and that it could probably be sold after that for about $30,000.

5. Ski Supplies - The company started with about $3,000 of ski supplies when they first opened and have about $4,000 on hand at year-end. All purchases of supplies are recorded immediately as expenses.

6. Interest - Interest on the $100,000 bank loan payable for the three months ending December 31, 2000, was not recorded or paid. The annual interest rate is 12 percent. No principal payments are due until the entire loan is due on February 1, 2006.

7. Advance Payments - During 2000 customers made advance payments of $30,000 to Upside-Down for ski lesson packages. These amounts were recorded as revenues in 2000 when the ski lesson packages were sold. About $18,000 of the ski lessons have not yet been given and will be provided in the next year.

8. Equipment Lease - On December 30, 2000, Upside-Down entered into a non-cancelable three-year lease for computer equipment expected to have a useful life of three years. Neither the equipment nor the lease payable was recorded. The lease liability is $25,000 and is the cash equivalent price of the new equipment.

9. Lawsuit - Upside-Down is being sued by a former employee for wrongful termination. The employee is seeking back wages in the amount of $50,000. Mr. Glib presented a letter to Ms. Cash from the corporation counsel stating that the suit is without merit and that the company is unlikely to be found liable.

10. Loan From Owner - Included in contributed capital is a promissory note payable to Mr. Often Glib in the amount of $50,000. This note originated on December 30, 2000, and is due December 30, 2001. The company needed cash to pay the overdue advertising bill. Mr. Glib loaned the $50,000 to the company.

11. Utility Bill - The company has not yet recorded its utility bill for December but estimates that it will be about $1,000. The bill usually arrives in the middle of the following month.

2000 is the first year of operations. Rent is paid at the beginning of the month for that month. Mr Glib provided the bank with the following income statement (which contains errors).

Upside-Down Ski School
Income Statement (Unaudited)
Year Ended December 31, 2000

Ski Lesson Revenue		$ 480,000
Expenses:		
Salaries	$ 213,500	
Building Rent	33,000	
Owner Withdrawal	24,000	
Supplies	23,000	
Utilities	10,000	
Interest	8,000	
Insurance	8,500	320,000
Net Income		$ 160,000

Requirements

1. Assume you are working for Ms. Countess, CPA. Using the spreadsheet template provided at the end of this case, enter the changes, if any, to the balance sheet accounts that each of the above items require. Remember to maintain the integrity of the balance sheet by maintaining the balance sheet equation on every row (perform an equality check). Item #1 has already been entered for you.

2. Prepare a revised balance sheet as of December 31, 2000. Be sure to include subtotals for current assets, fixed assets, current liabilities, and long-term liabilities (if needed).

3. Prepare a revised income statement for the year ending December 31, 2000.

4. Assume the role of the loan officer in this case. Apply to Upside-Down Ski School the Metropolis Commercial Bank's policy for qualifying loan applicants. What decision should Jacqueline Cash make? Write a memo to Mr. Glib informing him of your decision. Be sure to reference specific balance sheet and income statement information in support of your decision.

Template for Upside-Down Ski School

Adjustment Reference	Cash	Accounts Receivable	Advertising	Other Current Assets	Land	Equipment	Accounts Payable	Bank Loan Payable	Other Current Liabilities	Long-term Liabilities	Contributed Capital	Retained Earnings	Description of Adjustment	Equality Check
Unaudited Balance sheet	$ 30,000	$ 70,000	$ 50,000	$ -	$ 150,000	$ 150,000	$ 40,000	$ 100,000	$ -	$ -	$ 150,000	$ 160,000		0
Item #1		(4,000)										(4,000)	Bad debt expense	0
Item #2														
Item #3														
Item #4														
Item #5														
Item #6														
Item #7														
Item #8														
Item #9														
Item #10														
Item #11														
Other Items to Note														
Corrected Balance														

Group Assignment 2-7

Should Right-Side-Up Get The Loan?

Group Number _____   **Group members present and participating:**

_____

_____

Objectives

1. Understand the nature of assets, liabilities, and owner's equity of an economic entity.
2. Understand valuation of assets and liabilities in financial statements prepared in accordance with generally accepted accounting principles.
3. Understand the measurements of revenue and expenses and how the accrual basis of accounting causes accurate measurement of income.

Requirements

The Right-Side-Up Ski School has applied for a one-year loan of $90,000 beginning January 1, 2001 at Metropolis Bank because the company needs to purchase some equipment. Metropolis Bank's lending policy requires the loan applicant to have the following ratios:

    a. Current ratio of 1.5 or higher before the loan
    b. Debt ratio less than 50 percent before the loan
    c. Debt ratio less than 55 percent after the loan
    d. Return on equity greater than 10 percent

The bank explains that the debt ratio can be calculated by dividing total liabilities by total assets.

The current balance sheet and income statement (both unaudited) are shown at the end of this group assignment. Assume that you have determined that the balance sheet amounts are correct. After reviewing the income statement and revising it if necessary, come to a group consensus on the following requirements.

1. Compute the current ratio for Right-Side-Up before the $90,000 loan.

2. Compute the debt ratio before the $90,000 loan.

3. Compute the debt ratio after the $90,000 loan.

4. Compute the return on equity (ROE) for 2000 (assume beginning equity is $150,000):

5. What decision should the loan officer make regarding Right-Side-Up's loan application?

Right-Side-Up Ski School
Balance Sheet (Unaudited)
December 31, 2000

Assets			Liabilities and Owner's Equity		
Current Assets			Current Liabilities		
Cash		$ 50,000	Accounts Payable		$ 10,000
Accounts Receivable		70,000	Bank Loan Payable		100,000
Prepaid Insurance		45,000			
Total Current Assets		$ 165,000	Total Current Liabilities		110,000
Fixed Assets			Owner's Equity		
Land	$ 80,000		Contributed Capital	$ 150,000	
Equipment	20,000		Retained Earnings	5,000	
Total Fixed Assets		100,000	Total Owner's Equity		155,000
Total Assets		$ 265,000	Total Liabilities and Owner's Equity		$ 265,000

Right-Side-Up Ski School
Income Statement (Unaudited)
Year Ended December 31, 2000

Ski Lesson Revenue		$ 325,000
Expenses:		
Salaries	$ 213,500	
Building Rent	33,000	
Owner's Withdrawal	24,000	
Supplies	23,000	
Utilities	10,000	
Interest	8,000	
Insurance	8,500	320,000
Net Income		$ 5,000

Case Reading 2-8 Part A

USING PUBLISHED FINANCIAL STATEMENTS

INTRODUCTION

Many people are interested in the financial statements of publicly held corporations because they own stocks and bonds. When individuals buy stock they become part owners of the company, and when they buy bonds, they become creditors of the company. In either case, these purchasers will be interested in the financial health of the corporation.

In this case reading we will learn to interpret the types of information contained in the financial statements of publicly held companies, such as those contained in a prospectus, an annual report, or an auditor's report. Part B of this case includes references to the annual report of The Gap, Inc., which is included in Appendix A. Many companies also use the Internet to provide additional financial information, and you will learn how to use the Internet to obtain this information.

HOW SHAREHOLDERS ARE KEPT INFORMED

Publicly traded companies are companies whose shares are traded on organized stock exchanges such as the New York Stock Exchange or NASDAQ. The companies are required by law to keep their shareholders informed about their financial situation. Congress enacted laws giving the Securities and Exchange Commission (SEC) the responsibility of ensuring that the information provided by companies is accurate and complete, so that when investors buy stocks and bonds they know they can have confidence in the system. The SEC also has the responsibility of making sure companies follow certain rules on how stock exchanges take place.

Prospectus

One of the documents required by the SEC to be given to prospective purchasers of stocks and bonds is called a prospectus. There is an extensive list of topics mandated by SEC regulations when a company prepares a prospectus. For example, the section entitled "Selected Consolidated Financial Data" includes the income statement for the previous five years and such balance sheet data as:

- **Working Capital** (Current Assets Minus Current Liabilities)
- Total Assets
- Long-Term Debt
- Shareholders' Equity

In addition to these disclosures of financial information, there is a section (F-1) dedicated to presenting very detailed accounting information:

- Report of Independent Auditors
- Consolidated Balance Sheet
- Consolidated Statement of Operation (Income Statement)
- Consolidated Statement of Cash Flows
- Consolidated Statement of Parent Equity
- Notes to Consolidated Financial Statements

The term **consolidated** means joining together the financial statements of an entire family of separate legal corporations into a single financial statement. For example, if one corporation owns more than fifty percent of the voting stock of three other corporations, it is required to issue consolidated financial statements disclosing the assets, liabilities, revenues, expenses, etc., of all four companies as though it was one company. The SEC and the accounting profession has long held the need for companies to issue consolidated statements to fully disclose the subsidiary profits, losses, or other financial matters so investors can obtain an accurate report of the progress of the economic entity, the family of companies.

Annual Report

Companies also provide information to investors in their annual report. The **annual report** includes:

1. Some comments by the Chairman of the Board
2. Some comments by the Chief Executive Officer
3. A description of the company's new products, facilities, personnel, strategies, and similar items.
4. Management's discussion and analysis of operations
5. A financial section containing analyses, summaries, statements, footnotes, and the opinion of auditors on the fairness of the financial statements

We will focus on the financial section of the annual report. The financial statements are the primary component of the annual report. They tell the reader:

- The financial position by reporting the assets, liabilities, and owners' equity in the balance sheet.
- The results of operations by reporting the revenues and expenses for the year in the income statement.
- The change in the cash and cash equivalents by reporting the cash inflows or outflows from operating, investing, and financial activities.

There are also a variety of special disclosures that different companies find necessary. For example, IBM sells its products all over the world. Shareholders want to know how much sales revenue is generated in different parts of the world. Furthermore, present and prospective investors want to know how much profit and investment IBM is making in different parts of the world. Thus, IBM's annual report contains numerous tables and schedules to fully disclose the financial picture of the company. A much smaller company that sells only its products domestically would not require these extensive supplementary schedules in its annual report.

Publicly held companies need to communicate on an ongoing basis with their shareholders. The annual report is the most important means of accomplishing this need. Other important ways of communicating with shareholders include Form 10K filings with the SEC, meetings with securities analysts and reporters, and quarterly reports. Annual reports are also used to communicate with other corporate stakeholders, such as, prospective shareholders, creditors, employees, and customers. Also, Competing firms in the same industry may find annual reports of interest.

The beginning sections of most annual reports present an optimistic view of the company and its prospects for the future. These sections typically have numerous glossy pictures and highlight the company's achievements during the previous year. This section is not audited and managers are not precluded from painting an optimistic picture of the company's future. Despite its optimistic slant, this section is useful to investors. Readers can discover management's strategies, perceived progress toward implementing these strategies, and hopes for the future. These sections often discuss new product lines, programs to modernize or expand facilities, and progress toward long-term goals. All this information helps investors better estimate the company's future performance.

Auditor's Report

All companies whose stocks are traded publicly are required by the SEC to have their annual financial records audited by a certified public accounting (CPA) firm. The **auditor's report** (also called the **auditor's opinion**) expresses the CPA firm's opinion as to whether the financial statements present fairly in all material respects the financial position (balance sheet), results of operations (income statement), and cash flows (statement of cash flows) of the company audited. It also verifies that the financial statements were prepared in accordance with generally accepted accounting principles. The report identifies any uncorrected problems and material misstatements that the auditors have discovered. The report gives investors increased confidence that the financial statements present an honest reporting of the company's results but it *does not* advise the financial statement user as to whether or not the company is a good investment opportunity.

The auditor's report mentions that the financial statements are the responsibility of management. You will notice on page A10 of Appendix A that above the auditor's report for The Gap, Inc., is the "Management Report on Responsibility for Financial Reporting." It should be clear from these statements that management is responsible for preparing the financial statements and developing the internal controls needed to create accurate financial information.

The auditors' role is to assess the adequacy of the company's internal control system and test transactions to determine if the control system is operating properly. Because modern accounting systems operate on sophisticated computer systems, the CPA must be able to evaluate the integrity, security, and reliability of the data entering and exiting the system. The auditors also test the reasonableness of financial information given the economic environment and the company's level of sales and production. For large companies like The Gap, Inc., CPA firms perform tests during much of the year, and have a large team of accountants working on the audit just before and immediately after the fiscal year is over. Upon completion of the testing, auditors' issue a report called an auditors' opinion. An example of the opinion or report of the CPA firm which audits the ABC Corporation is shown in Exhibit 2-8A.1. Several portions of the opinion have been underlined for emphasis.

Exhibit 2-8A.1
Unqualified Auditors' Opinion

ANDERSON AND ZINDER
Certified Public Accountants
100 Park Plaza East
Denver, Colorado 80110
(555)358-8000

Independent Auditor's Report

To the Stockholders of ABC Corporation

We have audited the accompanying balance sheets of ABC Corporation as of December 31, 1999, and the related statements of income, retained earnings, and cash flows for the year then ended. These financial statements are the responsibility of the Company's management. Our responsibility is to express an opinion on these financial statements based on our audits.

We conducted our audits in accordance with generally accepted auditing standards. Those standards require that we plan and perform the audit to obtain reasonable assurance about whether the financial statements are free of material misstatement. An audit includes examining, on a test basis, evidence supporting the amounts and disclosures in the financial statements. An audit also includes assessing the accounting principles used and significant estimates made by management, as well as evaluating the overall financial statement presentation. We believe that our audits provide a reasonable basis for our opinion.

In our opinion, the financial statements referred to above present fairly, in all material respects, the financial position of ABC Corporation as of December 31, 1999 and the results of its operations and its cash flows for the year then ended in conformity with generally accepted accounting principles.

ANDERSON AND ZINDER, CPAs

March 5, 2000

The vast majority of auditors' opinions state that the financial statements are without material misstatements and fairly present the financial position of the companies being audited. These opinions are called **unqualified opinions**. This term may be misleading. It does not mean that the auditor is unqualified to give an opinion but rather it means that the financial statements of the company are fairly presented in all material respects. Even though most auditors' opinions are unqualified, you should not conclude that the auditors have not provided a valuable service. First, most audits generate a list of recommended adjustments to the financial statements and footnotes to the financial statements. The published statements always include these corrections because companies are anxious to avoid having the auditors report anything negative in their report. It may cause investors to lose confidence in the management and the company. Therefore, most companies agree to adjust their financial statements to reflect the work of the auditors.

Occasionally a company will refuse to comply with material changes that the auditor wants to make to the financial statements. In that case, if the auditor feels that, the financial statements do not fairly present the financial position, results of operation and cash flow of the business, the auditor will issue an **adverse opinion**. Management knows that an adverse opinion will cast a dark cloud over the company's reputation possibly hurting its stock price and creating obstacles to raising capital should there be a need for additional funds. Therefore, the incidence of an adverse opinion on financial statements is very rare.

Not as rare is a **qualified opinion** or an "exception" opinion on financial statements. This occurs when the CPA is in disagreement with just a small part of the financial statements. The misstated financial information is not material to the financial statements taken as a whole. In a qualified opinion, the CPA-auditor is stating that the reader can rely on all disclosures except for the one item he/she judges to be reported incorrectly. Usually a footnote to the financial statements explains the alternative way of handling the item which allows the reader to assess the gravity of the exception.

Because management knows that the financial statements will be audited, they have a strong incentive to develop adequate internal control systems and to avoid reporting inaccurate results. In spite of impending audits, most companies find that it is simply good business to have a reliable information system with safeguards to prevent the loss of either assets or data.

Footnotes to the Financial Statements

The **footnotes to the financial statements** (referred to simply as notes by The Gap, Inc.) are audited along with the financial statements and are considered to be an integral part of those statements. There are three main issues dealt with in the footnotes. First, footnote 1 presents a summary of significant accounting policies. This footnote is important because there is more than one way to account for many events. For example, companies are allowed to use various depreciation methods to measure the expense of using property and equipment. Footnote 1 tells the reader what alternate accounting method(s) the company uses. Financial statements of different companies cannot be compared intelligently unless significant accounting policy differences are understood. Although most companies number their footnotes, The Gap, Inc., uses letters instead of numbers. Appendix A (page A16) identifies the footnote showing the summary of significant accounting policies as Note A.

A second use of footnotes is to present detailed information about key numbers shown on the financial statements. The footnotes usually provide readers with detailed information explaining events that occurred during the year that affect items such as inventories, receivables, property and equipment, income tax expense and accruals, stock options and other management compensation plans, shareholders' equity, pension costs and accruals, and changes in accounting methods. The footnotes also contain information for the company broken down by industry segments. These footnotes provide the reader with sufficient information to spot problems at the company that are not apparent in the more summarized financial statements. Exhibit 2-8A.2 shows Note 3 from Nike's 1997 annual report.

The third type of information contained in the footnotes describes events that may have a significant impact on the company, but are difficult to quantify and put in the financial statements. These footnotes address commitments made by the company, contingent liabilities, and special risks faced by the company. Items reported in these footnotes can have a catastrophic impact on a company. For example, the possibility of large losses arising from asbestos lawsuits was disclosed in the footnotes of Johns-Manville Corporation and several other asbestos producers years before actual losses caused these firms to declare bankruptcy. More recently, in 1996, a Florida court ruled against a large tobacco company and ordered it to compensate a long-term smoker who contracted lung cancer. This exposure to liability will appear in the footnotes well before it appears in tobacco companies' financial statements.

Exhibit 2-8A.2

NOTE 3: PROPERTY, PLANT AND EQUIPMENT
Property, plant and equipment includes the following:
(in thousands)

May 31,	1997	1996
Land	$90,792	$75,369
Buildings	241,062	246,602
Machinery and equipment	735,739	572,396
Leasehold improvements	206,593	83,678
Construction in process	151,561	69,660
	1,425,747	1,047,705
Less accumulated depreciation	503,378	404,246
	$922,369	$643,459

Capitalized interest expense was $2,765,000, $858,000 and $261,000 for the fiscal years ended May 31, 1997, 1996 and 1995 respectively.

Management Discussion and Analysis of Operations

This section, although not audited, is where management presents its interpretation of the events that have occurred during the year that affect the financial statements. Financial results for the current and prior year are normally compared and causes of differences in performance explained. Changes in accounting standards that impacted the financial statements are presented. Discussions of production problems, addition of new plant capacity, the economic environment facing the firm, and problems with individual products are usually discussed here. Finally, events related to investing and financing activities, as well as any transactions that had a significant accounting impact, are explained.

In short, the purpose of this section is to give the reader an understanding of what events occurred during the year that impacted the financial statements. Knowledge of these underlying events is important if an investor is trying to estimate future profitability and cash flows for the firm. For example, if some unusual and nonrecurring events significantly impacted the financial statements, then the investor will want to take these into consideration when using current statements to estimate future financial performance.

IMPORTANCE OF FINANCIAL INFORMATION

Does the disclosure of audited financial information in annual reports and SEC Form 10K filings benefit you? Does it benefit society? The answer is yes and yes. The information benefits both you and society because it helps to expand the economy. An improved economy raises our standard of living, causes the creation of good, high-paying jobs, and provides the resources to address societal problems such as pollution.

In order to understand how audited financial information can improve economic performance, let's review the strengths of a market economic system. If people have an increased desire for a product or service with scarce availability, they will be willing to pay a price sufficient to create an attractive profit to producers. When producers see that it is profitable to create the goods or services demanded, they will shift resources into the production of the profitable items. For example, when demand for in-line skates exploded, companies realized that a good profit could be made at the current price. Based on the profit potential, manufacturers increased capacity and production to meet the huge increase in demand. Note that no government official or anyone else ordered companies to manufacture more skates; they simply responded to market signals. Financial information makes the reallocation of resources a rational process.

How do companies acquire capital to expand production when the market signals a profit opportunity? Two of the most important methods are the issuance of stock and the borrowing of money. How do stock and bond purchasers and other lenders such as banks decide if and at what rate of return they will provide funds to companies? A company's financial report is a key piece of information most investors use to make these decisions.

As a result of decisions made worldwide by millions of companies and millions of investors, companies with high future income and cash flow potential attract funding and grow. Conversely, firms with poor potential cannot attract capital and stagnate. Once again, the market has signaled where funds should be invested. No one has ordered banks, pension funds, and other investors to provide capital for certain companies or industries. The alternative to a market system is to let the government and politicians choose winners and losers. Most economists attribute the collapse of the Soviet Union and other Eastern European "planned" economies to woefully inefficient allocation of resources by politicians and bureaucrats making the investment decisions.

What role does *audited* financial information play? The ability to focus investments toward companies that show high potential is limited by the quality of information to which investors have access. Investors cannot, of course, acquire perfect information, but the better the information they have, the more funding high-potential companies will receive. If high-potential companies receive better funding, the economy will grow faster and consumer wants will be better satisfied at lower prices. Audited financial information gives investors more accurate, complete, and unbiased financial information than companies might provide in the absence of an audit. Thus, the improved quality of audited information used by investors creates a more efficient allocation of resources in the economy and increases the standard of living.

Financial information is limited in that it only reports what is measurable. It does not, for example, measure the impact of the company's business on society or evaluate the company as an employer. It is difficult to quantity the contributions that the company has made to the community or whether the company's products are environmentally friendly. This type of information may be important to the financial statement user but is not addressed in a company's annual report.

SUMMARY

Corporations which sell stock to the public are stewards of the investments entrusted to them. The management of companies are required by law to publicize timely financial information. The annual report is a key discharge of that responsibility. This case reading addressed the content of audited financial statements. A discussion of the various auditors' opinions was also presented. Part B of this case reading is a discussion of the financial information published by the Gap Inc.

EXERCISES

Exercises

Exercise 1 How are investors informed? Explain how present and prospective investors in publicly held companies are informed of the financial and other aspects of the corporation.

Exercise 2 Define *consolidated.* Define *consolidated* and the term's effect on financial statements.

Exercise 3 What information is in an annual report? What are the key components of the annual report of a corporation?

Exercise 4 CPA's opinion of financial statements. Write the paragraph of the independent auditor's report which you believe is the most important part of the report.

Exercise 5 Purpose of footnotes to financial statements. What is the purpose of footnotes to the financial statements?

Exercise 6 Use the Internet to find financial statements. Find the balance sheet of an airline company. Using the expanded equation of the balance sheet, compare the proportions of the six categories to those of The Gap, Inc. presented in Appendix A.

Exercise 7 Compare the terminology in three income statements. Find the income statements of three companies. Compare and contrast the terminology used for revenue, expenses, and net income.

Exercise 8 Earnings per share. Define earnings per share. How do investors use this financial disclosure?

Exercise 9 Equation for the cash flow statement. The cash flow statement details how the company's cash balance changed during the year. What are the components of this statement?

Exercise 10 Determine CFI and CFF. If a company's cash balance did not change from the beginning of the year to the end of the year and the CFO is $1 million, what inference can you make about CFI and CFF?

Case Reading 2-8 Part B

THE GAP, INC.
FINANCIAL STATEMENTS

INTRODUCTION

The annual report for Gap, Inc. is provided in Appendix A. Like all publicly held corporations, Gap's annual report consists of five main sections:

- A letter from the Chairman of the Board to Shareholders
- Summary of financial highlights for the previous ten years
- A description of the company's products, facilities, and advances during the year
- Management's analysis and discussion of the financial progress during the year
- Financial statements, footnotes, and auditors' report

The overall purpose of the annual report is to provide shareholders with a complete picture of the status of the company. The reader of annual reports must be a critical evaluator of what is presented. Often the annual report is a public relations document which avoids discussion of serious problems faced by the company. The tone in some of the verbiage may suggest that all is well in the company and its markets when, in fact, the financial statements reveal just the opposite is true. The Gap, Inc. annual report was chosen because it is an excellent example of superb reporting to shareholders and does not exaggerate its successes or diminish its failures.

THE GAP, INC. CONSOLIDATED INCOME STATEMENT

Besides the familiar stores called The Gap, The Gap, Inc., owns Banana Republic and Old Navy stores. The revenues and expenses of these separate units are consolidated into one income statement. Published income statements are usually condensed into just a few items. More detailed information is available to managers, such as sales and income from a region all the way down to certain product lines within a single store. Rarely is this level of detail made public because managers fear that to do so would reveal secret business strategy to competitors.

Please review The Gap, Inc.'s consolidated statement of earnings (another name for the income statement) shown in Exhibit 2-8B.1. Publicly held companies typically provide a comparison of the most recent income performance with that of previous years. One can easily infer from the trend whether the company is achieving improving or declining performance.

The discussion below is a brief explanation of the items in The Gap's statements of earnings.

Revenues

The revenues for The Gap, Inc. come from net sales. **Net sales** represent the revenue earned for the period of time stated in the heading of the income statement. For the 52 weeks ended January 31, 1998, The Gap, Inc., has had net sales of over $6.5 billion. The *net* in net sales refers to the normal retail practice of allowing customers to return merchandise for a refund. Therefore, the amount shown is actual sales made minus the amount of refunds. One reason that many retail companies end their fiscal year a month or so after the calendar year ends is to process the many returns made after the Christmas season. Companies in other industries often estimate the returns that are expected to be made by customers after the fiscal year ends. Those companies net the expected returns against their sales based upon historical data. The revenue to be reported is therefore a more accurate measure of the inflow of cash and other assets arising from transactions with customers.

Expenses

Expenses are defined as the cost of goods or services consumed in the generation of revenue.

Cost of Goods Sold and Occupancy Expenses

Cost of goods sold is the cost of the merchandise sold to customers. In many income statements this item is shown separately. The Gap combines it with the occupancy expenses. Occupancy expenses are the rental (lease) payments for all of its stores. More explanation of leases is provided in Note D of the financial statements.

Operating Expenses

Operating expenses are costs of running the business such as employee salaries, utility costs, insurance, advertising, depreciation of buildings and equipment, and distribution costs. This category collects expenses ranging from the top management salaries down to the electric bill at one of its many stores.

Net Interest Income

As you learned in the discussion of items in the balance sheet, The Gap makes major investments in short-term securities. The amount shown (almost $3 million) is revenue earned in the form of interest on those investments less interest expense on debt. The algebraic sign of this number is opposite the two expenses above. The Gap chose to display the interest revenue in this way to simplify the income statement.

Note that this item of income is much less than it was the year before. Referring back to the balance sheet shows that the short-term investments held at February 1, 1997 no longer appear on the current balance sheet. One can infer that the investments were sold to raise cash for other corporate projects deemed important by management of The Gap.

Calculation of Net Earnings and Earnings Per Share

After listing revenues and expenses, the company computes earnings before income taxes, income taxes, and then net earnings. Net earnings is also shown on a per share basis.

Earnings Before Income Taxes. Revenues minus expenses for the period gives us earnings before income taxes.

Exhibit 2-8B.1
The Gap, Inc. Income Statement

Consolidated Statements of Earnings

($000 except share and per share amounts)	Fifty-two Weeks Ended January 31, 1998	Percentage to Sales	Fifty-two Weeks Ended February 1, 1997	Percentage to Sales	Fifty-three Weeks Ended February 3, 1996	Percentage to Sales
Net sales	$ 6,507,825	100%	$ 5,284,381	100.00%	$ 4,395,253	100.0%
Costs and expenses						
Cost of goods sold and occupancy expenses	4,021,541	61.8	3,285,166	62.2	2,821,455	64.2
Operating expenses	1,635,017	25.1	1,270,138	24.0	1,004,396	22.9
Net interest income	(2,975)	0.0	(19,450)	(0.4)	(15,797)	(0.4)
Earnings before income Taxes	854,242	13.1	748,527	14.2	585,199	13.3
Income taxes	320,341	4.9	295,668	5.6	231,160	5.2
Net earnings	$ 533,901	8.2%	$ 452,859	8.6%	$ 354,039	8.1%
Weighted-average number of shares-basic	396,179,975		417,146,631		417,718,397	
Weighted-average number of shares-diluted	410,200,758		427,267,220		427,752,515	
Earnings per share-basic	$1.35		$1.09		$0.85	
Earnings per share-diluted	1.30		1.06		0.83	

See Notes to Consolidated Financial Statements.

Income Taxes. Taxes payable on the income reported to federal and state governments. Like individuals, corporations are subject to taxes on income. The effective tax rate on The Gap's income for the period is approximately 37 ½ percent calculated by dividing earnings before income tax by the income tax.

Net Earnings. Synonymous with net income, it is the addition to stockholders' equity arising from all operations of the business for the 52 weeks ended January 31, 1998. The earnings of $533,901,000 is the result of matching all expenses against all revenues for the fiscal year.

Weighted Average Number Of Shares. This is the number divided into net income to determine how much is attributable to each share of stock in the corporation. It is often a statistical calculation and not the actual number of shares at the end of the fiscal year. It gives a more accurate measurement when the number of shares has changed during the year as is true with The Gap.

Earnings Per Share. The net income (earnings) divided by the weighted average number of shares. This number is often used by investors when making an evaluation of market prices of various stocks they may consider purchasing.

Interpretation Of The Income Statement

The basis formula for the income statement is

$$\text{Revenues - Expenses} = \text{Net Income}$$

Alternatively,   Revenues = Expenses + Net Income

The alternate form can be expanded to better interpret The Gap's income statement:

$$\text{Net sales} = \text{Cost of goods sold} + \text{Operating expenses} + \text{Taxes} + \text{Net earnings}$$

If sales are equal to 100 percent, the above equation becomes

$$100\% = 61.8\% + 25.1\% + 4.9\% + 8.2\%$$

The net income percentage is the percentage of revenue that remains after deducting all costs and expenses and taxes. One way to view this percentage is that for every dollar of revenue which the Gap, Inc. earned in the year, 8.2 cents ended up as net income. The next question is, what will the Board of Directors decide to do with the income? Do they reinvest it in the business or do they pay it out to shareholders? This question will be addressed later in this reading.

Using the data from the Gap, the bar chart shown in Exhibit 2-8B.2 shows the items which make up the income statement equation in graphical form. In addition to showing the dollar amounts for the current year, the graph also shows the percentage of net income that each category represents. Net Income is 8.2 % of net sales. This is a ratio which is carefully watched by investors.

Exhibit 2-8B.2
The Income Statement Categories in Graphical Form

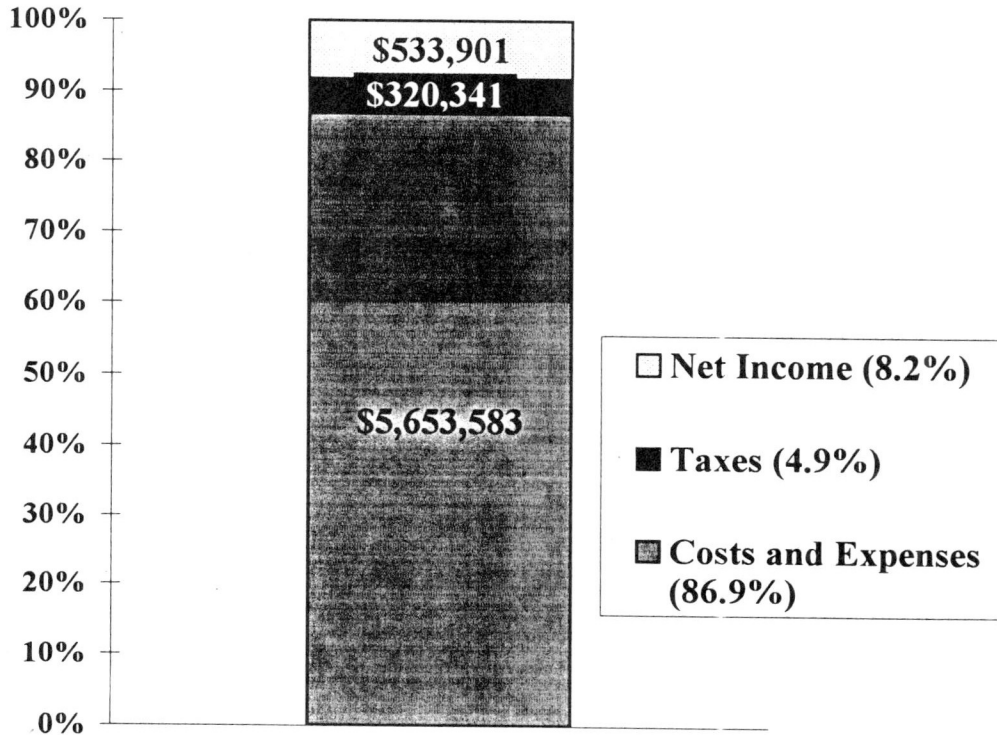

THE CONSOLIDATED BALANCE SHEET

The consolidated balance sheet (hereafter CBS) of The Gap, Inc., as of January 31, 1998, is shown in Exhibit 2-8B.3. The symbol ($000) at the top left corner of the statement signifies that all dollar amounts are rounded to the nearest thousand. For example, cash and equivalents at January 31, 1998, may have actually been $913,169,456.78 at that date. To make the reporting of financial information more readable, The Gap like most corporations rounds all numbers to the nearest thousand in financial reports. Therefore, the amount shown in the CBS is rounded down to $913,169,000. Some large companies round all amounts to the nearest million.

Your venture into the financial world by taking this course is somewhat like studying a new language. To permit you to understand what all of the numbers in the CBS mean, read the brief explanations that follow.

Assets

The assets for the Gap, Inc. include asset categories for current assets, and property and equipment as well as miscellaneous other assets.

Current Assets

Current assets are assets expected to be converted into cash within a year. The following descriptions explain the current assets for the Gap, Inc.:

Cash and Equivalents. Cash is money held in bank checking accounts that can be used immediately for any valid corporate purpose. Equivalents are high quality, low risk, short- term investments that can be converted into cash very quickly. Interest income is earned on equivalents but not on checking accounts.

Short-term Investments. Investments in securities of the government or other companies that have a maturity of more than three months but less than one year. An example might be a six-month Treasury bill issued by the U.S. Treasury.

Accounts Receivable. According to the CBS, The Gap does not have any material accounts receivable from customers. Customer purchases on credit are generally made with bank cards such as VISA rather than a credit card that is issued by The Gap. The bank issuing the credit card would show any unpaid credit purchases by Gap customers as accounts receivable in its financial statements.

Merchandise Inventory. The cost (not the selling price) of the items held for sale in all of The Gap's stores at this date. If items cannot be sold at or above cost, the amounts shown in the CBS include a reduction of these items to market value.

Prepaid Expenses And Other Current Assets. A prepaid expense is an asset because cash is paid for a future expense not yet incurred. An example is insurance premiums paid prior to the period of the insurance policy. Other current assets are miscellaneous assets that are expected to be converted into cash or preclude the need to pay out cash within the next year. An example is deposits on future purchases. It is also possible that the company might have an immaterial amount of miscellaneous receivables in this category.

Property and Equipment

Property and equipment are the long-lived assets used in the business.

Leasehold Improvements. The cost of remodeling stores and corporate facilities to meet the needs of The Gap. When a shopping mall leases space to The Gap it rents a basic shell which is decorated to its unique interior design specifications, usually at a significant cost. This cost is reported on the CBS and amortized over the expected occupancy in that mall.

Furniture and Equipment. The cost of acquiring the display fixtures, computer equipment, and cash registers to make all stores completely operational.

Exhibit 2-8B.3
The Gap, Inc. Consolidated Balance Sheets

Consolidated Balance Sheets ($000)	January 31, 1998	February 1, 1997
ASSETS		
Current Assets		
Cash and equivalents	$ 913,169	$ 485,644
Short-term investments	-	135,632
Merchandise inventory	733,174	578,765
Prepaid expenses and other current assets	184,604	129,214
Total current assets	1,830,947	1,329,255
Property and Equipment		
Leasehold improvements	846,791	736,608
Furniture and equipment	1,236,450	960,516
Land and buildings	154,136	99,969
Construction-in-progress	66,582	101,520
	2,303,959	1,898,613
Accumulated depreciation and amortization	(938,713)	(762,893)
Property and equipment, net	1,365,246	1,135,720
Long-term investments	-	36,138
Lease rights and other assets	141,309	125,814
Total assets	$ 3,337,502	$ 2,626,927
LIABILITIES AND SHAREHOLDERS' EQUITY		
Current Liabilities		
Notes payable	$ 84,794	$ 40,050
Accounts payable	416,976	351,754
Accrued expenses	389,412	282,494
Income taxes payable	83,597	91,806
Deferred lease credits and other current liabilities	16,769	8,792
Total current liabilities	991,548	774,896
Long-term Liabilities		
Long-term debt	496,044	-
Deferred lease credits and other liabilities	265,924	197,561
Total long-term liabilities	761,968	197,561
Shareholders' Equity		
Common stock $.05 par value		
Authorized 500,000,000 shares; issued 439,922,841		
and 476,796, 135 shares; outstanding 393,133,028		
and 411,775,997 shares	21,996	23,840
Additional paid-in capital	317,674	434,104
Retained earnings	2,392,750	1,938,352
Foreign currency translation adjustments	(15,230)	(5,187)
Deferred compensation	(38,167)	(47,838)
Treasury stock, at cost	(1,095,037)	(688,801)
Total shareholders' equity	1,583,986	1,654,470
Total liabilities and shareholders' equity	$ 3,337,502	$ 2,626,927

See Notes to Consolidated Financial Statements.

Construction In Progress. The cost invested in partially completed stores and company facilities as of the balance sheet date. When stores and facilities are opened for business, amounts from this category are reclassified to the two categories above.

Accumulated Depreciation and Amortization. The amount in parentheses signifies a subtraction from the three asset categories above and amount represents the cost of the years of usage of these assets in relation to the total useful life of the assets. The ratio of accumulated depreciation and amortization to the original cost of the long-lived assets is approximately 40 percent, indicating that, on average, 40 percent of the useful life of assets has expired. Therefore, if the store assets generally have a useful life of ten years, the CBS is telling us that on average such assets have been used for four years and can be used for six more years before replacement is necessary.

<u>Other Assets</u>

Other assets is a miscellaneous category which includes any other assets not listed in the remaining asset categories. The Gap does not show a separate line item for this category heading but just lists the other assets.

Long-term Investments. Long-term investments are investments in securities of other companies which have a maturity of from one to five years from the CBS date.

Lease Rights and Other Assets. Lease rights are the cost of the long-term, noncancelable contracts for the future occupancy of store locations in shopping malls and centers. Other assets added to the category are trademarks, copyrights, goodwill, patents, exclusive contracts. and other intangible legal rights reported at historical cost less write-downs due to usage or reduced future benefit.

Liabilities and Shareholders' Equity

The liabilities and shareholders' equity portion of the balance sheet include categories for current liabilities, long-term liabilities, and shareholders' equity.

<u>Current Liabilities</u>

Current liabilities are debts due for payment within one year.

Notes Payable. Debts which are evidenced by a legal document called a promissory note. The promissory note typically specifies an interest rate and a maturity date when the face amount of the note is due to the lender.

Accounts Payable. The Gap purchases its merchandise from many clothing manufacturers. Generally, payment for goods occurs 30-60 days after delivery to The Gap. During this period the merchandise inventory reflects the goods received and the accounts payable reflects the unpaid invoices of those goods.

Accrued Expenses. Amounts owed for labor and other operating expenses that have been incurred but not yet paid in cash. An example is the last two weeks of wages in the fiscal year which have been earned by employees but not yet paid. The wages expense of these two weeks is included in the fiscal year income statement and in this liability account until paid, i.e. wages payable.

Income Taxes Payable. The liability for taxes to be paid to the government based on taxable income.

Deferred Lease Credits And Other Current Liabilities. The amount owed for lease payments coming due in the next fiscal year. Other liabilities are miscellaneous items such as money owed to employees for reimbursement of travel expenses.

Long-term Liabilities

Long-term liabilities are debts with maturities beyond the next year.

Long-term Debt. This category generally includes long-term notes which are not due within the next year.

Deferred Lease Credits And Other Liabilities. The liability for lease payments scheduled beyond the next year. Other liabilities in this category are miscellaneous debts due beyond the next fiscal year.

Shareholders' Equity

Shareholders' equity is the claim which the owners have on the assets. It is the **net assets**, or the assets minus the liabilities, of the company.

Common Stock. The record of the number of shares issued at the par value per share. The Gap's par value per share is $.05. This is generally an arbitrary number, typically less than a dollar in most companies. It has no meaning in conveying the true value of the corporation.

Additional Paid-in Capital. Amounts in excess of par value paid to the corporation by investors purchasing shares usually pursuant to a stock offering to the public.

Retained Earnings. The accumulation of income or losses since the start of the corporation minus the dividends paid to stockholders. In its lifetime, The Gap has reported income of almost $2.4 billion more than it has paid out in dividends. Most of this $2.4 billion has been used to expand the business, to acquire other businesses, and to repurchase its own shares (see Treasury stock below).

Foreign Currency Translation Adjustment. An adjustment due to the fluctuation in foreign currency exchange rates for assets residing in foreign countries.

Restricted Stock Plan Deferred Compensation. The reduction in stockholders' equity resulting from granting employees the right to purchase shares of the company at below current market prices.

Treasury Stock, at Cost. The Gap, Inc., purchased shares in the open market, thereby reducing the number of shares outstanding. The actual cost of acquiring shares is almost $1.1 billion.

Interpretation Of The Balance Sheet

In Case Reading 1-1, we presented the equation which is the framework for the balance sheet:

$$\text{Assets} = \text{Liabilities} + \text{Shareholders' Equity}$$

We now expand this equation to examine the classified balance sheet of The Gap, Inc..

Current Assets + Property and Equipment + Other Assets = Current Liabilities + Long-term Liabilities + Shareholders' Equity.

Using The Gap, Inc. balance sheet data note the distribution of assets and equities in the graphs shown as Exhibit 2-8B.4

On the asset side, current assets represent over 54 percent of the total assets. This is common in retail companies such as The Gap because of the large investment in inventories. There is also a low investment in property because store locations are leased, not owned.

On the equity side, the shareholders have contributed 47 percent toward the assets and the creditors contribute the remaining 53 percent divided between current and long-term liabilities.

CONSOLIDATED STATEMENT OF CASH FLOWS

Our purpose in Case Reading 2-8, Part B is to give you an overview of the financial statements, so our discussion will deal with the major components of the statement of cash flows versus a line-by-line discussion. The statement of cash flows was discussed in depth in Case Readings 2-4 and 2-5. For this discussion, all cash flows are summarized into three categories:

- Operating Activities (CFO - cash flows from operating activities)
- Investing Activities (CFI - cash flows from investing activities)
- Financing Activities (CFF - cash flows from financing activities)

We can now represent the statement of cash flows in an equation as we did with the other financial statements:

$$\text{Beginning Cash} \pm \text{CFO} \pm \text{CFI} \pm \text{CFF} \pm \text{Exchange Rate Effects} = \text{Ending Cash}$$

The $\pm$ symbol means that the three main categories of cash flows can be positive or negative. The fourth item is relevant to only those companies with operations in foreign countries. Those who have traveled in foreign countries and converted U.S. currency into local currency may have experienced an exchange rate effect because of constantly fluctuating currency values.

Statement of Cash Flows for The Gap, Inc.

The statement of cash flows for The Gap is too complex to discuss in great detail. For now, focus on the major components of the cash flow statement for The Gap that are shown in Exhibit 2-8B.5. The operating section has been condensed to facilitate overall understanding of the components of the statement. The entire statement can be found in Appendix A on page A13.

Applying the equation to the Gap Consolidated Statement of Cash Flows gives:

Beginning Cash $\pm$ CFO $\pm$ CFI $\pm$ CFF $\pm$ Exchange Rate Effects = Ending Cash
$485,644 + 844,651 - 313,852 - 101,640 - 1,634 = \$913,169$ Ending Cash

Operating Activities

The cash flow statement shows that the company generated cash (and equivalents) of $844,651 as a result of day-to-day operations of the firm. Cash flow from operating activities consists of the net earnings figure of $533,901 from the consolidated statement of earnings (shown in Exhibit 2-8B.1) as well as some adjustments to adjust the income statement amounts to the cash basis. Further discussion of these types of adjustments can be found in Case Reading 2-5.

Cash Flow from Investing Activities

The company used its cash to invest in short-term investments, long-term investments, property and equipment, and to acquire lease rights and other assets. Net cash used for investing activities was $313,852.

Cash Flow from Financing Activities

The company borrowed more money (notes payable)and took on more long-term debt to raise cash so the company could buy back some of its own stock, thereby reducing the amount outstanding. Cash dividends were paid to the stockholders. Net cash used for financing activities was $101,640.

Effect of Exchange Rate Changes on Cash

This line item of The Gap financial statements shows that cash decreased by $1,634 as a result of exchange rate changes. Because The Gap, Inc., does business in foreign countries, and because of changes in the foreign currency translation rate, the company will need to adjust its cash balance for these exchange rate changes. During most of 1997, the U.S. Dollar increased in value against most foreign currencies. At January 31, 1998, cash deposits in foreign banks translated into lower amounts explaining the negative adjustment.

Exhibit 2-8B.4
Graphical Presentation of Balance Sheet Equation

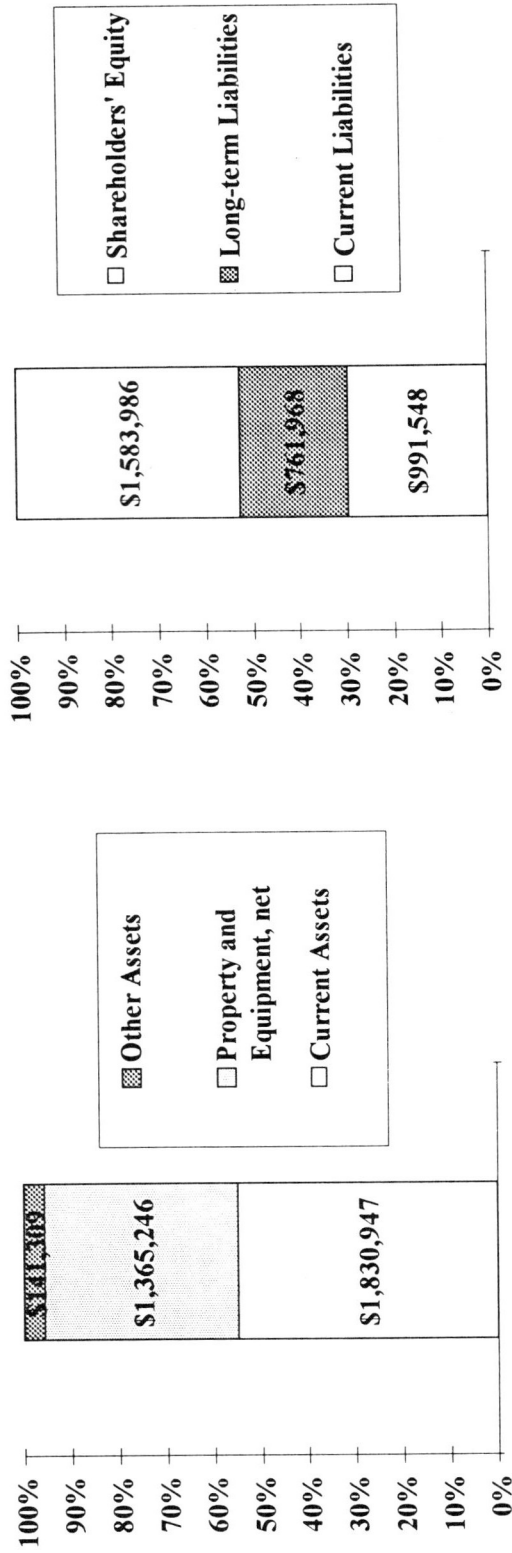

☐ Shareholders' Equity	
▓ Long-term Liabilities	
☐ Current Liabilities	

100%
90%
80%
70%
60%
50%
40%
30%
20%
10%
0%

$1,583,986

$761,968

$991,548

Total Liabilities and Shareholders' Equity
$3,337,502

Equal

=

▓ Other Assets	
☐ Property and Equipment, net	
☐ Current Assets	

100%
90%
80%
70%
60%
50%
40%
30%
20%
10%
0%

$141,309

$1,365,246

$1,830,947

Total Assets
$3,337,502

Exhibit 2-8B.5

Gap, Inc
Consolidated Statement of Cash Flows (Condensed)
Fifty Two Weeks Ended January 31, 1998

($000)

Operating Activities		
Net Earnings	$ 533,901	
Adjustments to cash basis	310,750	
Net Cash Provided by Operations		$ 844,651
Cash Flows from Investing Activities		
Purchase (maturities) of short term investments	174,709	
Purchase of long-term investments	(2,939)	
Purchase of property and equipment	(465,843)	
Acquisition of lease rights and other assets	(19,779)	
Net Cash Used for Investing Activities		(313,852)
Cash Flows from Financing Activities		
Net increase in notes payable	44,462	
Net issuance of long-term debt	495,890	
Issuance of common stock	30,653	
Net purchase of treasury stock	(593,142)	
Cash dividends paid	(79,503)	
Net Cash Used for Financing Activities		(101,640)
Effect of exchange rate changes on cash		(1,634)
Net increase (decrease) in cash and equivalents		427,525
Cash and equivalents at beginning of year		485,644
Cash and equivalents at end of year		$ 913,169

See Notes to Consolidated Financial Statements

Net Increase (Decrease) in Cash and Equivalents

This is the sum of the items explained above and shows the net increase or decrease to cash during the period. In the case of The Gap, Inc., cash increased by $427,525 during the accounting period.

Cash and Equivalents at Beginning of the Year

This amount of $485,644 represents the cash and cash equivalents on hand at the beginning of the year. Note that this amount will be the same amount as the ending balance of the previous year (February 1, 1997).

Cash and Equivalents at End of the Year

This amount of $913,169 is the same number that appears as the ending balance for that item on the consolidated balance sheet shown in Exhibit 2-8B.1. This will always be the case as the cash flow statement is an analysis of how the cash balance changed from the end of the previous year to the end of the most current year.

Availability of Financial Information on the Internet

Most corporations that have publicly traded stocks have extensive web sites. A search by company name should direct you to a particular company's web address. These sites generally include information about the company, including in many cases a history of the company, its current operating sites, and possibly its future goals. Most companies will generally put the most current financial information (including the annual report) on the web site as well.

SUMMARY

The Gap, Inc. publishes an annual report which is representative of most U.S companies. Because the financial statements and disclosures must meet various governmental, stock exchange, and audit requirements, the financial section of the annual report can be complex. This case reading discusses the general line-item descriptions in the primary financial statements of the Gap, Inc. After reading this case reading, you should be familiar with the wealth of information contained in corporate annual reports.

EXERCISES AND PROBLEMS

Exercises

Exercise 1 Management Discussion and Analysis. What was the percent net sales increase from the year ended February 1, 1997 to the year ended January 31, 1998?

Exercise 2 Management Discussion and Analysis. Explain in non-financial terms why sales increased from 1997 to 1998.

Exercise 3 Management Discussion and Analysis. What was the cost of adding new stores in 1997? How was the construction financed?

Exercise 4 Management Discussion and Analysis. How did the price of the Gap, Inc. stock perform in 1997?

Exercise 5 Auditor's Report. What do you infer from your reading of the Independent Auditors' Report?

Exercise 6 Consolidated Statements of Earnings (Income Statement). How much of every dollar of sales revenue did the Gap realize as net income in 1997? Did earnings per sales dollar increase or decrease from the year before? (This question is not asking for earnings per share.)

Exercise 7 Consolidated Balance Sheets. What is the amount of merchandise inventory of the Gap at January 31, 1998? Compute how much inventory on a per store basis is held on this date? (see ten-year summary for the number of stores.)

Exercise 8 Consolidated Balance Sheets. What proportion of the total assets is attributable to property and equipment?

Exercise 9 Consolidated Balance Sheets. What is the sum of current and long term liabilities? What proportion of the total assets is this sum?

Exercise 10 Consolidated Statement of Cash Flows. By how much did cash and equivalents increase (decrease) during the 52 weeks ended January 31, 1998? How does this compare to the previous years?

Problems

Problem 1 Shareholders' Equity. Using the information in the common stock "shares" column of the Consolidated Statements of Shareholders' Equity and Notes F and G to the financial statement, explain why the number of shares changed over the period January 28, 1995 to January 31, 1998.

Problem 2 Footnotes to the Financial Statements. From Footnote A, answer the following questions:

1. What is the Gap's definition of cash and equivalents?
2. How is property and equipment reported?
3. How are lease rights accounted for?
4. How are advertising related costs handled?
5. Does the Gap have operations in foreign countries? What evidence is there if it does or does not have business abroad?

Problem 3 Analysis. Of the six bar charts presented in the "Key Financial Statistics" section, which is the most positive and which is the most negative indication of financial performance of The Gap?

Case 2-8

USING FINANCIAL STATEMENTS OF PUBLICLY HELD CORPORATIONS

Case Objectives

1. Understand the main components of the balance sheet.
2. Understand the relationships of items on the income statement.
3. Understand how the CFO, CFI, and CFF cash flow categories combine to explain the change in cash and equivalents.

Decision: Using the most recent financial statements of two publicly held corporations, Lands' End and Wal-Mart, determine which has a greater investment in long-lived assets, which is more profitable on a per-share basis, and which has a larger positive cash flow for the year.

Requirements

1. a. Go to the web site for Lands' End and Wal-Mart. Obtain their financial statements. Using the balance sheets of Lands' End and Wal-Mart, write in the spaces provided below the dollar amounts corresponding to the six major categories of the balance sheet.

	Lands' End	Wal-Mart		Lands' End	Wal-Mart
Current Assets			Current Liabilities		
Property and Equip.			Long-term Liabilities		
Other Assets			Shareholders' Equity		
TOTAL			TOTAL		

b. Compute the <u>percentage</u> of each of the categories in Requirement 1a to the total. Complete the bar charts below. Label the segment of the bar and include the percentage of the total which that category represents.

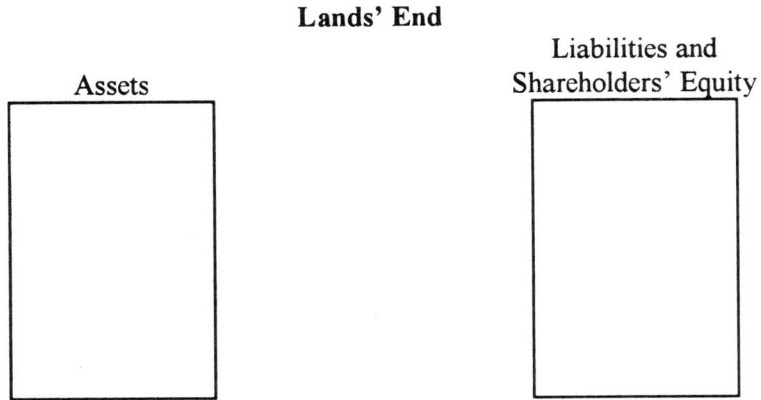

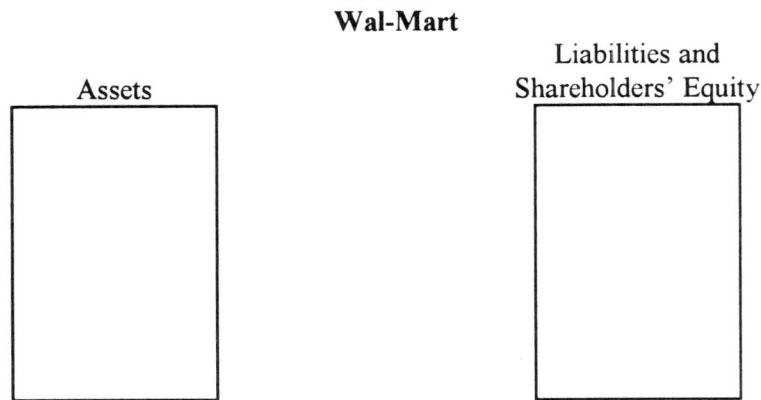

Lands' End

Assets

Liabilities and
Shareholders' Equity

Wal-Mart

Assets

Liabilities and
Shareholders' Equity

2. a. Using the income statements of Lands' End (they call it the statement of operations) and Wal-Mart, determine the following:

	Dollar Amounts		Percentage of Revenue	
	Lands' End	Wal-Mart	Lands' End	Wal-Mart
Costs and Expenses				
Taxes				
Net Income				

(hint: the percentages must add to 100)

b. Complete the bar charts as shown in Exhibit 2-8B.2 of Case Reading 2-8 Part B indicating the percentage of revenue that each category shown in Requirement 2a represents.

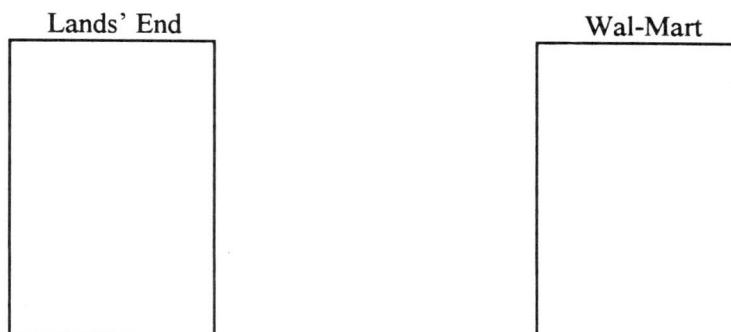

Lands' End

Wal-Mart

c. Enter the earnings per share (EPS) for each company:

EPS for Land's End =

EPS for Wal-Mart =

3. Using the cash flow equation shown below and in Case Reading 2-8 Part B, use the Statements of Cash Flow of Lands' End and Wal-Mart to verify the ending cash and equivalents reported on each company's balance sheet.

a. Cash and equivalents reported for Lands' End:

Beginning Cash ± CFO ± CFI ± CFF ± Exchange Rate Effects = Ending Cash

b. Cash and equivalents reported for Wal-Mart:

Beginning Cash ± CFO ± CFI ± CFF ± Exchange Rate Effects = Ending Cash

4. Which company is larger:

a. In terms of total assets?

b. In terms of total revenues?

c. In terms of cash and equivalents?

Group Assignment 2-8

BRIDGING "THE GAP"

Group Number _____ **Group members present and participating:**

_____

_____

Objectives

1. Understand the main components of the balance sheet
2. Understand the relationships of items on the income statement
3. Understand how the CFO, CFI, and CFF cash flow categories combine to explain the change in cash and equivalents.
4. Analyzing the changes from one year to another.

Case Reading 2-8 Part B discusses the financial statements of The Gap, Inc. for the fifty-two weeks ending January 31, 1998. This group assignment requires that you use the financial information for The Gap for the previous year which is provided in Appendix A at the end of the book.

Requirements

1. a. Using the balance sheets of The Gap, Inc., write on the spaces provided below the <u>dollar amounts</u> corresponding to the six major categories of the balance sheet.

	Fifty-Two Weeks Ending 2/1/97			Fifty-Two Weeks Ending 2/1/97
Current Assets			Current Liabilities	
Property and Equip.			Long-term Liabilities	
Other Assets			Shareholders' Equity	
TOTAL			TOTAL	

b. Compute the <u>percentage</u> of each of the categories above to the total computed in Requirement 1a. Complete the bar charts below. Label each section and include the percentage of the total which that category represents.

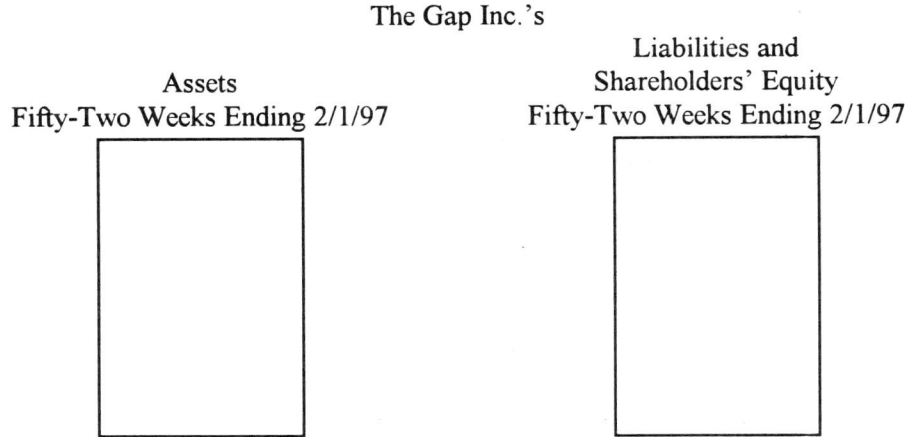

The Gap Inc.'s

Assets Fifty-Two Weeks Ending 2/1/97	Liabilities and Shareholders' Equity Fifty-Two Weeks Ending 2/1/97

2. a. Using the income statement of The Gap, Inc. determine the following:

	Fifty-Two Weeks Ending 2/1/97	
	Dollar Amounts	Percentage of Revenue
Costs and Expenses	_____	_____
Taxes	_____	_____
Net Income	_____	_____

b. Complete the bar chart below as shown in Exhibit 2-8B.2 of Case Reading 2-8 Part B for the fifty-two weeks ending 2/28/97 indicating the percentage of revenue that each category shown in Requirement 2a represents.

c. Enter the earnings per share (EPS) for The Gap, Inc.:

EPS for fifty-two weeks ending 2/1/97 =

3. What type of auditors' opinion did The Gap, Inc. receive for the fiscal year ending 1/31/98? (see the Auditors' Report for the current year)

4. How many new stores were added in that fiscal year? (see Management's Discussion and Analysis)

5. What is The Gap's definition of cash and equivalents? (see footnotes)

Modules 1 and 2

Peer Evaluation of Group Members	Class Section	Group No.

Evaluator's Name

_____

In the table below, please indicate your estimate, in percentage terms, of the contributions that individual group members made to each of the group assignments listed. Each column should add to 100 percent. For example, if there are five members in your group and all were present for group assignment 1-3, you would divide up the 100 percent among the five members, including yourself. If you felt that all group members were prepared to discuss the assignment and contributed equally to the solution, you would give each person 20 percent. If only four members were present, and you felt that one particular member contributed twice as much as the other three, you would give the heavy contributor 40 percent and the other three members 20 percent. The group member who was absent should be listed and given a zero percent.

Group Members (List)	Group Assignment Number						
	1-3	2-1	2-2	2-5	2-6	2-7	2-8
Myself							
Totals	100	100	100	100	100	100	100

Fill in this sheet after each group exercise is completed and turn in with the last group exercise in Module 2.

USING

Accounting Information

IN BUSINESS EXPANSION

00 $50.23 $4,356.00 $834.91 $12,937.89 $
00 $50.23 $4,356.00 $834.91 $12,937.89 $
00 $50.23 $4,356.00 $834.91 $12,937.89 $
00 $50.23 $4,356.00 $834.91 $12,937.89 $
00 $50.23 $4,356.00 $834.91 $12,937.89 $
00 $50.23 $4,356.00 $834.91 $12,937.89 $
00 $50.23 $4,356.00 $834.91 $12,937.89 $
00 $50.23 $4,356.00 $834.91 $12,937.89 $
00 $50.23 $4,356.00 $834.91 $12,937.89 $
00 $50.23 $4,356.00 $834.91 $12,937.89 $
00 $50.23 $4,356.00 $834.91 $12,937.89 $
00 $50.23 $4,356.00 $834.91 $12,937.89 $

Module 3 Introduction

USING ACCOUNTING INFORMATION IN BUSINESS EXPANSION

MODULE OVERVIEW

This module introduces concepts involved in business planning, including organizational forms and tax considerations. Planning tools involving cost (expense) behavior analysis and profitability analysis are examined. The module ends with a brief introduction to legal and tax considerations in the different forms of business organizations.

Two different decision contexts are used in this module to explore ideas:

* Should an investor start a small business?

This decision will be addressed by each group. It will involve library research, group oral presentations, and a visit to a local business if your instructor selects this alternative.

* Should John Miller add an interior decorating component to his painting business and if so, what form of business should he choose?

This decision represents a continuation of the "John's Painting Business" case introduced in Module 1.

Learning Objectives

After completing this module, a student should be able to:

1. Understand the nature of business planning involving the start-up of a new business.
   - Case Reading 3-1   Starting a Small Business
   - Group Assignment 3-1   Planning to Start a Business
   - Exercises and Problems   Exercises and Problems at the end of Case Reading 3-1

2. Understand the concepts of cost/expense behavior and classification of expenses into fixed, variable, and mixed categories; apply the high-low method to separate mixed expenses into fixed and variable components; and use a company's expense behavior information to determine contribution margin (total, per-unit, and ratio).
   - Case Reading 3-2   Planning for Variable and Fixed Expenses
   - Case 3-2   Identifying Expense Behavior
   - Exercises and Problems   Exercises and Problems at the end of Case Reading 3-2

3. Understand how to evaluate a proposed business by using contribution margin ratio, breakeven point, target profit, target profit after taxes, and return on equity. The module contains an example of how these techniques are used in the evaluation of the business of Corliss Accounting Firm.

     - Case Reading 3-3   Profitability Analysis
     - Case 3-3   The J & J Partnership
     - Group Assignment 3-3   What is Your Contribution?
     - Exercises and Problems   Exercises and Problems at the end of Case Reading 3-3

4. Describe how multiproduct firms plan and how to evaluate the start-up of a multiproduct company. Emphasis is on breakeven analysis, sensitivity analysis, sales mix, and operating leverage for multiproduct start-up firms.

     - Case Reading 3-4   Multiple Product Enterprises
     - Case 3-4   The J & J Corporation
     - Exercises and Problems   Exercises and Problems at the end of Case Reading 3-4

5. Describe the major characteristics of the three forms of business—proprietorship, partnership, corporation—apply different federal tax treatments to each of those forms. Understand preferred stock, common stock, additional paid-in capital, contributed capital, and dividends for the corporate form of organization.

     - Case Reading 3-5   Legal and Tax Considerations for Business Owners
     - Case 3-5   Different Tax Treatments for Different Forms of Business
     - Exercises and Problems   Exercises and Problems at the end of Case Reading 3-5

6. Understand the concepts of planning (static) budgets and performance budgets and their roles in planning and evaluating business performance.

     - Case Reading 3-6   Planning and Performance Budgets
     - Case 3-6   J & J Corporation - The Best Laid Plans...
     - Group Assignment 3-6   Did J & J Corporation Go Astray?
     - Exercises and Problems   Exercises and Problems at the end of Case Reading 3-6

Case Reading 3-1

STARTING A SMALL BUSINESS

INTRODUCTION

This case reading illustrates the basic procedures that should be followed when contemplating starting a new business. The main focus will be on gathering sufficient information in order to prepare financial statements based on future projections, and on gathering relevant information concerning the industry.

STARTING A BUSINESS

Two out of three new businesses fail within the first five years. Most fail because of inadequate research and planning and/or poor management. Given these terrifying statistics, why start a business? At first glance, it appears that one of the major motivations is profit. Further investigation suggests that there are many other reasons owners start their own businesses that might be equally as important, such as

> Making a living doing what they enjoy

> More flexible work hours

> Ability to work at home

> Having the independence and power to make their own business decisions

> Direct contact with customers, employees, suppliers, and others

> The personal satisfaction, sense of achievement, and recognition that comes with being successful

> The opportunity to create substantial wealth and job security for themselves and their family

> The opportunity to be creative in developing their own ideas, products, or services

> Contributing to their community and others in the form of employment, distribution of income, or possibly supporting a local charity

It sounds great, doesn't it? There is no question that there are some wonderful advantages to owning your own business. However, the disadvantages of starting your own business should be investigated as well.

> ➤ Owners no longer have only one boss; they now answer to their customers, to government agencies (local, state and federal), and possibly to some key suppliers.

> ➤ The financial risk is great and the failure rate of new businesses is high.

> ➤ As an owner, the hours will be long and hard. Owners often work 10 to 15 hour days, six to seven days a week.

> ➤ There will be limited time for family life or social engagements, and few, if any, vacations in the first few years.

> ➤ Income, unlike a salary, will fluctuate from month to month.

> ➤ If any problem arises, all the responsibility is yours; the cost comes out of your pocket, not your employer's.

> ➤ Owners may find that they do not like the work after all, and they will be stuck doing it for years until they can sell the business or find another way of satisfying their debts without a major financial loss.

> ➤ Owning a business is very risky due to the increasing amount of regulation and litigation. A lifetime of work building a business can be lost because of a lawsuit or a new law or regulation.

Starting a new business is not a decision to be taken lightly. What, then, can be done to increase the business's chance of success? The answer is research and planning.

The research and planning phase should take from six to twelve months, depending on the type of business. Professional advisors should be consulted during this process. Which advisors are sought will depend on the business, although all businesses should consult with an attorney and an accountant. Remember, the owner is the one who will be taking this major financial risk, and once the resources are committed, the decision is not easily reversed.

Choosing a Business

After making the decision to start a business, the next step is choosing the type of business. Should it be a manufacturing firm, or should it retail a product or service? Two further questions should be addressed before making this decision:

1. Does the owner have any experience in this business area?

It is possible for an owner to learn the business as he or she progresses, but it is advisable to have substantial experience in the business being proposed. The chances of operating successfully are increased if the owner has firsthand knowledge of the ins and outs of that particular type of business. Regardless, the amount of information the owner needs to learn will most likely be overwhelming.

2. Does the owner have a genuine interest in this type of business?

After making this commitment, the business will consume most of the owner's time for the next three to five years while it becomes established. Having a genuine interest in the field will make these years decidedly more enjoyable.

Market Research

After choosing the type of business, the owner will need to conduct market research. This may require the advice of a professional or a consulting firm. Additional information may be found in industry trade journals. There are many questions that need to be answered. Following are a few examples:

- Who is the competition? What is the size of the market?

- Why would a customer choose the new business over one he or she already patronizes? Can this new business provide the customer with better service or a better product than the competitor provides?

- How many of these businesses are in the area? (If the market is saturated with this type of business, are the products or services something new or unusual that will lure the customer into the establishment?)

- What is the predicted outlook for the products or services? Will there be an increase or decrease in demand?

- What is the future economic outlook for this area?

The success of the business depends on the answers to these extremely important questions about the market.

One other crucial factor to consider is location. In most cases, the location of a business has a large impact on the volume of business that the owner conducts. Most successful retail and services businesses are easy to locate and have visibility from the street in a high-traffic area. Research in this area can be conducted through local government agencies such as the planning commission or the economic development commission. A local chamber of commerce might also supply the owner with helpful information on established businesses in the area.

Which Legal Form of Business Should the Owner Choose?

There are primarily three legal forms of business—sole proprietorship, partnership, and corporation. Within these three categories are variations that should also be considered. The advantages and disadvantages of the three legal forms of business will be discussed at length in Case Reading 3-5. Right now, it is sufficient to say that a sole proprietorship has only one owner, a partnership has two or more owners, and a corporation can have any number of owners. The form of business chosen has a direct impact on financing the proposed business venture. The more owners, the more capital that is available to finance the start-up of the business. Having just one or a few owners means that a loan may need to be obtained from an outside creditor. A new form of business that is gaining popularity and legal status in some states is called the limited liability company. The limited liability company is intended to provide the limited liability of a corporation and the taxation of a partnership.

What Information Will the Owner Need to Obtain Financing for the Business Venture?

Providers of capital will require proof that the business can produce a profit and allow them to be compensated for their contribution. Documents and/or information that may be required are

- proof of the owner's knowledge or experience

- market feasibility studies

- industry/product forecasts

- marketing plans

- traffic patterns of the selected location

- legal form of business

- pro forma (projected) financial statements

Sources of capital include personal funds, funds of other existing or potential owners, and loans from outside creditors such as financial institutions. The advantages of debt versus equity financing (owners' contribution or withdrawals) will be discussed in a later case reading.

A Rose by Any Other Name . . .

Choosing a business name may seem like a simple task, but careful thought should be given to business image and legal considerations. The name should provide the public with a clear view of the business purpose. In addition, the owner cannot use a name already in use by another business or one that is similar, or that might confuse the customer. To prevent this, inquiries to the County Clerk and the Secretary of State's office should be made before making a final decision.

Legal Requirements

Legal requirements for starting a business vary with the type and legal form of business the owner plans to operate. The following categories of permits and licenses give a general idea of the red tape one can encounter prior to getting final approval by the government to open and operate a business. Be aware that each jurisdiction may require and follow different guidelines.

Local Licenses

City and/or county business licenses must be obtained prior to conducting business transactions. Local governments may also require special permits to operate. For example, a restaurant or food service provider needs to obtain special permits from the health department. In some cases, special permits will be required from the fire and/or police departments. If construction or remodeling is needed, a building permit must be obtained prior to commencing work. In addition, the owner should research zoning regulations to confirm that the proposed business is in compliance. In some cases, a special use permit may be required. Besides these permits, the local government might also impose a gross receipts, income, or payroll tax.

State Licenses

Many businesses and professions are regulated by the state and may not legally operate without being licensed. State licenses and permits are usually granted based on some combination of registration, bonding, education, experience, and passage of licensing examinations. States may vary in their licensing requirements. If the state has a sales tax, and the business sells tangible property such as merchandise, a sales and use tax permit must be obtained from the state sales tax agency. Most states also impose some form of income taxation.

Federal Licenses

The owner may be required to obtain a federal permit or license to operate. As stated earlier, laws and legislation governing businesses are constantly changing, so one should investigate the current regulations of the federal government. Once again, a professional advisor is strongly recommended.

Employees

The amount of red tape and government regulation increases dramatically if employees are hired. This includes a corporation with only one employee, the owner/president. The owner is required, as an agent of the government, to collect taxes from all employees, and to forward these taxes to the appropriate agencies. In addition, the owner needs to be current on the many rules and regulations governing employees. The following is a partial list of items that need to be considered

- Employer identification number
- Employer and employee Social Security (FICA) and Medicare taxes
- Federal income tax withholdings
- State income tax withholdings
- Federal unemployment tax
- State unemployment tax
- Workers' compensation or state disability insurance
- Group insurance
- Pension or profit-sharing plan
- Employee bonding
- Unions
- Federal OSHA (Occupational Safety and Health Administration) regulations
- State employee safety and health regulations
- Federal Fair Labor Standards Act
- Minimum wage requirement
- Overtime pay requirement
- Child labor laws
- Federal anti-discrimination laws
- Title VII of the Civil Rights Act of 1964
- Americans with Disabilities Act
- Sexual harassment

- Immigration law restrictions
- Deferred compensation plans
- Employee stock option plans

Even this partial list is long and cumbersome. If the owner has little or no knowledge of human resource management, it would be advisable to obtain this education. Legal encounters dealing with the hiring, firing, layoffs, or sexual harassment of an employee could cost the owner everything he or she has worked for, so it is important to understand these laws and regulations thoroughly.

Payroll Taxes

Payroll taxes are federal and state taxes that a business pays based on its payroll. They generally amount to approximately 14 percent of the total wage expense. If the owner plans to hire employees, he or she needs to know what these taxes are. Following is a list of payroll taxes with a brief description.

- Employer portion of the Social Security and Medicare Tax – In addition to withholding an employee's Social Security tax (FICA), an employer must also pay an equal amount of employer's Social Security tax. The employer's portion is currently about 7.65 percent of gross wages.

- Federal Unemployment Tax (FUTA) – Businesses are required to pay FUTA, and these taxes are imposed entirely upon the employer. To receive the most current laws regarding these taxes, contact your local IRS office. This tax is quite small—less than 1 percent.

- State Unemployment Tax – State governments also impose an unemployment tax. To receive the current rate for the state, contact the state government office responsible for tax collections. This tax usually approximates 2.7 percent. In some states, this tax depends on employment stability.

- Workers' Compensation Insurance – State law generally requires an employer to obtain workers' compensation insurance for their employees. This insurance covers employees who suffer a job-related injury or illness (this is not a group medical insurance plan). Failure to obtain workers' compensation insurance will result in legal sanctions.

Employee Benefits

If an employer provides employees with other benefits, such as group medical insurance or life insurance, the cost of these additional employer expenses must be considered. If pension or profit-sharing retirement programs are provided, the employer must follow the Employee Retirement Income Security Act of 1974 (ERISA). Failure to comply with ERISA, whether intentional or not, can result in criminal or civil penalties or both.

Financial Planning

Before beginning any financial planning, one must first prepare a **financial budget**. A financial budget is a projection of future financial statements or any of their components such as a cash budget. For example, before coming to college, most students estimated their cash expenses and prepared a budget to make sure they had sufficient funds to last through the school year. Starting a business requires careful financial planning and budgeting. Statistics support the notion that many small business failures are the direct result of failing to plan for the future financial and cash needs of the business.

Budgeting for a new business is a difficult task involving many uncertainties. The business does not have any past performance to use as a guideline. In addition, income will, in most cases, fluctuate from month to month until the business has established a solid customer base. Even though sales in the grand opening month may exceed all expectations, it would be overly optimistic to expect that level of sales to continue. Reasonable estimates of sales will provide the owner with the most accurate and reliable information to use in predicting profit and future cash flows.

Estimating Sales Revenue

So far this text has dealt with service companies. In this case reading a **retail business**, which is a company that sells a product versus a service, is introduced. **Sales revenue** is defined as the increase in the assets of the entity resulting from the sale of a product or service. The two components of revenue are quantity and price. For example, a certain number of items or services must be sold at a certain price to reach a projected sales forecast.

Projected sales revenue = Projected price × Projected quantity

A change in either price or quantity will affect the sales revenue achieved.

If a company is selling computer software packages for $300 each and 50 packages are sold, sales revenue is $15,000.

If the market becomes more competitive and the sales price is lowered to $250 per package but there is no increase in volume (quantity) sold, the total revenue is $12,500.

If the price remains at $300 throughout the year but the quantity sold increases to 75 packages, the total sales revenue equals $22,500.

There are many different combinations of these components that can affect the revenue of a business. All of these possibilities must be considered and anticipated.

What sales level does the owner need to make this business a "success"? This question can only be answered after a careful examination of the projected costs.

Estimating Costs

Following is a list of possible costs that a new company might encounter.

Start-Up Costs:

- Fixtures, equipment, and installation
- Decorating and/or remodeling
- Beginning inventory

- Personnel costs (hiring and training)
- Deposits (utilities, etc.)
- Licenses and permits
- Promotion for grand opening
- Organization costs (corporation)

Recurring Costs:

- Salary of manager
- Gross wages
- Repairs and maintenance
- Advertising
- Outside services (e.g., janitorial)
- Supplies
- Telephone/media expenses
- Other utilities
- Insurance
- Taxes (federal, state, local - for corporations only)
- Payroll taxes (if the company has employees)
- Automobile, delivery, and travel
- Professional fees (accounting and legal)
- Interest
- Rent
- Cost of goods sold
- Bad debt expense
- Miscellaneous expenses (other expenses related to the business)

Note that the list does not contain a salary for the work performed by the owner. In a sole proprietorship or a partnership, work performed by the owner is usually not shown on the income statement as a business expense. The owner withdraws funds from the business as needed. These withdrawals reduce retained earnings and are described as owner withdrawals. The only salary/wage expense shown on the income statement for these forms of business is that of employees. On the other hand, the corporate form of business recognizes the owner's salary as expense on the income statement.

Start-Up Costs vs. Recurring Costs

As shown above, the owner will encounter **start-up costs** (costs that will occur only once) and **recurring costs** (costs that will occur on a regular basis). All costs of a business are dealt with in one of two ways:

1. they are expensed during the year; or

2. they are recorded as assets of the business and expensed over several accounting periods.

The costs of the goods consumed in the process of generating revenue are called expenses. As stated in Module 2, the matching principle requires that all costs incurred in generating revenue be recognized as expenses in the same period as the related revenues.

Many start-up costs, such as personnel training costs, current year licenses/permits, and promotions for a grand opening, are expensed in the first year of business. Fixtures and equipment are considered to be fixed assets and are depreciated over the assets' useful lives.

Any decorating or remodeling charges are added to the cost of the fixed assets and depreciated as well. Refundable deposits are shown as an asset on the company's balance sheet. Inventory purchased during the period, even though a recurring cost, is recorded as an asset. The cost of inventory sold during the period is matched with the revenue generated by the sale. The cost of inventory sold is called **cost of goods sold**.

Because of the complexity of the corporate form of business, legal and professional fees, the cost of printing stock certificates, and other costs incurred to organize the business are considered intangible assets and are amortized (expensed) over a period not to exceed 40 years. These types of costs for a corporation are usually called **organization costs**.

Pro Forma (Projected) Statements

To estimate the profitability and financial condition of our proposed business, variations of the income statement and the balance sheet will be used. They are called **pro forma statements** and include projected or planned amounts rather than actual dollar amounts. Research will help immeasurably with the task of projecting financial information to prepare these statements. Fortunately, there are abundant research sources such as government agencies, professional services, and industry/trade publications that can help you with this information.

There are two alternatives to creating a pro forma income statement:

The **top-down approach** in which the owner estimates sales and works down to estimate the resulting profit.

The **bottom-up approach** in which the owner starts with profit and then determines what level of sales is needed to attain the profit goal.

Most businesses prefer the bottom-up approach because they can target a certain profit and then determine the level of sales required to attain this goal. The business then determines if its marketing plan can realistically achieve that level of sales. Carla's Copies, introduced in Group Assignment 3-1, illustrates the top-down approach. The following illustration, Jenny's Jewelry, will present the bottom-up approach.

JENNY'S JEWELRY EXAMPLE

Jennifer Weeks, a recent college graduate from the Midwest, wants to open a business selling bead jewelry. She recently inherited $50,000 from her grandmother and has decided that she will invest up to $40,000 of it. Her cousin opened a similar business in a nearby city and sales there are averaging $15,000 a month, which Jenny thinks is fantastic! Jenny plans on selling completed jewelry pieces as well as individual beads. She wants to hire one full-time employee. Besides offering bead classes, she plans to offer a special birthday party package for kids. She has also determined that she wants to run the business as a sole proprietorship.

Estimating Costs

Jenny has discussed her potential new business with several local merchants and professional advisors, and estimates the start-up costs as shown in Exhibit 3-1.1:

Exhibit 3-1.1
Start-up costs

Computer /Cash register	$5,000
Printer	350
Furniture and fixtures	4,500
Lease improvements (remodeling)	800
Professional services prior to opening	500
Start-up inventory - Beads/Bead supplies	15,000
Start-up office supplies	350
Advertisement for grand opening	800
Total start-up costs	**$27,300**

Accounting rules require that start-up costs such as the grand opening advertising ($800) and professional services ($500) prior to opening should be reported as expense in the first year. Jenny eliminated these two nonrecurring expenses from the expense estimate in Exhibit 3-1.2 as they are one-time-only costs and should not be included in an expense projection for an average month. The inventory of beads, bead supplies, and office supplies are assets until such time as they are used in the process of earning revenue. The first four items listed as start-up costs in Exhibit 3-1.1 are purchases of fixed assets which will benefit the business beyond the current year. Jenny feels that all fixed assets should be depreciated over a five-year life, and estimates a $700 salvage value. The last item in Exhibit 3-1.2 is depreciation expense of $166 to reflect the use of these assets for each monthly time period.

Exhibit 3-1.2
Monthly Expenses Regardless of Sales[1]

Store rent - lease	$1,100
Office supplies	80
Advertising	200
Utilities - per lease	350
Employee wages	1,120
Payroll taxes for employee (14% of wages)	157
Insurance	150
Professional services (accounting)	100
Business license	10
Depreciation of fixed assets	166
Total Expenses	**$3,433**

In addition to the above expenses, Jenny knows she will incur the expense of the beads used in the completed products sold as well as bead supplies. The cost of the beads sold and bead supplies expenses will depend on the amount of sales revenue. From discussions with other bead stores in the area and by doing research concerning industry norms, Jenny expects the cost of the beads sold to be about 40 percent of bead sales revenue and bead supplies to be about 8 percent of revenue.

Exhibit 3-1.3
Monthly Expenses Depending on Sales

Cost of Goods (Beads) Sold	40% of bead sales
Bead Supplies	8% of bead sales
Total	48% of bead sales

---

[1] To keep this example as simple as possible, the concepts of variable and fixed expenses and contribution margin are not introduced until Case Reading 3-2. The expenses in Exhibit 3-1.2 represent fixed expenses and the expenses shown in Exhibit 3-1.3 are variable expenses.

Determining Sales Needed to Earn Desired Profit

Jenny wants to invest in the business only if she can earn a $30,000 profit per year ($2,500 per month). This profit would compensate her for the many hours of work which she knows the business will demand, as well as give her a reasonable return on her investment. To calculate the monthly sales that would be required to generate a $2,500 profit, Jenny performs the following calculation:

Desired profit	$2,500
Monthly expenses per Exhibit 3-1.2	3,433
Amount Needed Before Considering Expenses in Exhibit 3-1.3	$5,933

The monthly expenses depending on sales shown in Exhibit 3-1.3 total 48% of sales; therefore the $5,933 amount calculated above must represent the other 52% of sales. Stated another way, for each sales dollar, 48% represents monthly expenses depending on sales, so the other 52% of each sales dollar must cover the $3,433 monthly expenses shown in Exhibit 3-1.2 and the desired profit of $2,500.

Amount needed to cover expenses from Exhibit 3-1.2 and desired profit are :

$$52\% \text{ of Sales} = \$5,933$$

$$\text{Sales} = \$5,933 \div 52\%$$

$$\text{Sales} = \$11,410$$

Once Jenny has determined the monthly sales required, it is easy to adapt the monthly figure to a yearly or daily sales figure. Seasonal fluctuations could also be factored in and the amount of sales required in a specific month of the year calculated. For example, if an average month had sales of $11,410 and, if sales around Christmas are expected to be 20 percent higher, then you could compute December's sales at 120 percent of $11,410, or $13,692.

What would the profit be in December?

Amount Needed	= 52% × sales of $13,692 = $7,120	
Less: Expenses per Exhibit 3-1.2		3,433
Profit		$3,687

Pro-Forma Income Statement

Jenny then prepares the pro forma income statement shown as Exhibit 3-1.4. Because Jenny's Jewelry sells a product and not a service, there are two profit computations: gross margin and net income. Each has a different function in measuring the success of the business.

The **gross margin** (also called **gross profit**) on sales is the difference between net sales and cost of goods sold. The gross margin figure is very important for a business. It is an indicator of how successful a business is in its

Gross Margin

industry. A high **gross margin percentage** (calculated by dividing the gross margin by sales) relative to the competition is an indication of the company's ability to (1) obtain high prices for its output, (2) control its expenses of production, and (3) maintain customer satisfaction. However, gross margin percentage does not take into consideration any expenses other than cost of goods sold. Inefficiency in controlling operating expenses will lower final net income even though the gross margin may be excellent.

The computation of net profit, or net income, reflects the true profitability of a business.

Net Income	Net income **(profit)** represents the increase in owners' equity from profitable operations; it is equal to net sales less all expenses.

Exhibit 3-1.4
Pro Forma Income Statement

Jenny's Jewelry	
Traditional Income Statement	
Average Month	
Sales Revenue	$ 11,410
Cost of Goods Sold	4,564
Gross Margin	6,846
Selling, General, and Administrative Expenses (SG&A)	4,346
Net Income	$ 2,500

Sales revenue is shown at the $11,410 computed on the previous page. Cost of goods sold is shown at 40 percent of sales or $4,564.

$$\text{Cost of Goods Sold (COGS)} = 40\% \times \$11,410 = \$4,564$$

Selling, general and administrative expenses (SG&A) include all expenses shown in Exhibit 3-1.2 as well as the bead supplies which are 8 percent of sales.

Expenses per Exhibit 3-1.2	$3,433
Bead Supplies 8% × $11,410	913
Total SG&A Expenses	$4,346

Pro Forma Balance Sheet

Jenny's insurance agent has told her that she must pay six months of insurance premiums in advance, and the landlord of the store demands the first and last months' rent in advance. Jenny notes that a one-year business license must also be purchased before she opens. The pro forma start-up balance sheet for Jenny's Jewelry is shown as Exhibit 3-1.5. The six months of advance insurance of $900 is shown as prepaid insurance. Two months of rent are listed as prepaid rent. The business license is also listed as an asset. Start-up inventory of beads and bead supplies is listed as $15,000, and office supplies on hand before the opening of the business are projected at $350. Current assets also include the start-up costs relating to professional fees of $500 and advertising of $800.

The fixed assets section contains all the long-term assets the company expects to use for the following five years. The owner does not project that the company will have any liabilities at the start-up date.

Notice that a start-up balance sheet does not have any retained earnings. That is because Jenny's Jewelry has not opened for business and no earnings have been generated to date.

Exhibit 3-1.5
Pro Forma Start-Up Balance Sheet

Jenny's Jewelry
Pro Forma Start-Up Balance Sheet
Average Month

Assets		Liabilities and Owner's Equity	
Current Assets		Liabilities	$ -
Cash	$ 9,480		
Office Supplies	350		
Prepaid Rent	2,200		
Prepaid Insurance	900		
Prepaid Advertising	800		
Prepaid Professional Fees	500		
Inventory	15,000		
Business License	120		
Total Current Assets	29,350		
Fixed Assets		Owner's Equity	
Computer/Cash drawer	5,000		
Printer	350	Contributed Capital	40,000
Furniture and Fixtures	4,500		
Lease Improvements	800		
Total Fixed Assets	10,650		
		Total Liabilities and	
Total Assets	$ 40,000	Owner's Equity	$ 40,000

Cash Flow Projections

Projecting cash flow is crucial for a start-up company. The start-up costs alone will require a large amount of cash. Jenny plans to contribute $40,000 to the business, but the start-up balance sheet shows that only $9,480 of that will be left in cash as of opening day. $30,520 cash ($40,000 – $9,480) would have been used to purchase the other assets which are reflected on the opening balance sheet. Jenny needs to be sure that the amount on hand is sufficient to pay suppliers and other bills in the next few months. Since the bead store is just starting out, Jenny can't really count on much cash coming in for the first few months. Even if sales are strong, many of the sales could be on credit and there may be a time lag between the sales date and the date of the cash collection. Exhibit 3-1.6 projects Jenny's potential cash budget for the first quarter.

Exhibit 3-1.6
Projected Cash Budget for Jenny's Jewelry

Jenny's Jewelry Projected Cash Budget - 1st Quarter	
Cash Inflows	
Cash from sales - first month at 65%	$ 7,417
Cash from sales - second month at 50%	5,705
Cash from sales - third month at 60%	6,846
Total cash inflow 1st quarter sales	19,968
Cash Outflows	
Cash for beads - 40% × $19,968 sales	(7,987)
Cash for bead supplies - 8% × $19,968 sales	(1,597)
Cash for wages (3 × $1,120)	(3,360)
Cash for payroll taxes (3 × $157)	(471)
Cash for professional services (3 × $100)	(300)
Cash for depreciation	N/A
Cash for business license	-
Cash for insurance	-
Cash for lease rent (2 × $1,100)	(2,200)
Cash for office supplies (3 × $80)	(240)
Cash for utilities (3 × $350)	(1,050)
Cash for advertising (3 × $200)	(600)
Total cash outflows in 1st quarter	(17,805)
Net cash inflow	$ 2,163

To keep it simple, this exhibit assumes cash sales only and that sales are 65 percent of the projected amount of $11,410 in the first month, 50 percent in the second month, and 60 percent in the third month. Since Jenny's business is new, she realizes she won't make her "average month" sales at first. Another assumption is that Jenny replaces any inventory items sold and any supplies used, paying cash to the supplier. No cash is needed for insurance or for a business license as these items were already purchased in advance. Also only two months of rent are needed as the first month was already paid in advance. Note that Exhibit 3-1.6 does not show any cash outflow for depreciation. Even though depreciation expense is needed to determine net income, it does not require the disbursement of cash. Cash is disbursed when fixed assets are purchased, not when used.

Even at the reduced sales levels, it appears that Jenny will have enough cash for the first quarter of operations. She did not, however, make any additional purchases of fixed assets or any owner's withdrawals of cash during the quarter. Does Jenny have enough cash to live on or must she take some out of the business? Remember, Jenny is not receiving any salary for her work.

The assumption was also made that all sales were for cash. What would happen if credit sales are 45 percent of total sales and there is a one-month time lag in the collection of all receivables (January's credit sales are collected in February, etc.)? How would this affect our cash projection?

Exhibit 3-1.7 shows the projected cash receipts given these estimates. Note that although total sales are the same as in Exhibit 3-1.6, cash received for those sales is less due to the fact that the company is now selling on credit and there is a time lag between the time of the sale and the time the cash is collected. Assuming that the cash outflows have not changed (the company is still paying cash to all the suppliers and is still immediately replacing any items sold), the cash needs for the first quarter are now different.

Exhibit 3-1.7
Jenny's Jewelry
Projected 1st Quarter Cash Receipts

	Cash Sales 55%	Credit Sales 45%	Total Sales per Exhibit 3-1.6	Cash Collections on Credit Sales	Total Cash Inflow
January	$4,079	$3,337	$7,416	0	$4,079
February	$3,138	$2,567	$5,705	$3,337	$6,475
March	$3,765	$3,080	$6,845	$2,567	$6,332
Total	$10,982	$8,984	$19,966	$5,904	$16,886

Cash Inflow per Exhibit 3-1.7 $16,886

Cash Outflow per Exhibit 3-1.6   (17,805)

Net cash outflow during 1st quarter   ($919)

Even under this scenario, it appears that Jenny has sufficient cash on hand to cover future expenditures, although she will be decreasing her cash on hand ($9,480 as of the start-up balance sheet date) by approximately $919 as a result of operations.

INDUSTRY NORMS AND RESOURCES

Throughout the planning process, it is advisable for the owner to research financial information concerning the industry in which he or she is potentially investing. The number and types of industry resources available are abundant and growing every day. Some potential resources include

Government Agencies

- Small Business Administration
- Chamber of Commerce
- Economic Development Commission
- Internal Revenue Service

Professional Services

- Attorney at Law
- Accountant
- Marketing Consultant
- Financial Consultant

Non-Profit Organizations

- SCORE (Service Corp of Retired Executives)
- Small Business Development Centers (1000 sites nationwide)

Industry Financial Ratios and Analysis Publications
- Dun & Bradstreet Key Business Ratios
- Manual of Performance Ratios for Business
- Almanac of Business and Industrial Financial Ratios
- Financial Ratio Analysis
- Elements of Financial Analysis (Schwartzman)
- Financial Studies of the Small Business
- Manufacturing USA
- Moody's Industry Review
- RMA Annual Statement Studies

Ratio Analysis

Whether planning a new business or evaluating an existing one, comparing the business performance of the company to industry norms is important because an owner can determine how the business is performing compared to other similar businesses. Financial institutions (banks), shareholders, and prospective investors will also want to compare the company's performance to industry norms. In the Jenny's Jewelry example, the cost of goods sold percentage, the gross margin percentage, and the net income as a percentage of sales should be compared with other jewelry companies. If there is a wide variance in the proposed venture and the industry norms, additional information should be gathered and reasonable explanations identified. It is important to consider all available information before committing oneself to a business venture.

Prior to searching for a business in the trade journals, it may be necessary to find the **standard industrial code (SIC)** number pertaining to the type of business. Many of the publications listed as industry sources are organized by SIC number. If the business has a unique product or service that does not have an SIC number listed, find a business that closely matches the business's operations. Often a listing of the various SIC numbers and the related industry can be found in the beginning or at the end of the industry publication.

Internet Sites

There are numerous Internet sources that should be consulted when starting a small business. Information and sites on the Internet are constantly changing. When searching the Internet, keep in mind that anyone can put information on the Internet, so make sure the information is from a reputable source. If the validity of the source is in question, do not use the information.

Many of the industry ratios available on the Internet are available for a fee, so obtaining free detailed industry information on the World Wide Web can be difficult. Standard industrial codes (SIC) are available on the Internet, however. After locating the Internet site, type in the name of the product being sold, and the Internet site will provide the numerical SIC code for the industry being researched.

Invest or Abandon

Many small business owners make the mistake of thinking that they are going to "get rich quick," but soon find themselves in financial trouble. Even if the owner has the "hottest" item in the market, he or she should not make the mistake of thinking that once the doors are open, he or she will be rolling in money. It could take several months or even years for the business to show a profit.

After the research and planning are completed, what decision should be made? The budgets will reflect the monetary impact of a decision to invest, but qualitative factors such as being one's own boss, etc., can't be quantified. As with any decision, weigh the advantages and disadvantages of the alternatives. Here are some questions to ask before committing to a business venture:

- Is the desired profit realistic?
- How sensitive is the profit to changes in sales volume?
- Are the sales goals attainable?
- How much time will it actually require to become profitable?
- Could the cash be invested somewhere else and yield a greater return?
- What are the risks and are they worth the gamble?
- Will the business be responsible for many sleepless nights?
- Will the time commitment be overwhelming?

Only after careful consideration of all important factors can the owner come to the "right" decision.

SUMMARY

In making the decision to open a new business, many factors must be considered. Among them is the legal form of organization under which the business operates. But just as important is the need to test one's business plan by preparing pro forma or projected financial statements. It is essential to see the opening balance sheet based upon the assumptions the owner is making concerning the start of the business. This task, properly done, will uncover any inconsistencies in the business plan, such as too little cash to get the business off the ground. Next it is essential that the prospective business owner prepare a projected income statement. Once projected sales are estimated, the question of whether it is possible to attain the necessary level of sales given the business location, products, competition, and other factors influencing the ultimate level of sales can be addressed. Finally, the cash flow must be determined, especially in the early months of the new business. Because many business fail due to lack of sufficient cash to sustain the business in the start-up phase, the forward view of cash coming in and going out based upon various assumptions will tell the new business owner what financial traps may lie ahead. When all these analyses are complete and positive, then it is time to turn to a number of qualitative questions. One such question is, is the owner really motivated enough to make the necessary commitment to make this business a success?

EXERCISES AND PROBLEMS

Exercises

Exercise 1 Motivation for Starting a Business. What two factors would motivate you to start a business? Explain briefly why each would motivate you to make a decision to start a business.

Exercise 2 Disadvantages of Starting a Business. What two factors would be most likely to keep you from starting a business? Explain briefly why each would deter you from making a decision to start a business.

Exercise 3 Using Market Research in Starting a Business. Why is market research so important in planning to start a business? Explain briefly.

Exercise 4 Financial Planning. How is financial planning used in deciding whether or not to start a business? Include an example in your answer.

Exercise 5 Start-Up Costs. How do start-up costs differ from recurring expenses? Explain briefly and give two examples of each.

Problems

Problem 1 Prepare a Start-Up Balance Sheet. Joni Garcia is planning to start a personal financial services practice. She has saved $66,000 during the last ten years while working for a large CPA firm in a major metropolitan area. She is evaluating the alternatives in establishing a personal financial services practice. Given below are her estimates of costs and expenses of opening the business and operating it during a typical month.

Start-up Costs:	
Computers (2) and office network	$10,000
Software	3,000
Office furniture and fixtures	4,000
Remodeling	1,700
Professional services prior to opening	1,400
Start-up office supplies	2,500
Advertising for grand opening and reception	1,600
Business license	200
Total Start-up Costs	**$24,400**

Monthly Recurring Expenses:	
Store rent - lease	$1,200
Office supplies	200
Advertising	250
Utilities - including telephone	300
Employee wages	1,300
Payroll taxes for employee (15%)	195
Insurance	200
Depreciation of fixed assets	255
Other fixed expenses	200
Total Fixed Expenses	**$4,100**

In addition to the listed expenses, Joni expects to incur additional expenses of about 10 percent of revenues. These expenses would be for such items as telephone toll charges, postage, travel to clients, and similar costs.

The depreciation of fixed assets was based on a 10 percent salvage value for each asset and useful lives of five years for the computer and network, three years for the software, and ten years for the office equipment.

If Joni starts the financial services practice, she will invest $50,000 of her savings into the business. The computer and software will be purchased for cash and the office furniture and fixtures will be purchased for 50 percent cash down and the remainder on open account (accounts payable).

Based on the above information, prepare a pro-forma start-up balance sheet for Joni Garcia Personal Financial Services Co.

Problem 2 Prepare a Pro-Forma Income Statement. Assume that Joni Garcia in Problem 1 would like to establish and open her business on September 1, 2000. During September she expects that she could earn $4,000 in personal services revenues, of which $2,000 would be collected in cash with the remainder in accounts receivable at September 30. Assume that all expenses would be incurred in the amounts planned. Based on this information, prepare a pro-forma income statement for September 2000 for Joni Garcia Personal Financial Services Co.

Problem 3 Calculate Necessary Profit Using Bottom-Up Approach. Assume that Joni Garcia in Problem 1 would like to establish and open her business on September 1, 2000. Assume that all expenses would be incurred in the amounts planned. Based on this information, if Joni wishes to be compensated $2,000 per month for the time she plans to devote to the business, what is the amount of revenue she needs to generate? (Hint: Use bottom-up approach.)

Problem 4 Library Research using Standard Industrial Codes (SIC). Go to your university or another library and locate information concerning industry norms for two industries. Use the standard industrial codes (SIC) to identify the industries. Select one code for a service industry and one for a manufacturing industry. For each of the two industry codes you select, report the following information:

- Current ratio
- Return on equity
- Profit before taxes percent, or earnings before interest and taxes

Group Assignment 3-1

PLANNING TO START A BUSINESS

Objectives

1. To understand the nature of business planning involving the start-up of a new business.
2. To understand how the concepts of expense behavior (variable, fixed, mixed) can be applied to a specific business entity.
3. To understand the notion of return on equity.
4. To enhance oral presentation skills.

Decision: Should the business investor set up this new business in your area?

Your group is to assume the role of a consultant to an investor who wishes to set up a new business in your locality. The objective for your group is to gather and analyze data on a business in order to decide whether that type of business is likely to be profitable for your investor. Assume that the investor whom you are representing has a profit goal of 12 percent of the initial capital investment. The investor has up to $100,000 in cash available to invest in the prospective business.[1] The investor does not want to work in the proposed business. Your findings will be presented to the class in an oral presentation at the end of Module 3.

An Approach to Profit Forecasting

One essential planning effort for starting a business is to assess whether the profit potential is sufficient to justify the risks and/or alternative uses of the money invested. Planning requires estimates of expected prices of proposed products or services and expected sales volumes, given a competitive environment. Planning also requires that the expenses of operating a business be intelligently forecasted. While no one can predict the future with 100 percent accuracy, it is nevertheless useful to engage in educated estimates of future revenues and expenses even though these estimates will turn out to be less than 100 percent accurate.

Your group is responsible for preparing a projected income statement for the business selected by your group. This estimated income statement (often called a profit projection) requires quantitative estimates. Several data sources can be drawn upon to make these estimates, including, but not limited to, the following:

1. Library research
2. Interviews with business owners/managers of a similar business establishment
3. Chamber of Commerce
4. Visits to other business establishments to compile competitive prices
5. Trade and business associations - journals and databases
6. Family, friends, or acquaintances who may be in the business
7. Your instructor

---

[1] Note: This is the maximum amount you have to invest. If your business doesn't require a $100,000 investment, you should use less. You must borrow if you need more than $100,000.

Throughout this group assignment you will notice that many schedules have been prepared that present and analyze data. These schedules have been surrounded with a box border so that you can easily identify them. The data was originally prepared using Microsoft Excel, a spreadsheet program, and then pasted into presentation software called Microsoft PowerPoint. The presentation software is relatively easy to learn and its use gives the presentation a more professional look. Each boxed schedule represents a slide in PowerPoint. If your school has computer facilities available on presentation days, your group may be able to present using a computer. If not, the slides can be printed and transparencies or handouts made.

To give you a brief idea of what is involved in this group assignment, a sample presentation has been prepared for you using a fictitious copy store named Carla's Copies. When you first view these slides, you may not understand the accounting concepts that they contain. These concepts will be covered in future case readings in Module 3. As mentioned previously, this presentation is not due until all Module 3 material has been thoroughly covered.

CARLA'S COPIES EXAMPLE

Drawing upon the data sources listed above, assume that your "consulting" group determines that Carla's Copies will offer three services at the prices shown below.

Services Provided

B/W Copies - Self Serve	$ 0.06	per page
B/W Copies - We Copy	0.08	per page
Color Copies	1.00	per page

To simplify your proposed business, try to limit your product/service line to three or four items. Carla's has the following machines available for use:

Copy Machines Available

2 Copy Machines - Self Serve
2 Copy Machines - We Copy
1 Color Copy Machine

The next step is to forecast the average monthly volume of the proposed copy store. After determining the sales price and volume for each product/service offered, you can compute a monthly sales forecast as shown in the following slide for Carla's Copies.

Monthly Sales Forecast

Copies	Revenue per Copy	B/W Self Serve	B/W We Copy	Color	Total
25,000	$ 0.06	$ 1,500.00			$1,500.00
35,000	0.08		$ 2,800.00		2,800.00
5,000	1.00			$ 5,000.00	5,000.00
Total		$ 1,500.00	$ 2,800.00	$ 5,000.00	$9,300.00

The copy store is also expected to incur cost of goods sold expense for the given sales volumes as shown in the next slide. Notice how the COGS (cost of goods sold) expense has been expressed as a percentage of sales. This calculation is ($4,550 ÷ $9,300) = 48.92 percent.

Monthly COGS Expense

Copies	COGS per Copy	B/W Self Serve	B/W We Copy	Color	Total
25,000	$ 0.02	$ 500.00			$ 500.00
35,000	0.03		$ 1,050.00		1,050.00
5,000	0.60			$ 3,000.00	3,000.00
Total		$ 500.00	$ 1,050.00	$ 3,000.00	$4,550.00
As a % of Revenue					48.92%

Besides cost of goods sold, Carla's Copies has many other expenses. All Carla's expenses must be classified as variable, fixed, or mixed as shown on the next slide.

Expected Classifications and Amounts

E x p e n s e s

Variable

Cost of Goods Sold	48.92% of revenue
Wages and Taxes	8.20% of revenue
Supplies	1.00% of revenue
Other	0.20% of revenue

Fixed

Manager's Salary and Tax	$ 1,186.50	per month
Advertising	250.00	per month
Building Rent	800.00	per month
Depreciation	366.50	per month
Equipment Rental	416.67	per month
Insurance	100.00	per month
Other Fixed Expenses	37.50	per month
Business License	8.33	per month

Mixed

Utilities	2% of revenue plus $150.00

Note how the variable expenses are expressed as a percentage of revenue. Alternatively, they could be expressed as a per-unit cost (as in the column "COGS per copy" in the Monthly COGS Expense slide). Fixed expenses are expressed as a fixed dollar amount because they do not change within the relevant range. Because mixed expenses include both a variable and a mixed component, they are expressed as a percentage of revenue and a fixed dollar amount.

You must have at least one mixed expense in your project.

We can further condense these three categories into two by breaking out the mixed expense for utilities into its variable and fixed component. The next slide shows that total variable expense is 60.33 percent of revenue.

Variable Expense Monthly and Yearly

	%	Monthly	Yearly
COGS	48.92%	$ 4,550.00	$ 54,600.00
Wages and Taxes	8.20%	762.75	9,153.00
Supplies	1.00%	93.00	1,116.00
Other	0.20%	18.60	223.20
Utilities	2.00%	186.00	2,232.00
Total Variable Expense *	60.33%	$ 5,610.35	$ 67,324.20

* Total percentage contains rounding differences.
Percentages are rounded to nearest hundredth.

Fixed expenses can be summarized in a similar manner:

Fixed Expense Summary

	Monthly	Yearly
Manager's Salary and Tax	$ 1,186.50	$ 14,238.00
Advertising	250.00	3,000.00
Building Rent	800.00	9,600.00
Depreciation	366.50	4,398.00
Equipment Rental	416.67	5,000.00
Utitities	150.00	1,800.00
Insurance	100.00	1,200.00
Other Fixed Expenses	37.50	450.00
Business License	8.33	100.00
Total Fixed Expenses	$ 3,315.50	$ 39,786.00

One of the more difficult expenses to calculate is salaries and wages because the employer must pay payroll taxes on all payroll. The payroll and tax information for Carla's Copies is shown below.

Monthly Payroll Summary

	#	Monthly Hours per Employee	Pay Rate	Monthly Wages	Tax @13%	Total Wages & Taxes
Manager	1	140	$ 7.50	$1,050.00	$136.50	$1,186.50
Employees	2	50	$ 6.75	$ 675.00	$ 87.75	$ 762.75

Note: The manager's salary is fixed. The employees' wages, including payroll taxes, are 8.20% (rounded) of sales revenue

Another expense that needs further explanation is depreciation. Carla's Copies has fixed assets, useful lives, and salvage values as shown in the next schedule. These amounts were used to calculate depreciation expense.

Equipment and Depreciation Summary

	Cost	Salvage	Life	Monthly Depreciation	Yearly Depreciation
Copy Machines	$ 33,000	$ 3,000	10 yrs.	$ 250.00	$ 3,000.00
Office Equipment	5,500	550	5 yrs.	82.50	990.00
Fixtures	1,200	-	10 yrs.	10.00	120.00
Furniture	3,200	320	10 yrs.	24.00	288.00
Total	$ 42,900	$ 3,870		$ 366.50	$ 4,398.00

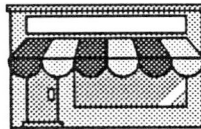

The variable and fixed expense information is then summarized in a projected contribution income statement as shown in the next slide.

Contribution Income Statement

	Monthly	Yearly
Sales	$ 9,300.00	$111,600.00
Variable Expenses	5,610.35	67,324.20
Contribution Margin	3,689.65	44,275.80
Fixed Expenses	3,315.50	39,786.00
Net Income	$ 374.15	$ 4,489.80

CMR = 39.67%

The Accounting Transaction Worksheet

At this point, all expenses have been identified and their proper yearly amounts calculated. The next step is to prepare an accounting transaction worksheet for the year similar to the one studied in Module 2. Two accounting transaction worksheets have been prepared for Carla's Copies, one for all start-up items and one for the transactions that occur after start-up and until the end of the first year of operations.

The start-up accounting transaction worksheet begins with all accounts having zero balances. The owner's contribution is recorded as well as any transactions involving start-up inventory, supplies, the purchase of fixed assets, a business license, prepaid rent, prepaid insurance, and so on. You will notice that there are no entries in the retained earnings column. Because operations have not started yet, there are no revenues or expenses. Revenues and expenses arise as a result of operations. This accounting transaction worksheet is shown on the next page as Exhibit G3-1.1.

The end of year 1 accounting transaction worksheet includes all transactions after opening until the end of the first year. The first row of the worksheet agrees with the ending balances per the start-up worksheet. You will notice that summary entries have been made for each item. For example, all sales revenues for the entire year were recorded in one row on the worksheet. Each expense the company incurred was recorded as a lump sum yearly amount on a separate row of the worksheet. After you have completed the worksheet, compare the balance in the Retained Earnings column with the net income on the contribution income statement presented earlier. In this case these two numbers should agree as the retained earnings column contains only income statement items (there are no owner's withdrawals). Exhibit G3-1.2 shows the worksheet at the end of the year.

Exhibit G3-1.1

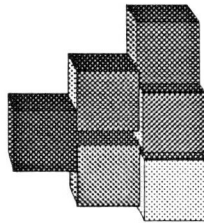

Start-up Worksheet

Transaction Description	Cash	Inventory	Supplies	Prepaid Insurance	Prepaid Rent	Business License	Copy Machines	Office Equipment	Fixtures	Furniture	Contributed Capital	Retained Earnings
Beginning Balance	$ -	$ -	$ -	$ -	$ -	$ -	$ -	$ -	$ -	$ -	$ -	$ -
Beg. Contribution by owner	70,000										70,000	
Purchase of 3 mos insurance	(300)			300								
Paid deposit on building rent	(800)				800							
Start Up Inventory	(13,880)	13,880										
Start Up Supplies	(500)		500									
Purchased color machines	(33,000)						33,000					
Bought Equipment	(5,500)							5,500				
Bought Fixtures	(1,200)								1,200			
Bought furniture	(3,200)									3,200		
Obtained Business License	(100)					100						
Total Start Up Costs	$ 11,520	$ 13,880	$ 500	$ 300	$ 800	$ 100	$ 33,000	$ 5,500	$ 1,200	$ 3,200	$ 70,000	$ -

Exhibit G3-1.2

End of Year 1 Worksheet

Transaction Description	Cash	Inventory	Supplies	Prepaid Insurance	Prepaid Rent	Business License	Copy Machines	Office Equipment	Fixtures	Furniture	Contributed Capital	Retained Earnings
Start Up Balance	$11,520	$13,880	$500	$300	$800	$100	$33,000	5,500	1,200	3,200	$70,000	$ -
Annual Revenue	111,600											111,600
Purchased Inventory	(54,100)	54,100										
Purchased supplies	(2,116)		2,116									
Supplies Used			(1,116)									(1,116)
Annual Bldg Rent	(9,600)											(9,600)
Annual Advertising	(3,000)											(3,000)
Cost of Goods Sold		(54,600)										(54,600)
Salary +taxes	(14,238)											(14,238)
Wages +taxes	(9,153)											(9,153)
Depreciation							(3,000)	(990)	(120)	(288)		(4,398)
Annual Insurance	(1,200)											(1,200)
Annual Utilities	(4,032)											(4,032)
Annual Equip. Rent	(5,000)											(5,000)
Other Fixed Expense	(450)											(450)
Other Variable Exp.	(223)											(223)
Business License	(100)											(100)
Balance - End Yr. 1	$19,908	$13,380	$1,500	$300	$800	$100	$30,000	4,510	1,080	2,912	$70,000	$4,490

Balance Sheets

Your group is required to prepare a start-up balance sheet and a balance sheet at the end of the first year of operations. The figures for the start-up assets and the end of the first year assets are shown in the schedule below. These numbers come from the ending account balances of their respective accounting transaction worksheets as shown in Exhibits G3-1.1 and G3-1.2. The assets need to be properly classified in their current and fixed classifications. When showing comparative statements at two different balance sheet dates, the most current amounts are generally shown to the left of older account balances.

Assets		End Year 1	Start Up
Current Assets			
	Cash	$19,908	$11,520
	Inventory	13,380	13,880
	Supplies	1,500	500
	Prepaid Insurance	300	300
	Prepaid Rent	800	800
	Business License	100	100
	Total Current Assets	35,988	27,100
Fixed Assets (net)			
	Copy Machines	$30,000	$33,000
	Office Equipment	4,510	5,500
	Fixtures	1,080	1,200
	Furniture	2,912	3,200
	Total Fixed Assets	38,502	42,900
	Total Assets	$74,490	$70,000

The owner's equity of Carla's Copies is shown in the next slide. The company does not have any liabilities. This is not very realistic, but to keep the example simple, that assumption will be made for this company.

Owner's Equity

	End Year 1	Start Up
Contributed Capital	$70,000	$70,000
Retained Earnings	4,490	-
Total Owner's Equity	$74,490	$70,000

Once again, all asset, liability, and owner's equity account balances on both the start-up balance sheet and the end of the first year balance sheet must agree with the corresponding balances on the accounting transaction worksheet.

Sensitivity Analysis

Your presentation should include a sensitivity analysis of your first year's profit projection and should consider several alternative volume estimates. An example for Carla's Copies appears below, in which the impact of changes in sales volume plus and minus 10 percent are examined.

Sensitivity Analysis

	90%	100%	110%
Sales	$100,440.00	$111,600.00	$122,760.00
Variable Expenses	60,591.78	67,324.20	74,056.62
Contribution Margin	39,848.22	44,275.80	48,703.38
Fixed Expenses	39,786.00	39,786.00	39,786.00
Net Income	$ 62.22	$ 4,489.80	$ 8,917.38

Breakeven and Target Profit Analysis

Your project should also include a **breakeven analysis** for your proposed business along with the appropriate calculations. The calculation for annual breakeven sales for Carla's Copies is shown on the next slide.

Breakeven Sales

$$\frac{\text{Fixed Expenses}}{\text{Contribution Margin Ratio}} = \frac{\$39,786}{39.67\%} = \$100,292$$

Additionally, the group assignment requires a computation to show the yearly sales needed to reach an annual target profit of 12 percent of beginning owner's equity. As shown in the start-up accounting transaction worksheet in Exhibit G3-1.1, Carla's initial capital contribution was $70,000. Therefore, a 12 percent profit would be $8,400.

Sales Needed to Reach Target Profit of 12% of beginning owner's equity

$$\frac{\text{Fixed Expenses} + \$8,400}{\text{Contribution Margin Ratio}} = \frac{\$48,186}{39.67\%} = \$121,467$$

Return on Equity Calculation

After preparing your balance sheets and your projected income statement for the first year of operations, you should calculate return on equity. The return on equity calculation requires the calculation of average equity for the first year. For this group assignment assume that average equity is the average of the start-up and ending balances for owner's equity. Be sure these amounts agree with your balance sheets.

Return on Equity

$$\frac{\text{Net Income}}{\text{Average O/E}} = \frac{\$4,490}{\$72,245} = 6.21\%$$

Average Owner's Equity (O/E) = ($70,000 + $74,490) ÷ 2

ASSIGNMENT RESOURCES

Library Research

Your initial source of information for this assignment should be the library where there is a wealth of information concerning industry norms. In most cases you will need to find the SIC (standard industrial code) for your business's industry. Information about SIC codes as well as the names of specific reference books can be found in Case Reading 3-1. Especially helpful would be items that pertain to small businesses. The library material should provide you with an idea of the major expense categories for the type of business you are considering as well as give you a perspective of what percentage of net sales each expense represents. For example, cost of goods sold might usually represent about 48 percent of net sales for the industry studied in your library research. The estimated expenses for your prospective business should reflect the research your group completed.

Library research often shows the income statement in a traditional format, so you will also need to prepare an income statement in that format. Instead of sorting the expenses into variable and fixed categories, the traditional format has a line item for cost of goods expense and selling, general, and administrative expenses (SG&A). Sometimes the SG&A expenses may be called operating expenses in resource material. The traditional format for Carla's Copies follows:

Yearly Income Statement
Traditional Format and Percentages

Sales	$111,600.00	100.00%
Cost of Goods Sold	54,600.00	48.92%
Gross Margin	57,000.00	51.08%
Selling, General and Administrative Expenses	52,510.20	47.05%
Net Income *	$ 4,489.80	4.02%

* Ignores Income Taxes and percentage column contains rounding differences.

GOAL

The next slide is a comparison of the contribution income statement and the traditional income statement for Carla's Copies.

Income Statement Comparison

	Traditional Format
Sales	$ 111,600.00
COGS	54,600.00
Gross Margin	57,000.00
Selling, General and Administrative Expenses	52,510.20
Net Income *	$ 4,489.80

Contribution Format	
Sales	$ 111,600.00
Variable Expenses	67,324.20
Contribution Margin	44,275.80
Fixed Expenses	39,786.00
Net Income *	$ 4,489.80

* Ignores Income Taxes

Once you have prepared an income statement in the traditional format, you need to show how your proposed company compares with other companies in the industry. An example of a tie-in to library research is presented below.

Library Research

	Carla's Copies	Source 1	Source 2
Revenue	100.00%	100.00%	100.00%
COGS	48.92%	48.80%	46.50%
Gross Margin	51.08%	51.20%	53.50%
Selling, General and Administrative Expenses	47.05%	45.90%	49.50%
Net Income *	4.02%	5.30%	4.00%

* Ignores Income Taxes and is rounded

Note how Carla's Copies figures are compared to figures obtained from the library research (shown above as Source 1 and Source 2). Photocopies from the sources found during the library research should be turned in with your project. Percentages used for comparative purposes should be circled on the photocopies. Be sure to identify the sources you used.

Chamber of Commerce

A local chamber of commerce is often a good source of information about businesses operating in the community. Often they have created business start-up kits to assist small businesses in their community. If so, obtain the kit to see what it has to say about starting a business in your locality.

Conclusion

Having completed all your analyses, your group should be ready to make the decision as to whether or not to invest in the company. Remember to use the investment criteria given in the problem.

Conclusion - DO NOT INVEST

Your net income of $4,490 is less than the $8,400 required. $8,400 is 12% of the beginning capital contribution

PREPARATION FOR PRESENTATION

Your group should meet outside of class as soon as possible to analyze any information that you have collected and to prepare for your presentation. The slides in your presentation should focus on your prospective new company and a projection of how the new company is expected to perform. The content of your presentation must include the following:

- A brief overview of the company you selected and the industry it serves.

- Your prospective company's major products/services and your approach for estimating revenues (limit to three or four products/services if possible).

- Your prospective company's major expenses and your approach for estimating variable expenses, fixed expenses, and mixed expenses (your company must have at least one mixed expense).

- Detailed schedules showing calculations for cost of goods sold, payroll, and depreciation.

- An estimated income statement (profit projection) using the contribution format for your prospective company's first year of operations and an analysis of the company's breakeven point and target sales level required to meet the investor's profit goal of 12 percent of beginning owner's equity.

- A schedule showing the sensitivity analysis.

- A comparison of income statements prepared using a contribution approach and a traditional approach.

- A tie-in of the traditional approach income statement to at least two sources reviewed in your library research (copies of the library research pages must also be turned in with appropriate percentages highlighted or circled).

- A start-up balance sheet and a balance sheet at the end of the first year of operations.

- Accounting transaction worksheets for recording transactions.

- Your proposed company's return on equity for the first year.

- Your conclusion as to whether to invest in your prospective company. Is it likely to succeed in your locality?

- Each member of your group must participate in your group's oral presentation, which should last 8-10 minutes with 2-3 minutes for follow-up questions by your assigned evaluation group(s), the class, and/or instructor. A sample list of questions that the instructor may ask is included at the end of this case. Before your presentation begins, your group must provide the instructor and your evaluation group(s) with a copy of the following:

  - Presentation outline
  - Schedules as stated above
  - Handouts to students during presentation (if any)
  - Thank-you note to business signed by all group members with a stamped addressed envelope (See requirements for options A and C)
  - Industry norms from library research

ADDITIONAL REQUIREMENTS

Your instructor may have additional requirements as follows:

Be sure to ask your instructor which option your school has chosen.

Option A : Visit Business - No Data Set Provided

Your group is required to select an existing business establishment in your locality to visit. Your purpose in visiting a real business is to collect data that will be useful in estimating income for your prospective business establishment. Each group in all sections of the course will analyze the data for a different business establishment. To avoid duplication of businesses, you must sign up for the business you would like to visit. Sign ups will be on a first-come, first-served basis. A sign-up sheet will be posted. You should meet with your group as soon as possible to select your company. A sample list of potential company types is presented below.

It is helpful to have the manager's agreement to participate in the project before completing the library research. If the manager refuses, you will need to select a new company which may be in a different industry. After selecting your company, complete the library research. Once you are familiar with the industry, you will be better able to communicate intelligently with the manager of the business you have chosen. Your library research should culminate in a written list of questions that your group will explore with the manager of your selected company. Ask your instructor when the list of questions needs to be handed in for approval.

Your instructor will provide your group with a letter of introduction addressed to the business manager whom you will be interviewing. This letter will help explain the purpose and thrust of the project. Keep in mind that the manager of the business will probably be hesitant about sharing financial information. **You do not need to see any financial reports.** You can pick up the necessary information by observation and by getting answers to specific questions you have prepared in advance. You may only have a chance to see the manager once! Perhaps your group could take the manager out to lunch. A luncheon meeting would provide you with a relaxed atmosphere in which to discuss your questions. Remember to keep this project simple. You need only look at three or four major products (services) and consider the major expenses.

At the end of your project, you will be expected to prepare a professionally written and carefully edited thank-you note to the manager of your selected business signed by all of the group members. You must also turn in a stamped envelope addressed to the manager of the business you visited. Your instructor will mail the thank-you letters after they have been approved.

Sample List of Types of Businesses

Drive-in oil change/lube	Convenience store	Take-out pizza
Hair salon	Travel agency	Video rental
Smog certificate shop	Bookstore (non-text)	Athletic/Fitness club
Bike shop	Radio station	Pet store
Women's clothing	Sandwich/Deli shop	Shoe repair
Record store	Computer store	Shoe store
Dry cleaners	Laundromat	Yogurt Store

Option B: No Business Visit - Data Set Provided

Your instructor will provide you with financial information that has already been gathered by the investor. Your role is to organize the data into the appropriate schedules required for the project. Your presentation will include a discussion of how these numbers were assembled as well as any additional research your group conducted to verify the numbers provided. No visit to a manager of an existing business is required but your instructor may require your group to prepare a written analysis of the investment opportunity.

Option C: Business Visit - Data Set Provided

Your instructor will provide you with financial information that has already been gathered by the investor. Your role is to organize the data into the appropriate schedules required for the project. You will then need to verify that information by visiting the manager of a similar small business in your community. Your group will ask the manager's input as to the reasonableness of the information your investor has provided. During the oral presentation, your group will show the figures and schedules you prepared related to the information provided by the investor. Your discussion, however, will not address how the schedules were prepared or how the numbers were calculated, but rather the reasonableness of the information provided by the investor as determined by your discussion with outside sources, including the manager. Your instructor may require your group to prepare a written analysis of the investment opportunity, which should include comments by the manager of the business visited.

Each group in all sections of the course will analyze the data for a different business establishment. To avoid duplication of businesses, you must sign up for the business you would like to visit. Sign ups will be on a first-come, first-served basis. A sign-up sheet will be posted. You should meet with your group as soon as possible to select your specific company.

Your next step is to complete the library research. Once you are familiar with the industry, you will be better able to communicate intelligently with the manager of the business you have chosen. Your library research should culminate in a written list of questions that your group will explore with the manager of your selected company. Ask your instructor when the list of questions needs to be handed in for approval.

Your instructor will provide your group with a letter of introduction addressed to the business manager whom you will be interviewing. This letter will help explain the purpose and thrust of the project. Keep in mind that the manager of the business may be hesitant about sharing financial information from the business. That is not a problem, because your task is to get the manager's opinion about whether an investment in a similar business is a good idea, not to obtain specific financial information about his/her business. You can pick up the necessary information by observation and by getting answers to specific questions you have prepared in advance. You may only have a chance to see the manager once! Perhaps your group could take the manager out to lunch. A luncheon meeting would provide you with a relaxed atmosphere in which to discuss your questions.

At the end of your project, you will be expected to prepare a professionally written and carefully edited thank-you note to the manager of your selected business signed by all of the group members. You must also turn in a stamped envelope addressed to the manager of the business you visited. Your instructor will mail the thank-you letters after they have been approved.

Continued on next page.

ORAL PRESENTATION EVALUATION

Your group's oral presentation will be graded both by the instructor and possibly by one or more of the other groups in your class. The evaluative criteria are shown on the following evaluation sheet. Each group member will receive the total points earned by the group, unless the group member's individual evaluation is significantly above or below the overall group evaluation (as determined jointly by the instructor and assigned evaluation group(s), in which case the individual's points will be adjusted accordingly).

Summary of Requirements and Points Assigned

	Points	Dates
1. Select company and sign up with instructor.	---	
2. Complete library research.		
3. Develop written list of questions (options A and C). Clear with instructor.		
4. Meet with business manager (options A and C)*.	---	
5. Complete analysis, prepare for oral presentation, and make presentation.		
* For option C, you may want to have some of the schedules completed before this step.		
Total Points		

SAMPLE LIST OF INSTRUCTOR QUESTIONS *

1. What was your contribution to the group?
2. Why was it important to do library research on the industry before meeting with your selected business?
3. What other resources did your group use and how useful were they?
4. What major assumptions did you make in developing your profit projection?
5. Why is it necessary to identify which expenses are variable vs. fixed?
6. How did your group handle seasonal fluctuations in your profit projections?
7. Why might the manager of your selected business feel very uncomfortable if you had asked to see his financial reports?
8. Did your selected business perform better or worse than industry norms?
9. What does the return on equity show you? How would you go about determining if the return on equity is reasonable for this type of business?
10. How did risk enter into your group's decision whether to invest or not?
11. How would the small business you are planning differ from the particular business you studied in your locality?
12. What other type of information would you try to obtain before making a final decision on whether to invest or not?
13. Where would you locate your new business and why? Do you think location is a key factor for your business?
14. How did the breakeven point you calculated enter into your decision whether to invest?
15. Would your profit be the same as your net cash flow from operations for the first year? Why or why not?
16. Why does your prospective company appear to have a lower (higher) breakeven point compared with one other group's proposed company (among other things, you need to be a good listener to answer this question!)?

* These are questions your instructor may ask you or members of your group during the oral presentation.

Oral Presentation Evaluation -Planning a Small Business

Group No.   **Section No.**

Your oral presentation will be graded according to the following criteria:

5= Excellent	3= Adequate
4= Good	2= Marginal
1= Inadequate	

> Note: Criteria are neither prioritized nor equally weighted.

Company/Industry Overview   1   2   3   4   5

- The overview provided an appropriate setting for the remainder of the presentation.
- The overview reflected multiple sources of information.
- The report showed a tie-in to at least two library research sources.
- Copies of the industry norms, obtained from the library research, were handed in with the report.

Estimating Revenues   1   2   3   4   5

- Prices shown were reasonable considering the small business studied and its industry.
- The high and low volume estimates were supported by the financial data given.

Estimating Expenses   1   2   3   4   5

- Collected data supported projections of variable expenses.
- Collected data supported projections of fixed expenses.
- Components of mixed expenses were separated reasonably.

Analysis   1   2   3   4   5

- The breakeven point and target sales were computed correctly.
- The return on equity was correctly computed.
- The start-up and end of year one balance sheets of the business were reasonable.
- The accounting transaction worksheet information agreed with other schedules prepared.

Other Oral Presentation Considerations   1   2   3   4   5

- · The presentation was well organized and presented.
- · The presentation was convincing and interesting.
- · There was appropriate and effective use of visuals and handouts.
- · The group stayed within time budget.
- · The group effectively responded to questions.
- · The group's decision to invest was reasonably supported by its analysis.
- · A well written, carefully edited thank-you letter was handed in with the report, complete with a stamped addressed envelope. All group members signed it. (Options A and C)

Overall Quality of Group Presentation   1   2   3   4   5

- · The total impact of the report

Total presentation points earned by group =

Overall Quality of Individual Presentations

Group Member		1	2	3	4	5
Group Member		1	2	3	4	5
Group Member		1	2	3	4	5
Group Member		1	2	3	4	5
Group Member		1	2	3	4	5
Group Member		1	2	3	4	5

Note: Each group member will receive the total points earned by the group unless the group member's evaluation is significantly above or below the group's overall evaluation, in which case the individual's points will be adjusted accordingly.

Case Reading 3-2

PLANNING FOR VARIABLE
AND FIXED EXPENSES

INTRODUCTION

This case reading introduces variable, mixed, and fixed expenses and shows how they are used along with revenue assumptions in the planning process. The high-low method is demonstrated as one alternative method used to separate mixed expenses into variable and fixed components. The importance of contribution margin and contribution margin ratio are emphasized, including examples of how these concepts are used in making short-term business decisions. This case reading also compares the contribution income statement format with a traditional income statement and describes when each format is used.

REVENUE PLANNING

The revenue that a company earns is determined by the unit price times the number of units sold. The price that a company charges for its products must be competitive unless that product is unique, and the buyer is willing to pay a premium to acquire it. In a department store, the price will depend on what the retailer paid to acquire the inventory plus what the retailer needs to cover other costs, such as advertising, salaries, supplies, insurance, and rent, etc., in addition to making a reasonable profit. If the product is widely distributed, the individual pricing of the product on any given day may depend on the price that a competitor charges for that item, any advertising specials, etc. For example, if a gas station operates in an area where there are many other gas stations, customers tend to be more price sensitive. As a result, the business may need to lower its price to attract customers. Unless the retailer is offering some additional services for the higher price, many customers will shop at the retailer that offers the lower price. Additional services may include window washing, tire checks, or the benefit of an easy access location.

Lowering the price on a product will usually increase the quantity sold. Understanding the effect a change in volume will have on profit is possible only if the planner understands the behavior of the company's various expenses.

EXPENSE PLANNING

The planned level of expenses will depend on the nature of each expense and its behavior in relation to sales volume. All expense behavior can be broken down into two categories: variable and fixed expenses. Some expenses are mixed expenses which have both a variable and a fixed component. An example is telephone expense, which includes a monthly fixed amount plus a variable charge for the minutes devoted to long distance calls. Further analysis of these expenses is needed to determine how much of the expense is variable and how much is fixed.

Variable Expenses

Variable expenses (VE) are expenses that, in total, vary in proportion to changes in sales volume. The calculation of the variable expense per unit is as follows:

Variable expense = Variable expense per unit × number of units

For example, let's assume that a college student has just written a book detailing all the different types of college scholarships available nationally, the requirements for each scholarship, and the details about the application process. The book sells for $40. Variable expenses include the cost of the paper, printing costs, and packaging. These variable expenses total $25 per book. Variable expenses for three books would be calculated as follows:

Variable expenses = $25 per book × 3 books = $75

Variable Expense

```
$
75-
50-
25-
      1   2   3
   Production or Sales Volume
```

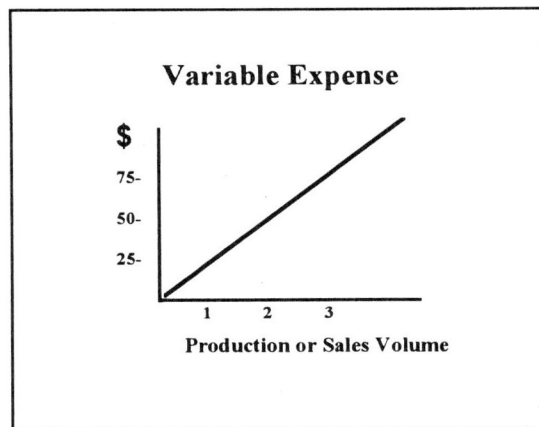

The variable expense graph shown above demonstrates that as the level of activity increases, the number of books produced or sold increases, the variable cost increases in a straight line. For example, if you sold one book your variable cost would be $25, for two books it would be $50, for three books $75, etc. A **level of activity** is an activity within an organization (e.g., sales activities, production activities, purchasing activities, etc.) which can be measured in terms of output, input, or a combination of the two. Examples of output measures are sales volume for a merchandising firm, or hours billed in a service firm. Labor hours is an example of an input measure.

Fixed Expenses

Fixed expenses are expenses which remain constant in total over a certain relevant range of activity, regardless of the activity level. For example, building rent is usually a fixed expense for most companies. Regardless of the number of units a company sells, the amount of rent expense for the building stays the same (until the company expands its facilities). The range of volumes over which fixed costs remain the same is known as a company's **relevant range**. Expanding to a new building would represent a new relevant range. The relevant range may differ for each type of fixed expense. Rent may not change, but the addition of a night shift could introduce additional fixed costs for supervision.

Going back to our book example, the graphic designer's fee would be the same regardless of how many books were sold (within the relevant range). Let's assume that the graphic designer's fee and other fixed expenses total $5,400. A graph showing these fixed expenses is shown on the next page. Notice how there is a horizontal line at the amount of $5,400, the fixed expenses. The horizontal line demonstrates that, regardless of the number of books produced or sold, the $5,400 would stay the same (within the relevant range).

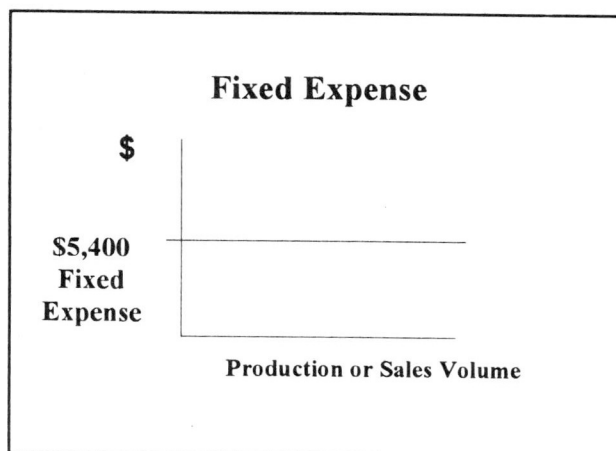

Fixed Expense

$

$5,400
Fixed
Expense

Production or Sales Volume

Mixed Expenses

Mixed expenses are expenses that are partially variable and partially fixed. The variable portion of the mixed expense varies with the activity level, and the remainder is fixed regardless of the activity level (within the relevant range). Good examples of mixed expenses are telephone or electric bills. Your bill is based on a flat fee per month regardless of use, plus a fee based on how much you used the utility.

A mixed expense graph for utility expense would look like this:

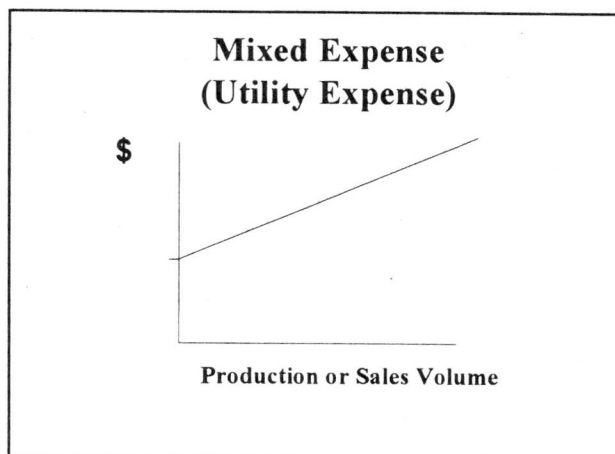

**Mixed Expense
(Utility Expense)**

$

Production or Sales Volume

Notice how the line does not go through the origin. The line will intersect the y axis at the amount of fixed expense.

There are several different methods for computing the amount of the variable and fixed expenses that make up a mixed expense. Only one of these methods, the high-low method will be presented.

High-Low Method

In the **high-low method**, mixed expenses are tracked as well as the activity level for a certain amount of time. The activity level for the high and the low expense can then be determined, and the following formula can be applied to compute the variable rate.

$$\text{Variable rate} = \frac{\text{High expense} - \text{Low expense}}{\text{High Activity} - \text{Low activity}}$$

Once that rate has been computed, that rate can be entered in the fixed expense equation to compute fixed expense.

$$\text{Fixed expense} = \text{Total expense} - (\text{Variable rate} \times \text{Activity})$$

The total expense figure would be the dollar amount for either the high or the low mixed expense. Whichever expense is selected, make sure to select the corresponding activity level.

The following example will give you an idea of how to apply the formulas to a real situation.

Month	Hours Worked	Phone Bill	
Jan.	180	$229	← Low Activity
Feb.	200	$260	
Mar.	250	$303	← High Activity
Apr.	225	$280	
May	190	$243	
June	240	$294	

1. First pick the high and low activity (hours worked). January is the low and March is the high.

2. Then compute the variable rate according to the formula:

$$\text{Variable rate} = \frac{\$303 - \$229}{250 - 180} = \$1.06 \text{ per hour}$$

3. Next compute the fixed expense using the equation for either the high activity or the low activity. The equation for both is shown below, although only one is necessary.

Fixed expense = Total expense – (Variable rate × Number hours)
Fixed expense = $303 – (1.06 × 250)   ← HIGH HOURS WORKED
Fixed expense = $303 – 265 = $38

Fixed expense = Total expense – (Variable rate × Number hours)
Fixed expense = $229 – (1.06 × 180)
Fixed expense = $229 – 191 = $38

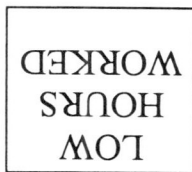

LOW HOURS WORKED

4. Express the mixed expense in a formula format:

Mixed expense = ($1.06 × Number hours) + $38

Variable expense   Fixed expense

This formula can then be used to project future expenses. For example, suppose that the employees worked 220 hours during the following month. We can expect the utility expense to be as follows:

Utility expense = ($1.06 × 220 hours) + $38 = $271

It is essential that the company separate all mixed expenses into their variable and fixed components in order to facilitate the planning process.

CONTRIBUTION MARGIN

The **contribution margin** (CM) is simply equal to sales minus variable expenses (VE). It is the part of sales revenue that is available to cover fixed expenses and to provide profit. An equivalent way of stating this is to say that contribution margin equals fixed expenses plus net income. Note that this calculation is made for a period of time such as a month, quarter, or fiscal year. The fixed expenses must relate to a specific time period. The variable expenses must relate to the volume of business planned in that same time period.

Sales – Variable expenses = Contribution margin

After identifying the variable expenses, the company can determine the contribution margin.

Sales = Unit selling price (SP) × Number of units sold
– Variable expense = Unit variable expense × Number of units sold
Contribution margin = Unit contribution margin × Number of units sold

Let's go back to our book example: As mentioned previously, the book sells for $40 and the variable expenses are $25 per book. What is the contribution margin (CM) per book?

Contribution margin = $40 Selling price – $25 Variable expense = $15 per book

We can use that same equation to calculate the contribution margin for 20 books.

Contribution margin for 20 books is 20 × $15 = $300

The **contribution margin ratio** (CMR) is the contribution margin divided by sales revenue. Exhibit 3-2.1 shows the contribution margin for one book, twenty books, and also the contribution margin ratio per book.

Exhibit 3-2.1

Contribution Margin Ratio (CMR)					
	Per Book		20 books		%
Revenues	$	40	$	800	100.00%
Variable Expenses		25		500	62.50%
Contribution Margin	$	15	$	300	37.50%

The above example shows that the contribution margin is $15 per book. To complete the table for sales revenue for 20 books, 20 is multiplied by each line item: sales price per book to arrive at sales, variable expense per book to arrive at variable expenses, and contribution margin per book to arrive at the contribution margin for twenty books. The contribution margin ratio can be calculated by using either $15 ÷ $40 or $300 ÷ $800. Either calculation will result in a contribution margin ratio of 37.5 percent.

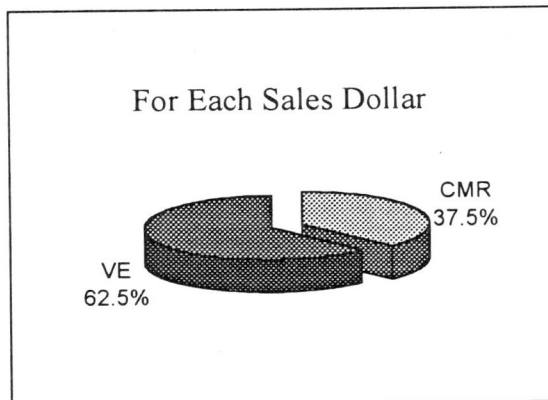

For Each Sales Dollar

CMR 37.5%

VE 62.5%

The contribution margin ratio indicates that for each sales dollar, 37.5 percent of that dollar is available to cover fixed expenses and to provide a profit. The **variable expense ratio** of 62.5 percent means that 62.5 percent of each sales dollar covers variable expenses.

THE CONTRIBUTION INCOME STATEMENT

The **contribution income statement** is designed to show, as a subtotal, the excess of revenue over variable expenses. Because the remaining deductions from revenue are fixed expenses, changes in contribution margin also explain the changes in net income. A contribution income statement format is presented in Exhibit 3-2.2.

Exhibit 3-2.2
Contribution Income Statement Format

Contribution Income Statement	
Revenues	Unit Selling Price × Units Sold
Variable Expenses	Unit Variable Expenses × Units Sold
Contribution Margin	Unit Contribution Margin × Units Sold
Fixed Expenses	Less Fixed Expenses
Net Income	Net Income

Returning to our book example, assuming a volume of 1,000 books, a completed contribution income statement would be as shown in Exhibit 3-2.3.

Exhibit 3-2.3
Contribution Income Statement - 1,000 Books Sold

Contribution Income Statement (Sales of 1,000 books)		
Revenues	$40 × 1,000 =	$ 40,000
Variable Expenses	$25 × 1,000 =	25,000
Contribution Margin	$15 × 1,000 =	15,000
Fixed Expenses		5,400
Net Income		$ 9,600

What does this statement reveal about the book company? It shows that $15 of each book's selling price is available to cover fixed expenses and to provide a profit. Suppose we sell one more book, how much more profit would there be?

The answer is $15, the amount of the contribution margin. Since fixed expenses have already been covered (i.e., the company is already making a profit), for each additional unit sold the contribution margin goes straight to profit.

THE CORLISS ACCOUNTING FIRM EXAMPLE

You were introduced to Corliss Accounting Firm and its activities for the month of June 2000 in Case Reading 2-1. This continues that example by taking the income statement information presented in Case Reading 2-3 and preparing a contribution income statement. The income statement for Corliss from Case Reading 2-3 is recreated in Exhibit 3-2.4.

Devenie Corliss, the owner, is trying to project what types of expenses and revenue she can expect for the month of July. In making this projection, her first step is to determine which of her expenses are variable expenses (vary directly with revenue) and which are fixed expenses (stay the same regardless of changes in sales volume). In making this assumption, Devenie is assuming that the sales volume is within the relevant range.

Exhibit 3-2.4
Corliss Accounting Firm Income Statement

Corliss Accounting Firm		
Income Statement		
Month Ended June 30, 2000		
Revenues		
Fees Revenue		$ 5,200
Expenses		
Wage Expense	$ 1,600	
Supplies Expense	750	
Interest Expense	733	
Depreciation Expense	200	
Insurance Expense	40	
Total Expenses		3,323
Net Income		$1,877

After considering her expenses, Devenie determines that her variable expenses include employee wages and supplies and that the remaining expenses are fixed. As mentioned previously, an income statement that sorts expenses into variable and fixed categories is called a contribution income statement. A contribution income statement for Corliss Accounting Firm is shown in Exhibit 3-2.5. You should notice the subtotal called contribution margin. This amount represents the amount of sales dollars that remain to cover fixed expenses and profit.

Exhibit 3-2.5
Contribution Income Statement

Corliss Accounting Firm		
Contribution Income Statement		
Month Ended June 30, 2000		
Revenues		
Fees Revenue		$ 5,200
Variable Expenses		
Wage Expense	$ 1,600	
Supplies Expense	750	
Total Variable Expenses		2,350
Contribution Margin		2,850
Fixed Expenses		
Depreciation Expense	200	
Insurance Expense	40	
Interest Expense	733	
Total Fixed Expenses		973
Net Income		$ 1,877

To aid in the planning process, it is helpful to express variable expenses and the contribution margin as a percentage of revenue as shown in Exhibit 3-2.6. Each of the line items below was divided by fees revenue to get the percentage indicated. For example, wage expense was calculated at 30.77 percent of revenue by taking the wage expense figure of $1,600 and dividing it by fees revenue of $5,200.

Exhibit 3-2.6
Contribution Margin in Dollars and Percentages

Revenues			$	%
Fees Revenue			$ 5,200	100.00%
Variable Expenses				
Wage Expense	$	1,600		30.77%
Supplies Expense		750		14.42%
Total Variable Expenses			2,350	45.19%
Contribution Margin			$ 2,850	54.81%

The percentage calculated above for the contribution margin is called the contribution margin ratio. This is a very important accounting term. In this example, a contribution margin ratio of 54.81 percent means that for every sales dollar, 54.81 percent of that dollar (or 55¢) is left to cover fixed expenses and profits. Once the company has covered its fixed expenses, for every additional dollar of revenue earned, the entire 55¢ will be profit!

TRADITIONAL VS. CONTRIBUTION INCOME STATEMENT

Many organizations prepare income statements in two different formats. Net income can be presented using a traditional income statement or a contribution income statement. The net income (profit) can be the same for both, but the information provided by the statements differs. The Corliss Accounting Firm example above showed a traditional and a contribution income statement for a service organization. Shown below as Exhibit 3-2.7 is a comparison of a traditional versus a contribution income statement for Jenny's Jewelry, the bead store introduced in Case Reading 3-1.

Exhibit 3-2.7
Comparison of Traditional vs. Contribution Income Statement

Jenny's Jewelry			
Pro Forma Income Statement - Average Month			
Traditional Income Statement		**Contribution Income Statement**	
Sales Revenue	$ 11,410	Sales Revenue	$ 11,410
Cost of Goods Sold	4,564	Less Variable Expenses:	
Gross Margin	6,846	Variable Cost of Sales	4,564
		Variable SG&A	913
Selling, General, and			
Administrative Expenses	4,346	Contribution Margin	5,933
		Fixed Expenses	3,433
Net Income	$ 2,500	Net Income	$ 2,500

Note that an income statement prepared under the contribution approach has the same net income as one prepared under a traditional approach.[1] In the **traditional income statement** the expenses for Jenny's Jewelry are broken down into cost of goods sold and selling general and administrative expenses. In the contribution format the expenses are broken down into variable and fixed categories.

Why Use Contribution Income Statements?

A traditional income statement is prepared for external reporting purposes. Generally accepted accounting principles require preparation of this type of income statement for all companies that are publicly traded. Most management accountants argue that the contribution income approach to income statements better supports management decisions than does the traditional approach. The primary advantage of the contribution approach is that, with fixed and variable costs readily determinable, "what if" questions managers use to assess risk are easily answered. For example, using a contribution approach, it is easy to determine the effect that an increase (or decrease) in sales of 20 percent would have on profit. These types of analyses cannot be done if only traditional income statement information is available.

Why is the traditional method required for external financial statements? The best answer is probably tradition. Many financial analysts and bankers argue that they also need cost information in a contribution income statement format so they can do "what if" analysis as well. To date, however, most users of external financial statements have had to "guesstimate" the companies' fixed and variable costs as only traditional income information has been provided.

SUMMARY

This case reading introduces the terms variable, fixed and mixed expenses. It explains that the separation of variable and fixed expenses is a powerful planning tool because it enables the planner to gain insight into the way in which income will change in relation to sales. The concepts of contribution margin, contribution margin ratio and the preparation of a contribution income statement are also presented. The Corliss Accounting Firm example is continued in this case reading. The income statement presented in Module 2 is reintroduced but in a contribution format. A discussion of the difference between a traditional and a contribution format income statement for a retail store is also presented with the benefits of the contribution approach highlighted.

EXERCISES AND PROBLEMS

Exercises

Exercise 1   Contribution Margin and Contribution Margin Ratio. Explain how contribution margin and contribution margin ratio are computed. Give one reason why the contribution margin and the contribution margin ratio is used in a business.

Exercise 2   Relating Contribution Margin and Contribution Margin Ratio. For a one-product company, would the contribution margin and the contribution margin ratio be the same for total sales and on a per-unit basis? Explain briefly.

---
[1] The net incomes will not be the same under the traditional and contribution format for manufacturing firms if they have a change in inventory levels during the accounting period.

Exercise 3 Expense Behavior Definitions. Define variable expense, fixed expense, and mixed expense two ways, in total and on a per-unit basis.

Exercise 4 Identifying Variable Expense Rate from Mixed Expense. Explain how the variable expense rate is computed from a mixed expense. Do not use numbers or computations; explain using only words.

Exercise 5 Contribution Income Statement Format. Explain how an income statement in the contribution format differs from a traditional income statement.

Problems

Problem 1 Contribution Margin. What is contribution margin? Explain how contribution margin can be used in evaluating whether or not to go into business.

Problem 2 Preparing a Contribution Margin Income Statement. Use the following data to prepare an income statement in good form using the contribution margin format for Safford Company for the month of September 2000.

Sales	$27,000
Fixed Expenses	$8,000
Contribution margin ratio	40%

Problem 3 Using the High-Low Method for Estimating Expenses. Vita Vista is trying to estimate her water cost for October 2000 for her produce business. During the last six months she has used the following quantities of water and incurred the related water costs.

Month	Quantity	Cost
April	110	$212
May	100	200
June	120	221
July	140	239
August	160	260
September	130	228

During October Ms. Vista expects to use 125 units of water. Determine her estimated water cost for October by using the high-low method of estimation.

Case 3-2

IDENTIFYING EXPENSE BEHAVIOR

Case Objectives

1. To understand the concepts of expense behavior and classification of expenses into variable, fixed, and mixed classifications.
2. To learn how to apply the high-low method to separate a mixed expense into fixed and variable components.

Requirements

1. As a student, you incur a variety of educational expenses, such as books, supplies, lab fees, computer fees, rent, parking, meal tickets, medical insurance, etc. Some of these expenses increase in proportion to the number of units for which you are enrolled and are called variable expenses. Other expenses are not dependent upon the specific number of units and are called fixed expenses. Drawing upon the above list of expense examples, identify in the spaces below three variable and three fixed expenses which are the result of your enrollment.

	Variable Expenses	Fixed Expenses
a.	_____	_____
b.	_____	_____
c.	_____	_____

2. Listed below are various expenses associated with a fleet of electric cars owned by City Courier Service, a company that delivers time-sensitive legal documents and small packages. Some of the listed expenses vary with the amount of service revenue earned by the company; others remain constant for changes in service revenue. For each expense item indicate whether it exhibits a fixed or variable expense behavior.

	Fixed	Variable
Electric power		
Depreciation		
Toll charges		
Battery maintenance		
Insurance premiums		
Tires		
Repairs and maintenance		

3. Some expenses behave in a mixed fashion, partly variable and partly fixed. The general manager of Movie-Ten, a multi-screen theater in Hollywood, has noticed that the monthly box office wage expense fluctuates significantly during the year. In general, wages appear to increase when ticket revenue increases, but not in direct proportion. The company's accountant has collected the following information for the previous six months (000's omitted). (When financial statements state "000's omitted", this means that the figures are stated in thousands. For example, revenue below for July is really $3,000,000 [3,000 thousands] and wages are really $33,000 [33 thousands].)

	Revenues	**Wages**
July	$3,000	$33.0
August	3,600	34.5
September	3,900	36.0
October	4,150	39.0
November	4,200	42.0
December	3,450	33.6

Using the high-low method illustrated in Case Reading 3-2, determine:

a. The variable portion of a monthly wage expense, expressed as a dollar rate per dollar of ticket revenue.

b. The fixed portion of a monthly wage expense, expressed as a lump sum amount.

c. Combine the results of (a) and (b) into a mixed expense formula of the following format:

Monthly wage expense = Fixed expense per month + (Variable rate × Ticket revenue)

d. Use the formula in (c) to calculate the expected wage expense for January of the following year when theater revenues are expected to be $5,000,000 due to the release of several Titanic-type movies.

4. Ice cream companies experience more business in the summer months than in the winter months. Using the graphs below with dollars on the vertical (y) axis and number of gallons of ice cream sold on the horizontal (x) axis, draw what you think would be the behavior of the following three expenses (costs):

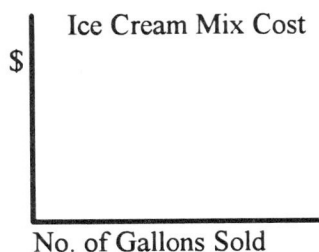

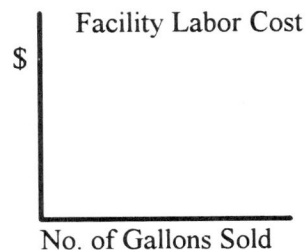

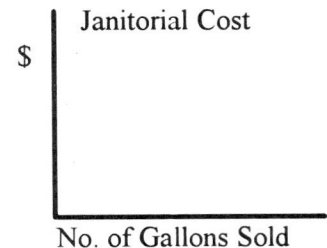

Ice Cream Mix Cost	Facility Labor Cost	Janitorial Cost
$	$	$
No. of Gallons Sold	No. of Gallons Sold	No. of Gallons Sold

Note: Assume that the above graphs are portraying the costs on a monthly basis. In the winter months, the number of gallons sold is toward the left end of the x axis. In the summer months, the number of gallons sold would tend toward the right side of the x axis.

Case Reading 3-3

PROFITABILITY ANALYSIS

INTRODUCTION

In Case Reading 3-2 the concept of cost behavior and how it is used for planning purposes was covered. In this case reading the contribution income statement will be revisited and the concepts of cost behavior will be extended to include breakeven analysis and target profit, both before and after taxes. The return-on-equity ratio will be reviewed again with emphasis on how this calculation might differ for the different forms of business.

BREAKEVEN ANALYSIS

Breakeven analysis is used to determine the amount of sales at which there is zero profit or a target profit. The amount of sales at which there is zero profit is called the **breakeven point** or **breakeven sales**. At this point revenues and expenses are equal. An example of a contribution margin income statement at breakeven sales is shown in Exhibit 3-3.1.

Exhibit 3-3.1
Contribution Income Statement at Breakeven Sales

Contribution Income Statement at Breakeven	
Revenues	Unit Selling Price × Units Sold
Variable Expenses	Unit Variable Expenses × Units Sold
Contribution Margin	Unit Contribution Margin × Units Sold
Fixed Expenses	Less Fixed Expenses
Net Income	0

Notice that this is the same contribution income statement format from Case Reading 3-2 but, instead of showing a net income, the statement shows a zero profit.

The equation can be rewritten as follows:

$$\text{Unit contribution margin} \times \text{Units sold} = \text{Fixed expenses}$$
or

Breakeven Sales in Units = Fixed Expenses ÷ Contribution Margin per Unit

Using the same book example from Case Reading 3-2, the sales price per book was $40, the variable expenses were $25 per book and the fixed expenses were $5,400. Using the equation above, the number of units that must be sold in order to breakeven can be calculated.

Unit breakeven = Fixed expenses ÷ Contribution margin per unit
= $5,400 ÷ $15
= 360 books

That means that if the student sells 360 books, he/she will have just enough to cover expenses but there will not be any profit. Can the amount of sales dollars it takes to breakeven be calculated also?

The breakeven sales dollars can be calculated in two different ways:

1. The 360 breakeven units can be multiplied by the selling price to calculate breakeven sales dollars.

    360 × $40 selling price per book = $14,400; or

2. The contribution margin ratio can be used to calculate the sales dollars to breakeven:

Breakeven Sales in Dollars = Fixed Expenses ÷ Contribution Margin Ratio

    Breakeven sales = $5,400 ÷ 37.5%
                    = $14,400

The contribution income statement shown as Exhibit 3-3.2 is prepared at the breakeven number of units—360 books. Note how, at this $14,400 level of sales activity, the profit is zero and revenues and expenses are equal.

Exhibit 3-3.2
Proof of Breakeven

Contribution Income Statement Proof of Breakeven (Sales of 360 books)		
Revenues	$40 × 360 =	$ 14,400
Variable Expenses	$25 × 360 =	9,000
Contribution Margin	$15 × 360 =	5,400
Fixed Expenses		5,400
Net Income		$ 0

Once the company has reached its breakeven sales, for each additional sale, the contribution margin goes straight to profit.

What is the profit if we sell 361 books? For 361 books, the profit would be the contribution margin for one book over breakeven, or $15.

What is the profit if we sell 400 books? For 400 books, the profit would be the contribution margin for 40 books over breakeven, or 40 × $15 = $600.

We can prove that these profit calculations are correct by going back to our original equation and substituting for the assumed number of units as shown in Exhibit 3-3.3.

Exhibit 3-3.3
What if One More is Sold?

	360	361	400
Revenues	$ 14,400	$ 14,440	$ 16,000
Variable Expenses	9,000	9,025	10,000
Contribution Margin	5,400	5,415	6,000
Fixed Expenses	5,400	5,400	5,400
Net Income	$ 0	$ 15	$ 600

Alternatively, we can use the contribution margin ratio. For each dollar over breakeven sales of $14,400, 37.5 percent goes to profit.

An extra $40 of sales would cause an additional $37.5\% \times \$40$, or $15 of profit.

An extra $1,600 of sales would create an additional profit of 37.5 percent of $1,600, or $600.

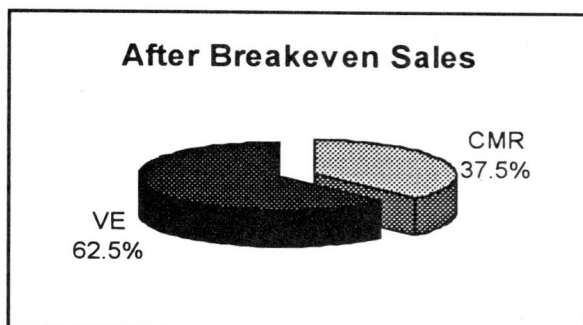

After Breakeven Sales

CMR 37.5%

VE 62.5%

After reaching breakeven sales, for every extra dollar of sales the percentage of the additional sales that will go toward profit is equal to the contribution margin ratio.

TARGET PROFIT

Most business owners want to earn a specific, realistic profit called a **target profit** and want to know the sales needed in order to obtain that target profit goal. This type of calculation is very similar to a breakeven calculation. The target profit that the company wants to make is added to the numerator of the equation. Suppose in our book example, the student wants to calculate how many books must be sold in order to earn a target profit of $17,100. The sales needed to attain a target profit are called **target sales**. The target sales can be calculated in units or in sales dollars.

$$\text{Target sales in units} = \frac{\text{Fixed expenses} + \text{Target profit}}{\text{Contribution margin per unit}} = \frac{\$5,400 + \$17,100}{\$15} = 1,500 \text{ units}$$

$$\text{Target sales in dollars} = \frac{\text{Fixed expenses} + \text{Target profit}}{\text{Contribution margin ratio}} = \frac{\$5,400 + \$17,100}{37.5\%} = \$60,000$$

We could also calculate the $60,000 by multiplying the 1,500 target sales units by the $40 sales price per unit.

Exhibit 3-3.4
Target Sales of $1,500 books

Contribution Income Statement (Target Sales of 1,500 books)		
Revenues	$40 × 1,500 =	$ 60,000
Variable Expenses	$25 × 1,500 =	37,500
Contribution Margin	$15 × 1,500 =	22,500
Fixed Expenses		5,400
Net Income		$ 17,100

Taxes and Target Profit

Because income taxes are an economic fact of life, the business owner must consider tax effects in planning. The assessment of income taxes on a business depends on the organizational form of business. Sole proprietorships or partnerships are not subject to federal income tax. The income from such businesses flows through to the owners and is reported on their personal tax returns. However, corporations are considered in the federal tax law to be taxpayers, and they are subject to federal income taxes.

Regardless of the form of organization, taxes fall on the owners. Therefore, target profit is usually thought of as the final return on equity (ROE) after taxes. To simplify this very complex area of the tax code, let us assume that our continuing example is one where the owner must pay 30 percent of the profit as taxes, whether it is paid by the owner or the owner's corporation. Recall that the target profit in the example was $17,100. What profit *before taxes* must be earned in order to have a profit of $17,100 *after taxes*? The formula is:

$$\text{Target profit before tax} = \frac{\text{Target profit after tax}}{1 - \text{Tax rate}}$$

$$\text{Target profit before tax} = \frac{\$17,100}{1 - .30} = \$24,429$$

To earn $17,100 after taxes, $24,429 must be the profit before tax. Thus the target sales necessary to reach this goal is computed as follows:

$$\text{Target sales} = \frac{\text{Fixed expenses} + \text{Target profit before tax}}{\text{Contribution margin ratio}}$$

$$\text{Target sales} = \frac{\$5,400 + \$24,429}{37.5\%} = \$79,544$$

Taxes must be considered in establishing target revenue; thus, business owners usually take taxes into account when setting profit goals that will provide a return on equity (ROE) which makes the investment reasonable in relation to opportunity cost and risk.

INDUSTRY CHARACTERISTICS

Some types of businesses, such as passenger air carriers, typically have low variable expenses. Processing tickets and in-flight food and drink are examples of common variable expenses. The contribution margin for the airlines is very high, but it needs to be because the airlines have very high fixed expenses such as salaries, depreciation on the airplanes, fuel, etc. Once a breakeven number of passengers are ticketed, every new passenger contributes his/her contribution margin directly to net income. In 1998, airline profits set new records largely because most planes flew at full capacity.

K-Mart is an example of a company that has high variable expenses mostly due to the cost of the inventory sold. Because of the high variable expenses, K-Mart has a low contribution margin. For this reason, the company needs to sell a large volume of merchandise to cover fixed expenses. Advertised specials sometimes are "loss leaders." which are designed to increase store traffic and thereby increase sales of regularly priced merchandise.

THE CORLISS ACCOUNTING FIRM

To continue the Corliss Accounting Firm example, the contribution income statement shown in Exhibit 3-2.4 from Case Reading 3-2 is reproduced below. The contribution margin ratio for Corliss was previously calculated at 54.81 percent.

$$\text{Contribution Margin Ratio} = \frac{\text{Contribution Margin}}{\text{Sales}} = \frac{\$2.850}{\$5.200} = 54.81\%$$

Corliss Accounting Firm Contribution Income Statement Month Ended June 30, 2000		
Revenues		
Fees Revenue		$ 5,200
Variable Expenses		
Wage Expense	$ 1,600	
Supplies Expense	750	
Total Variable Expenses		2,350
Contribution Margin		2,850
Fixed Expenses		
Depreciation Expense	200	
Insurance Expense	40	
Interest Expense	733	
Total Fixed Expenses		973
Net Income		$ 1,877

Devenie Corliss, the owner, is trying to determine the amount of fees she will need to generate in order to break even. As mentioned previously, the breakeven point is the point at which total revenues equal total expenses. In other words, it is the revenue amount at which there is zero profit. The following equation is needed to compute the breakeven revenue point.

$$\text{Breakeven revenue} = \frac{\text{Fixed expenses}}{\text{Contribution margin ratio}}$$

For Corliss Accounting Firm this equation would be

$$\text{Breakeven revenue} = \frac{\$973}{54.81\%} = \$1,775 \text{ per month}$$

This means that at revenue of $1,775 the company will have zero profit. A quick mathematical calculation can check to see if that amount is correct.

$$(\text{Contribution margin ratio} \times \text{Breakeven sales revenue}) - \text{Fixed Expenses} = 0$$

$$(54.81\% \times \$1,775) - \$973 = 0$$

$$\$973 - \$973 = 0$$

Target Revenue

Suppose that Devenie Corliss wants to compute how much revenue she would need in order to earn a profit of $2,000 per month after tax. Devenie has calculated that she will have an effective tax rate of 33.33 percent. Therefore, she will need to earn a profit before taxes of $3,000. That calculation is as follows:

$$\text{Target profit after tax} = \text{Target profit before tax} \times (1 - \text{tax rate of } 33.33\%)$$

$$\$2,000 = \text{Target profit before tax} \times 66.67\%$$

$$\text{Target profit before tax} = \$2,000 \div 66.67\% = \$3,000$$

The target revenue can be easily calculated by adding the target profit to the numerator as follows:

$$\text{Target revenue} = \frac{\text{Fixed expenses} + \text{Target profit before tax}}{\text{Contribution margin ratio}}$$

For Corliss the equation would be as follows:

$$\text{Target revenue} = \frac{\$973 + \$3,000}{54.81\%} = \$7,249$$

This shows that if revenue were $7,249, Corliss would earn a profit before tax of $3,000 and have net income of $2,000 after tax. This kind of information can be extremely helpful during the planning process.

RETURN ON EQUITY (ROE)

To determine how much of a return they have earned on their investment, owners can compute their **return on equity**. This is computed by dividing net income by average owners' equity. Average owners' equity is calculated by adding beginning and ending equity and dividing by two.

$$\text{Return on equity} = \frac{\text{Net income}}{\text{Average total owner's equity}}$$

Returning to the Corliss Accounting Firm example, the return on equity for the month of June can easily be calculated. In Case Reading 2-1, Corliss Accounting Firm had the following financial information for the month of June.

	May 31	June 30
Contributed capital	$50,000	$50,000
Retained earnings	0	877
Total owner's equity	$50,000	$50,877
Net income		$1,877

Remembering that May 31 figures become the beginning balances at June 1, return on equity (ROE) for Corliss is computed by completing the following calculation:

$$\text{ROE} = \frac{\$1,877}{(\$50,000 + \$50,877) \div 2} = 3.72\%$$

This calculation is only for the month of June. It can be annualized by multiplying it by 12.

$$3.72\% \times 12 = 44.64\% \text{ annual return}$$

In order to determine if this is a good return, a company will compare its current return with the past year's return on equity as well as look at the rate of return for other companies in the same industry. Several companies such as Dun and Bradstreet, Moody's, and others publish books which list financial figures, including ratios, for many different industries. These books should be readily available in your college library.

At first glance, a return of 44.64 percent looks excellent. Industry norms for accounting firms show that the average return on equity is 31 percent. Before we celebrate, however, let's discuss how salaries of the owner are treated for sole proprietorships and partnerships.

Salaries of Owners

Sole Proprietorships

The income statement of a sole proprietorship will usually not show any salaries expense related to work done by the owner. Any salaries or wages listed on the income statement are those of non-owners. It should be understood that some of the net income represents compensation for services provided by the owner—money that would have to be paid to someone else if the owner did not do the work. In our example, Corliss Accounting Firm is a sole proprietorship and Devenie Corliss, the owner, works in the business. Let's suppose a reasonable wage for the month for Devenie Corliss would be $1,800 ($21,600 per year). In that case, return on equity for the month after considering a reasonable salary for her work would be

$$\frac{\text{Net income} - \text{Reasonable salary}}{\text{Average owner's equity}} = \frac{\$1,877 - \$1,800}{\$50,439} = \frac{\$77}{\$50,439} = .0015 = .15\%$$

Annualized, that return on equity is .15% × 12 = 1.8%. Does that calculation make you less enthusiastic about the "success" of her accounting firm?

Partnerships

Partnerships are similar to sole proprietorships in that any work done by the partners in the business is not shown on the income statement as salaries expense. Generally, if one of the partners works in the business, the partnership agreement will state that the working partner will be compensated for his or her work first before any earnings (or losses) are distributed to the other partners. To determine a return on owners' equity for a partnership, you would consider the salary of the working partner in the same way as we did the salary of the owner of Corliss Accounting Firm.

Corporations

Owners of a corporation are called shareholders or stockholders. A corporation's income statement differs from that of a sole proprietorship or a partnership in that salaries expense on a corporation's income statement reflects the salaries for all people who work for the corporation, including any shareholders.

The return on owners' equity for a corporation is called return on stockholders' equity. The calculation of the return on stockholders' equity would already take into consideration the salaries of the owners as this expense was already deducted in the computation of net income. Corporations also have one additional expense called income tax expense. You will learn more about that in Case Reading 3-5.

Industry Norms

When using industry norms for comparison of one company's return on equity with another company's return, it is imperative that you determine first whether the company is a sole proprietorship, a partnership, or a corporation. Salaries of the owner are shown as expenses on the income statement only if the business is a corporation. For this reason, you would expect return on equity for a sole proprietorship to be higher than ROE for a comparable corporation, all other things being equal, because of the way owners' salaries are treated in the computation of net income. You can compensate for this by adjusting net income of a sole proprietor or a partnership for a reasonable amount of owner salaries before computing the return on equity and comparing it to industry data.

SUMMARY

This case reading begins with a discussion of breakeven sales. Target revenue is also explained as a useful aid in planning the future performance of the business. The effect of taxes when projecting target revenue is considered as well. When judging the performance of a company, one common measurement is the concept of return on equity. Return on equity depends on the calculation of net income, which can vary depending on the form of business organization. This case reading discusses how the return on equity of a partnership or proprietorship can be adjusted so that it is comparable to the return on equity for a corporation by adjusting for salaries of the owner. This additional analysis is needed to judge whether the business is earning a sufficient return on equity by including the opportunity cost of the owner working in another occupation.

EXERCISES AND PROBLEMS

Exercises

Exercise 1 Breakeven Point Evaluation. Explain what the breakeven sales point represents. How may breakeven sales be used in evaluating the business prospects of a company?

Exercise 2 Source of Breakeven Sales Information. What information from a contribution income statement is used to determine breakeven sales? How is this information used to determine breakeven sales?

Exercise 3 Using Target Profit in Determining Target Revenues. Target profit is often used to determine the target revenue needed to earn a certain profit goal. Explain how target revenue can be used in evaluating the prospects of a proposed new business.

Exercise 4 Sources of Data for Return on Equity Computation. Return on equity is the result of dividing one number by another. What are the sources of the two numbers? Be as specific as you can in identifying the sources of the numbers.

Exercise 5 Adjusting Return on Equity for Different Forms of Organizations. When comparing return on equity of a proprietorship and a corporation it is necessary to adjust the net income figure(s) to make them comparable. What adjustment is needed and why is it necessary to make this adjustment?

Problems

Problem 1 Determining Breakeven Sales Revenues. Following is a contribution income statement for Riesgo Company, a proprietorship. Based on this income statement, determine the breakeven sales revenue for the year.

Riesgo Company
Contribution Income Statement
For a Typical Month

Sales		$30,000
Variable Expenses:		
Salaries	$14,000	
Supplies	4,000	
Total Variable Expenses		18,000
Contribution Margin		12,000
Fixed Expenses:		
Depreciation	3,000	
Rent	3,500	
Other Fixed Expenses	1,500	
Total Fixed Expenses		8,000
Net Income (before taxes)		$ 4,000

Problem 2 Determining Target Revenue. Use the data in Problem 1 to determine the target revenue needed to earn net income of $7,500 a month. Show all computations.

Problem 3 Computing Return on Equity. Refer to the data in Problem 1. Assume that Riesgo Company had $98,000 of owner's equity at the beginning of the month and $102,000 at the end of the month. What was Riesgo Company's return on equity for the month? Show all computations.

Problem 4 Evaluating Return on Equity. Using the data in Problem 1, evaluate how well Riesgo Company is doing assuming Richard Riesgo, the owner, could earn $2,500 per month working for another company. How does this change the return on equity?

Problem 5 Estimating Breakeven Sales Revenues for a Year. Mr. I. R Green is planning to start a nursery business. He estimated that he can sell plants for an average of $5 each. His variable costs will average 60 percent of the plant sales revenues. He estimates his fixed expenses to be $3,000 a month. Based on this data, what is Mr. Green's breakeven revenue for a year?

Problem 6 Effect of Sales Beyond Breakeven Point. Refer to Problem 5. What is Mr. Green's expected net income if he sells one plant more than breakeven revenues? Show your reasoning. What net income or loss will result if 25,000 plant units are sold during a year?

Case 3-3

THE J & J PARTNERSHIP

Case Objectives

1. To understand how to develop a planned (estimated) contribution income statement broken down by business segments (departments).
2. To understand how to use the information in a contribution income statement to compute a breakeven point.
3. To understand the partnership form of business organization.

Decision: Should John and Joanna form a partnership?

During his sophomore spring break, John met Joanna at a ski resort in the Lake Tahoe area. Riding on the chairlift together, John learned that Joanna grew up in the same small town as he did. Halfway up the mountain, the lift came to a stop. While waiting for the lift to restart, their conversation spanned school, summer jobs, and career goals. Joanna mentioned that she had completed three courses in interior design and planned a career in that field. John described the painting business that he started the previous summer. He also indicated that he was studying business at his college.

At the bottom of the slope, Joanna began to think more about her plans for the following summer and whether she could set up a decorating and interior design business like John's. She wanted to accumulate enough money to continue her studies at the Evanston School of Architecture and Design. Instead of starting a business, a safer alternative would be to get a summer job.

That same evening, she came across a newspaper article that gave her an idea. The story stated that due to high real estate prices, many homeowners were remodeling and repairing their homes rather than moving to larger or newer homes. She wondered if John would be interested in a partnership that would offer both exterior house painting as well as interior decorating.

Joanna found John at the lodge. She showed him the article and told him of her idea for a business partnership. John offered the benefit of his experience. "The painting business was not lucrative, although I made a reasonable profit—better than a summer job." He remembered that about half his customers were also planning to do interior refurbishing of one type or another. Joanna hypothesized that her customers could also be in need of exterior painting. They agreed that the business partnership could consist of two departments that would complement each other.

The next day John and Joanna held a work session to try to decide whether this business venture had a good probability of financial success. John asked Joanna, "What is your estimate of how much business you could do June through August?" She jotted down the following:

Estimated number of projects:
Six new customers and six of John's previous customers.......... 12
Average fee per project.. $1,300

He then asked what expenses she expected to incur. After much discussion, she came up with the following list:

Expense of decorating materials..43% of the fee
Expense of consumable supplies .... 6% of the fee
Wages for hired help..11% of the fee

Joanna asked John, "Based on your experience, do you think these estimates are reasonable?" He thought they were.

"The key decision is whether our business venture will generate a profit that is better than what each of our summer jobs pay us," John added. "I know I could earn $900 per month for the three summer months. Let's assume you could earn the same."

Joanna responded, "That means the business must have a profit of at least $1,800 per month for three months to make this a beneficial venture."

"That's not all—what about the interest each of us could earn if the money invested in the business were in the bank instead, and need I mention that we have a lot more risk of losing our money in this business venture than if the money were tucked away in some big, solid bank," John said with a worried look.

With an optimistic tone Joanna stated, "OK, let's determine what interest we could earn from the bank and adjust that amount upward to compensate us for the added risk of the venture. The combined summer pay plus the lost interest will be the minimum amount of profit the business must generate in order for us to commit to the venture."

John and Joanna agreed that the next step was to gather data that would help them forecast the profit of their possible partnership. To add to the expense data supplied by Joanna, John produced the following income statement for the first summer of his painting business.

John's Painting Business Income Statement Three Months Ended August 31, 1999		
Fees Revenue		$11,800
Variable Expenses		
Paint	$3,850	
Supplies	430	4,280
Contribution Margin		$7,520
Fixed Expenses:		
Insurance	$ 550	
Interest (3 months)	74	
Advertising	990	
Depreciation (one year)	3,113	4,727
Net Income		$2,793

Joanna remarked that earning a profit of 24 percent of the fees revenue seemed pretty good. She wondered what the interior decorating profit would be.

John next presented his projected balance sheet as of May 31, 2000.

John's Painting Business **Projected Balance Sheet** **May 31, 2000**				
Assets		**Liabilities & Owner's Equity**		
Current Assets		Current Liabilities		
Cash	$ 6,061	Notes Payable		$ 3,300
Supplies	95	Interest Payable		223
Total Current Assets	6,156	Total Current Liabilities		3,523
Fixed Assets		Owner's Equity		
Ladders	$ 424	Contributed Capital	$ 11,600	
Compressors	1,696	Retained Earnings	120	
Trucks	6,967	Total Owner's Equity		11,720
Total Fixed Assets	9,087			
Total Assets	$ 15,243	Total Liabilities and Owner's Equity		$ 15,243

Calculations:

Ladders' book value = $600 – [($600 – $72) ÷ 3 years] = $424

Compressor's book value = $2,400 – [($2,400 – $288) ÷ 3 years] = $1,696

Truck's book value = $9,200 – [($9,200 – $2,500) ÷ 3 years] = $6,967

Interest payable = $3,300 × .09 × 9/12 = $223 (September through May)

Owner's equity = $13,193 – 1,250 – 223 = $11,720

Note: The cash balance at August 31, 1999, was $6,660 (see Case 2-6). In early September 1999, John paid his uncle the $74 interest owed at August 31. Also, in September and October, he collected the $1,300 in accounts receivable and paid the $575 in liabilities that appeared on his August 31, 1999, balance sheet (see Case 2-2). Finally, during the fall and winter, he withdrew a total of $1,250 in cash for personal uses. Hence, the cash balance at May 31 is $6,660 – $74 + $1,300 – $575 – $1,250 = $6,061.

John proposed that Joanna invest $11,720 in the business, the same amount that he will have invested as of June 1 (John's owner's equity at May 31, 2000) and that they share profits equally. Joanna agreed to both of these partnership provisions.

John expected Joanna to be startled by the amount of money she would have to invest. However, she remarked, "At least I'll be able to invest some of my Aunt Bertha's inheritance money at more than the 3 percent the bank has been giving me."

Joanna went on to suggest that she had only considered variable expenses in her projected list of expenses. "I wouldn't have the equipment needs your painting business does, but I would have advertising, insurance, a business license, and so forth," she said.

John replied that while his variable expenses (paint and supplies) were a constant percentage of sales and that the depreciation wouldn't change, some of his expenses would be affected by the combination of the two businesses. "My truck should be able to haul both my paint equipment and your decorating materials," he said. "We need to consider our shared costs of insurance and advertising, though. And I can't go another summer without a business license."

Together John and Joanna made careful estimates of the fixed expenses for their combined enterprise.

Projected Fixed Expenses for J & J Partnership

Depreciation (one year - straight line)	$3,113
Advertising	2,200
Insurance	1,100
Interest (3 months)	74
Annual business license	120
Equipment rental	1,550
Total	$8,157

John and Joanna agreed that they each had a lot of information to consider. They planned to meet later in the week to make a decision whether or not to pursue this business venture which would be called J & J Partnership.

Requirements

Use the contribution income statement format shown at the end of this case to complete the requirements below. You must use a computer spreadsheet to complete this problem. Round the percentages to the nearest hundredth (XX.XX%) of a percent and round dollars to the nearest dollar.

a.   John's income statement for 1999 shown in the case states that John's variable expenses are paint and painting supplies. State each of these variable expenses as a percentage of John's sales. Compute the contribution margin ratio for John's Painting Business for 1999.

b.   Record the variable expense percentage for Joanna's variable expenses in your spreadsheet as well. Assuming John and Joanna form a partnership, compute the projected contribution margin for the three months ended August 31, 2000, for the painting department and the decorating department. Assume that John's fees revenue are 40 percent more than those shown in the case due to an increase in painting volume (the number of paint jobs) and that the decorating fees and expense estimates made by Joanna are realistic. Compute the contribution margin ratio for each department.

c.   Assuming John and Joanna form a partnership, prepare a projected contribution income statement for the company as a whole for the three months ended August 31, 2000. The contribution income statement for the partnership is computed by summing the two departments. This income statement, however, should also include fixed expenses and the computation of net income. Use one year's depreciation and three month's interest.

d. Compute the contribution margin ratio for J & J Partnership.

e. Calculate breakeven sales for the partnership.

In completing this assignment, you will need to fill in all cells which have Xs in them. This assignment needs to be completed on a spreadsheet.

	A	B	C	D	E	F	G
1				Painting	PROJECTED PARTNERSHIP		
2			Variable Expense Percentage	8/31/99	Painting	Decorating	TOTAL
3		Fees Revenue		$ 11,800	$X,XXX	$X,XXX	$X,XXX
4		Variable Expenses					
5		Paint	XX.XX%	3,850	$X,XXX		$X,XXX
6		Painting Supplies	XX.XX%	430	$X,XXX		$X,XXX
7		Decorating Materials	XX.XX%			$X,XXX	$X,XXX
8		Wages	XX.XX%			$X,XXX	$X,XXX
9		Decorating Supplies	XX.XX%			$X,XXX	$X,XXX
10		Total Variable Expenses		4,280	$X,XXX	$X,XXX	$X,XXX
11		Contribution Margin		$ 7,520	$X,XXX	$X,XXX	$X,XXX
12		Fixed Expenses					
13		Depreciation					$X,XXX
14		Advertising					$X,XXX
15		Insurance					$X,XXX
16		Interest					$X,XXX
17		Annual Business License					$X,XXX
18		Equipment rental					$X,XXX
19							
20		Total Fixed Expenses					$X,XXX
21							
22		Net Income					$X,XXX
23							
24		Contribution Margin Ratio		XX.XX%	XX.XX%	XX.XX%	XX.XX%
25							
26		Breakeven Sales					$XX,XXX

After completing this homework assignment, make sure you save your file on a disk because you will be using this file again in Case 3-4 and Case 3-6.

Group Assignment 3-3

WHAT IS YOUR CONTRIBUTION?

Group Number _____ Group members present and participating:

_____

_____

Objectives

1. To understand how to develop a planned (estimated) contribution income statement broken down by business segments (departments).
2. To understand how to use the information in a contribution income statement to compute a breakeven point.
3. To understand the concept of return on equity.
4. To understand the partnership form of business organization.

Requirements

Based upon your group's deliberation of Case 3-3, record the consensus answers below.

1. What is your group's consensus answer for each department's projected contribution margin and J & J's total projected net income for the three summer months in 2000?

   Contribution Margin for Painting =   _____

   Contribution Margin for Decorating =   _____

   Projected Net Income for Partnership = _____

2. What is J & J's expected return on equity given your results in Requirement 1? (Assume that all profits are withdrawn by the partners, and therefore beginning and ending equity are each equal to $23,440.) Show all calculations.

_____

_____

_____

_____

3. Do you think that the J & J business is a good venture? Why? Would an economist who is concerned with opportunity costs agree? Supply supporting computations.

_____

_____

_____

_____

_____

_____

4. At what dollar level of sales, assuming a constant sales mix, will J & J break even?

Breakeven for J & J Partnership = _____

5. As part of their planning activities, John and Joanna are considering the possibility of increasing the planned amount to be spent on advertising from their original estimate of $2,200 to $3,400. If the additional $1,200 would lead to an additional $8,000 in sales in either department, which department should they choose to emphasize in the additional advertising? Explain.

_____

_____

_____

_____

_____

_____

Case Reading 3-4

MULTIPLE PRODUCT ENTERPRISES

INTRODUCTION

In Case Reading 3-3, the simple case of a business with a single product or service was introduced. In preparation for the case which follows a technique called sensitivity analysis is used. With the use of a computer spreadsheet, it is easy and interesting to experiment with different forecast assumptions. This type of analysis provides insight into the possible scenarios facing a business. Another challenge is introduced by considering the effect of sales mix on multiple product enterprises. A discussion of the concept of operating leverage, which tells how profits react to changes in sales revenue, is also presented. John and Joanna are contemplating a partnership. They need to very carefully forecast how the combination of the interior decorating and the exterior house painting businesses will perform to provide satisfactory returns on their equities.

SENSITIVITY ANALYSIS

In business planning, it is very helpful to prepare a contribution income statement at several different levels of sales volume. This type of analysis is called **sensitivity analysis**. It provides information showing how sensitive net income is to changes in sales volume. It also can give the business planner insight into how the operating leverage might be adjusted to achieve better financial results.

Assume the student government decides to publish a book of instructor evaluations by students at a university. The goal is to use profits from the book to pay for expenses for a rock concert. The variable expenses of the book are primarily printing; most of the labor is donated by volunteers. Data for the publication is provided as follows:

Exhibit 3-4.1
Contribution Income Statement

	50 units	%
Sales	$ 150	100%
Variable Expense	30	20%
Contributed Margin	120	80%
Fixed Expenses	100	
Net Income	$ 20	

The variable expense ratio is calculated by dividing the variable expense of $30 by the sales amount of $150. The contribution margin ratio is calculated in a similar manner. Divide the contribution margin of $120 by sales of $150.

Suppose the student government thinks that the sales goal for next month should be $300. What would net income be then? Since sales would double, will net income double as well?

Exhibit 3-4.2 shows contribution income statement at the $300 sales amount.

Exhibit 3-4.2
Effect of Doubling Sales

	100 units	%
Sales	$ 300	100%
Variable Expense	60	20%
Contributed Margin	240	80%
Fixed Expensse	100	
Net Income	$ 140	

Net income at sales of $300 is actually seven times net income ($140 net income versus $20 net income in Exhibit 3-4.1) at sales of $150. This is primarily because the variable expense ratio is so low. Once the students have earned a profit for each publication after that, only 20 percent of it goes to variable expenses. The remaining 80 percent of it goes directly to profit because all fixed expenses have already been covered!

The variable expense of $60 in Exhibit 3-4.2 is calculated by multiplying the 20 percent variable expense ratio times the $300 sales amount. The contribution margin ratio can be calculated either by subtracting variable expense from sales or by multiplying the 80 percent contribution margin ratio by the sales amount.

What would net income be if it only reached 95 percent of the $300 goal? Suppose it exceeded that goal by 5 percent, what would net income be then?

Computer spreadsheets can be very helpful in calculating profit at these different sales levels. Once an income statement has been prepared at one level on a spreadsheet, the formulas can easily be copied for the new sales level. A sensitivity analysis for $300 in sales and for 95 and 105 percent of that sales amount is shown below as Exhibit 3-4.3.

Exhibit 3-4.3
Sensitivity Analysis

	95%	100%	105%
Sales	$ 285	$ 300	$ 315
Variable Expense	57	60	63
Contribution Margin	228	240	252
Fixed Expenses	100	100	100
Net Income	$ 128	$ 140	$ 152

To calculate the $285 sales, multiply the $300 sales times 95 percent. The same holds true for variable expenses. To calculate the $57 in variable expense, multiply 95 percent times the $60 variable expense. This expense would be 95 percent of the 100 percent variable expense because sales are 95 percent of that sales level. Alternatively, we can calculate the $57 by using the same variable expense percentage used at the 100 percent sales amount. When sales were $300, variable expenses were $60, or 20 percent of sales, so that same percentage must exist at all other sales levels as well. If sales are $285, variable expenses must be 20 percent of that amount, or $57.

To calculate sales in the 105% column, multiply 105 percent times the 100 percent sales of $300. For the variable expense of $63, multiply the 100 percent variable expense of $60 by 105 percent. Alternatively, this same amount could be computed by multiplying the 20 percent variable expense percentage by the sales amount of $315. Variable expense will always be 20 percent of the sales amount.

The fixed expense does not change; it remains fixed for all sales levels within the relevant range.

Is there a quicker way to compute profit at a given sales level without having to do a sensitivity analysis?

For any given company, after reaching the breakeven sales level, the contribution margin ratio can be multiplied by the sales amount over breakeven to determine the effect on profit of the increase in sales. For this company, which has a contribution margin ratio of 80 percent, every additional dollar of sales after breakeven will result in $.80 more profit. The other 20 percent or $.20 of the additional sales dollar goes toward variable expenses. In other words, for $15 more in sales, 80 percent of $15 or $12 goes to increase the profit.

What would net income be if sales were $400? $600?

A sensitivity analysis could be prepared for these two sales projections but is there a faster way to compute net income?

$$(\text{Contribution margin ratio} \times \text{Sales}) - \text{Fixed expenses} = \text{Net income}$$

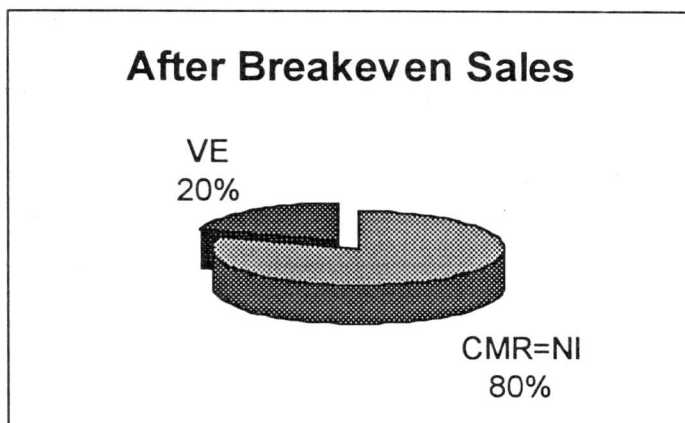

After Breakeven Sales

VE 20%

CMR=NI 80%

At $400 of sales, net income would be (80% × $400) – $100 = $220

At $600 of sales, net income would be (80% × $600) – $100 = $380

CORLISS ACCOUNTING FIRM EXAMPLE

Below is the contribution income statement for Corliss presented as Exhibit 3-2.4 from Case Reading 3-2.

Corliss Accounting Firm Contribution Income Statement Month Ended June 30, 2000		
Revenues		
Fees Revenue		$ 5,200
Variable Expenses		
Wage Expense	$ 1,600	
Supplies Expense	750	
Total Variable Expenses		2,350
Contribution Margin		2,850
Fixed Expenses		
Depreciation Expense	200	
Insurance Expense	40	
Interest Expense	733	
Total Fixed Expenses		973
Net Income		$ 1,877

Suppose Corliss wanted to know what net income would be if sales were 20 percent more or less than predicted. Exhibit 3-4.4 shows that sensitivity analysis. Once again, note that fixed expenses do not change. Also notice that each variable expense is the same percentage of revenue regardless of the sales level. In other words:

Wage expense percent = $1,280 ÷ $4,160 = $1,600 ÷ $5,200 = $1,920 ÷ $6,240 = 30.77%

Exhibit 3-4.4
Corliss Sensitivity Analysis

Corliss Accounting Firm Sensitivity Analysis			
	80%	100%	120%
Revenues			
Fees Revenue	$ 4,160	$ 5,200	$ 6,240
Variable Expenses			
Wage Expense	(1,280)	(1,600)	(1,920)
Supplies Expense	(600)	(750)	(900)
Total Variable Expenses	(1,880)	(2,350)	(2,820)
Contribution Margin	2,280	2,850	3,420
Fixed Expenses			
Depreciation Expense	(200)	(200)	(200)
Insurance Expense	(40)	(40)	(40)
Interest Expense	(733)	(733)	(733)
Total Fixed Expenses	(973)	(973)	(973)
Net Income	$ 1,307	$ 1,877	$ 2,447

ASSUMPTIONS USED IN OUR ANALYSIS

In the examples used to demonstrate profitability analysis, we have made several assumptions which are discussed in further detail below.

1. All expense behavior is either variable or fixed.
2. The company sells only one product.
3. There is no change in sales price during the period.

All Expense Behavior Is Either Variable Or Fixed

It is often difficult to classify specific expenses as variable or fixed all the time. In many situations, the graph of a specific variable or fixed expense may not be a straight line. For this reason, it is helpful to look at these expenses over the long-term versus a very short time span. For a short period such as a week it is difficult to turn the flow of expenses on or off with changes in sales. The time required to respond to changes in sales revenue is simply longer than one week. For a period of one month, it might be possible to control material costs in the planned relationship to sales, such as in a restaurant business. However, it may be difficult to control labor cost on a short-term basis simply because work schedules are set in advance. In spite of these practical difficulties, if the expense seems to vary proportionately with sales over the relevant range, then classify that expense as a variable expense. Managers and owners must then control the expenses accordingly. If the expense doesn't seem to vary in proportion to sales over the relevant range, then classify it as a fixed expense.

The Company Sells Only One Product

The previous examples were simplified in that they assumed that the company sells only one product. Most companies sell multiple products, but they are still able to use the cost-volume-**profit (CVP) analysis** model after some modifications. CVP analysis includes the set of techniques, including breakeven analysis, used in this case reading as well as Case Reading 3-3 to project levels of profitability and assess risk. If the company sells multiple products and wants to compute a breakeven point for the company as a whole, then it is meaningless to compute breakeven in units as there are many different product units being sold, all with their own set of expenses. In such cases, you first need to compute the monthly sales for all of your products combined.

In Group Assignment 3-1, Carla's Copies was introduced as a copy store offering three different products: black and white copies made by the customer, black and white copies made by Carla's employees, and color copies. The total sales for these products were presented in a monthly sales forecast, repeated below in Exhibit 3-4.5.

Exhibit 3-4.5
Sales Revenue by Product

Copies	Revenue per Copy	B/W Self Serve	B/W We Copy	Color	Total
25,000	$ 0.06	$ 1,500.00			$ 1,500.00
35,000	0.08		$ 2,800.00		2,800.00
5,000	1.00			$ 5,000.00	5,000.00
Total		$ 1,500.00	$ 2,800.00	$ 5,000.00	$ 9,300.00

Cost of goods sold was also presented and is repeated in Exhibit 3-4.6 below

Exhibit 3-4.6
Cost of Goods Sold by Product

Copies	COGS per Copy	B/W Self Serve	B/W We Copy	Color	Total
25,000	$ 0.02	$ 500.00			$ 500.00
35,000	0.03		$ 1,050.00		1,050.00
5,000	0.60			$ 3,000.00	3,000.00
Total		$ 500.00	$ 1,050.00	$ 3,000.00	$ 4,550.00
As a % of Revenue					48.92%

Cost of goods sold is one of several variable expenses. At almost 50 percent of sales, it clearly is a major expense that must be carefully controlled.

The table shown below as Exhibit 3-4.7 summarizes the relationships between cost of goods sold (a variable expense) and sales for each product line. Note that the color copies have a considerably higher cost of goods sold ratio.

Exhibit 3-4.7
Group Assignment 3-1 Cost of Goods Sold Relationships

Group Assignment 3-1 Cost of Goods Sold Relationships				
	B/W Self Serve	B/W We Copy	Color	Total
Sales	$ 1,500	$ 2,800	$ 5,000	$ 9,300
Cost of Goods Sold (COGS)	500	1,050	3,000	$ 4,550
COGS as % sales	33.33%	37.50%	60.00%	48.92%

The monthly information for individual sales and cost of goods sold can be annualized by multiplying by twelve as shown in Exhibit 3-4.8. The contribution margin ratio by product can then be computed.

Exhibit 3-4.8
Contribution Income Statement by Product

	B/W Self Serve	B/W We Copy	Color	Total
Sales	$ 18,000.00	$ 33,600.00	$ 60,000.00	$ 111,600.00
Variable Expenses				
Cost of Goods Sold	6,000.00	12,600.00	36,000.00	54,600.00
Wages and Taxes	1,476.29	2,755.74	4,920.97	9,153.00
Utilities	360.00	672.00	1,200.00	2,232.00
Supplies	180.00	336.00	600.00	1,116.00
Other	36.00	67.20	120.00	223.20
Total Variable Expenses	8,052.29	16,430.94	42,840.97	67,324.20
Contribution Margin	9,947.71	17,169.06	17,159.03	44,275.80
Fixed Expenses				39,786.00
Net Income				$ 4,489.80
Contribution Margin Ratio	55.27%	51.10%	28.60%	39.67%
Breakeven Sales				$ 100,292

The cost of goods sold percentage for black and white copies - self serve is 33.33 percent of sales. Yearly sales for this product are $18,000, therefore cost of goods sold is $6,000, computed by taking 33.33 percent times the $18,000 sales of that product. Similar calculations are made for the other two products. Total cost of goods sold is the sum of cost of goods sold for all products.

The remaining variable expenses are assumed to have the same variable expense relationships as in Group Assignment 3-1; that is, for each product, wages and taxes are 8.2 percent (This is a rounded percentage. The actual percentage used is 8.2043%.) of sales for each product, utilities are 2 percent, supplies are 1 percent and other variable expenses are .2 percent. Given these relationships, the contribution margin ratio for each product and for the company as a whole is then calculated. Exhibit 3-4.8 shows that the black and white self serve copies has the highest contribution margin ratio (55.27%) and that the color copies have the lowest contribution margin ratio (28.60%). The contribution margin ratio of 39.67 percent used in the breakeven calculation is a weighted average of contribution margin ratio of the three products.

In Group Assignment 3-1, breakeven sales for Carla's Copies were calculated to be $100,292 per year. The computation for breakeven sales is as follows:

$$\frac{\text{Fixed Expenses}}{\text{Contribution Margin Ratio}} = \frac{\$39,786}{39.67\%} = \text{Breakeven sales of } \$100,292$$

This breakeven calculation is for total company sales (all products). It is often more helpful to know the sales that are expected in each product line. For example, how many color copies do I need to sell? Black and white self-serve? Black and white we copy? This individual product line information can be computed after a calculation of the company's sales mix, explained next.

Sales Mix

A company's **sales mix** includes the combination of products that make up a company's total sales. If a company has more than one product, the breakeven sales dollars for the company as a whole are allocated to the individual products based on that product's percentage of total sales. For example, if one product generates 40 percent of the total company sales, that product would be responsible for generating 40 percent of breakeven sales.

For Carla's Copies, the forecast sales mix is as shown in Exhibit 3-4.9 follows:

Exhibit 3-4.9
Sales Mix for Carla's Copies
for Group Assignment 3-1

	Dollars	Percent
B/W copies - self serve	$ 18,000	16.13%
B/W copies - we copy	33,600	30.11%
Color copies	60,000	53.76%
Total Sales	$ 111,600	100.00%

Given these percentages, breakeven sales of $100,292 will be allocated to each product using those same sales mix percentages as shown in Exhibit 3-4.10.

Exhibit 3-4.10
Allocation of Breakeven to Individual Product Lines

	Dollars	Percent	Breakeven
B/W copies - self serve	$ 18,000	16.13%	$ 16,177
B/W copies - we copy	33,600	30.11%	30,198
Color copies	60,000	53.76%	53,917
Total Sales	$ 111,600	100.00%	$100,292

Because black and white copies self-serve represented 16.13 percent of the total sales, that product was given 16.13 percent of the breakeven sales, or $16,177. Note how the column for breakeven must total the total breakeven sales of $100,292. If actual total sales reached that amount, but the sales mix shifted in favor of color copies, a product with a much lower contribution margin ratio, a loss would result. In contrast, if more of the actual sales occurred in black and white copies self serve, a profit would result.

For multi-product companies, the sales mix computed is assumed to continue when the company performs profitability analysis using the contribution margin ratio. To illustrate the impact of sales mix changes on profit, let us suppose Carla's copies had sales of $102,000, which is greater than the breakeven of $100,292, previously calculated but that the sales mix changed as follows:

	Actual Sales of $102,000	Actual Sales Mix Percentage	Sales Mix Percentage per Exhibit 3-4.9
B/W Self Serve	$12,750	12.50%	16.13%
B/W We Copy	20,859	20.45%	30.11%
Color	68,391	67.05%	53.76%
Total	$102,000	100.00%	100.00%

Cost of goods sold can then be calculated by using the relationship as shown in Group Assignment 3-1. The cost of goods sold for the sales volume of $12,750 for black and white self-serve would result in a cost of goods sold of $4,250, computed by taking 33.33 percent times the $12,750 sales of that product. Similar calculations can be made for the other two products. Total cost of goods sold is merely the sum of cost of goods sold for all products.

The remaining variable expenses in Exhibit 3-4.11 are assumed to have the same variable expense relationships as in Group Assignment 3-1; that is, wages and taxes are 8.2 percent (rounded) of sales for each product, utilities are 2 percent, supplies are 1 percent, and other variable expenses are .2 percent. Fixed expenses are fixed so they do not change from the amount given in Exhibit 3-4.8. Net income (loss) can then be calculated for the $102,000 sales volume. This is computed in Exhibit 3-4.11 as a loss of $2,522.

Exhibit 3-4.11
Revised Sales Mix for Carla's Copies

	B/W Self Serve	B/W We Copy	Color	Total
Sales	$ 12,750.00	$ 20,859.00	$ 68,391.00	$ 102,000.00
Variable Expenses				
Cost of Goods Sold	4,250.00	7,822.13	41,034.60	53,106.73
Wages and Taxes	1,045.71	1,710.77	5,609.17	8,365.65
Utilities	255.00	417.18	1,367.82	2,040.00
Supplies	127.50	208.59	683.91	1,020.00
Other	25.50	41.72	136.78	204.00
Total Variable Expenses	5,703.71	10,200.39	48,832.28	64,736.38
Contribution Margin	7,046.29	10,658.61	19,558.72	37,263.62
Fixed Expenses				39,786.00
Net Income				$ (2,522.38)
Contribution Margin Ratio	55.27%	51.10%	28.60%	36.53%
Breakeven Sales				$ 108,913

Analysis of Sales Mix Changes

Exhibit 3-4.11 shows that even though the company had sales greater than the breakeven sales of $100,292 calculated in Group Assignment 3-1, they still incurred a net loss. The net loss is because the sales mix changed and the company is selling more color copies and less black and white copies than originally planned. This lowered the weighted average of the three contribution margins. Note that the color copies have a 28.6 percent contribution margin ratio, while the black and white copies have a 55.27 percent and a 51.10 percent contribution margin ratio for self serve and we copy respectively. A lower contribution margin ratio means that there are fewer dollars available to cover fixed expenses, because more of the sales revenue was absorbed by variable expenses.

The sales mix is very important in that some products contribute more dollars towards fixed expenses and profit (higher contribution margin ratio), while other products contribute less (lower contribution margin ratio). If your sales mix includes more of the higher contribution margin ratio products than originally planned, your breakeven sales will go down, but the opposite is also true. You will note that the sales mix changes also affect the contribution margin ratio for the company as a whole. The contribution margin ratio is 39.67 percent under the initial sales mix assumption, but under this sales mix assumption it is 36.53 percent. The revised breakeven is

Fixed Expenses ÷ Contribution margin ratio = $39,786 ÷ 36.53% = $108,913

Since the total sales of $102,000 were less than the revised breakeven sales of $108,913, the company had a net loss.

There is No Change in Sales Price During the Period

In our examples so far, only changes in sales volume and sales mix have been considered. In each instance, it was assumed that the sales price during the period did not change. In reality, sales prices are constantly changing and each increase or decrease of sales price has an effect on breakeven sales. If the sales price goes down but volume remains constant, the variable expense percentage will go up and the contribution margin ratio will go down. The result of this decrease in price will mean that more units have to be sold to break even. For example, lets go back to our example earlier in this case reading.

The contribution martin ratio is $2.40 ÷ $3 or 80 percent of book sales. Breakeven sales are $125 calculated by dividing fixed expenses of $100 by 80 percent, the contribution margin ratio. What happens if the sales price falls to $2.80 but the remaining expenses stay the same?

	Original $ per Unit	%	Revised $ per unit	%
Sales price	$3.00	100.00%	$2.80	100.00%
Variable exp.	.60	20.00%	.60	21.43%
CM	$2.40	80.00%	$2.20	78.57%

The revised contribution margin will be $2.20 ($2.80 − .60) and the revised contribution margin ratio will be 78.57 percent ($2.20 CM ÷ $2.80 sales). The new breakeven will be

$$\text{Breakeven} = \frac{\text{Fixed expenses}}{\text{Contribution margin ratio}} = \frac{\$100}{78.57\%} = \$127$$

If the sales price per unit falls to $2.80, the company needs sales of $127 to break even. The increase in the sales needed to break even ($127 vs. $125) is due to a change in the selling price of the product.

OPERATING LEVERAGE

In the previous examples the various effects of changes in sales revenue and variable expenses were analyzed. The company's ratio of fixed to variable expenses is also important. Companies with high fixed expenses and low variable expenses are said to be highly leveraged. **Operating leverage** is the degree to which profits or losses are magnified by changes in sales. This means that a small change in sales will have a large effect on net income. A company that has lower fixed expenses and higher variable expenses, that is, a company with less leverage, is not affected nearly as much by changes in sales volume. A business with a high operating leverage will see profits and losses increase and decrease disproportionately with similar changes in revenue. This occurs in businesses having a relatively low variable expense ratio.

High Operating Leverage

Exhibit 3-4.12 shows the Delta Company that has a variable expense ratio of 20 percent, which means the contribution margin ratio is 80 percent. The example shows the unit sales increasing by 20 percent from 50 to 60. However, the increase in income is 120 percent {($44 − $20) ÷ $20}. Income more than doubled. This is due to the very high contribution margin ratio of 80 percent.

Exhibit 3-4.12
Delta Company
High Operating Leverage

Contribution Income Statement				
	50 units	%	60 units	%
Revenues	$ 150	100%	$ 180	100%
Variable Expenses	30	20%	36	20%
Contribution Margin	120	80%	144	80%
Fixed Expenses	100		100	
Net Income	$ 20		$ 44	

Since most individuals have experience operating an automobile, think about the transmission as an analogy. If the car is kept in first gear, an increase in the throttle quickly accelerates the car. The reverse is also true. When the throttle is released, the car decelerates very quickly. This is analogous to a high operating leverage business whereby a small increase in sales generates a large increase in profit. In contrast, if the car is in the highway gear, a large change in the throttle will have some minor effect on the acceleration or deceleration; the response will not be nearly as sharp as the car in low gear. This is similar to a business with low operating leverage as illustrated in Exhibit 3-4.13. The diagram below shows that a company with high operating leverage will have higher highs but also lower lows.

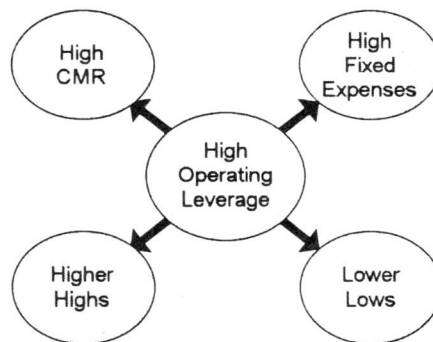

Low Operating Leverage

The Gamma Company's contribution income statement is shown in Exhibit 3-4.13. This company has a 60 percent variable expense ratio and $40 fixed expenses per month. The contribution margin of 40 percent and the fixed expenses of $40 are much lower than the previous example. Note that the $20 net income is the same as Delta's for the same level of sales, 50 units.

Exhibit 3-4.13
Gamma Company
Low Operating Leverage

Contribution Income Statement				
	50 units	%	60 units	%
Revenues	$ 150	100%	$ 180	100%
Variable Expenses	90	60%	108	60%
Contribution Margin	60	40%	72	40%
Fixed Expenses	40		40	
Net Income	$ 20		$ 32	

The same increase in sales of 10 units or 20 percent produces an increase in net income but one not nearly as dramatic as Delta's. Specifically, the increase in net income is 60 percent {($32 – $20) ÷ $20}. Income is only $32 as opposed to $44 for the Delta Company shown in Exhibit 3-4.12.

Many managers place the lowering of their company's breakeven point as a major goal of the organization. Why? Because, by lowering the breakeven sales level, there is less risk of a company reporting a net loss (or at least losing large amounts of net income) in an economic downturn. The airline industry is one example where managers work to lower breakeven sales levels. They have reduced counter and gate space in airports by entering into sharing arrangements with other airlines. Also, to improve operating leverage many airlines have reduced or eliminated food service during flight. A third strategy of some airlines, Southwest Airlines for example, is to minimize the time that the jet is on the ground. Southwest's success at doing this has reduced the variable cost per passenger dollar compared to other air carriers.

Software companies are good examples of companies with high operating leverage. For example, Microsoft's Windows 98 costs consumers about $95 to upgrade from Windows 95. No doubt Microsoft spent huge amounts to develop the improvements in the new release. These were fixed expenses under the category of research and development expense. The variable cost to produce and distribute a unit of the Windows 98 operating system is very likely less than $5. In other words, the contribution margin ratio for the Windows 98 product is extremely high (90 ÷ 95 = 94.7%). This is undoubtedly true of most of Microsoft's products. Microsoft Corporation is clearly a high operating leverage company, which could explain why Bill Gates' shares in Microsoft Corporation make him the wealthiest individual in the world.

In contrast, the fast food restaurant business is an example of a low operating leverage industry. Industry statistics show that food supplies, labor, and other variable expenses are approximately 80 percent of sales revenue. This means that the contribution margin ratio is a mere 20 percent, making for a higher breakeven point and slower profits growth. Perhaps this in part explains why restaurants are the types of businesses that are most likely to fail.

SUMMARY

Multi-product businesses require a special type of analysis to plan for target profits and breakeven points. Sales mix is a critical variable in evaluating actual performance versus the planned performance. A sales shift toward higher margin products will lower breakeven points, while a sales shift toward lower margin products will raise the breakeven point. The sales mix can also affect the operating leverage of a company. Its weighted-average contribution margin ratio is the result of the actual sales mix achieved. Industries exhibit vastly different operating leverage characteristics. Some have cost structures which are high fixed cost and low variable cost, while others have the reverse. Profit response to changes in sales revenue, up or down, can have dramatically different profit outcomes. In the case that follows John and Joanna must consider the sales mix that is likely if they merge their two businesses. You will be asked to decide if they are making the right decision.

EXERCISES AND PROBLEMS

Exercises

Exercise 1 Sensitivity Analysis. Define sensitivity analysis. Explain how sensitivity analysis may be used to make a business decision.

Exercise 2 Applying Sensitivity Analysis. Assume that Petite Company sells one product at a price of $10 per unit and that it has a contribution margin ratio of 30 percent. Petite also incurs $2,400 fixed expenses per month, which results in a breakeven point of $8,000 of monthly revenues. Using the simplest approach you can, what is the monthly profit if sales are expected to be $9,000? If sales are expected to be $12,000?

Exercise 3 Assumptions Used in Breakeven Analysis. In breakeven analysis and target profit analysis we have used three simplifying assumptions. Explain why we used these assumptions in our analysis.

Exercise 4 Sales Mix and Breakeven Analysis. In this case reading we introduced the concept of sales mix when doing breakeven analysis. How does sales mix change our breakeven point analysis? Explain briefly.

Exercise 5 Effects of High Operating Leverage. What is a major advantage of a company having high operating leverage? What is a major disadvantage of a company having high operating leverage?

Problems

Problem 1 Applying Sensitivity Analysis. Bumble Company had the following unit sales, revenues, and expenses for its first year of operations:

Units	500
Sales Revenues	$50,000
Variable Expenses	20,000
Contribution Margin	30,000
Fixed Expenses	42,000
Operating Loss	($12,000)

Betty Bumble is planning for her second year of operations. She has hired you to perform sensitivity analysis for her. She believes that she can sell 1,000 units during her second year of operations. She wants you to prepare an analysis for 1,000 units of sales and for sales of plus and minus 10 percent from the 1,000 units. Your analysis should be in a format similar to the income (loss) computation above.

Problem 2 Applying Operating Leverage. Refer to Problem 1. Is Bumble Company a highly leveraged company? For each $10,000 increase in revenues, how much can you expect net income to increase? Show computations and explain briefly.

Problem 3 Working with Sales Mix Breakeven. David Leon sells two types of electric golf carts. He purchases the carts new and then does some custom painting and minor modifications for the purchaser. One model, the Easy Rider, is sold for $2,000. The other model, the Double Eagle, is sold for $3,000. During 1999 he had the following sales and expenses.

	Easy Rider	Double Eagle	Total
Units Sold	100	60	160
Sales Revenues	$200,000	$180,000	$380,000
Variable Expenses:			
Purchase Cost of Carts	130,000	96,000	226,000
Modification Costs	20,000	20,000	40,000
Total Variable Expenses	150,000	116,000	266,000
Contribution Margin	$ 50,000	$ 64,000	114,000
Fixed Expenses			69,000
Net Income			$ 45,000

Based on the above information for the Leon Golf Cart, Ltd., determine (1) the breakeven sales for the company for 2000 assuming the same cost structure for the next year, and (2) how many units of each cart, the Easy Rider and the Double Eagle, will be sold at the breakeven point. Be sure to show your computations and reasoning.

Problem 4 Changes in Sales Mix Breakeven. Use the information from Problem 3 and assume that Leon Golf Cart, Ltd., sold 90 Easy Rider and 70 Double Eagle carts in 2000. Prepare (1) an income statement in the same format as the one in Problem 3 to determine how much net income was earned in 2000, and (2) determine the breakeven point for the company with the new sales mix.

Problem 5 Understanding Operating Leverage. Operating leverage concerns the relationship between revenue changes and changes in net income. An income statement is presented below for Riesgo Company. Using this data, determine whether Riesgo Company has high or low operating leverage. Explain your answer assuming a 10 percent increase in sales revenue.

Riesgo Company
Contribution Income Statement
For a Typical Month

Sales		$30,000
Variable Expenses:		
Salaries	$14,000	
Supplies	4,000	
Total Variable Expenses		18,000
Contribution Margin		12,000
Fixed Expenses:		
Depreciation	3,000	
Rent	3,500	
Other Fixed Expenses	1,500	
Total Fixed Expenses		8,000
Net Income (before taxes)		$ 4,000

Case 3-4

THE J & J CORPORATION

Case Objectives

1. To understand differences between the partnership and corporate forms of business organization and impacts on income measurement.
2. To gain practice in the use of sensitivity analysis in formulating a business plan.

Decision: Should John and Joanna form a corporation?

John was excited at the prospect of going into the painting and decorating venture with Joanna. But he still was unsure of what his decision would be. He sought out the advice of his uncle, Ernie Miller, who had loaned him the $3,300 to start his house painting business. Clearly John valued his uncle's input. Miller is employed by General Equipment Corporation as executive director of the Computer Assisted Design (CAD) Division. The division makes state-of-the-art manufacturing systems.

When John phoned Ernie, he described the details of his and Joanna's business idea and financial projections. "Well, Uncle, what do you think I should do?"

Ernie, known for being direct and somewhat opinionated, replied: "John, the number one rule in business is to make decisions based upon a clear and stated set of goals. Don't mix up economic reality with the delusion that this business venture could be fun, exciting, or even romantic. Most small businesses fail because the goals are more personal than economic. Now for a few specifics. First, in preparing a forecast of business profit, think of the worst-case scenario and run the numbers to see if the business still makes sense. For example, see what profits will be if your revenues are only 90 percent of the forecast."

"Second, make sure you have enough working capital to keep the business running. You'll probably have to pay for all of your supplies and labor up front, but your customers won't pay you until the job is done."

"Third, think hard about the partnership setup. If a conflict arises, you have one vote and your partner has one vote. How do you get past that point? Also, if one partner wants out, the business may have to be liquidated. Here's my solution: incorporate! Have J & J conduct its business as a corporation."

John thanked his uncle for the advice. He started to think about how his business would grow larger if it were organized as a corporation. He pondered the advice and concluded that he must come up with a counter proposal for Joanna. He continued to believe that the complementary lines of painting and decorating made good sense, were less risky, and offered more profit.

As John dialed Joanna's number, he reviewed the following points of his revised business plan:

1. A corporation should be formed as the legal entity providing painting and decorating services for clients.

2. He would invest the net assets of his sole proprietorship into the corporation (see Case 3-3, The J & J Partnership). Assume that the fair market value of the assets and liabilities is the same as that listed on the balance sheet for John's Painting Business.

3. The corporation would be capitalized as follows:

    John's investment of net assets $11,720
    Joanna's investment of cash... $11,720

4. The corporation will pay John and Joanna $2,700 each for their summer compensation ($900 per month, which they could have earned elsewhere).

Joanna answered on the second ring.

"Hello, Joanna, this is John. Do you have a few minutes?"

"Sure, John, what's up?" Joanna replied.

"I have a suggestion about our business venture." he said. "Can we meet tomorrow?"

Requirements

1. Open the spreadsheet file you used in Case 3-3. Use the Save As command to save the file under a different filename. What changes to projected income would there be if John and Joanna decided to incorporate? Assume that John and Joanna are each paid a salary of $2,700, which is a fixed expense. Make all necessary changes on the spreadsheet to reflect the incorporation.

2. On the same spreadsheet, prepare projected statements (income before taxes) for the corporation in total for the three month period June-August, 2000, under each of the following assumptions:

    a. 100 percent of the sales estimated in Case 3-3 will be realized. Also, salaries of $5,400 will be deducted as an additional corporate (fixed) expense.

    b. 90 percent of the sales estimated in Case 3-3 will be realized. Also, salaries of $5,400 will be deducted as an additional corporate (fixed) expense.

    c. 110 percent of the sales estimated in Case 3-3 will be realized. Also, salaries of $5,400 will be deducted as an additional corporate (fixed) expense.

3. What is the new breakeven point (in sales dollars) for the corporation as a whole? What amount of dollar sales must each department have to reach this breakeven point? (Hint: After computing the breakeven sales dollars for the corporation as a whole, allocate the breakeven sales dollars to each department on the basis of that department's percentage of total sales.) For example, if the painting department's sales were 70 percent of the total sales, then they would be allocated 70 percent of the breakeven point. Show computations on your computer's spreadsheet.

4. Use a spreadsheet to prepare a projected beginning balance sheet for the J & J Corporation as of May 31, 2000, to reflect incorporation and the addition of Joanna as a shareholder. Specify any assumptions you make in drafting the balance sheet.

5. Compute the return on equity for J & J Corporation at each of the different sales volume levels considered in Requirement 2. Use the equity computed in Requirement 4 as your average equity. Ignore income taxes.

Save this spreadsheet file because it will be used again for Case 3-6.

Case Reading 3-5

LEGAL AND TAX CONSIDERATIONS FOR BUSINESS OWNERS

INTRODUCTION

The owners' equity section of the balance sheet is a primary report to investors communicating the status of their financial stake in the business. The presentation of that part of the balance sheet depends on the type of legal organization the owners have chosen. The overall business strategy is the product of many decisions, among them are tax consequences and exposure of personal assets to business losses. This case reading is intended to prepare you for the following case in which investors need to determine the best legal form of organization to select.

FORMS OF BUSINESS ORGANIZATION

There are three basic forms of business organizations: sole proprietorships, partnerships, and corporations. According to the entity concept, all forms of businesses are considered to be entities separate and distinct from their owners. This accounting principle requires the financial statements of the business to reflect only the activities of that business. For example, Devenie Corliss owns personal assets separate and distinct from Corliss Accounting Firm. Any financial statement prepared for her business will not include her personal assets or personal liabilities. The name of the entity for which the statements have been prepared will be clearly identified in the heading of the financial statement. Regardless of the organization's form, financial transactions for the business are kept separate from those of its owner(s).

To fully understand the unique characteristics of the three business forms, the following factors need to be considered:

- The number of owners
- Life of the entity
- Owner's personal liability for the business's debts
- Ease of accumulating capital
- Income statement presentation of owners' salaries
- Federal income taxes
- Government regulation

Sole Proprietorship

A **sole proprietorship**, also called a **proprietorship**, is a business entity owned by only one person. This owner usually works in the business and is very involved in its day-to-day activities. Most business organizations are sole proprietorships. The popularity of this business form is due to the ease with which the business can be established. There is limited government regulation and paperwork to file. In fact, obtaining a business license may be the main interaction you have with the government before opening your place of business. The owner may dissolve the business at will, or it will be automatically dissolved upon the sale of the business or upon the owner's death.

Under a sole proprietorship, resources are difficult to obtain because there is only one owner who can contribute financially. The owner's options for obtaining capital are limited to additional personal contributions and outside creditors. Before an outside creditor will consider financing the business, the creditor will demand assurance that the loan will be repaid on time with acceptable interest. The owner may have to pledge additional personal assets as collateral for the business debts. This means that if the business fails to pay the loan, the collateral pledged could be seized and sold to satisfy the debt.

The government does not recognize a sole proprietorship as a separate **legal entity**. This distinction means that from a legal perspective, the owner and the business are one and the same. The sole proprietorship cannot be a defendant in a lawsuit; the lawsuit must be filed against the business owner. Consequently, the owner's personal assets are at risk to satisfy business liabilities.

Taxation

Since a sole proprietorship is not considered a separate legal entity, the government cannot tax the business. In fact, the business does not file a business tax return. Any business income is reported on **Schedule C** of the owner's personal 1040 income tax return. Schedule C lists the revenues and the expenses of the sole proprietorship. The income from the business is then added to any other taxable income the owner may have received and the appropriate personal income tax rate is then applied. This is an advantage to many owners because their personal income tax rates are often less than the corporate tax rates (the major advantage is single versus double taxation, which is discussed later in the chapter).

Because business income is taxed on the owner's personal tax return, the business income statement does not recognize any salary expense for the owner's work. Only the wages of employees will be shown as wage or salaries expense. Because the law considers the sole proprietorship and the owner to be one and the same, the owner/sole proprietorship cannot be an employer and an employee simultaneously. A sample income statement for a sole proprietorship is shown below as Exhibit 3-5.1. Note that the income statement does not show any salaries expense for the owner's work. Also, the income statement will not reflect any income taxes.

Proprietor's Compensation

From an accounting standpoint, consider the implications on business net income if the owner could determine a salary for his or her work and record it in the financial statements. This figure could be easily manipulated to increase or decrease net income at the will of the owner. By eliminating this figure, the financial statements are much more objective and trustworthy. When comparing the operating results of a sole proprietorship with that of a corporation, however, make sure to adjust for the fact that the work of the owner is not reflected in the financial statement figures of a sole proprietorship (but it is in a corporation). An example of how to make the adjustment is shown in Case Reading 3-3.

Exhibit 3-5.1
Income Statement for a Sole Proprietorship

Mac's Produce Business
Income Statement
Year Ended December 31, 2000

Revenues		
Sales		$ 120,000
Expenses		
Cost of Produce Sold	$ 80,000	
Salaries (other than owner)	12,000	
Supplies	2,000	
Other Expenses	5,000	
Total Expenses		99,000
Net Income		$ 21,000

The owner's equity section of a sole proprietorship generally contains one account called **contributed capital** or **capital**. This account contains not only the capital contributed by the owner, but also any profits, losses, or withdrawals of the owner. Instead of a statement of retained earnings, a sole proprietorship prepares a statement of owner's equity in addition to the remaining financial statements at the end of the accounting period. The following statement of owner's equity shown as Exhibit 3-5.2 is for the first year of business for Mac's Produce Business.

Exhibit 3-5.2

Mac's Produce Business
Statement of Owner's Equity
Year Ended December 31, 2000

Mac Capital, January 1, 2000		$ -
Add:		
Investments by Owner	$ 30,000	
Net Income	21,000	
Subtotal		51,000
Less Withdrawals by Owner		12,000
Mac Capital, December 31, 2000		$ 39,000

This statement shows that the capital account increases by the amount of net income and capital contributions during the period and decreases by the amount of withdrawals. If the company had incurred a net loss instead of a net income, that amount would have been deducted on the statement.

The balance sheet for a sole proprietorship usually does not have a separate account such as retained earnings to reflect the earnings kept in the business. Instead, it includes the earnings not withdrawn by the owner in the contributed capital account as shown above. (The authors, however, believe that it is important for the student to be able to differentiate between the concepts of contributed capital and retained earnings. For this reason, we will assume that all forms of business use contributed capital *and* retained earnings accounts even though the corporate form is the only type of business entity that actually uses both of these accounts.)

In summary, the sole proprietorship form of business has several advantages and disadvantages. It is the easiest to form, there is very little government regulation, the owner can work in the business and be his or her own boss, and, in many cases, there can be tax advantages over a corporation. On the other hand, there are many risks involved. The sole proprietor has **unlimited liability**. This means that personal assets of the owner are at risk to satisfy business debts. The availability of outside financing is also more limited than for other forms of business.

Partnership

A **partnership** is a business entity owned by two or more individuals in which the level of each partner's interest in the company is legally defined in a partnership agreement. This agreement defines the role that each partner will play in the day-to-day operations of the partnership. A well-written partnership agreement also states how the profits of the partnership will be allocated among the partners. If the partnership agreement is mute on this point, the income of the partnership is divided equally. The following example assumes that the partnership agreement for Ross and Mac's Produce Business states that Ross is to receive 60 percent of the profits and Mac receives 40 percent. This distribution of net income is shown at the bottom of the company's income statement. The income statement for Ross and Mac's Produce Business shows how the profit of $21,000 is allocated 60 percent, or $12,600, to Ross and 40 percent, or $8,400, to Mac.

Exhibit 3-5.3
Income Statement for a Partnership

Ross & Mac's Produce Business Income Statement Year Ended December 31, 2000		
Revenues		
Sales		$ 120,000
Expenses		
Cost of Produce Sold	$ 80,000	
Salaries (other than partners')	12,000	
Supplies	2,000	
Other Expenses	5,000	
Total Expenses		99,000
Net Income		$ 21,000
Distribution of Net Income:		
Ross, 60%	$ 12,600	
Mac, 40%	8,400	$ 21,000

Distribution of Income to Partners

This income statement is similar to that of a sole proprietorship in that it does not reflect any salaries of the owners. Partners who work in the business are usually compensated for their time by receiving additional income at the time of distribution. For example, suppose that Ross works in the business on a daily basis and the partnership agreement states that he will receive the first $10,000 of distribution before any other distributions to the owners, and that the remaining net income (loss) will be allocated 60 percent to Ross and 40 percent to Mac. The distribution of the $21,000 income in this case would be as follows:

Income to distribute	$21,000
Salary of Ross	(10,000)
Left to distribute	11,000
Ross's portion (60%)	(6,600)
Mac's portion (40%)	$4,400

In this example, Ross will receive $16,600 of the $21,000 income and Mac will receive $4,400. Ross's profit includes the $10,000 for his work in the business and the $6,600 for his remaining distribution of profit. The $10,000 "salary" is not a true expense. Instead it is just a way to divide income.

Taxation

Like a sole proprietorship, a partnership is not a taxable entity so the income of the partners is taxed on their personal tax returns. The partnership sends a Schedule K-1 (Form 1065) to the partner; this reflects the amount of income that was earned by that partner. The partner then includes this amount on the applicable schedule of his or her individual 1040 tax return (usually Schedule E). The partnership as a business entity is required to report to the government for information purposes the total amount of income earned by the business and how this income was allocated among the partners. The Internal Revenue Service (IRS) can then compare the amount of income reported by the partnership for that partner with the amount of income reported by the partner on the 1040 tax return.

Resources are easier to obtain for partnerships than for sole proprietorships because there are more partners as financial contributors. If there are only two partners, the resources will be significantly more limited than if there are thirty partners, depending on the initial level of capital contribution demanded for a partnership interest. Once again, a partnership may need to obtain outside financing and may have to pledge personal assets as collateral for partnership debt.

Legal Considerations

Partnerships are not nearly as popular as sole proprietorships. (About 70% of businesses are sole proprietorships, 20% corporations, and 10% partnerships.) A partner shares decision making with other partners. Many start-up business owners want to be "on their own" to make their own choices, right or wrong. Even though there is little government regulation involved in forming a partnership, a lawyer should be consulted to draw up the partnership agreement and to ensure that the interest of all parties is represented. Just like sole proprietorships, partnerships are not considered separate legal entities. The partnership as a business entity cannot be sued. Partners are individually listed as defendants in lawsuits, and the partner's personal assets are generally at risk to satisfy business obligations. For this reason, you need to trust your business partners implicitly and think highly of their business expertise. Your personal assets may be directly tied to their business judgment.

The life of a partnership is generally relatively short. Anytime there is a change in partner membership, the old partnership is dissolved and a new partnership is formed. For this reason, it is critical for the partnership to keep accurate records of the capital balances of each partner. The financial statements of a partnership will include a statement of partners' capital. This statement reflects all changes that occurred in each partner's capital balance during the accounting period. A partnership, like a sole proprietorship, usually does not have a retained earnings account but includes all capital contributions, owner withdrawals, and income in the individual partners' capital account.

Returning to the original example in which neither partner worked in the business, a statement of partner's capital is shown as Exhibit 3-5.4 for Ross and Mac's Produce Business. This statement assumes that Ross invested $18,000, or 60 percent, of the $30,000 capital invested in the business, whereas Mac invested only $12,000, or 40 percent, of the total invested.

Exhibit 3-5.4

Ross and Mac's Produce Business Statement of Partnership Capital Year Ended December 31, 2000			
	Ross	Mac	Total
Capital, January 1, 2000	$ -	$ -	$ -
Add:			
Investments by Partner	18,000	12,000	30,000
Net Income	12,600	8,400	21,000
Subtotal	30,600	20,400	51,000
Less Withdrawals by Partner	7,200	4,800	12,000
Capital, December 31, 2000	$ 23,400	$ 15,600	$ 39,000

Although this example does assume that the income is split in the same ratio as the capital investment, that is not a necessity. As mentioned previously, the partnership agreement can define the income split in any manner that is agreeable to all partners. The withdrawals for the business are assumed to be a 60/40 ratio, although the partnership agreement can dictate any withdrawal policy. As you can see, there are many similarities between this statement and a statement of owner's equity for a sole proprietorship.

Limited Partnership

A **limited partnership** is a partnership that defines different levels of liability for different partners. Partners within a limited partnership are either general partners or limited partners. General partners are jointly and wholly liable for partnership obligations (meaning that their personal assets are at risk). Limited partners are liable only to the extent of their equity contribution in the partnership. General partners usually participate in the business; limited partners do not. Each limited partnership is required to have at least one general partner.

Corporations

A **corporation** is a legal entity chartered by a state; it has one or more owners. The owners of a corporation are called **stockholders** or **shareholders** and they are issued stock certificates as evidence of their ownership. Although there are more sole proprietorships in sheer number, the dollar amount of contributed capital for corporations far exceeds any other form of business. Because of the vast amount invested in corporations, this form of business must comply with a much more rigid set of government restrictions, both federal and state. A corporation must have a charter approved by the state in which it is organized. The **corporate charter** specifies the capital stock authorized. Any companies that are publicly traded on a stock exchange must follow the rules of the SEC Acts of 1933 and 1934 which require audits of the financial statements.

The shareholders of a corporation elect a board of directors who are responsible for the hiring/firing of top management. Managers usually have extensive professional experience and training. They may or may not be stockholders in the business. Because decisions are made by people with more professional expertise, many shareholders expect these companies to perform better financially and to earn a higher return for their owners. Managers are considered to be employees and, as such, their salaries are reflected on the income statement of a corporation even if they are shareholders. The life of a corporation is considered to be continuous; unless stated otherwise in its corporate charter the corporation continues to exist regardless of changes in the ownership of the business.

Resources are easier to obtain for a corporation than for any other form of business. The corporation can issue additional authorized stock if more capital is needed. Because the assets of the business are usually large, creditors are more willing to lend the company additional funds. In addition, the corporation itself can be sued just like an individual, for example, for default on a loan.

Taxation

The corporation is the only form of business legally considered a separate **taxable entity** from its owners. Unlike a sole proprietorship and partnership, owners of a corporation are not personally responsible for the debts incurred by the corporation beyond the amount of their investment. As a separate legal and taxable entity, the business itself must pay a **corporate income tax**. This tax varies depending on the income earned by the corporation, but for income above $335,000 is approximately 34 percent.

Many shareholders feel the tax burden of being a shareholder in two ways. First, the corporation (which the shareholders own) is taxed on its corporate income; second, the after-tax income that is distributed to the shareholders as dividends is taxed on Schedule B of each individual's personal 1040 tax return. This concept is called **double taxation**. In a sole proprietorship, all profit is taxed on the individual's tax return, whether distributed or not. Under the corporate form, only dividends (the profits distributed to shareholders) are taxed on the individual's 1040 form. The amount of after-tax income retained in the business is not taxed a second time.

Consider the following example. Blaster Pro Corporation has many shareholders. The company has taxable income of $500,000 and the corporate tax rate is 34 percent. The company plans to distribute all of its after-tax income to the shareholders as dividends. How much tax have the stockholders paid, in total, assuming a corporate tax rate of 34 percent and an average individual tax rate of 25 percent?

Blaster Pro Corp. taxable income	$500,000
Corporate tax at 34%	(170,000)
After-tax income	$330,000
Dividends (all after-tax income)	$330,000
Average individual tax rate	25%
Individual tax for shareholders	$ 82,500

Corporate tax	$170,000	←	Paid on corporate tax return
Individual tax	82,500	←	Paid on individual tax return
Total tax (double tax)	$252,500		

Although the corporation actually prepared the corporate tax return and wrote the check from a corporate bank account, as owners of the corporation the shareholders have indirectly paid the corporate tax of $170,000. The individual tax of $82,500 was paid directly by shareholders. The total effect of the double taxation to the shareholders is $252,500. What is the effective tax rate on the corporate income, given the double taxation?

$$\frac{\text{Total tax}}{\text{Income before tax}} = \frac{\$252,500}{\$500,000} = 50.5\% \text{ effective rate}$$

Shareholders' Equity on the Balance Sheet

The owners' equity section of a corporation is usually called **stockholders'** (or shareholders') **equity**. This section of the balance sheet in its simplest form contains captions for contributed capital and retained earnings. Contributed capital includes all capital contributions of the owner and the retained earnings account contains all of the net earnings that have not been distributed to the shareholders in the form of dividends since the business began.

The stockholders' equity section of the balance sheet (also termed the book value of the company) is the accounting valuation accruing to the preferred and common shareholders. It is composed primarily of the following four categories:

1. **Preferred stock** is the par value of the preferred shares outstanding at the balance sheet date. **Par value** is an arbitrary valuation assigned to the stock at the time the stock is initially authorized (created). In the event of bankruptcy or liquidation of the corporation, preferred shareholders stand ahead of common shareholders in recovering their investment. A usual feature of preferred stock is a stated dividend amount per preferred share, which is established at the time of stock issuance. Preferred dividends must be paid before any common share dividends can be paid. Not all corporations choose to issue preferred stock, but many corporations use this type of security to raise capital for the corporation. If the caption "preferred stock" does not appear on the balance sheet, it means the corporation has not issued this class of stock.

2. **Common stock** is the par value assigned to the common shares outstanding at the balance sheet date. The dollar amount is the number of shares issued times the par value per share. Par value is typically a small number such as $.05 and is obviously an arbitrary amount having no correspondence with the intrinsic value of the company. In recent years many companies have engaged in buyback programs whereby the corporation purchases its shares in the open market. The repurchased shares are called **treasury stock**. The number of treasury shares is subtracted from the numbers of shares issued to determine how many shares are outstanding. The number of outstanding shares is important because it represents the ownership shares and the number of votes that can be cast at the annual shareholders' meeting.

3. **Additional paid-in capital** (also referred to as **contributed capital in excess of par**) is the difference between the par values of the preferred and common shares outstanding and the actual amount received by the company when the shares were issued (sold). For example, in a recent initial public offering (IPO) the company issued its shares for $10 after commissions were paid to the underwriter, but the par value was arbitrarily set at $.10. Therefore, $9.90 of the net proceeds to the corporation were recorded in "Additional paid-in capital."

4. **Retained earnings** is the sum of all net income less operating losses reported by the company over the period of its existence less dividends declared over the same period.

Preferred Stock. Preferred stock is listed first in the stockholders' equity section because it is preferred in the event of a liquidation of the company. As mentioned above, if the company ceases to exist, after all creditors have been repaid, the preferred shareholders, to the extent of their capital contribution, may receive the business assets before the common shareholders. The preferred shareholders are also preferred when dividends are declared. These shareholders receive their dividends before any dividends are paid to common shareholders.

> *Why then would anyone want to be a common shareholder when it seems*
> *that the preferred shareholder gets all the benefits?*

Preferred shareholders usually have limited, if any, voting rights. By not being able to vote on all matters, they limit their voice in company-related matters such as management strategy and future goals. Consent of two-thirds of the preferred shareholders is required, however, in any matter that might affect the seniority of their claim on the company's assets. In addition, even though preferred shareholders receive assets and dividends before common shareholders, the amount they receive is limited and usually has a ceiling.

Preferred stock can be either cumulative or noncumulative. **Cumulative preferred stock** accumulates dividends if a year goes by and a dividend is not declared. Any shareholders who hold **noncumulative preferred stock** lose their rights to a dividend if none is declared in that year. For example, assume that the preferred stock has the right to receive the first $100 in dividends a year, but this year the company does not declare any dividends. Next year the company declares a dividend on common stock of $40. If the preferred stock was cumulative, the preferred shareholders must first receive $200, which includes $100 from this year and $100 from last year. Common shareholders could then receive their $40 dividend. If the preferred stock was noncumulative, however, the $100 from last year is lost forever and the preferred shareholders receive only this year's $100 before the common shareholders receive their $40 dividend. Preferred shareholders receive only the amount of the promised dividend that year, regardless of the size of any dividend declared on common stock.

The amount of the preferred stock dividend is usually expressed as either a dollar amount or as a percentage of par. This percentage or dollar amount is detailed in the description of the preferred stock. For example, if the description of the preferred stock reads

> Preferred Stock, cumulative, 10%, $50 par

you can conclude that the annual dividend requirement is $5 or 10 percent of the $50 par value each year. If the shareholder did not receive that dividend this year, it would carry over until next year because the stock is cumulative. When a dividend is finally declared, the previous dividends must first be paid before any current year dividends are distributed to either preferred or common shareholders. Undeclared previous years' dividends on cumulative preferred stock are called **dividends in arrears**. This is disclosed in a footnote to the financial statements. The rights of the preferred shareholder in dividends are important because such amounts are subtracted from net income in computing earnings per share, a very popular financial measure of publicly held companies which is watched very closely. Earnings per share will be discussed in more depth in a future case reading.

Common Stock. As mentioned previously, common stock is the voting stock of the company. For this reason, every corporation has common stock. These shareholders have a residual interest in the company after all claims of creditors and preferred shareholders have been paid. This means that common shareholders receive whatever is left if the company liquidates. In most cases of bankruptcy, common shareholders recover none of their investment.

Common shareholders also have the right (called a **preemptive right**) to maintain their percentage of ownership in the company. That means that if the company issues additional shares, the shares are offered to existing shareholders first so that they can maintain their percentage of ownership in the business.

The board of directors, elected by the shareholders, is the group that actually declares the dividends to be paid to shareholders. The dividend becomes a liability on the date the dividend is announced (called the **declaration date**) and remains such until the dividend has been paid to the shareholders. The dividend announcement states that any **shareholder of record,** who is anyone who has recorded his or her legal ownership of the shares with the company, will receive the dividend as of a certain future date, called the **date of record**. For example, a dividend may be declared on December 2nd to anyone who owns shares as of December 4th but not be paid until December 31st. December 2nd is the declaration date, December 4th is the date of record and the 31st is the date of payment. Not all dividends are cash dividends. Some dividends are paid with shares of stock and are called **stock dividends**.

Not all companies declare dividends on their common stock. Some companies choose to retain all profits for internal growth. If you are looking for a company in which to invest and you want to receive dividend income, make sure to check the company's dividend history. The significant appreciation in the value of stocks in the latter half of the 90s without a proportionate increase in dividend amounts by corporations has reduced the average dividend yield of the thirty major corporations comprising the Dow Jones Industrial Average to be only around 2 percent. The **dividend yield** is merely the annual dividend divided by the current market price.

The amount listed in the stockholders' equity section for common and preferred stock is usually the par value amount of the shares and is calculated by multiplying the par value times the number of shares issued. If the shareholder paid more for his or her shares than the par amount (which is usually the case), this extra amount is recorded in an account called contributed capital in excess of par. Preferred stock usually sells at an amount fairly close to its par value, but common stock almost always sells at amounts greater than its par value. The par value amount is not related in any way to the market price of the stock. As stated before, par value is an arbitrary valuation assigned to the stock at the time the stock is initially authorized.

When the corporate charter is approved, it authorizes a certain number of shares to be issued. **Authorized shares** are merely the shares that the company can issue to the public without any further approval from the state of incorporation. However, the SEC must approve all issuance of publicly traded securities in the U.S. Just because shares are authorized doesn't mean that they are issued. The **issued shares** are the shares that have been sold. Often a company will repurchase its own stock in order to resell it later when the company needs money. Common stock that has been repurchased by the company and held in its treasury is called treasury stock. Treasury stock is not considered in voting, paying dividends, or when calculating earnings per share. Stockholders do not vote on the resale of treasury stock and they do not have preemptive rights on the stock. The issued shares less the treasury stock represent the shares currently held by shareholders. These shares are called **outstanding shares**.

Exhibit 3-5.5 shows a sample stockholders' equity section for a corporation. After reviewing this exhibit you should be able to answer the following questions:

1. How many shares of preferred stock have been sold?

    There are 1,000 issued shares of preferred stock. Issued shares are shares which have been sold.

Exhibit 3-5.5
Stockholders' Equity Section for Corporation

Produce Inc. Stockholders' Equity Section of the Balance Sheet December 31, 2000		
Preferred Stock, $100 Par Value, 7% Cumulative, 1,800 Shares Authorized, 1,000 Shares Issued & Outstanding	$100,000	
Contributed Capital in Excess of Par Value, Preferred Stock	5,000	
Total Capital Contributed by Preferred Stockholders		$105,000
Common Stock, $15 par value, 12,000 shares Authorized, 10,000 Shares Issued & Outstanding	150,000	
Contributed Capital in Excess of Par value, Common Stock	110,000	
Total Capital Contributed by Common Stockholders		260,000
Total Contributed Capital		365,000
Retained Earnings		82,000
Total Stockholders' Equity		$447,000

2. How many additional shares of preferred stock can be issued without further approval?

    There are 1,800 shares authorized but only 1,000 shares issued, which means that the company can issue an additional 800 shares without further approval.

3. What was the average selling price for a share of preferred stock?

    The total capital contributed by preferred shareholders is $105,000, which means that the average issuance price for each preferred share must be $105,000 ÷ 1,000, or $105 per share.

4. What amount is the annual dividend requirement for the preferred stock?

    The annual dividend requirement on the preferred stock is 7 percent of $100, or $7 per share. The total dividend is $7,000.

5. If a dividend on the preferred stock was not declared last year, and this year's common and preferred dividend is $16,000, how much of that dividend would be paid to the preferred stockholders?

   The description says that the preferred stock is cumulative. If a dividend was not declared last year, the preferred stockholders would need to receive last year's dividend of $7,000 and this year's dividend of $7,000 before any dividend goes to common stockholders. The preferred stockholders will receive $14,000 and the common stockholders will receive $2,000.

6. How many shares of common stock have been sold? How many are outstanding?

   10,000 shares of common stock have been issued. The description says all issued shares are also outstanding, which means that there is no treasury stock.

7. What was the average issuance price for a share of common stock?

   The average issuance price per share of common stock is calculated by taking the total capital contributed by the common shareholders of $260,000 and dividing it by the number of issued shares of 10,000. The average issuance price is $26 per share.

8. How many additional shares of common stock can be issued without further approval?

   Produce Inc. can issue an additional 2,000 shares of common stock without further authorization. This is computed by subtracting the issued shares from the authorized shares.

As an investor, a good understanding of the stockholder's equity section of a balance sheet is essential. To make a decision about whether or not to invest in a company, you need to address the following questions:

- Should I buy preferred or common stock?

- What voting rights, if any, do preferred shareholders have?

- What are the dividend yields and how certain am I that dividends will be paid on time?

- How many shareholders are there in the company and how diverse is the ownership?

- Who are the majority stockholders?

- What is the annual dividend requirement on the preferred stock?

- Is the preferred stock cumulative or noncumulative? If cumulative, are there any dividends in arrears?

- What dividends have common shareholders received in the last few years?

- What markets does the company serve and are they growing? Is income growth a probable future for the company?

After answering these questions, you should have a better understanding of the current ownership of the company and the implications it has for you as a future investor.

Alternate Business Forms

Before making a final decision on the business form to select, be sure to weigh all of the advantages and disadvantages. There are good and bad points to consider for all three business forms. Some of the negative aspects might be addressed by adopting one of the variations of the traditional business forms.

Limited Liability Partnership/Limited Liability Corporation (LLP/LLC)

A **limited liability partnership/limited liability corporation** is one in which all owners materially participate in the business. This type of business is ideal for professional service organizations (e.g., accounting firms, law firms, public relations firms, ad agencies). The key issue in a limited liability partnership/corporation is professional liability. Professional liability insurance is needed by both the company and the individual owners. All of the business' assets are subject to judgment, but only the owners who are directly involved in an alleged "tort" are personally liable. Owners who are not directly involved are not *personally* liable.

Subchapter S Corporation

A **Subchapter S corporation** is much like a limited liability corporation (LLC). An LLC is slightly more flexible than a Subchapter S corporation, but it is more expensive to establish. As in an LLP/LLC, the net income or net loss of the Subchapter S corporation "passes through" to the owners.

SUMMARY

U.S. tax law considers both shareholders and corporations as separate taxable entities. Individual shareholders are required to complete an individual income tax return (Form 1040) and corporations are required to complete a corporate tax return (Form 1120). Sole proprietorships and partnerships are not tax-paying entities. Therefore, a sole proprietorship entity does not file a business tax return at all, the owner does. However, a partnership must file an information return (Form 1065), which tells the government how much income the partnership made and how it was allocated among the partners. The partners then report their shares of partnership income on their individual income tax returns.

Business income earned by the owners of a sole proprietorship or a partnership (whether distributed or not) is reported on their individual 1040 income tax returns. Sole proprietors report their income on Schedule C of their 1040 form, while partners report their income on Schedule E. Distributions of profit from corporations are called dividends. Unlike sole proprietorships or partnerships, shareholders are taxed only on the amount of profit which the corporation distributes to them. Often the corporation retains much of the profit. The amount of net income not distributed is not taxable to the shareholders. One thing to note is that dividends are not expenses. The definition of an expense is that it is a cost incurred in order to generate revenue. Dividends do not generate revenue. Since dividends are not an expense, they are not listed on a corporation income statement and they are not deducted to arrive at taxable income. Therefore, it can be said that dividends are paid out of after-tax profit. Many people feel that the shareholders are subject to double taxation. This term reflects the fact that the corporation first must pay corporate tax on its earnings (shareholders own the company so they are really paying this corporate tax) and then the individuals must pay individual taxes on the amount of cash dividends that is distributed to them out of the corporation's net income (after tax).

Exhibit 3-5.6 summarizes the different factors to consider when selecting a form of business. Before making a final decision on the business form to select, be sure to weigh all of the advantages and disadvantages. There are good and bad points to consider for all three business forms. Some of the negative aspects might be addressed by adopting one of the variations of the traditional business forms.

Exhibit 3-5.6

	Sole Proprietorship	Partnership	Corporation
Resource availability	Hard to obtain	Hard to obtain	Easier to obtain
Life of entity	Limited	Limited	Unlimited
Owner's liability for business debts	Unlimited	Unlimited	Limited
Government regulation	Not much	Not much	Much more
Income taxation	Once	Once	Twice

In the case which follows, you are asked to calculate the return on equity on an after-tax basis. The prospective investors are asking you to advise them on the better organizational form to select based upon the tax consequences of each alternative.

EXERCISES AND PROBLEMS

Exercises

Exercise 1 Characteristics of Different Business Forms. List how a proprietorship, partnership, and corporation differ for the following three characteristics: (1) number of owners, (2) life of entity, and (3) federal income taxes.

Exercise 2 Characteristics of a Sole Proprietorship. List three advantages and three disadvantages of the sole proprietorship form of organization.

Exercise 3 Characteristics of a Partnership. List three advantages and three disadvantages of the partnership form of organization.

Exercise 4 Characteristics of a Corporation. List three advantages and three disadvantages of the corporate form of organization.

Exercise 5 Distribution of Net Income to Partners. In the partnership form of organization, how is net income distributed among the partners, that is, what factors may be used to allocate net income to partners?

Exercise 6 Characteristics of a Limited Partnership. Identify and explain the characteristics that make a limited partnership different from a regular partnership.

Exercise 7 Why the Corporate Form of Organization is Popular. Explain why the corporate form of business organization is popular.

Exercise 8 Taxation of Corporate Earnings. What is "double taxation" of corporate profits? Why don't proprietorships and partnerships also have double taxation of earnings?

Exercise 9 Preferred Stock and Common Stock Differences. List and explain two significant differences between preferred stock and common stock.

Problems

Problem 1 Distribution of Partnership Net Income. Donna, Ed, and Frank are partners in DEF Partnership, which earned $60,000 in 1999. Distribute the partnership net income to the partners if (1) there was no mention in the partnership agreement of how profits were to be divided among the partners, and (2) the partnership agreement states that Donna is to have a salary allowance of $20,000 and Frank is to have a salary allowance of $25,000, and the remaining amount is to be divided equally among the three partners.

Problem 2 Statement of Partnership Capital. Use the partnership data in Problem 1 and assume that the partners shared the $60,000 net income equally, that 1999 was the first year of operations, and that each of the partners contributed $30,000 in capital at the beginning of 1999. Withdrawals for 1999 were $18,000 for Donna, $24,000 for Frank, and $0 for Ed. Based on this information, prepare a statement of partnership capital for 1999 for DEF Partnership. Assume the partnership year ends on December 31.

Problem 3 Effective Income Tax Rate for Corporate Earnings. Bejay, Inc., has $1,000,000 net income before tax for year 2000. Assume Bejay, Inc., pays 34 percent tax on its taxable income, that all the net income (after tax) is distributed to stockholders as dividends, and that the average income tax rate for all the stockholders is 30 percent. What is the effective income tax rate on the income earned for 2000? Show all computations.

Problem 4 Dividends in Arrears. Jerge Corporation had 1,000 shares each of common stock and preferred stock outstanding for 2000. The preferred stock is $100 par value, 6%, cumulative with dividends in arrears for 1998 and 1999. If Jerge Corporation wants to declare total dividends of $30,000 at the end of 2000, how much will preferred stockholders receive before common stockholders receive any dividend?

Problem 5 Stockholders' Equity Section of the Balance Sheet. Samantha Corporation had the following stockholders' equity section in its balance sheet at December 31, 2000.

Samantha Corporation
Stockholders' Equity Section of Balance Sheet
December 31, 2000

Preferred Stock, $60 Par Value, 8% Cumulative, 10,000 Shares Authorized, 1,500 Shares Issued And Outstanding	$ 90,000
Common Stock, $1 Par Value, 50,000 Shares Authorized, 30,000 Issued And Outstanding	30,000
Contributed Capital In Excess Of Par Value (All From Common Stock)	270,000
Total Contributed Capital	$390,000
Retained Earnings	110,000
Total Stockholders' Equity	$500,000

Use the information on the previous page to answer the following questions.

1. What was the average issue price per share for preferred stock?

2. What amount of dividends per share will be paid to the preferred stockholders if dividends are declared?

3. What was the average issue price per share for common stock?

4. How many additional common stock shares can be issued by Samantha Company?

5. If preferred stock dividends are in arrears for 1999, how much will the preferred stockholders be paid in total before common stockholders can receive a dividend for 2000?

Problem 6   Effective Income Tax Rates with Multiple Income Tax Rates. Minilate Company has just completed its first year of operations, 1999, with net operating income of $200,000. Assume that the operating income is also its taxable income and that it is subject to the following corporate income tax rates:

Income Over	But Not Over	Tax is	Of the amount over
$0	$ 50,000	15%	$0
50,000	75,000	$ 7,500 + 25%	50,000
75,000	100,000	13,750 + 34%	75,000
100,000	335,000	22,250 + 39%	100,000
335,000	----	34%	335,000

Assume that Minilate Company wants to distribute to stockholders all the net income (after tax) as dividends and that the average individual income tax rate for all stockholders is 28 percent. What is the effective income tax rate on the income earned for 1999? Show all computations.

Case 3-5

DIFFERENT TAX TREATMENTS FOR DIFFERENT FORMS OF BUSINESS

Case Objective

To understand the different federal tax treatments of partnerships vs. corporations.

Decision: Based on return on equity, is the partnership or corporation form of business better for the group which is opening the new business?

Sam decided to open a restaurant in Las Vegas. With the assistance of Ms. Drivon, CPA, he has developed a financial plan which projects a pre-tax profit of $800,000 in the first year, before considering his own salary. Sam's problem is that he does not have the personal wealth to invest the $3,000,000 it will take to open the restaurant. Also, because of some past difficulties with law enforcement authorities, he expects most banks will be disinclined to lend him $2,400,000 to supplement $600,000 of his own money.

Sam sends the financial plan prepared by Ms. Drivon along with the architectural design of the proposed restaurant to Hank and Judy. He asks each of them to join him in this venture by investing $1,200,000 each. He further proposes two alternative arrangements:

Alternative 1. Partnership: Each partner will have an interest in the business proportional to each person's capital (equity). Therefore:

Sam's contribution	$600,000	20%
Hank's contribution	$1,200,000	40%
Judy's contribution	$1,200,000	40%
Total partnership equity	$3,000,000	100%

Sam proposes that he be credited with a $100,000 salary because he will manage the restaurant. Distributions of remaining income after the salary will be made in the same ratio as the above percentages. Based upon Sam's projected income, the distribution to each partner for financial reporting and tax purposes (Form K-1) will be:

	Sam	Hank	Judy	Total
Salary	$100,000			$100,000
Residual	140,000	$280,000	$280,000	700,000
K-1 distribution	$240,000	$280,000	$280,000	$800,000

Alternative 2. Corporation: Each owner will own voting stock in proportion to the original amount invested. Sam suggests that the corporation issue a total of 1,000,000 shares to the three shareholders as follows:

	Amount Invested	%	No. of Shares Issued
Sam	$600,000	20	200,000
Hank	$1,200,000	40	400,000
Judy	$1,200,000	40	400,000
Total shareholders' equity	$3,000,000	100	1,000,000

Sam points out that his $100,000 salary will be an expense in computing taxable income for the corporation, thus requiring the corporation to be taxed on $700,000 of income. Sam further proposes that the corporation's entire net income after taxes be distributed as a cash dividend to shareholders in proportion to the number of shares held.

Compare the two alternatives proposed by Sam by determining the after-tax income to the investors. Use the following corporation and individual tax rates.

Corporation Tax Rate Schedule			
Income Over	But Not Over	Tax is	Of the amount over
$0	$50,000	15%	$0
50,000	75,000	$7,500 + 25%	50,000
75,000	100,000	13,750 +34%	75,000
100,000	335,000	22,250 + 39%	100,000
335,000	--	34%	0

Individual Income Tax Rates	
Hank	31%
Judy	31%
Sam	28%

Requirements

1. a. Calculate each partner's income and income tax liability (the income tax shown on each partner's individual tax return).

   b. What is each partner's return on equity based on income after taxes? (Use each partner's capital contribution as his or her average equity.)

2. a. Calculate the corporate income tax liability which would appear on the corporate tax return, and a computation of the net income available for dividends.

   b. Calculate each stockholder's dividend and total tax liability shown on his or her individual tax return (assume the corporation distributes all net income to shareholders as dividends).

   c. What is the return for each shareholder after all taxes are paid? (Use each shareholder's capital contribution as his or her average equity).

3. Compare the total return on equity under scenario 1b and scenario 2c for each shareholder. From a tax perspective, which form of business organization do you recommend? Why?

Show all supporting computations in a spreadsheet format.

Case Reading 3-6

PLANNING AND
PERFORMANCE BUDGETS

INTRODUCTION

The term "budget" is used in the financial planning process to describe projected financial statements and their supporting schedules. Organization budgets serve the dual purpose of providing 1) a framework to forecast future financial performance of the enterprise, and 2) managers with a tool to control revenue and expenses. In a sense the budget is like the instruments in the cockpit of an airplane. The budget (instruments) tells the managers (pilots) the performance of the business (aircraft) against a predetermined standard or goal. On an aircraft, usually a buzzer or a warning light will tell the pilot when there is a deviation or a variation from what is normally expected. In business, however, these warning signs may be much more difficult to identify. Once alerted to the deviations from the plan, pilots and managers can make decisions to get back on course.

John and Joanna set their financial profit goal by creating a budget in Case 3-3. Case 3-6 is designed to evaluate the performance of their new venture against the plan they set earlier. The resulting analysis will provide insight into the successes and failures in their first full year in business.

PLANNING BUDGETS

A **planning budget** is the translation of the company's operating plan into a forecast of revenues and expenses and the consequence of those economic factors on assets and liabilities. Recall that the operating plan specifies how an enterprise will employ humans, machines, knowledge, and other resources to create value for customers. To construct an operating plan, many decisions must be made. Examples are: how many hours will the store be open, how many employees will be hired, what price should be set on the product or service, how much advertising will be done, what media will be used for advertising, and so on. Once all these operational decisions are made, the first draft of the planning budget can be prepared. If the results indicate a flaw in the plan, additional decisions may be necessary. The flaw could be the shortage of cash to carry out the operating plan. One such decision might be to raise additional capital by borrowing funds or by issuing stock. Another draft of the planning budget is then made to incorporate new assumptions or decisions.

In Case Reading 3-2 we discussed the concepts of variable and fixed expenses as well as the concepts of contribution margin. Case Reading 3-3 discussed breakeven sales and target sales. These are important concepts because the planning budget incorporates the ways in which expenses behave in relation to sales volume. These concepts were applied to the Corliss Accounting Firm. Sensitivity analysis was used by J & J for planning purposes. The changes in income that resulted from changes in sales revenue were more easily identified because variable expenses were separated from the fixed expenses.

In this case reading, assume that Devenie Corliss has decided that the most realistic expectation for July's revenue is that it will be 20% greater than June's revenue. Recall that variable expenses were 45.19% of sales revenue. The relationship of variable expenses to sales revenues, in this situation

$.45/sales dollar (rounded), is referred to as the **budgeted variable rate** (per unit of the activity). Another way of saying this, is that for each $1 increase in revenue, we can expect to incur an additional 45¢ (rounded) in variable expenses. Also recall that fixed expenses remain the same because they are fixed over the relevant range of activity.

Applying these concepts, we can prepare a planning budget for July. Below, Exhibit 3-6.1 shows the planned figures for July. This budget is often referred to as a **static budget** or "before-the-fact" budget since it has been prepared before the period (i.e., July) has begun to unfold. You will notice that these figures agree with the applicable calculations we made for a 20% increase in revenues when we did a sensitivity analysis in Case Reading 3-3.

Exhibit 3-6.1

Corliss Accounting Firm Planning Budget Month Ended July 31, 2000			
Fees Revenue	100.00%		$ 6,240
Variable Expenses			
Wage Expense	30.77%	$ 1,920	
Supplies Expense	14.42%	900	
Total Variable Expense	45.19%		2,820
Contribution Margin	54.81%		3,420
Fixed Expenses			
Depreciation Expense		200	
Insurance Expense		40	
Interest Expense		733	
Total Fixed Expenses			973
Net Income			$ 2,447

Now that Devenie has a budget for July, she can use this budget for planning, motivation, coordination, and communication purposes; in other words she will be more effective at managing the business. One month is for all practical purposes the shortest period of time in which to exert control over the business. Devenie would be well-advised to make weekly observations of the level of spending to ascertain that she is staying on the course to earn the desired level of income. When the month is completed, it is time to evaluate performance.

PERFORMANCE BUDGET

Suppose that the Corliss Accounting Firm has now completed the month of July and that its actual fees revenue turned out to be $6,100. Given these actual revenue results, what amount of variable expenses should have been incurred during the month? The budgeted variable expense relationship and our knowledge of the way fixed costs behave may be used to prepare a **performance budget**, which is based on the actual volume of revenue. The performance budget is sometimes called a **flexible budget** or an "after-the-fact" budget because it is prepared after the actual revenue results have been determined. The performance budget is presented in Exhibit 3-6.2.

The budgeted variable rate for wage expense in the planning budget shown in Exhibit 3-6.1 was 30.77% of fees revenue . The performance budget wage expense maintains that same variable rate percentage and is computed by multiplying 30.77% times the actual fees revenue of $6,100.

$$30.77\% \times \$6,100 = \$1,877$$

Exhibit 3-6.2

Corliss Accounting Firm Performance Budget for July Month Ended July 31, 2000			
Fees Revenue	100.00%		$ 6,100
Variable Expenses			
Wage Expense	30.77%	$ 1,877	
Supplies Expense	14.42%	880	
Total Variable Expenses	45.19%		2,757
Contribution Margin	54.81%		3,343
Fixed Expenses			
Depreciation Expense		200	
Insurance Expense		40	
Interest Expense		733	
Total Fixed Expenses			973
Net Income			$ 2,370

The supplies expense is calculated in a similar manner. Supplies would be 14.42% of the actual fees revenue. Notice how the fixed expenses in the performance budget are identical to the fixed expenses in the planning budget. This is because fixed expenses stay the same within the relevant range.

One can characterize the performance budget as "20-20 hindsight." If Devenie knew that revenues for July would be exactly $6,100, she would have budgeted all the variable expenses ($2,757) as shown in the above exhibit. Of course no one can forecast the future with 100% accuracy, and in business unforeseen factors can cause fluctuations in revenues and expenses. What is important now is for Devenie to compare the performance budget to the actual income statement to determine whether her variable expenses were in fact 45% of revenue and whether her fixed expenses were $973 for the month. After analyzing any deviations from the plan, Devenie can alter her operational decisions so that the following months will achieve a financial result which is consistent with her goals.

PERFORMANCE VARIANCES

Exhibit 3-6.3 is a comparison of the performance budget with the actual results for the period of July. The exhibit shows the Planning Budget, the Performance Budget, and the Actual Results taken from the income statement for the Corliss Accounting Firm for the month of July. Performance variances have also been calculated. These variances from planned amounts are labeled "F" or "U" to indicate favorable or unfavorable, respectively.

One way the analysis can be used is to evaluate the performance of those individuals who are in charge of expenses. For example, let's suppose actual wages for July turned out to be $2,100 or 34.43% of actual fees revenue of $6,100. This means that the variable expense rate (30.77%) used for wages (planned wage expense/planned sales) was too low. Increased wages could be due to an increase in the wage rate for employees or an increase in the number of hours worked. This difference should be investigated and the reason should be taken into consideration when making a budget for August. Similar computations could be made for other variable expenses.

This same type of reasoning can be applied to fixed expenses as well. By definition, budgeted fixed expenses are remained constant over a relevant range of revenues. If actual fixed expenses differ from the budgeted amount, this variance would be due to increases or decreases in the actual amounts of the fixed expense incurred. For example, actual insurance rates may have increased, or actual building rent may have decreased in relation to amounts estimated in the fixed expense budget. Any differences noted between the performance budget and the actual operating results are called **performance variances**. The variances are further described as being favorable or unfavorable.

Exhibit 3-6.3

	Planning Budget	Performance Budget	Actual Results	Performance Variance	F /U
Corliss Accounting Firm **Calculation Of Performance Variance** **Month Ended July 31, 2000**					
Revenues					
Fees Revenue	$ 6,240	$ 6,100	$ 6,100	$ -	
Variable Expenses					
Wage Expense	1,920	1,877	2,100	(223)	U
Supplies Expense	900	880	850	30	F
Total Variable Expenses	2,820	2,757	2,950	(193)	U
Contribution Margin	3,420	3,343	3,150	(193)	U
Fixed Expenses	-	-			
Depreciation Expense	200	200	280	(80)	U
Insurance Expense	40	40	40	-	
Interest Expense	733	733	733	-	
Total Fixed Expenses	973	973	1,053	(80)	U
Net Income	$ 2,447	$ 2,370	$ 2,097	$ (273)	U

An **unfavorable variance** causes a decrease in net income and a **favorable variance** results in an increase in net income. Variances should be reviewed by appropriate company personnel, the reasons for the variances should be investigated, and corrective action taken, if necessary. A one or two percent variance is probably too small to warrant investigation. A good threshhold for deciding when to probe into the cause of a variance is when the variance is over 5% of planned net income. The unfavorable variance in wage expense of $223 should be investigated because that variance caused net income to decline by 9.4% (calculated by $223 variance/$2,370 net income in the performance budget).

Depreciation expense is the only fixed expense variance shown in the exhibit. The explanation for this $80 variance could be as simple as new equipment installed at the beginning of July was not included in the planning budget. For integrity of future planning budgets the underlying cause of this variance should be determined.

PLANNING VARIANCES

For most enterprises the actual level of sales revenue compared to plan is of vital importance. Even if expenses are tightly controlled and thus meet planned rates, a significant sales decline will still negatively impact profits. Therefore it is incumbant upon managers to carefully monitor the rate at which revenues are being earned. The operating plan should contain a process to generate sales at the level necessary to attain the desired profit. Similar to expenses, if sales show a negative variance of more than five percent from planned level, steps should be taken by management to determine the causes and to the extent possible, corrective action taken.

One way to measure the effect of the actual sales increase/decrease versus the planned sales activity on profit is called a **planning variance**. This variance is calculated by taking the difference between the contribution margin per the planning budget and the contribution margin per the performance budget. Assuming that sales prices remain constant, the root cause of this variance is a change in sales volume. For Corliss Accounting Firm, the planning variance would be:

Planning variance = CM per planning budget − CM per performance budget
                  = $3,420 − $3,343 = $77

This unfavorable variance indicates that net income went down by $77 because of a decrease in fees revenue.

SUMMARY

The planning budget, the after-the-fact performance budget, and actual income statement should be compared to determine the causes of income declines. This exercise will undoubtedly provide insights that will enable managers or owners to make better business decisions. John and Joanna are disappointed in the results of their first year in business together. In Case 3-6, you are asked to prepare an analysis as shown in this reading.

EXERCISE AND PROBLEMS

Exercises

Exercise 1 Primary Purposes of Budgets. Identify the two primary purposes of budgets. Select one of the two primary purposes and explain how it is used or benefits management in making decisions.

Exercise 2 Planning Budget. Define planning budget. How is a planning budget typically used in an organization?

Exercise 3 Performance Budget. Define performance budget. How is a performance budget typically used in an organization?

Exercise 4 Performance Variances. What is a performance variance? Explain which variances should be (require) follow up by a manager.

Problems

Problem 1 Understanding the Performance Report. Refer to Exhibit 3-6.3 for the Corliss Accounting Firm in this Case Reading. Explain 1) why $6,100 was used in the Performance Budget column for Fees Revenues and 2) how the $1,877 for Wage Expense and the $880 for Supplies Expense was computed. Be specific in your comments.

Problem 2 Prepare a Planning Budget. Juan's Clip Joint is a hair salon in a suburban mall. Juan Rodriguez, the owner, is planning operations for the year ending December 31, 2000 and has developed the following expense items and behavior:

Wages	40% of revenues
Supplies	8% of revenues
Utilities	5% of revenues
Rent	$9,600 for the year
Insurance	1,200 for the year
Utilities	1,500 for the year
Other	900 for the year

Juan expects revenues for 2000 to be about $60,000. Based on this information, prepare a planning budget income statement using the contribution margin format for Juan's Clip Joint for 2000.

Problem 3 Prepare a Performance Report. In solving this problem, use the same expense items and behavior as given in Problem 2 above for Juan's Clip Joint. Also, assume Juan had the following revenues and expenses for 2000:

Services Revenues	$62,300
Expenses:	
Wages	25,000
Supplies	5,000
Utilities (variable)	3,300
Rent	9,600
Insurance	1,250
Utilities (fixed)	1,620
Other	966

Prepare a performance report for Juan's Clip Joint for 2000. Your report should be similar in form to Exhibit 3-6.3 in this Case Reading. When you have completed your performance report, write a note to Juan explaining which variances (expenses) probably need to be closely looked at by him.

Problem 4 Looking Behind the Numbers. Gail Lee has just returned from a 4 week vacation. During the vacation she was concerned that the sales projection for August of $20,000 would not be met. During a meeting with her manager, she was given the following condensed monthly report for August 2000:

Lee's Lube Shop
Monthly Report
Month Ended August 31, 2000

	Performance Budget	Actual Results	Performance Variances	Variance %
Revenues	$ 18,000	$ 18,000	0	0.0%
Variable Expense (30%)	5,400	5,500	$100U	1.9%
Contribution Margin	12600	12500	100U	0.8%
Fixed Expenses	6,200	6,150	50F	0.8%
Net Income	$ 6,400	$ 6,350	$50U	0.8%

Ms. Lee read the condensed statement and said "All the variances are well within our 5% limit so I guess things went very well while I was on vacation."

How is it that Ms. Lee's statement is incorrect? Explain what is hidden (missing) from the condensed monthly report above that would be of interest to Ms. Lee?

Case 3-6

J & J CORP. -THE BEST LAID PLANS...

Case Objective

To understand the concepts of planning (static) budgets and performance (flexible) budgets and their roles in evaluating business performance

It is September, 2000. We look in on John and Joanna to see if their corporation is a success. They have just received the income statement from Axel, Rose, and Hammer, Certified Public Accountants, shown below as Exhibit C3-6.1.

Exhibit C3-6.1
Income Statement

J & J Corporation Income Statement Three Months Ended August 31, 2000			
	Painting	Decorating	TOTAL
Fees Revenue	$ 11,000	$ 17,500	$ 28,500
Variable Expenses			
Paint	4,000		4,000
Painting Supplies	450		450
Decorating Materials		7,325	7,325
Wages		2,000	2,000
Decorating Supplies		1,450	1,450
Total Variable Expenses	4,450	10,775	15,225
Contribution Margin	$ 6,550	$ 6,725	13,275
Fixed Expenses			
Depreciation			3,113
Advertising			2,700
Insurance			1,050
Interest			74
Annual Business License			120
Equipment Rental			1,300
Salaries Expense			5,400
Total Fixed Expenses			13,757
Income (loss) before tax			$ (482)

John and Joanna are perplexed. Joanna said, "I recall that when we prepared our planning (static) budget for the corporation (shown below as Exhibit C3-6.2), we needed to reach $25,971 in sales to break even. Our income statement (Exhibit C3-6.1) shows that we beat that sales number and yet we lost $482! What went wrong?"

Exhibit C3-6.2
Planning Budget

J & J Corporation
Planning (Static) Budget
Three Months Ended August 31, 2000

	Painting	Decorating	TOTAL
Fees Revenue	$ 16,520	$ 15,600	$ 32,120
Variable Expenses			
Paint	5,390		5,390
Painting Supplies	602		602
Decorating Materials		6,708	6,708
Wages		1,716	1,716
Decorating Supplies		936	936
Total Variable Expenses	5,992	9,360	15,352
Contribution Margin	$ 10,528	$ 6,240	16,768
Fixed Expenses			
Depreciation			3,113
Advertising			2,200
Insurance			1,100
Interest			74
Annual Business License			120
Equipment Rental			1,550
Salaries Expense			5,400
Total Fixed Expenses			13,557
Income Before tax			$ 3,211
Breakeven Sales			$ 25,971

"Let's look at the planning budget we prepared last May," said John. "Notice that we had originally expected sales to be $32,120. Unfortunately, this target was not met. The income statement prepared by our CPAs (Exhibit C3-6.1) shows total sales of only $28,500."

"John, given that our income statement reported actual sales revenue as only $28,500, shouldn't our expenses have been *less than the amounts appearing in our original budget?*" asked Joanna.

"I think you're right," said John. "Let's try to figure out what our expenses *should have been*, given that sales amounted to only $28,500."

Requirements

1. Use the same spreadsheet file you used in Case 3-4 to complete this assignment. Prepare 3 schedules as follows:

   Schedule 1: For the painting department, prepare a schedule with the format shown below as Exhibit C3-6.3. The planning budget and the actual results column have already been completed for you. You need to complete the performance budget, calculate the performance variance and state if the variance is favorable or unfavorable (F or U).

Exhibit C3-6.3
Format for Painting Department

	Painting				
	Planning Budget	Performance Budget	Actual Results	Performance Variance	F or U
Fees Revenue	$ 16,520		$ 11,000	N/A	N/A
Variable Expenses:					
Paint	5,390		4,000		
Painting Supplies	602		450		
Decorating Materials					
Wages					
Decorating Supplies					
Total Variable Expenses	5,992		4,450		
Contribution Margin	$ 10,528		$ 6,550		

   Schedule 2: For the decorating department, complete a schedule with the same format as above.

   Schedule 3: For J & J Corporation, as a whole, complete a schedule with the same format as above but extend the income statement to include fixed expenses and net income. **The figures for the company as a whole are merely the sum of the two departments.**

2. The difference between the planning budget contribution margin and the performance budget contribution margin is called a planning variance.

   a) Compute the planning variance for J & J corporation as a whole. Show all computations.

   b) What is the primary cause of this planning variance?

Group Assignment 3-6

DID J & J CORP. GO ASTRAY?

Group Number _____ **Group members present and participating**:

_____

_____

Objective

To understand the concepts of planning (static) budgets and performance (flexible) budgets and their roles in evaluating business performance.

Requirements

1. Suppose you are the manager in charge of revenue and variable expenses for J & J Corp. What would the planning variance tell you? In general terms, what causes this variance and what action would you take, if any, as a result of this variance? Assume that sales prices remain constant during the year.

_____

_____

_____

_____

2. Assume you are the manager in charge of the variable expenses for the painting and decorating departments. In general terms, what information would the performance variances give you? What action might you take to investigate the variances?

_____

_____

_____

_____

3. Would you want these variable expense performance variances to be favorable or unfavorable? Explain.

_____

_____

_____

4. Which variable expenses would you focus your attention on as a result of computing these performance variances for the painting department? For the decorating department?

_____

_____

_____

5. What would the fixed expense performance variance be for J & J Corp. as a whole? Explain how you calculated this amount. What kind of events would cause this type of variance?

_____

_____

_____

_____

6. Explain why J & J did not break even despite surpassing its anticipated breakeven sales volume of $25,971 as computed in Case 3-4, Part 3. Support your answer with computations. (Hint: Compute a revised break-even point based on the actual results per the income statement before you give your explanation).

Revised breakeven point: _____

Explanation: _____

_____

_____

_____

Module 3

Peer Evaluation of Group Members	Class Section	Group No.

Evaluator's Name _____

In the table below, please indicate your estimate, in percentage terms, of the contributions that individual group members made to each of the group assignments listed. Each column should add to 100 percent. For example, if there are five members in your group and all were present for Group Assignment 3-1, you would divide up the 100 percent among the five members, including yourself. If you felt that all group members were prepared to discuss the assignment and contributed equally to the solution, you would give each person 20 percent. If only four members were present, and you felt that one particular member contributed twice as much as the other three, you would give the heavy contributor 40 percent and the other three members 20 percent. The group member who was absent should be listed and given a zero percent.

| Group Members (List) | Group Assignment Number | | |
	3-1	3-3	3-6
Myself			
Totals	100	100	100

Fill in this sheet after each group exercise is completed and turn in with the last group exercise in Module 3.

MODULE FOUR

USING

Accounting Information

TO EVALUATE BUSINESSES

Module 4 Introduction

USING ACCOUNTING INFORMATION TO EVALUATE BUSINESSES

MODULE OVERVIEW

Module 4 begins with coverage of accounting documentation and internal control. The module then changes its focus to the long-term consequences of decision making and the time value of money. This module examines decisions involving accounts receivable, inventory, long-lived assets, and the use of long-term liabilities and/or equity to finance those assets. Valuation issues associated with each type of asset are also examined. The module concludes with a discussion on making decisions using financial statement analysis with both domestic and foreign companies.

The decision context that is the focus of this module involves a continuation of the "John the Painter" case. John and Joanna evaluate and make decisions based on the financial information provided by the owner of a paint and wallpaper retail store. In addition, the concept of financial statement analysis is introduced by evaluating the financial statements of Steve's Stereos, a company which is planning on expanding into the international marketplace. The two decision contexts used in this module are:

- Should J & J expand its existing business by purchasing a retail store and, if so, how should it finance the purchase?
- Which company should Steve's Stereos target for its expansion into the international marketplace?

Learning Objectives

After completing this module, a student should be able to:

1. Understand the nature of internal control and the documentation needed to support a good system of internal controls, understand the components of good internal control, and understand how to correct relatively simple deficiencies in internal control.

2. Understand the nature of accounts receivable and how receivables are valued at net realizable value, understand the linkage between accounts receivable and sales, understand various approaches for establishing an allowance for bad debts, and use various ratios to evaluate the reasonableness of a company's allowance for bad debts.

- Case 4-4	J & J Corporation: Purchase of a Retail Store—Part I
- Group Assignment 4-4	Thompson vs. the Industry
- Group Assignment 4-5	To Err is Human
- Exercises and Problems	Exercises and Problems at the end of Case Readings 4-2 and 4-4

3. Understand the nature of merchandise inventories and how the perpetual and periodic systems track inventory; understand and apply the specific identification, FIFO, and LIFO costing methods; understand the linkage between inventories and cost of goods sold; and understand the requirement for inventories to be valued at the lower of cost or market and the impact of writedowns on the balance sheet and income statements.

- Case Reading 4-3	Decisions Involving Inventory
- Case Reading 4-4	Buying an Existing Business
- Case 4-3	Kris' Crafts
- Case 4-4	J & J Corporation: Purchase of a Retail Store—Part I
- Group Assignment 4-3	Stand Up and Be Counted
- Group Assignment 4-4	Thompson vs. the Industry
- Group Assignment 4-5	To Err is Human
- Exercises and Problems	Exercises and Problems at the end of Case Readings 4-3 and 4-4

4. Understand the nature of long-lived assets and how those assets are accounted for at the date of purchase and during their useful lives.

- Case Reading 4-4	Buying an Existing Business
- Case Reading 4-5	Decisions Involving Property and Equipment
- Case 4-5	J & J Corporation: Purchase of a Retail Store—Part II
- Group Assignment 4-4	Thompson vs. the Industry
- Group Assignment 4-5	To Err is Human
- Exercises and Problems	Exercises and Problems at the end of Case Reading 4-4 and 4-5

5. Understand the nature of long-term liabilities and the significance of the time value of money in measuring those liabilities at their present values, identify cash flows by time period and discount those cash flows to obtain a net present value, determine the internal rate of return associated with a set of cash flows, prepare a mortgage amortization schedule for a mortgage loan at a specified interest rate and number of loan payments, and understand how the liability and related interest arising under a capital lease is treated on the lessee's balance sheet and income statement.

- Case Reading 4-6	Decisions Involving Debt and Equity
- Case Reading 4-7	Decisions Involving Leases and Mortgages
- Case 4-6	Pine Acquires Mahogany - "Wood" You?
- Case 4-7	J & J Corporation: Purchase of a Retail Store—Part III
- Group Assignment 4-7	What is Your Best Option?
- Exercises and Problems	Exercises and Problems at the end of Case Reading 4-6 and 4-7

6. Understand how to analyze financial statements of U.S. companies using horizontal, vertical, trend analysis and ratio analysis; understand where and how to find industry data for comparison purposes; and understand how to analyze financial statements of foreign companies; understand the typical difficulties encountered when analyzing foreign company financial statements.

- Case Reading 4-8	Analysis of Financial Statements
- Case Reading 4-9	Analyzing Foreign Company Financial Statements
- Case 4-8	Financial Statement Analysis: Food for Thought
- Case 4-9	Steve's Stereos Goes International
- Group Assignment 4-8	Through the Looking Glass
- Group Assignment 4-9	What in the World?
- Exercises and Problems	Exercises and Problems at the end of Case Readings 4-8 and 4-9

Case Reading 4-1

ACCOUNTING DOCUMENTATION
AND INTERNAL CONTROL

INTRODUCTION

The newspaper headline read:

> "25-year Employee Embezzles $2 Million"

In disbelief, the owners had no choice but to press charges against their trusted employee. They pondered how it was possible for an employee to steal so much money without being discovered. As the story goes, it was not the owners of the business who uncovered the embezzlement but a new employee who questioned why the return on equity was not improving since the revenues were increasing at a 30 percent rate.

This case reading introduces the concept of internal control. Internal control is the set of procedures and policies which ensures that assets are safe from unauthorized use or theft and that the financial statements are reliable measures of the economic status of the business. An understanding of internal control requires a basic knowledge of the operating cycle of a retail business as well as the accounting documents used and the flow of these documents within the organization.

OPERATING CYCLE OF A BUSINESS

The **operating cycle** for a merchandising company (a company which purchases goods for resale) is the time that it takes to buy inventory, sell the inventory to the customer, and collect the cash. For example, let's suppose Jenny's Jewelry buys beads from a manufacturer on June 1, sells the beads to a customer on credit on June 26, and collects the cash from the customer on July 3. For Jenny's Jewelry, the operating cycle for this transaction was from June 1 to July 3, or 33 days.

Purchase Inventory → Sell Inventory to Customer on Credit → Collect Cash from Customer

A short operating cycle is best because it means that inventory on average is sold more often, which generally means more operating profits. A short operating cycle is often looked at as a measure of efficiency for a company.

The Purchasing of Inventory

For larger merchandising companies, the purchasing of inventory normally involves the use of a **purchase requisition**. The requisition is prepared by an individual in the department requesting the merchandise. The requisition lists the item requested, the quantity desired, the person requesting the purchase, and possibly a suggested vendor. Often purchase requisitions are sequentially numbered so that the company can keep track of how many purchase requisitions are outstanding and how many have been filled. After the requisition is prepared, it is forwarded to the purchasing department. The requisitioning department keeps a copy of the requisition for its files.

When the purchasing department reviews and approves the purchase requisition, a **purchase order** is generated. Purchase orders (POs) are sequentially numbered and contain similar information to the purchase requisition. The sequential numbering ensures that all purchase orders can be accounted for, and that no one can improperly use one to make a purchase for personal use. Additionally, the purchase order contains the name of the vendor (seller), any shipping instructions, shipping terms, and the date by which the delivery is required. Exhibit 4-1.1 shows a sample purchase order for Jenny's Jewelry. The company is ordering three items from Beads 'N Such, a vendor.

The purchase order is approved by Cindy Ferrini. Requiring written approval of purchase orders and other accounting documents before processing is an internal control measure. Internal control measures are procedures companies undertake to safeguard their assets. A more thorough discussion appears later in this case reading.

A copy of the purchase order is kept in the purchasing department and filed numerically. The original is sent to the vendor and another copy is sent to the accounting department where it is eventually matched with the vendor's invoice when received. An additional copy may also be sent to the receiving department, which is the department that receives all inventory deliveries.

Exhibit 4-1.1
Purchase Order

Jenny's Jewelery
123 Leather Lane
Cincinnati, Ohio 45243

Purchase Order

To:	Date:	6/2/97	PO #	788423
	Terms	2/10, net 30		
Beads 'N Such	Ship By:	Express Trucking		
817 Larkspur Lane	Instructions:	FOB Shipping Point		
Crown Point, Indiana 46307	Date Required:	6/22/97		

Item #	Quantity	Description	Unit price	Amount
582	60	5 pack blue oval beads	$ 1.22	$ 73.20
373	24	Pointed tweezers	3.45	82.80
921	36	60 ft. 1 lb. gauge wire	6.90	248.40

Approved by *Cindy Ferrini*

	TOTAL	$ 404.40

The purchase order is number 788423 and it requests shipping by Express Trucking. Jenny's needs the items by June 22. The items are to be shipped FOB shipping point. FOB is an abbreviation for Free on Board. **FOB shipping point** means that the title to the goods passes to the buyer when the item leaves the shipping point (the vendor). This means that during shipment the buyer holds title to the goods. **FOB destination** means that the title passes at the destination point, which would be the buyer's place of business. During transit, the seller owns the goods. Usually the company which owns the goods during shipment is responsible for payment of freight charges.

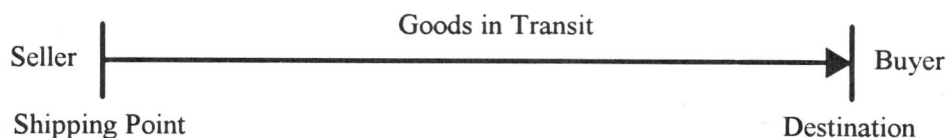

```
                            Goods in Transit
Seller   |─────────────────────────────────────────────────▶|   Buyer

Shipping Point                                              Destination
```

FOB Shipping Point – Title transfers at shipping point and buyer pays freight.

FOB Destination – Title transfers at destination and seller pays freight.

After the purchase order has been sent to the vendor, the buyer waits for the merchandise to be delivered. For larger merchandising companies, the goods are generally received in the company's receiving department. When the goods arrive, the receiving clerk inspects the merchandise and completes a **receiving report** which lists the item received, the quantity and date received, plus any additional information the company might desire. Companies using computerized accounting software packages can have the system generate a receiving report from the purchase order. This form lists the vendor and the items ordered but not the quantity. The receiver is expected to count each item and fill in the quantity actually received. It is important that the receiving clerk accept shipments only for items that have been ordered by the company. Like purchase orders, receiving reports are numbered sequentially so that the company can account for each report issued. One copy of the receiving report is filed numerically and a second copy is forwarded to the accounting department.

The **vendor invoice** is the seller's bill. It is usually received in the mail and sent to the accounting department. It is critical that the invoice not be paid until the accounting department has verified that the goods ordered were in fact received. The accounting department does this by matching all the information on the purchase order with that on the receiving report. Comparing these two documents with the vendor's invoice ensures that the company is only billed for what was ordered and received. The accounting clerk normally initials the invoice as evidence that this comparison check has been performed. The invoice is also clerically checked for accuracy before it is forwarded to the finance department for payment. Documented evidence of the clerical check can be shown with the checker's initials as well.

The finance department clerk prepares a check along with a **remittance advice**. The remittance advice is attached to the check and states the check amount and its purpose. The treasurer signs the check after reviewing the supporting documentation, which usually includes the purchase order, invoice, and receiving report. Checks are sequentially numbered and have several carbon copies. One copy is filed numerically and a second copy is attached to the supporting documentation. The original check is mailed to the vendor.

The check is prepared in the finance department instead of the accounting department in order to separate the cash handling duties from the recordkeeping duties. By separating these two functions, the company is safeguarding its assets. The company needs to ensure that an employee with cash handling responsibilities does not have the ability to cover up a mishandling of cash by recording a bogus transaction in the accounting records.

The purchase of inventory is recorded in the accounting records as of the date the buyer obtains legal title. That date depends on whether the item was shipped FOB shipping point or FOB destination. Recording inventory on the correct date is very important in accounting. As mentioned previously, accountants consider the matching of expenses during the period with the revenues of the period to be critical. A proper matching can occur only if inventory items are properly reflected in the accounting records. If inventory is purchased on credit, then a misstatement in recording inventory will also result in a misstatement of accounts payable and potentially a misstatement of cost of goods sold.

The Sale of Inventory

A merchandising company is in business to sell inventory. The sale can be a cash sale or a credit sale. For a cash sale, the inventory is given to the buyer and cash is received for the selling price of the goods. If the sale is made on credit, the sales process becomes more complex.

Credit Checks

Before the sale is approved, a credit check must be performed on the customer. Most companies require customers to provide financial information which the seller will then review and analyze to determine how much, if any, credit the customer should be granted. Additional outside sources such as the TRW credit bureau may also be consulted. These outside sources maintain credit backgrounds on virtually every individual and business. They then sell these credit reports to inquiring companies for a fee. Once the customer has been deemed creditworthy, a credit limit is assigned. A customer's credit limit represents the maximum accounts receivable balance that customer can maintain. It is the seller's responsibility to maintain adequate records so that the outstanding balance in a particular customer's account is known at any given point in time. By keeping up-to-date records, the company will recognize immediately if customers exceed their credit limits.

Sales Order

When a purchase order is received from a customer and the credit check is complete, the company will issue a **sales order**. The sales order communicates the description and quantity of the item(s) ordered by the customer. In many companies a preparation of a sales order also represents that a credit check has been performed and the shipment of goods is authorized. Once again, initials on the sales order could be one way that the seller documents credit approval. One copy of the sales order is sent back to the customer as a verification of the receipt of the purchase order. A second copy is filed numerically and a third copy is filed by customer name. The last copy of the sales order is sent to the shipping department to be used as a basis for preparing the shipping document. By accounting for a copy of the sales orders numerically, the company can ensure that all sales orders are accounted for.

Shipping Document

Shipping documents are particularly important because companies generally use them to update inventory information. One copy of the shipping document is sent to the customer, one is filed numerically, and one copy is sent to the accounting department as a signal to prepare a sales invoice. The shipping document usually contains information about the type of inventory shipped, the quantity shipped, and the shipping terms. In some cases, a shipping document is also called a **bill of lading,** which is the legal shipping document for common carriers. The shipping document is matched with the customer purchase order in the accounting department and the sales records are updated based on the information provided in these documents. The sale should be recorded on the date that the title passes to the customer. When the customer receives the merchandise, the receiving clerk will sign the bill of lading, a copy of which will be returned to the seller. The accounting department will make an entry to increase accounts receivable and record the sales revenue as of the date of receipt noted by the customer. An additional entry to reduce inventory and record cost of goods sold will also be made if a perpetual inventory system is used (see Case Reading 4-3 for a thorough discussion of a perpetual inventory system).

Sales Invoice

A **sales invoice** is the bill that is sent to the customer. Exhibit 4-1.2 shows a sample invoice for Jenny's Jewelry. Sales invoices, like most accounting documents, are prenumbered. The sales invoice shown is invoice #6621. The customer's name is Lorie Lovejoy. Jenny's Jewelry, the seller, received PO# 45876 from Lovejoy, as shown on the invoice. Lovejoy ordered two inventory items A423, identified as bead earrings, for $32 each. The invoice shows that the shipping terms are FOB destination, which means Jenny's Jewelry intends to pay for the freight and owns the goods during shipment.

Exhibit 4-1.2
Sales Invoice

Jenny's Jewelery *123 Leather Lane* *Cincinnati, Ohio 45243*		Invoice		
		Date	Invoice #	
		6/1/97	6621	

Bill To:			Ship To:		
Lorie Lovejoy 967 Garrison Drive Lexington, KY 48761			Same		

P.O. Number	Terms:	Rep:	Ship	VIA	F.O.B.
45876	2/10, Net 30	Jenny	6/3/97	UPS	Destination

Quantity	Item Code	Description	Unit Price	Amount
2	A423	Bead Earrings	$32.00	$64.00
				$64.00

The **sales terms** on the invoice are listed as 2/10, net 30. This means that Lorie Lovejoy will receive a 2 percent discount off the $64 selling price if she pays within 10 days of the invoice date of June 1. If she does not, the entire amount is due within 30 days of the invoice date. How much should Lovejoy expect to pay on June 6?

Lovejoy can expect to pay 98 percent of $64, or $62.72.

Most companies have software programs that generate their sales invoices. The software programs ensure that the total amount on the invoice is correct unless there is an error in the quantity or price. Still, it would be wise for Lorie Lovejoy to clerically check the invoice before rendering payment for the earrings.

ELEMENTS OF INTERNAL CONTROL

A successful business is one where well thought-out procedures and systems are in place to transact business. **Internal controls** are the policies and procedures adopted to safeguard an entity's assets and to ensure accuracy and reliability in its financial records. Owners, management, and employees should all be cognizant of the checks and balances within a company. This lessens the chance that an employee will embezzle or defraud the business of money or other assets.

The following list represents the key attributes of a good internal control system:

- Proper authorization of transactions
- Proper segregation of employee duties
- Safeguarding of assets and accounting records
- Independent verification
- Adequate documents and records
- Independent monitoring of controls

Proper Authorization of Transactions

Designated individuals are assigned the responsibility for the proper authorization of transactions. For example, the purchase order in Exhibit 4-1.1 for Jenny's Jewelry lists Cindy Ferrini as the individual authorized to approve this transaction. Before signing the purchase order, Cindy would check the information from the purchase requisition to ensure that there was a need for the ordered item, that Beads 'N Such was an authorized vendor (seller), and that the price of the items ordered were on the approved price list. Cindy would also be knowledgeable about the various shipping arrangements with the approved vendors. The vendor would notify Cindy if there were any problem with the order.

Proper Segregation of Employee Duties

In any business it is important to separate the custody of the assets from the recordkeeping or accounting for the assets, thus ensuring a proper segregation of employee duties. Additionally, if an individual is designated as one who authorizes a given transaction, that individual should not be responsible to account for the transaction. In our illustration, the purchase of an item was authorized in the purchasing department by Cindy Ferrini, recorded in the accounting department, and paid for in the finance department. If these functions were not separated, an employee could potentially authorize a purchase from a bogus vendor, record the fictitious transaction in the accounting records, and pay the bogus vendor, keeping the money for himself or herself.

Safeguarding of Assets and Accounting Records

The assets of the business and the accounting documents need to be physically safeguarded. These safeguards might include a fireproof safe to lock up accounting documents and records, an alarm system to protect the warehouse from theft, and password protection to access accounting software and data files. By safeguarding the assets and accounting records, the company protects them from being stolen, damaged, altered, or lost. In the manufacture of small high-tech parts which can easily be stolen, a few pounds of stolen computer chips can be worth thousands of dollars. Sophisticated procedures and systems must be installed to prevent loss of inventory.

Independent Verification

Independent verification is the process of one employee checking another employee's work. For example, one employee might be responsible for reviewing the vendor's invoice. This review may include clerically checking the invoice. If after checking the invoice another employee repeats this procedure, it is called internal verification. Internal verification increases the chance that the procedure was accurately performed. An employee checking another employee's work often documents this internal verification by placing his or her initials or signature on the appropriate document.

Adequate Documents and Records

Adequate documents and records include purchase orders, receiving reports, sales invoices, and other accounting documents as well as accounting records such as the general ledger and the various accounting journals. The documents and records should be easy to understand and designed to meet the information needs of the company. Multiple copies of the documents should be created if necessary. For example, the purchase order used by Jenny's Jewelry had several copies which were distributed to different departments of the business. The records should be created at the time the transactions take place to minimize errors or omissions. Most accounting documents are prenumbered and issued in sequence to facilitate control over the issuance and use of the documents. For example, by prenumbering and issuing sales invoices in sequence, the accountant could easily identify a sales invoice that had not been entered in the accounting records. This assumes that when recording the sale, the sales invoice number is also recorded. Companies which use prenumbered documents usually maintain a numerical file of the particular document.

In a recent case, a check for $5,000 cleared a company's checking account. This was a check number which a year earlier was presumed to have been lost or destroyed. Unfortunately, the embezzler still had possession of the signed check. The embezzler waited until the "lost check" had long been forgotten and then successfully cashed it. The mistake in this story is that a missing or unaccounted check number is always cause for suspicion. An inexpensive insurance policy is to immediately notify the bank and place a stop payment on the check number. Banks have the ability to suspend payment of a check pending further authorization when circumstances suggest that fraud may be involved.

Independent Monitoring of Controls

Larger companies have internal audit departments that are responsible for making sure that the policies and procedures of the company are enforced. The internal audit staff are employees of the company so they are not independent of the company, but they do exist independently of any other department. The internal audit staff is responsible for maintaining and evaluating the current internal control system, making corrective changes as necessary.

External auditors also evaluate the internal control system as part of the audit of a company's financial statements. The external auditors are generally hired by the Board of Directors and are not employees of the company that they audit. Their purpose is to give an opinion as to the fairness of the financial statements. In order to fulfill this purpose, the auditors perform a thorough evaluation of the internal control system to determine if the system can be relied upon to generate financial statements that are free of material misstatements. At the completion of the audit, the external auditors provide the company with suggestions for improvement of the company's internal control system.

The **Foreign Corrupt Practices Act** is a U.S. law that was enacted in 1977 that makes it the responsibility of management to report on the adequacy of internal control. This act was passed because of the increasing number of bribes that were being paid to foreign governments to encourage them to do business with U.S. companies. The act made the payment of such bribes illegal. As a result, most publicly traded companies have a system of internal control that results in the safeguarding of assets and the preparation of reliable financial statements. In most cases, the management of a company will publicly acknowledge its responsibility by issuing a Report of Management, which is generally included in the company's annual report. The Report of Management reinforces the policy that management is responsible for safeguarding the assets and for the reliability of the financial statements.

It is quite common in publicly held companies for the Board of Directors to appoint an audit committee, usually consisting of outside board members. That is, they are not members of management. Typically the **audit committee** is a group of individuals that reviews, recommends, and reports to the Board on (1) the independent auditors, (2) the quality and effectiveness of internal controls, (3) the engagement or discharge of the independent certified public accountants, (4) the professional services provided by the independent accountants, and (5) the review and approval of major changes in the accounting practices and principles used by the company in publishing its financial reports. In essence, the audit committee works on behalf of the shareholders to make sure that the controls which facilitate sound business and reporting practices are maintained.

WHEN THERE ARE NO CONTROLS

This is an example of a business situation which had a reasonable rationale but where management forgot to install normal internal controls. It concerns a food service operation at a university. The food service management had the idea that if they sold for $20 food cards having a redemption value of $25, the food service revenues would increase and the operation would be more profitable. They printed simple cards which had many cells with denominations of $1.00, $.50, $.25, etc., which totaled $25. The printing was of a generic quality and the cards were not sequentially numbered.

When a customer would purchase the card for $20 at any one of several locations, the revenue would be recorded as a sale of food, just like that of a cash customer. When a customer presented the card when making a purchase, the cash register clerk would use a hole punch to cancel the value of the items being purchased. For example, if a customer presented a card with $21.50 remaining value on it, and the purchase amounted to $3.50, the clerk would punch out the cells on the card totaling $3.50, leaving $18.00 of redemption value on the card. The clerk would not key in the purchase amount when a food card was used.

As you are probably aware by now there are several major internal control flaws in this situation. It illustrates how a promising promotional strategy can go awry because controls were not installed when the program was launched. We will analyze this situation using the elements of internal control discussed above.

Proper Authorization of Transactions

The food cards could be sold by virtually any employee of the food service. Most employees were trained to operate the cash register so that when long lines formed at peak times of the day, various food service personnel could open cash register stations. With many people involved, it was not possible to reconcile cash received with the unsold cards. If there existed a shortage of cards, it would not be possible to identify which clerk was responsible for the shortage.

Proper Segregation of Duties

In cash businesses such as restaurants and bars there is a greater vulnerability to theft by employees. In some cash businesses, computers are used to track the items sold to customers, which then sets up a control of how much cash should be collected at the end of the shift. What could have been done in the food card case is to sell the cards at the cashier's window. This would have limited the number of individuals who had access to the unsold cards and afforded the chance to track the total amount of sales of cards for later analysis of the profit or loss of the program.

Safeguarding of Assets and Accounting Records

The unsold cards are as much an asset as the cash in the register or the food inventory. The casual manner in which the unsold cards were controlled invited theft. If cards were stolen no one would know it. A dishonest employee could sell cards to friends or use the card for personal purchases. Also, the lack of controls made it possible to sell a customer a food card for $20 and pocket the money when no one was looking.

With regard to the accounting records, a system would be needed to know two summary amounts: how much revenue was obtained by selling the cards and the total redemption amount. In theory, the total redemption should never be more than 25 percent above the sale of food cards ($5 ÷ $20). If this occurred it would be evidence that cards are being stolen. However, management never set up a system to track the flow of activity associated with the food card program. They would forever be in the dark.

Independent Verification

Normally, a manager verifies that the amount entered in a cash register agrees with the cash collected during that employee's shift. Even with this procedure, the nonexistent controls with respect to the unsold cards rendered this control meaningless. The employee could give the food card to a customer, place the $20 in the register, and not ring it up. Unless the customer was an astute internal control expert, it is not likely that he or she would suspect anything irregular in the food card transaction.

Adequate Documents and Records

The fatal flaw in the food card program was the lack of prenumbered cards. Not only did this preclude safeguarding the assets, it opened the door to counterfeiting the cards. Recall that they were the product of a generic printing job, easy to duplicate on a copy machine. From a purely practical point of view, the only control of unsold cards that could be accomplished, absent the sequential prenumbering, was to repeatedly count the number of unsold cards and to compare that to the same number the previous day. With many employees dispensing the cards, this procedure, while grossly inefficient, would still be unmanageable due to unrestricted authorization to make transactions. It should be mentioned that an important control procedure of prenumbered documents is that they are not used out of sequence. The rule must be set and communicated to the appropriate employees. An independent check that this rule is being observed must be done by a manager who is not involved in the daily transactions.

Independent Monitoring of Controls

As alluded to above, it is incumbent upon management to design a system that safeguards the assets and ensures that the accounting records are reliable. Management must identify the risks inherent in a particular business situation and set up a way to monitor its operation to uncover irregularities or errors. In a large company, internal auditors test the operation to determine whether the controls are being applied. In a small company the risks increase because fewer people are available to separate duties and authorizations. In such cases it is even more important that the owner think through the risks and periodically perform an audit to assure that procedures are being followed.

SUMMARY

This case reading introduced and explained many of the documents used in the operating cycle of the business. Proper documents and records are essential elements in a good internal control system. An adequate control system must safeguard the assets from misuse or theft and ensure that the accounting records contain accurate measures of the economic status of the enterprise. Internal control will take unique forms in different business. However, there are basic principles and attributes of a good internal control system. Many years ago Congress, seeing the importance of internal controls to the economy of the country, passed legislation which required public companies to have adequate controls. Independent certified public accountants were required to test the adequacy of the internal controls. Even a business which is successful in terms of its products or customer satisfaction can fail because inadequate controls preclude the management from having an accurate picture of the company's financial position and the safety of its assets.

EXERCISES AND PROBLEMS

Exercises

Exercise 1 Understanding The Operating Cycle. Explain the term operating cycle. Is it better to have a short or long operating cycle? Explain.

Exercise 2 Purchase Requisitions and Purchase Orders. Distinguish between a purchase requisition and a purchase order.

Exercise 3 Understanding FOB. In Exhibit 4-1.1 the instructions state "FOB Shipping Point." What is meant by FOB and why is it significant?

Exercise 4 Relating Receiving Report and Vendor Invoice. How are a receiving report and a vendor invoice related?

Exercise 5 Understanding Sales Terms. What do sales terms of 3/10, net 30 mean? When purchasing goods, would you prefer terms of 1/10, net 30 or 3/10, net 30? Explain.

Exercise 6 Explaining an Attribute of Good Internal Control. Select one of the six key attributes of a good internal control system and explain how it can be used to strengthen internal controls in an organization.

Exercise 7 Explaining How to Circumvent an Attribute of Internal Control. Select one of the six key attributes of a good internal control system and explain how someone could circumvent (get around) it to weaken a corporation's internal control system.

Exercise 8 Responsibility for Internal Control System. Who is primarily responsible for an adequate system of internal controls in an organization? In a typical large corporation, how is this responsibility discharged?

Problems

Problem 1 Library Research on Internal Control Defects. Go to your university library or another library to find a news article in a business publication (*The Wall Street Journal*, *Business Week*, or another publication) concerning a breakdown in internal control. Write a one-page summary of the article, including what key attributes of a good internal control system were violated.

Problem 2 Corporate Annual Report Research on Internal Control. Find the annual report for a large publicly traded corporation. You may find these reports in your library or check with your professor for other sources of published annual reports. In the annual report, find at least two mentions of the corporate internal control system. Report where you found the references in the annual report and the significance of its mention.

Problem 3 Identifying an Internal Control Weakness. Periodically a news article will appear in the financial press about a long-term trusted employee who has robbed his or her company of a few hundred thousand dollars. Usually, the fraud was covered by an employee who was working for a small bank and who had not taken a vacation for five or ten years.

Based on this information, explain what key internal control attributes probably were circumvented by the employee. Be as specific as you can in your explanation.

Problem 4 Identifying Weaknesses in an Existing Internal Control System. To increase textbook sales at the college bookstore at California University, general manager Kelly Taylor introduced a time payment plan for textbooks. When students pre-register for classes 60 days prior to the start of the semester, the registrar's office provides the bookstore with a computer file of the pre-registered students' class schedules. The bookstore uses its textbook database to develop a list of required textbooks for each student. The bookstore sends an offer letter to pre-registered students stating that all books will be delivered to their dorm room or apartment by the first day of classes. The list of textbooks and the total price is included in the letter. To take advantage of the offer, the student must sign the attached agreement and return it with payment by check or credit card for 25 percent of the total. The agreement specifies that three installments of 25 percent each must be paid at 30-day intervals.

The order-fulfillment process begins about two weeks before the start of the school term. University students are employed to gather the texts ordered by students and shrink-wrap the set for easier handling. Fifteen students work on this project for the two weeks prior to the start of the term. No specific duties are assigned to individuals since they are supposed to work as a team. Consequently, deliveries to dorm and apartments are made by everyone, depending on who feels like getting out of the order-picking detail. Sometimes the students flip a coin to determine who does what.

Kelly is concerned that her plan to boost sales might have a glitch. During the first week of the term she has heard from her staff that a lot of students who paid the 25 percent down payment never got their books and had to fight the long lines at the bookstore to get them during the first week of classes. Some missed assignments as a result. One student whose father is a class-action attorney has threatened to sue for a refund and punitive damages!

Requirements

Identify three of the six internal control characteristics that are absent in the book ordering and delivery process. For each of the three characteristics explain how the weakness can result in either loss of assets or loss of managerial control of the business operation. What procedures should be implemented to improve internal control?

Case 4-1

INTERNAL CONTROL LAPSES

Case Objective

To apply the attributes of a sound internal control structure to two situations in which there exists a major flaw in the design of the system.

Decision: How can the company's internal control be improved?

Case Reading 4-1 listed six characteristics of a good internal control system. Examples of how these controls would operate were also discussed. In this case we present three business situations in which the company may be vulnerable to loss of assets or inadequate knowledge of the true state of the business due to poor documentation. Your job is to identify the characteristics which are absent in each of the following three situations and to recommend a remedy to improve internal control.

Situation A. This is a warehouse membership store that is a high-volume merchandiser of a variety of product categories including food, housewares, electronic appliances, jewelry, clothing, tires, and seasonal items. The marketing strategy is to sell many items in larger quantities than competitors and at somewhat lower profit margins. Additionally, the strategy is to merchandise many innovative items as impulse purchases. To attain the very high sales volume required by this strategy, the company has a liberal "no questions asked" return policy.

To reduce operating expenses, the company runs its stores as cash-and-carry retail. Customers pay in cash or by check. A customer returning an item is given cash for the item. The process works as follows: The customer enters the store showing the club card. The attendant at the entrance gives the customer an adhesive tag which is affixed to the item being brought back to the store for return. When the customer arrives at the merchandise return counter, the clerk removes the tag and tosses it in the waste basket. The clerk asks the customer the reason for the return and, based on the answer, enters a check mark next to the appropriate category in a return log. The categories are as follows:

1. Customer did not need the product
2. Customer purchased the wrong size
3. Customer found the product defective
4. Customer found the product of low quality
5. Customer can buy the product elsewhere at a lower price
6. Customer refused to state the reason for the return or other reason

Next the customer is asked for the cash register receipt. If the customer has it, the refund is based upon the amount paid. If the customer fails to produce it the clerk refers to a book of prices (updated weekly) to determine the current price of the item. If the item is found in the price book, the customer will be told of the refund amount.

If the customer disagrees with the refund amount, the clerk asks when the item was purchased and at what price. It is possible that the current price is lower than a previous price because of markdowns intended to clear that item out of inventory to make room for new items to be promoted. If the clerk determines the explanation to be reasonable, the customer's assertions are accepted and the refund is based on the price claimed by the customer.

The refund counter is equipped with a cash register and is stocked with $1,000 in currency every four hours. The clerk making the refund enters the refund amount. The cash register computes the sales tax and the total cash amount to be refunded is handed to the customer.

The clerk inspects the returned merchandise. If the clerk finds the item to appear to be merchantable and the customer's reason for return was other than being defective, the item is returned to the display shelves in the store.

For items returned due to the product being defective, the clerk completes a defect form documenting the make, model, description, and other relevant data that the clerk deems important. The company policy is to give all nonfood defective merchandise to an agency that employs physically challenged workers to repair and refurbish the returned items. Food items are thrown out. The return clerk is expected to make a daily delivery of the defective merchandise to the repair facility. Upon making the delivery, the clerk is given a receipt for the items delivered. The next day the clerk attaches this receipt to the group of defect forms prepared the previous day. Occasionally the store manager reviews the receipt from the repair agency to check that defect forms match the items on the receipt.

Requirements

Identify three of the six internal control characteristics that are absent in the refund and inventory process. For each of the three characteristics explain how the weakness can result in either loss of assets or loss of managerial control of the business operation. What procedures should be implemented to improve internal control?

Situation B. This is a small neighborhood liquor store owned and operated by Mr. and Mrs. Romano. Unfortunately, Mr. Romano needed bypass surgery and is recuperating at home for six months. Mrs. Romano helped out in the liquor store business handling the accounting, banking, vendor payment, and tax filings. Mr. Romano handled the ordering of inventory, organizing backroom stock, designing shelf displays, and cashiering the sales.

Because Mr. Romano's illness struck suddenly, the couple had no time to recruit someone they felt they could trust with the management and operation of the store. They felt that seeking the services of a temporary employment agency was a reasonable alternative. The agency sent Manfred Schnapps, who had just moved into town from Las Vegas. On his application he indicated that he worked part time as a bartender while he was in school.

Mrs. Romano agreed to the six-month contract with the temporary agency. Manfred seemed to be trustworthy and had a pleasant disposition of which customers would approve. Mrs. Romano gave Manfred a list of functions he is to perform:

1. Ring up all cash, check, and credit card sales in the cash register. Mrs. Romano would take the deposit to the bank each day.

2. Stock all of the shelves from backroom inventory and place orders with the appropriate liquor and beer distributors for replenishment of stock.

3. When deliveries on credit are made, verify that everything billed has been received. Sign the invoice to indicate the shipment is complete and put the invoice in the office.

4. When deliveries are to be paid C.O.D., verify as above that all items to be paid for have been received. Pay the route salesperson cash out of the register. Sign and place the invoice in the cash register.

5. Monitor prices by comparing our prices to distributor suggested prices. Change prices when the distributor recommends changes. Also mark down prices by no more than 10 percent for slow-moving items.

6. Use your judgment when repairs or janitorial services are required by choosing someone listed in the phone book. If necessary, pay for these services out of the cash register and place the bill in the cash register with the day's receipts. Otherwise, place the bills for these services in the office.

Requirements

Identify three of the six internal control characteristics that are absent in the overall store management. For each of the three characteristics explain how the weakness can result in either loss of assets or loss of managerial control of the business operation. What procedures should be implemented to improve internal control?

Case Reading 4-2

DECISIONS INVOLVING
ACCOUNTS RECEIVABLE

INTRODUCTION

This case reading analyzes the issues involved in granting credit to customers and monitoring their credit history. The impact of bad debts (uncollectible accounts) on the financial statements is presented and examples given. The case reading concludes with the financial statement presentation of accounts receivable. The auditor's role in reviewing the estimates made by management is also emphasized.

DECISIONS INVOLVED IN ISSUING CREDIT

Because most businesses sell their goods and services by accepting a short-term account receivable in exchange, accounting information is needed to manage the credit-granting function. The **credit policy** of a company will determine who will receive credit from the company, based on information such as past credit history, how long in business or work history, and other factors. Case Reading 4-1 mentioned how a company obtains credit information about its customers. In determining a reasonable credit limit for any individual customer, the company wants to set a limit high enough to encourage the customer to buy, but also to set it at a level so that the sales amount is collectible within a reasonable period of time. Companies extending credit to customers usually experience increased sales. Granting credit to customers gives customers more freedom in financing their purchases, so they tend to buy more. On the other hand, a business may incur significant losses due to customers' inability to pay their bills. Determining the point at which sales are maximized and bad debts are at an acceptable level requires sound accounting information and management vigilance.

During the normal course of business, the company will encounter accounts receivable which are questionable. In fact, if a company doesn't have any bad accounts, it is probably not maximizing its sales potential. To remain competitive, a seller must provide credit to worthy customers. In most cases it is a win-win situation for both the company and the customer.

What Are the Options If a Customer Doesn't Pay?

If the customer does not pay within a reasonable period of time it usually means that the customer is unable or unwilling to pay. A customer who is unwilling to pay should be questioned further. Why would a customer risk his or her credit rating by not paying if he or she were able to pay? One possible answer is that the customer is dissatisfied with the product for some reason. Any customer dissatisfaction should be immediately investigated. Management would want to be sure that the problem is an isolated incident and not an indication of a poor quality product or service.

If the customer is unable to pay because of limited funds, the company has several options:

1. Keep the accounts receivable in the accounting records for a while longer, hoping the customer will eventually pay.
2. Write the account balance off (write-offs are discussed later in this case reading).
3. Convert the account receivable into a note receivable. The customer would need to sign a written promise to pay (a promissory note). This note would state an interest rate and a due date.

ESTIMATING THE EXPENSE OF UNCOLLECTIBLE ACCOUNTS RECEIVABLE

Recall the revenue recognition principle which states that a company records a sale when the earnings process is substantially complete, never earlier. This is usually when the title of the goods passes to the customer. An additional requirement is that costs associated with the sale are known or can be estimated with reasonable accuracy. If the company sells on credit there may be losses due to uncollectible accounts. **Uncollectible accounts** are accounts that the company is unable to collect, for whatever reason. Such losses should be shown as an expense in the same accounting period as the one reporting the sales revenue. To do otherwise would overstate net income in one accounting period (the period of the sale) and understate income in the following period(s) when the expense of uncollectible accounts becomes an established fact. There are two methods of recognizing the expense related to uncollectible accounts. These methods are called the direct write-off method and the allowance method.

Direct Write-Off Method

In the **direct write-off method**, an expense called **bad debt expense** (also called **uncollectible accounts expense**) is recorded when the company determines that a customer's accounts receivable is uncollectible. A notice of bankruptcy or any other event which suggests a low probability of collecting the account receivable triggers the recording of the expense. At the same time the expense is recorded, accounts receivable is reduced by the same amount.

The direct method is easier to use, but a problem arises because this method violates the matching principle. As you will recall, the matching principle says that expenses must be recorded in the same period as the revenues to which they relate. In this case, however, the bad debt expense is not recorded until it is actually determined that the specific account receivable is uncollectible. This could be in an entirely different accounting period from the one in which the sales revenue was recorded. In that case, the bad debt expense would not be properly matched with the sales revenue. This method is primarily used by companies that are not required to follow generally accepted accounting principles (GAAP) or companies that rarely have an uncollectible accounts receivable. It is also the only method that is allowed for the calculation of bad debts for income tax purposes and therefore it must be used when preparing tax returns.

An example is a medical practice. The doctor is not bound by GAAP since it is assumed that there are no other investors or major creditors. The typical creditors of a medical practice would not demand audited financial statements prepared in accordance with GAAP. Suppose the doctor has revenues in 2000 of $500,000 and ends the year with accounts receivable of $200,000. Further let us assume net income is $250,000. Is the direct write-off method correctly measuring the doctor's true expenses for 2000? Is the doctor's income really $250,000? There is a strong probability that contained in the $200,000 of accounts receivable are some accounts that will never be collected; assume that amount is $20,000. The direct write-off method will reflect these losses in the year 2001 or later. The result of the misalignment of revenues and expenses is that income for 2000 is overstated and income for 2001 is understated, giving the doctor a false picture of the true income of the practice for each year.

Allowance Method

The **allowance method** requires a company to *estimate* the uncollectible accounts rather than wait for an account to actually be identified as uncollectible. This estimate is made in the same period as the sale is made and therefore a proper matching of revenues and expenses is achieved. The estimate is based upon the entire pool of receivables; no individual accounts are identified as uncollectible in the estimate. The company creates an account called allowance for uncollectible accounts (often abbreviated an allowance account). The allowance method usually results in a more conservative determination of net income than the direct write-off method.

Companies that trade their stock in the open market (public companies) are required by the Securities Exchange and Commission (SEC) to use GAAP in their annual reports. The direct write-off method is not considered to be GAAP, primarily because of the lack of good matching of revenues and expenses, and thus the SEC will not allow it to be used for company reporting purposes. Accordingly, public companies need to use the allowance method for reporting uncollectible accounts.

Allowance for uncollectible accounts (also called **allowance for doubtful accounts**) represents the amount of accounts receivable the company estimates will be uncollectible. The account is a **contra account,** or to be more precise, a contra-asset account. A contra-asset account is found in the asset section of the worksheet (and therefore in the asset section of the balance sheet) but has a negative balance. During an accounting period, the allowance account is increased by the amount of bad debt expense and decreased by the amount of write-offs.

The amount recorded for **bad debt expense** depends on which approach the company uses to estimate uncollectible accounts. There are two common approaches to estimating uncollectible amounts: the percentage of sales approach and the aging of accounts receivable approach. Both of these approaches calculate bad debt expense in a unique way and will be discussed later in this case reading. Regardless of the approach used, the amount recorded for bad debt expense would be shown on the transaction worksheet as a negative amount in both the Retained Earnings and Allowance for Uncollectible Accounts columns. Since allowance for uncollectible accounts is a contra-asset account, a negative amount in that column increases that account balance.

When a particular account receivable is determined to be uncollectible the company records the **write-off** on the worksheet by a decrease to accounts receivable and allowance for uncollectible accounts. A decrease to the allowance account is recorded as a positive dollar amount on the worksheet because the allowance is a contra-asset account.

The partial transaction worksheet shown as Exhibit 4-2.1 demonstrates how to record entries on the transaction worksheet for bad debt expense and write-offs. As mentioned previously, the accounts affected are the same, regardless of the allowance approach used. In this example, the company is recording $5,000 of bad debt expense for accounts that the company estimates will be uncollectible in the future. Additionally, the company has identified $3,000 of accounts receivable from individual customers that are uncollectible. Note that the company has reduced accounts receivable by this amount, so that the specific account deemed uncollectible is no longer included in the accounts receivable account. The third entry assumes a **recovery of bad debts** which means that an account we had written off in the past was subsequently collected. The result of this entry is to reverse the previous write-off entry in the amount of the recovery. An additional entry (not shown in the exhibit) to record the collection of the accounts receivable with cash is also required. The collection entry would be recorded as an increase to cash and a decrease to accounts receivable.

Exhibit 4-2.1
Worksheet Entries for Bad Debts, Write-offs and Recoveries

	Accounts Receivable	Allowance for Uncollectible Accounts	Retained Earnings
To record bad debt expense		$ (5,000)	$ (5,000)
To write-off an account	$ (3,000)	3,000	
To recover a bad debt	1000	(1,000)	

One of the objectives of accounting for uncollectible accounts is to report the best estimate of the amount of cash that will ultimately be realized from the receivable asset. Regardless of the allowance approach used, the balance in the allowance account at the end of the accounting period is subtracted from accounts receivable to compute the collectible portion of the accounts receivable as shown in the example below. The following excerpt is from the balance sheet of QRS Inc. as of Dec. 31, 2000.

Accounts receivable	$25,000
Less: Allowance for uncollectible accounts	3,000
Net accounts receivable	$22,000

In the above presentation, QRS, Inc. expects to collect $22,000 of its $25,000 accounts receivable balance. The company has not specifically identified which individual accounts receivable will be uncollectible but estimates they will total about $3,000. The $3,000 was calculated by algebraically adding together the amounts in the allowance for uncollectible accounts column of the accounting transaction worksheet shown in Exhibit 4-2.1. The financial statement presentation came from a transaction worksheet where the accounts receivable had an ending balance of $25,000 and the allowance for uncollectible accounts had a balance of ($3,000).

The net accounts receivable of $22,000 is also called the **net realizable value** of accounts receivable. This amount represents the accounts receivable that the company expects to collect in the future. It is the net amount that is added to the balance of the other current asset accounts to get total current assets. QRS Inc.'s December 31, 2000 current asset section of the balance sheet is illustrated below.

Current Assets	
Cash	$ 8,000
Accounts receivable, net	22,000
Inventory	65,000
Total Current Assets	$95,000

The easiest way to understand the difference between the two approaches to the allowance method of accounting for bad debts is to use an example. Consider the following information.

ABC Company is a consulting business that began operations on January 1, 2000. At that time, the owner invested $70,000 cash in the business. Exhibit 4-2.2 shows accounts receivable information for 2000 and 2001.

Exhibit 4-2.2
Sample Problem Data for ABC Company

	Yr. 2000	Yr. 2001
Total sales, all on credit	$ 110,000	$ 120,000
Collections on accounts receivable	87,300	116,000
Write-off of bad debts	2,700	4,900

The credit sales, collections on accounts receivable, and write-offs are recorded identically regardless of which approach the company utilizes.

Percentage of Sales Approach

In the **percentage of sales** approach management estimates the bad debts by multiplying credit sales by an estimated bad debt expense percentage. This approach is also called the income statement approach. In our example, let's suppose that management estimates that 5 percent of the credit sales of $110,000 will be uncollectible.

5% × $110,000 = $5,500	←——————————	Management's Estimate

The company will record an entry to increase the allowance account and decrease retained earnings by recording bad debt expense. The increase to the allowance account is shown in brackets because this account is a contra-asset account with a negative balance. In this case we are adding to the negative balance. The write-off of $2,700 is shown as a decrease to the allowance account (the negative balance is now smaller than before) and a decrease to accounts receivable. Because the company has determined that these specific accounts are uncollectible, they are deleted from the accounts receivable balance.

Keep in mind that the bad debt expense of $5,500 was management's estimate of the credit sales which would be uncollectible. The write-off identifies $2,700 of specific credit sales during the year which were, in fact, uncollectible. The balance in the allowance for uncollectible accounts shows that the company still anticipates $2,800 of year 2000 sales to be uncollectible in the year 2001 or later. The partial transaction worksheet for 2000 using the percentage of sales approach is shown in Exhibit 4-2.3.

Exhibit 4-2.3
Percentage of Sales Approach - Year 2000

Explanation	Cash	Accounts Receivable	Allowance for Uncollectible Accounts	Contributed Capital	Retained Earnings
Beg. Bal. 2000	$ 70,000	$ -	$ -	$ 70,000	$ -
Sales on credit		110,000			110,000
Collections on A/R	87,300	(87,300)			
Bad debt expense			(5,500)		(5,500)
Write-off		(2,700)	2,700		
End. Bal. 2000	$ 157,300	$ 20,000	$ (2,800)	$ 70,000	$ 104,500

The financial statement presentation for the balance sheet at the end of 2000 is as follows:

Accounts Receivable	$20,000
Less: Allowance for uncollectible accounts	2,800
Net Accounts Receivable	$17,200

The income statement for 2000 would show bad debt expense, which is usually considered to be a selling expense, of $5,500. The bad debt expense is reflected in the retained earnings account on the worksheet.

To extend our example, assume that in 2001 credit sales were $120,000 and cash collections were $116,000. Again, management estimates that 5 percent of the $120,000 ($6,000) would be uncollectible. In 2001, several specific accounts receivable balances totaling $4,900 were determined to be uncollectible. These customers' accounts were written off. The partial worksheet for 2001 is shown in Exhibit 4-2.4.

Exhibit 4-2.4
Percentage of Sales Approach -Year 2001

Explanation	Cash	Accounts Receivable	Allowance for Uncollectible Accounts	Contributed Capital	Retained Earnings
Beg. Bal. 2001	$ 157,300	$ 20,000	$ (2,800)	$ 70,000	$ 104,500
Sales on credit		120,000			120,000
Collections on A/R	116,000	(116,000)			
Bad debt expense			(6,000)		(6,000)
Write-off		(4,900)	4,900		
End. Bal. 2001	$ 273,300	$ 19,100	$ (3,900)	$ 70,000	$ 218,500

The ending balances from year 2000 became the beginning balances for year 2001. The bad debt expense was recorded at the same 5 percent of credit sales rate as in 2000.

5% × $120,000 = $6,000	⟵	Management's Estimate

In general, for any given accounting period, the allowance account is increased by the amount of bad debt expense (in this case $6,000) and decreased by the amount of the write-off ($4,900 for year 2001). The net increase in allowance during the year of $1,100 is added to the beginning balance in the allowance account to calculate the ending allowance balance of $3,900.

What is the net realizable value of accounts receivable at the end of 2001? The net realizable value is estimated to be $15,200. This means that the company anticipates collecting cash of $15,200 related to its accounts receivable in the future.

Accounts Receivable	$ 19,100
Less: Allowance for Uncollectible Accounts	3,900
Net Accounts Receivable	$ 15,200

Aging of Accounts Receivable Approach

In this approach to the allowance method, the company prepares an aging of accounts receivable report. An **aging of accounts receivable report** is a list of all customers and their outstanding accounts receivable balances sorted by invoice due dates. Invoices are typically placed in categories according to whether they are current, 1-30 days overdue, 31-60 days overdue, 61-90 days overdue, 91-120 days overdue and more than 120 days overdue. A sample aging report is provided in Exhibit 4-2.5.

Exhibit 4-2.5
Aging Schedule - Year 2000

	Total	Current	1-30	31-60	61-90	91-120	over 120
Adams, Stuart	$1,794.81	$986.00	$468.92	$339.89			
Harder, Linda	1,736.80	480.35			$ 958.00	$ 298.45	
Lee, Peter	1,178.76	265.00	368.76				$ 545.00
Praeten, Polly	1,232.01		452.67	779.34			
Thwartall, Helen	1,619.88	923.89	243.76		452.23		
Others *	12,437.74	6,182.56	869.33	550.23	877.43	413.00	3,545.19
	$20,000.00	$8,837.80	$2,403.44	$1,669.46	$2,287.66	$711.45	$4,090.19

* In reality, the aging would include an individual listing for each customer but
the remaining customers are summarized here for simplicity.

The aging shows that the accounts receivable outstanding balance at the end of 2000 is $20,000. Exhibit 4-2.6 shows that management has estimated the percentages of uncollectible accounts in each aging category. In deciding the percentage, management takes into consideration how long the receivable has been outstanding. If you look at the percentages, they range from 5 percent for accounts currently due to 35 percent for accounts over 120 days overdue. The assumption in this approach is the older the receivable, the greater the chance that it will be uncollectible.

The aging schedule shows that the company needs an allowance of $3,000 at the end of 2000 as calculated in Exhibit 4-2.6. As an example, the allowance needed for the 1-30 category is calculated by multiplying the ending accounts receivable balance for that category by the percentage given for that category, 10 percent. This calculation results in an allowance of $240 for that 1-30 day category. A similar process is performed for all other categories. The allowances for each category are then totaled.

Exhibit 4-2.6
Aging of Accounts Receivable Approach
Calculation of Allowance - Year 2000

	Total	Current	1-30	31-60	61-90	91-120	over 120
Accounts Receivable Ending Balance	$ 20,000	$ 8,838	$ 2,403	$ 1,669	$ 2,288	$ 711	$ 4,090
Estimated % uncollectible			5%	10%	15%	20%	25%	35%
Allowance needed	$3,000	$442	$240	$250	$458	$178	$1,432

After applying the appropriate percentages, the allowance is totaled and the total of $3,000 becomes the ending worksheet balance for the allowance account. The bad debt expense is "plugged," meaning that it is the adjustment to the allowance account that is necessary to get the allowance balance to the estimated amount of $3,000.

Beginning allowance	($0)	
Add: Bad debt expense	(?)	Need to solve for this (?)
Less: Write-offs	2,700	
Ending allowance	($3,000) ◄—	Management's Estimate

Bad debt expense = (?) = ($5,700)

The partial accounting transaction worksheet using the aging approach for 2000 is shown in Exhibit 4-2.7. Notice that the sales, collections, and write-off entries are identical to the percentage of sales approach. The entry to record bad debt expense affects the allowance account and retained earnings account in the same manner as it did in the sales approach, but the amounts for both bad debt expense and the amount for the ending balance in the allowance account differ under the two approaches. The sales approach recorded bad debt expense of $5,500 (vs. $5,700 in the aging method) and resulted in an ending allowance balance of $2,800 (vs. $3,000). The minor differences in amounts are due to the way the expense is calculated. Over the long run, both approaches should result in similar amounts of expense.

Exhibit 4-2.7
Aging of Accounts Receivable Approach - Year 2000

Explanation	Cash	Accounts Receivable	Allowance for Uncollectible Accounts	Contributed Capital	Retained Earnings
Beg. Bal. 2000	$ 70,000	$ -	$ -	$ 70,000	$ -
Sales on credit		110,000			110,000
Collections on A/R	87,300	(87,300)			
Bad debt expense			(5,700)		(5,700)
Write-off		(2,700)	2,700		
End. Bal. 2000	$ 157,300	$ 20,000	$ (3,000)	$ 70,000	$ 104,300

The accounts receivable for 2000 will be reported on the balance sheet in the same way as the percentage of sales approach, but note the different allowance balance.

Accounts Receivable	$ 20,000
Less: Allowance for uncollectible accounts	3,000
Net Accounts Receivable	$ 17,000

In the following year, 2001, the company has sales of $120,000, collections of accounts receivable of $116,000, and write-offs of $4,900. At the end of the year, the company would prepare another aging schedule as it did in 2000 and apply the appropriate percentages to the different categories. Assume the company did this and determined that an allowance for uncollectible accounts of $3,600 was needed at the end of the year.

To compute the amount of the bad debt expense, compute the amount of expense necessary so that the ending allowance balance is $3,600.

Beginning allowance	($3,000)	
Add: Bad debt expense	(?)	Need to solve for this (?)
Less: Write-offs	4,900	
Ending allowance	($3,600) ←	Management's Estimate

Bad debt expense = (?) = ($5,500)

At the end of 2001, accounts receivable will be shown on the balance sheet as follows:

Accounts Receivable	$ 19,100
Less: Allowance for uncollectible accounts	3,600
Net Accounts Receivable	$ 15,500

Exhibit 4-2.8 shows a partial accounting transaction worksheet for 2001.

Exhibit 4-2.8
Aging of Accounts Receivable Approach - Year 2001

Explanation	Cash	Accounts Receivable	Allowance for Uncollectible Accounts	Contributed Capital	Retained Earnings
Beg. Bal. 2001	$ 157,300	$ 20,000	$ (3,000)	$ 70,000	$ 104,300
Sales on credit		120,000			120,000
Collections on A/R	116,000	(116,000)			
Bad debt expense			(5,500)		(5,500)
Write-off		(4,900)	4,900		
End. Bal. 2001	$ 273,300	$ 19,100	$ (3,600)	$ 70,000	$ 218,800

Evaluating Management's Estimate

Both the percentage of sales and the aging of accounts receivable approaches depend on percentages that are estimated by management. How does management determine these percentages? These percentages are determined by past experience in the company. If the company is in its early years, management will have to base the percentages on prior experience with different companies or perhaps on industry norms. In any case, management needs to keep a close watch on the percentages to see if the estimates are reasonable. Over time, bad debt expense should approximate the write-offs. The data is now available for ABC Company for 2002 and sales for all three years totaled $360,000. The allowance account information for the three-year period has been summarized in Exhibit 4-2.9 for the percentage of sales approach.

Exhibit 4-2.9
Analysis of the Allowance Account
Percentage of Sales Approach

	2000	2001	2002	2000-2002
Beg. allowance	$ -	$ (2,800)	$ (3,900)	$ -
Bad debt expense	(5,500)	(6,000)	(6,500)	(18,000)
Write-offs	2,700	4,900	6,800	14,400
Ending allowance	$ (2,800)	$ (3,900)	$ (3,600)	$ (3,600)

The bad debt expense, as we already know, is 5 percent of sales for the three year period. Sales for that period were $360,000, so bad debt expense for the three years was $18,000.

$$\$360,000 \times 5\% = \$18,000$$

Write-offs of accounts totaled $14,400 for the same three year period and write-offs were 4 percent of credit sales.

$$\text{Write-offs} \div \text{Credit sales} = \$14,400 \div \$360,000 = 4\%$$

Management should consider this three-year history and consider revising the percentage, perhaps to around 4.5 percent of sales. In the long run, write-offs should approximate bad debt expense, regardless of the approach used.

Evaluation of Accounts Receivable

There are several ways investors as well as managers can evaluate the accounts receivable of a company. The evaluation process looks at the accounts receivable balance over the history of the company as well as compares the receivable information gathered with other companies in the same industry.

Accounts Receivable Turnover

One of the most popular ways to evaluate accounts receivable is to calculate the **accounts receivable turnover**. The turnover is illustrated below.

Assume that last year's ending accounts receivable balance was $5,000 and this year's ending balance was $5,500. Credit sales for the year were $45,000. The first step in the process is to calculate average accounts receivable by adding the beginning and ending accounts receivable balances and then dividing by two to compute the average.

$$\text{Accounts receivable turnover} = \frac{\text{Net credit sales}}{\text{Average accts. receivable}} = \frac{\$45,000}{(\$5,000 + \$5,500) \div 2} = 8.57 \text{ times per year}$$

This means that the average accounts receivable is collected 8.57 times per year. The accounts receivable turnover is more easily understood if we take one further step and compute the **accounts receivable collection period**.

$$\text{Accts. rec. collection period} = \frac{365 \text{ days}}{\text{Accts. rec. turnover}} = \frac{365}{8.57 \text{ times}} = 43 \text{ days}$$

This means that the average collection time is 43 days. The company can use this information to predict when the cash will be collected from an account receivable to facilitate cash planning. The information can also be used to evaluate the company's credit terms. For example, let's suppose that the company's credit terms are 1/10, n/30. This means that the buyer can take a 1 percent discount if he or she pays within 10 days. If not paid within 10 days, the full amount (net) is due within 30 days.

If the collection period is 43 days, the credit terms are not effective as 43 days is longer than the 30 days allowed. First of all, a 1 percent discount would not be sufficient to encourage payment within the first 10 days as the long average collection period indicates.

If the company offers a 1 percent discount for payment in 10 days, what is the equivalent annual interest rate? The logic behind the 1 percent discount terms is that the discount is available to those purchasers who are willing to forego the additional twenty days (30–10) of free credit by paying before day 10, rather then before day 30. One way to compare the discount to annual interest is to annualize the 1 percent.

$$\text{Number of 20-day intervals in a year} = \frac{365}{20} = 18.25$$

$$\text{Annualized interest rate} = 18.25 \times 1\% = 18.25\%$$

How does 18.25 percent compare to credit card interest? Most credit cards charge interest rates higher than 18.25 percent. If the customer has a choice between paying a credit card bill versus the company's bill, in most cases the customer will choose to pay off the bill that charges the highest interest—the credit card. Perhaps if the company offered a 2 or 3 percent discount the buyers might be encouraged to pay earlier.

Secondly, the net 30 portion of the terms is also not effective. If the average collection period is 43 days, then perhaps the company is too lax in the granting of credit or perhaps their collection department does not emphasize the importance of payments on time. Both of these possibilities should be investigated thoroughly by the company.

Relative Age of the Accounts in Accounts Receivable

Another way to evaluate accounts receivable is to look at the changes over time in the relative amounts in the various aging categories (e.g., current, 1-30 days past due, 31-60 days past due, etc.). The company would certainly want to investigate further if they noticed that their receivables were getting older. Exhibit 4-2.5 presented an aging schedule for ABC Company. Exhibit 4-2.10 takes the figures from the aging schedule and shows the total receivables in each aging category as a percentage of total receivables. The benefits of such a presentation are that comparisons between years can be easily made and a manager can see if the receivables in general are getting "older" or not, allowing him or her to locate problem areas before they get out of control.

Assume that the percentages for 2001 and 2002 were calculated in a manner similar to the ones for year 2000. Is there a pattern emerging?

Exhibit 4-2.10
Aging Categories as a Percentage of Total Receivables

	Yr. 2000 Accounts Receivable Balance	Yr. 2000 Percentage of Total A/R	Yr. 2001 Percentage of Total A/R (Assumed)	Yr. 2002 Percentage of Total A/R (Assumed)
Currently due	$ 8,837.80	44.19%	34.23%	25.98%
1-30 days overdue	2,403.44	12.02%	15.02%	17.34%
31-60 days overdue	1,669.46	8.35%	10.45%	13.21%
61-90 days overdue	2,287.66	11.44%	13.89%	15.01%
91-120 days overdue	711.45	3.56%	5.46%	6.33%
over 120 days overdue	4,090.19	20.45%	20.95%	22.13%
Total Accounts Receivable*	$20,000.00	100.00%	100.00%	100.00%

* Columns may not add to amounts shown due to minor differences in rounding.

The exhibit shows that the receivables are getting older over the three-year period of time. Notice that the current receivables are 44.19 percent of total receivables in 2000 but only 25.98 percent of total receivables in 2002. Additionally, the percentages in the older aging categories are growing over time. This should send out an alarm.

Importance of Industry Data

Usually you can locate industry norms for the company you are analyzing. While the data for the aging of accounts receivable is rarely available, the accounts receivable turnover is a frequently listed ratio. A comparison of your company to the industry norms will give you information about how your company is doing in comparison to other companies in the same industry.

Annual Reports

Some annual reports might show the accounts receivable net of the allowance account as follows:

    Accounts receivable, net $17,000

This shows that the company expects to collect $17,000 cash from the current receivables.

Additionally, most companies do not show bad debt expense as a separate line item on their income statements, but rather combine this expense with other expenses in the caption "selling expenses," or, if expenses are even more summarized, "operating expenses."

Users of the financial statements want to be sure that management's estimates are reasonable. Otherwise, if management wanted to show an inflated net income, bad debt expense could be underestimated. One way that users of the financial statements can ensure that the estimates are reasonable is to determine if the financial statements have been audited. An audit of the financial statements includes, among other things, a review of the estimates made by management. In this case, the auditor reviews management's calculation of bad debt expense and the reasonableness of the allowance for uncollectible accounts. In addition to reviewing the management estimates, the auditor analyzes the recent history related to accounts receivable and in some cases contacts customers of disputed large accounts. A typical footnote of a publicly traded corporation points out that management has made estimates in preparing the financial statements (emphasis added).

"The preparation of financial statements in conformity with generally accepted accounting principles requires management to make *estimates* and *assumptions* that affect the reported amounts of assets and liabilities and disclosure of contingent assets and liabilities at the date of the financial statements and the reported amounts of revenue and expenses during the reporting period. Actual results could differ from those estimates."

The auditors' opinion states that (emphasis added):

"An audit includes examining, on a test basis, evidence supporting the amounts and disclosures in the financial statements. An audit also includes *assessing the accounting principles used and significant estimates made by management*, as well as evaluating the overall financial statement presentation."

These statements give assurance to the user of audited financial statements that management's estimates have been reviewed and are reasonable. Reported income therefore can be relied upon as a fair measurement of the economic gains of the previous fiscal year.

SUMMARY

Selling on credit is a common business practice. The risk of granting credit to customers is manageable if the customers' credit information is carefully scrutinized. However, there is the probability that a small percentage of customers will be unable to pay their debts. This fact requires that estimates of bad debts likely to occur be entered into the financial statements on a timely basis. The matching principle applied to uncollectible accounts receivable means that a special contra account called allowance for uncollectible accounts is netted against the asset accounts receivable to report the net realizable value of the asset and a reasonable estimate of bad debt expense. Published financial reports must follow GAAP, which gives the investor greater assurance as to the fairness of the statements. The audit of a CPA culminating in an unqualified (clean) opinion on the financial statements implies that the CPA has reviewed estimates and has concluded that they are based upon objective evidence.

EXERCISES AND PROBLEMS

Exercises

Exercise 1   Reasons for Extending Credit to Customers. When a company extends credit to customers it knows some accounts receivables will become uncollectible. Why, then, would a company decide to extend credit to customers?

Exercise 2   Why Use Uncollectible Accounts? Why do companies estimate uncollectible accounts? Wouldn't it be simpler to wait until an account receivable becomes bad and then write it off as an expense? Explain briefly.

Exercise 3   Advantages and Disadvantages of Direct Write-Off Method. Give two advantages and two disadvantages of the direct write-off method of accounting for uncollectible accounts.

Exercise 4   Accounts Receivable Disclosure in the Balance Sheet. How are accounts receivable disclosed in the balance sheet when the allowance for uncollectible accounts is used? Give an illustration of balance sheet disclosure using assumed numbers.

Exercise 5   Evaluating Accounts Receivable. What is accounts receivable turnover? What does the accounts receivable collection period refer to? How are turnover and collection period used in evaluating accounts receivable?

Exercise 6   Use of Allowance Method by Publicly Traded Companies. Why do all publicly traded stock companies use the allowance method to account for uncollectible accounts? Explain briefly.

Exercise 7   Two Approaches to Using Allowance Method. Differentiate between the percentage of sales approach and the aging of accounts receivable approach to estimating the uncollectible accounts expense.

Problems

Problem 1   Allowance with Percentage of Sales Approach. The following information pertains to Shelby Company for 2000:

Sales	$200,000
Accounts receivable, December 31, 2000	30,000
Allowance for uncollectible accounts, January 1, 2000	4,000
Accounts receivable written off during 2000	3,700

Shelby Company uses the percentage of sales approach to estimate bad debt expense.

   a. Determine the amount of bad debt expense for 2000 if Shelby expects 1.5 percent of sales to become uncollectible.

   b. Compute the balance of Shelby's allowance for uncollectible accounts account at December 31, 2000.

Problem 2   Allowance with Aging of Accounts Receivable Approach. Use the information in Problem 1, except assume that Shelby Company uses aging of accounts receivable to estimate bad debt expense. The aging of accounts receivable schedule shows that $4,200 of the ending receivable will likely become uncollectible.

   a. Determine the amount of bad debt expense for 2000. Show supporting computations.

   b. What should be the balance of the allowance for uncollectible accounts at December 31, 2000?

Problem 3   Aging of Accounts Receivable Approach with Receivable Recovered. Aumend Company had the following data for 2000:

Sales	$500,000
Accounts receivable, January 1, 2000	70,000

Accounts receivable, December 31, 2000	80,000
Allowance for uncollectible accounts, January 1, 2000	9,000
Accounts receivable written off during 2000	9,700

The aging of accounts receivable show that $10,000 of accounts receivable at December 31, 2000, will likely not be collectible.

a. How much bad debt expense should be recorded for Aumend Company in 2000?

b. Explain the effect of the write-off of an account receivable that has become uncollectible for Aumend Company in regard to the net realizable value of the accounts receivable as shown in the balance sheet.

c. Would your answer to part a change if there was a recovery of the write-off (part of the amount written-off was subsequently collected) in the amount of $1,200? Explain.

Problem 4 Evaluating Credit Terms. Determine the accounts receivable collection period for Bastion Company for 2000. Assume that the company had sales for the year of $500,000. Accounts Receivable at January 1, 2000 was $70,000 and they were $80,000 on December 31, 2000. If the company had credit terms of 2/10, net 45 days, how effective is their credit and collections policy? Show computations and explain briefly.

Problem 5   Interpreting Accounts Receivable Ratios. Donaldson Company has been in business for many years and is proud of its customer relations. Judie Quick has been hired as the new credit manager for Donaldson Company. Her analysis of accounts receivable for the most recent 12 months with comparable industry information follow:

	Donaldson Co.	Industry Norm
Accounts receivable turnover	8 times	10.5 times
Accounts receivable collection period	45.6 days	34.8 days
Credit terms	2/10, n/30	2/10, n/30
Sales revenues	$960,000	$800,000

After reviewing the above data, Ms. Quick became concerned. What concerns did she probably have? What additional data would you like to have to better evaluate the situation concerning receivable collections?

Case 4-2

LENNY'S LUMBER: CREDIT POLICY AND ACCOUNTS RECEIVABLE VALUATION

Case Objectives

1. To understand the nature of accounts receivable and how receivables are valued at net realizable value.
2. To understand the linkage between accounts receivable and sales.
3. To understand various approaches for establishing an allowance for uncollectible accounts.
4. To be able to use various ratios to evaluate the reasonableness of a company's allowance for uncollectible accounts.
5. To be able to use various ratios to evaluate the effectiveness of a company's credit terms.

Decision: What should Lenny's Lumber do with respect to its credit policy, discount terms, and accounting for bad debts?

Lenny's Lumber sells most of its retail merchandise on credit to local home builders and remodeling contractors. For the past three years ending December 31, 2002, Lenny's has been encouraging credit sales through its liberal credit policy, although it has maintained its 1/10, n/60 credit terms. Credit sales have been increasing each year since the company's first year in 2000. Lenny's controller, Dave Dismal, is not pleased. "Our liberal credit policy is making collection difficult. Many of our credit customers are deadbeats who just don't pay," says Dave. The company president, I. M. Rosey, disagrees. "I believe our collection experience compares favorably with the rest of the industry."

The summary data for sales, accounts receivable, and bad debts for the three-year period 2000-2002 is shown in Exhibit C4-2.1. Each year, Lenny's recognizes bad debt expense (uncollectible accounts expense) in the amount of 3 percent of credit sales. This amount represents the portion of current period receivables that are estimated to become uncollectible. Write-offs involve specific customer accounts that have been identified as not collectible.

Exhibit C4-2.1
Summary Data for Sales, Accounts Receivable, and Bad Debts

Year	Credit Sales	Write-Offs	Year-End Accounts Receivable Balance	Allow. for Uncoll. Accts.
2000	$ 4,500,000	$ 89,569	$ 765,000	$45,431
2001	4,600,000	136,451	824,000	46,980
2002	4,700,000	142,000	828,000	45,980

A detailed aging of the entire list of its customer accounts receivable at the end of each of the last three years is shown in Exhibit C4-2.2.

Exhibit C4-2.2
Aging of Accounts Receivable

Days Past Due	2000	2001	2002
Current	$ 491,150	$ 516,456	$ 490,658
1-30	102,950	113,982	100,689
31-60	88,500	88,490	92,623
61-90	30,090	43,261	51,329
91-120	27,760	33,645	49,777
over 120	24,550	28,166	42,924
Total	$ 765,000	$ 824,000	$ 828,000

Lenny's Lumber is a member of a regional trade association which collects financial information from nearly all of its members and publishes an annual survey. The following data for companies with annual sales in the range of $2 to $5 million were shown in the annual survey for 2001 and 2002:

Annual Survey Industry Data

Gross Sales $2 - $5 Million	2001	2002
Allowance for bad debts ÷ Accounts receivable	.061	.062
Accounts receivable collection period	34 days	40 days

Based on your review of all the data provided, who do you think is right, Dave Dismal or I.M. Rosey?

Requirements

1. Compute the following for Lenny's Lumber for 2000, 2001, and 2002. Exhibit C4-2.3 is a template for your solutions. Please show all calculations in space provided.

    a. Bad debt expense

    b. Net realizable value of accounts receivable

    c. Allowance for bad debts ÷ Accounts receivable

    d. Accounts receivable turnover

    e. Accounts receivable collection period

2. What does the term "net realizable value" mean?

3. Prepare a schedule showing an aging of accounts receivable shown as a percentage of total accounts receivable as discussed in Exhibit 4-2.10 in Case Reading 4-2. Use the information provided in Exhibit C4-2.2 to complete the template shown in Exhibit C4-2.4 at the end of this case.

4. Analyze the above data to determine whether:

    a. Lenny's experience with bad debts is getting better or worse over the three-year period.

    b. Lenny's experience with bad debts is better or worse than industry norms for 2001 and 2002.

5. Are Lenny's credit terms of 1/10, n/60 effective? Explain and discuss.

6. What do you think Lenny's Lumber should do with respect to its credit policy, discount terms, and accounting for bad debts?

7. If credit sales were $4.9 million in 2003 and write-offs were $143,500 during the year, what would the allowance for uncollectible accounts balance be at the end of 2003, assuming bad debt expense during the year is still 3 percent of credit sales?

Exhibit C4-2.3
Template for Requirement 1

	A	B	C	D	E	F	G	H	I	J
1	Year	Credit Sales	Write-Offs	Year-End Accounts Receivable Balance	Allow. for Uncoll. Accts.	Bad Debt Expense	Net Realizable Value	% Allowance ÷ Accounts Receivable	Accounts Receivable Turnover	Accounts Receivable Collection Period
2	2000	$ 4,500,000	$ 89,569	$ 765,000	$ 45,431					
3	2001	4,600,000	136,451	824,000	46,980					
4	2002	4,700,000	142,000	828,000	45,980					

Calculations:

Column F:

Column G:

Column H:

Column I:

Column J:

Exhibit C4-2.4
Template for Requirement 2

Days Past Due	2000	2001	2002
Current			
1-30			
31-60			
61-90			
91-120			
over 120			
Total	100.00%	100.00%	100.00%

Case Reading 4-3

DECISIONS INVOLVING INVENTORY[1]

INTRODUCTION

The relationship of cost of goods sold to sales revenue is a key indicator of profitability. A company whose products are differentiated from those of the competition will generally enjoy a low cost ratio to sales price. This is referred to as the gross margin. When the gross margin is rising it suggests that the company is improving its position in that market. Conversely, when the gross margin is declining it suggests that the competition is eroding the advantages once held in that market. This case reading explores the impact which inventory valuation methods have on the gross margin. Because there are several acceptable methods of arriving at cost of goods sold, knowing the impact of the alternate approaches will help one to competently analyze the gross margin trends. The reading will also explore the effect of errors that can distort the gross profit measurement.

GROSS PROFIT MARGIN

The **gross margin** (also called gross profit or **gross profit margin**) on sales can best be described as the difference between net sales and cost of goods sold. Although the gross margin figure is very important for a business, it does not take into consideration any expenses other than cost of goods sold.

A common ratio used by companies is the **gross margin ratio** (also called the **gross profit ratio**) calculated by dividing the gross margin by sales. Another closely related ratio is the cost of goods sold ratio which is computed by dividing cost of goods sold by sales. The sum of the cost of goods sold ratio and the gross margin ratio must add to one hundred percent. Consider the following example which shows a gross profit ratio of 52.7 percent calculated by dividing $548,500 by $1,040,000.

Sales revenue	$1,040,000	100.0%
Cost of goods sold	491,500	47.3
Gross margin	548,500	52.7%

This analysis enables managers and investors to monitor the margin rate. Some stock market analysts rely on profit margin percentages to forecast future income and earnings per share.

Note that B & B Corporation's income statement shown in Exhibit 4-3.1 reports a gross margin of $548,500 for the year ended December 31, 2000.

---

[1] The authors thank Brock Murdoch from California State University, Chico for his major contributions to this Case Reading.

Exhibit 4-3.1
Traditional Vs. Contribution Income Statement

B & B Corporation Traditional Income Statement Year Ended December 31, 2000		B & B Corporation Contribution Income Statement Year Ended December 31, 2000	
Sales Revenue	$ 1,040,000	Sales Revenue	$ 1,040,000
Cost of Goods Sold	491,500	Less Variable Expenses:	
Gross Margin	548,500	Variable Cost of Sales	491,500
Selling, General, and Administrative Expenses (SG&A)	459,000	Variable SG&A	68,000
Interest Expense	10,000	Contribution Margin	480,500
		Fixed SG&A + Interest	401,000
Income before IncomeTax	79,500	Income before IncomeTax	79,500
Income Taxes	31,800	Income Taxes	31,800
Net Income	$ 47,700	Net Income	$ 47,700

Generally accepted accounting principles require preparation of this traditional type of income statement for all companies which are publicly traded. The traditional format income statement contains these major headings: sales revenue; cost of goods sold; gross margin; selling, general, and administrative expenses (often shortened to selling and administrative or SG&A); interest expense; income before income tax; income taxes; and net income. Most companies add more detail within some of these categories, but the format is similar.

The major division of expenses in a traditional income statement is between cost of goods sold listed above gross margin ("above the line") and selling, general, and administrative (SG&A) and other expenses listed below gross margin ("below the line"). Expenses included in cost of goods sold are often referred to as product costs because these costs are assigned to products (unlike SG&A expenses) and do not show up on the income statement until the product is sold. Notice in Exhibit 4-3.1 that the cost of goods sold is the same in each format. This is because, for a retail business, cost of goods sold consists entirely of variable expenses. In a manufacturing business, however, cost of goods sold will also include fixed manufacturing expenses. Therefore, in the traditional approach, fixed and variable costs are often mixed together in both the cost of goods sold and SG&A categories.

Showing the relationship of each expense item to sales is part of vertical analysis. For example, selling, general, and administrative expenses are $459,000. This is clearly a major expense of B & B Corporation. It is 44.1 percent of sales calculated by dividing $459,000 by $1,040,000. Included in this category could be advertising, salaries, commissions, and just about every expense of running the corporation that is not part of the direct costs of the product or service. If management of B & B set a target of SG&A expenses at only 40 percent of sales revenue, it would be seeking ways to reduce the overspending which occurred in this category. Investors too can use vertical analysis (all items in the income statement are shown as a percent of sales) to make a judgment of whether the company's expenses are being properly controlled. Vertical analysis will be discussed in greater detail in Case Reading 4-8.

RETURN ON SALES

The computation of net profit, or net income, reflects the profitability of a business. The ratio of net income to sales is of prime importance, especially to investors. An improving trend in income as a percentage of sales is a positive factor in improving stock prices and possibly dividends.

The **return on sales ratio** (ROS) for B & B is computed as follows:

$$\text{Return on sales} = \frac{\text{Net income}}{\text{Sales}} = \frac{\$47,700}{\$1,040,000} = .0459 \text{ or } 4.59\%$$

There are two important comparisons to make with respect to the return on sales ratio: (1) the comparison to the previous year's ratio and (2) the comparison of the ratio to that of similar businesses in the same industry. Comparing a company with other similar companies in the same industry is called a comparison with the **industry norms**.

The following information is obtained from the income statements of B & B Corporation for the previous three years.

Year	Sales	Net Income	Ratio	%
1997	$1,460,000	$131,000	.0897	8.97
1998	1,370,000	112,000	.0818	8.18
1999	1,110,000	84,000	.0757	7.57
2000	1,040,000	47,700	.0459	4.59

The return on sales ratio can be viewed as how many pennies of each dollar of sales revenue result in net income. For B & B, the trend is undesirable. The return on sales ratio has been consistently declining. The next step for B & B is to reverse this trend. The root causes of declining income may result from a wide range of events. Some events could be internal to the company, such as the loss of key employees, or bankruptcy of a primary supplier necessitating finding a new one with possibly higher prices. Often the negative events are the result of external factors, such as a poor economic climate in other parts of the world which may affect the customers of B & B who in turn reduce their purchases. Finally, the data illustrate the twofold problem facing B & B. Sales are declining rapidly, and the ratio of income is also declining. Note that the dollar amount of income is about one-third of the level three years earlier.

MANAGING INVENTORY ASSETS

There are many decisions that internal and external users of financial statements must make regarding inventory. Decisions involve interpreting the different types of businesses and their inventory, periodic vs. perpetual inventory systems, physical inventory methods, inventory cost flow assumptions, and the lower of cost or market rule impact on presentation and disclosure of inventories in the financial statements.

Importance of Inventory Assets

Inventory is one of the most significant assets of many business. For example, DuPont reported 3.737 billion dollars of inventory in its December 31, 1995 balance sheet, which amounted to more than 34 percent of its current assets. On this same date, Ford Motor Company reported $7.162 billion dollars of inventory, amounting to more than 26 percent of its current assets.

> Inventories are defined as assets held for sale in the ordinary course of business or goods that will be used or consumed in the production of goods to be sold.

Types of Businesses and Their Inventory

Thus far, this text has focused primarily on service organizations which typically have no significant inventory assets. Service organizations generate revenue by selling or providing a service. Painters, doctors, lawyers, automotive repairmen, and accountants are examples of individuals who often do business as service organizations. Service organizations do not sell inventory.

Of course, many organizations sell products rather than services. Some purchase products with the intention of reselling the merchandise to customers. These businesses are called merchandising organizations and may operate as retailers or wholesalers. Examples of merchandising companies are Bloomingdales, Sears, Sam's Club, and Costco/Price Club. Other companies manufacture the products they sell and are referred to as manufacturing organizations. Boeing, General Motors, Kellogg's, and Compaq are examples of manufacturing companies.

The merchandise purchased by merchandising organizations is in a form that is ready for resale. A **manufacturing company**, however, purchases raw materials that are used to produce goods that may be sold to a final consumer, merchandising companies, or other manufacturers. Consequently, manufacturers have three types of inventory: raw materials, work-in-process, and finished goods. Raw materials inventory consists of the commodities or parts that are used in the production of finished goods. Finished goods inventory is merchandise that is ready to sell. Work-in-process inventory refers to goods that are only partially completed at the end of the accounting period. Manufacturers must report the cost of each of the three types of inventory in their financial statements. Merchandising companies, on the other hand, only report inventory that is ready for sale, so their inventory is simply described and reported as merchandise inventory.

Current Assets	
Cash	$ 20,000
Accounts Receivable (net)	10,000
Merchandise Inventory	**4,000**
Prepaid Expenses	500
Total Current Assets	$ 34,500

This case reading will focus on accounting information relevant to inventories of merchandising organizations. Accounting for the inventories of manufacturing organizations is beyond the scope of this course[2].

PERIODIC VS. PERPETUAL INVENTORY SYSTEMS

A merchandising company must choose the type of system it will use to account for its inventory. Traditionally, most merchandising organizations used a periodic inventory system. Unless a company had a relatively small number of sales of high value merchandise (such as a car dealership), it was too time-consuming for the company to look up in its inventory records the cost of each unit sale. Prior to modern information system technology, it was simply too expensive for most organizations to use a perpetual inventory system.

Periodic Inventory Systems

In a **periodic inventory system**, the company maintains a record of the cost of each purchase of merchandise. When sales are made, however, the company does not attempt to determine the cost of the merchandise that was sold. On the sale date, it records the sale at the retail price, but makes no entry to record the reduction of inventory or the decrease in retained earnings caused by cost of goods sold.

At the end of the accounting period, the company takes a **physical inventory** (also called a **physical count**), which means that all the inventory owned by the company is counted to determine the units on hand and their cost. (Cost is determined according to the inventory cost flow assumption used by the company; this topic will be discussed later in this case reading.) It then subtracts the cost of the ending inventory from the cost of goods available for sale (i.e., beginning inventory plus purchases made during the period) to determine the cost of goods sold. A partial income statement illustrating the computation of cost of goods sold for a merchandising business is displayed below.

Sales		$ 100,000
Cost of Goods Sold:		
Beginning Inventory	$ 5,000	
Purchases	65,000	
Cost of Goods Available for Sale (GAFS)	70,000	
Ending Inventory	(18,000)	
Cost of Goods Sold		52,000
Gross Margin		$ 48,000

Under the periodic inventory system, it is assumed that if merchandise is not on hand at the end of the period (in ending inventory), it must have been sold. If some of the merchandise was stolen rather than sold, its cost will be buried in cost of goods sold.

At the end of the period, the inventory is adjusted to its correct amount as determined from the physical count. Consequently, the inventory account is only *periodically* up to date.

---

[2] This topic is discussed extensively in the book *Using Management Accounting Information: A Decision Case Approach,* Adams, Pryor, Keller, and Harston, South-Western College Publishing, 1999.

Perpetual Inventory Systems

Modern information technology has made it possible for the perpetual inventory system to be used by many more types of companies. Bar code systems allow merchandising companies (drug stores, department stores, and auto parts stores, for example), that once used periodic systems to use perpetual systems. In a **perpetual inventory system**, the business keeps track of the cost of each purchase and records the cost of each sale (and the corresponding reduction to inventory) at the time

Perpetual Inventory

- Keeps track of <u>each</u> purchase and sale made to-date through INVENTORY
- Used by businesses because their inventory can be easily tracked with the bar code system

(Each purchase is added to "Inventory". The cost of each sale is subtracted from "Inventory" and "Retained Earnings")

the sale occurs. Bar code systems give a company the ability to efficiently and inexpensively track the cost of their sales on a timely basis. Consequently, the inventory account is *perpetually* up to date. Since the number of companies using perpetual systems is increasing because of new technology, and the number of companies using periodic systems is declining, only the perpetual system is presented in detail.

Exhibit 4-3.2 illustrates how the accounting transaction worksheet is affected by purchases and sales of merchandise in a perpetual inventory system. Assume a company has beginning inventory of $20,000.

Exhibit 4-3.2
Accounting Transaction Worksheet - Perpetual Method

Dates	Cash	Inventory	Accounts Payable	Contributed Capital	Retained Earnings	Explanation Of Transaction
12/1/00	$ 176,000	$ 20,000	$ 40,000	$ 86,000	$ 70,000	
12/2/00		5,000	5,000			Inventory Purchase
Various	24,000				24,000	Sales
Various		(15,000)			(15,000)	COGS Expense
12/31/00	$ 200,000	$ 10,000	$ 45,000	$ 86,000	$ 79,000	

Purchases are recorded in Inventory

The cost of inventory sold is subtracted from Inventory and Retained Earnings (COGS Exp.)

On December 2, 2000, the company purchases merchandise costing $5,000 on credit. The purchase is recorded by increasing inventory and accounts payable by the $5,000 cost of the merchandise.

Also during December the company sold merchandise with a $15,000 cost for $24,000 cash. The cash sales increase cash and retained earnings (sales revenue). Inventory is simultaneously decreased for the $15,000 cost of the merchandise that was sold and retained

hand at the end of December.

earnings is also decreased by $15,000 because of the cost of goods sold.[3] The remaining (ending) balance in inventory of $10,000 represents the cost of the merchandise that is still on

Taking a Physical Inventory in a Perpetual System

When financial statements are audited, sample inventory counts are made to verify the correctness of the inventory value appearing on the balance sheet. It is a recommended procedure even if no financial statement audit is performed. A physical inventory is taken annually at the end of the fiscal year even when a perpetual inventory system is in use. The physical count of the inventory on hand verifies the inventory balance or allows the company to correct the cost of the merchandise recorded in the inventory account. Typically, there is some adjustment to be made in the amount of cost assigned to inventory, since some theft, spoilage, or breakage in the handling of merchandise is likely to occur.

For instance, assume that the physical count of the inventory on hand at the end of December in the previous example indicated the cost of that ending inventory was $9,850. The inventory account in the transaction worksheet shows a balance of $10,000. There is an inventory shortage, which may have been caused by theft, spoilage, errors, or breakage, of $150. In this situation, the accountant would make an entry to record an expense (inventory shortage) by decreasing retained earnings by $150 and would record a corresponding decrease in inventory.

INVENTORY COST FLOW

In valuing its inventory, a company must choose from among different generally accepted inventory cost flow methods. A company is free to choose whichever generally accepted method it wishes to use. The industry, the business cycle, tax considerations, and management preferences are some of the factors which dictate a specific method to be used. However, a company is expected to be consistent in its use of the method it chooses. It is not allowed to switch methods frequently.

If a company does decide to change its cost flow method, it is required to explain why it is changing, disclose the effect of the change on its earnings and, in some cases, change its prior years' financial statements (included in the current annual report for comparative purposes) to reflect the new inventory cost flow assumption.

There are three generally accepted cost flow methods for inventory and cost of goods sold. These three methods are (1) specific identification, (2) first-in, first-out (FIFO), and (3) last-in, first-out (LIFO). Companies may also use a fourth method, weighted average, but the study of that method is beyond the scope of this text.

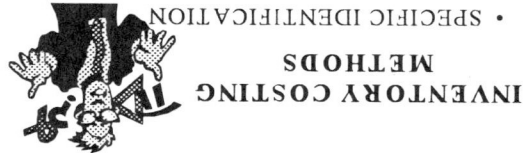

INVENTORY COSTING METHODS

- SPECIFIC IDENTIFICATION – unique items—trace cost to invoice
- FIRST-IN, FIRST-OUT (FIFO) – like an escalator: first on, first off!
- LAST-IN, FIRST-OUT (LIFO) – like an elevator: last in, first out!

---

[3] The reader should note that individual entries that, in total, increase cash and retained earnings (sales) by $24,000 and decrease inventory and retained earnings (increase cost of goods sold) by $15,000 would be made. These entries are summarized for the purposes of the illustration.

The inventory activity for Delpa Company is shown in Exhibit 4-3.3 and will be used to explain the difference in the three cost flow methods.

Exhibit 4-3.3
Schedule of Inventory Activity for January

Date	Explanation	Units	Unit Cost	Total Cost
1/1/00	Beg. Inventory	400	$ 20.00	$ 8,000
1/8/00	Units sold	(300)	?	?
1/10/00	Purchase	200	$ 21.00	$ 4,200
1/19/00	Units sold	(200)	?	?
1/25/00	Purchase	100	$ 22.00	$ 2,200
	End. inventory	200		?

When the Delpa Company sells the 300 units on January 8 and the 200 units on January 19, what should it record for the cost of those units sold? The answer to that question depends on the inventory cost flow method chosen by the company.

Specific Identification

The most intuitive cost flow method tracks each specific unit of merchandise so that each unit's actual cost is assigned to cost of goods sold when that specific unit is sold. This method is called **specific identification**. It is the only cost flow method that must correspond to the actual physical flow of the merchandise. This method is only practical when there are relatively low volume sales of high-priced merchandise. It is too costly to track the individual units for companies with a large volume of sales of low-priced merchandise. Car, yacht, aircraft dealerships, and custom jewelry retailers are examples of businesses that could use the specific identification method. An example is a Chevrolet dealer who has three 1999 Corvettes in inventory just prior to selling one. Even if it is assumed that the three are identical vehicles, the serial number of the Corvette sold would dictate the dealer's invoice cost to use in determining the cost of goods sold. The unsold units' invoice cost becomes the inventory cost for the balance sheet at that date.

Suppose the Delpa Company knew that on January 8, it sold 300 units that had an invoice cost of $20. The cost of goods sold recorded at that date using the specific identification method would be $6,000 (300 × $20).

If on January 19, the company identified that it sold 50 of the units that cost $20 and 150 that had cost $21, the cost of goods sold at that date would be $4,150 calculated as follows:

$$50 \text{ units @ } \$20 = \$1,000$$
$$150 \text{ units @ } \$21 = \underline{3,150}$$
$$200 \text{ units} \qquad \$4,150$$

The ending inventory would consist of the remaining units for a total cost of $4,250 (50@$20 + 50@$21 + 100@$22).

If Delpa Company used the specific identification method, it would know exactly what units were sold on each of the January dates because the units sold had a uniqueness (such as a serial number) which allowed the company to trace the cost of the units sold to the specific invoice when the item was purchased.

First-In, First-Out (FIFO)

The **first-in, first-out (FIFO)** method results in transferring the oldest purchase costs to cost of goods sold and leaving the most recent purchase costs in inventory for the balance sheet. Other than the specific identification method, FIFO corresponds most closely to the actual physical flow of merchandise for most businesses. In most cases, it is logical that the older merchandise is sold prior to selling newer merchandise. To demonstrate how inventory is computed under the FIFO method, refer again to the inventory activity for the month of January shown in Exhibit 4-3.3.

To illustrate how computer software performs this function, the perpetual inventory card shown in Exhibit 4-3.4 is used to illustrate inventory transactions.

Exhibit 4-3.4
Perpetual Inventory Card - FIFO

	Purchases			Sales			Balance		
Date	Units	Unit Cost	Total Cost	Units	Unit Cost	Total Cost	Units	Unit Cost	Total Cost
1/1/00							400	$20	$8,000
1/8/00				300	$20	$6,000	100	$20	$2,000
1/10/00	200	$21	$4,200				100	$20	$2,000
							200	$21	$4,200
1/19/00				100	$20	$2,000			
				100	$21	$2,100	100	$21	$2,100
1/25/00	100	$22	$2,200				100	$21	$2,100
							100	$22	$2,200
	Purchases		$6,400	COGS		$10,100	End. Inv		$4,300

FIFO assigns the earlier costs to cost of goods sold and the later costs to inventory. A detailed explanation of the perpetual inventory card follows. *Note that the perpetual inventory card tracks only the cost of the sale, not the selling price of the goods sold.*

Date	Explanation
January 1	The first entry on the FIFO inventory card is for the beginning inventory— 400 units at $20 per unit, or $8,000.
January 8	300 units were sold. FIFO dictates that the cost of the first units purchased are the first transferred to cost of goods sold, so FIFO assumes the units sold must have been 300 of the 400 beginning inventory units. Note how the $20 cost per unit is entered in the Sales Unit Cost column. A new inventory balance of the remaining inventory on hand is then computed—100 units at $20 per unit.

January 10   The company made a purchase of 200 units at $21 each; these units are entered in the Purchases columns and a new inventory balance is again computed. The company now has 100 units at $20 and 200 units at $21 on hand. It is common for the Balance columns to list the older units first.

January 19   The company made a sale of 200 units. Since FIFO states the older units are transferred first, the cost of goods sold for that sale would consist of 100 of the remaining beginning inventory units at $20 and 100 units at $21 from the January 10 purchase. A new inventory balance is then computed.

January 25   The company made a purchase of 100 units at $22 each; these units are entered in the Purchases columns and a new inventory balance is again computed.

After entering all the monthly inventory activity on the perpetual inventory card, the cost of goods sold (COGS) for the month can be computed by summing the amounts in the Total Cost column for Sales. In other words, cost of goods sold would be equal to $6,000 + $2,000 + $2,100 = $10,100. The cost of the ending inventory is the ending inventory balance on the perpetual inventory card. For our example, the ending inventory is made up of 100 units at $21 each and 100 units at $22 each for a total cost of $4,300.

Besides recording the activity in the perpetual inventory records, the company must also record the activity in the various worksheet accounts as well. An accounting transaction worksheet using the perpetual inventory system and a FIFO cost flow assumption is illustrated in Exhibit 4-3.5. The beginning inventory is shown on the worksheet at $8,000 along with other related account balances. For simplicity's sake, only a few accounts are shown and only inventory-related activity is illustrated on this worksheet.

Exhibit 4-3.5
Accounting Transaction Worksheet
Perpetual Inventory System - FIFO

Date	Cash	Inventory	Contributed Capital	Retained Earnings	Explanation Of Retained Earnings
1/1/00	$ 9,000	$ 8,000	$ 14,500	$ 2,500	Assumed beg.bal.
1/8/00	9,000			9,000	Sales revenue
1/8/00		(6,000)		(6,000)	COGS expense
1/10/00	(4,200)	4,200			
1/19/00	6,000			6,000	Sales revenue
1/19/00		(4,100)		(4,100)	COGS expense
1/25/00	(2,200)	2,200			
1/31/00	$ 17,600	$ 4,300	$ 14,500	$ 7,400	Ending Balance

When 300 units of merchandise are sold for $30 each on January 8, the $9,000 received for these sales is recorded as an increase to cash and an increase in retained earnings (sales). On that same date, the cost of goods sold from the perpetual inventory card of $6,000 is recorded as a decrease in retained earnings due to cost of goods sold expense and a $6,000 reduction in inventory.

The January 10 purchase is then recorded, increasing inventory and decreasing cash by $4,200.

The sale of 200 units at $30 each on January 19 is recorded as an increase to cash and retained earnings (sales) for $6,000. The reduction in retained earnings due to the cost of the goods sold and the corresponding reduction to inventory once again is taken from the amount computed on the perpetual inventory card, $4,100.

Finally, the transaction worksheet shows the January 25 purchase of inventory for cash of $2,200.

The ending balances for all the accounts are calculated by summing all the amounts in the worksheet columns.

Last-In, First-Out (LIFO)

The **last-in, first-out (LIFO)** method of determining cost of goods sold and inventory matches the cost of the most recent purchases against the sales revenue. It is the opposite of FIFO. It is important to note that *the actual physical flow of the merchandise does not correspond to the way the costs are assumed to flow when using LIFO.*[4] There are financial and tax reasons for the acceptance of LIFO as an inventory method. These reasons are discussed in a later section in conjunction with the advantages and disadvantages of both FIFO and LIFO. Exhibit 4-3.6 illustrates a LIFO perpetual inventory card.

With LIFO, as the name implies, the cost of the earliest purchases are assigned to the inventory on hand at the end of the period. The most recent costs are allocated to cost of goods sold.

Exhibit 4-3.6
Perpetual Inventory Card - LIFO

	Purchases			Sales			Balance		
Date	Units	Unit Cost	Total Cost	Units	Cost per Unit	Total Cost	Units	Unit Cost	Total Cost
1/1/00							400	$20	$8,000
1/8/00				300	$20	$6,000	100	$20	$2,000
1/10/00	200	$21	$4,200				100	$20	$2,000
							200	$21	$4,200
1/19/00				200	$21	$4,200	100	20	$2,000
1/25/00	100	$22	$2,200				100	$20	$2,000
							100	$22	$2,200
	Purchases		$6,400	COGS		$10,200	End. Inv		$4,200

---

[4] This may be true for FIFO also, although with FIFO the cost and physical inventory flow are typically very close. Specific identification is the only method for which the flow of costs and the physical flow are identical. With LIFO, the flow of costs and the physical flow rarely, if ever, correspond.

The beginning balance and the January 8 sales are recorded on the perpetual inventory card as shown above. You will notice that there is only one possible source of inventory on hand (the units at $20) to sell on January 8, which is why the LIFO and FIFO cost of goods sold are identical on that date.

After the purchase on January 10, the company had 100 units at $20 and 200 units at $21 available to sell. When the company sells 200 units on January 19, the cost of the last 200 units purchased ($4,200 from January 10) are transferred to cost of goods sold. The cost of the 100 units at $20 remain in inventory.

The January 25 purchase is recorded in the perpetual inventory records in the same way as FIFO.

The LIFO accounting transaction worksheet is presented in Exhibit 4-3.7. All sales and purchases are recorded identically regardless of the cost flow method chosen. The shaded rows are the cost of goods sold entries which may differ depending on the method (LIFO, FIFO, specific identification) selected. The information for the cost of goods sold comes from the LIFO perpetual inventory card. The ending balances for all the accounts are calculated by summing the amounts in the worksheet columns.

Exhibit 4-3.7
Accounting Transaction Worksheet
Perpetual Inventory System - LIFO

Date	Cash	Inventory	Contributed Capital	Retained Earnings	Explanation Of Retained Earnings
1/1/00	$ 9,000	$ 8,000	$ 14,500	$ 2,500	Assumed beg. bal.
1/8/00	9,000			9,000	Sales revenue
1/8/00		(6,000)		(6,000)	COGS expense
1/10/00	(4,200)	4,200			
1/19/00	6,000			6,000	Sales revenue
1/19/00		(4,200)		(4,200)	COGS expense
1/25/00	(2,200)	2,200			
1/31/00	$ 17,600	$ 4,200	$ 14,500	$ 7,300	Ending Balance

Advantages and Disadvantages of LIFO and FIFO

When using LIFO, the actual physical flow of the merchandise usually does not correspond to the way costs are assumed to flow. For most companies, the physical flow of their products is such that the earliest purchases of merchandise are usually the first to be sold. That is, very few industries would actually sell the last merchandise purchased before selling the earliest purchases.[5] Why would a method such as LIFO, in which costs are assumed to flow in the

---

[5] One example of a true LIFO flow is a company that sells coal. When the coal is purchased, it is dumped into a large bin. Sales are made from the most recent purchases because they are on top in the storage bin.

opposite direction of the actual physical flow of the merchandise, be an acceptable method of accounting for inventory?

The answer lies in how accountants define income and the impact of how the different acceptable flow methods affect the measurement of net income. Accountants have generally adopted the definition of J.R. Hicks, the noted economist, who stated that income is the amount an entity can consume during a given period and still leave the entity as well off at the end of the period as it was at the beginning.[6] Which of these polar methods, LIFO or FIFO, most closely adheres to Hicks' definition? Exhibit 4-3.8 illustrates that the LIFO method is the preferred measure of income, given Hicks' definition.

A company buys a unit of inventory on the first day of the accounting period for $20 and sells it on the last day of the accounting period for $30. Also on the last day of the accounting period, the company purchases a unit to replace the one just sold at a cost of $24 (i.e., cost has increased 20 percent).

Under FIFO, the company recognizes $10 gross margin while under LIFO it is $6. Which of the two methods does a better job of matching current costs with current revenues on the income statement? The answer is that LIFO usually does a better job of matching current costs with current revenues. In this example, LIFO matches the most recent cost of $24 with the sales revenue of $30. As you can see in our example, FIFO matched the older cost of $20 with the revenue of $30 resulting in a gross margin of $10.

Exhibit 4-3.8
Comparison of FIFO vs. LIFO

	FIFO	LIFO
Income Statement		
Sales revenue	$ 30	$ 30
Cost of goods sold	20	24
Gross margin	$ 10	$ 6
Balance Sheet		
Inventory	$ 24	$ 20

The difference between the two cost of goods sold amounts of $20 for FIFO and $24 for LIFO is often called inventory profit or inventory holding gain. **Inventory profit** arises when a company holds inventory in a period of rising prices. The additional $4 gross margin shown under FIFO is misleading, however. If the company were to distribute the entire FIFO gross margin of $10 to its owners and also replace the inventory unit sold at a cost of $24, the company would have $4 less in cash than it had at the beginning of the period, whereas under LIFO the amount of cash would not have changed, as shown in Exhibit 4-3.9.

---

[6] J.R. Hicks, *Value and Capital* [Oxford: Clarendon Press, 1946], p. 172.

Exhibit 4-3.9
FIFO vs. LIFO Cash Analysis

	FIFO	LIFO
Cash sale	$ 30	$ 30
Purchase of inventory for cash	(24)	(24)
Payment to owners of gross margin	(10)	(6)
Net cash flow during period	$ (4)	$ -

The balance sheet also differs in the amount shown for ending inventory. In a period of rising prices, LIFO inventory balances will consist of inventory costs that are significantly lower than the costs the company will need to incur to replace the inventory units. Since the impact of using LIFO for inventory valuation is cumulative, the balance sheet of an organization that has used LIFO for many years may significantly understate the current replacement cost of inventory. FIFO's advantage is that it reports the inventory on the balance sheet very close to its current replacement cost ($24 for inventory vs. $20 under LIFO). FIFO is the preferred method of inventory valuation for the balance sheet. As mentioned previously, however, FIFO does not match current costs with current revenues but rather matches the oldest costs with current revenues.

The advantages of FIFO versus LIFO discussed above are related to financial reporting goals. That is, FIFO results in a preferred amount for inventory on the balance sheet, while LIFO yields an income number that is more representative of the amount that can be distributed to owners. LIFO, though, has an additional tax advantage in periods of rising prices.

LIFO is acceptable and is used by many companies for income tax reporting. Because it normally results in a lower income and therefore a lower tax, a company using LIFO will postpone the payment of taxes because it reports lower income to tax authorities. In the example above, LIFO would mean taxes are paid on $6 of income rather than $10 of income. Many companies have adopted the LIFO method chiefly for its tax benefits. Income tax regulations require a company that uses LIFO for tax purposes to also use LIFO in its financial statements.

Inventory Errors

When a company takes its physical inventory at the end of the accounting period, there is a risk that errors may occur in counting or costing the inventory. If an error is undetected before the financial statements are prepared, the amount of the error will affect the income reported in both the current and succeeding year. This two-year effect occurs because the ending inventory for one year is the beginning inventory for the following year.

In a periodic inventory system, there is less probability that an error in taking the physical inventory will be discovered before the financial statements are prepared. This is because in a periodic inventory system there is no current inventory balance in the accounting records to compare to the cost computed after taking a physical inventory. In a perpetual system, however, a large difference between the recorded amount and the amount obtained in the physical inventory count may cause the company to question either the physical inventory count or the perpetual inventory records. The company may investigate and discover the error. Whether the undetected error in valuing the inventory occurs in a periodic or perpetual inventory system, it has a direct impact on the current and following years' reported cost of goods sold, gross margin, and net income.

Consider the example shown in Exhibit 4-3.10 in which the ending inventory was recorded at $3,880 when the correct amount was actually $4,300—an understatement in inventory of $420. During any accounting period, the **cost of the goods available for sale** is equal to the beginning inventory and the purchases. The goods available for sale can be sold (reported as cost of goods sold) or can be on hand at the end of the period (reported as ending inventory). Consequently, if ending inventory is understated by $420, then cost of goods sold must be overstated by that same amount (cost of goods sold is reported as $10,520 when the correct amount is $10,100). Since cost of goods sold is an expense that is subtracted on the income statement to arrive at net income, if the expense is overstated, then gross margin and net income are understated.

Exhibit 4-3.10
Inventory Errors–January

	Incorrect		Correct	
Sales		$ 15,000		$ 15,000
Cost of Goods Sold:				
Beginning Inventory	$ 4,000		$ 4,000	
Purchases	10,400		10,400	
Cost of Goods Available for sale	14,400		14,400	
Ending Inventory	3,880		4,300	
Cost of Goods Sold		10,520		10,100
Gross Margin		$ 4,480		$ 4,900

In the following period, the opposite effects will occur as is shown in Exhibit 4-3.11.

Exhibit 4-3.11
Inventory Errors–February

	Incorrect		Correct	
Sales		$ 16,000		$ 16,000
Cost of Goods Sold:				
Beginning Inventory	$ 3,880		$ 4,300	
Purchases	12,100		12,100	
Cost of Goods Available for sale	15,980		16,400	
Ending Inventory	5,200		5,200	
Cost of Goods Sold		10,780		11,200
Gross Margin		$ 5,220		$ 4,800

Because the ending inventory of the previous period was understated, this period's beginning inventory will be understated as well. The understated beginning inventory is added to the period's purchases to arrive at the cost of goods available for sale. This will cause the cost of goods available for sale to be too low as well. In the month of February, the ending inventory was correctly recorded at $5,200, resulting in an $420 understatement of cost of goods sold and an overstatement of gross margin and net income.

An error in taking the physical inventory will correct itself within two accounting periods. However, don't interpret the fact that the error self-corrects within two periods to mean that the consequences of the error are lessened. Rather, it means that two periods' financial statements (rather than one) are reported incorrectly. The overall effect on gross margin over the two accounting periods is shown in Exhibit 4-3.12.

Exhibit 4-3.12
Two-Month Overview of Gross Profit Margin

	Incorrect	Correct
Gross margin—January	$ 4,480	$ 4,900
Gross margin—February	5,220	4,800
Total for Two Months	$ 9,700	$ 9,700

Inventory Disclosures

All businesses must disclose in footnotes to their financial statements that inventories are reported at the lower of cost or market and the inventory flow assumption used in valuing inventories (i.e., specific identification, FIFO, LIFO, etc.). Manufacturers must either report materials, work-in-process, and finished goods inventories separately in their balance sheet or in a separate schedule in the notes to the financial statements.

Today, many firms that use LIFO present supplementary FIFO balance sheet disclosures as an objective means of presenting the value of their inventory at or near its current replacement cost.[7] Such disclosures are clearly in the best interests of financial statement users so that they can compare the financial statements of companies using different inventory methods.

SUMMARY

Inventory is a major asset of merchandising and manufacturing companies. Applying the cost principle to inventory has a direct consequence on the amount shown as cost of goods sold, a major determinant of net income. LIFO, FIFO, and specific identification are three acceptable methods of determining the reported cost of inventory at a balance sheet date. In an environment of changing prices for new purchases of inventory, the cost of goods sold and therefore income can vary significantly depending on which inventory costing method is used. Another decision context introduced is the effect of errors in determining inventory. Because the ending inventory of one year becomes the beginning inventory of the next year, errors in the first year will be offset in the following year. Corrections once discovered can result in a restatement of the previous year's net income.

EXERCISES AND PROBLEMS

Exercises

Exercise 1   Importance of Gross Margin. What is gross margin? Why is gross margin important to a retail business?

Exercise 2   Relationship of Gross Margin to Income-to-Sales Ratio. Is it possible for a company to have an increasing gross margin ratio and a decreasing income-to-sales ratio? Explain your reasoning.

Exercise 3   Inventories of Different Organizations. Explain how service companies, merchandising companies, and manufacturing companies differ regarding inventories.

[7] Brock Murdoch, Lee Pryor, and Paul Krause, "A Study of the Usefulness of FIFO Inventory Disclosures," *Midwestern Journal of Business and Economics* (Winter 1991), p. 16.

Exercise 4 Periodic Inventory System and Perpetual Inventory System. Explain how the periodic inventory system differs from the perpetual inventory system.

Exercise 5 Inventory Cost Flow Assumptions. List the three inventory cost flow assumptions discussed in this case reading and explain how costs flow in each.

Exercise 6 FIFO Inventory Advantages and Disadvantages. List two advantages and two disadvantages of the FIFO inventory costing method.

Exercise 7 Inventory Errors. Year 1 ending inventory is overstated by $1,000. Explain why and how this error will affect year 1 and year 2 net income.

Problems

Problem 1 Income Statement Ratio Analysis. The income statement for Yetzer Company for 2000 is given below.

Yetzer Company
Income Statement
Year Ended December 31, 2000

Sales	$ 600,000
Cost of goods sold	450,000
Gross margin	150,000
Operating expenses	120,000
Earnings before income tax	30,000
Income taxes	10,500
Net income	$ 19,500

Use the above information to determine:

a. The gross profit ratio.

b. The income-to-sales ratio.

c. The average income tax rate for 2000.

d. Return on equity (after tax) assuming $200,000 of average owners' equity for 2000.

Problem 2 Computing FIFO and LIFO Inventory. Lake Company had the following transactions relating to inventory for July 2000:

	Units	Unit Cost	Total Cost
Beginning inventory	200	$100	$20,000
July 5 purchase	300	101	30,300
July 8 sale	250	---	---
July 19 purchase	500	105	52,500
July 23 sale	100	---	---
July 29 sale	350	---	---

Assuming Lake Company uses a perpetual inventory system, determine:

a. The number of units in the July 31 ending inventory.

b. FIFO inventory cost at July 31.

   c. LIFO inventory cost at July 31.

Problem 3 Prepare Income Statement and Effects of Error.

   a. Use the information in problem 2 above to prepare a traditional income statement for Lake Company for July 2000 assuming the sales price per unit is $150 and they use the FIFO inventory method. Operating expenses were $20,000 and the income tax rate was 30% for year 2000.

   b. If the ending inventory was understated by $10,500 because of an error, explain which amounts in your income statement will be different and by how much they will differ.

Case 4-3

KRIS' CRAFTS

Case Objectives

1. To understand the nature of merchandise inventories and how the perpetual inventory system tracks inventory.
2. To understand and apply the specific identification, FIFO, and LIFO costing methods.
3. To understand the linkage between merchandise inventory and cost of goods sold.

Decision: Which method, FIFO or LIFO, should the company use if it wants to record the highest net income?

Kristen Scott, "Kris," started Kris' Crafts with a personal investment of $350,000 in cash. The company began operations as a retail distributor of cabin cruisers on January 1, 2000, renting showroom space costing $40,000 per year (including utilities) and launching an aggressive advertising and promotional program costing $48,000 per year. One salesperson was hired, agreeing to be compensated on a commission basis at the rate of 12 percent of sales. All expenses mentioned above are paid in cash in the year incurred. The company paid a $6,000 dividend to Kristen each year.

All boat purchases and boat sales are for cash only. A review of Kris' perpetual inventory records indicates that boat purchases and sales during 2000, 2001 and 2002 are as presented in Exhibit C4-3.1 (dollar amounts in 000's).

Exhibit C4-3.1
Inventory Data for 2000-2002

Date	Purchases		Sales	
	Quantity	Cost/Unit*	Quantity	Sales Price/Unit*
1/31/00	2	$110		
2/15/00			1	$170
2/28/00	2	$115		
3/15/00			2	$170
1/31/01	2	$118		
2/28/01			2	$175
3/15/01	2	$122		
4/01/01			1	$175
2/28/02	2	$125		
3/15/02			3	$180
Totals	10		9	

* Cost and sales price per unit information is given in thousands. For example, on 1/31/00 the company purchased 2 units at $110,000 each.

Yearly income is taxed at the rate of 34 percent of net operating income. All the cabin cruisers purchased over the three year period are identical and increases in purchase prices are due to inflation.

Requirements

Prepare the following for Kris' Crafts assuming the company uses the perpetual system to record inventory.

1. Exhibit C4-3.2 illustrates a completed perpetual inventory card prepared using FIFO cost information. Accumulate the LIFO cost information on the blank LIFO perpetual inventory card provided in Exhibit C4-3.3 at the end of the case.

2. Record all transactions for Kris' Crafts for the second and third year on an accounting transaction worksheet assuming a FIFO inventory cost flow. Use the information given in Exhibit C4-3.2 to record cost of goods sold. All other variable expenses should be entered using a formula (percentage of sales) rather than a specific dollar amount. Make sure to use the sum formula to compute ending account balances after each year end. A template for the accounting transaction worksheet format is illustrated in Exhibit C4-3.4. The first year has already been entered for you. After completing the template, save the spreadsheet. Print the FIFO spreadsheet to hand in. Do not close the file but use it to complete Requirement 3.

3. Using the same accounting transaction worksheet template as Requirement 2, revise transactions to reflect a LIFO inventory cost flow. Use the Save As command to save this file under a different name than your original spreadsheet. (Alternatively, you can record the LIFO information in a new worksheet in the same workbook file.) Print the LIFO spreadsheet to hand in. A blank template for a LIFO accounting transaction worksheet has been provided as Exhibit C4-3.5.

   Be sure to tear out and attach the LIFO perpetual card you completed in Requirement 1 as supporting documentation for the purchases and COGS figures in your LIFO accounting transaction worksheet.

4. Compute net income for each year under both FIFO and LIFO by looking at the spreadsheet. Which method has the highest net income for 2000? 2001? 2002?

Exhibit C4-3.2
Perpetual Inventory Card — FIFO

Date	Purchases			Sales			Inventory		
	Number of Units	Unit Cost	Total Cost	Number of Units	Unit Cost	Total Cost	Number of Units	Unit Cost	Total Cost
1/31/00	2	$110,000	$220,000				2	$110,000	$220,000
2/15/00				1	$110,000	$110,000	1	$110,000	$110,000
2/28/00	2	$115,000	$230,000				1	$110,000	$110,000
							2	$115,000	$230,000
3/15/00				1	$110,000	$110,000			
				1	$115,000	$115,000	1	$115,000	$115,000
1/31/01	2	$118,000	$236,000				1	$115,000	$115,000
							2	$118,000	$236,000
2/28/01				1	$115,000	$115,000			
				1	$118,000	$118,000	1	$118,000	$118,000
3/15/01	2	$122,000	$244,000				1	$118,000	$118,000
							2	$122,000	$244,000
4/1/01				1	$118,000	$118,000	2	$122,000	$244,000
2/28/02	2	$125,000	$250,000				2	$122,000	$244,000
							2	$125,000	$250,000
3/15/02				2	$122,000	$244,000			
				1	$125,000	$125,000	1	$125,000	$125,000

Exhibit C4-3.3
Template for Requirement 1
Perpetual Inventory Card — LIFO

Date	Purchases			Sales			Inventory		
	Number of Units	Unit Cost	Total Cost	Number of Units	Unit Cost	Total Cost	Number of Units	Unit Cost	Total Cost
1/31/00									
2/15/00									
2/28/00									
3/15/00									
1/31/01									
2/28/01									
3/15/01									
4/1/01									
2/28/02									
3/15/02									

Exhibit C4-3.4
Accounting Transaction Worksheet Template - FIFO Assumption

	A	B	C	D	E	F
1	Date	Cash	Inventory	Contributed Capital	Retained Earnings	Explanation
2	1/1/00	350,000		350,000		Beg. balance
3	2000	(40,000)			(40,000)	Rent expense
4	2000	(48,000)			(48,000)	Advertising expense
5	1/31/00	(220,000)	220,000			Purchases
6	2/15/00	170,000			170,000	Sales revenue
7			(110,000)		(110,000)	Cost of goods sold
8	2/28/00	(230,000)	230,000			Purchases
9	3/15/00	340,000			340,000	Sales revenue
10			(225,000)		(225,000)	Cost of goods sold
11	2000	(61,200)			(61,200)	Commissions expense
12	2000	(8,772)			(8,772)	Income tax expense
13	2000	(6,000)			(6,000)	Dividend
14		246,028	115,000	350,000	11,028	12-31-00 BALANCES
15	2001					Rent expense
16	2001					Advertising expense
17	1/31/01					Purchases
18	2/28/01					Sales revenue
19						Cost of goods sold
20	3/15/01					Purchases
21	4/1/01					Sales revenue
22						Cost of goods sold
23	2001					Commissions expense
24	2001					Income tax expense
25	2001					Dividend
26						12-31-01 BALANCES
27	2002					Rent expense
28	2002					Advertising expense
29	2/28/02					Purchases
30	3/15/02					Sales revenue
31						Cost of goods sold
32	2002					Commissions expense
33	2002					Income tax expense
34	2002					Dividend
35						12-31-02 BALANCES
36						

Note: The figures for COGS and inventory purchases come from the FIFO perpetual card in Exhibit C4-3.2.

Exhibit C4-3.5
Accounting Transaction Worksheet Template - LIFO Assumption

	A	B	C	D	E	F
1	Date	Cash	Inventory	Contributed Capital	Retained Earnings	Explanation
2	1/1/00					Beg. balance
3	2000					Rent expense
4	2000					Advertising expense
5	1/31/00					Purchases
6	2/15/00					Sales revenue
7						Cost of goods sold
8	2/28/00					Purchases
9	3/15/00					Sales revenue
10						Cost of goods sold
11	2000					Commissions expense
12	2000					Income tax expense
13	2000					Dividend
14						12-31-00 BALANCES
15	2001					Rent expense
16	2001					Advertising expense
17	1/31/01					Purchases
18	2/28/01					Sales revenue
19						Cost of goods sold
20	3/15/01					Purchases
21	4/1/01					Sales revenue
22						Cost of goods sold
23	2001					Commissions expense
24	2001					Income tax expense
25	2001					Dividend
26						12-31-01 BALANCES
27	2002					Rent expense
28	2002					Advertising expense
29	2/28/02					Purchases
30	3/15/02					Sales revenue
31						Cost of goods sold
32	2002					Commissions expense
33	2002					Income tax expense
34	2002					Dividend
35						12-31-02 BALANCES
36						

Group Assignment 4-3

STAND UP AND BE COUNTED

Group Number _____**Group members present and participating**:

_____

_____

Objectives

1. To understand the nature of merchandise inventories and how the perpetual inventory system tracks inventory.
2. To understand and apply the specific identification, FIFO, and LIFO costing methods.
3. To understand the linkage between merchandise inventory and cost of goods sold.

Requirements

1. Assuming Kristen needs a bank loan at the end of 2000 and will use inventory as collateral, which inventory method would you recommend? Why?

_____

_____

_____

2. Assuming Kristen wants to report the highest net income in the early years of the company in order to attract investor interest, which inventory method do you recommend? Why? What direction (up or down) of inventory costs are you assuming in your answer? Explain.

_____

_____

_____

3. Assuming Kristen wants to maximize net cash flows over the three-year period, does the choice of inventory cost flow assumption make a difference? Is there any reason she should prefer one set of cash flows to the other? Explain.

_____

_____

_____

_____

_____

4. What if Kristen had purchased four boats on February 28, 2002 instead of two boats, but still sold the same amount in 2002? Assuming a LIFO inventory cost flow, what effect would this have on the following. Please circle the correct response for (a) and (b).

    a.   Year 2002 net income? Up or Down?

    b.   Inventory balance shown on the balance sheet at December 31, 2002? Inventory balance Up or Down?

    c.   Based on your calculations in (a) and (b), can management manipulate income and ending inventory by purchasing/not purchasing near year end?

_____

_____

_____

5. Our problem assumes that all the cabin cruisers were identical. In most cases, cabin cruisers would be unique. What inventory method would Kristen probably use in reality? Explain why.

_____

_____

_____

_____

Case Reading 4-4

BUYING AN EXISTING BUSINESS

INTRODUCTION

When starting a business, it may not be necessary to build the business from the ground up. An existing business may be for sale that meets the buyer's needs. Purchasing an established business offers several important advantages over a start-up company, but there are considerable disadvantages and pitfalls one must be aware of before finalizing the decision. At a minimum, the services of an attorney and an accountant should be sought. Even for these professionals, buying an existing business can be complicated, but they are trained to recognize potential problems.

When buying an existing business, apply the well-known phrase:

"CAVEAT EMPTOR"

or

"LET THE BUYER BEWARE"

Because the asking price of an existing business will be based largely upon the information contained in financial statements, it is important that the prospective purchaser understand how the values shown in the balance sheet were derived. If the financial statements were audited by a CPA and the resulting opinion clearly stated that the statements present fairly the financial position, results of operation (income), and cash flow in accordance with GAAP, the purchaser can place reliance on the statements. This in not to suggest that audited values are the sole basis of arriving at a fair price for an existing business. An auditor's opinion does not suggest that the business is a good investment; only that the statements depict an economic reality, good or bad.

This case reading is prompted by the fact that J & J Corporation is contemplating the purchase of an existing business, Thompson's Paint and Wallpaper. In the case which follows, you will be asked to evaluate the financial statements of Thompson's to determine whether the various assets are properly presented. In addition, Thompson's operating results will be compared with industry norms. If John and Joanna make a mistake at this point in their embryonic business venture, such as paying too high a price for Thompson's or being mislead as to the trend of its sales revenue, the error could lead to business failure.

VALUE OF BUSINESS ASSETS

What exactly is the buyer purchasing and what should the buyer be looking for when researching the business? The buyer is purchasing the **net assets**, the owner's equity, of the business. In other words, he or she is purchasing 100 percent ownership in the business which consists of all the assets less all the liabilities.

Net Assets = Assets – Liabilities = Owner's equity

When evaluating the assets of a company the buyer needs to be cautious and objective. The amount recorded in the seller's financial statements (historical cost) may not reflect the true value of the asset since the current market value of an asset often differs from its historical cost. In addition, the seller of the business will probably be more optimistic than the buyer about the value of the business assets. The process of selling a business can be compared to the sale or purchase of a used car. Generally there are three facts that occur during this process:

1. The price ultimately depends on a process of negotiation and some people are better negotiators than others;

2. The seller will think that the car (business) is worth more than the buyer does; and

3. Since the seller knows more about the car (business) than does the buyer, some negative information may be concealed or misrepresented.

Before purchasing any assets, a careful analysis of the market value of the assets should be undertaken. Additionally, the ownership of the assets should be investigated by an attorney to make sure that there are no undisclosed liens.

In the following section the advantages and disadvantages of purchasing accounts receivable, inventory, fixed assets, intangible assets (patents, trademarks) and assuming (accepting the responsibility for) the liabilities will be reviewed.

Accounts Receivable

When purchasing accounts receivable, there are several factors that must be considered:

1. What percentage of the existing accounts receivable are collectible?

2. Has the amount of credit sales versus cash sales increased recently?

3. Are the existing credit terms reasonable and effective or do they need to be changed?

What Percentage of the Existing Accounts Receivable are Collectible?

As mentioned previously, the seller of the business will probably be more optimistic than the buyer concerning the collectibility of the accounts receivable. All accounts receivable need to be reviewed carefully. An aging of accounts receivable, like that described in Exhibit 4-2.4, should be completed. An aging schedule summarizes all accounts receivable in categories depending on the length of time each account receivable has been outstanding. This tool was illustrated in detail in Case Reading 4-2. The general rule is *the longer the account has been outstanding the less chance there is of collecting it.* Slow payment by customers may indicate unresolved disputes. When buying an existing business, the buyer should look carefully at these older accounts to be sure that he or she is not buying uncollectible accounts. Most accounting software packages can maintain detailed account information for each customer. If the current owner uses such software, he or she should be able to provide the buyer with the customers' credit histories with the business.

Has the Amount of Credit Sales Versus Cash Sales Increased Recently?

Information about the proportion of cash versus credit sales is valuable since it will be useful in making future cash flow projections. Cash sales are immediately collectible, while credit sales are collectible at a future date, and sometimes not at all. If the proportion of credit sales versus cash sales has notably increased in the last period, perhaps the company has relaxed its credit standards and sold on credit to customers who were previously deemed not creditworthy. Because sales revenue is recorded on the date that the exchange of goods took place (according to the revenue recognition principle), the company could show increased income from these sales without a corresponding increase in cash. This type of activity would result in the recording of questionable accounts receivable that may be uncollectible. In anticipation of selling the business, the seller may be motivated to show increased sales to make the business look more attractive to the buyer.

Are the Existing Credit Terms Reasonable and Effective or do They Need to be Changed?

To determine if the company's credit terms are effective, the company will generally compute the accounts receivable turnover for the year. The turnover calculation can then be used to calculate the average collection period of an accounts receivable. The collection period can then be compared with the sales terms to see if those terms are effective. This process was discussed in depth in Case Reading 4-2 and will not be repeated here.

A complete review and analysis should be completed on all credit terms, special pricing, or discounts available. Once the buyer has completed the evaluation, he or she will have to decide what to do if the credit terms are too lenient. If stricter standards are imposed, will the existing customers continue to do business with the company?

Horizontal (Year-to-Year) Analysis

It is often beneficial to compare the current year figures with the previous year to determine the percentage increase or decrease for that item during the year. This process is called horizontal analysis. For example, a growth of receivables from $90,000 in 2000 to $110,000 in 2001 would be computed as follows:

$$\frac{\text{2001 Receivables}}{\text{2000 Receivables}} - 1.00 = \frac{\$110,000}{\$90,000} - 1.00 = 22.22\%$$

Alternatively, this could be computed:

$$\frac{\text{2001 Receivables} - \text{2000 Receivables}}{\text{2000 Receivables}} = \frac{\$110,000 - \$90,000}{\$90,000} = 22.22\%$$

Both computations indicate that receivables grew 22 percent during 2001. This trend in receivables can then be compared with other companies in the industry and reasons can be obtained for any major differences. For example, if sales revenue did not grow at approximately the same or a greater percentage than the industry, it could mean that uncollectible accounts are piling up in accounts receivable. The buyer of these receivables must guard against an excessive bad debt (uncollectible accounts) rate. Horizontal analysis will be discussed in greater detail in Case Reading 4-8.

Inventory

Purchasing the inventory of an existing business should be done only after addressing the following issues.

1. Does the company have the correct product mix for the buyer's needs?

2. Is the amount of inventory on hand reasonable?

3. Is the current inventory outdated or obsolete?

Does the Company have the Correct Product Mix?

When considering purchasing another company's inventory, it is important that the buyer is purchasing the right product mix for his or her needs. For example, if the previous owner was a furniture salesperson and sold all types of furniture, but the new owner intends to specialize in bedroom furniture, then the product mix might not be right. The buyer will want to determine if the purchase agreement includes all inventory items, "a package deal," or if he or she can select what to buy. If the product mix is acceptable for his or her needs, it will facilitate the purchase.

Is the Amount of Inventory on Hand Reasonable?

Inventory levels will already be established for the needs of the existing business, but the potential buyer will need to evaluate the existing levels in terms of the proposed business. The existing business can provide additional supplemental information highlighting any seasonal product fluctuations. This information will also assist the buyer in projecting future cash disbursements relating to inventory purchases.

One tool used to control the inventory is the **inventory turnover ratio,** which is the inventory level in relation to sales. A merchandising organization must try to control its inventory in order to maximize profits. To control inventory, the company attempts to carry an optimal amount of merchandise. Not carrying enough inventory may cause a company to lose sales by not having the merchandise on hand when customers demand it. On the other hand, carrying too much inventory may cause a company to incur additional inventory carrying costs such as insurance, storage, interest, and obsolescence costs. Technology has helped many companies reduce the level of inventory and the consequent carrying costs. For example, Wal-Mart stores are linked to regional distribution centers via satellite for the purpose of transmitting sales and inventory data. The instantaneous transfer of sales data cuts down the time between sales at an individual Wal-Mart store and the replenishment of the fast-moving stock.

As an example, assume that the company had beginning inventory of $75,000 and ending inventory of $85,000. Cost of goods sold (COGS) for the year was $400,000. Inventory turnover would be computed as follows:

$$\text{Inventory turnover} = \frac{\text{Cost of Goods Sold}}{(\text{Beg. Inv.} + \text{End. Inv.}) \div 2} = \frac{\$400,000}{(\$75,000 + \$85,000) \div 2} = 5 \text{ times}$$

The inventory calculation shows that inventory turns over five times per year. An alternative, and perhaps easier to understand, ratio is the average number of **days sales in inventory**, computed by dividing 365 (the number of days in a year) by the turnover. This indicates the average number of days it takes a company to sell its inventory.

$$\text{Days sales in inventory} = \frac{365 \text{ days}}{\text{Inventory turnover}} = \frac{365}{5} = 73 \text{ days}$$

This means that the average item in inventory takes about 73 days to be sold. To determine if this is a good or bad result, the 73 days should be compared to previous years for the same company to see if the number of days was increasing or decreasing. The inventory turnover ratio can also be compared to other companies in the same industry. Generally speaking, companies would like to have a faster inventory turnover compared to previous periods (or other companies), which would result in a fewer number of days sales in inventory.

Of course, not all companies or industries would have the same inventory turnover target. Companies should monitor the inventory turnover or average number of days sales in inventory over several periods and observe whether significant changes occur. If the turnover declines or the average number of days increases significantly, a need to improve inventory control may be indicated. Some possible reasons for such changes in these ratios are an increase in obsolete merchandise included in inventory, carrying too much inventory, or reduced sales activity.

Is the Current Inventory Outdated or Obsolete?

When buying another business's inventory, the buyer must make sure that the inventory is marketable. For example, if purchasing a computer store, do all computers have the most current microprocessor installed, or will the inventory need to be sold at a lower price? Outdated or obsolete inventory must be identified prior to the purchase since these items may be overvalued in the company's records. A tour of the company's premises will allow the purchaser to view the inventory items for sale. The buyer should look for outdated models and boxes which are especially old, dusty, or possibly damaged.

Valuation of Inventory to Lower of Cost or Market. Merchandising companies take a risk that while they hold merchandise for resale it may decline in value. This may occur because merchandise becomes obsolete or demand declines for some other reason. Generally accepted accounting principles require that at each financial statement date the company compare the recorded cost of its inventory to its current market price. By "market," accountants mean current replacement cost. The company must reflect the lower of the cost or market amount on its balance sheet. If that amount is cost, no adjustment needs to be made; but if that amount is market, an adjustment is needed to reduce inventory to its lower replacement cost. This is known as the **lower of cost or market rule**.

An entry would be made in the accounting transaction worksheet to reduce both inventory and retained earnings. The decrease to retained earnings would be reflected on the income statement as a "Loss on write-down of inventory." Similar to receivables, the older the inventory, the more likely a portion of it is obsolete and cannot be sold at a price that permits a profit margin to be earned.

Physical Inventory Count. One way the cost of goods sold expense (COGS) in the income statement can be determined is by counting the physical inventory at the end of the fiscal year and then applying a unit cost to the items counted. As mentioned in Case Reading 4-3, the formula for cost of goods sold is:

$$COGS = Beginning\ inventory + Net\ purchases - Ending\ inventory$$

The proper measurement of both beginning inventory and ending inventory is critical to the correct cost of goods sold and therefore the net income for the period. When a company takes its physical inventory at the end of the accounting period, there is a risk that errors may occur in counting or costing the inventory. If an error is not detected before the financial statements are prepared, the amount of the error will affect the income reported in both the current and succeeding year. This two-year effect occurs because the ending inventory for one year is the beginning inventory for the following year. Consequently, the error will make both the ending inventory for the current year and the beginning inventory for the following year incorrect. This was discussed in more depth in Case Reading 4-3.

In a periodic inventory system, there is a greater chance that a mistake in counting and costing the inventory will distort the income statement and balance sheet. This is because in a periodic inventory system, there are no inventory records used to keep track of daily inventory changes. The risk to the prospective purchaser of existing inventory is that the inventory asset is overstated. If the negotiated purchase price is based upon the erroneous inventory value, losses could result in later accounting periods. More important, perhaps, is that the expected cash to be realized from the sale of the existing inventory could be significantly less than expected, thereby triggering a cash shortage.

Fixed Assets

According to the historical cost principle, fixed assets should be recorded in the accounting records at their historical cost, which is the amount paid to acquire the asset. During the years that the asset is in use, the company records depreciation each accounting period to allocate that acquisition cost over the estimated useful lives of the assets. The net amount recorded in the financial statements for fixed assets is therefore the cost less the depreciation accumulated since the acquisition date. This net amount, also called the **book value**, will rarely reflect the market value of the various fixed assets.

The buyer should expect to pay the current market value for any assets purchased, so hiring an outside appraiser to evaluate the assets is a necessity. If the financial statements are not audited, a seller may be more prone to violate the historical cost principle by writing up an asset in the financial statements to what he or she believes is the current market value. The independent appraisal of the current market value of assets will help the buyer avoid overpaying for the assets of an existing business.

Land and Buildings

If purchasing an existing business, the land and buildings are already in place and ready to accommodate the needs of the business. Does the business have the ability to expand at its present location or will it need to be moved to accommodate an increase in business? Is the business already at capacity? If the site is unable to expand at its present location or if it is already at capacity it may be a wise decision not to buy. If the property is acceptable, a title search should be performed to ensure that there are no liens filed against the property. A lien allows a creditor to assume ownership of the property if an outstanding liability is not repaid. The buyer may also want to employ the services of a surveyor to validate the established property lines.

Environmental laws are becoming more rigid every day and the buyer must be aware of these laws. If contamination is a concern, research and testing should be conducted to ensure the site is not contaminated by toxic substances. It is becoming customary to require the sellers to make detailed representations and warranties concerning environmental matters and to undertake extensive and costly environmental audits as a condition to buying a business. This matter should be taken seriously because the clean-up costs of a contaminated site may be more than the land is worth.

Equipment and Machinery

Any used fixed assets the buyer is purchasing should be scrutinized in the same manner as when buying a used car. The assets must be dependable. If they are unable to perform their function, the buyer will not realize any profit from their use. Following are some questions the purchaser may want to have answered regarding these assets.

1. How old are the fixed assets and what is their estimated life expectancy at the time of purchase?

2. Have the assets had preventive maintenance and are all maintenance records available?

3. Has this model been replaced by a more efficient model rendering this model obsolete?

4. Is this brand a reliable one and is the company that made it trustworthy?

If the business is a manufacturing concern, purchasing a business that is capable of production from day one is an enormous advantage. Not only are all fixtures and equipment in place but the added knowledge of known production capacity is also available. This information will definitely help in making future planning budgets more reliable.

Intangible Assets

An **intangible asset** is an asset that does not have a physical form. The value of intangible assets derives from the future benefit expected from the intangible asset. Examples of intangible assets include trademarks, copyrights, and patents. If the seller has any of these already in place and they are still bona fide legal and/or economic rights, the buyer will benefit. If these items are included in the sale, the legal expiration date of the intangible assets will need to be known. An intangible asset that expires soon will be of little value to the buyer. It is difficult to assess the market value of an intangible asset; professionals should be consulted. Like fixed assets, intangible assets are initially recorded in the accounting records at cost and that cost is allocated over all periods benefited. This allocation is called

amortization. The amount shown at any given point in time for the intangible asset would be its cost less the accumulated amortization. Once again, this does not correspond in any way to market value.

Another example of an intangible asset that could appear on the balance sheet of an existing business is goodwill. Proper accounting practice restricts the recording of goodwill on a balance sheet to purchase transactions. If the amount paid for an existing business exceeds the fair market value of the net assets acquired, then the excess is classified as an intangible asset called goodwill. Presumably the buyer, seeking his or her own best interest, would be willing to pay a premium over fair market value only when indications are that the business will earn above-average profits in the future. Above-average profits can result from the business having a unique competitive advantage such as proprietary technology, extraordinary employees, a strong customer base, a very desirable location, etc. The buyer must be wary of the fact that the goodwill appearing on the balance sheet of an existing business may no longer be something of value. This is an intangible asset which the seller purchased when he or she bought the business, whenever that may have been! As a general rule, goodwill appearing on the balance sheet is not severable from the other assets; its value is highly suspect.

Liabilities

Before purchasing an existing business, the buyer needs to look carefully at the obligations and debts of the business. A decision needs to be made as to whether the liabilities will be assumed (they become the buyer's liabilities) or if all or many of the liabilities will be paid off. For example, there may be a mortgage on the building that has a low interest rate that the buyer may want to assume.

Be sure to look for unrecorded liabilities as well. Are there any amounts still due the utility company, suppliers, or back taxes due, etc.? A thorough review of the company's financial information should provide answers to these questions.

Operating Results

All current and previous financial statements should be provided by the seller and thoroughly analyzed by the buyer. Performing vertical and horizontal analysis on a company's statements should point out areas to be investigated further. An example of horizontal analysis was provided earlier in this case reading. A more thorough example of both horizontal and vertical analysis can be found in Case Reading 4-8.

Current financial information for the existing company can be used to estimate future operating results. Maintaining the existing inventory level will reduce the probability that the business will experience a shortage or overstock of product. This, in turn, will reduce the risk of losing a customer due to product unavailability, or necessitating mark downs due to over-ordering. A major advantage of purchasing an existing business is that relationships with customers and suppliers are already established, a customer base is provided, and suppliers are familiar with the business's needs. Because of these factors, the business can open right away without a shutdown and profit can be earned immediately.

By looking at the past financial statements of the business, future performance will be easier to predict. Past performance in a company is a reasonable indicator of future performance. For example, rent or lease payments along with past utilities expense bills should be available to be used in planning future operations. In addition, more accurate cash budgeting is provided by using past cash flow analyses as a guide. Therefore, a better overview of cash requirements is possible, including cash needed for inventory purchases, slow periods, promotional seasons, or other reasons.

Accuracy of the Financial Information

Are the financial statements provided by the seller accurate and reliable? When purchasing a business it is preferable to have an independent accountant review the financial statements for adherence to generally accepted accounting principles. Additionally, the accountant, called an auditor, will review any estimates made by management to make sure they are reasonable. For example, is the life of the equipment reasonable? Is there an adequate bad debt allowance for uncollectible accounts? Are sales recorded on the proper date and are expenses matched with those sales to reflect the proper amount of profit? The independent auditor will address all these issues and will issue an opinion on the financial statements. Users of financial statements worldwide rely on auditors' opinions in making business decisions.

OTHER CONSIDERATIONS

Other considerations also need to be addressed because they will have an impact on the purchase of an existing business. For example, when buying an existing business, the accounting system is in place and ready to record transactions immediately. This eliminates the need to adopt and set up another accounting software package. This will save the buyer hours of planning. Once again, the buyer can begin making and recording sales almost immediately after the purchase is finalized.

What is the Real Reason the Previous Owner is Selling?

A common reason given for selling is poor health or retirement. Is this an honest answer? At this point it would be a good idea to develop some detective skills to make sure that all underlying issues have surfaced. Sources for further information are employees, neighboring businesses, the county planning commission or economic development team, and the chamber of commerce. Additional reasons for selling could include limited growth in the area, a declining neighborhood, competition in the area, demographic changes (the customer base left the area), diversion of customer traffic due to new highway construction, or a large chain store building in the area within the year.

Location

In purchasing the land and buildings the buyer is also purchasing the location of the business. This is a definite advantage to the new business owner because customers are already aware of its existence and location. Some business leaders believe that location is one of the most important predictors of success for any business. For example, a bar or pizza parlor located adjacent to a college campus would probably be a reasonable location. The location dictates the customer base which can then be targeted for marketing. For the bar or pizza parlor example, most members of the target audience would probably consist of students.

The competition can also be readily identified and future business sites should be identifiable with some research.

Is the location in an area that is growing or declining? Wherever the business locates, there needs to be room for growth and the area should not be in a declining part of town. If the business is located in a declining neighborhood, future sales may be affected and the business may need to relocate to be profitable. Are other businesses leaving this area and, if so, why? The business could be for sale for no other reason than a large discount retail store is building a few blocks away. What are the current or future zoning laws regarding this site? Make sure that the business is currently in compliance with these laws and that the zoning laws are consistent with the future plans for the business.

Does the previous owner have a good reputation with customers and the surrounding area? If not, can the reputation be overcome and new customers attracted, or will it be too difficult? Identify the customers' perception of the business; the buyer does not want to take over a business that has the reputation of being of low value or inherit the previous owner's bad will. Will customer dissatisfaction result from the sale, new product mix, or new pricing structure? Poll the community. Take a random sample to find the answers to these questions because each of these points could contribute to the loss of potential customers.

Employees

One advantage of buying an existing business is that the work force is already in place to take care of customers from day one. No additional funds need to be spent on training existing employees; they already know their roles and responsibilities. In addition, employees can assist in acquainting the new owner with details of the business's operation.

A new owner may run into problems, however. Are the employees comfortable with the change? Current employees may resist the change in ownership and not cooperate, continuing to prefer the way things were in the past. Do the current employees fit into the buyer's plans for the future? Are they professional in what they do and can they help the purchaser achieve his or her goals? In accepting the current employees, the buyer is also accepting their personalities, professionalism, etc. If any doubts exist, it may be a good idea to hire an outside source to review and evaluate their performance. If employees are terminated, anticipate that their coworkers may show resentment and also feel that their own position is in jeopardy.

SUMMARY

The prospective buyer of an existing business must scrutinize financial statements produced by the seller to determine that they are a fair representation of the economic facts. Audited financial statements are certainly preferred over unaudited statements. However, the differences between historical cost and current market value must be kept in mind when reviewing a balance sheet. It may be possible that fair market value of the assets is less than even those contained in an audited statement. In all cases, the past performance of the business must be compared to industry norms to assess its future profit potential. Finally, there are always qualitative issues which must be understood before leaping into the transaction to purchase an existing business. For example, the plan to close the road in front of the business for two years while a major highway project is underway will not appear in the financial statements.

EXERCISES AND PROBLEMS

Exercises

Exercise 1 Sources of Information/Help in Purchasing a Business. When purchasing a business, where does much of the information come from that the purchaser is to rely upon? What two professional people will the purchaser likely rely upon to help him or her evaluate the business prospects of the target business?

Exercise 2 Net Assets and Value. What does the term "net assets" refer to? What is likely to be the single biggest question in the purchaser's mind when purchasing the net assets of another business?

Exercise 3 Factors in Determining Business Price. In purchasing a business, what are the three factors that generally determine the final price to be paid for the business? Select one of the three factors and explain how it can affect the negotiations.

Exercise 4 Valuing Accounts Receivable. If accounts receivable are included in the net assets purchased, how are the accounts receivable valued? How does the aging of accounts receivable help in valuing them?

Exercise 5 Industry Data and Horizontal Analysis. How are industry data and horizontal analysis used in the evaluation of accounts receivable? Explain briefly.

Exercise 6 Factors in Purchasing Inventory. List three significant factors to consider when purchasing inventory of another company as part of a package purchase of the whole company.

Exercise 7 Evaluating Inventory. Explain the significance of days sales in inventory when evaluating the purchase of inventory.

Exercise 8 Inventory Errors. Why do businesspeople and auditors put so much emphasis on determining the correct ending inventory? What is the effect on the financial statements if an incorrect ending inventory is recorded?

Exercise 9 Valuing Fixed Assets. Explain how you would determine the fair market value of fixed assets on the balance sheet.

Exercise 10 Valuing Intangible Assets. Why are intangible assets so difficult to value? List four intangible assets that may be purchased when purchasing another business.

Exercise 11 Assuming Liabilities. When purchasing a business where liabilities are going to be assumed, what are the most important questions that need to be answered? Explain briefly.

Exercise 12 Advantages and Disadvantage of Existing Work Force. List two advantages and two disadvantages of having a work force in place when purchasing an existing business.

Problems

Problem 1 Accounts Receivable and Inventory Ratios. Listed below are selected data for the McNutt Company balance sheets for 1999 and 2000 and its income statement for 2000.

From the balance sheet:

	2000	**1999**
Cash	$ 12,000	$ 10,000
Accounts Receivable	34,000	30,000
Inventory	70,000	60,000
Prepaid Rent	6,000	6,000
Total Current Assets	$122,000	$106,000

From the income statement:

Sales	$320,000
Cost of Goods Sold	260,000
Gross Margin	$ 60,000

Use the information above to answer the items below.

a. Determine the accounts receivable turnover and the accounts receivable collection period.

b. Determine the inventory turnover and the days sales in inventory.

Case 4-4

J & J CORPORATION: PURCHASE OF A RETAIL STORE – PART I

Case Objectives

1. To understand the content of a balance sheet and income statement and the relationships between the two financial statements.
2. To understand specific types of assets (accounts receivable, merchandise inventory, fixed assets) and liabilities (accounts payable, long-term liabilities) that appear on a balance sheet.
3. To understand specific categories in an income statement (revenues and expenses).

Decision: Should J & J buy Thompson's Paint and Wallpaper Store?

INTRODUCTION

You are a financial consultant who has been retained (hired) by J & J Corporation to assist John and Joanna in their deliberations about whether to purchase Thompson's Paint & Wallpaper.

BACKGROUND

John and Joanna continued their summer business until John graduated from college, at which point they carefully reviewed their options. They both decided that their best course of action was to expand J & J Corporation into a full-time, year-round business. Accordingly, during the next couple of years, they aggressively pursued new business, hired several employees, and experienced significant growth in sales, net income, and net assets.

Near the end of 2002, John and Joanna met to discuss next year's plans. "With the growth that we are experiencing, we need more space," observed John. "Our current lease will expire on March 31, 2003, and I would like to see us move to a new facility as soon as possible. I need a warehouse for my equipment and supplies, and you need a showroom for your interior design customers. Also, I think that our profits could be improved if we didn't have to pay retail prices for our paint, wallpaper, and supplies."

"I agree completely, John, and I've been looking for showroom space for the last few weeks," responded Joanna. "Luckily, I think I may have stumbled onto just the space we need. Yesterday, I learned from one of my home remodeling contractors that the owner of Thompson's Paint and Wallpaper has been talking about retiring and selling his retail paint and wallpaper store. The building is on 7th and Main, which is an excellent location. Also, the building appears to have enough floor space to meet both our needs for the next five to ten years."

"Joanna, that's terrific news!" John explained. "Let's stop in and talk with the owner tomorrow. Do you know anything about him?"

"Not really," said Joanna. "We've never done business at Thompson's, and I've never heard anything good or bad about the business."

INITIAL MEETING WITH BUD THOMPSON

John and Joanna had an excellent first meeting with Bud Thompson, who was pleased to find out that his store was of great interest to J & J Corporation. He immediately agreed to share with them his financial information about the store as soon as 2002 results were available.

As John and Joanna drove back to their office, they began to speculate about the store purchase. "You know, John, merging our current business with the store is bound to have a positive impact on your painting business and on my interior design services," Joanna stated. "I would expect that Bud has many loyal contractors in both construction and remodeling businesses. Those contractors could definitely use our services."

"That's true," said John. "I also think that we can do a lot with Bud's store that he's not doing. For instance, Bud does very little advertising. With the right approach, I bet we could generate significant growth in the store's sales and profits. I wonder what his competitors are doing in terms of sales and profits?"

"I think you're right," replied Joanna. "I wonder what Bud's sales and profits are currently? I'm certainly anxious to see his financial information. Incidentally, we need to talk to Fidelity Bank as soon as possible to determine what kind of financing they can give us for this deal."

"I'll stop by at the bank early next week," said John. "In the meantime, can you try to find some industry data on retail paint and wallpaper stores that we could use to evaluate Thompson's store?"

FOLLOW-UP MEETING WITH BUD THOMPSON

In early January 2003, Bud dropped off a package of information for John and Joanna that included the following items. As noted below, some of this information has been included in this case for your review.

- Unaudited income statements and balance sheets for the last three years (included).

- Sales breakdown for the last three years by major customer category and product line (included). Assume that all of Thompson's sales are made on credit terms of net 30 days.

- A complete listing of all customers who had an outstanding balance at December 31, 2002 (not included), which added to the $56,000 shown on the December 31, 2002 balance sheet for accounts receivable. Bud indicated that all receivables were "solid" (i.e., fully collectible in a few weeks).

- A detailed listing of all merchandise inventory, showing the quantity of each item on hand at December 31, 2002, multiplied by Bud's estimate of each item's current market price (not included). This list added to the $94,000 shown on the December 31, 2002 balance sheet for merchandise inventory.

- Bud's estimate of the current market value of his land and store building, indicating a value of $130,000 for the land and $320,000 for the building. No purchases of land or building were made in 2002.

- A list of all furniture and fixtures that included Bud's best guess as to each item's current, second-hand market value (not included). This list totaled $30,000. No purchases of furniture or fixtures were made in 2002.

- A brief "bio" for each of Bud's five current employees, who all indicated a strong interest in working for J & J Corporation if the company purchased the store (not included).

Before leaving, Bud indicated, "I sure hope we can strike a deal. I'd like to settle this before the end of January. I want to sell all of the net assets. Of course, I'll just keep the cash that's on hand at the closing. If it would help you, I would be willing to lease the land and building for fifteen years rather than sell them to you outright. I wouldn't mind receiving a monthly lease payment. It would be a nice alternative to the monthly salary of $3,000 that I presently take out of the business as an administrative expense."

J & J'S NEED FOR ASSISTANCE

"John, I've looked over the information that Bud has given us, and I have begun to make some industry comparisons, but frankly I'm a little overwhelmed with all of this data," remarked Joanna. "Have you made any headway in your analysis?"

"Not really, Joanna. In fact, I've got more questions than answers," said John. "I think we need help before we go much further with this store purchase decision. Let's prepare a list of questions and issues that need to be addressed and then seek help from our CPA consultant."

CASE EXHIBITS

The following information is provided for use in Case 4-4, Group Assignment 4-4, Case 4-5 and Group Assignment 4-5.

Exhibit C4-4.1
Unaudited Income Statements

Thompson's Paint & Wallpaper
Unaudited Income Statements
Years Ended December 31

	2002	2001	2000
Sales	$330,000	$265,000	$270,000
Cost of Goods Sold	165,000	151,000	154,000
Gross Margin	165,000	114,000	116,000
Operating Expenses			
Selling Expenses [a]	21,000	20,000	19,000
Administrative Expenses [b]	47,000	49,000	45,000
Total Operating Expenses	68,000	69,000	64,000
Income Before Taxes	$ 97,000	$ 45,000	$ 52,000

[a] Includes bad debt expense of $1,500 for 2002, 2001, and 2000.
[b] Includes Bud Thompson's salary of $36,000 and depreciation expense of $5,000 for 2002, 2001, and 2000. Of the $5,000, $4,000 applied to the building and $1,000 to the furniture and fixtures.

Exhibit C4-4.2
Unaudited Balance Sheets

Thompson's Paint & Wallpaper
Unaudited Balance Sheets
December 31st

	2002	2001	2000
Assets			
Cash	3,000	5,000	4.500
Accounts Receivable	56,000	34,000	32.000
Merchandise Inventory	94,000	53,000	49.000
Prepaid Expenses	1,000	700	900
Total Current Assets	154,000	92,700	86.400
Land	55,000	5,000	5.000
Building, net	195,000	39,000	43.000
Furniture and Fixtures, net	30,000	12,000	11.000
Total Fixed Assets	280,000	56,000	59,000
Total Assets	$ 434,000	$ 148,700	$ 145.400
Current Liabilities			
Accounts Payable	36,000	36,000	35.000
Accrued Payroll Taxes	3,000	3,000	3.500
Total Current Liabilities	39,000	39,000	38.500
Owner's Equity			
Bud Thompson, Capital	395,000	109,700	106.900
Total Liabilities and Owner's Equity	$ 434,000	$ 148,700	$ 145.400

Exhibit C4-4.3
Thompson's Paint and Wallpaper
Sales Breakdown

	2002	2001	2000
Total Sales	$ 330,000	$ 265,000	$ 270,000
Home building contractors	$ 100,000	$ 70,000	$ 72,000
Paint	65,000	55,000	50,000
Wallpaper and supplies	35,000	15,000	22,000
Home remodeling contractors	$ 85,000	$ 65,000	$ 67,000
Paint	35,000	20,000	22,000
Wallpaper and supplies	50,000	45,000	45,000
Retail customers	$ 145,000	$ 130,000	$ 131,000
Paint	120,000	115,000	115,000
Wallpaper and supplies	25,000	15,000	16,000

Exhibit C4-4.4
Thompson's Paint and Wallpaper
Industry Norms

Trade Association Data			
Retail Paint and Wallpaper Stores			
Sales range: $250,000 - $750,000			
	2002	2001	2000
Average sales growth	12.00%	9.00%	10.00%
Average gross margin percentage	45.00%	43.00%	41.00%
Average accounts receivable turnover	7.5	7.9	7.6
Average inventory turnover	4.7	4.5	4.6
Average growth in fixed assets	9.00%	6.00%	7.00%
Average current ratio	1.85	1.90	1.88
Average return on equity	22.00%	21.00%	20.00%

Requirements

As part of your assignment, you will need to address various financial evaluation issues related to the store purchase by preparing written responses to the questions listed below, drawing upon information shown in this case and the case readings. Financial information is provided in the exhibits included in this case. Your responses to these questions should be word processed and should include supporting numerical computations.

Sales and Accounts Receivable

1. What was Thompson's growth in sales (in percent) in 2002 compared to 2001? 2001 compared to 2000?

2. In general, what events should take place before a company recognizes a sale in its income statement? Explain.

3. What was Thompson's accounts receivable turnover in 2002, 2001, and 2000? What is the average collection period for those years in days?

4. In general, at what value should accounts receivable be shown on a company's balance sheet? Explain.

Ending Inventory, Cost of Goods Sold, and Gross Margin

5. Complete the schedule for cost of goods sold for 2002 shown below.

Beginning inventory	
Add: Purchases	
Deduct: Ending inventory	
Cost of goods sold	

6. What were Thompson's cost of goods sold percentages and gross margin percentages (as a percent of sales) in 2002, 2001, and 2000?

7. What was Thompson's inventory turnover in 2002, 2001, and 2000? How many days will inventory remain in stock before it is sold each year?

8. In general, at what value should merchandise inventory be shown on a retail company's balance sheet?

Group Assignment 4-4

THOMPSON VERSUS THE INDUSTRY

Group Number _____ **Group members present and participating**:

_____

_____

Objectives

1. To understand the content of a balance sheet and income statement and the relationships between the two financial statements.
2. To understand specific types of assets (accounts receivable, merchandise inventory, fixed assets) and liabilities (accounts payable, long-term liabilities) that appear on a balance sheet.
3. To understand specific categories in an income statement (revenues and expenses).
4. To understand how to evaluate a company's financial information by means of comparisons to industry norms.

Requirements

1. Is Thompson's sales growth consistent with the industry? If not, what possible explanations might be given for Thompson's differences? Explain and give supporting figures.

_____

_____

_____

_____

_____

2. Is Thompson's accounts receivable turnover consistent with the industry? If not, what possible explanations might be given for Thompson's differences? Explain and give supporting figures.

_____

_____

_____

_____

_____

3. Are Thompson's gross margin percentages consistent with the industry? If not, what possible explanations might be given for Thompson's differences? Explain and give supporting figures.

_____

_____

_____

_____

4. Is Thompson's inventory turnover consistent with the industry? If not, what possible explanations might be given for Thompson's differences? Explain and give supporting figures.

_____

_____

_____

_____

_____

Case Reading 4-5

DECISIONS INVOLVING PROPERTY, PLANT, AND EQUIPMENT[1]

INTRODUCTION

This case reading presents the many decisions involved in recording the purchase and use of property, plant, and equipment items. Examples of several alternate methods of depreciation are presented and the concept of deferred taxes is introduced. The reading concludes by discussing how fixed assets and depreciation are recorded and presented in the financial statements.

PROPERTY, PLANT, AND EQUIPMENT

Previous readings have focused on current assets; however, organizations must also invest in long-term assets in order to provide goods or services. The category of long-term assets discussed in this case reading is property, plant, and equipment (sometimes referred to as fixed assets). Property, plant, and equipment, or PPE for short, consists of tangible property with a life extending beyond one year that will be used in the operation of the organization and is not held for resale to customers. These assets are expected to provide benefits to the organization for several future periods. Examples include land, warehouses, factory buildings, machines, delivery vehicles, and office furniture.

The acquisition and use of property, plant, and equipment in the operation of the business requires that management answer the following five questions:

1. What is the cost of the asset when it is acquired?
2. What is the asset's estimated useful life?
3. How much will the asset be worth at the end of its useful life?
4. What depreciation method should be used to depreciate the asset?
5. How should the asset be reported in the financial statements?

The answer to the first question determines the cost of the asset that will be recorded in the accounting records. Answers to the next three questions will determine how much of the asset is expensed each year through the process of depreciation. The final answer will show how property, plant, and equipment is presented in the balance sheet, income statement, and cash flow statement. The remainder of this case reading will consider the answers to each of these questions and the effect of each decision on the financial statements. Janet's Greenhouse, a small business specializing in plant seedlings, will be used throughout the discussion as an illustration.

---

[1] The authors thank Angele Brill from Castleton State College for her major contribution to this Case Reading.

DETERMINING THE COST OF PROPERTY, PLANT, AND EQUIPMENT

What is the Cost of the Asset When it is Acquired?

Assets are recorded at historical cost. Historical cost is defined as the purchase price (the invoice cost) plus any costs incurred to acquire the asset and get it ready for use. This is referred to as the cost principle and is one of the major principles comprising generally accepted accounting principles. Valuing assets at historical cost helps to ensure that the amounts shown in the financial statements are based on objective evidence (e.g., a purchase invoice), not on management's estimate. Expenditures that are included in the cost of a fixed asset are said to be capitalized.

To illustrate, Janet's Greenhouse purchases a tractor. The purchase price of the tractor as listed on the purchase invoice is $30,000. The invoice also shows a charge of $1,500 for sales tax and $500 for delivery. Janet paid $1,000 to have a trailer hitch installed. One month later Janet pays $200 to have the oil changed. Which expenditures does Janet need to capitalize?

Purchase price	$ 30,000
Sales tax	1,500
Delivery	500
Installation of trailer hitch	1,000
Total cost	$ 33,000

Janet should capitalize the $33,000; the tractor account should be increased by $33,000 for the purchase of the tractor. Other accounts affected will depend on how the tractor is financed. The oil change is not capitalized because the benefits from the expenditure will be used up in the current period. Instead, the oil change becomes an expense of the current period (probably repairs and maintenance expense).

Often several assets will be acquired at the same time for one combined purchase price. For example, Janet might purchase a piece of land with a greenhouse on it for $250,000. This is called a **basket purchase**. It is necessary to allocate the basket purchase price to each asset purchased because each asset may have a different useful life and salvage value. The allocation of this cost is based on the appraised value of each asset. The appraisal was $120,000 for the land and $180,000 for the greenhouse. The allocation of the cost to the assets purchased is shown below in Exhibit 4-5.1.

Exhibit 4-5.1
Basket Purchase

	Appraised Value	Percentage of Total	Allocation of Cost
Land	$ 120,000	40.00%	$ 100,000
Greenhouse	180,000	60.00%	150,000
Total	$ 300,000	100.00%	$ 250,000

Since the land is 40 percent of the $300,000 appraised value, it is allocated 40 percent of the $250,000 purchase price, or $100,000. The remaining 60 percent or $150,000 would be allocated to the greenhouse.

DEPRECIATING PROPERTY, PLANT, AND EQUIPMENT

Before the remaining questions are answered, it is first necessary to discuss the concept of depreciation. Property, plant, and equipment assets are used by an organization in the production of revenue over the assets' estimated useful life. As mentioned earlier, costs incurred to produce revenue are considered expenses in the period used. This is the matching principle. In order to properly determine net income, revenues must be offset by the costs incurred in earning the revenue. Therefore, expenses must be matched to the revenues produced.

What does all this have to do with depreciation? Remember, fixed assets are used in the organization's operations; it is the land, building, and equipment owned by the organization. These assets are used to produce revenue. The cost of the assets must become an expense because the usefulness of the asset is used up in the process of earning revenues. This process is called depreciation. **Depreciation** is the systematic allocation of the cost of an asset to expense over the periods that the asset is used to produce revenue. Depreciation is **not** an attempt to match the cost of the asset to its current market value. It is merely a process to comply with the matching principle.

In order to compute an organization's annual depreciation expense, answers to the remaining three questions must be determined.

What is the Asset's Estimated Useful Life?

In order to depreciate a fixed asset, its estimated useful life must be determined. The estimated **useful life** is the period of time that the organization expects to receive benefits from the asset; in other words, the length of time the organization expects to use the asset to produce revenue. Land does not have an estimated useful life since it is not normally used up; therefore, land is not depreciable.

The estimated useful life can be determined in a number of ways. Published industry standards exist for most industries. Alternatively, at the time of purchase, management may ask the manufacturer of the asset for an estimate of its life. Internal Revenue Service publications and guidelines may be consulted, though this is useful mainly for tax purposes. Finally, management may have experience with similar assets.

Often when one of these sources is consulted, management will be given a range of time, not a specific number of years. For instance, if Janet asks the manufacturer of the tractor what its useful life is, she may be told "anywhere from 7 to 10 years." Which estimate should she use? The answer is the life that best matches the number of years she expects to use the tractor before it becomes obsolete, inadequate, or deteriorates too much. Useful life depends on four factors:

1. **Usage** (The more intensely an asset is used the faster it will be used up.)
2. **Passage of Time** (Some components deteriorate over time as they are exposed to the elements.) To illustrate this point consider the following story.

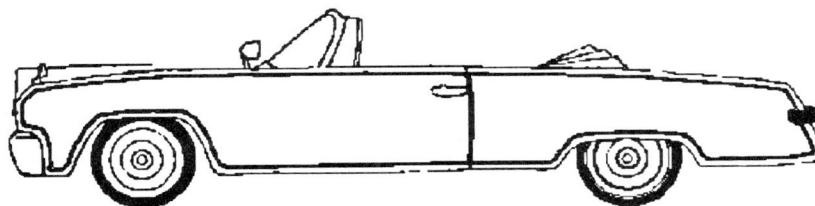

In 1976, Cadillac announced that it was building the last American convertible. There was a man who was very fond of Cadillac convertibles and to ensure that he would have one for the remainder of his life he purchased seven 1976 models. His plan was to use one and put the others in storage until needed.

What sound do you suppose he heard in 1999 when he turned the ignition key on the last of the seven Cadillac convertibles?

This story is intended to demonstrate that the passage of time (even in the absence of usage) results in the deterioration of some fixed assets. In all probability the man heard nothing because the battery and engine had deteriorated in storage for over 20 years.

3. **Obsolescence** (For example, technological advances result in a very short life for computers and software.)
4. **Management Policy** (Major car rental companies and public utilities use the same type of vehicles, yet the useful lives are very different.)

Therefore, it is reasonable to assume that different people will arrive at different determinations of estimated useful life. In other words, it is a matter of professional judgment.

How Much Will the Asset Be Worth At the End of Its Useful Life?

Depreciation allocates the cost of the asset used to expense. If the asset will still have value at the end of its life, then the asset has not been completely "used up" by the organization. Instead, management expects to recover some of the cost of the asset when it is sold. The estimated value of the asset at the end of its useful life is referred to as **salvage value** (also know as scrap value). If salvage value is expected to be insignificant, it will be ignored in the depreciation computation.

Salvage value is determined in much the same way as the estimated useful life except that there are no Internal Revenue Service publications or guidelines for salvage value. As with estimated useful life, consulting sources will often provide a range of possible salvage values. If you have ever tried to trade in a used car for a new car, you may have experienced this. Different dealers will offer you different trade-in values for the same car, providing you with the range of possible salvage values on your used car.

Since salvage value is expected to be recovered when the asset is sold, depreciation is computed using only the value of the asset that the organization expects to use up; this is referred to as its **depreciable cost**. Therefore, before Janet can depreciate the tractor, she needs to determine its salvage value. Janet asks the manufacturer and is told that the tractor will have a value of $3,000 to $5,000 at the end of its useful life. Which is the "right" value for Janet to use? Again, the answer is the value that most realistically reflects what she believes she can sell the tractor for, based on the amount of use and regular maintenance it will receive. This is a matter of professional judgment, and the determination of salvage value may vary.

Which Depreciation Method Should Be Used?

Generally accepted accounting principles allow management the choice of several methods of computing depreciation. These methods fall into two categories: straight-line depreciation and accelerated depreciation. Management may choose either of the accepted methods as long as the method is applied consistently over the asset's useful life. Management may also use a different method for each plant and equipment asset. For example, Janet may decide to use straight-line depreciation for the building and an accelerated method for the tractor.

Straight-Line Depreciation

Straight-line depreciation is the easiest and most widely used method of depreciation for financial reporting purposes. Under this method, an equal portion of the asset's depreciable cost is recognized each year as depreciation expense until the asset is fully depreciated. An asset is fully depreciated when its book value (original cost - accumulated depreciation) is equal to its salvage value. Straight-line depreciation should be chosen if the asset is expected to be used evenly over its useful life. Depreciation is computed by taking the asset's cost less salvage value and dividing the remaining depreciable cost by the estimated useful life.

Assume Janet decided to use a 10-year estimated useful life and a $5,000 salvage value for the tractor. She would compute annual depreciation expense using straight-line as follows:

$$\frac{\text{Cost} - \text{Salvage value}}{\text{Useful life}} = \frac{\$33,000 - \$5,000}{10 \text{ years}} = \$2,800 \text{ per year}$$

Every year for 10 years, Janet will expense 10 percent of the depreciable cost of the asset, or $2,800, to depreciation expense.

Accelerated Methods of Depreciation

Accelerated depreciation methods expense a larger portion of the cost of the asset in the early years and a smaller portion in the later years. Management would choose to use accelerated depreciation methods if they expected the asset to have greater and better usage in the early years and larger repair bills in the later years of the asset's life. By using accelerated depreciation, the total expense of using the asset would remain relatively constant over the years; as depreciation expense declines, it is replaced by higher repair and maintenance expenses.

The **double-declining-balance (DDB) method** is the most widely used of the accelerated depreciation methods. It is based on an annual depreciation rate that is twice the straight-line rate. For example, Janet previously determined that the tractor had a 10-year useful life. If straight-line depreciation is used, the straight-line rate would be 10 percent (each year one tenth of the asset is expensed). If double-declining balance is used, the annual depreciation rate would be 20 percent—twice (double) the straight-line rate of 10 percent.

The computation of depreciation using the double-declining-balance method differs from straight-line depreciation in two important ways. First, salvage value is ignored in the computation, except that depreciation will cease when the book value of the asset equals salvage value. Second, the depreciation rate is multiplied by the cost of the asset less accumulated depreciation (the amount of depreciation taken to date); the difference between cost and accumulated depreciation is referred to as **book value** or carrying value.

$$\boxed{\text{Book Value}} = \text{Cost} - \text{Accumulated depreciation}$$

Assume Janet believes that she will obtain the best use of the tractor during the early years, so she chooses to use the double-declining-depreciation method. Depreciation expense, accumulated depreciation, and book value will be computed as shown in Exhibit 4-5.2 for the first three years of usage.

Exhibit 4-5.2
Double-Declining-Balance Method

Year	Computation	Depreciation Expense	Accumulated Depreciation	Book Value
				$ 33,000
1	$33,000 × 20%	$ 6,600	$ 6,600	26,400
2	$26,400 × 20%	5,280	11,880	21,120
3	$21,120 × 20%	4,224	16,104	16,896

To compute depreciation in year 1, Janet multiplies twice the straight line rate (10 percent in this example) by the cost. Notice how the salvage value was *not* subtracted from the cost to compute depreciation as in straight-line depreciation. Depreciation in the second year is calculated by multiplying the 20 percent rate by the book value at the end of year 1.

Accumulated depreciation is merely the sum of all depreciation expenses recorded for the asset so far. For example, accumulated depreciation of $16,104 in year 3 is the sum of the depreciation expenses for years 1–3 ($6,600 + $5,280 + $4,224). The book value is computed by subtracting accumulated depreciation from the original cost.

What effect will the use of accelerated depreciation have on net income in the early years of an asset's life? Remember, the annual depreciation expense on the tractor using straight-line depreciation was $2,800 per year. Compare that to the first year of depreciation expense of $6,600 computed using the accelerated method of double-declining balance. If Janet desired to maximize profit, which method would she prefer to use? The double-declining-balance method computes a larger depreciation expense in the early years; therefore, reported profit would be less than if straight-line depreciation were used.

To illustrate this comparison, assume Janet's Greenhouse had total sales of $25,000 in the first year. Cost of sales was $12,000 and operating expenses other than depreciation were $5,000. The income tax rate is 30 percent.

> What is net income if Janet uses (1) straight-line depreciation or (2) double-declining-balance accelerated depreciation?

A comparison of the two methods is shown in Exhibit 4-5.3.

Exhibit 4-5.3
Straight-Line Depreciation Versus Double-Declining Balance

	Straight-Line	200% DDB Accelerated
Sales	$ 25,000	$ 25,000
Cost of sales	12,000	12,000
Gross Margin on Sales	13,000	13,000
Operating expenses (except depreciation)	5,000	5,000
Depreciation expense	2,800	6,600
Income from operations	5,200	1,400
Income tax expense (30%)	1,560	420
Net income	$ 3,640	$ 980

Understanding the effect of accelerated depreciation on net income is important for one other reason—it is the method currently used to compute depreciation for tax purposes. The Internal Revenue Code specifies the method and rate of depreciation and the life of the asset. The Code also disregards salvage value in the computation of depreciation.

Depreciation for Tax Purposes

Depreciation is computed for tax purposes using the **modified accelerated cost recovery system**, abbreviated as **MACRS**. For most equipment assets, MACRS uses the double-declining-balance method and specifies the depreciation rate in published tables. A partial rate table is presented below.

Depreciation Rate for Recovery Period

Year	3-year Life	5-year Life	7-year Life
1	33.33%	20.00%	14.29%
2	44.45	32.00	24.49
3	14.81	19.20	17.49
4	7.41	11.52	12.49
5		11.52	8.93
6		5.76	8.92
7			8.93
8			4.46

MACRS also specifies the estimated useful life of an asset. The tractor purchased by Janet's Greenhouse would have a 7-year estimated useful life for tax purposes. Janet would compute the amount of depreciation to report on the corporate income tax return (assuming the business is a corporation) by applying the rate for each year to the cost of the tractor. For the first three years of the tractor's life, depreciation expense using MACRS would be computed as shown in Exhibit 4-5.4.

Exhibit 4-5.4
Computation of MACRS Depreciation

Year	Computation	MACRS Depreciation
1	$33,000 × 14.29%	$4,716
2	$33,000 × 24.49%	$8,082
3	$33,000 × 17.49%	$5,772

Notice in this example that the depreciation expense taken in the first year is less than the amount computed for the next two years. Using MACRS, only a half year of depreciation can be deducted in the first year. This half-year convention is built into the tables published by the Internal Revenue Service. This also explains why an asset with a 7-year life will be depreciated over eight years (one-half year's depreciation is recognized in year 1 and year 8 for tax purposes).

A business must use MACRS to depreciate business assets for income tax reporting purposes; it will probably use a different method for financial reporting purposes. In other words, a business is not required to use the same method of depreciation for income tax purposes that it uses for financial reporting purposes. In fact, most businesses will not; the most widely used method for financial reporting is straight-line. Because businesses use different methods, the income tax expense computed on the income statement will differ from the income tax liability computed on the tax return. Businesses will recognize an additional liability for this difference called deferred taxes. **Deferred taxes** represent an estimated future tax liability because taxable income differs from net income.

RECORDING DEPRECIATION
IN THE ACCOUNTING RECORDS

Property, plant, and equipment assets are initially recorded at historical cost. When the asset is originally acquired, the specific property, plant, and equipment account is increased. Other accounts affected in the transaction will be determined based on how the asset is acquired. If the asset is acquired with cash, then the cash account is decreased. If a liability is incurred for either all or part of the cost, then the liability account will be increased. If the asset is contributed by the owner, then the contributed capital account is increased.

Janet's Greenhouse acquires the tractor on January 10 by paying cash of $3,000 and signing a 10 percent note payable for the remaining $30,000 balance. On December 31, after using the tractor for a full year, depreciation expense must be recorded. Remember, the purpose of recording depreciation is to match the expense of the asset used against the revenues it helped to generate in order to achieve a fair measure of net income. When the topic of depreciation was first introduced in Module 2, depreciation expense was recorded as a deduction to the related property, plant, and equipment account and to retained earnings as shown in Exhibit 4-5.5 below. No accumulated depreciation account was used.

Exhibit 4-5.5
Partial Accounting Worksheet - No Accumulated Depreciation - Year 1

Date	Cash	Equipment	Notes Payable	Contributed Capital	Retained Earnings
1/10	($3,000)	$33,000	$30,000		
12/31		(2,800)			(2,800)

Accumulated Depreciation

The above method is efficient and achieves the purpose of reducing the equipment account by the amount of annual depreciation. Additional information is needed by financial statement users, however. They want to be able to determine how old the assets are so that they can predict when these assets will need to be replaced. They also want to know the original cost of the assets so they have an idea of the approximate cost of replacement. Accountants solve these two problems by creating a special account called accumulated depreciation.

Accumulated depreciation represents the total of depreciation expense taken to date; in other words, it is the total amount of the property, plant, and equipment asset that has been written off as an expense (or "used up") since the asset was placed in service. Accumulated depreciation is a contra asset account, which means that it will reduce the cost of the related asset account. It is sometimes referred to as a valuation account since it reduces the recorded "value" of an asset. The recording of depreciation using an accumulated depreciation account would appear as shown in Exhibit 4-5.6.

Exhibit 4-5.6
Partial Accounting Worksheet With Accumulated Depreciation - Year 1

Date	Cash	Equipment	Accumulated Depreciation	Notes Payable	Contributed Capital	Retained Earnings
1/10	($3,000)	$33,000		$30,000		
12/31			(2,800)			(2,800)

Note that when depreciation is recorded, cash is not affected. Depreciation is one of the few noncash expenses, which means that the expense does not affect the balance of cash at any time. Almost all other expenses will require a payment of cash at some point; depreciation does not. Instead, the cash payment is recorded when the property, plant, and equipment asset is acquired.

How Does Property, Plant, and Equipment Appear on the Balance Sheet?

Property, plant, and equipment accounts appear on the balance sheet at book value. Book value, as mentioned previously, is cost minus accumulated depreciation and represents the portion of the asset that has not yet been "used up." It is the portion of the cost of the asset that still has future economic benefit to the organization. Book value for the tractor for year 1 is computed as follows:

Equipment (tractor)	$33,000	What the tractor originally cost
Less: Accumulated depreciation	(2,800)	The portion expensed to-date
Book value	$30,200	Fixed asset remaining for future operations

Organizations disclose the book value of property, plant, and equipment on the balance sheet in several ways. In all cases, it will be shown as a long-term asset. Janet's Greenhouse can decide to detail the major categories of property, plant, and equipment assets and then subtract the amount of accumulated depreciation. In the example below, it is assumed that depreciation expense on the greenhouse building is $7,500 for the second year. Accumulated depreciation for the two-year period would be $10,300 ($2,800 + $7,500).

Property, Plant, and Equipment

Land	$100,000
Building	150,000
Equipment	33,000
Less: Accumulated depreciation	(10,300)
	$272,700

More common balance sheet presentations include reporting the total of property, plant, and equipment net of accumulated depreciation in one of the two following formats:

Property, plant, and equipment, net of accumulated
depreciation of $10,300 $272,700

OR

Property, Plant, and Equipment, net $272,700

Frequently the reader will be referred to a specific footnote number for more detail. Footnote disclosure is discussed later in this case reading.

How is Depreciation Expense Shown on the Income Statement?

Depreciation expense usually is not separately stated on the income statement. Instead, it is included in either cost of goods sold, operating expenses, general and administrative expenses, or any combination of the three. To determine the amount of depreciation expense taken for the year, consult the footnote disclosure.

How is Property, Plant, and Equipment Shown on the Statement of Cash Flows?

Remember, the statement of cash flows explains the sources and uses of cash. The various sources and uses of cash are categorized into operating activities, investing activities, and financing activities. The acquisition, disposition, and depreciation of property, plant, and equipment assets may affect operating and investing activities.

The operating activities section reports the inflows and outflows of cash from producing goods and services. This section can be prepared either using the direct or indirect method. If the organization uses the direct approach, depreciation expense will not affect the statement. *Depreciation is neither a source nor a use of cash.* However, if the organization uses the indirect approach, an adjustment must be made to net income for the amount of depreciation expense incurred for the year. Since depreciation expense reduced net income, it must be added back in order to compute cash flows from operating activities.

Acquisitions and dispositions of property, plant, and equipment assets for cash are reported in the investing activities section. Only the amount of cash actually paid for the asset is reported in the investing section, not the total cost of the asset. For example, Janet's Greenhouse acquired the tractor by paying $3,000 in cash and signing a note for $30,000. In the investing activities section, only the $3,000 will be shown as a cash use for the purchase of the tractor. This will be reported on the statement of cash flows as follows:

> Cash flows from investing activities
>> Cash paid for equipment   ($3,000)

By computing the increase or decrease in the cost of the property, plant, and equipment assets as shown on the balance sheet and comparing that to the amount of cash paid to acquire the assets, one may gain some insight into the amount of asset acquisitions that the organization financed. The footnote disclosure for liabilities can assist the financial statement reader in verifying the amount of financing used to acquire assets.

What is the Required Footnote Disclosure for Property, Plant, and Equipment?

Generally accepted accounting principles require that all information relevant to financial decision making be disclosed either in the financial statements themselves or in the notes to the financial statements. The notes to the financial statements are an integral part of the statements and must be studied before making any decisions based on the financial statements. Organizations must disclose in footnotes the basis used for valuing the property, plant, and equipment assets; in most cases this will be historical cost. The company must also disclose assets pledged as collateral for debt.

Required disclosure for property, plant, and equipment and depreciation in the financial statements includes:

1. the amount of depreciation expense for the period;
2. balances for the major categories of fixed assets;
3. accumulated depreciation; and
4. general description of the method or methods used to compute depreciation. This is usually done in two separate notes—note 1, which discloses significant accounting policies, and a second note, which discusses property, plant, and equipment assets.

SUMMARY

The nature of many industries requires a significant investment in property, plant, and equipment. The reporting of this key group of assets is based upon the historical cost to bring the asset into operating usefulness. The depreciable cost is allocated to expense over the useful life of the asset. A number of depreciation methods are acceptable. If the method chosen is a fair measurement of the share of capitalized cost assigned to an accounting period, then the net income will be a reliable measure of the company's economic progress (or decline) for the accounting period.

Because the acquisition and accounting for long-term assets is complex, footnotes providing a more detailed explanation of transactions involving property, plant, and equipment items are generally found in published financial statements.

EXERCISES AND PROBLEMS

Exercises

Exercise 1 Asset Basis. What is the basis for recording long-term assets for a business? Explain.

Exercise 2 Depreciation and the Matching Principle. Define depreciation as used in accounting. How do depreciation and the matching principle relate to each other?

Exercise 3 Useful Lives for Depreciable Assets. What are the four factors that determine useful life for a depreciable asset? Explain which of the four factors is likely to be most important in determining the useful life of a computer.

Exercise 4 Determining Salvage Value. Define salvage value. How does management determine salvage value for a fixed asset, for example, a delivery truck?

Exercise 5 Straight-Line Depreciation Characteristics. List two advantages and two disadvantages of the straight-line method of depreciation.

Exercise 6 Advantages of MACRS. What are two significant advantages of using MACRS for income tax purposes?

Exercise 7 Understanding Accumulated Depreciation. What is accumulated depreciation? How is the balance of accumulated depreciation disclosed in the financial statements?

Exercise 8 Disclosing Long-Lived Assets in the Financial Statements. For most companies, property, plant, and equipment is disclosed in one or two lines on the balance sheet. What additional disclosure is needed for property, plant, and equipment in the financial statements?

Problems

Problem 1 Determining Cost of a Purchased Vehicle. Champion Company purchased a car for its top outside salesperson. The following items relate to the car:

Car list price	$27,000	Sales tax paid on car purchase	$1,750
Car purchase price	25,000	Vehicle registration for one year	75
First tank of gasoline	30	Vehicle license fee for one year	500
Insurance for one year	800	Sound reduction undercoating for car	400
Radio upgrade to a CD	300	Traffic ticket while on business trip	140

a. What amount should be capitalized as the cost of the car on Champion Company books?
b. For any item not capitalized, explain how it should be handled in the accounting records.

Problem 2 Computing Depreciation Using Three Methods. On January 2, 2000, Dronebarger Company purchased a computer network system for $44,000. It is estimated that the system will have a five-year useful life and a $4,000 salvage value at the end of five years. Based on this information, determine depreciation for Dronebarger Company for 2000 using:

a. Straight-line method of depreciation.
b. Double-declining-balance method of depreciation.
c. MACRS depreciation (For income tax purposes the system has a five-year life.)

Problem 3 Illustrating Financial Statement Disclosure of Long-Lived Assets. Use the information from Problem 2 to illustrate how the computer network system and related depreciation would be disclosed in the balance sheet, income statement, and a footnote to the financial statement assuming Dronebarger Company used straight-line depreciation.

Case 4-5

J & J CORPORATION: PURCHASE
OF A RETAIL STORE—PART II

Case Objectives

1. To understand the content of a balance sheet and income statement and the relationships between the two financial statements.
2. To understand specific types of assets (accounts receivable, merchandise inventory, fixed assets) and liabilities (accounts payable, long-term liabilities) that appear on a balance sheet.
3. To understand specific categories in an income statement (revenues and expenses).
4. To understand how to evaluate a company's financial information by means of comparisons to industry norms.

Decision: Should J & J buy Thompson's Paint and Wallpaper Store?

This case is a continuation of Case 4-4. Students will need to use financial information provided in Case 4-4, specifically Exhibits C4-4.1 through C4-4.4, to complete the case.

Requirements

Prepare responses to the questions listed below, drawing upon information from Case 4-4 and Case Reading 4-5. Your responses should be word processed and include supporting numerical computations.

1. What was Thompson's growth in fixed assets (in percent) in 2002 compared to 2001? 2001 compared to 2000?

2. Is Thompson's fixed asset growth consistent with the industry each year? If not, what possible explanations might be given for Thompson's differences? Explain.

3. Assuming that the amounts for fixed assets were properly stated at December 31, 2001, what is the proper amount that should be shown for the book value of the land, building, and the furniture and fixtures at December 31, 2002?

4. Is Thompson's Paint and Wallpaper a sole proprietorship or a corporation? Explain your reasoning by specific references to case information given. (There should be at least three items you can reference as an answer for this requirement).

5. Assuming that Thompson's is a corporation, what was the return on equity for Thompson's Paint and Wallpaper in 2002 and 2001? (Use net income after tax as the numerator in the ROE calculation; assume a 27 percent tax rate on income).

6. Was Thompson's return on equity consistent with the industry in both years? If not, what possible explanations might be given for Thompson's differences? Explain.

7. What was Thompson's current ratio in 2002? 2001? 2000? (The current ratio was originally covered in Case Reading 2-2).

8. Was Thompson's current ratio consistent with the industry in each of the three years? If not, what possible explanations might be given for Thompson's differences? Explain.

9. As consultants to J & J, are you concerned about the value that Bud has placed on his accounts receivable, inventory, and fixed assets at December 31, 2002? What advice would you give to J & J about the purchase of these major assets? Explain. (Note: accounts receivable and inventory were investigated in Case 4-4 and Group Assignment 4-4.)

Group Assignment 4-5

TO ERR IS HUMAN...

Group Number _____ **Group members present and participating**:

_____

_____

Objectives

1. To understand the content of a balance sheet and income statement and the relationships between the two financial statements.
2. To understand specific types of assets (accounts receivable, merchandise inventory, and fixed assets) that appear on a balance sheet.
3. To understand specific categories in an income statement (revenues and expenses).
4. To understand the effect of errors and omissions on the financial statements.

Requirements

Answer the following questions after completing Case 4-4 and 4-5 by checking the appropriate column.

1. Suppose Thompson is overly optimistic regarding the collectibility of his year-end (December 31, 2002) accounts receivable. For each financial statement item below, indicate if it would be overstated, understated, or not affected.

	Overstated	Understated	Not Affected
Gross margin			
Net income			
Total assets			
Total liabilities			
Owner's equity			

2. Suppose Thompson has failed to recognize a significant inventory obsolescence problem that exists in his year-end inventory at December 31, 2002. For each financial statement item shown in the table, indicate if the item would be overstated, understated, or not affected as a result of the inventory obsolescence.

	Overstated	Understated	Not Affected
Gross margin			
Net income			
Total assets			
Total liabilities			
Owner's equity			

3. Suppose that at the end of 2002, Thompson had his bookkeeper "adjust" fixed assets appearing in the December 31, 2002 balance sheet to reflect current market value. Show the impact that this bookkeeping adjustment would have on each financial statement item listed below. Indicate if the item would be overstated, understated, or not affected as a result of the bookkeeping adjustment by checking the appropriate column.

	Overstated	Understated	Not Affected
Gross margin			
Net income			
Total assets			
Total liabilities			
Owner's equity			

4. Suppose that at the end of 2002, Thompson's bookkeeper forgot to record the utilities bill for the current month, which totaled $1,300. The bill applied to utilities used in December but not paid for until January. Show the impact that this bookkeeping error would have on each financial statement item listed below. Indicate if the item would be overstated, understated, or not affected as a result of the bookkeeping adjustment by checking the appropriate column.

	Overstated	Understated	Not Affected
Gross margin			
Net income			
Total assets			
Total liabilities			
Owner's equity			

Case Reading 4-6

DECISIONS INVOLVING
DEBT AND EQUITY

INTRODUCTION

One of the most important decisions that owners, managers, and investors can make concerns the relative proportions of long-term debt and shareholders' equity on the balance sheet of the companies in which they have an interest. As business expansion opportunities present themselves, a decision on how to finance the needed assets must be made. Since total assets are equal to creditor and shareholder claims on the balance sheet, the business's capital structure is a key strategic problem to solve if the business is to be profitable for its owners. A wrong decision regarding alternative financing strategies could increase the risk of poor financial performance. This case reading will present the characteristics of long-term debt, shareholders' equity, and resultant financial leverage.

CAPITAL STRUCTURE

Capital structure is the relative proportion of liabilities and shareholders' equity which appear on the right side of the balance sheet. Recall the balance sheet equation:

$$\text{Assets} = \text{Liabilities} + \text{Shareholders' equity}$$

If the company has a high proportion of debt in contrast to equity, then it relies more on debt financing than equity financing. **Debt financing** is the financing of business needs through the use of creditors' funds rather than owners' funds. **Equity financing**, on the other hand, is the financing of business needs through the use of contributed capital or retained earnings.

A company has a higher **financial risk** (likelihood of going bankrupt) if it relies more on debt than equity. One way to assess the financial risk of a company is to compute the **debt-to-equity ratio** (DER).

$$\text{DER} = \frac{\text{Ending liabilities}}{\text{Ending shareholders' equity}}$$

An increase in the company's debt-to-equity ratio or a high ratio relative to the industry indicates higher financial risk and greater use of debt financing. This ratio is particularly important to bankers, bondholders, and other creditors.

DEBT VERSUS EQUITY

To understand the advantages and disadvantages of financing with debt versus equity, it is imperative that we have a better understanding of the two terms. The following issues will be discussed:

- control over the company
- interest payments vs. dividends
- corporate income taxes
- effect on earnings per share
- effect on return on equity

Control Over the Company

Creditors have no voice in the management of the business, but they may place restrictions on the borrower through loan covenants. A **loan covenant** is restrictive wording in the loan document that puts responsibilities on the borrower, such as requiring the borrower to maintain certain ratios, certain account balances, or possibly restricting the payments of dividends if income is below a certain dollar amount. For example, many creditors include in the loan document a covenant dictating that the company maintain a 2 to 1 current ratio. This means that the current ratio (defined as current assets ÷ current liabilities) must be 2, or current assets must be twice current liabilities. Creditors want to ensure that the company has sufficient cash available in future months to make the loan payments, including interest. If the company does not adhere to this covenant, the creditor can call the entire loan be paid before its due date.

On the other hand, if the company issues stock there will be an increased number of shareholders, each having a vote in the management of the company equal to the number of shares owned. These additional shareholders could eventually alter the existing company focus, much to the chagrin of the original shareholders. Each additional share of stock issued changes the shareholder mix.

Interest Payments vs. Dividends

Borrowing cash from a creditor increases liabilities. Creditors will demand that the principal of the loan be repaid as well as interest according to a certain agreed-upon schedule. This schedule must be adhered to whether or not the company is earning a profit. This could create a hardship if the industry experiences a slowdown. Creditors can demand missed payments and force the company into bankruptcy if the company cannot raise sufficient cash to satisfy the debt.

Dividends to common shareholders, on the other hand, are not mandatory. A company's dividend policy is at the discretion of the board of directors.

Corporate Income Taxes

Interest is a business expense that is deductible in computing taxable income. Dividends to stockholders, on the other hand, are not expenses but are distributions of after-tax profits. Because dividends are not expenses, they are not deductible in the computation of taxable income. Exhibit 4-6.1 shows an analysis of two options a company might encounter when trying to raise $600,000: borrowing $600,000 at 12 percent interest or issuing 10,000 shares of stock at $60 a share. Assume that the company currently has 20,000 shares outstanding.

Exhibit 4-6.1
Effects of Borrowing Versus Issuing Stock

	Borrow $600,000 at 12% interest	Issue 10,000 shares of stock at $60 per share
Income Before Interest and Income Tax	$ 250,000	$ 250,000
Less: Interest Expense ($600,000 × .12)	(72,000)	-
Income Before Income Tax	178,000	250,000
Less: Income Tax Expense (35%)	(62,300)	(87,500)
Net Income	$ 115,700	$ 162,500
Earnings Per Share		
Debt ($115,700 ÷ 20,000 shares)	$5.79	
Equity ($162,500 ÷ 30,000 shares)		$5.42

As you can see from studying the example, income tax expense for the debt alternative is $25,200 less ($87,500 – $62,300) than the stock alternative. By borrowing, the company has, in essence, routed the $25,200 reduction in taxes (called a *tax savings* because the money would have gone to the government in taxes under the stock alternative) to creditors to pay for interest. The net effect is that, by choosing the debt alternative, the company only incurs an additional cash outflow of $46,800 ($72,000 – $25,200) to pay for the interest.

Effect on Earnings Per Share

Earnings per share (EPS) is a common calculation used to compare a company's performance from one year to another, as well as to compare one company with another within the same industry. In its simplest form, and assuming a company issues only common stock (no preferred stock), earnings per share can be calculated by dividing net income by the average number of common shares outstanding.

$$EPS = \frac{\text{Net income}}{\text{Common stock outstanding}}$$

Usually the number of outstanding shares is adjusted or weighted according to how long the shares were outstanding during the year. To keep our example simple, we will assume that if additional common stock is issued, it would be outstanding for the entire year. The example in Exhibit 4-6.1 assumes that the company already has 20,000 shares of common stock outstanding before analyzing the effect of the debt vs. equity financing alternatives on the company's earnings per share. The earnings per share calculation would be:

      <u>Long-term note alternative:</u>
      EPS = $115,700 ÷ 20,000 shares = $5.79

      <u>Stock alternative:</u>
      EPS = $162,500 ÷ 30,000 shares = $5.42

Although net income is reduced by $46,800 in the long-term debt alternative, earnings per share is $.37 ($5.79 less $5.42) higher under that financing plan. From the shareholders' point of view this would be slightly more attractive, because there are fewer shareholders and earnings per share are slightly greater. Before making any decisions on whether to issue stock or to incur a long-term note payable, a company should prepare pro forma (projected) calculations of net income and earnings per share as shown in Exhibit 4-6.1 to determine the tax savings and how the ultimate decision would affect shares outstanding and earnings per share. Different hypotheses will result in different outcomes.

Earnings per share is not the same as dividends per share. As mentioned earlier, the company does not have any obligation to distribute the net income of the company as dividends unless the dividends have been declared (announced) to the public.

Effect on Return on Equity

Return on equity is also affected by the decision on whether to finance with debt versus equity. Before looking at the impact of a financing decision on this important ratio, a more thorough discussion of types of debt is required. The topic of return on equity will be revisited later in this case reading.

TYPES OF DEBT FINANCING

Current Liabilities

Current liabilities are debts and other obligations that will be paid in cash or satisfied with other assets or services within one year. The most prevalent current liability is accounts payable. Recall from previous cases that the accounts payable originates when the business makes purchases of inventory or other items on credit. The vendor selling to the business delivers the items ordered and extends interest-free credit for a limited amount of time, usually 30 days. An invoice is a formal bill issued to the buyer which specifies the items ordered, the unit price, the quantity delivered, the shipping charges, taxes, the total amount due, and various terms of the transaction. A sample invoice was presented in Exhibit 4-1.2 of Case Reading 4-1 and is reproduced here as Exhibit 4-6.2.

Exhibit 4-6.2
Sales Invoice

Jenny's Jewelery 123 Leather Lane Cincinnati, Ohio 45243		Invoice	
		Date	Invoice #
		6/1/97	6621

Bill To:	Ship To:				
Lorie Lovejoy 967 Garrison Drive Lexington, KY 48761	Same				

P.O. Number	Terms:	Rep:	Ship	VIA	F.O.B.
45876	2/10, Net 30	Jenny	6/3/97	UPS	Destination

Quantity	Item Code	Description	Unit Price	Amount
2	A423	Bead Earrings	$32.00	$64.00
				$64.00

Before the sale, the buyer and the seller must agree on the terms of the purchase transaction. The typical terms explain:

- Who pays freight and shipping charges?
- At what location(s) will the delivery be made?
- What mode of transportation will be utilized?
- Who pays for insurance of the goods while in transit?
- Is the purchase to be paid for on delivery or will the purchaser be invoiced?
- In how many days must the invoice be paid?
- What is the interest rate assessed on invoices not paid by the due date?
- What discount is offered if the invoice is paid promptly?

Vendors often provide an incentive for their customers to pay invoices within the discount period by offering a cash discount. It is in the interest of vendors to have the invoice paid quickly because on their books this transaction is an account receivable until paid by the buyer. Recall the earlier discussion in Case Reading 4-2 on the aging of receivables. All businesses are intent on managing their accounts receivable assets with the goal of minimizing the average collection period. One technique to accomplish this is the cash discount.

To illustrate the cash discount incentive, suppose the terms of the sale are quoted in the following shorthand manner: "3/10, n/30, FOB shipping point, 1½ percent per month interest on invoices over 30 days (overdue)". The translation of this code is:

- A 3 percent discount can be taken if the invoice is paid in full within 10 days of the invoice date.
- n/30 reads "net 30," meaning that the full amount of the invoice must be paid if payment is made 11 to 30 days after the invoice date.
- "FOB shipping point" means that title to the goods transfers to the buyer at the vendor's dock. Freight and insurance during transit are the responsibility of the buyer. "FOB destination" means that title passes at the buyer's dock in which case the seller is responsible for freight and insurance during transit.
- Another incentive that vendors create is the interest charges on overdue invoices. Overdue invoices are invoices that have not been paid within the period allowed. If the terms are 3/10, n/30, the invoice would become overdue on day 31. Therefore, if the invoice is 30 days overdue, that means it must be at least 60 days old. If paid after that date, a 1½ percent interest charge will be assessed on the open balance (which would be the outstanding balance including interest). This "late charge" is reported on the monthly statements vendors customarily send to their customers.

Purchase Discount Example

Assume that Tahoma Ski Emporium purchases $500,000 of assorted snow-related merchandise inventory from Sierra Sports. The terms are 3/10, n/30. Tahoma's controller, Suzy Sweet, is contemplating whether it is prudent to pay the invoice within the 10-day discount period. The discount would be significant; 3 percent of $500,000 is $15,000. The logic behind the terms is that the discount is available to those purchasers who are willing to forego the additional 20 days of free credit by paying in 10 days rather then in 30 days.

One way to compare the discount to annual interest is to annualize the 3 percent.

$$\text{Number of 20-day intervals in a year} = \frac{365}{20} = 18.25 \text{ intervals}$$

$$\text{Annualized interest rate} = 18.25 \text{ intervals} \times 3\% = 54.75\% \text{ per year}$$

The generous discount compares to almost a 55 percent annual rate, which is too good a deal to pass up. Even if Suzy has to borrow the necessary funds in order to pay the bill during the discount period, there are no banks that charge interest rates as high as the effective interest of 55 percent that the supplier is giving her. Suzy is inclined to pay the invoice immediately, which after the 3 percent discount would require cash of $485,000.

$$\$500,000 - (\$500,000 \times 3\%) = \$485,000$$

If the decision is made to forego the discount, the entire $500,000 amount would be due in 30 days. Sufficient cash may still be unavailable to pay the invoice at that time. According to the terms, if the bill is not paid within 30 days of the invoice date, Suzy would be charged 1½ percent interest on the unpaid balance. Suzy is cognizant that the 1½ percent monthly interest charge is equivalent to 18 percent annual interest expense (calculated by multiplying 1½ percent by 12). Foregoing the discount may only postpone her cash flow problem. Instead it may require borrowing from the bank to avoid the 18 percent effective interest should the invoice be overdue for more than 30 days.

Long-Term Debt

Long-term debt is frequently used to finance the purchase of long-lived assets. Long-term debt is a liability with a maturity date longer than one year. Typical long-term liabilities are notes payable, bonds payable, and certain leases. Notes payable and bonds payable are discussed in this case reading. Leases are presented in Case Reading 4-7.

Notes Payable

Notes payable are legal obligations. A promissory note is a legal document executed by the borrower which provides the lender with evidence of the financial obligation. The note payable carries a stated interest rate or a variable rate formula based upon market rates. A fixed rate, such as 7 percent, means that interest must be paid annually at the rate of 7 percent of the face value of the note.

It is common for banks and other financial institutions to lend businesses the money needed to finance the purchase of assets or to repay maturing debt. For example, if Sutherland borrowed $10 million from its bank at a fixed annual interest rate of 7 percent, it would have an interest expense on its income statement of $700,000 per year and pay that amount to the lender.

$$\$10,000,000 \times 7\% = \$700,000$$

Assuming a maturity of five years, Sutherland also would need to have cash of $10 million to repay the note on the maturity date. If Sutherland and its lender negotiated a variable rate agreement, it might find that the interest rate for the first year is 6 percent, the second year 8 percent, the third year 9 percent, etc. Increasing (or decreasing) rates would be the result of market rates increasing (or decreasing) over the three-year period.

Another common characteristic of notes payable is the lender's requirement for collateral. **Collateral** is an asset or group of assets which the lender can take possession of and legal title to if the borrow defaults on the note. For instance, if the loan agreement defined a default condition as the current ratio falling below 1.0, and the company's current ratio was .8, the lender could demand immediate payment of the liability.

When funds are borrowed to purchase real estate assets, the note is referred to as a **mortgage note payable.** Mortgage notes often require periodic payments on the principle in addition to the interest on the remaining balance. Default on this type of note can trigger foreclosure of the real estate property. Mortgage payables are more thoroughly discussed in Case Reading 4-7.

Footnotes to the financial statements tell the reader the details regarding the note payable. An example from an annual report might be:

> The Company has a loan agreement with its banking group to borrow up to $250 million at 12 percent annual interest. Borrowings under this loan agreement are subject to the Company maintaining certain levels of shareholders' equity and financial ratios. Based upon current capital structure and restrictions contained in the loan agreement, the Company is precluded from declaring dividends to common shareholders.

When a long-term note is within one year of its maturity, the face value of the note must be reclassified to the current liability category of the balance sheet. If a company has a mortgage note payable, the amount of mortgage principle due within the subsequent year is shown as a current liability. The logic behind this reclassification is to provide readers with accurate information on the cash requirements of the company in the next year.

Bonds Payable

A **bond** is a contract which evidences an agreement between the corporation issuing the bond and the investors who bought the bond. The agreement specifies all of the terms of the transaction. An example of some of the key terms are the interest rate to be paid on the bond, the maturity date, the right of the corporation to call (pay off) the bond before maturity, and the maintenance of certain balance sheet relationships, such as the debt-to-equity ratio. The bondholders are creditors and as such can demand that certain conditions be met to maintain their creditor status. The failure of the corporation to meet the terms of the agreement is termed **default**. For example, a company with a series of large losses for several years saw its shareholders' equity total on its balance sheet fall below 25 percent of the assets. This outcome violated one of the terms of the bond issue. Bondholders then have the right to receive immediate payoff of the bonds they are holding.

The issuance of bonds brings an obligation to use future cash flows to make periodic interest payments. This is generally perceived to be a higher risk alternative. Common features of a corporate bond are as follow:

- A face value of $1,000
- A fixed rate of interest to be paid on the face value
- A fixed term such as ten or twenty years
- A specific maturity date when the bonds will be redeemed
- Whether the bonds are callable or not (most corporate bonds are callable)
- The call price if the bonds are callable
- Whether the bonds are convertible into common stock
- If convertible how many shares per bond the bondholder can receive

Example. Assume the Eldorado Corporation is planning to open a new manufacturing operation which will cost $10 million. To raise the necessary funds to pay for $8 million of equipment, it issues bonds to the public with a 10-year term and a 10 percent annual interest rate.

Accounting for the bonds in their first year will have the following impact on financial statements:

- Cash will increase and liabilities will increase.
- When assets are purchased those categories will rise and cash will decline.
- Interest expense and interest payable will increase.
- Cash will decrease when the liability for interest is paid.

These entries to the accounting worksheet are shown in Exhibit 4-6.3,

Exhibit 4-6.3
Accounting Transaction Worksheet - Bond Transactions

Explanation of Transaction	Cash	Equipment	Interest Payable	Bonds Payable	Contributed Capital	Retained Earnings
Bonds issued	$10,000,000			$ 10,000,000		
Equipment Purchased	(8,000,000)	8,000,000				
Interest Accrued @ 10%			1,000,000			(1,000,000)
Interest Paid	(1,000,000)		(1,000,000)			

The entry to record the issuance of the bonds, purchase of equipment, and the cash payment of interest will be recorded on the dates the transactions occurred. The entries to record the interest accrual will be made at the end of the accounting period.

Leases

Another form of long-term financing is a capital lease. This topic is not addressed here but will be discussed in detail in Case Reading 4-7.

CAPITAL STRUCTURE DECISIONS

Returning to the discussion of capital structure, suppose Sutherland Company is planning to begin a business in the manufacturing of fiber optic data transmission devices. This new venture will require a $100 million investment in plant and equipment. Sutherland's chief financial officer has provided three alternative capital structure proposals. In terms of the balance sheet equation, they are (in millions):

$$A \ = \ L \ + \ SE$$

Alternative 1 Low Risk $100 = $10 + $90

Alternative 2 Medium Risk $100 = $50 + $50

Alternative 3 High Risk $100 = $90 + $10

Risk is based upon the implications that each alternative has on future profitability and return on equity. Alternative 3 has been classified as high risk due to its high debt component.

To compare and contrast the three alternatives (low, medium, and high risk) the following additional facts of the case must be considered:

- Borrowed funds will carry a 10 percent rate of interest

- The expansion will require $100 million of cash

- Sutherland is able to issue additional shares of common stock

- Income before taxes is 5 million, the tax rate is 40 percent, net income is $3 million from operations already existing ($5 million – $2 million tax = $3 million)

- Current return on equity = Net Income ÷ Shareholder equity = $3 million ÷ $25 million = 12%

- The income before interest and taxes from the expansion is forecast at $20 million

One way to evaluate each of the three capital structure alternatives is to analyze each in terms of the return on equity as shown in Exhibit 4-6.4.

Exhibit 4-6.4
Analysis of Return on Equity Under Alternative Capital Structures

	Risk		
	Low	Medium	High
Existing Income Level	$ 5,000,000	$ 5,000,000	$ 5,000,000
Income from expansion	20,000,000	20,000,000	20,000,000
Income before interest & taxes	$ 25,000,000	$ 25,000,000	$ 25,000,000
Long-term debt - bonds	$ 10,000,000	$ 50,000,000	$ 90,000,000
Interest expense @ 10%	1,000,000	5,000,000	9,000,000
Income before taxes	$ 24,000,000	$ 20,000,000	$ 16,000,000
Taxes @ 40%	9,600,000	8,000,000	6,400,000
Net income	$ 14,400,000	$ 12,000,000	$ 9,600,000
Existing Shareholders' Equity	$ 25,000,000	$ 25,000,000	$ 25,000,000
New Shareholders' Equity	90,000,000	50,000,000	10,000,000
Total after expansion	$ 115,000,000	$ 75,000,000	$ 35,000,000
Comparative return on equity	12.52%	16.00%	27.43%

The top three lines of Exhibit 4-6.4 are a calculation of the income before interest and taxes expected after the expansion is completed. The fourth line represents the increase in various debt levels under each financing alternative. The interest expense at 10 percent per year on the bonds or other long-term debt to be issued is shown on line five. Because interest expense reduces income, line six is labeled income before taxes.

The assumed tax rate of 40 percent is used to compute the tax expense on the projected income, which is then subtracted from income before taxes in order to arrive at net income. Note that the net income is inversely correlated with the amount of debt. The higher the debt level, the higher the interest expense, and this causes a lower net income. Is the alternative with the highest dollar net income the best one?

Not necessarily. From the viewpoint of the pre-expansion shareholders of Sutherland, the low-risk strategy would produce the lowest return on equity. Further, the low-risk strategy requires the issuance of a significant number of new shares which could dilute the interests of existing shareholders. The prospects for future dividend increases and appreciation (increasing) of stock prices are likely to be diminished by this strategy. Conversely, the high-risk strategy adds significantly fewer new shares but raises the needed funds by issuing bonds. This strategy is an example of financial leverage. **Financial leverage** is the use of long-term debt to finance the acquisition of operating assets with the goal of paying interest cost in an amount less than the assets will earn. When the financial leverage strategies are successful, the return on equity is enhanced more than it is in strategies utilizing shareholder equity rather than long-term debt.

In the high-risk alternative of Exhibit 4-6.4, Sutherland pays interest to bondholders in the amount of $9,000,000. However, the interest expense reduces income and therefore reduces the income tax expense. Many financial analysts consider the effective interest cost to be (1 - tax rate) × interest expense. In Sutherland's case the $9,000,000 actually paid to bondholders each year becomes a net cash outflow of only $5,400,000 after considering the $3,600,000 of reduced taxes for that alternative.

Another way of describing that same example is that without the $9,000,000 in interest expense, income before taxes would have been $25,000,000. After applying a 40 percent tax rate, taxes would have been $10,000,000. Exhibit 4-6.4 shows taxes of only $6,400,000 because of the interest expense. The difference in taxes between the two scenarios is $3,600,000 ($10,000,000 – $6,400,000).

Financial leverage in the high-risk alternative produces an improved return on equity, because the assets acquired with borrowed funds increase income significantly more than the interest expense.

Financing Alternatives - Low, Medium, or High Risk?

Financial leverage is like the proverbial two-edged sword. It has benefits as seen in Exhibit 4-6.4 but it can also have negative attributes which cut into profitability. To illustrate, Exhibit 4-6.5 is the same analysis as Exhibit 4-6.4 except that for various reasons such as competition, strikes, or managerial failure, the income from the expansion (before interest and tax) is only $5 million instead of the $20 million that was originally forecast. Exhibit 4-6.5 illustrates that the high-risk alternative produces a return on equity less than the other alternatives. The highly leveraged balance sheet means that the proportion of long-term debt to assets is very high. With the long-term debt comes the cost of servicing the debt, namely interest expense.

Exhibit 4-6.5
Analysis of Return on Equity Under Alternative Capital Structures

	Risk		
	Low	Medium	High
Existing Income Level	$ 5,000,000	$ 5,000,000	$ 5,000,000
Income from expansion	5,000,000	5,000,000	5,000,000
Income before interest & taxes	$ 10,000,000	$ 10,000,000	$ 10,000,000
Long-term debt - bonds	$ 10,000,000	$ 50,000,000	$ 90,000,000
Interest expense @ 10%	1,000,000	5,000,000	9,000,000
Income before taxes	$ 9,000,000	$ 5,000,000	$ 1,000,000
Taxes @ 40%	3,600,000	2,000,000	400,000
Net income	$ 5,400,000	$ 3,000,000	$ 600,000
Existing Shareholders' Equity	$ 25,000,000	$ 25,000,000	$ 25,000,000
New Shareholders' Equity	90,000,000	50,000,000	10,000,000
Total after expansion	$ 115,000,000	$ 75,000,000	$ 35,000,000
Comparative return on equity	4.70%	4.00%	1.71%

You learned in Module 3 about the difference between fixed and variable expenses. Interest on notes or bonds payable is a fixed annual expense. It will not change because of changes in volume of business transacted. Sales revenue can fluctuate from year to year but the interest expense on the outstanding debt will not change unless part or all of the debt is paid off. Given the forecast of much lower income from the expansion, the low-risk alternative is a better strategy. Return on equity of the low risk capital structure is 4.7 percent while that of the high-risk strategy is only 1.7 percent.

It should be noted that another alternative is not to expand the business given the forecast of meager profits. Recall the original assumptions that Sutherland had net income of $3 million and shareholders' equity of $25 million, or a return on equity of 12 percent. In Exhibit 4-6.5 even the best return on equity is 4.7 percent, which means simply that the expansion is dragging down the performance of the company.

SUMMARY

Decisions involving liabilities have implications for future profitability. Most businesses are able to purchase inventory and services on credit, thereby creating a liability on the balance sheet called accounts payable. Many vendors provide an incentive to pay off accounts payable quickly by offering a discount from invoice amounts. Accounts payable are current liabilities.

Common long-term liabilities are notes payable and bonds payable. Lenders are financial institutions and investors who purchase such interest-bearing securities. An important strategic decision is how to finance the purchase of assets or the repayment of maturing debt. Issuing more shares or issuing long-term debt are two options available to define the company's capital structure. The issuance of long-term debt is a decision which is based upon the concept of financial leverage. When financial leverage is effective, return on equity, the return to common shareholders, is improved. When profitability of the business declines and fixed interest expenses associated with long-term debt must be paid, return on equity declines and the common shareholders have experienced the risk of financial leverage.

EXERCISES AND PROBLEMS

Exercises

Exercise 1 Capital Structure. Define capital structure. Why is capital structure important to investors and managers?

Exercise 2 Explaining Invoice Terms. Carlsbad Beach Club purchases supplies from a vendor with terms 2/10, net 45, FOB destination. Explain what these terms mean.

Exercise 3 Financial Leverage and Return on Equity. What is the relationship between financial leverage and return on equity?

Exercise 4 Using Bonds in Business Expansion. List two advantages and two disadvantages of issuing bonds instead of common stock to finance a business expansion.

Exercise 5 Bond Cost and Income Tax. How do income taxes affect the effective interest cost for bonds? Give a simple illustration.

Problems

Problem 1 Purchase Discounts. August Company purchases inventory from their supplier on terms 2/10, net 45. Based on this information, determine:

a. What options does August Company have in regard to paying a $1,000 invoice?

b. What is the effective annual interest rate for paying in 45 days instead of 10 days?

c. What is your advice to August Company in regard to when it should pay its $1,000 invoice?

Problem 2 Financing a Business Expansion. Gigantic Fitness Club has been successfully operating for six years. The Club has $8,000,000 of assets, $4,000,000 of liabilities, and $4,000,000 of shareholders' equity. They are planning a very large expansion that will cost $10,000,000. Use this information to answer the following:

a. What factors should be considered if the entire expansion would be financed by issuing 10 percent, 20-year bonds?

b. What factors should be considered if the entire expansion would be financed by issuing 200,000 shares of common stock to the general public? Currently, there are 100,000 shares of common stock outstanding, all held by the three founders of Gigantic Fitness Club.

c. What factor(s) would likely decide how the planned expansion will be financed? Be as specific as the data permit.

Problem 3 Risk in Business Expansion. Monica Mill Works, Inc. (MMW) manufactures metal parts primarily for the auto industry. MMW has an excellent reputation for quality work and timely production. Their only factory is in California, but an increasing proportion of their business is in the Midwest. MMW is planning to expand into the Midwest by opening a plant in Ohio. The plant would cost $60,000,000 to build, equip, and make ready for production.

The California operations produced $975,000 of net income for the most recent year of operations, and management expects about the same level of earnings for the next few years. Currently, MMW has no long-term debt outstanding and has $10,000,000 total equity including 100,000 shares of $40 par value common stock outstanding. MMW management is considering either issuing $50 million of bonds and $10 million of stock (80,000 shares) or issuing $10 million of bonds and $50 million of stock (400,000 shares) to finance the expansion.

Additional information concerning the expansion include:

- Borrowed funds will carry a 9 percent interest rate
- The expansion will cost $60 million
- There will be a ready market for both the bonds or stock when issued
- Income before taxes is $1,500,000, the tax rate is 35 percent, net income is $975,000
- The current return on equity is 9.75 percent ($975,000 net income ÷ $10,000,000 total equity)

- The earnings before interest and taxes from the planned expansion is forecast at $10,000,000

Based on the information above for MMW, determine the following:

a. Which method of financing the expansion will result in the largest return on equity for MMW? Prepare a solution similar to Exhibit 4-7.1 in this case reading.

b. Write a letter to Monica William, president of MMW, explaining why you think one proposal is better than the other. Be sure to include a discussion of risk in your letter.

Case 4-6

PINE ACQUIRES MAHOGANY - "WOOD" YOU?

Case Objective

To understand the effect of alternate balance sheet capital structures on profitability and return on equity.

Decision: Which levels of long-term debt versus shareholders' equity meet target return on equity?

Pine Company desires to increase sales and net income. Like many corporations, it wants to expand by acquiring other corporations. Pine's chief financial officer, Harvey Holstrom, has become aware that Mahogany Corporation is interested in being acquired. Mahogany's business is similar to Pine's and consolidation of the two businesses could produce efficiencies by eliminating duplicate administrative and manufacturing functions. Holstrom has learned that Mahogany can be acquired for a price between $6 and $15 million.

When Harvey presented Mahogany's financial statements (see Exhibit C4-6.1) to Pine's chief executive officer, Geoffrey Gavin, they both pondered whether the price range of $6–$15 million was low enough to allow Pine to maintain its return on equity. (Pine's financial statements are presented as Exhibit C4-6.2). Pine's acquisition strategy is to maintain or improve return on equity. Also, Pine does not wish to issue more shares in the corporation than necessary because to do so would dilute the ownership interest that current shareholders have in the corporation. Gavin and several others in the top management currently have controlling interest in Pine as together they own more than 51 percent of the stock. Issuing more stock could mean that their combined percentage would fall below 50 percent.

You should assume the role as assistant to Pine's chief financial officer and, using a spreadsheet, perform the various analyses specified in the requirements of this case. The case involves three scenarios:

1. Purchase price of $8 million; Long-term debt and common stock will be issued. Debt will have an interest rate of 10 percent.
   a. Long-term debt of $2 million and common stock of $6 million
   b. Long-term debt of $4 million and common stock of $4 million
   c. Long-term debt of $6 million and common stock of $2 million

2. Purchase price of $10 million and various interest rates; Only long-term debt will be issued in the amount of the purchase price.

3. Various purchase prices and various interest rates; Only long-term debt will be issued in the amount of the purchase price.

Pine's chief executive officer does not want to acquire Mahogany unless the resulting return on equity is greater than or equal to Pine's current return on equity.

Exhibit C4-6.1
Financial Statements of Mahogany Corporation

Mahogany Corporation Balance Sheet (In Millions) December 31, 2000			
Current Assets	$ 2.0	Current Liabilities	$ 2.0
Plant and Equipment	5.0	Shareholders' Equity	
Other Assets	1.0	Common Stock	1.0
		Retained Earnings	5.0
		Total Liabilities and	
Total Assets	$ 8.0	Shareholders' Equity	$ 8.0

Mahogany Corporation Income Statement (In Millions) Year Ended December 31, 2000	
Sales	$ 6.0
Cost of goods sold	4.0
Gross profit margin	2.0
Selling and administrative exp.	1.0
Income before taxes	1.0
Income tax	0.4
Net income	$ 0.6

Exhibit C4-6.2
Financial Statements of Pine Company

Pine Company Balance Sheet (In Millions) December 31, 2000			
Current Assets	$ 5.0	Current Liabilities	$ 1.0
Plant and Equipment	20.0	Long-Term Debt	10.0
		Shareholders' Equity	
		Common Stock	4.0
		Retained Earnings	10.0
		Total Liabilities and	
Total Assets	$ 25.0	Shareholders' Equity	$ 25.0

Pine Company Income Statement (In Millions) Year Ended December 31, 2000	
Sales	$ 20.0
Cost of goods sold	12.0
Gross profit margin	8.0
Selling and administrative exp.	4.0
Interest expense	1.0
Income before tax	3.0
Income tax	1.2
Net income	$ 1.8

Requirements

1. Using the financial statements presented in Exhibits C4-6.1 and C4-6.2, calculate the return on equity for each company at December 31, 2000.

2. Gavin instructs Holstrom to develop three financing strategies which are a combination of long-term debt and common stock assuming an $8 million dollar price and a 10 percent interest rate. Holstrom suggests three alternate long-term debt levels of $2, $4, and $6 million with the remainder of the $8 million in each alternative raised through the issuance of common stock. Your job as the assistant chief financial officer is to prepare the spreadsheet analysis requested by Gavin. Use the template provided in Exhibit C4-6.3 to calculate the return on equity for each alternative. Assume the revenues and expenses for 2000 will continue into 2001. Note: We have entered the income figures for the low risk alternative in the spreadsheet for you to help you get started.

3. Suppose Pine plans to acquire Mahogany by using a financial leverage strategy of issuing only long-term debt (no stock) to raise the necessary funds. Holstrom has asked you to prepare an analysis assuming a $10 million dollar price for each interest rate alternative given in Exhibit C4-6.4. One column of the exhibit has been completed as an example for you although the price in that column was assumed to be $8 million (vs. $10 million). Assume that the net income (after interest and taxes) of Pine and Mahogany are $1.8 and $.6 million respectively.

4. Gavin instructs Holstrom to prepare an analysis showing the price and interest rate alternatives which allow Pine to acquire Mahogany and still have a return on equity equal to or greater than what was calculated in Requirement 1. After completing Requirement 3, transfer the return on equity information for the $10 million dollar price into the schedule prepared by Holstrom shown as Exhibit 4-6.5. Highlight or list the price/interest combinations which you would recommend.

Exhibit C4-6.3
Requirement 2
Effect of Financing Strategies on Return on Equity

	RISK		
	Low	Medium	High
Existing income level	$ 3,000,000		
Income from expansion	1,000,000		
Income before interest and taxes	$ 4,000,000		
New long-term debt - bonds			
Interest expense @ 10%			
Income before taxes			
Taxes @ 40%			
Net income			
Existing shareholders' equity			
New shareholders' equity			
Total after expansion			
Comparative return on equity			

Exhibit C4-8.6
Template for Requirement 2
Horizontal Analysis

(000s omitted)	Midwest Foods			National Foods		
	2000	1999	% Change	2000	1999	% Change
Assets						
Current Assets	$ 270,167	$ 244,965		$ 384,744	$ 387,918	
Long-Term Investments	2,000	2,000		-	-	
Property Plant and Equipment	255,763	241,791		209,561	201,021	
Total Assets	$ 527,930	$ 488,756		$ 594,305	$ 588,939	
Liabilities and Stockholders' Equity						
Current Liabilities	$ 177,387	$ 153,444		$ 143,205	$ 145,853	
Long-Term Liabilities	34,883	34,883		75,000	75,000	
Total Liabilities	212,270	188,327		218,205	220,853	
Stockholders' Equity	315,660	300,429		376,100	368,086	
Total Liabilities and Stockholders' Equity	$ 527,930	$ 488,756		$ 594,305	$ 588,939	

Exhibit C4-6.5
Requirement 4
Return on Equity under Different Interest and Price Strategies

INT. RATES	6.00%	8.00%	10.00%	12.00%
PRICES				
$6 million	15.60%	15.09%	14.57%	14.06%
8 million	15.09%	14.40%	13.71%	13.03%
10 million				
11 million	14.31%	13.37%	12.43%	11.49%
12 million	14.06%	13.03%	12.00%	10.97%
13 million	13.80%	12.69%	11.57%	10.46%
14 million	13.54%	12.34%	11.14%	9.94%
15 million	13.29%	12.00%	10.71%	9.43%

Case Reading 4-7

DECISIONS INVOLVING
MORTGAGES AND LEASES[1]

INTRODUCTION

This case reading introduces concepts relating to the time value of money and then applies these techniques to accounting for mortgages and long-term leases. The **time value of money** concept, also called moving money through time, is often used in business and can be used in making many personal financial decisions. It is based on the theory that money received today is more valuable than money received at some time in the future. In other words, one would prefer to receive $1 today than $1 a year from now. This case reading explains the concept of the time value of money and how it is applied to selected long-term liabilities.

PRESENT VALUE CONCEPTS

If someone gave you $100 today, you could invest it for one year at a certain interest rate, 5 percent for example, and at the end of one year it would have grown or "compounded" to $105.

$$\$100 + (\$100 \times 5\%) = \$105$$

The $100 you have today would be called the **present value**. The $105 would be called the **future value** at the end of time period 1 (in this case one year). If you keep that $105 invested for another year, it will grow to $110.25 at the end of the second year (the $110.25 would be called the future value at the end of time period 2). Not only is the original $100 earning 5 percent in the second year, but the $5 interest you earned in the first year is also earning interest at 5 percent in the second year.

$$\$100 + [(\$100 \times 5\%) \times (\$105 \times 5\%)] = \$110.25$$

This is the concept of **compound interest** (the interest earns interest).

We can generalize this relationship between the present value of a $1 and the future value ($1.05 at n=1, $1.1025 at n=2) as follows:

FV	=	future value (the value at the end of n periods)
PV	=	present value (the value today)
n	=	the number of compounding periods
i	=	the interest rate per compounding period

[1] The authors thank Wesley E. Harder and Leslie B. Thengvall from California State University, Chico for their major contributions to this Case Reading.

$$PV_0 = FV_n \times \frac{1}{(1+i)^n}$$

e.g., $PV_0 = \$105 \times (1 \div 1.05) = \$100$

e.g., $PV_0 = \$110.25 \times (1 \div (1.05^2)) = \$100$

$\dfrac{1}{(1+i)^n}$ is what we call the **present value factor.**

For example, suppose that Robbie Daniels is fourteen and he is saving to buy a car when he is eighteen. He wants to know how much money he has to deposit in the bank today (the present value) so that at the end of four years he will have $10,000 (the future value) to buy a car. He knows that his bank pays 6 percent annual interest, compounded annually.

$$PV_0 = \$10,000 \times \frac{1}{(1+6\%)^4} = \$7,920.94$$

Robbie would find that he would have to invest $7,920.94 today at 6 percent annual interest in order to have $10,000 at the end of year 4. The future value is said to be "discounted to the present".

What if the interest was compounded semiannually? The number of interest periods would be doubled (eight interest periods) and the annual interest rate would be halved to get the semiannual rate.

$$PV_0 = \$10,000 \times \frac{1}{(1+3\%)^8} = \$7,894.09$$

Robbie would find that he would have to invest $7894.09 today at 6 percent annual interest, compounded semiannually, to have $10,000 at the end of year 4.

There is a much simpler way to perform these calculations on the computer by using the net present value formula and Excel.

NET PRESENT VALUE

Net present value (NPV) is defined as the difference between the sum of future cash inflows discounted to the present time at the required interest rate and the initial cash outflow made at time 0. The purpose of determining present value is to better understand the financial effects of transactions in today's dollars (the present worth of cash inflows and outflows).

It is especially helpful when using the net present value formula to have a time line which organizes the cash flows. For example, going back to the original example in which the annual interest rate was 6 percent and the number of interest periods were 4, the time line for Robbie would appear on a computer spreadsheet as shown in Exhibit 4-7.1.

Exhibit 4-7.1
Time Line With Single Future Cash Flow

	A	B	C	D	E	F
1	Period	0	1	2	3	4
2	Cash flow	$ -	$ -	$ -	$ -	$ 10,000.00

The time line shows that there were no receipts today or in periods 1–3 but in period 4 there is a cash receipt of $10,000. It is important to show time 0, which represents today on the time line. We can then input the equation for the net present value, which in general is:

=NPV(interest rate, sum of cash flows from time 1 to time n) + cash flow at time 0

Exhibit 4-7.2 shows the net present value for this series of cash flows:

Exhibit 4-7.2
Net Present Value for Single Future Cash Flow

	A	B	C	D	E	F
1	Period	0	1	2	3	4
2	Cash flow	$ -	$ -	$ -	$ -	$ 10,000.00
3						
4	NPV	$7,920.94				

In this case the formula for cell B4 would be: =NPV(6%,C2:F2)+B2

This formula results in a net present value of $7,920.94. This is the same amount we computed previously by hand.

The net present value formula is often used to compare a cash outflow in time 0 (today) with a cash inflow in the future. For example, suppose Robbie has a cash outflow (putting the money in a bank) of $7,920.94 in time 0 and has no cash flows in years 1–3 but receives $10,000 at the end of year 4. The time line and calculation of the net present value of the cash flows are shown in Exhibit 4-7.3.

Exhibit 4-7.3
Net Present Value of $0

	A	B	C	D	E	F
6	Period	0	1	2	3	4
7	Cash flow	($7,920.94)	$ -	$ -	$ -	$ 10,000.00
8						
9	NPV	$0.00				

The net present value formula is the same as in Exhibit 4-7.2 but the amount of net present value computed is now $0. A net present value of $0 means that, at 6 percent interest, the sum of the present values of the amounts in cells B7:F7 will equal zero. In other words, an individual should be indifferent to receiving $7,920.94 today versus $10,000 at the end of four years, assuming a 6 percent interest rate compounded annually.

PRESENT VALUE OF AN ANNUITY

An **ordinary annuity** is a series of equal cash flows that are received or paid at the end of each time period in the series. (Cash flows occurring at the beginning of each period constitute an "**annuity due**" and require different applications of these principles. These will not be discussed here.) The following example illustrates an ordinary annuity.

Ray Block has just won the $1 million lottery (ignore taxes for this illustration). He will receive $200,000 a year for the next five years. The cash receipt of $200,000 would be called an annuity.

Let's look at these cash flows on a time line in Exhibit 4-7.4 and see, by computing the net present value, if Ray has really won $1 million today in the lottery. The example assumes a 7 percent interest rate compounded annually.

Exhibit 4-7.4
Net Present Value of an Annuity

	A	B	C	D	E	F	G
1	Period	0	1	2	3	4	5
2	Cash flow	$ -	$ 200,000	$ 200,000	$ 200,000	$ 200,000	$ 200,000
3							
4	NPV	$820,039.49					

The formula for cell B4 would be: =NPV(7%,C2:G2)+B2

Even though Ray won five cash receipts of $200,000 each, the present value of those future cash receipts is only $820,039.49. The difference between the present value of $820,039.49 and the $1 million is made up of interest.

Exhibit 4-7.5
Analysis of Lottery Fund

	A	B	C	D	E	F
1	Time Period	End-of-Year Payment to Ray	Interest Earned on Fund Balance	Reduction of Fund	Lottery Fund Balance	
2	0				$820,039.49	
3	1	$ 200,000.00	$ 57,402.76	$142,597.24	677,442.25	
4	2	200,000.00	47,420.96	152,579.04	524,863.21	
5	3	200,000.00	36,740.42	163,259.58	361,603.63	
6	4	200,000.00	25,312.25	174,687.75	186,915.89	*
7	5	200,000.00	13,084.11	186,915.89	0.00	
8	Totals	$ 1,000,000.00	$179,960.51	$820,039.49		*
9						
10	* Differences due to rounding					

If the lottery trustee puts $820,039.49 as shown in cell E2 in the fund and it earns annual interest at the rate of 7 percent per year compounded annually, the fund will earn $57,402.76 ($820,039.49 x 7%) in interest for the first year as shown in cell C3.

If at the end of the year the fund makes a payment to Ray of $200,000 (cell B3), the net decrease to the fund for the year is $142,597.24 calculated by the formula "=B3–C3".

The new fund balance is then calculated by subtracting the current year reduction of fund from the lottery fund balance at the end of the last period (=E2–D3).

The interest earned by the fund over the five-year period is summed in cell C8 and accounts for the difference between the $1 million in payments shown in cell B8 and the present value of those payments of $820,039.49 shown in D8.

Expanding our lottery example, let's suppose that Ray wants to buy a house in Beverly Hills, California. The house is listed at $842,472.76 and Ray has offered the owner, Chase Tyler, his future cash receipts of $200,000 a year for five years for the house. To evaluate this alternative, it may be helpful for Chase to use a concept called the internal rate of return.

INTERNAL RATE OF RETURN

Internal rate of return (IRR) is the interest rate that will cause the net present value of an investment to equal zero. Thus, the internal rate of return is where the present value of cash outflows exactly equals the present value of the cash inflows.

A time line showing the cash flows of the possible purchase is shown in Exhibit 4-7.6.

Exhibit 4-7.6
Calculation of Internal Rate of Return

	A	B	C	D	E	F	G
1	Period	0	1	2	3	4	5
2	Cash flow	($842,472.76)	$ 200,000	$ 200,000	$ 200,000	$ 200,000	$ 200,000
3							
4	IRR	6.00%					
5	NPV	($0.00)					

The general formula for the internal rate of return formula entered in B4 is as follows:

IRR = (cell addresses of all the cash flows including time 0, interest rate guess)

For Exhibit 4-7.6, the formula is: =IRR(B2:G2,5%)

The computer will accept the 5 percent guess as long as it's reasonable. For example an interest rate guess of 4 percent to 16 percent or even higher would be appropriate here. When making the interest rate guess, be sure to consider whether the interest rate should be an annual rate, semiannual rate, quarterly rate, or monthly rate. For example, if the payments were quarterly payments instead of yearly payments, an appropriate interest rate guess might be 2 percent.

The formula output in Exhibit 4-7.6 as shown in cell B4 is that the internal rate of return is 6 percent. That means that the net present value of the cash flows is zero (see cell B5) assuming an interest rate of 6 percent compounded annually. If Chase feels that a 6 percent interest rate is reasonable, he should be indifferent to those two cash flow alternatives and should be willing to accept the offer (all other things being equal).

Now that we understand the concepts of net present value, internal rate of return, and how to utilize a time line to chart cash flows, we will see how these terms apply to long-term liabilities.

CASH FLOW ANALYSIS AND LONG-TERM LIABILITIES

Sometimes cash flows can be numerous and varied. In general, long-term liabilities are characterized by a significant net cash inflow at time 0, followed by a succession of net cash outflows during the life (term) of the long-term liability (as is the case when a loan is taken out). It is helpful to have a systematic way to lay out the cash flows. Let's look at a general cash flow analysis model that can be used for all long-term liabilities. A term loan example is used to illustrate these concepts.

Term Loan Example

The LeBlond Company is considering the purchase of a new machine to use in production to replace several manual tasks presently performed by factory workers. The plant manager has the following information regarding the proposed machine purchase:

- Purchase price of the machine (including installation costs) is $100,000
- Useful life of the machine is 6 years
- Financing arrangements:
  - 6-year term loan for $100,000
  - interest of $10,000 per year for years 1–3
  - 50% repayment of principal at the end of year 3
  - interest of $5,000 per year for years 4–6
  - final 50% principal payment at the end of year 6

The cash flow analysis for this problem is shown in Exhibit 4-7.7. The cash inflows and outflows are identified for each year of the loan, including time 0 (today). The cash flows are then totaled. These totals are used to compute the internal rate of return (**effective interest rate**) of this loan using the same spreadsheet layout as illustrated in Exhibit 4-7.6.

Exhibit 4-7.7
Time Line, Net Present Value, and Internal Rate of Return for Term Loan

	A	B	C	D	E	F	G	H
1	Time Period	0	1	2	3	4	5	6
2	Inflows: Loan proceeds	$100,000						
3	Outflows: Yearly interest		($10,000)	($10,000)	($10,000)	($5,000)	($5,000)	($5,000)
4	Principal Repayments				($50,000)			($50,000)
5	Yearly net cash inflow (outflow)	$100,000	($10,000)	($10,000)	($60,000)	($5,000)	($5,000)	($55,000)
6								
7	Internal Rate of Return (IRR)	10.00%						
8	=IRR(B5:H5,8%)							
9	Net Present Value (NPV)	$0.00						
10	=NPV(10%,C5:H5)+B5							

In Exhibit 4-7.7, it was first necessary to summarize the annual cash flows before calculating the internal rate of return and the net present value.

The numerical result of the internal rate of return formula is shown as 10 percent in cell B7. The text for the formula is recreated in cell A8 so that you can understand the cell references. The IRR formula asks the computer to do three things:

1. Compute the present value of all the cash flows in row 5 (cells B5 through H5) using an interest rate guess of 8 percent.

2. Having learned from that interest rate guess and the resulting present value, find the interest rate that will make the present value of the cash inflows equal to the present value of the cash outflows. In other words, find the interest rate at which the net present value of the cash flows in row 5 is zero.

3. Enter the result in cell B7.

The numerical value for the net present value is shown in cell B9 and the text for the formula is recreated for your benefit in cell A10. The formula entered for net present value in this equation asks the computer to do three things as well.

1. Compute the present value of all the cash flows in row 5 except cell B5 (cells C5 through H5) using the internal rate of return of 10 percent.

2. Add that result to the amount in cell B5.

3. Enter the result in cell B9.

The future cash outflows in Exhibit 4-7.7 total $145,000 (cells C5:H5). The cash inflow from the loan proceeds in time 0 is $100,000 (cell B5). Given that the net present value of the cash flows in cells B5:H5 is zero (shown in cell B9), then the cash flows for the time periods 1-6 must have a present value equal to ($100,000). This assumes an annual rate of interest of 10 percent (the internal rate of return).

PV of ($145,000) cash outflows in time period 1-6 (cells C5:H5)	($100,000)
PV of loan proceeds in time 0 (cell B5)	100,000
Net Present Value (cell B9)	-0-

Mortgages

A mortgage is a type of long-term note payable. In this particular type of note, the payments made on the note can be made monthly or yearly and each payment contains both principal and interest portions. In addition, the property that is being purchased is pledged as collateral for the debt. This means that the borrower promises to transfer title to the property to the lender if the mortgage payments cannot be made.

As an example, suppose that we purchase property costing $120,000 on which we are required to make a 20 percent down payment. We will take out a loan for the remaining 80 percent. Monthly payments of $772.44 at the end of each month for thirty years are required. Exhibit 4-7.8 shows the calculation of the internal rate of return. Because there are so many interest periods due to the fact that the payments are monthly, it is often easier to prepare a time line with the periods and payments shown vertically versus horizontally because the row numbers in an Excel spreadsheet can help keep track of the period number.

For example, in this mortgage, there would be 360 monthly interest periods (12 × 30 years). Our cash flows will then use rows 1 to 361. The reason we need to go to row 361 and not 360 is because row 1 is used for time 0 (so row 2 would be time 1, row 361 would be time 360). You can see from the cell addresses that rows 6 through 358 on the spreadsheet have been hidden to save space in this exhibit. (To learn how to hide rows and columns see Excel instructions in Appendix C). The cash inflow in time 0 is $120,000 × 80 percent, or $96,000, the amount of the loan after the $24,000 downpayment. The $96,000 is shown as an inflow because the mortgage gives us the cash to purchase the property. The monthly cash outflow is placed in cell A2 and is copied and pasted through cell A361.

Exhibit 4-7.8
Time Line and Internal Rate of Return for Monthly Mortgage

	A	B
1	$ 96,000.00	
2	(772.44)	
3	(772.44)	
4	(772.44)	
5	(772.44)	
359	(772.44)	
360	(772.44)	
361	(772.44)	
362		
363	0.75%	IRR

The formula in cell A363 that was input to calculate the internal rate of return was:

=IRR(A1:A361,1%)

Note how the interest rate guess was a monthly interest rate because the payments were made monthly. If the guess had been 12 percent instead of 1 percent, the computer may have given an error message reading "#NUM!". To correct the error message, enter a monthly interest rate guess. The importance of the accuracy of the interest rate guess (or whether a guess is required at all) is dependent on the version of Excel you are using.

A monthly internal rate of return of .75 percent is equivalent to an annual interest rate of 9 percent (12 × .75%). Once the interest rate of a series of cash flows is known, that internal rate of return can be compared with the interest rate of other alternative uses of money to find the best uses of funds.

Exhibit 4-7.9 illustrates a mortgage amortization table. A **mortgage amortization table** shows the details of the mortgage payments to be made over the entire life of the mortgage. The format is similar to the lottery fund example in Exhibit 4-7.5. Once again, rows 6 through 358 have been hidden to save room in this exhibit.

Exhibit 4-7.9
Mortgage Amortization Table

	A	B	C	D	E
1	Monthly Payment	Interest Expense	Reduction of Principal	Mortgage Principal Balance	
2				$ 96,000.00	
3	$ 772.44	$ 720.00	$ 52.44	95,947.56	
4	772.44	719.61	52.83	95,894.73	
5	772.44	719.21	53.23	95,841.51	*
359	772.44	22.75	749.69	2,282.99	
360	772.44	17.12	755.32	1,527.67	
361	772.44	11.46	760.98	766.69	
362	772.44	5.75	766.69	0.00	

* Penny difference in this row due to rounding

Notice how rows 1 through 362 were used in this exhibit. Once again the row labels can be used to keep track of the time period number. Row 1 was used for headings, row 2 for time period 0, and rows 3 through 362 for time periods 1 to 360.

Exhibit 4-7.9 shows the original principal balance is $96,000 (cell D2). The monthly payments are shown in column A and are constant at $772.44. The interest expense for each interest period is based on the previous period's principal balance. For example, the interest expense shown in cell B3 is calculated as follows:

$$\$96,000 \times .75\% = \$720.00$$

The formula entered in cell B3 would be: =D2*.75%

The interest expense is then subtracted from the monthly payment to determine the amount of the monthly payment to be applied to principal. For cell C3 the formula would be:

=A3-B3

The new principal balance can then be computed by subtracting the reduction of principal for the period from the principal balance. The following formula should be entered in cell D3.

=D2-C3

Because the amortization table has been prepared at the internal rate of return (in this case .75 percent), it should show an ending principal balance of $0 as shown in cell D362.

Exhibit 4-7.10 shows the formulas for the mortgage amortization table.

Exhibit 4-7.10
Formulas for Mortgage Amortization Table

	A	B	C	D
	Monthly Payment	Interest Expense	Reduction of Principal	Mortgage Principal Balance
1				
2				96000
3	772.44	=D2*0.75%	=A3-B3	=D2-C3
4	772.44	=D3*0.75%	=A4-B4	=D3-C4
5	772.44	=D4*0.75%	=A5-B5	=D4-C5
359	772.44	=D358*0.75%	=A359-B359	=D358-C359
360	772.44	=D359*0.75%	=A360-B360	=D359-C360
361	772.44	=D360*0.75%	=A361-B361	=D360-C361
362	772.44	=D361*0.75%	=A362-B362	=D361-C362

Once the formulas have been entered in row 3, the row can be copied and pasted to rows 4 through 362 to expedite the placement of formulas in the remaining rows.

The formula in cell B3 is the one which multiplies the internal rate of return times the previous principal balance. If that interest rate has been rounded to the nearest percent, the mortgage amortization table may not end with a zero balance due to rounding. To keep the calculations as accurate as possible, round the interest rate to the nearest hundredth of a percent as shown in cell B3 in Exhibit 4-7.10.

It is interesting to note in Exhibit 4-7.9 that, as the outstanding principal balance decreases over the life of the mortgage, less of each monthly payment goes to interest and more goes to a reduction of principal. This is because the interest amount is based on the decreasing principal balance. Because the monthly payments remain the same over the mortgage life, if the amount applied to interest decreases, the amount applied to principal increases by the same amount.

Financial Statement Presentation for Mortgages

Suppose the mortgage loan in Exhibit 4-7.8 began on November 1, 2000 and that the property being mortgaged is a building with an estimated 40-year life and no salvage value. The financial statements would reflect the following information relating to the property and mortgage.

The balance sheet will reflect the book value of the property purchased (historical cost less accumulated depreciation) and the principal amount of the mortgage due as of the balance sheet date. The liability for the mortgage principal will generally be broken down into its current and long-term components with the current portion reflecting the amount of the principal within a year from the balance sheet date and the long-term portion being the remaining portion of the principal balance. Exhibit 4-7.11 shows the mortgage amortization table with the cells highlighted to help in the computations. A date column has also been added.

Exhibit 4-7.11
Interest and Liability Calculations for Financial Statements

	A	B	C	D	E
		Monthly	Interest	Reduction of	Mortgage Principal
1	Date	Payment	Expense	Principal	Balance
2					$ 96,000.00
3	11/30/00	$ 772.44	$ 720.00	$ 52.44	95,947.56
4	12/31/00	772.44	719.61	52.83	95,894.73
5	1/31/01	772.44	719.21	53.23	95,841.51
6	2/28/01	772.44	718.81	53.63	95,787.88
7	3/31/01	772.44	718.41	54.03	95,733.85
8	4/30/01	772.44	718.01	54.43	95,679.42
9	5/31/01	772.44	717.60	54.84	95,624.58
10	6/30/01	772.44	717.19	55.25	95,569.32
11	7/31/01	772.44	716.77	55.67	95,513.66
12	8/31/01	772.44	716.36	56.08	95,457.57
13	9/30/01	772.44	715.93	56.51	95,401.06
14	10/31/01	772.44	715.51	56.93	95,344.14
15	11/30/01	772.44	715.08	57.36	95,286.78
16	12/31/01	772.44	714.65	57.79	95,228.99

There are numerous rounding differences in the mortgage amortization table above. If you note that your calculations do not agree to the penny with the exhibit above, it is possibly due to rounding. Keep in mind that the computer stores the entire amount in a cell even though for presentation purposes the amounts are rounded to the nearest penny. The only way to ensure that your mortgage amortization table is correct is to prepare the table for the entire mortgage. If prepared correctly, the ending principal balance at the end of the mortgage will be zero.

Balance Sheet at December 31, 2000:

Assets

Fixed Assets:

Building	$120,000
Accumulated depreciation	(500)
	$119,500

Liabilities

Long-term Liabilities:

Mortgage Payable[2] $95,895

---

[2] To keep the example simple, the mortgage payable will not be divided into its current and long-term portion but rather will be shown as all long-term. The current liability, however, is the portion of the mortgage principal due in the next year, 2001. This is the sum of cells D5 through D16 in Exhibit 4-7.11. The long-term portion is the amount of the principal due after 2001. This can be found in cell E16. The sum of the current portion and the long-term portion must total the mortgage payable liability at December 31, 2000 ($666 + $95,229 = $95,895 shown in cell E4).

Calculations for Balance Sheet:

The accumulated depreciation for the building is for two months of depreciation. The property was purchased November 1 so there is two months or $500 of accumulated depreciation (assuming no salvage value), computed as follows:

Building cost ÷ useful life = $120,000 ÷ 40 years = $3,000 year or $250 per month

The mortgage payable amount comes from cell D4 on the mortgage amortization table in Exhibit 4-7.11.

The income statement will reflect the interest expense for the number of months that the mortgage has been outstanding during the year (in this case the months of November and December). This amount can be gathered from cells C3 and C4 of the mortgage amortization table in Exhibit 4-7.11. Depreciation expense for the property will also be shown for the number of months that the property has been in service during the year.

Income Statement for 2000:

Interest expense (sum of cells C3+C4) $1,440

Depreciation expense: Building (November and December)   500

Leases

There are two types of leases: operating leases and capital leases. The owner of the leased property is called the **lessor** and the individual who is leasing the property is called the **lessee**. **Operating leases** are short-term and/or cancelable and the risks of ownership remain with the lessor. Operating leases are recorded on the transaction worksheet in the same manner as rent expense. The company would decrease cash by the amount of the lease payment and decrease retained earnings by the same amount for lease expense. An example of an operating lease would be the lease on your apartment. **Capital leases**, on the other hand, are long-term and noncancelable leases. FASB Statement No. 13 states that if one of the following criteria are present, the lease is classified as a capital lease.

1. The title of the leased asset transfers to the lessee at the end of the lease.
2. The lease contains a bargain purchase option.
3. The lease term is greater than 75 percent of the useful life of the leased asset.
4. The present value of the lease payment is equal to or greater than 90 percent of the value of the leased asset.

Accounting for a capital lease is very similar to accounting for the purchase of an asset. The leased asset is recorded on the worksheet of the lessee at its fair market value on the date of the lease and the lessee also records a liability (**lease obligation**) equal to the present value of the future lease payments. Each lease payment contains an interest expense component and a reduction of the principal of the lease obligation. This process is very similar to what we saw when we learned about mortgages. The lessee also records depreciation expense on the leased asset. An example of a capital lease follows.

Machine Leasing Example

Aragon Company is considering leasing a machine. The lease provisions are shown below and the NPV and IRR are calculated in Exhibit 4-7.12.

- Lease term is 6 years from November 1, 2000

- Yearly lease payment is $23,333 and due on October 31 of each year

- Ownership of the machine is transferred to Aragon Company at the end of the 6th year on October 31, 2006, after the last payment is made.

- Machine has a 16-year life and an estimated salvage value of $4,000

- Fair market value of the lease is $100,000

Exhibit 4-7.12
Calculation of Internal Rate of Return and Net Present Value for Lease

	A	B	C
1	$100,000		
2	($23,333)		
3	($23,333)		
4	($23,333)		
5	($23,333)		
6	($23,333)		
7	($23,333)		Formulas
8	10.55%	IRR	=IRR(A1:A7,8%)
9	$0	NPV	=NPV(A8,A2:A7)+A1

The effective interest rate (IRR) has been computed as 10.55 percent (rounded) in cell A8. As a reminder, to compute this, the present value of the cash flows in cells A1 to A7 was initially computed at the provided interest rate guess–8 percent in this example. The computer then learned from the interest rate guess and determined the exact interest rate that would make the present value of the cash inflows equal to the present value of the cash outflows. That interest rate is the IRR rate of 10.55 percent.

The computer calculated the net present value in cell A9. Based on the formula, the cash flows in cells A2 through A7 have been discounted at the internal rate of return computed in cell A8. These discounted cash flows have been totaled and added to the amount in cell A1. If the cash flows are discounted at the internal rate of return, the net present value should always be zero, as it is in cell A9. This added step is a proof of the IRR = 10.55 percent (rounded).

Note that at time 0 shown in cell A1, the net cash flow is $100,000. when in fact no cash was received; rather a machine worth $100,000 was received. Since $100,000 of value was received, it is the equivalent of a $100,000 cash flow. In effect, $100,000 cash was borrowed and used to purchase the machine for cash.

Exhibit 4-7.13 shows an amortization table for the life of the capital lease. The table is set up similarly to the mortgage amortization table in Exhibit 4-7.9. Each payment (column B) is split as to the interest (column C) and principal portions (column D). The outstanding lease obligation (principal balance shown in column E) is reduced by the principal portion of the payment each year until the obligation is satisfied at the end of year 6.

Exhibit 4-7.13
Lease Amortization Schedule

	A	B	C	D	E	F
1	Date	Yearly Payment	Interest Expense	Payment Applied to Lease Obligation	Lease Obligation	
2	11/1/00				$100,000.00	
3	10/31/01	$23,333.00	$10,551.41	$12,781.59	$87,218.41	
4	10/31/02	23,333.00	9,202.77	14,130.23	73,088.19	*
5	10/31/03	23,333.00	7,711.84	15,621.16	57,467.02	*
6	10/31/04	23,333.00	6,063.58	17,269.42	40,197.60	
7	10/31/05	23,333.00	4,241.41	19,091.59	21,106.02	*
8	10/31/06	23,333.00	2,226.98	21,106.02	0.00	
10	Total	$139,998.00	$39,998.00	$100,000.00		*
11	* Includes minor rounding differences					

Each year interest expense is calculated by multiplying the internal rate of return times the lease obligation at the end of the previous year. Although Exhibit 4-7.12 showed an interest rate of 10.55 percent, that was a rounded figure. In fact the interest rate was closer to 10.55141 percent. To avoid these types of rounding problems and to make sure that your lease obligation in column E ends with a zero dollar amount, it is helpful to avoid rounding the interest rate if possible. Even without rounding, the interest rate in the amortization table may include minor rounding differences.

Financial Statement Presentation by Lessee

The lease obligation and the expenses associated with it will be reflected in Aragon's financial statements at the end of the first year as follows (including references to Exhibit 4-7.13):

Balance Sheet at December 31, 2000:

Assets
Fixed assets:
Leased machinery $100,000
Accumulated depreciation: Leased machinery   (1,000)
                                                                                        $99,000
Liabilities
Current Liabilities:
Interest payable $1,759

Long-term Liabilities:
Lease obligation[3]   100,000

Calculations for Balance Sheet:

The company would depreciate the leased machine in the same manner as if it were owned and not leased, based on a cost of $100,000. The computation is as follows:

_____

[3] The lease obligation should be split between the current and the long-term portion. This gets rather complex because the lease term differs from a calendar year end. For this reason, it is beyond the scope of this text.

Machine cost, $100,000 – Salvage value, $4,000

$$\frac{\text{Machine cost, \$100,000 – Salvage value, \$4,000}}{\text{Useful life of 16 years}} = \$6,000 \text{ per year} = \$500 \text{ per month}$$

Because the machine lease began on November 1, two months of depreciation will be recognized totaling $1,000.

As of December 31, 2000, because we have not made any principal payments as of that date, the lease obligation contains the original lease obligation of $100,000. The current liability for the unpaid interest of $1,759 is calculated below.

Income Statement:

Interest expense (see calculation below)	$1,759
Depreciation expense: Leased machinery	1,000

Calculations for the Income Statement:

The interest expense shown in cell B3 of Exhibit 4-7.13 of $10,551 applies to interest for the period November 1, 2000 to October 31, 2001. Because these financial statements are for the year 2000 only, the income statement will reflect only the interest expense for the months of November and December.

$$\$10,551 \times (2 \div 12) = \$1,759$$

Depreciation expense was previously explained under balance sheet calculations.

SUMMARY

Understanding how to use present value and future value concepts in a variety of cash flow situations is a must for present-day managers. Identifying cash flows to determine net present value or the internal rate of return for a proposed project can be a tedious task. Fortunately, computer programs and spreadsheets are a significant help in evaluating long-term cash flow projects. Accounting for mortgages, notes, and long-term leases are common examples of where present value concepts are needed.

EXERCISES AND PROBLEMS

Exercises

Exercise 1. Relating Present Value and Future Value with Compound Interest. If you have $1,000 today, how does compound interest get you to the future value of the $1,000 three years from today? Explain briefly.

Exercise 2 Present Value Components. What three factors are necessary to determine the present value of an amount? Give a short explanation for each of the three factors.

Exercise 3 Net Present Value. Define net present value. If an investment has a positive net present value, what does that mean?

Exercise 4   Ordinary Annuity.   Define ordinary annuity.   What are the two primary components of an annuity?

Exercise 5   Internal Rate of Return.   Define internal rate of return.   When IRR is calculated on a computer spreadsheet, what net present value will show on the same spreadsheet?

Problems

Problem 1   Present Value of an Amount.   You have just finished your freshman year at Anywhere University.   You were telling your Uncle Bob about your college experiences and how pleased you are with your grades.   Your uncle, a jovial and affluent person, decided to give you a challenge.   His challenge was: "I will put enough money in a mutual fund tomorrow to grow at 6 percent a year so that $3,000 is in the fund three years from now when you graduate, but you need to determine how much I need to invest now.   You have 15 minutes to give me your correct answer."   Will your Uncle Bob be proud of you because you determined the correct amount or will you lose this chance for a "really nice" graduation present?   Show your reasoning/computations.

Problem 2   Present Value of an Annuity.   You are about to begin your senior year of high school.   Your parents have set aside $40,000 for your college education in a fund that is earning 7 percent per year.   The program you plan to enroll in at college is a 5-year course of study.   If you need $10,000 each year for tuition, books, and living expenses, have your parents set aside enough money for you to take out $10,000 for college expenses each year beginning one year from today?   Prepare a net present value annuity time line and explain your answer.

Problem 3   Determine Net Present Value and Internal Rate of Return for Bonds.   Padre Company issued $200,000, 4-year, 10 percent bonds at par on July 1, 2000.   Interest is payable on December 31 and June 30 each year until the bonds mature on July 1, 2004.   Prepare a time line for the life of the bonds with net present value and internal rate of return for Padre Company in a form similar to Exhibit 4-7.7.

Problem 4   Mortgage Amortization Table.   You have purchased a home for $150,000, paid $30,000 down, and financed $120,000 for 15 years at 7 percent interest.   Payments of $13,176 on the loan are to be made annually at the end of each year.   Prepare an amortization table for this loan (mortgage) in a form similar to Exhibit 4-7.11.   What is the unpaid balance of the loan at the end of three years?   How much interest expense is expected to be paid on the loan for year 5?

Problem 5   Capital Lease Computations and Disclosure.   This case reading contained a machine leasing example for the Aragon Company.   Using the information contained in that example, determine the following for the year 2001:

a.   Indicate how the leased machinery will be disclosed in the balance sheet at December 31, 2001.   Show supporting computations.

b.   Determine the amount of the lease obligation that should be shown in the balance sheet at December 31, 2001.   Show supporting computations.

c.   Determine what expenses and the amounts for each that should be disclosed in the income statement for 2001.

Case 4-7

J & J CORPORATION: PURCHASE OF A RETAIL STORE – PART III

Case Objectives

1. To understand the nature of long-term liabilities and the significance of the time value of money in measuring those liabilities at their present values.
2. To be able to identify cash flows by time period, discount those cash flows to obtain a net present value, and determine the internal rate of return associated with those cash flows.
3. To be able to prepare an amortization table for a liability at a specified interest rate and number of loan payments.
4. To understand how the liability and related interest arising under a capital lease are treated on the lessee's and lessor's balance sheet and income statement.

Decision: If J & J buy Thompson's Paint and Wallpaper Store, how should they finance the purchase?

After reviewing the concerns raised by their CPA consultant regarding the credibility/reliability of Thompson's unaudited financial statements for the year ended December 31, 2002 (presented in Case 4-4 as Exhibits C4-4.1 and C4-4.2), John and Joanna, as a condition of the sale, requested that Thompson provide audited statements. In early February, Thompson delivered a revised set of financial statements including the audited balance sheet for the year ended December 31, 2002 and the audited income statement. These are shown in Exhibit C4-7.1 and C4-7.2. The audited financial statements were accompanied by the auditors' opinion shown in Exhibit C4-7.3.

Exhibit C4-7.1

Thompson's Paint & Wallpaper
Balance Sheets
December 31st

	2002	2001	2000
Assets			
Cash	$ 3,000	$ 5,000	$ 4,500
Accounts receivable, net	29,000	34,000	32,000
Merchandise inventory, at LCM	55,000	53,000	49,000
Prepaid expenses	1,000	700	900
Total Current Assets	88,000	92,700	86,400
Fixed Assets			
Land	5,000	5,000	5,000
Building, net	35,000	39,000	43,000
Furniture and fixtures, net	11,000	12,000	11,000
Total Fixed Assets	51,000	56,000	59,000
Total Assets	$ 139,000	$ 148,700	$ 145,400
Liabilities			
Accounts payable	37,300	36,000	35,000
Accrued payroll taxes	3,000	3,000	3,500
Total Liabilities	40,300	39,000	38,500
Owner's Equity			
Bud Thompson, Capital	98,700	109,700	106,900
Total Liabilities and Owner's Equity	139,000	$ 148,700	$ 145,400

Exhibit C4-7.2

Thompson's Paint & Wallpaper
Income Statement
Years Ended December 31

	2002	2001	2000
Sales	$ 330,000	$ 265,000	$ 270,000
Cost of goods sold	204,000	151,000	154,000
Gross margin	126,000	114,000	116,000
Operating Expenses			
Selling expenses (a)	48,000	20,000	19,000
Administrative expenses (b)	48,300	49,000	45,000
Total operating expenses	96,300	69,000	64,000
Income before taxes	$ 29,700	$ 45,000	$ 52,000

(a) Includes bad debt expense of $1,500 for 2002, 2001, and 2000.
(b) Includes Bud Thompson's salary of $36,000 and depreciation expense of $5,000 for 2002, 2001, and 2000. Of the $5,000, $4,000 applied to the building and $1,000 to the furniture and fixtures.

Exhibit C4-7.3
Auditors' Opinion

Anderson and Jones
Certified Public Accountants
101 Tower Circle #3A

Independent Auditors' Report

We have audited the accompanying balance sheet of Thompson's Paint & Wallpaper as of December 31, 2002 and the related income statement for the year ended December 31, 2002. These financial statements are the responsibility of the company's management. Our responsibility is to express an opinion on these financial statements based on our audit.

We conducted our audit in accordance with generally accepted auditing standards. Those standards require that we plan and perform the audit to obtain reasonable assurance about whether the financial statements are free of material misstatement. An audit includes examining, on a test basis, evidence supporting the amounts and disclosures in the financial statement. An audit also includes assessing the accounting principles used and significant estimates made by management, as well as evaluating the overall financial statement presentation. We believe that our audit provides a reasonable basis for our opinion.

In our opinion, the financial statements referred to above present fairly, in all material respects, the financial position of Thompson's Paint & Wallpaper as of December 31, 2002 and the results of their operations for the year ended December 31, 2002 in conformity with generally accepted accounting principles.

Anderson and Jones, CPAs
February 4, 2003

OFFER PRICE

After carefully reviewing Bud's revised financial statements and taking into account future growth and profitability prospects, John and Joanna decided, with the help of their CPA consultant, to offer Bud a price of $296,500 determined as follows:

Accounts Receivable (collectible portion)	$29,000
Inventory	55,000
Prepaid Expenses	1,000
Land (per appraisal information given later in case)	50,000
Building (per appraisal information given later in case)	190,800
Furniture and Fixtures (at depreciated cost)	11,000
Less:	
Accounts payable	37,300
Accrued payroll taxes	3,000
Fair Market Value of Net Assets	$296,500

John noted, "The offer price assumes that Bud keeps the $3,000 cash on hand shown on the audited balance sheet as he requested (in Case 4-4)." John and Joanna next turned to a consideration of financing options.

FINANCING OPTIONS

"Bud's offer to lease his land and building seems like a good idea," said Joanna. "This would allow us to keep our current cash balance for other expenditures. Yesterday, I checked further with Bud about details of the lease, and he outlined the following provisions:"

- Term: 15 years (begins March 1, 2003, noncancelable)

- Yearly payment: $34,000 (due at the end of each year, first payment due on February 28, 2004)

- Interest rate (to be computed using internal rate of return function)

- Taxes, insurance, repairs and maintenance: to be paid by the lessee (J & J)

- Ownership: transfers to lessee at end of fifteenth year when final payment is made

John was skeptical of the lease because the yearly payments seemed so high. "Joanna, if I take the yearly payment of $34,000 and multiply it by 15, I come up with a total of $510,000, which far exceeds the current fair market value of the land and building. I just don't understand how Bud came up with such a large yearly lease payment. Furthermore, I stopped in at Fidelity Bank this morning and picked up our loan commitment documents. The bank's monthly mortgage payment seems quite reasonable, and we get twenty years to pay off the loan. Also, if I multiply the monthly payment of $1,949.89 by 240 monthly payments, I come up with approximately $467,973.60, which is much lower than the total amount involved in the lease. Here's what Fidelity Bank is offering:

- Appraised values:

Land	$50,000
Building	190,800
Total	$240,800

- Mortgage loan on the real estate:

  - Down payment: 10 percent of $240,800 = $24,080
  - Loan amount: $216,720 ($240,800 – $24,080)
  - Term: 20 years (begins March 1, 2003)
  - Interest rate (to be computed)
    - Monthly payment: $1,949.89 (interest and principal)

The bank provided me with the mortgage amortization table in Exhibit C4-7.4." (Note that rows 15 through 237 have been hidden to save space. To learn how to hide and unhide rows, see Appendix C at the back of the book).

Exhibit C4-7.4
Mortgage Amortization Table

	A	B	C	D	E
1	Date	Monthly Payment	Interest Expense	Reduction of Principal	Mortgage Principal Balance
2	3/1/03				$ 216,720.00
3	3/31/03	$ 1,949.89	$ 1,625.40	$ 324.49	216,395.51
4	4/30/03	1,949.89	1,622.97	326.92	216,068.59
5	5/31/03	1,949.89	1,620.51	329.37	215,739.22
6	6/30/03	1,949.89	1,618.04	331.84	215,407.38
7	7/31/03	1,949.89	1,615.56	334.33	215,073.05
8	8/31/03	1,949.89	1,613.05	336.84	214,736.21
9	9/30/03	1,949.89	1,610.52	339.36	214,396.85
10	10/31/03	1,949.89	1,607.98	341.91	214,054.94
11	11/30/03	1,949.89	1,605.41	344.47	213,710.46
12	12/31/03	1,949.89	1,602.83	347.06	213,363.41
13	1/31/04	1,949.89	1,600.23	349.66	213,013.75
14	2/29/04	1,949.89	1,597.60	352.28	212,661.46
238	10/31/22	1,949.89	71.50	1,878.38	7,655.47
239	11/30/22	1,949.89	57.42	1,892.47	5,763.00
240	12/31/22	1,949.89	43.22	1,906.66	3,856.33
241	1/31/23	1,949.89	28.92	1,920.96	1,935.37
242	2/28/23	1,949.89	14.52	1,935.37	0.00
243					
244	Total	$ 467,972.66	$ 251,252.66	$ 216,720.00	
245	Note: Table contains minor rounding differences.				

"What is the interest rate that the bank is offering?" asked Joanna.

"I'm not sure. Maybe our CPA consultant can help us calculate it," replied John.

Requirements

1. Using the information provided in the amortization table shown in Exhibit C4-7.4, calculate the **annual** interest rate on the mortgage. (Hint: You do not need to do an IRR calculation here but rather think about how interest expense is calculated on a monthly basis. Once you have calculated the monthly interest rate you can compute the yearly interest rate)

2. Write a one-paragraph explanation to John to help him understand why his comparison of the $467,973.60 (total mortgage payments) to today's fair market value of the land and the building is an incorrect analysis of the problem.

3. Using the internal rate of return (IRR) function of a computer spreadsheet as shown in Exhibit 4-7.12 in Case Reading 4-7, determine the implicit annual interest rate involved in the lease offered by Bud Thompson.

4. Prepare a lease amortization table for the fifteen-year lease period using a format similar to Exhibit 4-7.13 in Case Reading 4-7.

5. After reviewing the following assumptions, fill in the requested dollar amounts for the lease on the partial balance sheet and income statement projections as of December 31, 2003. A template has been provided for you in Exhibit C4-7.5.

- The building has a remaining 25-year life as of March 1, 2003 with no salvage value.

- The lease begins on March 1, 2003. The first lease payment, however, will not be made until February 28, 2004 (at the end of the first year of the lease).

Exhibit C4-7.5
Template for Requirement 5

	Lease Option
Partial Balance Sheet at 12/31/2003	
Fixed Assets	
Land	_____
Building	_____
Less: Accumulated Depreciation	_____
Building, net	_____
Total Fixed Assets	_____
Liabilities:	
Current Liabilities	
Interest Payable	_____
Long-term Liabilities	
Lease Obligation	_____
Income Statement for 2003	
Depreciation Expense	_____
Interest Expense	_____

Calculations:

Group Assignment 4-7

WHAT IS YOUR BEST OPTION?

Group Number _____ Group members present and participating:

_____

_____

Objectives

1. To identify the pros and cons of various long-term debt financing options.
2. To understand how the liability and related interest arising under a mortgage option is treated on the borrower's balance sheet and income statement.

Requirements

1. The mortgage in Case 4-7 begins March 1, 2003. The first monthly payment is due March 31, 2003. Fill in the requested dollar amounts for the mortgage option on the partial balance sheet and income statement projections as of December 31, 2003. Assume the building has a remaining 25-year life as of March 1, 2003 with no salvage value.

Partial Balance Sheet at 12/31/2003		
Fixed Assets:		
Land		
Building		
Less: Accumulated Depreciation		
Building, net		
Total Fixed Assets		
Current Liabilities		
Interest Payable		
Long-term Liabilities		
Mortgage Payable		
Income Statement for 2003		
Depreciation Expense		
Interest Expense		

2. Briefly identify the differences between the mortgage and the lease financing option in Case 4-7. Look at interest rates, length of time of liability, ownership of assets during the term of the liability, the yearly cash payments required, and the timing of cash payments.

Interest rates: _____

_____

Length of time of liability: _____

_____

Ownership of assets during debt term: _____

_____

_____

Yearly cash payment: _____

_____

_____

Timing of cash payments: _____

_____

_____

_____

3. Make a recommendation for an appropriate course of action.

_____

_____

_____

_____

Case Reading 4-8

ANALYSIS OF FINANCIAL
STATEMENTS[1]

INTRODUCTION

Prudent investment decisions are based upon an objective analysis of what the financial statements reveal about a company. Such an analysis frequently involves the comparison of several investment alternatives. It is difficult to make an investment decision when the sizes of the companies being compared are diverse. Comparing a multi-billion dollar global company to a small startup company without an analytical approach may lead one to make incorrect inferences.

This case reading introduces horizontal analysis, vertical analysis, and key financial ratios. An explanation of how to compare and contrast the financial information of more than one company is illustrated, including the limitations inherent in such comparisons. The following pages present various analytical methods using the financial information for a fictitious company, Steve's Stereos.

COMPARATIVE FINANCIAL STATEMENT ANALYSIS

Changes in particular items in financial statements can be more clearly identified when two or more successive accounting periods are placed side by side on a single statement. Financial statements of this type are called **comparative financial statements**. Comparative financial statements provide the data necessary to analyze percentage changes of certain line items or to plot the current trend in any one category.

Horizontal Analysis

Horizontal analysis presents both dollar and percentage changes in income statement and balance sheet items for two or more years. When two statements are used in a comparison, the earlier financial statement is used as the base year. If the analysis is comprised of more than two statements there are two methods which may be used: (1) the earliest financial statement may be used as the base for comparison or (2) each statement may be compared with the immediately preceding year. Exhibit 4.8.1 is an example of the latter approach.

---

[1] The authors thank Steven J. Adams of California State University, Chico for his major contributions to this Case Reading.

Exhibit 4-8.1
Steve's Stereos
Comparative Income Statements–Horizontal Analysis

	2000	1999	1998	Increase (Decrease) 2000 versus 1999		Increase (Decrease) 1999 versus 1998	
				Amount	Percent	Amount	Percent
Net Sales	$ 545,000	$ 505,000	$ 486,000	$ 40,000	7.92%	$ 19,000	3.91%
Cost of Goods Sold	330,000	304,000	286,000	26,000	8.55%	18,000	6.29%
Gross Margin on Sales	215,000	201,000	200,000	14,000	6.97%	1,000	0.50%
Operating Expenses	133,000	93,000	89,000	40,000	43.01%	4,000	4.49%
Interest Expense	9,450	8,320	8,380	1,130	13.58%	(60)	-0.72%
Earnings Before Income Tax	72,550	99,680	102,620	(27,130)	-27.22%	(2,940)	-2.86%
Income Tax at 30%	21,765	29,904	30,786	(8,139)	-27.22%	(882)	-2.86%
Net Income	$ 50,785	$ 69,776	$ 71,834	$ (18,991)	-27.22%	$ (2,058)	-2.86%

In comparing net sales for 2000 to 1999, we can see that net sales increased by $40,000. This increase can also be expressed as a percentage by performing the following calculation:

$$\frac{\text{Net sales 2000} - \text{Net sales 1999}}{\text{Net sales 1999}} = \frac{\$545,000 - \$505,000 = \$40,000}{\$505,000} = 7.92\%$$

Likewise we can complete a similar computation when comparing 1999 to 1998:

$$\frac{\text{Net sales 1999} - \text{Net sales 1998}}{\text{Net sales 1998}} = \frac{\$505,000 - \$486,000 = \$19,000}{\$486,000} = 3.91\%$$

Although not shown in the table, we could also calculate the change from 1998 to 2000:

$$\frac{\text{Net sales 2000} - \text{Net sales 1998}}{\text{Net sales 1998}} = \frac{\$545,000 - \$486,000 = \$59,000}{\$486,000} = 12.14\%$$

Note that in each case the base year is the denominator of the equation. Summarizing this information, we can see that net sales increased 3.91 percent in 1999 and 7.92 percent in 2000 for an overall increase of 12.14 percent for the two-year period. A similar calculation for the year-to-year changes has also been done for other line items in Exhibit 4-8.1.

Having completed the mathematical calculations, the information should be analyzed. For example, our sales increased 7.92 percent during 2000 but cost of goods sold, a variable expense that should vary in proportion to sales, increased 8.55 percent during that time period. We would expect a 7.92 percent increase. What caused the additional change? Possible answers could be increased prices from our suppliers, increased freight charges on the merchandise purchased, or other factors.

Other items to note in the analysis include the increase of 43.01 percent in operating expenses. One would anticipate some increase in operating expenses since some of these expenses are probably variable expenses but this increase is significant. The 13.58 percent increase in interest expense is also significant. With such a change, one would expect that the company has borrowed additional funds. In looking at the balance sheet in Exhibit 4-8.2, current notes payable has increased from $30,050 to $40,050, whereas long-term notes payable has increased from \$130,000 to \$176,000 in 2000. In fact, we might actually expect a larger increase in interest expense than 13.58 percent in 2000. Possibly, the additional funds were not borrowed until late in the year. In that case, we should expect an even larger amount of interest expense next year. The same type of analysis could be performed on the income statement figures to compare the 1999 results with the 1998 amounts.

Exhibit 4-8.2 shows the horizontal analysis for 1998 through 2000 for balance sheet accounts.

Exhibit 4-8.2
Steve's Stereos
Comparative Balance Sheets–Horizontal Analysis

	2000	1999	1998	Increase (Decrease) 2000 versus 1999		Increase (Decrease) 1999 versus 1998	
				Amount	Percent	Amount	Percent
Assets							
Current Assets							
Cash	\$ 48,500	\$ 58,000	\$ 52,000	\$ (9,500)	-16.38%	\$ 6,000	11.54%
Accounts Receivable, net	89,000	76,000	68,000	13,000	17.11%	8,000	11.76%
Merchandise Inventory	162,000	154,000	150,000	8,000	5.19%	4,000	2.67%
Prepaid Expenses	29,450	28,650	28,650	800	2.79%	-	0.00%
Total Current Assets	328,950	316,650	298,650	12,300	3.88%	18,000	6.03%
Property and Equipment							
Land	93,000	68,000	68,000	25,000	36.76%	-	0.00%
Building	325,000	154,000	154,000	171,000	111.04%	-	0.00%
Equipment	96,000	62,030	61,040	33,970	54.76%	990	1.62%
	514,000	284,030	283,040	229,970	80.97%	990	0.35%
Accumulated Depreciation	(122,000)	(86,120)	(86,000)	(35,880)	41.66%	(120)	0.14%
	392,000	197,910	197,040	194,090	98.07%	870	0.44%
Long-term Investments	13,320	13,320	13,320	-	0.00%	-	0.00%
Total Assets	\$ 734,270	\$ 527,880	\$ 509,010	\$ 206,390	39.10%	\$ 18,870	3.71%
Liabilities and Stockholders' Equity							
Current Liabilities							
Notes Payable	\$ 40,050	\$ 30,050	\$ 10,000	\$ 10,000	33.28%	\$ 20,050	200.50%
Accounts Payable	64,000	59,000	61,000	5,000	8.47%	(2,000)	-3.28%
Accrued Expenses	28,060	27,650	28,450	410	1.48%	(800)	-2.81%
Income Taxes Payable	36,000	34,210	35,550	1,790	5.23%	(1,340)	-3.77%
Total Current Liabilities	168,110	150,910	135,000	17,200	11.40%	15,910	11.79%
Long-term Liabilities							
Long term Notes Payable	176,000	130,000	130,000	46,000	35.38%	-	0.00%
Stockholders' Equity							
Common Stock, par \$1	80,000	50,000	50,000	30,000	60.00%	-	0.00%
Additional Paid-In Capital	150,000	70,000	70,000	80,000	114.29%	-	0.00%
Retained Earnings	160,160	126,970	124,010	33,190	26.14%	2,960	2.39%
	390,160	246,970	244,010	143,190	57.98%	2,960	1.21%
Total Liabilities and Stockholders' Equity	\$ 734,270	\$ 527,880	\$ 509,010	\$ 206,390	39.10%	\$ 18,870	3.71%

The computations are very similar to those for the income statement. For example, to calculate the increase/decrease in cash for 2000 versus 1999, the calculation would be

$$\frac{\text{Cash } 2000 - \text{Cash } 1999}{\text{Cash } 1999} = \frac{\$48,500 - \$58,000 = (\$9,500)}{\$58,000} = -16.38\%$$

Noting that cash decreased by 16.38 percent, a reader of the balance sheet might ask how this could happen when the company was making a $50,785 profit in 2000, as shown on the income statement. The financial statement user must refer to the statement of cash flows to see what transactions caused the changes in cash for 2000.

Other items to note in 2000 include the 17.11 percent increase in accounts receivable. What caused that increase? Sales did increase 7.92 percent, but certainly not all of those additional sales are in accounts receivable. This increase could indicate a change in the credit policy of the company. Have they relaxed their credit terms? Did they not have a sufficient allowance for bad debts? These would all be concerns that users of the financial statements might have.

Land and building increased 36.76 percent and 111.04 percent, respectively, in 2000. Equipment also increased 54.76 percent. Why did the company make these extra expenditures? Are they expanding? How did they finance these new purchases? As mentioned previously, current notes payable increased by $10,000 and long-term notes payable increased by $46,000. The increase in fixed assets was probably financed in part by increased debt. The cash flow statement, not given here, should provide us with additional details concerning the financing. Accumulated depreciation increased 41.66 percent in 2000. Given the fixed asset purchases, this amount seems reasonable. We can plan for at least this amount or more of depreciation in future years as some of the new fixed asset purchases may have been late in the year.

Accounts payable increased by $5,000, or 8.47 percent, in 2000. Some of this increase might be due to the fact that we have increased the amount of inventory on hand. Note that inventory on hand is $8,000 more or 5.19 percent higher in 2000. The increase in accounts payable could be explained by unpaid inventory purchases late in the year.

Income taxes payable increased 5.23 percent from 1999 to 2000. An observant student might wonder why this liability has increased, given that the net income actually declined over the same period. Accounting records are kept according to generally accepted accounting principles, as we have noted previously. However, the tax liability of the business is governed by federal tax laws, which might be different than GAAP, so it is possible to have an increased tax liability even when net income is decreasing.

The stockholders' equity section also has some changes in 2000. The company's stock issuance caused a total increase in common stock and paid-in capital of $110,000. The issuance of additional stock was probably necessary to help finance the fixed asset purchases. Once again, the cash flow statement would give us more information on the inflows and outflows of cash during the period. Retained earnings increased by $33,190 during the year. Why did retained earnings only increase $33,190 when net income for 2000 was $50,785? The most plausible explanation is dividends. This information can be confirmed by looking at the financing cash outflows on the cash flow statement to determine the amount of cash expended for dividends. A reconciliation of the retained earnings account for the year 2000 is as follows:

Retained Earnings, 1/1/2000	$126,970
Add: Net income	50,785
Subtotal	$177,755
Less: Dividends	17,595
Retained Earnings, 12/31/2000	$160,160

Most comparisons shown in this illustration were for the years 2000 and 1999. The figures are available to review changes between 1999 and 1998. For example, was the amount of dividends in 1999 more or less than the $17,595 computed for 2000?

A similar reconciliation of retained earnings for 1999 would show that dividends in 1999 were $66,816. We can calculate the dividend per share for 1999 by dividing the cash dividend by the number of shares outstanding as follows:

$$\frac{\text{1999 Dividend}}{\text{\# shares outstanding}} = \frac{\$66,816}{\$50,000 \div \$1.00 \text{ par} = 50,000 \text{ shares}} = \$1.34 \text{ per share}$$

What is the dividend per share for 2000? 80,000 shares are outstanding at the end of 2000 due to more shares being issued during 2000. The cash dividend is equally divided among the shares, which amounts to $.22 per share. **Dividends per share** is a ratio that is commonly published and may be compared to other companies in the industry. The users of the financial statement information might be concerned about the reduction in the dividend per share from $1.34 in 1999 to $.22 per share in 2000. Their concern could be reflected in a lower market price if the stock is publicly traded.

Vertical Analysis

Vertical analysis is used to analyze the relative size of various balance sheet or income statement items in relationship to a base amount within a given year. Some analysts prepare common-size statements, which are used in vertical analysis. Common-size statements translate all dollar amounts on the given statement into percentages of the total, such as total assets on the balance sheet or net sales on the income statement. By doing this, the size of the company becomes irrelevant. It therefore becomes meaningful to compare a company the size of United Airlines, for example, to a small regional commuter airline since absolute dollars are removed from the analysis. This type of analysis is especially helpful when comparing numerous companies in the same industry.

In the following example we will again use Steve's Stereos. In a vertical analysis of the income statement (statement of earnings) each item is stated as a percentage of net sales. Regardless of the year, net sales is always 100 percent and all of the other revenues and expenses are shown as a percentage of net sales of that same year. This allows comparisons across time as well.

Exhibit 4-8.3
Steve's Stereos
Comparative Income Statements–Vertical Analysis

	2000	%	1999	%	1998	%
Net Sales	$545,000	100.00%	$ 505,000	100.00%	$ 486,000	100.00%
Cost of Goods Sold	330,000	60.55%	304,000	60.20%	286,000	58.85%
Gross Margin on sales	215,000	39.45%	201,000	39.80%	200,000	41.15%
Operating Expenses	133,000	24.40%	93,000	18.42%	89,000	18.31%
Interest Expense	9,450	1.73%	8,320	1.65%	8,380	1.72%
Earnings Before Income Tax	72,550	13.31%	99,680	19.74%	102,620	21.12%
Income Tax at 30%	21,765	3.99%	29,904	5.92%	30,786	6.33%
Net Income	$ 50,785	9.32%	$ 69,776	13.82%	$ 71,834	14.78%

Looking at Exhibit 4-8.3, we see that cost of goods sold was 58.85 percent of sales in 1998. In 1999, it was 60.20 percent of net sales, and in 2000, it was 60.55 percent of net sales. Why, if cost of goods sold is variable, is its percentage of sales increasing over time? You will remember that variable costs increase in total as volume increases, but the proportion of variable costs in relation to sales should stay the same. One possible answer is higher costs paid to the suppliers. Internally, the cost accountant might be considering a decision as to whether or not the sales price should be adjusted to reflect those higher costs.

Operating expenses have increased dramatically in 2000 as a percentage of sales. In 1999, operating expenses were 18.42 percent of sales and in 2000, they were 24.40 percent. Considering the large increase in depreciation expense this year due to additional fixed asset purchases, this increase in operating expenses is not a surprising discovery. Can the amount of depreciation expense be computed? Assuming there are no plant and equipment sales or retirements during the year, depreciation expense for Steve's Stereos must have been $35,880, calculated from the information in Exhibit 4-8.4 as follows:

Accumulated depreciation, 1/1/99	$ 86,120
Plus: Depreciation expense	35,880 (by inference)
Accumulated depreciation, 12/31/99	$122,000

Interest increased slightly as a percentage of sales from 1999 to 2000, but did not change over the two-year period as a whole. Income taxes have been decreasing for the last few years as a percentage of sales. Net income as a percentage of sales reflects a downward trend due to steadily increasing cost of good sold and operating expenses from 1998 to 2000. Other reasons for this include additional depreciation and interest in 2000 versus 1999.

When performing vertical analysis on balance sheet figures, each line item is stated as a percentage of total assets; liabilities and stockholders' equity items are stated as percentages of total liabilities and stockholders' equity. In other words, total assets are defined as 100 percent and total liabilities and owners' equity are defined as 100 percent.

Exhibit 4-8.4 shows a vertical analysis for 2000, 1999, and 1998 balance sheets for Steve's Stereo. As shown in the exhibit, cash for 2000 is 6.61 percent of total assets. This is calculated by dividing cash of $48,500 by total assets of $734,270. Cash is a much lower percentage of total assets in 2000 than in the previous two years, when it was approximately 10–11 percent of total assets. This is probably because of large cash disbursements on property and equipment expenditures in 2000.

All of the current assets have decreased as a percentage of total assets during 2000 as compared with the previous two years. This is not surprising since total assets have increased by 39.10 percent in 2000, as previously noted in the horizontal analysis in Exhibit 4-8.2. Building has increased from 29.17 percent in the previous year to 44.26 percent in 2000, probably due to a building purchase. Changes in other fixed asset accounts are not noteworthy.

The accounts shown as current liabilities have fluctuated as a percentage of total liabilities and stockholders' equity over the three-year period. This is fairly common and there is no notable pattern. Overall, current liabilities have decreased in the current year.

Exhibit 4-8.4
Steve's Stereos
Comparative Balance Sheets–Vertical Analysis

	2000	%	1999	%	1998	%
Assets						
Current Assets						
Cash	$ 48,500	6.61%	$ 58,000	10.99%	$ 52,000	10.22%
Accounts Receivable, net	89,000	12.12%	76,000	14.40%	68,000	13.36%
Merchandise Inventory	162,000	22.06%	154,000	29.17%	150,000	29.47%
Prepaid Expenses	29,450	4.01%	28,650	5.43%	28,650	5.63%
Total Current Assets	328,950	44.80%	316,650	59.99%	298,650	58.67%
Property and Equipment						
Land	93,000	12.67%	68,000	12.88%	68,000	13.36%
Building	325,000	44.26%	154,000	29.17%	154,000	30.25%
Equipment	96,000	13.07%	62,030	11.75%	61,040	11.99%
	514,000	70.00%	284,030	53.81%	283,040	55.61%
Accumulated Depreciation	(122,000)	-16.62%	(86,120)	-16.31%	(86,000)	-16.90%
	392,000	53.39%	197,910	37.49%	197,040	38.71%
Long-term Investments	13,320	1.81%	13,320	2.52%	13,320	2.62%
Total Assets	$ 734,270	100.00%	$ 527,880	100.00%	$ 509,010	100.00%
Liabilities and Stockholders' Equity						
Current Liabilities						
Notes Payable	$ 40,050	5.45%	$ 30,050	5.69%	$ 10,000	1.96%
Accounts Payable	64,000	8.72%	59,000	11.18%	61,000	11.98%
Accrued Expenses	28,060	3.82%	27,650	5.24%	28,450	5.59%
Income Taxes Payable	36,000	4.90%	34,210	6.48%	35,550	6.98%
Total Current Liabilities	168,110	22.89%	150,910	28.59%	135,000	26.52%
Long-term Liabilities						
Long term Notes Payable	176,000	23.97%	130,000	24.63%	130,000	25.54%
Stockholders' Equity						
Common Stock, par $1	80,000	10.90%	50,000	9.47%	50,000	9.82%
Additional Paid-In Capital	150,000	20.43%	70,000	13.26%	70,000	13.75%
Retained Earnings	160,160	21.81%	126,970	24.05%	124,010	24.36%
	390,160	53.14%	246,970	46.79%	244,010	47.94%
Total Liabilities and Stockholders' Equity	$ 734,270	100.00%	$ 527,880	100.00%	$ 509,010	100.00%

In reviewing liabilities and owners' equity over the three-year period, a shift is evident in 2000 from debt financing to equity financing. For example, in 1998 and 1999 total liabilities (current plus long-term liabilities) are about 52–53 percent of total liabilities and stockholders' equity while equity financing is approximately 47 percent of total liabilities and stockholders' equity. In 2000, the reverse is true; equity financing now accounts for 53 percent while debt financing accounts for 47 percent (22.89% + 23.97%). This might signal a change in the company's financing philosophy.

A further analysis as shown in Exhibit 4-8.5 could be prepared at this point to reveal how each of the current assets has changed in comparison to total current assets. This additional analysis shows us that the makeup of current assets has changed in 2000. Cash has decreased as previously mentioned but, more importantly, accounts receivable is a greater percentage of current assets each year. This in itself is not alarming, but once again the collectability of the accounts receivable and a thorough review of credit policy might be warranted. Inventory and prepaid expenses have remained about the same percentage of current assets over the last few years.

Exhibit 4-8.5
Steve's Stereos
Vertical Analysis of Current Assets

	2000	%	1999	%	1998	%
Assets						
Current Assets						
Cash	$ 48,500	14.74%	$ 58,000	18.32%	$ 52,000	17.41%
Accounts Receivable, net	89,000	27.06%	76,000	24.00%	68,000	22.77%
Merchandise Inventory	162,000	49.25%	154,000	48.63%	150,000	50.23%
Prepaid Expenses	29,450	8.95%	28,650	9.05%	28,650	9.59%
Total Current Assets	$ 328,950	100.00%	$ 316,650	100.00%	$ 298,650	100.00%

A further analysis of the makeup of current liabilities, similar to Exhibit 4-8.5 for current assets, could be performed, but is not illustrated here.

Horizontal and vertical analysis are used both internally and externally by users of the financial statements. Companies that are publicly traded on stock exchanges are required to include income statements for the most recent three years and balance sheets for the last two years in external reports. Internal users analyze the financial statements for budgeting and diagnostic purposes. External users of the financial statements use these analyses to identify trends from year to year and to highlight potential problem areas for investment purposes.

RATIO ANALYSIS

Users of financial information typically employ ratio analysis to better assess a company's performance. Several key ratios have been discussed elsewhere in the text but are repeated here for your convenience. Additional ratios are introduced in this section so that you can expand the scope of your analysis.

The financial statement ratios which follow are categorized into three groups:

- **Profitability** - Ratios which measure income in relation to revenue, assets, or shareholders' equity.

- **Liquidity** - Ratios which measure the ability of the company to meet short-term debts.

- **Risk** - Ratios which measure the vulnerability of the company to negative events such as default on debt contracts, breach of bond covenants, cancellation of dividends to shareholders, forced sale of assets, and insolvency.

The ratios which follow are designed to be used for comparative purposes. When an investor is contemplating the investment in a certain company, it is possible to compare its financial ratios with those of companies in the same industry to determine if the profitability, liquidity, and risk compares favorably to other companies.

Profitability Ratios

Return on Equity (ROE)

Return on equity is computed by dividing net income by average shareholders' (or stockholders') equity. Average equity is the sum of the beginning equity balance and ending equity balance divided by 2. In equation form,

$$\text{ROE} = \frac{\text{Net income}}{(\text{Beginning equity} + \text{Ending equity}) \div 2}$$

For stockholders, return on equity is usually considered to be the primary measure of overall company performance. A high return on equity compared to previous years and to companies that face similar risks is an indication of good performance.

Return on Assets (ROA)

Return on assets is computed by dividing net income by average total assets. It gives insight into how efficiently the company is using its assets and is probably the best measure of a company's operating performance. The higher the value of the ratio the more net income per dollar of assets is exhibited.

$$\text{ROA} = \frac{\text{Net income}}{(\text{Beginning total assets} + \text{Ending total assets}) \div 2}$$

Return on Sales (ROS)

Return on sales is computed by dividing net income by sales revenue. In equation form,

$$\text{ROS} = \frac{\text{Net income}}{\text{Sales revenue}}$$

Return on sales ratio is a measure of the profit earned on each sales dollar. An increasing or high ratio relative to other companies in the same industry is usually an indication of efficient operations and good cost control. It is important to compare only companies in the same industry, because the return on sales ratio will vary greatly from industry to industry. For example, a reasonable ratio might be 2 percent for a supermarket, but 10 percent or more for a jewelry store. One reason for the difference in these amounts is that supermarkets might generate two or three times the level of sales per dollar of investment than do jewelry stores. As a result, supermarkets need only earn half as much per dollar of sales in order to generate the same return on equity.

Gross Profit Margin (GPM)

The gross profit margin ratio (gross profit ratio) is a percentage of sales revenue which remains after deducting cost of goods sold. It is a key measure of profitability. If the ratio is declining for a retail store it is indicative that the company is facing increased competition or possibly cost of good sold is rising faster than the sales price.

$$GPM = \frac{\text{Gross profit on sales}}{\text{Sales}}$$

Earnings Per Share (EPS)

Earnings per share is computed by dividing net income (less any preferred stock dividends) by the average number of common stock shares outstanding during the year. In its simplest form, the equation is:

$$EPS = \frac{\text{Net income} - \text{Preferred stock dividends}}{\text{Average number of common stock shares outstanding}}$$

Earnings per share is usually computed for you, generally at the bottom of the income statement. It is a number almost all analysts focus on.

Earnings per share is often used instead of total income in vertical analysis because it adjusts a company's income for an increasing or decreasing number of shares outstanding. For example, assume that a company's net income increases from $1,000,000 in 1999 to $1,200,000 in 2000. Assume that, during the same period, common stock increases from 50,000 shares to 100,000 shares because the company issues more shares. Does this increase in income represent good performance from a common stockholder's perspective? No, because earnings per share declined from $20 in 1999 to $12 in 2000.

Liquidity Ratios

Current Ratio (CR)

The current ratio is computed by dividing current assets by current liabilities.

$$CR = \frac{\text{Current assets}}{\text{Current liabilities}}$$

It is a measure of liquidity or solvency. As you may have noticed, all accounts on the balance sheet are listed in order of liquidity. Liquidity refers to how quickly a company can convert its assets to cash and the length of time until its liabilities mature. In other words, cash is listed first as it is considered to be the most liquid asset. The company wants to have a current ratio which indicates that the current assets are sufficient to cover the current liabilities when they come due. This would suggest that the current ratio must be at least 1. Most companies like to maintain a higher current ratio, usually between 1.5 or 2 because, in some cases, certain current assets, such as inventory, might not be converted to cash very easily. Exhibit 4-8.5 earlier in this case reading illustrated the type of analysis that might be performed to evaluate the composition of current assets more closely. Loan covenants sometimes require a company to maintain at least a minimum specified current ratio.

Accounts Receivable Turnover Ratio (ART)

The accounts receivable turnover ratio is computed by dividing net sales by average accounts receivable. This is calculated as follows:

$$ART = \frac{\text{Net sales}}{(\text{Beginning accounts receivable} + \text{ending accounts receivable}) \div 2}$$

The accounts receivable turnover calculation helps financial statement users to monitor the accounts receivable collection process. The higher the ratio, the more quickly the accounts receivable are being collected.

Oftentimes the accounts receivable turnover is converted into another ratio called days sales outstanding or the accounts receivable collection period. This calculation is made by dividing 365 by the accounts receivable turnover. A more thorough discussion of both of these ratios can be found in Case Reading 4-2.

Inventory Turnover Ratio (ITR)

The inventory turnover ratio is computed by dividing cost of goods sold by average inventory. In equation form,

$$ITR = \frac{\text{Cost of goods sold}}{(\text{Beginning inventory} + \text{Ending inventory}) \div 2}$$

Inventory turnover ratio is a measure of how efficiently inventory is managed. An increasing or high ratio relative to other companies in the same industry is usually an indication of efficient inventory management. Companies often divide 365 by the inventory turnover ratio in order to compute the number of days that an average inventory item will remain in inventory before it is sold. Both of these calculations are discussed more thoroughly in Case Reading 4-4.

Risk Ratios

Debt-to-Equity Ratio (DER)

The debt-to-equity ratio is computed by dividing ending total liabilities by ending total shareholders' equity. In equation form,

$$DER = \frac{\text{Ending liabilities}}{\text{Ending shareholders' equity}}$$

The debt-to-equity ratio is a measure of a company's financial risk (likelihood of going bankrupt) and the extent to which a company is taking advantage of cheaper debt financing. Both a relatively high and a relatively low ratio are undesirable. Therefore, companies strive to achieve an optimum debt-to-equity ratio. An increasing or high ratio relative to the industry indicates higher financial risk and greater use of debt financing. The debt-to-equity ratio varies greatly from industry to industry. For example, utilities companies, with a stable demand in monopoly markets, normally have a much higher ratio than electronics firms, which face intense competition and short, risky product life cycles. The debt-to-equity ratio is particularly important to bankers, bondholders, and other creditors.

Times Interest Earned (TIE)

Because default on a company's indebtedness brings the possibility of being forced into bankruptcy, a measure of how many times the income of the business will pay the interest on the debt helps assess risk. The formula for **times interest earned ratio** is:

$$\text{TIE} = \frac{\text{Income before interest and taxes}}{\text{Interest expense}}$$

A company whose income is barely enough to pay the interest is one with low profitability and/or a high debt-to-equity ratio. For example, if Company A had interest expense of $1 million and income before interest and taxes of $1.2 million, it would be a much greater risk than Company B with $10 million in income and only $1 million is interest expense. It would have a times interest earned ratio of 1.2 while Company B has a ratio of 10. The investor and creditor would favor Company B.

OBTAINING CURRENT INFORMATION

Financial information concerning publicly traded companies is often publicized in newspapers. *The Wall Street Journal* provides a section called "Explanatory Notes" which aids in the understanding of how to read stock market information. Stock information helps current and potential investors evaluate a corporation. Market price of the stock, price-earnings ratio (P/E) and earnings per share (EPS) are some indicators of the health of a corporation. The following is a reproduction of The Gap, Inc. stock listing as of August 13, 1998.

52 Weeks					Yld		Vol	Current week			Net
Hi	Lo	Stock	Sym	Div	%	P/E	100s	Hi	Lo	Close	Chg
67.44	28.04	Gap, Inc.	GPS	.20	.3	46	15,096	66.63	63.56	66.56	+ 4.06

The 52-week high and low columns show the highest and lowest price of the stock during the previous 52 weeks. The high for The Gap, Inc. for the previous year was $67.44.

The dividend column shows the latest annual dividend which is $.20 per share.

The yield column (dividend yield) indicates the rate of return that a stockholder would receive if the stock were purchased at its latest price. It is the dividends or other distributions paid by a company on its securities, expressed as a percentage of price. (Note: The yield is calculated by dividing the annual dividend by the current market price.)

The **price/earnings ratio (P/E)** is computed by dividing the current market price of the stock by the most recent primary earnings per share. In equation form,

$$P/E = \frac{\text{Common stock price}}{\text{Primary earnings per share}}$$

All other things being equal, a high price/earnings ratio means that investors have a favorable opinion of a company compared to other companies in the same industry which have a lower ratio. A company with a high price/earnings ratio is also considered "expensive" because a high price is being paid for the stock compared to the company's earnings. Conversely, a low price/earnings ratio often occurs when a company is out of favor with investors.

The volume (100s) column is the unofficial daily total shares traded. in hundreds.

The Close column reflects the last price the stock was traded for during the trading session. In this case it was $66.56.

The Current week high and low columns show the highest and lowest price of the stock during the current week. The high for The Gap for the week was $66.63 and the low was $63.56. The net change shows that the closing price of $66.56 was up $4.06 from the last price during the previous trading session.

One additional computation that has not been discussed so far is the **book value per share**. The book value per share (BV/S) is computed by dividing total shareholders' equity attributable to common shareholders by the number of common shares outstanding at the balance sheet date.

In equation form,

$$BV/S = \frac{\text{Total shareholders' equity (common)}}{\text{Common stock shares outstanding}}$$

Book value per share is a number frequently used by analysts, particularly in horizontal analysis. A book value per share that is near or above the stock price indicates that investors are not enthused by the company's performance. It could mean that the earnings are weak, there is little confidence in management, the company has created little goodwill or value through product and personnel development, or the company has negative uncertainties facing it. Conversely, a low book value per share compared to the stock price means that investors see favorable attributes that are not reflected by the financial statements.

Industry Norms Comparison

By utilizing industry norms a company can compare its performance with similar companies in the same industry. Industry norms can also be used to interpret or judge trends in one's industry. These ratios are extremely useful in determining whether a company is performing at a desirable level. However, there are several limitations to using industry norms that must be considered when researching any particular industry.

- Even though two companies are in the same industry, they might not be comparable. For example, consider two companies said to be in the computer industry. One is retailing products it buys from other producers. The other develops, produces, and markets its own products.

- Most large companies today can be described as diversified companies, sometimes called conglomerates. In other words, they operate in many unrelated industries. When using the consolidated financial statements of these companies for financial analysis, it is often impossible to use industry norms as the standard.

- Companies in the same industry and very similar in appearance might use different accounting procedures. The impact of alternate inventory methods such as FIFO and LIFO on the computation of net income may distort the comparisons. Each alternate method is acceptable under GAAP, but the use of different methods will complicate comparisons between companies in the same industry which use these different methods.

- Inflation might be the cause of increases in line item amounts over time. In other words, the company might not actually be doing better; increased dollar amounts could be due to inflation. Auto companies, for example, report changes in unit sales rather than dollar sales. A percentage increase is thus a real increase in business activity, not just due to a price increase.

When using industry norms it is important to find companies that most closely match the industry characteristics in order to find the most accurate information available. Each industry will have different standards of performance and must not be compared with other industries in evaluation of performance. For example, it would not be useful to compare the ratios used for the retail grocery industry with that of the retail electronics industry. Both are retail outlets, but take into consideration the amount of labor involved for each operation. A grocery store does not need salespeople to secure a sale, whereas to sell most electronics you not only need the normal support staff, but will also require the employment of knowledgeable salespeople to promote the product.

Other Industry Sources

The Market Guide Inc.[2] provides company snapshots free on the internet. Information provided for The Gap, Inc. as of August 13, 1998, is shown later in this case reading. The information differs in some cases from the information obtained from *The Wall Street Journal* because the snapshot for The Gap, Inc. was on a different date.

The Market Guide service also provides some industry comparisons. A few pages of these industry comparisons follow as well. Much of the information available at these types of web sites are part of a service which one can obtain for a certain fee. The pages provided here are free of charge.

American Online, Microsoft Network, Compuserve, and Prodigy all have financial services available for free to their customers. These internet providers give their customers access to the financial information of many publicly traded stocks.

---

[2]The following five pages are reprinted with the permission of The Market Guide Inc. This information is available at the web site: http://www.marketguide.com

Comparison for The Gap, Inc.   Page 1 of 3

The Gap, Inc.
NYSE: GPS
Sector: Services
Industry: Retail (Apparel)

Market Guide
The Benchmark for Quality Financial Information

Comparison

RATIO COMPARISON

Valuation Ratios	Company	Industry	Sector	S&P 500
P/E Ratio (TTM)	42.19	31.54	30.47	29.70
P/E High - Last 5 Yrs.	40.24	41.95	37.56	38.66
P/E Low - Last 5 Yrs.	14.32	12.12	15.90	13.64
Beta	0.69	0.81	0.79	1.00
Price to Sales (TTM)	3.54	2.08	3.43	3.85
Price to Book (MRQ)	14.50	8.91	5.16	7.63
Price to Tangible Book (MRQ)	16.03	9.81	8.41	10.73
Price to Cash Flow (TTM)	28.39	20.34	18.05	21.95
Price to Free Cash Flow (TTM)	59.13	43.17	41.10	41.89
% Owned Institutions	52.09	62.06	48.90	61.98

Dividends	Company	Industry	Sector	S&P 500
Dividend Yield	0.32	0.69	1.86	1.67
Dividend Yield - 5 Year Avg.	1.00	0.94	1.50	2.07
Dividend 5 Year Growth Rate	13.39	10.84	6.29	9.82
Payout Ratio (TTM)	13.49	13.61	23.33	32.60

Growth Rates(%)	Company	Industry	Sector	S&P 500
Sales (MRQ) vs Qtr. 1 Yr. Ago	39.68	26.57	21.30	11.16
Sales (TTM) vs TTM 1 Yr. Ago	29.50	21.82	21.10	11.76
Sales - 5 Yr. Growth Rate	17.06	16.81	20.99	14.06
EPS (MRQ) vs Qtr. 1 Yr. Ago	67.46	53.72	24.17	9.99
EPS (TTM) vs TTM 1 Yr. Ago	38.21	33.17	15.94	9.10
EPS - 5 Yr. Growth Rate	21.41	17.00	18.40	18.33
Capital Spending - 5 Yr. Growth Rate	17.65	18.56	26.36	11.12

Financial Strength	Company	Industry	Sector	S&P 500
Quick Ratio (MRQ)	0.84	0.74	0.89	0.95
Current Ratio (MRQ)	1.85	2.03	1.50	1.50
LT Debt to Equity (MRQ)	0.29	0.26	0.88	0.61
Total Debt to Equity (MRQ)	0.35	0.30	0.97	0.94
Interest Coverage (TTM)	NM	10.44	8.14	10.52

Profitability Ratios (%)	Company	Industry	Sector	S&P 500
Gross Margin (TTM)	39.06	34.91	43.28	48.38
Gross Margin - 5 Yr. Avg.	36.86	33.13	42.92	47.88

8/13/98   4:19:34 PM

Comparison for The Gap, Inc.

EBITD Margin (TTM)	17.52	13.30	21.70	21.86
EBITD - 5 Yr. Avg.	17.85	12.71	21.22	21.51
Operating Margin (TTM)	13.40	10.13	11.17	17.83
Operating Margin - 5 Yr. Avg.	13.54	9.35	11.02	17.86
Pre-Tax Margin (TTM)	13.39	9.98	10.06	16.12
Pre-Tax Margin - 5 Yr. Avg.	13.54	9.35	9.63	15.71
Net Profit Margin (TTM)	8.37	6.11	7.32	10.60
Net Profit Margin - 5 Yr. Avg.	8.25	5.73	6.09	10.21
Effective Tax Rate (TTM)	37.50	39.24	37.86	35.94
Effective Tax Rate - 5 Yr. Avg.	39.04	39.01	36.46	35.55

Management Effectiveness (%)	Company	Industry	Sector	S&P 500
Return On Assets (TTM)	19.36	14.99	5.07	8.28
Return Of Assets - 5 Yr. Avg.	17.17	12.49	5.61	8.12
Return On Investment (TTM)	27.42	22.48	7.03	13.48
Return Of Investment - 5 Yr. Avg.	23.33	19.60	7.79	13.02
Return On Equity (TTM)	36.93	26.99	14.51	22.95
Return Of Equity - 5 Yr. Avg.	27.04	20.66	14.57	21.63

Efficiency	Company	Industry	Sector	S&P 500
Revenue/Employee (TTM)	863,747	456,294	2,478,749	397,584
Net Income/Employee (TTM)	72,304	34,071	123,066	59,116
Receivable Turnover (TTM)	NM	55.10	15.22	9.45
Inventory Turnover (TTM)	5.39	4.86	14.34	9.24
Asset Turnover (TTM)	2.31	2.39	1.19	1.09

Companies in the Retail (Apparel) Industry are listed from left to right in order of descending market capitalization.

GPS	TJX	LTD	NOBE	ANF	PSS	ROST	BCF	SUIT
AEOS	CLE	IBI	GDYS	TLB	FTS	ANN	PSUN	FEET
BKE	DBRN	SMRT	CHRS	WTSLA	BEBE	SGE	CACOA	URBN
GCO	FINL	PLCE	SYM	GYMB	MENS	URGI	JBAK	WLSN
SCVL	DEBS	PAUH	CHCS	GADZ	BSMT	SKFB	CATH	CACH
BDOG	TMAN	BFCI	SHOE	JOSB				

Alphabetical Listing of all Industries in the Services Sector.
Advertising
Broadcasting & Cable TV
Business Services
Casinos & Gaming
Communications Services
Hotels & Motels
Motion Pictures
Personal Services
Printing & Publishing
Printing Services
Real Estate Operations
Recreational Activities
Rental & Leasing
Restaurants
Retail (Apparel)
Retail (Catalog & Mail Order)
Retail (Department & Discount)
Retail (Drugs)
Retail (Grocery)

Comparison for The Gap, Inc.
Page 3 of 3

Retail (Home Improvement)
Retail (Specialty)
Retail (Technology)
Schools
Security Systems & Services
Waste Management Services
Glossary of financial terms.

[Home] [Research] [What's Hot] [Screening] [About] [Help]

100hot

Snapshot for The Gap, Inc.   Page 1 of 2

SEARCH FOR
◉ Symb ○ Name

[   ]

[Find Report]

▶ Snapshot
▶ Quotes
▶ News
▶ Charts
▶ Highlights
▶ Performance
▶ Comparison
▶ Projections
▶ Ownership
▶ Financials

▶ More Research

The Gap, Inc.
NYSE: GPS
Sector: Services
Industry: Retail (Apparel)

Market Guide
The Benchmark for Quality Financial Information

Snapshot

The Gap, Inc. is an international specialty retailer operating 2143 stores selling casual apparel, personal care and other accessories for all age groups. GPS's brands include Gap, GapKids, babyGap, Bannana Republic & Old Navy. For the 13 weeks ended 5/2/98, net sales rose 40% to $1.72B. Net income rose 61% to $136.1M. Revenues reflect increased retail selling space and comparable store sales. Earnings reflect an increase in merchandise margins.

The Gap, Inc.
One Harrison Street
San Francisco, CA 94105
Phone: (415) 952-4400
Fax: (415) 427-7007

Sector: Services

Industry: Retail (Apparel)

Employees: 8,100

Market Cap (Mil) $: 24,724.75

Complete Financials: Apr 1998

Updated: 08/15/98

Earnings Announcement: Jul 1998

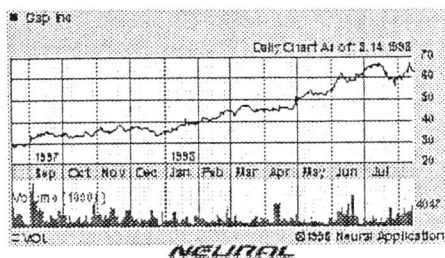

Earnings Announcement: For the 13 weeks ended 08/01/98, revenues were 1,904,970; after tax earnings were 136,874. (Thousands)

OFFICERS: M.S. Drexler, Pres./CEO, D.G. Fisher, Chmn., R.J.Fisher, Exec. VP/COO, John B. Wilson, Exec. VP/COO, Anne B.Gust, Sr. VP/Counsel/Secy., W.R. Hashagen, Sr. VP-Fin./CFO.TRANSFER AGENT: Harris Trust Co. of CA. Co. reinc. 1988 inDE. Direct inquiries to: Director of Investor Relations.

Key Ratios & Statistics

Price & Volume		Valuation Ratios	
Recent Price $	62.94	Price/Earnings (TTM)	38.12*
52 Week High $	68.00	Price/Sales (TTM)	3.30*
52 Week Low $	28.04	Price/Book (MRQ)	14.59
Avg Daily Vol (Mil)	1.02	Price/Cash Flow (TTM)	28.56
Beta	0.69	**Per Share Data**	
Share Related Items		Earnings (TTM) $	1.65*
Mkt. Cap. (Mil) $	24,724.75	Sales (TTM) $	19.09*
Shares Out (Mil)	392.84	Book Value (MRQ) $	4.32
Float (Mil)	255.30	Cash Flow (TTM) $	2.20

Snapshot for The Gap, Inc.

Dividend Information		Cash (MRQ) $	2.13
Yield %	0.32	**Mgmt Effectiveness**	
Annual Dividend	0.20	Return on Equity (TTM)	41.39*
Payout Ratio (TTM) %	12.11	Return on Assets (TTM)	20.70
Financial Strength		Return on Investment (TTM)	29.55*
Quick Ratio (MRQ)	0.84	**Profitability**	
Current Ratio (MRQ)	1.85	Gross Margin (TTM) %	39.06
LT Debt/Equity (MRQ)	0.29	Operating Margin (TTM) %	13.40
Total Debt/Equity (MRQ)	0.35	Profit Margin (TTM) %	8.64*

Mil = Millions MRQ = Most Recent Quarter TTM = Trailing Twelve Months

Glossary of financial terms.

SUMMARY

Analysis of financial statements is a way to gain insights into the relative strength of a company. The statements reveal the effect of management's decision making and the resultant company's performance. The comparison of financial ratios to those of other companies in the same industry will be further evidence of the relative strength or weakness of a company which is being considered for investment or credit. The profitability, liquidity, and risk ratios can provide an early warning of financial trouble ahead. Given the information in this case reading, would you invest in Steve's Stereos?

EXERCISES AND PROBLEMS

Exercises

Exercise 1 Horizontal Analysis. Define horizontal analysis. What is the major benefit of horizontal analysis?

Exercise 2 Vertical Analysis. Define vertical analysis. What is the major benefit of vertical analysis?

Exercise 3 Three Groups of Financial Statement Ratios. List the three groups of financial statement ratios and explain the significance of each group.

Exercise 4 Relating Return on Equity and Return on Assets. What is the major difference between return on equity and return on assets? Which is a better measure of overall company performance? Explain.

Exercise 5 Times Interest Earned Ratio. In the times interest earned ratio, why is earnings before interest and taxes used instead of net income as the numerator ? Explain briefly.

Problems

Problem 1 Library or Web Research. Find in *The Wall Street Journal,* some other financial section of a paper, or on the web, a New York Stock Exchange listing for a large oil company. Then, answer the following questions:

    A. What is the annual dividend paid (per share) for the most recent year?

    B. What is the company's price/earnings ratio?

    C. What was the closing price for the stock you selected and on what date was that?

    D. What is the 52-week high and low price for the company stock you selected?

Problem 2 Library Research on Industry Norms. Go to your college library and find industry norms for either (1) petroleum refining, (2) electronic components and accessories manufacturing, or (3) grocery and meats retailing and find the following:

A. Current ratio

B. Return on sales

C. Debt-to-equity ratio

D. Return on assets

E. Inventory turnover ratio

F. Gross margin ratio

Problem 3 Ratio Analysis for Steve's Stereos. The following ratios have been calculated for Steve's Stereos for the year 2000 based on the information provided for the company in this case reading. Assume that the average common shares outstanding were 65,000 during the year.

Ratio Description	2000
Times Interest Earned (TIE)	8.68 times
Return on Equity (ROE)	15.94%
Return on Assets (ROA)	8.05%
Current Ratio (CR)	1.96
Accounts Receivable Turnover (ART)	6.61 times
Inventory Turnover (ITR)	2.09 times
Return on Sales (ROS)	9.32%
Debt to Equity Ratio (DER)	.88
Earning per Share (EPS)	$.7813

Recompute the ratios shown above, showing the calculation for each ratio. Give a short one-or two-sentence explanation as to the meaning of the ratio.

Problem 4. Horizontal and Ratio Analysis. Shelby Company's condensed income statement and balance sheet for the years 2000 and 1999 follow.

Shelby Company Comparative Income Statement Years Ended December 31		
	2000	**1999**
Net Sales	$ 308,000	$ 242,000
Cost of Sales	200,200	169,400
Gross Margin on Sales	107,800	72,600
Operating Expenses	72,952	45,855
Interest Expense	980	1,078
Earnings Before Income Tax	33,868	25,667
Income Tax at 34%	11,515	8,727
Net Income	$ 22,353	$ 16,940

```
┌─────────────────────────────────────────────────────────────────────────────┐
│                            Shelby Company                                      │
│                       Comparative Balance Sheet                                │
│                            December 31                                         │
```

	2000	1999
Assets		
Current Assets		
Cash	$ 2,156	$ 1,972
Accounts Receivable, net	15,960	9,389
Merchandise Inventory	33,401	35,091
Prepaid Expenses	2,076	2,876
Total Current Assets	53,593	49,328
Property and Equipment		
Land	63,200	63,200
Building	169,600	169,600
Equipment	28,400	13,872
	261,200	246,672
Accumulated Depreciation	(166,800)	(159,688)
Total Property & Equip.	94,400	86,984
Long-Term Deposits	1,398	487
Total Assets	$ 149,391	$ 136,799
Liabilities & Stockholders' Equity		
Current Liabilities		
Accounts Payable	$ 8,029	$ 7,027
Current Portion Long-term Debt	1,000	1,000
Accrued Expenses	5,054	4,031
Income Taxes Payable	6,881	2,469
Total Current Liabilities	20,964	14,527
Long-term Liabilities		
Long-term Notes Payable	10,000	11,000
Total Liabilities	30,964	25,527
Stockholders' Equity		
Common Stock, par $100	12,000	12,000
Retained Earnings	106,427	99,272
Total Stockholders' Equity	118,427	111,272
Total Liabilities & Stockholders' Equity	$ 149,391	$ 136,799

Use the information in Shelby Company's financial statements to do the following:

A. Perform a horizontal analysis of the income statement.

B. For 2000 determine the (1) return on assets, (2) current ratio, (3) gross profit margin ratio, (4) inventory turnover ratio, and (5) debt-to-equity ratio.

C. From your analysis above, what three items create concerns for you?

Problem 5   Vertical Analysis.   Using the information given in Problem 4 for Shelby Company complete the following:

A. Perform a vertical analysis for Shelby Company's balance sheet.

B. From your analysis above, what three items create concerns for you?

Case 4-8

FINANCIAL STATEMENT ANALYSIS: FOOD FOR THOUGHT

Case Objectives

1. Learn horizontal analysis of financial statements.
2. Learn vertical analysis of financial statements.
3. Evaluate profitability of companies using financial statement ratios.
4. Evaluate liquidity of companies using financial statement ratios.
5. Evaluate financial risk using financial statement ratios.

Decision: Based upon an analysis of financial statements using key ratios, which company appears to be a better investment?

Rachel and Martin are college students who are planning to invest $500 each in a stock investment. They plan to pool their funds to purchase the shares of one company, although they are cognizant of the added risk of not diversifying their investments. Rachel and Martin expect to maintain their investment for one to three years. They have narrowed their search for a company in which to invest to two companies in the food industry.

Exhibits C4-8.1 and C4-8.2 contain the financial statements of Midwest Food Company, which supplies restaurants and institutions (schools, hospitals, and prisons) with various processed food products. Exhibits C4-8.3 and C4-8.4 contain the financial statements for National Food Corporation, a maker of breakfast cereals and baking products.

Note that all of the numbers are in thousands as indicated by the notation (000s omitted). This simplifies the financial statement presentation. The rounding to the nearest thousand is not considered a material distortion of the actual values contained in the company records.

Both company's shares are publicly traded and have a price-earnings ratio of 10. Rachel and Martin want to invest $1,000 in the shares of one of the two companies. They ask you to recommend which company is a better investment.

Exhibit C4-8.1
Midwest Food Company
Comparative Balance Sheets
December 31

(000s Omitted)	2000	1999
Assets		
Current Assets		
Cash	$ 32,154	$ 37,865
Accounts Receivable, net	123,460	100,643
Merchandise Inventory	102,013	96,452
Other Assets	12,540	10,005
Total Current Assets	270,167	244,965
Long-Term Investments	2,000	2,000
Property and Equipment		
Land	40,826	40,826
Building	197,846	192,846
Equipment	28,023	17,984
	266,695	251,656
Accumulated Depreciation	(10,932)	(9,865)
Total Property & Equipment	255,763	241,791
Total Assets	$ 527,930	$ 488,756
Liabilities & Stockholders' Equity		
Current Liabilities		
Short Term Debt	$ 42,646	$ 36,200
Accounts Payable	108,452	90,971
Accrued Expenses	13,951	14,578
Accrued Income Taxes	12,338	11,695
Total Current Liabilities	177,387	153,444
Long-Term Debt	34,883	34,883
Total Liabilities	212,270	188,327
Stockholders' Equity		
Common Stock, par $1.00	181,750	181,750
Contributed Capital	116,646	116,646
Retained Earnings	17,264	2,033
Total Stockholders' Equity	315,660	300,429
Total Liabilities & Stockholders' Equity	$ 527,930	$ 488,756

Exhibit C4-8.2
Midwest Food Company
Comparative Income Statements
Years Ended December 31

(000s omitted)	2000	1999
Net Sales	$816,564	$792,648
Cost of Goods Sold	563,743	555,323
Gross Margin on Sales	252,821	237,325
Selling and Administrative	129,859	127,983
Interest Expense	12,652	10,852
Earnings Before Income Tax	110,310	98,490
Income Tax at 40%	44,124	39,396
Net Income	$ 66,186	$ 59,094

Exhibit C4-8.3
National Food Corporation
Comparative Income Statements
Years Ended December 31

(000s omitted)	2000	1999
Net Sales	$ 1,465,823	$ 1,325,080
Cost of Sales	1,068,744	960,323
Gross Margin on Sales	397,079	364,757
Operating Expenses	215,969	210,574
Interest Expense	20,645	18,659
Earnings Before Income Tax	160,465	135,524
Income Tax at 40%	64,186	54,210
Net Income	$ 96,279	$ 81,314

Exhibit C4-8.4
National Food Corporation
Comparative Balance Sheets
December 31

(000s Omitted)	2000	1999
Assets		
Current Assets		
Cash	$ 31,649	$ 18,526
Accounts Receivable, net	149,658	165,836
Merchandise Inventory	189,647	185,323
Prepaid Expenses	13,790	18,233
Total Current Assets	384,744	387,918
Property and Equipment		
Land	56,254	56,254
Building	158,642	148,423
Equipment	18,647	15,987
	233,543	220,664
Accumulated Depreciation	(23,982)	(19,643)
Total Property & Equipment	209,561	201,021
Total Assets	$ 594,305	$ 588,939
Liabilities & Stockholders' Equity		
Current Liabilities		
Accounts Payable	$ 81,325	$ 88,225
Current Portion Long-term Debt	22,000	22,000
Accrued Expenses	30,235	25,977
Income Taxes Payable	9,645	9,651
Total Current Liabilities	143,205	145,853
Long-term Notes Payable	75,000	75,000
Total Liabilities	218,205	220,853
Stockholders' Equity		
Common Stock, par $1.00	195,000	195,000
Contributed Capital	148,972	148,972
Retained Earnings	32,128	24,114
Total Stockholders' Equity	376,100	368,086
Total Liabilities & Stockholders' Equity	$ 594,305	$ 588,939

Requirements

1. Prepare a vertical analysis of both company's income statements for the year 2000. A format has been provided in Exhibit C4-8.5. Are there any items for either company that need to be investigated further?

2. Prepare a horizontal analysis for the main categories of both company's balance sheets for changes from 1999 to 2000. A format has been provided in Exhibit C4-8.6. Are there any items for either company that need to be investigated further?

3. Calculate the return on equity, accounts receivable turnover, debt-to-equity, and earnings per share ratios for both companies.

4. Assume that both company's shares have a price/earnings ratio of 10. Write a two-to three-paragraph statement to Rachel and Martin concluding in a purchase recommendation.

Exhibit C4-8.5
Template for Requirement 1

Midwest Food Company				
Vertical Analysis of the Income Statement				
Years Ended December 31				
(000s omitted)	**2000**	**1999**	**Vertical Analysis 2000**	**Vertical Analysis 1999**
Net Sales	$ 816,564	$ 792,648		
Cost of Goods Sold	563,743	555,323		
Gross Margin on Sales	252,821	237,325		
Selling and Administrative	129,859	127,983		
Interest Expense	12,652	10,852		
Earnings Before Income Tax	110,310	98,490		
Income Tax at 40%	44,124	39,396		
Net Income	$ 66,186	$ 59,094		

National Food Corporation				
Vertical Analysis of the Income Statement				
Years Ended December 31				
(000s omitted)	**2000**	**1999**	**Vertical Analysis 2000**	**Vertical Analysis 1999**
Net Sales	$ 1,465,823	$ 1,325,080		
Cost of Sales	1,068,744	960,323		
Gross Margin on Sales	397,079	364,757		
Operating Expenses	215,969	210,574		
Interest Expense	20,645	18,659		
Earnings Before Income Tax	160,465	135,524		
Income Tax at 40%	64,186	54,210		
Net Income	$ 96,279	$ 81,314		

Exhibit C4-8.6
Template for Requirement 2
Horizontal Analysis

(000s omitted)	Midwest Foods			National Foods		
	2000	1999	% Change	2000	1999	% Change
Assets						
Current Assets	$ 270,167	$ 244,965		$ 384,744	$ 387,918	
Long-Term Investments	2,000	2,000		-	-	
Property Plant and Equipment	255,763	241,791		209,561	201,021	
Total Assets	$ 527,930	$ 488,756		$ 594,305	$ 588,939	
Liabilities and Stockholders' Equity						
Current Liabilities	$ 177,387	$ 153,444		$ 143,205	$ 145,853	
Long-Term Liabilities	34,883	34,883		75,000	75,000	
Total Liabilities	212,270	188,327		218,205	220,853	
Stockholders' Equity	315,660	300,429		376,100	368,086	
Total Liabilities and Stockholders' Equity	$ 527,930	$ 488,756		$ 594,305	$ 588,939	

Group Assignment 4-8

THROUGH THE LOOKING GLASS

Group Number _____ **Group members present and participating:**

_____

_____

Objectives

1. To be able to evaluate companies based on the dividends per share.
2. To be able to identify other factors which might be considered important to potential investors.

Requirements

1. Assume that Midwest Food Company paid one dividend during the year to the shareholders who owned shares at December 31, 2000. Using the information provided in Case 4-8, calculate the amount of the dividend per share. Show all computations.

_____

_____

_____

_____

2. Using the information provided in Case 4-8, calculate the amount of the current ratio for year 2000 for each company. Which company has the best current ratio?

_____

_____

_____

_____

3. There are many publicly traded companies that have maintained a policy of paying either a very minor dividend or no dividend at all but still these companies have many investors. Why might investors want to invest in such companies?

_____

_____

_____

_____

_____

Case Reading 4-9

ANALYZING FOREIGN COMPANY
FINANCIAL STATEMENTS[1]

INTRODUCTION

This case reading introduces how financial statements of foreign companies may differ from those of U.S. companies. Some of these differences are discussed below, along with some of the possible approaches for dealing with those differences. The exercises, problems, and case for this case reading assume that you have read the material in Case Reading 4-8 concerning financial statement analysis.

LANGUAGE

Many foreign company financial statements and their footnotes are in the language of the home country. Some companies may be able to provide an English translation upon request. Otherwise the reader may need to arrange locally for a translation. Translation services may be available through university language departments. Commercial translation businesses are generally listed in the phone book yellow pages.

Even if the reader has some familiarity with the language of the country, the foreign company financial statements may use specialized business and accounting terms that the reader does not understand. Even financial statements in English may present a language problem; terminology used by British companies differs in several respects from terms used by U.S. companies. For instance, the U.S. "Sales Revenue" is comparable to the British "Turnover." The reader is advised to become better acquainted with such terminology differences; business reference librarians may be able to suggest possible printed and electronic resources.

GENERALLY ACCEPTED ACCOUNTING
PRINCIPLES (GAAP)

Many foreign company financial statements are prepared according to the generally accepted accounting principles of the home country, rather than U.S. GAAP. Foreign GAAP may be absolutely appropriate and legally required for the foreign company, but the GAAP differences may undermine a reader's ability to meaningfully compare U.S. companies with the foreign company. Some foreign company financial statements may provide a reconciliation to U.S. GAAP in a footnote. If the foreign company has shares of its stock listed on one of the U.S. stock exchanges, the company is required to file a Form 20-F with the Securities and Exchange Commission. The foreign company must either (a) prepare its financial statements according to U.S. GAAP or (b) explain the differences between the foreign accounting principles and U.S. GAAP and then calculate what its net income would have been if U.S. accounting principles had been followed. This reconciliation might enable the reader to calculate what adjustments to the balance sheet would be implied so that the foreign

---

[1] This Case Reading was written by Dianna R. Coker of St Mary's University in San Antonio, Texas.

company's balance sheet numbers would also be comparable to one prepared using U.S. GAAP.

The reader of the statements may wonder whether it would be cost-beneficial to research the GAAP differences between the U.S. and the foreign country of interest. Such a comparison would be worthwhile only if one were going to frequently analyzing financial statements of that country. Some financial statements state that the reports have been prepared in agreement with International GAAP, which is a voluntary set of accounting principles developed by the International Accounting Standards Committee. The Committee is made up of accounting organization representatives of many nations. International GAAP is comparable in many, but not all, ways to U.S. GAAP. The reader may decide it would be cost-beneficial to take the time to research the differences between U.S. and International GAAP if he or she expects to encounter many such statements. If, however, the reader is interested only in a specific foreign company, the possibility of hiring a local office of an international CPA firm to analyze the differences should be investigated.

One particularly interesting difference between U.S. GAAP and the accounting principles of a foreign country is the Mexican requirement for companies to prepare reports using inflationary accounting because of recurring periods of severe inflation and the continued devaluation of the Mexican peso. The majority of Mexican accounting principles followed throughout the year are comparable to U.S. GAAP; however, before the year-end publication of Mexican financial statements all primary financial statements must be restated to show the effects of inflation. Among other things, financial statement amounts are reported in pesos of current purchasing power by applying factors derived from the Mexican National Consumer Price Index. Because of hyperinflation, many countries in Central and South America use inflation-adjusted financial statements for external reporting purposes.

Inflationary accounting is very complicated, and restating peso amounts makes the absolute values reported difficult to interpret. The reader may, however, use ratios to analyze the relative size of the restated peso amounts. Because reported amounts for all years (as in comparative balance sheets) are restated using the same index, the amounts still retain some of their original relationship to each other, which can be revealed through common ratio analysis by applying the concepts discussed in Case Reading 4-8.

DISCLOSURE LEVELS

Some foreign company financial statements, even though prepared in accordance with U.S. GAAP or reconciled to U.S. GAAP, may not provide the wealth of disclosures common to U.S. companies. Because of international differences in disclosure requirements, it is not safe to assume that the absence of disclosure about a certain topic (such as potential losses from pending lawsuits) indicates that the company in question has no such potential losses. In this case no news may *not* be good news. The reader is advised to stay current with business news in the foreign country of interest and do a search for news articles about the company of interest. It may be possible to discuss disclosure concerns with a business reference librarian, an accountant familiar with the foreign GAAP in question, or someone familiar with the particular industry of the foreign company in question.

CURRENCY

Many foreign company financial statements are denominated in the currency of the home country, such as new pesos in Mexico, franc in France, and yen in Japan. If the statements have been prepared according to U.S. accounting principles but is in a foreign currency, the reader may still calculate the common ratios and perform vertical and horizontal analysis as explained in Case Reading 4-8. The results should be the same as if these underlying numbers had all been translated into U.S. dollars. If the reader still wishes to see the financial statements in U.S. dollars to get a better feel for the relative size of the companies being compared, he or she can ask the company whether there is an available version of the statements denominated in U.S. dollars. If the company has filed a Form 20-F with the Securities and Exchange Commission, check it to see if the financial statement information in the Form 20-F has been converted into U.S. dollars. Form 20-F is available through Lexis-Nexis[2] on EDGARP, a Securities and Exchange Commission database. If no U.S. dollar version is available, the reader may translate the currency using appropriate currency exchange rates. The balance sheet normally uses the exchange rate in effect at the balance sheet date and the income statement and statement of cash flows generally use the average exchange rate for the year.[3] These rates are available through past issues of the *The Wall Street Journal* or on the internet.

Another aspect of foreign company financial statements that should be disclosed is the extent to which the foreign company may have receivables or payables denominated in a currency other than its home currency. If a receivable or payable is denominated in a foreign currency (receivable or payable in other than the home currency), the company has a potential gain or loss that may not be disclosed in the financial statements. For example, a French company could sell materials to a Japanese company and agree to be paid in yen, the Japanese currency. On the French company books the receivable will be stated at the value of yen translated into francs at the date of sale. However, if the receivable is collected 60 days later when the yen has fallen 10 percent in value to the franc, the French company will have a foreign exchange loss of 10 percent of the sales price of the materials. Companies that conduct large amounts of business denominated in foreign currencies will usually hedge the foreign currency exposure so that large currency losses cannot happen. This topic will be more thoroughly discussed in the second semester book of this series, *Using Management Accounting Information: A Decision Case Approach.*

FORMAT OF FINANCIAL STATEMENTS

Although most foreign company financial statements will report a balance sheet and income statement, and many will prepare a statement of cash flows, these reports may be in an unfamiliar format. For instance, on British balance sheets assets are listed in order of ascending liquidity so that cash is listed last, whereas cash is listed first in U.S. reports. Although thoughtful examination of most foreign company statements will reveal many format differences, the reader may also wish to consult a business reference for sources discussing international report formats.

UNDERLYING DIFFERENCES IN BUSINESS PRACTICES

Even if a foreign company financial statement is in English, U.S. dollars, and a standard format prepared using U.S. GAAP, there still may be important differences about how business was actually transacted. Not being familiar with the business practices and the culture of a foreign country, a reader may inappropriately interpret a given statement. This misinterpretation occurs because underlying events and business practices may have a

---

[2] Lexis-Nexis is often available in college libraries.
[3] Some items on the balance sheet may be translated using rates other than those on the date of the balance sheet. Income statement and statement of cash flows items may be translated using rates other than the average for the year. Such complexity is beyond the scope of this course.

significance for the foreign company quite different from the significance they would have for a U.S. company. One example is debt in Japanese companies. Japanese companies tend to belong to one of several "keiretsus" or affiliated groups of companies, each keiretsu generally including a bank which is particularly interested in providing loans to its fellow keiretsu members. Much of the money borrowed and reported by Japanese companies is considered by them to be short-term loans, but in fact these short-term loans are likely to be renewed. A nine-month loan, for instance, is likely to be converted to another nine-month loan on its due date, which makes the loan economically equivalent to long-term debt. Also, carrying a large amount of debt is seen in Japan as a good thing, signifying lenders' confidence in the ability of the company to repay large amounts. The accepted business practice in Japan, therefore, is to carry much long-term debt while classifying it as short-term debt. This should be kept in mind when interpreting ratios that examine the debt structure of a Japanese company, particularly if the ratios are compared with ratios of other non-Japanese companies.

Another example of business practice differences is related to the differences in assets and liabilities which may result from differences in foreign laws and regulations. For instance, if a foreign country does not require companies to remediate (clean up) toxic waste dumps which they have created, then the foreign company may not consider that it even has a liability to report. A comparable U.S. company, however, knowing that the Environmental Protection Agency requires such remediation, would report a liability for the amount required to clean up the toxic site. It is advisable to become familiar with business differences and laws affecting businesses. Keeping current on international business news and researching the particular business practices of the country of interest are essential. Various texts are available on the finer points of analyzing foreign company financial statements. Several sources should be consulted before reaching a conclusion about any given ratio you have calculated.

SUMMARY

This case reading discusses complications inherent in the analysis of foreign company financial statements and suggests possible approaches that readers of these financial statements may take to address such complications. The student is encouraged to approach the analysis of foreign statements with a healthy understanding of the many potential problems arising from the more obvious distinctions from domestic (U.S.) financial statements (language, terminology, report format, and currencies), as well as underlying differences in accounting principles, disclosure levels, and business practices. In dealing with foreign companies, foreign exchange, and foreign company financial statements there are many risks that are not present when dealing only with U.S. companies and dollars.

EXERCISES AND PROBLEMS

Exercises

Exercise 1   Understanding Foreign Company Financial Statements.   Comment on the accuracy of the following statement: "Once foreign company financial statements are translated into English, a knowledgeable businessperson should be able to understand the foreign company financial statements as well as he or she understands U.S. company financial statements."

Exercise 2   Different Generally Accepted Accounting Principles.   Foreign company financial statements may be prepared under different sets of generally accepted accounting principles (GAAP). A foreign company could prepare its financial statements under at least three different sets of GAAP. What are the three sets of GAAP, and which set would be most difficult to understand/interpret?

Exercise 3 Differences Between U.S. and Foreign Company Financial Statements. List and explain five significant differences between financial statements prepared in the United States and foreign company financial statements, i.e., what typically are the most significant differences between these financial statements?

Problem

Problem 1 Library or Web Research. Find a foreign company financial statement in your library, on the web, or at a large brokerage house office. List the three most significant questions you have after reviewing the foreign company financial statements. Be specific.

Case 4-9

STEVE'S STEREOS GOES
INTERNATIONAL[1]

Case Objectives

1. To understand the nature of foreign companies and how the operations of foreign entities can be compared to each other.
2. To be able to use horizontal and vertical analysis to compare the financial information of businesses.
3. To be able to use ratio analysis to compare the financial information of businesses.

Decision: Which company should Steve Stereos target for its expansion into the international marketplace, Tokyo Trendy or Ruidoso Stereo?

1. Case Reading 4-8 illustrates trend and ratio analysis using the comparative financial statements of Steve's Stereos. At the beginning of year 2000, Steve's Stereos is considering expansion of its operations to other countries in order to improve its operating performance ratio and return on equity. To gain better insight about the existing competition, the vice president of finance for Steve's Stereos has suggested examining the financial statements of two successful ventures, one in Tokyo, Japan, and one in Mexico City, Mexico. She selected these two cities because they possess the largest markets in their respective countries for electronic equipment. Both operations are family owned and have several store locations within the cities.

2. Exhibits C4-9.1 and C4-9.2 show the comparative income statements for Tokyo Trendy and Ruidoso Stereos, respectively. The balance sheet for Tokyo Trendy is shown in Exhibit C4-9.3; and Exhibit C4-9.4 shows the balance sheet for Ruidoso Stereo. Notice that the financial statements for the Tokyo company, Tokyo Trendy Electronic Equipment, are in yen and those for the Mexican entity, Ruidoso Stereos, are in new pesos.

3. Steve's Stereos hopes for great success with its future international expansion, but needs your help in analyzing these foreign companies to determine which of the two companies it should target for future expansion into the international marketplace.

---

[1] This Case was written by Mary E. Harston of St. Mary's University in San Antonio, Texas.

Exhibit C4-9.1
Tokyo Trendy
Income Statement

Tokyo Trendy Electronic Equipment Comparative Income Statements in Yen Years Ended December 31		
	2000	**1999**
Net Sales	66,217,500	61,357,500
Cost of Goods Sold	39,068,325	36,936,000
Gross Margin on Sales	27,149,175	24,421,500
Selling and Administrative	10,605,023	11,071,700
Interest Expense	1,402,822	1,238,680
Earnings Before Income Tax	15,141,330	12,111,120
Income Tax at 40%	6,056,532	4,844,448
Net Income	9,084,798	7,266,672

Exhibit C4-9.2
Ruidoso Stereo
Income Statement

Ruidoso Stereos Comparative Income Statements in New Pesos Years Ended December 31		
	2000	**1999**
Net Sales	1,308,000	1,212,000
Cost of Sales	863,280	848,400
Gross Margin on Sales	444,720	363,600
Operating Expenses	166,952	163,855
Interest Expense	9,800	10,780
Employees' Statutory Profit Sharing	16,168	11,997
Earnings Before Income Tax	251,800	176,968
Income Tax at 34%	85,612	60,169
Net Income	166,188	116,799

Exhibit C4-9.3
Tokyo Trendy
Balance Sheets

Tokyo Trendy Electronic Equipment Comparative Balance Sheets in Yen December 31		
	2000	1999
Assets		
Current Assets		
Cash	6,297,282	5,047,000
Notes & Accounts Receivable, net	9,185,384	8,012,318
Merchandise Inventory	2,626,412	2,644,600
Other Assets	6,689,834	3,480,973
Total Current Assets	24,798,912	19,184,891
Long-term Investments	3,000,000	3,000,000
Property and Equipment		
Land	11,625,627	8,262,000
Building	25,557,133	18,711,000
Equipment	9,032,671	7,536,646
	46,215,431	34,509,646
Accumulated Depreciation	(11,132,788)	(6,728,565)
	35,082,643	27,781,081
Total Assets	62,881,555	49,965,972
Liabilities & Stockholders' Equity		
Current Liabilities		
Short Term Debt	11,912,437	9,200,900
Accounts Payable	1,235,576	1,216,118
Accrued Expenses	1,391,596	864,545
Accrued Income Taxes	3,028,266	2,422,224
Total Current Liabilities	17,567,875	13,703,787
Long-Term Liabilities		
Long-Term Debt	6,288,156	4,996,597
Retirement Benefits	1,296,591	1,286,005
Total Long-Term Liabilities	7,584,747	6,282,602
Total Liabilities	25,152,622	19,986,389
Stockholders' Equity		
Common Stock, par 100	6,075,000	6,075,000
Capital Surplus	8,368,728	8,368,728
Legal Reserve	136,272	109,000
Retained Earnings	23,148,933	15,426,855
Total Stockholders' Equity	37,728,933	29,979,583
Total Liabilities & Stockholders' Equity	62,881,555	49,965,972

Exhibit C4-9.4
Ruidoso Stereos
Balance Sheets

Ruidoso Stereos Comparative Balance Sheets in New Pesos December 31	2000	1999
Assets		
Current Assets		
Cash	21,566	19,726
Accounts Receivable, net	159,600	133,899
Merchandise Inventory	334,012	165,091
Prepaid Expenses	20,760	28,760
Total Current Assets	535,938	347,476
Property and Equipment		
Land	163,200	163,200
Building	369,600	369,600
Equipment	230,400	118,872
	763,200	651,672
Accumulated Depreciation	(267,800)	(206,688)
Total Property and Equipment	495,400	444,984
Guarantee Deposits	3,986	2,487
Total Assets	1,035,324	794,947
Liabilities & Stockholders' Equity		
Current Liabilities		
Accounts Payable	188,029	123,027
Current Portion Long-Term Debt	10,000	10,000
Accrued Expenses	50,541	40,314
Income Taxes Payable	7,134	5,014
Employees' Statutory Profit Sharing	16,168	11,997
Total Current Liabilities	271,872	190,352
Long-term Liabilities		
Long-Term Notes Payable	100,000	110,000
Total Liabilities	371,872	300,352
Stockholders' Equity		
Common Stock, par $100	120,000	120,000
Legal Reserve	54,497	49,867
Retained Earnings	488,955	324,728
Total Stockholders' Equity	663,452	494,595
Total Liabilities & Stockholders' Equity	1,035,324	794,947

Requirements

Prepare the following for the foreign companies, using either a spreadsheet or word processor. If you use a spreadsheet, also print out cell formulas with row and column labels. If you use a word processor show all computations and equations used to obtain your answer. Assume each set of comparative financial statements is presented in the local currency of each entity's country, the yen for the Japanese company and new peso for the Mexican company.

1. For both companies analyze the case data to determine whether the gross margins, operating expenses, cash, accounts receivable, and accounts payable are improving or deteriorating. What is the specific amount of growth or decline of each item? A template has been provided in Exhibit C4-9.5 as one possible way to gather the information needed to answer the questions.

2. Are the gross margins and net incomes for both companies similar in 2000? What income statement items might be causing any noted differences? A template has been provided in Exhibit C4-9.6 as one possible way to gather the information needed to answer the questions.

3. Compute the following ratios for each entity for the year 2000:

   a. Return on Equity
   b. Accounts Receivable Turnover
   c. Debt-to-Equity
   d. Earnings Per Share

4. Based upon your analysis above, what do you think are the greatest problem areas for the Tokyo company? the Mexican company?

5. Explain which company you think Steve's Stereos should select for their expansion into the international marketplace.

Exhibit C4-9.5
Template for Requirement 1

Tokyo Trendy

	2000	1999	Change	%	Comments
Gross Margin on Sales					
Selling and Administrative					
Cash					
Notes and Accounts Receivable, net					
Accounts Payable					

Ruidoso Stereos

	2000	1999	Change	%	Comments
Gross Margin on Sales					
Operating Expenses					
Cash					
Accounts Receivable, net					
Accounts Payable					

Exhibit C4-9.6
Template for Requirement 2

Tokyo Trendy Electronic Equipment
Comparative Income Statements in Yen
Years Ended December 31

	2000	1999	Vertical Analysis 2000
Net Sales	66,217,500	61,357,500	
Cost of Goods Sold	39,068,325	36,936,000	
Gross Margin on Sales	27,149,175	24,421,500	
Selling and Administrative	10,605,023	11,071,700	
Interest Expense	1,402,822	1,238,680	
Earnings Before Income Tax	15,141,330	12,111,120	
Income Tax at 40%	6,056,532	4,844,448	
Net Income	9,084,798	7,266,672	

Ruidoso Stereos
Comparative Income Statements in New Pesos
Years Ended December 31

	2000	1999	Vertical Analysis 2000
Net Sales	1,308,000	1,212,000	
Cost of Sales	863,280	848,400	
Gross Margin on Sales	444,720	363,600	
Operating Expenses	166,952	163,855	
Interest Expense	9,800	10,780	
Employees' Statutory Profit Sharing	16,168	11,997	
Earnings Before Income Tax	251,800	176,968	
Income Tax at 34%	85,612	60,169	
Net Income	166,188	116,799	

Group Assignment 4-9

WHAT IN THE WORLD?[1]

Group Number _____ Group members present and participating:

_____

_____

Objectives

1. To understand the nature of foreign companies and how foreign operations can be compared to each other and a U.S. company.
2. To be able to use horizontal and vertical analysis to compare the financial information of foreign businesses with that of a U.S. company.
3. To be able to use ratio analysis to compare the financial information of foreign businesses with that of a U.S. company.

Requirements

1. Refer to the financial information from Case Reading 4-8 regarding Steve's Stereos and your prior individual analysis of the two foreign companies. Complete Exhibit G4-9.1.

Exhibit G4-9.1

	Tokyo Trendy Electronic Equipment	Ruidoso Slick Stereos	Steve's Stereos
Gross Margin Trend		22.31%	6.97%
Operating Expenses Trend		1.89%	43.01%
Accounts Receivable Trend		19.19%	17.11%
Accounts Payable Trend		52.84%	8.47%
Gross Margin %		34.00%	39.45%
Net Income %		12.71%	9.32%
Return on Equity		28.70%	15.94%
Accounts Receivable Turnover		8.91	6.61
Debt-to Equity Ratio		56.05%	88.20%
Earnings per Share		138.49	$ 0.78

The earnings per share calculation for Steve's Stereos assumes that there are an average of 65,000 shares outstanding during the year.

---

[1] This Group Assignment was written by Mary E. Harston of St. Mary's University in San Antonio, Texas.

2. Are the operations of Tokyo Trendy Electronic Equipment as successful as those of Steve's Stereos? Are the operations of Ruidoso Stereos as successful as those of Steve's Stereos? Why or why not? Use the data in Exhibit G4-9.1 to substantiate your conclusions.

_____

_____

_____

_____

_____

_____

_____

_____

_____

_____

_____

3. During your comparison of the foreign financial statements with those of Steve's Stereos, did you notice any differences in the format or accounts of the financial reports? List four of the differences you noticed.

_____

_____

_____

_____

_____

Module 4

Peer Evaluation of Group Members	Class Section	Group No.

Evaluator's Name _____

In the table below, please indicate your estimate, in percentage terms, of the contributions that individual group members made to each of the group assignments listed. Each column should add to 100 percent. For example, if there are five members in your group and all were present for group assignment 4-3, you would divide up the 100 percent among the five members, including yourself. If you felt that all group members were prepared to discuss the assignment and contributed equally to the solution, you would give each person 20 percent. If only four members were present, and you felt that one particular member contributed twice as much as the other three, you would give the heavy contributor 40 percent and the other three members 20 percent. The group member who was absent should be listed and given a zero percent.

Group Members (List)	Group Assignment Number					
	4-3	4-4	4-5	4-7	4-8	4-9
Myself						
Totals	100	100	100	100	100	100

Fill in this sheet after each group exercise is completed and turn in with the last group exercise in Module 4.

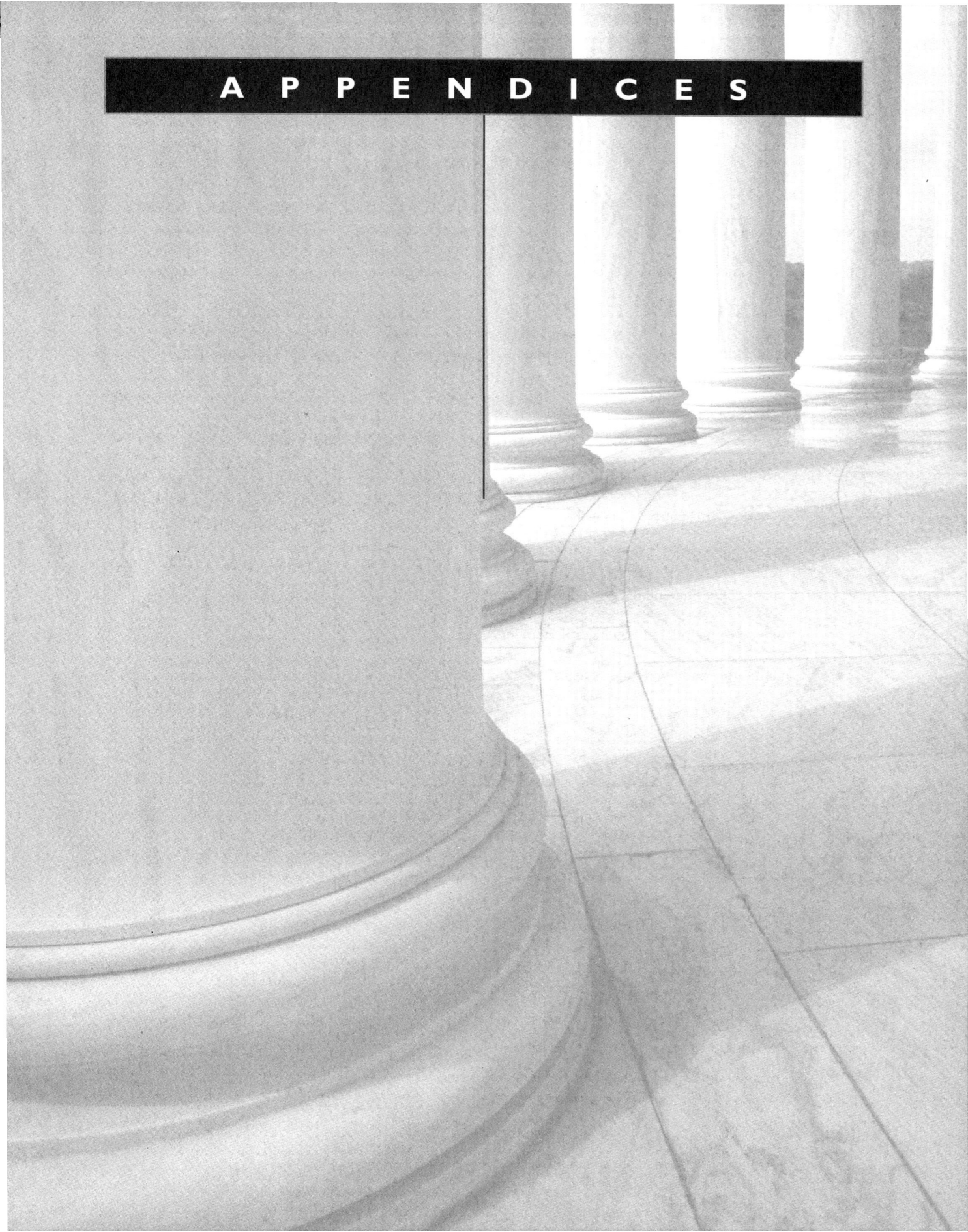

APPENDICES

Appendix A

GAP INC. ANNUAL REPORT

Financial Contents

Net Sales

88: 1.3 | 89: 1.6 | 90: 1.9 | 91: 2.5 | 92: 3.0 | 93: 3.3 | 94: 3.7 | 95: 4.4 | 96: 5.3 | 97: 6.5

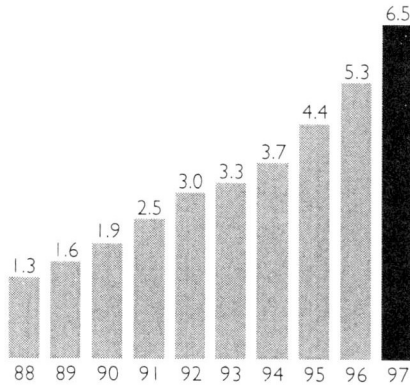

Net Sales
(in billions of dollars)
10-year CAGR=20%

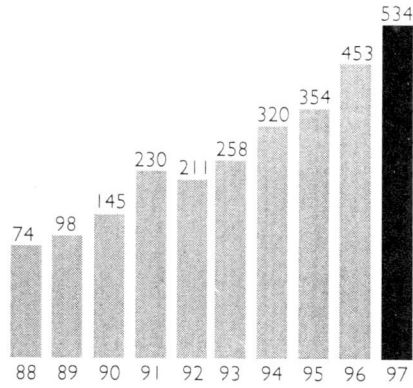

Net Earnings

88: 74 | 89: 98 | 90: 145 | 91: 230 | 92: 211 | 93: 258 | 94: 320 | 95: 354 | 96: 453 | 97: 534

Net Earnings
(in millions of dollars)
10-year CAGR=23%

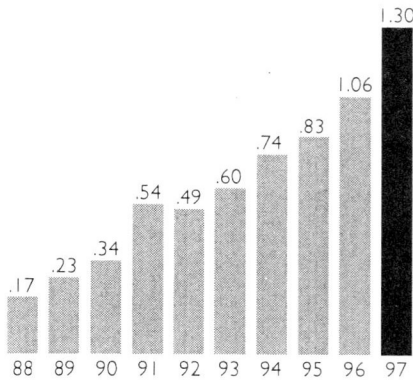

Earnings Per Share

88: .17 | 89: .23 | 90: .34 | 91: .54 | 92: .49 | 93: .60 | 94: .74 | 95: .83 | 96: 1.06 | 97: 1.30

Earnings Per Share–Diluted
(in dollars)
10-year CAGR=23%

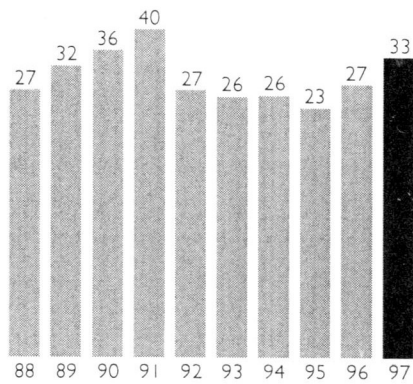

Return on Average Shareholders' Equity

88: 27 | 89: 32 | 90: 36 | 91: 40 | 92: 27 | 93: 26 | 94: 26 | 95: 23 | 96: 27 | 97: 33

Return on Average Shareholders' Equity
(percent)

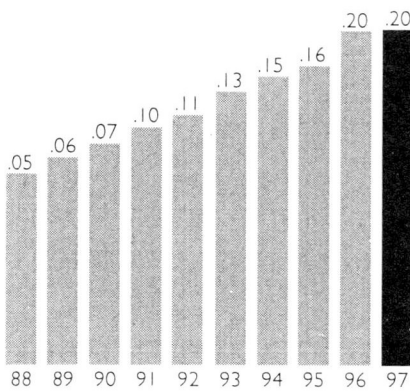

Dividends Per Share

88: .05 | 89: .06 | 90: .07 | 91: .10 | 92: .11 | 93: .13 | 94: .15 | 95: .16 | 96: .20 | 97: .20

Dividends Per Share
(in dollars)

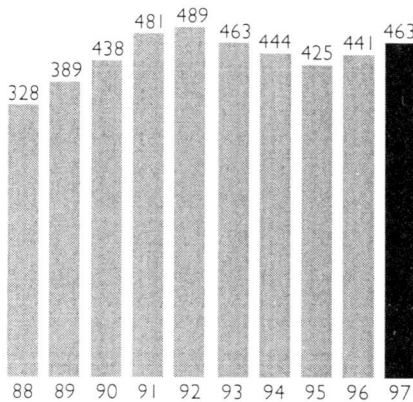

Sales Per Average Gross Square Foot

88: 328 | 89: 389 | 90: 438 | 91: 481 | 92: 489 | 93: 463 | 94: 444 | 95: 425 | 96: 441 | 97: 463

Sales Per Average Gross Square Foot[1]
(in dollars)

Ten-Year Selected Financial Data

	Compound Annual Growth Rate			1997 52 weeks	1996 52 weeks
	3-year	5-year	10-year		
OPERATING RESULTS ($000)					
Net sales	21%	17%	20%	$6,507,825	$5,284,381
Cost of goods sold and occupancy expenses, excluding depreciation and amortization	—	—	—	3,775,957	3,093,709
Percentage of net sales	—	—	—	58.0%	58.5%
Depreciation and amortization[a]	—	—	—	$ 245,584	$ 191,457
Operating expenses	—	—	—	1,635,017	1,270,138
Net interest (income) expense	—	—	—	(2,975)	(19,450)
Earnings before income taxes	17	20	21	854,242	748,527
Percentage of net sales	—	—	—	13.1%	14.2%
Income taxes	—	—	—	$ 320,341	$ 295,668
Net earnings	19	20	23	533,901	452,859
Percentage of net sales	—	—	—	8.2%	8.6%
Cash dividends	—	—	—	$ 79,503	$ 83,854
Capital expenditures	—	—	—	483,114	375,838
PER SHARE DATA					
Net earnings–basic[b]	21%	21%	23%	$1.35	$1.09
Net earnings–diluted[c]	21	22	23	1.30	1.06
Cash dividends	—	—	—	.20	.20
Shareholders' equity (book value)[d]	—	—	—	4.03	4.02
FINANCIAL POSITION ($000)					
Property and equipment, net	18%	16%	24%	$1,365,246	$1,135,720
Merchandise inventory	26	15	14	733,174	578,765
Total assets	19	19	23	3,337,502	2,626,927
Working capital	15	19	21	839,399	554,359
Current ratio	—	—	—	1.85:1	1.72:1
Total long-term debt, less current installments	—	—	—	$ 496,044	—
Ratio of long-term debt to shareholders' equity	—	—	—	.31:1	N/A
Shareholders' equity	5	12	19	$1,583,986	$1,654,470
Return on average assets	—	—	—	17.9%	18.2%
Return on average shareholders' equity	—	—	—	33.0%	27.5%
STATISTICS					
Number of stores opened	20%	21%	10%	298	203
Number of stores expanded	—	—	—	98	42
Number of stores closed	—	—	—	22	30
Number of stores open at year-end[e]	12	10	10	2,130	1,854
Net increase in number of stores	—	—	—	15%	10%
Comparable store sales growth (52-week basis)	—	—	—	6%	5%
Sales per square foot (52-week basis)[f]	—	—	—	$463	$441
Square footage of gross store space at year-end	19	19	15	15,312,700	12,645,000
Percentage increase in square feet	—	—	—	21%	14%
Number of employees at year-end	14	16	18	81,000	66,000
Weighted-average number of shares–basic[b]	—	—	—	396,179,975	417,146,631
Weighted-average number of shares–diluted[c]	—	—	—	410,200,758	427,267,220
Number of shares outstanding at year-end, net of treasury stock	—	—	—	393,133,028	411,775,997

(a) Excludes amortization of restricted stock, discounted stock options and discount on long-term debt.
(b) Based on weighted-average number of shares excluding restricted stock.
(c) Based on weighted-average number of shares adjusted for dilutive effect of stock options and restricted stock.
(d) Based on actual number of shares outstanding at year-end.
(e) Includes the conversion of GapKids departments to their own separate stores. Converted stores are not classified as new stores.
(f) Based on weighted-average gross square footage.

	Fiscal Year						
1995 53 weeks	1994 52 weeks	1993 52 weeks	1992 52 weeks	1991 52 weeks	1990 52 weeks	1989 53 weeks	1988 52 weeks
$4,395,253	$3,722,940	$3,295,679	$2,960,409	$2,518,893	$1,933,780	$1,586,596	$1,252,097
2,645,736	2,202,133	1,996,929	1,856,102	1,496,156	1,187,644	1,006,647	814,028
60.2%	59.2%	60.6%	62.7%	59.4%	61.4%	63.4%	65.0%
$ 175,719	$ 148,863	$ 124,860	$ 99,451	$ 72,765	$ 53,599	$ 39,589	$ 31,408
1,004,396	853,524	748,193	661,252	575,686	454,180	364,101	277,429
(15,797)	(10,902)	809	3,763	3,523	1,435	2,760	3,416
585,199	529,322	424,888	339,841	370,763	236,922	162,714	125,816
13.3%	14.2%	12.9%	11.5%	14.7%	12.3%	10.3%	10.0%
$ 231,160	$ 209,082	$ 166,464	$ 129,140	$ 140,890	$ 92,400	$ 65,086	$ 51,585
354,039	320,240	258,424	210,701	229,873	144,522	97,628	74,231
8.1%	8.6%	7.8%	7.1%	9.1%	7.5%	6.2%	5.9%
$ 66,993	$ 64,775	$ 53,041	$ 44,106	$ 41,126	$ 29,625	$ 22,857	$ 18,244
309,599	236,616	215,856	213,659	244,323	199,617	94,266	68,153
$ .85	$ .76	$ .62	$ .51	$ .56	$ .36	$.24	$.18
.83	.74	.60	.49	.54	.34	.23	.17
.16	.15	.13	.11	.10	.07	.06	.05
3.80	3.17	2.59	2.05	1.59	1.10	.80	.65
$ 957,752	$ 828,777	$ 740,422	$ 650,368	$ 547,740	$ 383,548	$ 238,103	$ 191,257
482,575	370,638	331,155	365,692	313,899	247,462	243,482	193,268
2,343,068	2,004,244	1,763,117	1,379,248	1,147,414	776,900	579,483	481,148
728,301	555,827	494,194	355,649	235,537	101,518	129,139	106,210
2.32:1	2.11:1	2.07:1	2.06:1	1.71:1	1.39:1	1.69:1	1.70:1
—	—	$ 75,000	$ 75,000	$ 80,000	$ 17,500	$ 20,000	$ 22,000
N/A	N/A	.07:1	.08:1	.12:1	.04:1	.06:1	.08:1
$1,640,473	$1,375,232	$1,126,475	$ 887,839	$ 677,788	$ 465,733	$ 337,972	$ 276,399
16.3%	17.0%	16.4%	16.7%	23.9%	21.3%	18.4%	16.2%
23.5%	25.6%	25.7%	26.9%	40.2%	36.0%	31.8%	27.0%
225	172	108	117	139	152	98	106
55	82	130	94	79	56	7	N/A
53	34	45	26	15	20	38	21
1,680	1,508	1,370	1,307	1,216	1,092	960	900
11%	10%	5%	7%	11%	14%	7%	10%
0%	1%	1%	5%	13%	14%	15%	8%
$425	$444	$463	$489	$481	$438	$389	$328
11,100,200	9,165,900	7,546,300	6,509,200	5,638,400	4,762,300	4,056,600	3,879,300
21%	21%	16%	15%	18%	17%	5%	6%
60,000	55,000	44,000	39,000	32,000	26,000	23,000	20,000
417,718,397	421,644,426	417,905,336	412,629,996	407,007,521	401,965,082	399,847,754	410,942,274
427,752,515	431,619,827	428,937,902	427,068,347	423,687,625	419,978,006	420,619,541	434,112,567
431,621,976	434,294,247	435,746,184	432,555,714	427,570,002	423,792,090	421,654,212	421,576,368

Management's Discussion and Analysis
of Results of Operations and Financial Condition

The information below and elsewhere in this Annual Report contains certain forward-looking statements which reflect the current view of Gap Inc. (the "Company") with respect to future events and financial performance. Wherever used, the words "expect," "plan," "anticipate," "believe" and similar expressions identify forward-looking statements.

Any such forward-looking statements are subject to risks and uncertainties that could cause the Company's actual results of operations to differ materially from historical results or current expectations. Some of these risks include, without limitation, ongoing competitive pressures in the apparel industry, risks associated with challenging international retail environments, changes in the level of consumer spending or preferences in apparel, and/or trade restrictions and political or financial instability in countries where the Company's goods are manufactured and other factors that may be described in the Company's filings with the Securities and Exchange Commission. Future economic and industry trends that could potentially impact revenues and profitability remain difficult to predict.

The Company does not undertake to publicly update or revise its forward-looking statements even if experience or future changes make it clear that any projected results expressed or implied therein will not be realized.

Results of Operations

NET SALES

	Fifty-two Weeks Ended Jan. 31, 1998	Fifty-two Weeks Ended Feb. 1, 1997	Fifty-three Weeks Ended Feb. 3, 1996
Net sales ($000)	$6,507,825	$5,284,381	$4,395,253
Total net sales growth percentage	23	20	18
Comparable store sales growth percentage (52-week basis)	6	5	0
Net sales per average gross square foot (52-week basis)	$463	$441	$425
Square footage of gross store space at year-end (000)	15,313	12,645	11,100
Number of:			
New stores	298	203	225
Expanded stores	98	42	55
Closed stores	22	30	53

The total net sales growth for all years presented was attributable primarily to the increase in retail selling space, both through the opening of new stores (net of stores closed) and the expansion of existing stores. An increase in comparable store sales also contributed to net sales growth in 1997 and 1996.

The increase in net sales per average square foot in 1997 and 1996 was primarily attributable to increases in comparable store sales.

COST OF GOODS SOLD
AND OCCUPANCY EXPENSES

Cost of goods sold and occupancy expenses as a percentage of net sales were 61.8 percent in 1997, 62.2 percent in 1996 and 64.2 percent in 1995.

The .4 percentage point decrease in 1997 from 1996 was primarily attributable to a .6 percentage point decrease in occupancy expenses, partially offset by a decrease in merchandise margin. The decrease in occupancy expenses as a percentage of net sales was primarily attributable to leverage achieved through comparable store sales growth.

The 2.0 percentage point decrease in 1996 from 1995 was due to a 1.2 percentage point increase in merchandise margin combined with an .8 percentage point decrease in occupancy expenses as a percentage of net sales. The increase in merchandise margin was driven by increases in initial merchandise markup and in the percentage of merchandise sold at regular price. The decrease in occupancy expenses was primarily attributable to the effect of the growth of the Old Navy division, which carries lower occupancy expenses as a percentage of net sales when compared to other divisions, and leverage achieved through comparable store sales growth.

The Company reviews its inventory levels in order to identify slow-moving merchandise and broken assortments (items no longer in stock in a sufficient range of sizes) and uses markdowns to clear merchandise. Such markdowns may have an adverse impact on earnings, depending upon the extent of the markdown and the amount of inventory affected.

OPERATING EXPENSES

Operating expenses as a percentage of net sales were 25.1 percent for 1997, 24.0 percent for 1996 and 22.9 percent for 1995.

In 1997, the 1.1 percentage point increase was primarily attributable to an .8 percentage point increase in advertising/marketing costs as part of the Company's brand development efforts. An increase in the write-off of leasehold improvements and fixtures associated with the remodeling, relocation and closing of certain stores planned for the next fiscal year accounted for .4 percentage point of the increase.

In 1996, the 1.1 percentage point increase was primarily attributable to a .3 percentage point increase in advertising/marketing costs to support the Company's brands and a .5 percentage point increase in incentive bonus expense.

NET INTEREST INCOME

Net interest income was $3.0, $19.5 and $15.8 million for 1997, 1996 and 1995, respectively. The decrease in 1997 was due to the interest expense related to the long-term debt securities issued during the third quarter, as well as to a decrease in gross average investments. The change in 1996 from 1995 was primarily attributable to an increase in gross average investments.

INCOME TAXES

The effective tax rate was 37.5 percent in 1997 and 39.5 percent in 1996 and 1995. The decrease in the effective tax rate in 1997 was a result of the impact of tax planning initiatives to support changing business needs.

Liquidity and Capital Resources

The following sets forth certain measures of the Company's liquidity:

| | Fiscal Year | | |
	1997	1996	1995
Cash provided by operating activities ($000)	$844,651	$834,953	$489,087
Working capital ($000)	839,399	554,359	728,301
Current ratio	1.85:1	1.72:1	2.32:1

For the fiscal year ended January 31, 1998, the increase in cash provided by operating activities was due to an increase in net earnings offset by investments in merchandise inventory and the timing of payments for income taxes and certain payables. For the fiscal year ended February 1, 1997, the increase in cash provided by operating activities was attributable to an increase in net earnings and the timing of certain year-end payables and accrued expenses.

The Company funds inventory expenditures during normal and peak periods through a combination of cash flows provided by operations and normal trade credit arrangements. The Company's business follows a seasonal pattern, peaking over a total of about ten to twelve weeks during the Back-to-School and Holiday periods. During 1997 and 1996, these periods accounted for approximately 35 and 33 percent, respectively, of the Company's annual sales.

The Company has committed credit facilities totaling $950 million, consisting of an $800 million, 364-day revolving credit facility, and a $150 million, 5-year revolving credit facility through June 30, 2002. These credit facilities provide for the issuance of up to $450 million in letters of credit. The Company has additional uncommitted credit facilities of $300 million for the issuance of letters of credit. At January 31, 1998, the Company had outstanding letters of credit of approximately $498 million.

To provide financial flexibility, the Company issued $500 million of 6.9 percent, 10-year debt securities in fiscal 1997. The proceeds from this issuance are intended to be used for general corporate purposes, including store expansion, brand investment, development of additional distribution channels and repurchases of the Company's common stock pursuant to its ongoing repurchase program.

Capital expenditures, net of construction allowances and dispositions, totaled approximately $450 million in 1997. These expenditures resulted in a net increase in store space of approximately 2.7 million square feet or 21 percent due to the addition of 298 new stores, the expansion of 98 stores and the remodeling of certain stores. Capital expenditures for 1996 and 1995 were $359 million and $291 million, respectively, resulting in a net increase in store space of approximately 1.5 million square feet in 1996 and approximately 1.9 million square feet in 1995.

The increase in capital expenditures in 1997 from 1996 was primarily attributable to the number of stores opened, expanded and remodeled, as well as the expansion of headquarters facilities. The increase in capital expenditures in 1996 from 1995 was primarily attributable to the construction of two distribution centers and a headquarters facility. Expenditures in 1997, 1996 and 1995 also included costs for equipment.

For 1998, the Company expects capital expenditures to total approximately $700 million, net of construction allowances. This represents the addition of 300 to 350 new stores, the expansion of approximately 80 to 90 stores and the remodeling of certain stores, as well as amounts for headquarters facilities, distribution centers and equipment. The Company expects to fund such capital expenditures with cash flow from operations and other sources of financing. Square footage growth is expected to be 18 to 20 percent before store closings. New stores are generally expected to be leased.

In 1997, the Company completed construction of a headquarters facility in San Bruno, California for approximately $60 million. The facility became fully operational in October 1997. To further support its growth, the Company continues to explore alternatives for additional headquarters facilities in San Francisco and San Bruno, California. The Company acquired land in 1997 in San Francisco and in the fourth quarter entered into a purchase contract to acquire additional land in San Bruno.

Also during 1997, the Company commenced construction on a distribution center in Fresno, California for an estimated cost at completion of $60 million. The majority of the expenditures for this facility will be incurred in 1998. The facility is expected to begin operations in early 1999.

On November 24, 1997, the Company's Board of Directors authorized a three-for-two split of its common stock effective December 22, 1997, in the form of a stock dividend for shareholders of record at the close of business on December 8, 1997. Share and per share amounts herein and in the accompanying consolidated financial statements have been restated to reflect the stock split.

In October 1996, the Board of Directors approved a program under which the Company may repurchase up to 45 million shares of its outstanding common stock in the open market over a three-year period. As of January 31, 1998, 28 million shares had been repurchased for $744 million. The program announced in October 1996 follows an earlier 27 million share repurchase program which was completed in November 1996 at a cost of approximately $450 million.

During fiscal 1997, the Company entered into various put option contracts in connection with the share repurchase program to hedge against stock price fluctuations. The Company also continued to enter into foreign exchange forward contracts to reduce exposure to foreign currency exchange risk involved in its commitments to purchase merchandise for foreign operations. Additional information on these contracts and agreements is presented in the Notes to Consolidated Financial Statements (Note E). Quantitative and qualitative disclosures about market risk for financial instruments are presented on page 38.

The Company pursues a diversified global import operations strategy which includes relationships with vendors in over 40 countries. These sourcing operations may be adversely affected by political instability resulting in the disruption of trade from exporting countries, significant fluctuation in the value of the U.S. dollar against foreign currencies, restrictions on the transfer of funds and/or other trade disruptions. The current financial instability in Asia is an example of this instability, which could affect some suppliers adversely. Although to date the instability in Asia has not had a material adverse effect on the Company's ability to import apparel, and therefore on the Company's results of operations and financial condition, no assurances can be given that it will not have such an effect in the future.

The Company is addressing the need to ensure that its operations will not be adversely impacted by software or other system failures related to year 2000. A program office was established in 1997 to coordinate the identification, evaluation and implementation of any necessary changes to computer systems, applications and business processes. The costs associated with this effort are expected to be incurred through 1999 and are not expected to have a material impact on the results of operations, cash flows or financial condition in any given year. However, no assurances can be given that the Company will be able to completely identify or address all year 2000 compliance issues, or that third parties with whom the Company does business will not experience system failures as a result of the year 2000 issues, nor can the Company fully predict the consequences of noncompliance.

Per Share Data

Fiscal	1997	1996	1997	1996	Market Prices				Cash Dividends	
					High	Low	High	Low		
1st Quarter					$24 1/8	$19 1/16	$20 5/16	$15 7/16	$.05	$.05
2nd Quarter					29 13/16	20 9/16	24 1/16	18 1/8	.05	.05
3rd Quarter					35 3/4	28	24 5/16	17 5/16	.05	.05
4th Quarter					41 1/4	32 15/16	22 5/16	18 9/16	.05	.05
Year									$.20	$.20

The principal markets on which the Company's stock is traded are the New York Stock Exchange and the Pacific Exchange. The number of holders of record of the Company's stock as of March 9, 1998 was 7,108.

Management's Report on Financial Information

Management is responsible for the integrity and consistency of all financial information presented in the Annual Report. The financial statements have been prepared in accordance with generally accepted accounting principles and necessarily include certain amounts based on Management's best estimates and judgments.

In fulfilling its responsibility for the reliability of financial information, Management has established and maintains accounting systems and procedures appropriately supported by internal accounting controls. Such controls include the selection and training of qualified personnel, an organizational structure providing for division of responsibility, communication of requirement for compliance with approved accounting control and business practices and a program of internal audit. The extent of the Company's system of internal accounting control recognizes that the cost should not exceed the benefits derived and that the evaluation of those factors requires estimates and judgments by Management. Although no system can ensure that all errors or irregularities have been eliminated, Management believes that the internal accounting controls in use provide reasonable assurance, at

reasonable cost, that assets are safeguarded against loss from unauthorized use or disposition, that transactions are executed in accordance with Management's authorization and that the financial records are reliable for preparing financial statements and maintaining accountability for assets. The financial statements of the Company have been audited by Deloitte & Touche LLP, independent auditors. Their report, which appears below, is based upon their audits conducted in accordance with generally accepted auditing standards.

The Audit and Finance Committee (the "Committee") of the Board of Directors is comprised solely of directors who are not officers or employees of the Company. The Committee is responsible for recommending to the Board of Directors the selection of independent auditors. It meets periodically with Management, the independent auditors and the internal auditors to assure that they are carrying out their responsibilities. The Committee also reviews and monitors the financial, accounting and auditing procedures of the Company in addition to reviewing the Company's financial reports. Deloitte & Touche LLP and the internal auditors have full and free access to the Committee, with and without Management's presence.

Independent Auditors' Report
To the Shareholders and Board of Directors of The Gap, Inc.:

We have audited the accompanying consolidated balance sheets of The Gap, Inc. and subsidiaries as of January 31, 1998 and February 1, 1997, and the related consolidated statements of earnings, shareholders' equity and cash flows for each of the three fiscal years in the period ended January 31, 1998. These financial statements are the responsibility of the Company's management. Our responsibility is to express an opinion on these financial statements based on our audits.

We conducted our audits in accordance with generally accepted auditing standards. Those standards require that we plan and perform the audits to obtain reasonable assurance about whether the consolidated financial statements are free of material misstatement. An audit includes examining, on a test basis, evidence supporting the amounts and disclosures in the financial statements. An audit also includes assessing the accounting principles used and significant estimates made by

management, as well as evaluating the overall financial statement presentation. We believe that our audits provide a reasonable basis for our opinion.

In our opinion, such consolidated financial statements present fairly, in all material respects, the financial position of the Company and its subsidiaries as of January 31, 1998 and February 1, 1997, and the results of their operations and their cash flows for each of the three fiscal years in the period ended January 31, 1998 in conformity with generally accepted accounting principles.

Deloitte & Touche LLP

San Francisco, California
February 27, 1998

Consolidated Statements of Earnings

($000 except share and per share amounts)	Fifty-two Weeks Ended January 31, 1998	Percentage to Sales	Fifty-two Weeks Ended February 1, 1997	Percentage to Sales	Fifty-three Weeks Ended February 3, 1996	Percentage to Sales
Net sales	$6,507,825	100.0%	$5,284,381	100.0%	$4,395,253	100.0%
Costs and expenses						
Cost of goods sold and occupancy expenses	4,021,541	61.8	3,285,166	62.2	2,821,455	64.2
Operating expenses	1,635,017	25.1	1,270,138	24.0	1,004,396	22.9
Net interest income	(2,975)	0.0	(19,450)	(0.4)	(15,797)	(0.4)
Earnings before income taxes	854,242	13.1	748,527	14.2	585,199	13.3
Income taxes	320,341	4.9	295,668	5.6	231,160	5.2
Net earnings	$ 533,901	8.2%	$ 452,859	8.6%	$ 354,039	8.1%
Weighted-average number of shares—basic	396,179,975		417,146,631		417,718,397	
Weighted-average number of shares—diluted	410,200,758		427,267,220		427,752,515	
Earnings per share—basic	$1.35		$1.09		$.85	
Earnings per share—diluted	1.30		1.06		.83	

See Notes to Consolidated Financial Statements.

Consolidated Balance Sheets

($000)	January 31, 1998	February 1, 1997
ASSETS		
Current Assets		
Cash and equivalents	$ 913,169	$ 485,644
Short-term investments	—	135,632
Merchandise inventory	733,174	578,765
Prepaid expenses and other current assets	184,604	129,214
Total current assets	1,830,947	1,329,255
Property and Equipment		
Leasehold improvements	846,791	736,608
Furniture and equipment	1,236,450	960,516
Land and buildings	154,136	99,969
Construction-in-progress	66,582	101,520
	2,303,959	1,898,613
Accumulated depreciation and amortization	(938,713)	(762,893)
Property and equipment, net	1,365,246	1,135,720
Long-term investments	—	36,138
Lease rights and other assets	141,309	125,814
Total assets	$ 3,337,502	$ 2,626,927
LIABILITIES AND SHAREHOLDERS' EQUITY		
Current Liabilities		
Notes payable	$ 84,794	$ 40,050
Accounts payable	416,976	351,754
Accrued expenses	389,412	282,494
Income taxes payable	83,597	91,806
Deferred lease credits and other current liabilities	16,769	8,792
Total current liabilities	991,548	774,896
Long-Term Liabilities		
Long-term debt	496,044	—
Deferred lease credits and other liabilities	265,924	197,561
Total long-term liabilities	761,968	197,561
Shareholders' Equity		
Common stock $.05 par value		
Authorized 500,000,000 shares; issued 439,922,841 and 476,796,135 shares; outstanding 393,133,028 and 411,775,997 shares	21,996	23,840
Additional paid-in capital	317,674	434,104
Retained earnings	2,392,750	1,938,352
Foreign currency translation adjustments	(15,230)	(5,187)
Deferred compensation	(38,167)	(47,838)
Treasury stock, at cost	(1,095,037)	(688,801)
Total shareholders' equity	1,583,986	1,654,470
Total liabilities and shareholders' equity	$ 3,337,502	$ 2,626,927

See Notes to Consolidated Financial Statements.

Consolidated Statements of Cash Flows

($000)	Fifty-two Weeks Ended January 31, 1998	Fifty-two Weeks Ended February 1, 1997	Fifty-three Weeks Ended February 3, 1996
CASH FLOWS FROM OPERATING ACTIVITIES			
Net earnings	$ 533,901	$ 452,859	$ 354,039
Adjustments to reconcile net earnings to net cash provided by operating activities:			
Depreciation and amortization[a]	269,706	214,905	197,440
Tax benefit from exercise of stock options by employees and from vesting of restricted stock	23,682	47,348	11,444
Deferred income taxes	(13,706)	(28,897)	(2,477)
Change in operating assets and liabilities:			
Merchandise inventory	(156,091)	(93,800)	(113,021)
Prepaid expenses and other	(44,736)	(16,355)	(15,278)
Accounts payable	63,532	88,532	1,183
Accrued expenses	107,365	87,974	9,427
Income taxes payable	(8,214)	25,706	24,806
Deferred lease credits and other long-term liabilities	69,212	56,681	21,524
Net cash provided by operating activities	844,651	834,953	489,087
CASH FLOWS FROM INVESTING ACTIVITIES			
Net maturity (purchase) of short-term investments	174,709	(11,774)	116,134
Net purchase of long-term investments	(2,939)	(40,120)	(30,370)
Net purchase of property and equipment	(465,843)	(371,833)	(302,260)
Acquisition of lease rights and other assets	(19,779)	(12,206)	(6,623)
Net cash used for investing activities	(313,852)	(435,933)	(223,119)
CASH FLOWS FROM FINANCING ACTIVITIES			
Net increase in notes payable	44,462	18,445	20,787
Net issuance of long-term debt	495,890	—	—
Issuance of common stock	30,653	37,053	17,096
Net purchase of treasury stock	(593,142)	(466,741)	(71,314)
Cash dividends paid	(79,503)	(83,854)	(66,993)
Net cash used for financing activities	(101,640)	(495,097)	(100,424)
Effect of exchange rate changes on cash	(1,634)	2,155	(465)
Net increase (decrease) in cash and equivalents	427,525	(93,922)	165,079
Cash and equivalents at beginning of year	485,644	579,566	414,487
Cash and equivalents at end of year	$ 913,169	$ 485,644	$ 579,566

See Notes to Consolidated Financial Statements.

(a) Includes amortization of restricted stock, discounted stock options and discount on long-term debt.

Consolidated Statements of Shareholders' Equity

($000 except share and per share amounts)	Common Stock Shares	Common Stock Amount
Balance at January 28, 1995	**470,918,331**	**$23,546**
Issuance of common stock pursuant to stock option plans	1,491,558	75
Net issuance of common stock pursuant to management incentive restricted stock plans	1,547,070	77
Tax benefit from exercise of stock options by employees and from vesting of restricted stock		
Foreign currency translation adjustments		
Amortization of restricted stock		
Purchase of treasury stock		
Reissuance of treasury stock		
Net earnings		
Cash dividends ($.16 per share)		
Balance at February 3, 1996	**473,956,959**	**$23,698**
Issuance of common stock pursuant to stock option plans	2,386,761	119
Net issuance of common stock pursuant to management incentive restricted stock plans	452,415	23
Tax benefit from exercise of stock options by employees and from vesting of restricted stock		
Foreign currency translation adjustments		
Amortization of restricted stock		
Purchase of treasury stock		
Reissuance of treasury stock		
Net earnings		
Cash dividends ($.20 per share)		
Balance at February 1, 1997	**476,796,135**	**$23,840**
Issuance of common stock pursuant to stock option plans[a]	2,848,567	142
Net cancelations of common stock pursuant to management incentive restricted stock plans	(946,861)	(47)
Tax benefit from exercise of stock options by employees and from vesting of restricted stock		
Foreign currency translation adjustments		
Amortization of restricted stock and discounted stock options		
Purchase of treasury stock		
Reissuance of treasury stock		
Retirement of treasury stock	(38,775,000)	(1,939)
Net earnings		
Cash dividends ($.20 per share)		
Balance at January 31, 1998	**439,922,841**	**$21,996**

See Notes to Consolidated Financial Statements.
(a) Includes payout of cash for fractional shares resulting from the three-for-two split of common stock effective December 22, 1997.

Additional Paid-in Capital	Retained Earnings	Foreign Currency Translation Adjustments	Deferred Compensation	Treasury Stock		Total
				Shares	Amount	
$282,716	$1,282,301	$ (8,320)	$(54,265)	(36,624,084)	$ (150,746)	$1,375,232
9,591						9,666
19,531			(16,191)			3,417
11,444						11,444
		(751)				(751)
			21,721			21,721
				(6,289,200)	(72,717)	(72,717)
4,012				578,301	1,403	5,415
	354,039					354,039
	(66,993)					(66,993)
$327,294	$1,569,347	$ (9,071)	$(48,735)	(42,334,983)	$ (222,060)	$1,640,473
19,694			(9,648)			10,165
32,799			(12,903)			19,919
47,348						47,348
		3,884				3,884
			23,448			23,448
				(23,284,650)	(468,246)	(468,246)
6,969				599,495	1,505	8,474
	452,859					452,859
	(83,854)					(83,854)
$434,104	$1,938,352	$ (5,187)	$(47,838)	(65,020,138)	$ (688,801)	$1,654,470
47,963			(18,166)			29,939
(10,452)			3,869			(6,630)
23,682						23,682
		(10,043)				(10,043)
			23,968			23,968
				(21,190,300)	(598,149)	(598,149)
7,344				645,625	5,007	12,351
(184,967)				38,775,000	186,906	0
	533,901					533,901
	(79,503)					(79,503)
$317,674	$2,392,750	$(15,230)	$(38,167)	(46,789,813)	$(1,095,037)	$1,583,986

Notes to Consolidated Financial Statements

For the Fifty-two Weeks ended January 31, 1998 (fiscal 1997), the Fifty-two Weeks ended February 1, 1997 (fiscal 1996) and the Fifty-three Weeks ended February 3, 1996 (fiscal 1995)

NOTE A: SUMMARY OF SIGNIFICANT ACCOUNTING POLICIES

Gap Inc. (the "Company") is an international specialty retailer which operates stores selling casual apparel, personal care and other accessories for men, women and children under a variety of brand names including: Gap, GapKids, babyGap, Banana Republic and Old Navy. Its principal markets consist of the United States, Canada, Europe and Asia with the United States being the most significant.

On November 24, 1997, the Company's Board of Directors authorized a three-for-two split of its common stock effective December 22, 1997, in the form of a stock dividend for shareholders of record at the close of business on December 8, 1997. Share and per share amounts in the accompanying consolidated financial statements for all periods have been restated to reflect the stock split.

The consolidated financial statements include the accounts of the Company and its subsidiaries. Intercompany accounts and transactions have been eliminated.

The preparation of financial statements in conformity with generally accepted accounting principles requires Management to make estimates and assumptions that affect the reported amounts of assets and liabilities and disclosure of contingent assets and liabilities at the date of the financial statements and the reported amounts of revenue and expenses during the reporting period. Actual results could differ from those estimates.

Cash and equivalents represent cash and short-term, highly liquid investments with original maturities of three months or less.

Short-term investments include investments with an original maturity of greater than three months and a remaining maturity of less than one year. Long-term investments include investments with an original and remaining maturity of greater than one year. Effective July 1997, the Company's short- and long-term investments, which consist primarily of debt securities, are classified as available for sale and are carried at fair market value. Any unrealized gains or losses computed in marking these securities to market are reported within shareholders' equity. Prior to July 1997, such securities were classified as held to maturity and were carried at amortized cost.

Merchandise inventory is stated at the lower of FIFO (first-in, first-out) cost or market.

Property and equipment are stated at cost. Depreciation and amortization are computed using the straight-line method over the estimated useful lives of the related assets.

Lease rights are recorded at cost and are amortized over 12 years or the lives of the respective leases including option periods, whichever is less.

Costs associated with the opening or remodeling of stores, such as pre-opening rent and payroll, are expensed as incurred. The net book value of fixtures and leasehold improvements for stores scheduled to be closed or expanded within the next fiscal year is charged against current earnings.

Costs associated with the production of advertising, such as writing copy, printing and other costs, are expensed as incurred. Costs associated with communicating advertising that has been produced, such as magazine and billboard space, are expensed when the advertising first takes place. Advertising costs were $175 million, $96 million and $64 million in fiscal 1997, 1996 and 1995, respectively.

Deferred income taxes arise from temporary differences between the tax basis of assets and liabilities and their reported amounts in the consolidated financial statements.

Translation adjustments result from the process of translating foreign subsidiaries' financial statements into U.S. dollars. Balance sheet accounts are translated at exchange rates in effect at the balance sheet date. Income statement accounts are translated at average exchange rates during the year. Resulting translation adjustments are included in shareholders' equity.

The Company accounts for stock-based awards using the intrinsic value-based method under Accounting Principles Board (APB) Opinion No. 25, *Accounting for Stock Issued to Employees*, and has provided pro forma disclosures of net earnings and earnings per share in accordance with the provisions of Statement of Financial Accounting Standards (SFAS) No. 123, *Accounting for Stock-Based Compensation*. Restricted stock and discounted stock options represent deferred compensation and are shown as a reduction of shareholders' equity.

In the fourth quarter of 1997, the Company adopted SFAS No. 128, *Earnings per Share*, which requires dual presentation of basic earnings per share (EPS) and diluted EPS. All prior periods have been restated to conform with the new statement. Basic EPS is computed as net earnings divided by the weighted-average number of common shares outstanding, excluding restricted stock, for the period. Diluted EPS reflects the potential dilution that could occur from common shares issuable through stock-based compensation including stock options, restricted stock and other convertible securities.

The Financial Accounting Standards Board issued SFAS No. 130, *Reporting Comprehensive Income*, which requires that an enterprise report, by major components and as a single total, the change in its net assets during the period from non-owner sources; and SFAS No. 131, *Disclosures About Segments of an Enterprise and Related Information*, which establishes annual and interim reporting standards for an enterprise's operating segments and related disclosures about its products, services, geographic areas and major customers. Adoption of these standards will not impact the Company's consolidated financial position, results of operations or cash flows, and any effect will be limited to the form and content of its disclosures. SFAS No. 130 and SFAS No. 131 are effective for the Company's fiscal years ending after January 31, 1998.

Certain reclassifications have been made to the 1995 and 1996 financial statements to conform with the 1997 financial statements.

NOTE B: DEBT AND OTHER CREDIT ARRANGEMENTS

The Company has committed credit facilities totaling $950 million, consisting of an $800 million, 364-day revolving credit facility, and a $150 million, 5-year revolving credit facility through June 30, 2002. These credit facilities provide for the issuance of up to $450 million in letters of credit. The Company has additional uncommitted credit facilities of $300 million for the issuance of letters of credit. At January 31, 1998, the Company had outstanding letters of credit of $498,256,000.

Borrowings under the Company's credit agreements are subject to the Company not exceeding a certain debt ratio. The Company was in compliance with this debt covenant at January 31, 1998.

During fiscal 1997, the Company issued long-term debt which consists of $500 million of 6.9 percent unsecured notes, due September 15, 2007. Interest on the notes is payable semi-annually. The fair value at January 31, 1998 of the notes was approximately $526 million, based on the current rates at which the Company could borrow funds with similar terms and remaining maturities. The balance of the debt is net of unamortized discount.

Gross interest payments were $8,399,000, $2,800,000 and $2,274,000 in fiscal 1997, 1996 and 1995, respectively.

NOTE C: INCOME TAXES

Income taxes consisted of the following:

($000)	Fifty-two Weeks Ended Jan. 31, 1998	Fifty-two Weeks Ended Feb. 1, 1997	Fifty-three Weeks Ended Feb. 3, 1996
Currently Payable			
Federal	$279,068	$266,063	$176,200
State	33,384	36,167	40,111
Foreign	21,595	22,335	17,348
Total currently payable	334,047	324,565	233,659
Deferred			
Federal	(14,832)	(23,980)	(7,169)
State and foreign	1,126	(4,917)	4,670
Total deferred	(13,706)	(28,897)	(2,499)
Total provision	$320,341	$295,668	$231,160

The foreign component of pretax earnings before eliminations and corporate allocations in fiscal 1997, 1996 and 1995 was $84,487,000, $82,220,000 and $71,545,000, respectively. No provision was made for U.S. income taxes on the undistributed earnings of the foreign subsidiaries as it is the Company's intention to utilize those earnings in the foreign operations for an indefinite period of time or repatriate such earnings only when tax effective to do so. Undistributed earnings of foreign subsidiaries were $218,113,000 at January 31, 1998.

The difference between the effective income tax rate and the United States federal income tax rate is summarized as follows:

	Fifty-two Weeks Ended Jan. 31, 1998	Fifty-two Weeks Ended Feb. 1, 1997	Fifty-three Weeks Ended Feb. 3, 1996
Federal tax rate	35.0%	35.0%	35.0%
State income taxes, less federal benefit	3.2	4.4	5.0
Other	(.7)	.1	(.5)
Effective tax rate	37.5%	39.5%	39.5%

Deferred tax assets (liabilities), reported in other assets in the Consolidated Balance Sheets, consisted of the following at January 31, 1998 and February 1, 1997:

($000)	Jan. 31, 1998	Feb. 1, 1997
Compensation and benefits accruals	$ 31,367	$ 31,640
Scheduled rent	44,451	40,834
Inventory capitalization	28,776	16,459
Nondeductible accruals	20,003	18,705
Other	17,854	24,224
Gross deferred tax assets	142,451	131,862
Depreciation	(9,553)	(13,611)
Other	(6,345)	(5,404)
Gross deferred tax liabilities	(15,898)	(19,015)
Net deferred tax assets	$126,553	$112,847

Income tax payments were $320,744,000, $249,968,000 and $197,802,000 in fiscal 1997, 1996 and 1995, respectively.

NOTE D: LEASES

The Company leases most of its store premises and head-quarters facilities and some of its distribution centers. These leases expire at various dates through 2013.

The aggregate minimum non-cancelable annual lease payments under leases in effect on January 31, 1998 are as follows:

Fiscal Year	($000)
1998	$ 409,607
1999	403,285
2000	387,668
2001	364,270
2002	332,364
Thereafter	1,172,849
Total minimum lease commitment	$3,070,043

Many leases entered into by the Company include options, which are generally exercised, that may extend the lease term beyond the initial commitment period, subject to terms agreed to at lease inception. Some leases also include early termination options which can be exercised under specific conditions. If conditions did not warrant invoking early termination of any leases, and all renewal options were exercised for current lease agreements, the total lease commitment for the Company would be approximately $4.1 billion.

For leases that contain predetermined fixed escalations of the minimum rentals, the Company recognizes the related rental expense on a straight-line basis and records the difference between the recognized rental expense and amounts payable under the leases as deferred lease credits. At January 31, 1998 and February 1, 1997, this liability amounted to $129,981,000 and $110,633,000, respectively.

Cash or rent abatements received upon entering into certain store leases are recognized on a straight-line basis as a reduction to rent expense over the lease term. The unamortized portion is included in deferred lease credits.

Some of the leases relating to stores in operation at January 31, 1998 contain renewal options for periods ranging up to 25 years. Many leases also provide for payment of operating expenses, real estate taxes and for additional rent based on a percentage of sales. No lease directly imposes any restrictions relating to leasing in other locations (other than radius clauses).

Rental expense for all operating leases was as follows:

($000)	Fifty-two Weeks Ended Jan. 31, 1998	Fifty-two Weeks Ended Feb. 1, 1997	Fifty-three Weeks Ended Feb. 3, 1996
Minimum rentals	$391,472	$337,487	$300,171
Contingent rentals	38,657	30,644	22,464
Total	$430,129	$368,131	$322,635

NOTE E: FINANCIAL INSTRUMENTS

Foreign Exchange Forward Contracts

The Company enters into foreign exchange forward contracts to reduce exposure to foreign currency exchange risk. These contracts are primarily designated and effective as hedges of commitments to purchase merchandise for foreign operations. The market value gains and losses on these contracts are deferred and recognized as part of the underlying cost to purchase the merchandise. At January 31, 1998, the Company had contracts maturing at various dates through 1998 to sell the equivalent of $123,230,000 in foreign currencies (20,200,000 British pounds, 46,200,000 Canadian dollars, 62,625,260,078 Italian lire, 1,543,000,000 Japanese yen and 1,234,884,074 Spanish pesetas) at the contracted rates. The deferred gains and losses on the Company's foreign exchange forward contracts at January 31, 1998 are immaterial.

Put Options

At January 31, 1998, the Company had various put option contracts to repurchase up to 3,050,000 shares of its common stock. The contracts have exercise prices ranging from $32.95 to $38.37, with expiration dates extending to the third quarter of fiscal 1998.

Interest Rate Swaps

During fiscal 1997, the Company entered into interest rate swap agreements in order to reduce interest rate risk on a substantial portion of its long-term debt. The swap agreements, which were issued at an aggregate notional amount of $400 million, were settled in September 1997 at an interest rate of 6.7 percent. The gains on the interest rate swaps were deferred and are being amortized to reduce interest expense over the life of the debt.

NOTE F: EMPLOYEE BENEFIT
AND INCENTIVE STOCK COMPENSATION PLANS
Retirement Plans

The Company has a qualified defined contribution retirement plan, called GapShare, which is available to employees who meet certain age and service requirements. This plan permits employees to make contributions up to the maximum limits allowable under the Internal Revenue Code. Under the plan, the Company matches all or a portion of the employee's contributions under a predetermined formula. The Company's contributions vest over a seven-year period. Company contributions to the retirement plan in 1997, 1996 and 1995 were $12,907,000, $11,427,000 and $9,839,000, respectively.

A nonqualified Executive Deferred Compensation Plan was established on January 1, 1994 and a nonqualified Executive Capital Accumulation Plan was established on April 1, 1994. Both plans allow eligible employees to defer compensation up to a maximum amount defined in each plan. The Company does not match employees' contributions.

A Deferred Compensation Plan was established on August 26, 1997 for nonemployee members of the Board of Directors. Under this plan, Board members may elect to defer receipt on a pre-tax basis of eligible compensation received for serving as nonemployee directors of the Company. In exchange for compensation deferred, Board members are granted discounted stock options to purchase shares of the Company's common stock. All options are fully exercisable upon the date granted and expire seven years after grant or one year after retirement from the Board, if earlier. The Company may issue up to 300,000 shares under the plan.

Incentive Stock Compensation Plans

The 1996 Stock Option and Award Plan (the "Plan") was established on March 26, 1996. The Board authorized 41,485,041 shares for issuance under the Plan, which includes shares available under the Management Incentive Restricted Stock Plan ("MIRSP") and an earlier stock option plan established in 1981, both of which were superseded by the Plan. The Plan empowers the Compensation and Stock Option Committee of the Board of Directors to award compensation primarily in the form of nonqualified stock options or restricted stock to key employees. Stock options generally expire ten years from the grant date or one year after the date of retirement, if earlier. Stock options generally vest over a three-year period, with shares becoming exercisable in full on the third anniversary of the grant date. Nonqualified stock options are generally issued at fair market value but may be issued at prices less than the fair market value at the date of grant or at other prices as determined by the Compensation and Stock Option Committee. Total compensation cost for those stock options issued at less than fair market value under the Plan and for the restricted shares issued under MIRSP was $17,170,000, $22,248,000 and $23,743,000 in 1997, 1996 and 1995, respectively.

Employee Stock Purchase Plan

The Company has an Employee Stock Purchase Plan under which all eligible employees may purchase common stock of the Company at 85 percent of the lower of the closing price of the Company's common stock on the grant date or the purchase date on the New York Stock Exchange Composite Transactions Index. Employees pay for their stock purchases through payroll deductions at a rate equal to any whole percentage from 1 percent to 15 percent. There were 645,625 shares issued under the plan during fiscal 1997, 599,495 during 1996 and 578,301 during 1995. All shares were acquired from reissued treasury stock. At January 31, 1998, there were 4,176,579 shares reserved for future subscriptions.

NOTE G: SHAREHOLDERS'
EQUITY AND STOCK OPTIONS
Common and Preferred Stock

The Company is authorized to issue 60,000,000 shares of Class B common stock which is convertible into shares of common stock on a share-for-share basis; transfer of the shares is restricted. In addition, the holders of the Class B common stock have six votes per share on most matters and are entitled to a lower cash dividend. No Class B shares have been issued.

The Board of Directors is authorized to issue 30,000,000 shares of one or more series of preferred stock and to establish at the time of issuance the issue price, dividend rate, redemption price, liquidation value, conversion features and such other terms and conditions of each series (including voting rights) as the Board of Directors deems appropriate, without further action on the part of the shareholders. No preferred shares have been issued.

In October 1996, the Board of Directors approved a share-buyback program under which the Company may repurchase up to 45,000,000 shares of its outstanding stock in the open market over a three-year period. As of January 31, 1998, 28,184,650 shares were repurchased for $743,805,000 under this program.

Stock Options

Under the Company's Stock Option Plans, nonqualified options to purchase common stock are granted to officers, directors and key employees at exercise prices equal to the fair market value of the stock at the date of grant or at other prices as determined by the Compensation and Stock Option Committee of the Board of Directors.

Stock option activity for all employee benefit plans was as follows:

	Shares	Weighted-Average Exercise Price
Balance at January 28, 1995	11,619,816	$10.18
Granted	14,226,600	11.94
Exercised	(1,491,558)	6.48
Canceled	(894,222)	12.27
Balance at February 3, 1996	23,460,636	$11.41
Granted	9,364,110	20.60
Exercised	(2,386,761)	8.30
Canceled	(1,198,608)	14.85
Balance at February 1, 1997	29,239,377	$14.46
Granted	11,392,531	21.62
Exercised	(2,849,034)	10.65
Canceled	(2,559,295)	16.01
Balance at January 31, 1998	35,223,579	$16.97

Outstanding options at January 31, 1998 have expiration dates ranging from March 20, 1998 to January 29, 2008 and represent grants to 2,347 key employees.

At January 31, 1998, the Company reserved 60,083,011 shares of its common stock, including 14,996 treasury shares, for the exercise of stock options. There were 24,859,432 and 32,745,096 shares available for granting of options at January 31, 1998 and February 1, 1997, respectively. Options for 4,299,847 and 4,373,222 shares were exercisable as of January 31, 1998 and February 1, 1997, respectively, and had a weighted-average exercise price of $11.66 and $9.01 for those respective periods.

The Company accounts for its Stock Option and Award Plans in accordance with APB Opinion No. 25, under which no compensation cost has been recognized for stock option awards granted at fair market value. Had compensation cost for the Company's stock-based compensation plans been determined based on the fair value at the grant dates for awards under those plans in accordance with the provisions of SFAS No. 123, *Accounting for Stock-Based Compensation*, the Company's net earnings and earnings per share would have been reduced to the pro forma amounts indicated below. The effects of applying SFAS No. 123 in this pro forma disclosure are not indicative of future amounts. SFAS No. 123 does not apply to awards prior to fiscal year 1995. Additional awards in future years are anticipated.

	Fifty-two Weeks Ended Jan. 31, 1998	Fifty-two Weeks Ended Feb. 1, 1997	Fifty-three Weeks Ended Feb. 3, 1996
Net earnings ($000)			
As reported	$533,901	$452,859	$354,039
Pro forma	507,966	437,232	348,977
Earnings per share			
As reported–basic	$1.35	$1.09	$.85
Pro forma–basic	1.28	1.05	.84
As reported–diluted	1.30	1.06	.83
Pro forma–diluted	1.24	1.02	.82

The weighted-average fair value of the stock options granted during fiscal 1997, 1996 and 1995 was $8.76, $7.47 and $4.18, respectively. The fair value of each option granted is estimated on the date of the grant using the Black-Scholes option-pricing model with the following weighted-average assumptions for grants in 1997: dividend yield of .7 percent; expected price volatility of 31 percent; risk-free interest rates ranging from 5.9 percent to 7.0 percent and expected lives between 3.9 and 5.8 years. The fair value of stock options granted prior to 1997 was based on the following weighted-average assumptions: dividend yield of 1.0 percent; expected price volatility of 30 percent; risk-free interest rates ranging from 5.5 percent to 6.5 percent; and expected lives between 3.6 and 5.8 years.

The following table summarizes information about stock options outstanding at January 31, 1998:

			Options Outstanding			Options Exercisable	
Range of Exercise Prices			Number Outstanding at Jan. 31, 1998	Weighted-Average Remaining Contractual Life (in years)	Weighted-Average Exercise Price	Number Exercisable at Jan. 31, 1998	Weighted-Average Exercise Price
$ 3.86	to	$11.29	8,215,077	5.10	$10.12	1,995,467	$ 8.39
11.40	to	13.03	7,454,625	5.75	12.96	210,600	11.79
13.42	to	20.88	10,688,682	8.08	19.13	2,077,095	14.68
20.89	to	39.00	8,865,195	8.66	24.10	16,685	25.79
$ 3.86	to	$39.00	35,223,579	7.04	$16.97	4,299,847	$11.66

NOTE H: EARNINGS PER SHARE

Under SFAS No. 128, the Company provides dual presentation of EPS on a basic and diluted basis. The Company's granting of certain stock options and restricted stock resulted in potential dilution of basic EPS. The following summarizes the effects of the assumed issuance of dilutive securities on weighted-average shares for basic EPS.

	Fifty-two Weeks Ended Jan. 31, 1998	Fifty-two Weeks Ended Feb. 1, 1997	Fifty-three Weeks Ended Feb. 3, 1996
Weighted-average number of shares–basic	396,179,975	417,146,631	417,718,397
Incremental shares from assumed issuance of:			
Stock options	10,037,700	5,597,219	1,939,485
Restricted stock	3,983,083	4,523,370	8,094,633
Weighted-average number of shares–diluted	410,200,758	427,267,220	427,752,515

The number of incremental shares from the assumed issuance of stock options and restricted stock is calculated applying the treasury stock method.

Excluded from the above computation of weighted-average shares for diluted EPS were options to purchase 440,063 shares of common stock during fiscal 1997, 5,084,978 during 1996 and 3,087,269 during 1995. Issuance of these securities would have resulted in an antidilutive effect on EPS.

NOTE I: RELATED PARTY TRANSACTIONS

The Company has an agreement with Fisher Development, Inc. (FDI), wholly owned by the brother of the Company's chairman, setting forth the terms under which FDI may act as general contractor in connection with the Company's construction activities. FDI acted as general contractor for 266, 177 and 204 new stores' leasehold improvements and fixtures during fiscal 1997, 1996 and 1995, respectively. In the same respective years, FDI supervised construction of 97, 38 and 54 expansions, as well as remodels of existing stores and headquarters facilities. Total cost of construction was $233,777,000, $111,871,000 and $164,820,000, including profit and overhead costs of $16,845,000, $10,751,000 and $11,753,000 for fiscal 1997, 1996 and 1995, respectively. At January 31, 1998 and February 1, 1997, amounts due to FDI were $10,318,000 and $6,456,000, respectively. The terms and conditions of the agreement with FDI are reviewed annually by the Audit and Finance Committee of the Board of Directors.

NOTE J: QUARTERLY FINANCIAL INFORMATION (UNAUDITED)

Fiscal 1997 Quarter Ended

($000 except per share amounts)	Thirteen Weeks Ended May 3, 1997	Thirteen Weeks Ended Aug. 2, 1997	Thirteen Weeks Ended Nov. 1, 1997	Thirteen Weeks Ended Jan. 31, 1998	Fifty-two Weeks Ended Jan. 31, 1998
Net sales	$1,231,186	$1,345,221	$1,765,939	$2,165,479	$6,507,825
Gross profit	442,060	462,135	721,266	860,823	2,486,284
Net earnings	84,304	69,458	164,523	215,616	533,901
Earnings per share–basic	.21	.17	.42	.55	1.35
Earnings per share–diluted	.20	.17	.40	.53	1.30

Fiscal 1996 Quarter Ended

($000 except per share amounts)	Thirteen Weeks Ended May 4, 1996	Thirteen Weeks Ended Aug. 3, 1996	Thirteen Weeks Ended Nov. 2, 1996	Thirteen Weeks Ended Feb. 1, 1997	Fifty-two Weeks Ended Feb. 1, 1997
Net sales	$1,113,154	$1,120,335	$1,382,996	$1,667,896	$5,284,381
Gross profit	413,840	400,170	545,221	639,984	1,999,215
Net earnings	81,573	65,790	134,310	171,186	452,859
Earnings per share–basic	.19	.16	.32	.42	1.09
Earnings per share–diluted	.19	.15	.32	.41	1.06

Quantitative and Qualitative Disclosures About Market Risk

The table on the right provides information about the Company's market sensitive financial instruments as of January 31, 1998 and constitutes a forward-looking statement. The Company operates in foreign countries which exposes it to market risk associated with foreign currency exchange rate fluctuations. The Company's policy is to hedge substantially all merchandise purchases for foreign operations through foreign exchange forward contracts. These contracts are entered into with large reputable financial institutions, thereby minimizing the risk of credit loss. Further discussion of these contracts appears in the Notes to Consolidated Financial Statements (Note E).

The Company issued unsecured notes payable with a fixed interest rate of 6.9 percent. By entering into the fixed-rate notes, the Company avoided interest rate risk from variable rate fluctuations.

A portion of the Company's fixed-rate short-term borrowings used to finance foreign operations are denominated in foreign currencies. By borrowing and repaying the loans in local currencies, the Company avoided the risk associated with exchange rate fluctuations.

($000)	Average Contract Rate[a]	Notional Amount of Forward Contracts in U.S. Dollars	Fair Value at Jan. 31, 1998[b]
Foreign exchange forward contracts[c]			
British pounds	.60	$33,394	$ 33,269
Canadian dollars	1.40	32,984	31,757
Italian lire	1,743.25	35,924	35,383
Japanese yen	120.52	12,803	12,266
Spanish pesetas	151.98	8,125	8,112
Total foreign exchange forward contracts		$123,230	$120,787

($000)	Fixed Interest Rate	Carrying Amount in U.S. Dollars	Fair Value at Jan. 31, 1998[d]
Notes payable[e]	6.9%	$496,044	$526,128

(a) Currency per U.S. dollar.

(b) Calculated using spot rates at January 31, 1998.

(c) All contracts mature within one year.

(d) Based on the rates at which the Company could borrow funds with similar terms and remaining maturities at January 31, 1998.

(e) Principal amount $500 million due September 15, 2007.

Appendix B

EXCEL FORMULAS FOR CORLISS FINANCIAL STATEMENTS

INTRODUCTION

This appendix shows the accounting transaction worksheet for June, 2000 for the Corliss Accounting Firm and the related financial statements that were presented in various case readings in Module 2. As you learned in Module 2, the financial statements are prepared from information obtained from the accounting transaction worksheet. Following each financial statement, the cell formulas that were typed into Excel to produce the correct value in that statement will be shown. This will help you understand the links between the accounting transaction worksheet and the financial statements. All exhibits in this appendix will retain their original numbering scheme so that you can easily identify the case reading in which the statement was first presented. (For example, Exhibit 2-1.5 represents Exhibit 5 from Case Reading 2-1). Therefore, the exhibits will not be sequentially numbered and may come from several different case readings. The best way to use this appendix is to review the formulas for the statements as you learn those statements in Module 2.

CORLISS COMPANY FORMULAS

The spreadsheet program you are using should have the ability to print cell formulas. (Printing cell formulas in Excel is covered in Appendix C along with linking worksheets together.) By printing the formulas, one can easily see the cell formulas that are in each cell. You will notice when you print the formulas that the spreadsheet software disregards all cell formatting such as alignment, dollar signs, and so on. Also, column widths will generally be considerably wider. Some spreadsheet programs will allow you to adjust the column widths if you wish to print out the formulas but if this is not the case, you can always print in condensed mode to get the entire spreadsheet on one page. Column widths were adjusted for this appendix to make them easier to read and to ensure that the entire formula is visible.

On the next page you will see a reprint of the accounting transaction worksheet shown as Exhibit 2-1.5 in Case Reading 2-1. All the Corliss financial statements that follow are prepared from this worksheet.

Exhibit 2-1.5
Corliss Accounting Firm
June Accounting Transaction Worksheet

	A	B	C	D	E	F	G	H	I	J	K	L
1		ASSETS						LIABILITIES + OWNER'S EQUITY				
2	Date	Cash	Accounts Receivable	Supplies	Prepaid Insurance	Land	Building	Accounts Payable	Mortgage Payable	Contributed Capital	Retained Earnings	Explanation of Retained Earnings
3	Beg.Bal. 6/1/00	$ 29,300	$ -	$ 1,000	$ -	$ 30,000	$ 100,000	$ 300	$ 110,000	$ 50,000	$ -	
4	6/1/00	(960)			960							
5	6/4/00	(300)						(300)				
6	6/15/00	2,000	1,000								3,000	Fees Revenue
7	6/16/00	(1,000)									(1,000)	Owner Withdrawal
8	6/30/00	1,100	1,100								2,200	Fees Revenue
9	6/30/00	(1,600)									(1,600)	Wage Expense
10	6/30/00						(200)				(200)	Depreciation Expense
11	6/30/00				(40)						(40)	Insurance Expense
12	6/30/00			(750)							(750)	Supplies Expense
13	6/30/00	(806)							(73)		(733)	Interest Expense
14	End.Bal. 6/30/00	$ 27,734	$ 2,100	$ 250	$ 920	$ 30,000	$ 99,800	$ -	$ 109,927	$ 50,000	$ 877	

Note how this worksheet has been printed with row and column labels. If you are printing formulas, you must also print row and column labels. Appendix C explains how to print a spreadsheet with formulas and with row and column labels.

As the individual financial statements are discussed, you will see the references to the June worksheet cells. For example, assume we are preparing the balance sheet shown in Exhibit 2-1.8. The accounts on the balance sheet as well as their balances should be linked to the June worksheet. Look at the cash balance on the balance sheet. The June worksheet shows the cash balance as $27,734, and it is mandatory that the cash balance on the balance sheet agrees with the cash balance on the June worksheet. However, do not type in the June worksheet dollar amount for cash. Instead do the following:

1. Set up your worksheets so that the accounting transaction worksheet is on one worksheet and the balance sheet is on another. (Eventually you will have a different worksheet tab for each financial statement but this example will only deal with the June worksheet and the balance sheet.) If you need help with these directions, see the section, "Workbooks and Worksheets," in Appendix C and also see Figure C9 in that appendix. The worksheet tabs in Figure C9 correspond to the exhibit numbers of their respective financial statements.

2. Complete the June accounting transaction worksheet by entering the transactions.

3. Go to the balance sheet worksheet by clicking on your worksheet tab for the balance sheet.

4. In the balance sheet worksheet, go to the cell that will contain the amount for Cash. For the Corliss balance sheet shown in Exhibit 2-1.8 this would be cell D8. Click in that cell.

5. While in the cell, hit the **equals** key.

6. At the bottom of your screen, click on the June worksheet tab.

7. Click the mouse in cell B14, which is the ending balance amount of cash.

8. Hit **Enter.** You should be back in the balance sheet file.

When the formulas are printed out, note that the workbook file name and the worksheet name has been added to each cell reference. For example, the printout of the formulas for cell D8, the cash balance of the balance sheet, showed:

	D
8	=[C3.xls]JWksh!B14

"[C3.xls]" is a reference to the workbook name, "JWksh" is a reference to the worksheet name, and "B14" is the cell reference on the worksheet. The workbook file name may not be visible on the screen while you are viewing the formulas but appears when they are printed out.

Exhibit 2-1.8

	A	B	C	D	E	F	G	H	I
1							Corliss Accounting Firm		
2							Balance Sheet		
3							June 30, 2000		
4									
5		Assets					Liabilities and Owner's Equity		
6									
7		Current Assets					Current Liabilities		
8		Cash		$ 27,734			Accounts Payable	$	-
9		Accounts Receivable		2,100			Long Term Liabilities		
10		Supplies		250			Mortgage Payable		
11		Prepaid Insurance		920					109,927
12		Total Current Assets		31,004					
13							Total Liabilities		109,927
14		Fixed Assets					Owner's Equity		
15		Land	$ 30,000				Contributed Capital	$ 50,000	
16		Building	99,800				Retained Earnings	877	
17		Total Fixed Assets		129,800			Total Owner's Equity		50,877
18									
19									
20		Total Assets		$ 160,804			Total Liabilities and Owner's Equity		$ 160,804
21									

Shown to the right is Exhibit 2-1.8, the balance sheet for Corliss as of June 30, 2000. The related formulas are shown on the following page. You will notice that the account descriptions in columns B and G from Exhibit 2-1.8 are not typed in. They are merely the cell addresses for the account names on the June accounting transaction worksheet (all from row 2 of that worksheet). The account balances are also formulas. They are taken from the ending balance row of the worksheet (row 14 of the June worksheet).

Oftentimes, text or formulas on the worksheet will not be reflected in their entirety as shown on the next page. The heading "Liabilities and Owner's Equity" is missing from the balance sheet on the next page. Do not be alarmed. That heading was entered in cell F5 of Exhibit 2-1.8 and then centered across columns G, H and I.

When the cell formulas on the next page were printed, the cell width was not wide enough to show this particular heading. (As mentioned previously, the cell widths were widened intentionally so all *formulas* could be viewed but some text may not be readable). Although the headings are there it is not important to see them and widening the column would make the printed output smaller and therefore harder to read.

Cell Formulas for the Balance Sheet Shown in Exhibit 2-1.8

	A	B	C	D	E	F	G	H	I
1				Corliss Accounting Firm					
2				Balance Sheet					
3				June 30, 2000					
4									
5		Assets							
6									
7	Current Assets					Current Liabilities			
8		=[C3.xls]JWksht!B2		=[C3.xls]JWksht!B14				=[C3.xls]JWksht!H2	=[C3.xls]JWksht!H14
9		=[C3.xls]JWksht!C2		=[C3.xls]JWksht!C14					
10		=[C3.xls]JWksht!D2		=[C3.xls]JWksht!D14		Long Term Liability			
11		=[C3.xls]JWksht!E2		=[C3.xls]JWksht!E14				=[C3.xls]JWksht!I2	=[C3.xls]JWksht!I14
12	Total Current Assets			=SUM(D8:D11)					
13						Total Liabilities			=SUM(I8:I12)
14	Fixed Assets					Owner's Equity			
15		=[C3.xls]JWksht!F2	=[C3.xls]JWksht!F14				=[C3.xls]JWksht!J2	=[C3.xls]JWksht!J14	
16		=[C3.xls]JWksht!G2	=[C3.xls]JWksht!G14				=[C3.xls]JWksht!K2	=[C3.xls]JWksht!K14	
17	Total Fixed Assets			=SUM(C15:C16)					
18						Total Owner's Equity			=SUM(H16:H17)
19									
20	Total Assets			=D12+D17		Total Liabilities and Owner's Equity			=I13+I18
21									

Exhibit 2-3.3

	A	B	C	D
1		**Corliss Accounting Firm**		
2		**Income Statement**		
3		**Month Ended June 30, 2000**		
4	Revenues			
5		Fees Revenue		$ 5,200
6				
7	Expenses			
8		Wage Expense	$ 1,600	
9		Supplies Expense	750	
10		Interest Expense	733	
11		Depreciation Expense	200	
12		Insurance Expense	40	
13	Total Expenses			3,323
14	Net Income			$1,877
15				

The income statement shown in Exhibit 2-3.3 and its related formulas are shown to the right and on the following page. Note that the revenues and expenses are all referenced to column K (the retained earnings column) of the June worksheet. The revenue and expense descriptions are all referenced to column L, which explains the retained earnings column. Individual expense amounts are generally shown as positive amounts on formal financial statements. Because in the June worksheet these are negative amounts (reductions), a minus sign in front of the cell addresses adjusts the negative amounts to positive amounts. The net income computation is Revenues – Expenses = Net Income.

The cell formulas for Exhibit 2-3.3 follow. Once again, the columns have been widened so that the entire formula is visible. The full income statement heading is in cell A1:A3 but only A2 appears in the formulas because column A is not wide enough to accommodate the heading in cell A1 and A3. The Centering Across Columns command that was used on the statement does not work when formulas are printed. You will notice that each cell with a formula references first to the workbook file (in this case C3.xls), then to the worksheet within the workbook (in this case JWksht), and then to the individual cell reference within that worksheet (e.g., the cell reference for the word "Fees Revenue" is L8).

Cell Formulas for the Income Statement Shown in Exhibit 2-3.3

	A	B	C	D
1				
2			Income Statement	
3				
4				
5	Revenues	=[C3.xls]JWksht!L8		=[C3.xls]JWksht!K6+[C3.xls]JWksht!K8
6				
7	Expenses			
8		=[C3.xls]JWksht!L9	=-[C3.xls]JWksht!K9	
9		=[C3.xls]JWksht!L12	=-[C3.xls]JWksht!K12	
10		=[C3.xls]JWksht!L13	=-[C3.xls]JWksht!K13	
11		=[C3.xls]JWksht!L10	=-[C3.xls]JWksht!K10	
12		=[C3.xls]JWksht!L11	=-[C3.xls]JWksht!K11	
13	Total Expenses			=SUM(C8:C12)
14	Net Income			=D5-D13
15				

Following is the retained earnings statement of the Corliss Accounting Firm shown in Exhibit 2-1.6. Even though the statement wording in cell A8 states that the owner's withdrawal is subtracted, you can see that the amount taken from the June worksheet is already negative and is added to the subtotal to get to Retained Earnings, June 30, 2000.

Exhibit 2-1.6

	A	B
1	**Corliss Accounting Firm**	
2	**Statement of Retained Earnings**	
3	**Month Ended June 30, 2000**	
4		
5	Retained Earnings, June 1, 2000	$ -
6	Add Net Income	1,877
7	Subtotal	1,877
8	Less Withdrawals by Owner	(1,000)
9	Retained Earnings, June 30, 2000	$ 877
10		

The cell formulas for the Retained Earnings Statement come primarily from column K of the June worksheet. Cell address K3 is the beginning balance in the retained earnings column and K7 is the owner withdrawal. As mentioned earlier, it is not necessary to subtract the owner's withdrawals because the cell amount is already negative on the June worksheet. The amount of net income comes from the income statement. Note that D14 is the cell address for the net income amount in Exhibit 2-3.3.

Cell Formulas for the Statement of Retained Earnings shown in Exhibit 2-1.6

	A	B
1	**Corliss Accounting Firm**	
2	**Statement of Retained Earnings**	
3	**Month Ended June 30, 2000**	
4		
5	Retained Earnings, June 1, 2000	=[C3.xls]JWksht!K3
6	Add Net Income	='[C3.xls]Ex 2-3.3'!D14
7	Subtotal	=SUM(B5:B6)
8	Less Withdrawals by Owner	=[C3.xls]JWksht!K7
9	Retained Earnings, June 30, 2000	=B7+B8
10		

The statement heading for the Corliss Accounting Firm is evident on the spreadsheet above because column A was widened to accommodate the remaining text in that column and therefore was wide enough to accommodate the heading.

Exhibit 2-4.2

	A	B	C	D
1		**Corliss Accounting Firm**		
2		**Statement of Cash Flows- Direct Method**		
3		**Month Ended June 30, 2000**		
4		Operating Activities		
5		Cash Inflows		
6		Fees collected		$ 3,100
7		Cash Outflows		
8		Cash paid for wages	$ (1,600)	
9		Cash paid for interest	(733)	
10		Cash paid for insurance	(960)	
11		Cash paid for supplies	(300)	
12		Total Cash Outflows		(3,593)
13		Net Cash Flow from Operations		(493)
14		Investing Activities		-
15		Financing Activities		
16		Cash paid for principal on loan	(73)	
17		Cash withdrawn by owner	(1,000)	
18		Net Cash Flow from Financing Activities		(1,073)
19		Net Decrease in Cash During June		(1,566)
20		Add Cash Balance, June 1, 2000		29,300
21		Cash Balance, June 30, 2000		$ 27,734
22				

The direct method of the statement of cash flows is comprised of cash inflows and cash outflows. These cash flows come directly from the cash column, which is column B in our June accounting transaction worksheet. The cash outflow for principal and interest on the note (cell B13 on the June worksheet) must be separated into its financing and operating components. The total payment (cell B13) less the reduction of the principal (I13) is shown as the cash paid for interest in cell C9 of the statement of cash flows. This is the operating portion of the cash flow. The total payment (cell B13 on the June worksheet) less the interest portion (cell K13 on the June worksheet) is shown as the cash paid for the principal on the loan (cell C16). Cash paid for principal is in the financing portion of the statement of cash flows.

Cell Formulas for the Statement of Cash Flows—Direct Method Shown in Exhibit 2-4.2

	A	B	C	D
1		Corliss Accounting Firm		
2		Statement of Cash Flows - Direct Method		
3		Month Ended June 30, 2000		
4	Operating Activities			
5	Cash Inflows			
6		Fees collected		=[C3.xls]JWksht!B6+[C3.xls]JWksht!B8
7	Cash Outflows			
8		Wages paid	=[C3.xls]JWksht!B9	
9		Interest paid	=[C3.xls]JWksht!K1	
10		Insurance paid	=[C3.xls]JWksht!B4	
11		Cash paid for supplies	=[C3.xls]JWksht!B5	
12	Total Cash Outflows			=SUM(C8:C11)
13	Net Cash Flow from Operations			=SUM(D6:D12)
14	Investing Activities			0
15	Financing Activities			
16		Cash paid for principal on loan	=[C3.xls]JWksht!I13	
17		Cash withdrawn by owner	=[C3.xls]JWksht!B7	
18	Net Cash Flow from Financing Activities			=SUM(C16:C17)
19	Net Decrease in Cash During June			=SUM(D13+D18)
20	Add Cash Balance, June 1, 2000			=[C3.xls]JWksht!B3
21	Cash Balance, June 30, 2000			=SUM(D19:D20)
22				

Exhibit 2-5.3

	A	B	C	D
1		**Corliss Accounting Firm**		
2		**Statement of Cash Flows - Indirect Method**		
3		**Month Ended June 30, 2000**		
4		Operating Activities		
5		Net Income		$ 1,877
6		Add (deduct) adjustment to cash basis:		
7		Depreciation expense	$ 200	
8		Increase in accounts receivable	(2,100)	
9		Increase in prepaid insurance	(920)	
10		Decrease in supplies	750	
11		Decrease in accounts payable	(300)	(2,370)
12				
13		Net Cash Flow from Operations		(493)
14		Investing Activities		-
15		Financing Activities		
16		Cash paid for principal on loan	(73)	
17		Cash withdrawn by owner	(1,000)	
18		Net Cash Flow from Financing Activities		(1,073)
19		Net Decrease in Cash During June		(1,566)
20		Add Cash Balance, June 1, 2000		29,300
21		Cash Balance, June 30, 2000		$ 27,734
22				

The operating section of the indirect method of the statement of cash flows starts with net income. The net income comes from cell D14 of the income statement shown in Exhibit 2-3.3. As explained in Case Reading 2-5, a generalized format for the operating activities section is :

Net income
+ Depreciation expense
+ Decreases in current assets
– Increases in current assets
+ Increases in current liabilities
– Decreases in current liabilities

Net cash flow from operations

The increases (decreases) in the current asset and current liability accounts are calculated by subtracting the beginning balance from the ending balance in the account. For example, the increase in accounts receivable is calculated by subtracting the beginning balance in accounts receivable (cell C3 on the June worksheet) from the ending balance (cell C14 on the June worksheet). Depreciation Expense was taken from column K on the June worksheet. Since an expense is by nature a negative amount in retained earnings, we must subtract the contents of the cell so that the end result is adding depreciation expense back to net income (subtracting a negative is the mathematical equivalent to adding).

Cell Formulas for the Statement of Cash Flows—Indirect Method Shown in Exhibit 2-5.3

	A	B	C	D
1		Corliss Accounting Firm		
2		Statement of Cash Flows - Indirect Method		
3		Month Ended June 30, 2000		
4	Operating Activities			
5	Net Income		=-[C3.xls]JWksht!K10	='[C3.xls]Ex 2-3.3'!D14
6	Add (deduct) adjustment to cash basis:			
7		Depreciation expense	=-[C3.xls]JWksht!K10	
8		Increase in accounts receivable	=-([C3.xls]JWksht!C14-[C3.xls]JWksht!C3)	
9		Increase in prepaid insurance	=-([C3.xls]JWksht!E14-[C3.xls]JWksht!E3)	
10		Decrease in supplies	=-([C3.xls]JWksht!D14-[C3.xls]JWksht!D3)	
11		Decrease in accounts payable	=([C3.xls]JWksht!H14-[C3.xls]JWksht!H3)	
12				
13	Net Cash Flow from Operations			=D5+D11
14	Investing Activities			0
15	Financing Activities			
16		Cash paid for principal on loan	='[C3.xls]Ex 2-4.2'!C16	
17		Cash withdrawn by owner	='[C3.xls]Ex 2-4.2'!C17	
18	Net Cash Flow from Financing Activities			=SUM(C16:C17)
19	Net Decrease in Cash During June			=SUM(D13+D18)
20	Add Cash Balance, June 1, 2000			=[C3.xls]JWksht!B3
21	Cash Balance, June 30, 2000			=SUM(D19:D20)
22				

Appendix C

INSTRUCTIONS FOR MICROSOFT EXCEL

INTRODUCTION

Microsoft Excel is a powerful spreadsheet software with many complex capabilities. Although you may be familiar with this spreadsheet software, the Excel instructions assume no previous exposure to spreadsheets. These instructions will not make you an expert in using Microsoft Excel, but provide enough information such that you can complete the spreadsheet assignments in the course. To understand the instructions completely read the text and follow the directions while sitting at a computer. These instructions assume a Windows 95 operating system and Microsoft Excel version 7 or 8.

BASIC WINDOWS COMMANDS

Before using Microsoft Excel, it is necessary to be familiar with some basic Windows 95 commands. First, turn on the computer and the monitor (TV screen). Windows will start up after some preliminary operating system procedures which are automatic. Figure C1 shows how the windows desktop might look after starting up. There should be several icons and a menu bar at the bottom. If you are not familiar with maneuvering around in Windows or do not know how to use the mouse, Microsoft Windows has a quick tutorial lesson that can be accessed in the following way:

1. While on the Windows desktop (see Figure C1), move the mouse to the "Start" button in the lower left-hand corner and click on the left mouse button to select.

2. Click on the "Help" option from the menu that appears.

3. Click on "Tour: Ten minutes to using Windows."

4. Click the "Display" button.

The term **click** is mouse terminology for pressing and releasing the left mouse button.

Computer Hardware Terminology

After completing the tutorial, you will be familiar with the Windows desktop. Figure C1 shows a sample desktop with the window called "My Computer" open. This window shows the basic drives available on this computer. This computer has a 3 ½ inch floppy disk (drive A:), a hard disk (drive C:), and a CD ROM (drive D:). The following section will explain the meaning of those terms and how to use the drives.

Figure C1 - Windows Desktop

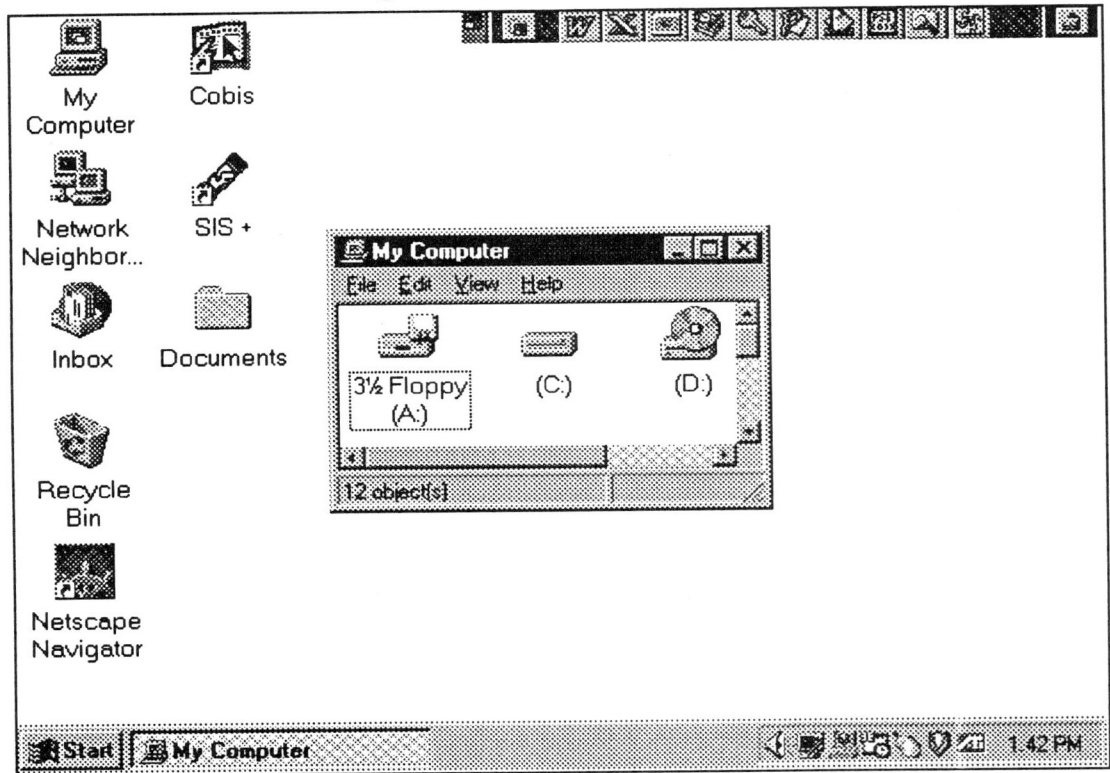

Floppy Drives and Disks

The 3 ½ inch floppy drive is Drive A on this computer. The floppy diskette drives on a personal computer (PC) are referenced as Drive A (typically the top drive) and Drive B. If a PC only has one floppy drive, it is Drive A. A **floppy drive** is used to read and write to a **floppy diskette (disk)**. A floppy diskette is easily transportable and is used to store files so that they can be read by the computer. Most computers use 3 ½ inch disks that have two different storage capacities:

> 720 K capacity
>> Marked DD (double density)
>> A square in lower left corner

> 1.44 MB (megabytes) capacity
>> Marked HD (high density)
>> A square in both lower corners

Floppy disks, nicknamed "floppies," can be purchased in your student bookstore or in a variety of other places (probably even in the supermarket). The high-density disk is preferable because it has a larger storage capacity. Before using a floppy disk for the first time, you may need to format the disk.

Formatting a Floppy Diskette. Formatting is a process that establishes sectors on the diskette and performs other functions that allow the diskette to store files. Formatting is generally performed only on brand new diskettes. Check the packaging before purchasing, because most diskettes will generally come preformatted. If so, they are ready to use, and you do not need to format them again. Do not format a diskette that has data on it because formatting erases the data.

To format a disk using Windows 95:

1. Double click on the "My Computer" group icon on the Desktop.

2. Select the "3 ½ Floppy (A:)" icon by clicking it once.

3. From the File menu select "Format".

4. Choose the appropriate Capacity:, select the "Quick (erase)" Format Type (you will be prompted if the disk needs a more complete format) and click on "Start."

5. When the format is complete you will get a Summary dialog box. Click on "Close." You can then either exit the Format box, or insert another disk, and press "Start." To close the Format window: Either press the "Close" button or click the "x" in the upper right corner.

When the computer is accessing the floppy drive, a light will come on. It is very important *not* to remove the floppy disk from the drive when it is in use.

Hard Drives

The **hard disk** (also called a fixed disk) drive is the main storage device of the computer. The hard disk has a much larger capacity than a floppy disk. Whereas the floppy may store 1.44 MB of information, a hard disk drive may store two gigabytes (GB). (A gigabyte is equivalent to 1,000 megabytes) of information or even more. Computers can have many hard drives but the one on our windows desktop in Figure C1 shows just one drive, (C:). Note how the picture of the hard drive differs from the picture of the floppy drive and the CD-ROM drive. Hard-disk drives come preformatted and *you do not want to format your hard drive* without discussing it first with a computer consultant (and even then only in very rare circumstances because formatting a hard disk will erase all information stored on your hard drive). While a floppy disk is removable from the computer, the hard disk is more permanent. Because the hard disk stores so much information, software programs are copied from floppies or CD-ROMS onto the hard drive. Hard disk drives are much faster to store information on and to access than floppy drives, so most PC owners use their hard drive almost exclusively. Floppy disks are used only to transport files, read in or copy files to the hard drive after purchasing software, or as a back up of file information on the hard drive. If you are using a school computer, however, you will probably be required to store all your personal files on a floppy disk. This allows the hard-disk storage capacity on the school computer to be used for program software (like Microsoft Excel) that benefits everyone.

CD-ROMS

A **compact disk read-only memory (CD ROM) drive** is very similar to the CD ROM drive that is used by stereo systems to play music. In fact, many CD ROM drives on computers will play music CDs. The CDs that are generally used by the computer, however, store computer file information. The most common CDs are readable but not writeable although even that is changing with current technology. A readable CD means that the computer reads all the information that is stored on the CD and can either copy that information to the hard drive or, in many cases, can run the program from the CD itself. A writeable CD means that the user can change or add to the information stored on the CD. Blank CDs are relatively cheap to purchase, and one CD can store about 600 megabytes of information (more than 400 times the information that can be stored on a floppy disk).

Network Drives

A computer *network* is a collection of computers that are linked together. The computers each use network software that allows each networked computer to access the information on the hard drives of a larger computer called a *file server*.

Using Windows Explorer

Windows Explorer is a program in the Windows 95 operating system that allows you to view and copy files.

Viewing Files

To view the directory of the files stored on any of the following, use the guidelines that follow them:

- ♦ Floppy disk (drive A or B)
- ♦ Hard-disk drive (the internal drive in your PC is typically drive C)
- ♦ CD-ROM disk drive (typically drive D)
- ♦ Network disk drives (typically drives F to Z)

1. Start Windows Explorer. (Click on the "Start" button on the menu bar, choose "Programs," and find the Windows Explorer listing, usually towards the end.)

2. Click on the appropriate Drive icon on the left hand side of the screen (as shown in Figure C2). Your file or files will appear in a list in the right half of the Explorer window. (If viewing files on a floppy disk, remember to put the diskette in the disk drive.)

3. To view the subdirectories, click on the + signs to expand the listing.

4. To view files in a subdirectory (note "Expanded Subdirectory Listing" in Figure C2) click on the *subdirectory name*.

Figure C2 - Windows Explorer

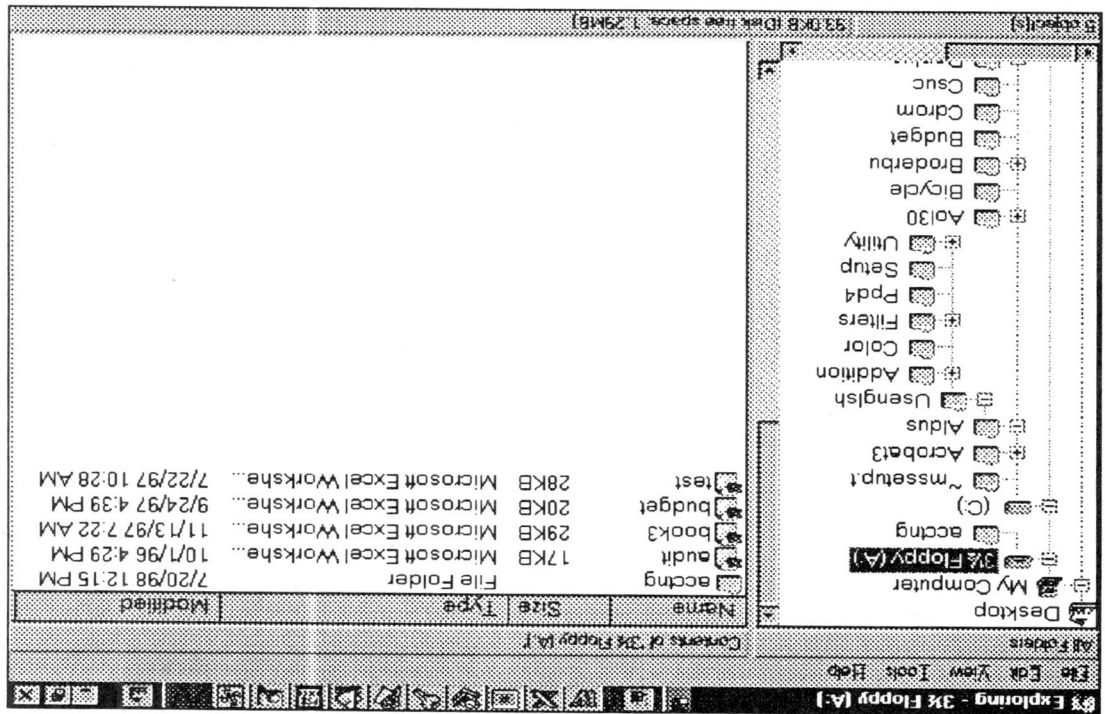

Copying a File

The copy procedure allows you to make a duplicate or back up of a file or files from one disk location to another. Two typical examples follow:

1. Copy "audit" (currently on the disk in drive A) to the disk in drive C.

   a. Start Windows Explorer (as explained above).

   b. Click on the Drive icon for drive A. This will give you a listing of the files on drive A.

   c. Click and drag (hold down the mouse button) the icon for "audit" to the Drive icon for drive C. A "+" sign should be added to your cursor to show that you are copying the file.

   d. Release the mouse button, and the words "Copying audit . . . " will appear while the file is being copied from the A drive to the C drive.

   e. You now have the file on both disk drives.

2. Copy "book3" and "test" from the A drive to the budget subdirectory on drive C.

   a. Start Windows Explorer.

   b. Click on the Drive icon for drive A to see a listing of the files on drive A.

   c. To copy multiple files at once: Hold down the Ctrl key and click on "book3" and "test" on the A drive and drag to the subdirectory "budget" located on drive C. This will copy both files to your C drive.

   d. Click on the subdirectory listing "budget" on Drive C to ensure that the copied files are listed in that subdirectory.

MICROSOFT EXCEL—A GENERAL OVERVIEW

Note: These instructions can be used for Microsoft Excel version 7.0 (Windows 95) and Excel 8.0 also called Excel 97 (Windows 97). *Any differences in instructions for Excel 97 are noted in italics and bold.*

Accessing Microsoft Excel

1. Turn on the computer as described above under Basic Windows Commands.

2. Once Windows has started, select the "Start" button, then "Programs." The Excel icon may be on the main menu, or it may be in a submenu. Try "MS Office," "Office 95," "Office 97," or similar folders. If you hold the left mouse button down and slowly move down the menu, you will be able to see what is in each subheading, or, depending on the software loaded, the Microsoft Office toolbar may be floating somewhere on the desktop.

   If so, you may select the Excel icon from there to start the program.

3. Place your formatted disk in the appropriate disk drive. This disk is where you will save your Excel spreadsheets.

4. After you open Microsoft Excel, a blank workbook should appear on the screen. If not, see Illustration 1 later in this appendix on how to open a new file.

You are now ready to learn some of the basic functions and commands of the spreadsheet, which will allow you to complete your assignments. Below are some basic instructions on the purpose of the spreadsheet and how to get started using it.

Figure C3-Basic Excel

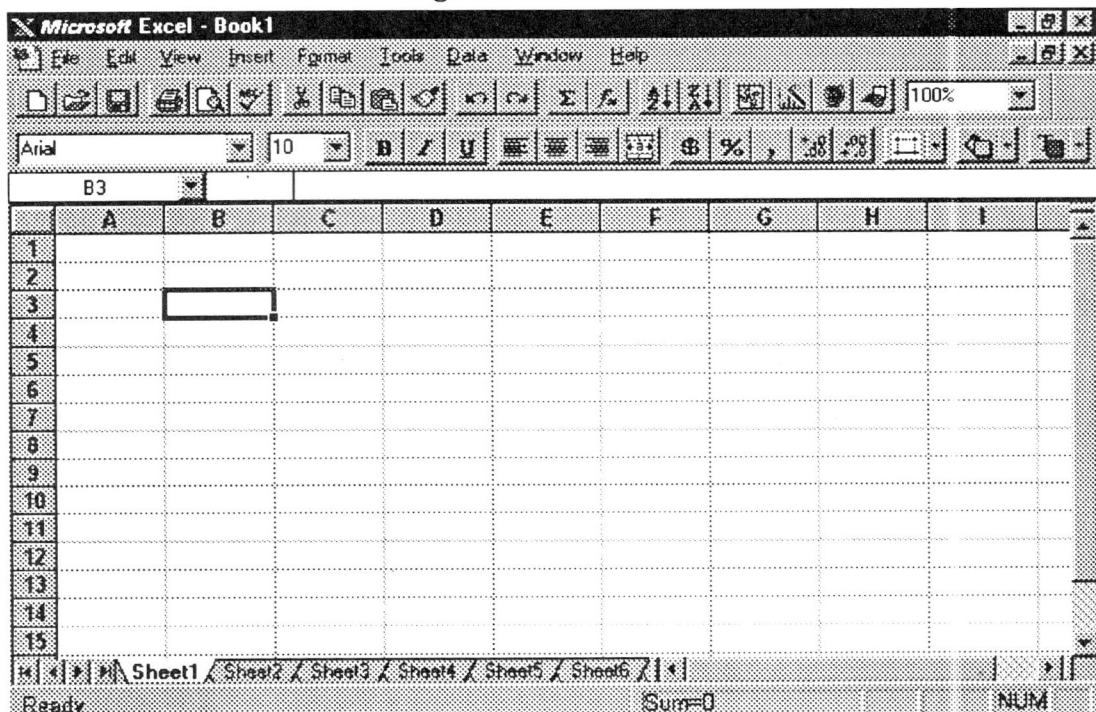

Moving Around the Workbook

The input area of Excel consists of a workbook that contains several worksheets (or spreadsheets). By clicking on the workbook tabs at the bottom of the display you can move from one worksheet to another. A spreadsheet consists of a matrix of columns and rows. The intersection of each column and row is referred to as a cell. In Figure C3 notice that the active cell is B3, as noted in the reference area or cell reference. The mouse pointer appears in Microsoft Excel as a small cross. To make a cell the active cell, position the mouse pointer on that cell and click once.

Although you can see only a small portion of the spreadsheet on the screen, there are 16,384 rows and 256 columns in Microsoft Excel. To see other parts of the spreadsheet, click either on the up or down arrows in the vertical scroll bar or on the left or right arrows in the horizontal scroll bar.

In Excel 97 there are 65,536 rows possible in the spreadsheet. This may cause problems if you switch back and forth between Windows 95 and 97. See the Excel 97 Help documentation for more information.

To move within the spreadsheet, you can use the Tab key or the Arrow keys. The Tab key moves the selection one cell to the right. Pressing Shift + Tab moves the selection one space to the left. The Arrow keys move the selection in the direction indicated. The Enter key may or may not move the selection, depending on the option you have designated. From the Tools menu, select "Options." On the "Edit" tab, there is an option that allows you to designate if the selection moves when "Enter" is pressed and which direction it will move. You can set this option to your liking. Pressing Shift + Enter will move the cell selection in the opposite direction from what is designated here. (If the selection normally moves down when you press Enter, pressing Shift +Enter will move it up one cell.)

Entering Data in the Spreadsheet

You can enter data into any cell in the spreadsheet. There are four types of data you will need to enter: text, numbers, formulas, and functions. Each one is discussed below.

Text

Text may include alpha, numeric, or other characters, although alpha characters are the most common ones. Two of the most common types of text are the column headings at the top of the spreadsheet or the row descriptions to the left of the spreadsheet. For example, you will learn how to use spreadsheets to track changes caused by transactions in the financial position of the firm. You will enter text for the different types of assets, liabilities, and owner's equity in the columns at the top of the spreadsheet; you will describe the transaction entered in each row on the left side of the spreadsheet.

To enter text in a particular cell, move the cursor to the cell in which you want the text to appear, click, and then type the text. The text will appear justified to the left side of the cell. Cells can contain 255 characters, but if the text is over 8 characters long, it will appear to continue into the next cell. (You can see about 8 characters in a cell unless you change the cell width. Changing the cell width and aligning text are addressed later in this appendix.)

Numbers

Spreadsheets are designed to hold matrices of numerical data. To enter a number in a cell, simply click the mouse in the cell in which you want the number to appear and use either the numeric characters above the QWERTYUIOP alpha characters or the numeric characters in the number pad at the right-hand side of the keyboard. (Laptop computer keyboards may not have numerical keys on the right side.) Enter numbers without commas or dollar signs, but include decimal points. If you wish to enter a negative number, precede the number you wish to enter with the minus (-) sign.

Formulas

By entering a formula in a cell, the spreadsheet becomes a more flexible tool for analyzing and arraying data. A formula allows you to perform arithmetic operations on the number in one cell and then enter the result in another cell. To tell Microsoft Excel that you are entering a formula in a cell, you precede the formula with an equals (=) sign. You then follow this sign with the formula. Cell locations referred to in a formula are designated with the column letter(s) first, followed by the row number. Arithmetic operators are + for addition, − for subtraction, * for multiplication, / for division, and ^ for exponentiation. The standard order of operations is in effect in Microsoft Excel (calculations in parentheses first, then exponentiation, then multiply/divide, and finally add/subtract.)

For example, suppose as a manager you need to calculate the depreciation for a new piece of equipment costing an estimated $100,000 with an eight-year life and a $10,000 salvage value. You might enter the cost, 100000, in cell D7. In cell D8 you want to compute the annual depreciation. You would enter the following formula in cells D8 to show that depreciation is equal to cost less salvage value divided by the useful life:

        Enter in cell D8:   =(D7−10000)/8

Depreciation of 11250 would appear in cell D8. If, upon purchase, the actual cost of the equipment is $99,000, rather than $100,000, entering the new 99000 cost in D7 would automatically cause a depreciation amount of 11125 to appear in cell D8.

Now let's do another example. First let us exit this workbook. To do so, click on "File" (at the top, in the menu bar), and click on "Close." A dialog box will appear asking if you want to "Save changes in Book1?". In this case you do not want to save your worksheet, click on "No."

By using the following small example you can become aware of what Microsoft Excel can do for you.

Illustration 1. John Goodman is a sole proprietor, and he has an average revenue each month of $3,000 from business operations, $1,200 from securities, and $300 from rental property. What is his monthly revenue ?

This is an example of addition. To compute the total we need to enter the data first. If you make a mistake when entering data, make the cell that needs correction the active cell, then press the F2 key. You will notice that the previously typed item is up in the Formula Bar for editing.

Figure C4

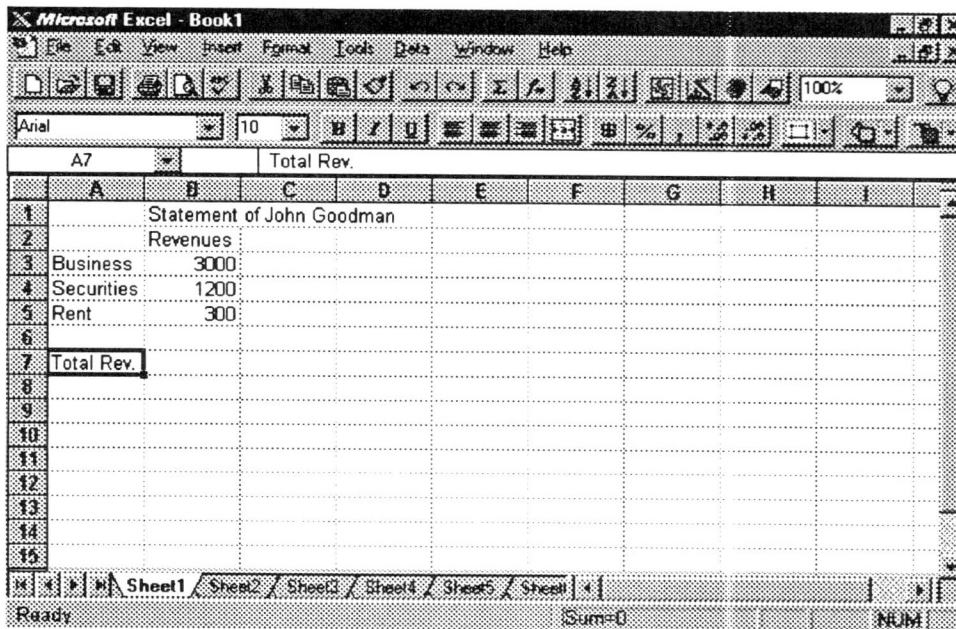

Notice the amounts entered do not have any commas and $ signs. They can be entered by using the formatting commands, which are explained later.

To start a new workbook, after using the "Close" command (like you did above), click on "File." Click on "New." Click on the "General" tab, then select the "Workbook" icon (if it's not already highlighted). Click on "OK."

After entering the data in Figure C4, place the cursor at B7. Enter a formula starting with a = sign followed by B3+B4+B5. The = sign indicates to the software that a math operation has to be performed. After typing the formula press Enter.

Figure C5 shows the formula bar after the formula has been entered in cell B7. Note that cell B7 contains the amount 4500 but what the computer has really stored in that cell is the formula, not the numerical amount. If the contents of cell B3 were changed to 4000, the contents of cell B7 would automatically change to 5500.

Figure C5

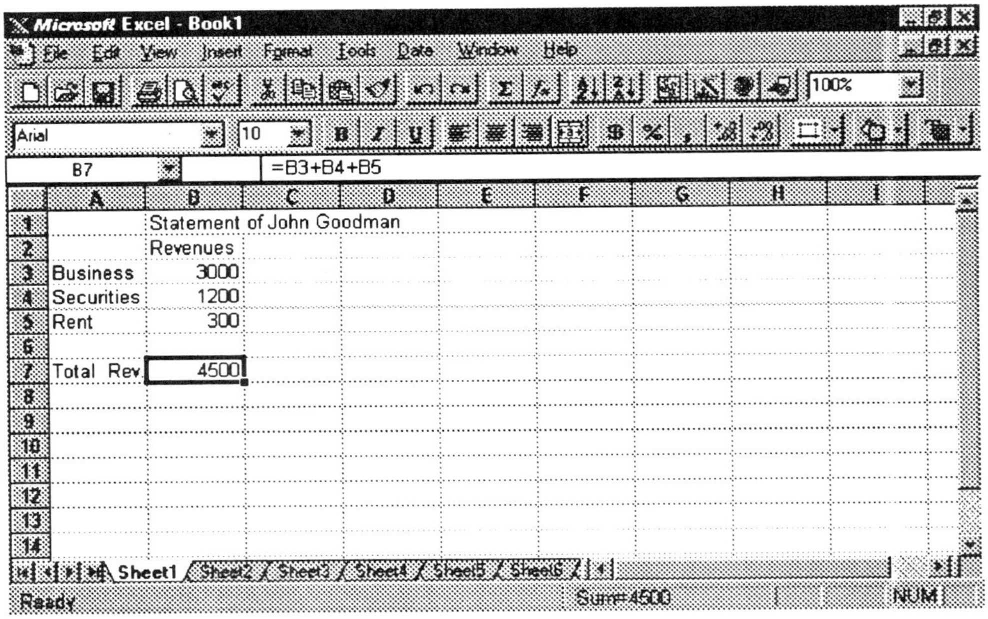

Illustration 2. Suppose John Goodman spent $3,200 in expenses to help generate the $4,500 in revenues. What is his net income for the month?

This is an example of subtraction, another operation that can be performed easily. As always, the data needs to be entered before computing. Figure C6 shows the spreadsheet that results from the following entries.

First, type in the word "Expenses" in cell B9, "Total Exp." in cell A10, and "Net. Inc." in cell A12.

Placing your cursor in cell B12 and therefore making it the active cell, type the following formula "=B7-B10" and press Enter.

Illustration 3. Suppose John Goodman believes he can improve revenue from business operations by 10 percent next month. His net income in this case will be what, assuming expenses remain the same ?

This is an example of multiplication. First make B3 the active cell and you shall see 3000. Type "=3000*1.10" and press Enter.

You will notice the amount in cell B3 changes to 3300, Total Rev. changes to 4800, and Net Inc. changes to 1600. This is one of the most powerful features of spreadsheets. By changing one figure all the connected figures are also changed. A word of caution: this can happen only if the formulas are properly constructed. These changes are all shown in Figure C7.

Figure C6

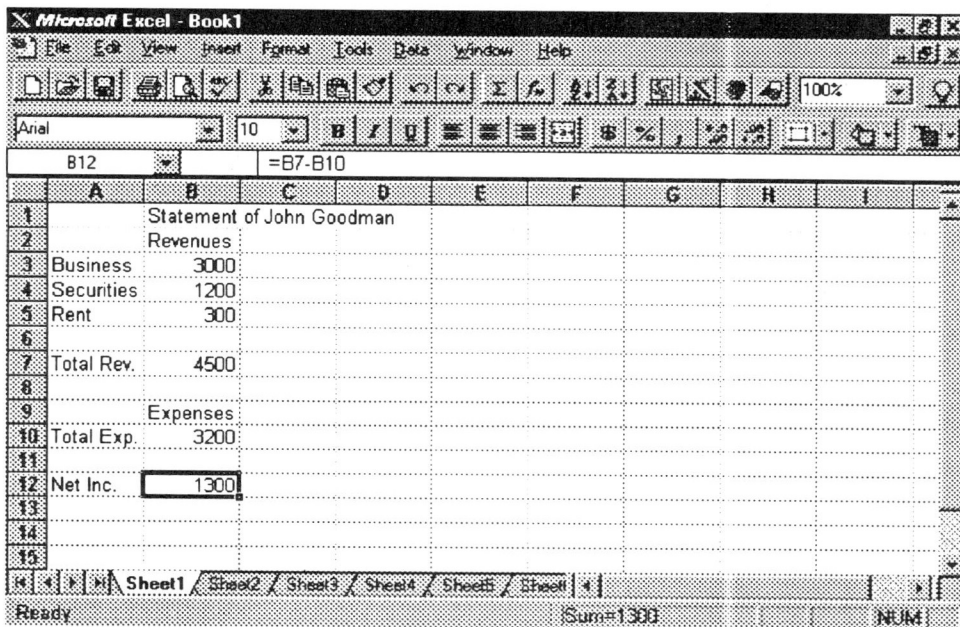

Figure C7

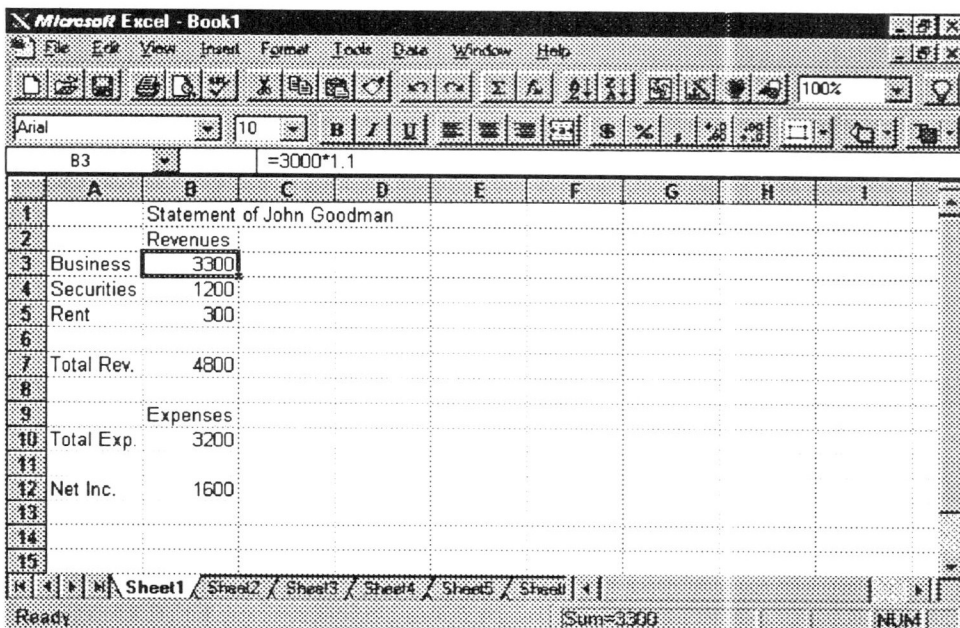

Illustration 4. John Goodman would like to know the relationship of his net income to total revenue.

This is an example of division. Move the cursor to B13 and type "=B12/B7" and press Enter. As usual the = sign indicates to the program that it is a math operation.

The screen for this is shown as Figure C8.

Figure C8

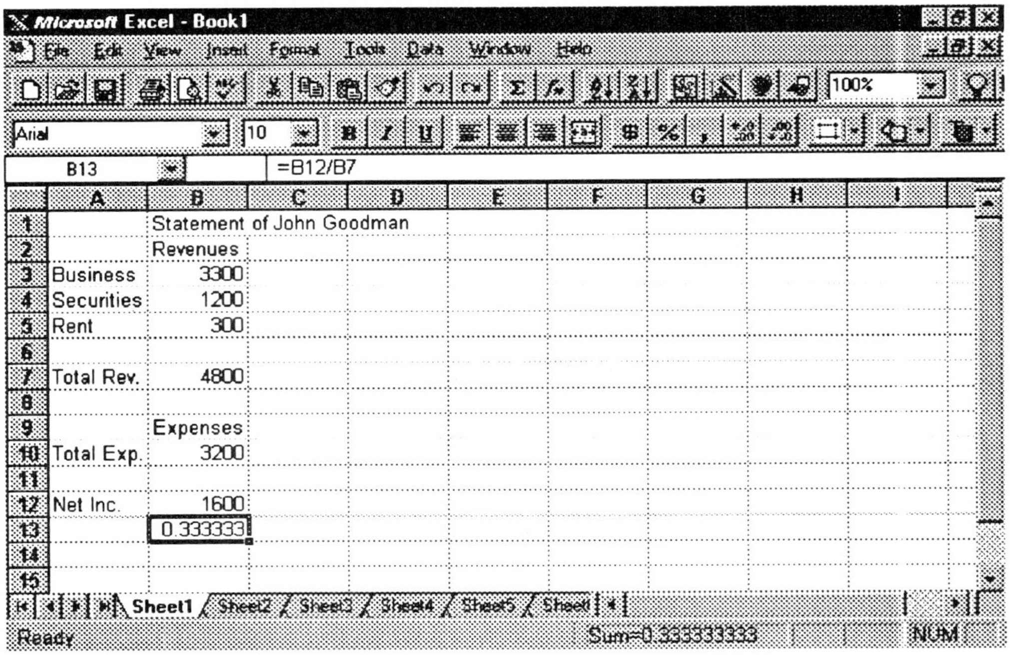

Workbooks and Worksheets

When you open a new file within Excel, that file is called an *Excel workbook file*. The workbook itself has many different worksheets. Each worksheet in the workbook can be used and given an identifying name by the worksheet preparer. For example, Figure C9 shows the author's workbook file for the many Corliss financial statements that appear in Module 2. The workbook file name is C3, as shown in the top left-hand corner of Figure C9. In this file, the various worksheets have been named by their exhibit numbers. For example, the worksheet named Ex 2-1.8 would contain the balance sheet for the Corliss Accounting Firm for June 2000 as shown in Exhibit 2.1-8 from Case Reading 2-1.

The worksheet that is currently displayed is named JWksht because it contains the June worksheet for the Corliss Accounting Firm.

When a new workbook file is opened, all worksheets within the workbook have preassigned names such as Sheet1, Sheet2, Sheet3, and so on. To rename a particular worksheet, double click on the open worksheet tab at the bottom of the workbook. (The open worksheet tab is white whereas the other worksheet tabs are a darker color, usually gray.) A menu will pop up with a box called "Rename Sheet." Putting the mouse cursor within the box, delete the current sheet name, and type in the name you want to assign to the sheet. Then click "OK." If done correctly, your sheet should now have a new name. (Alternatively, you can get the same effect by selecting the Format menu, "Sheet," and then "Rename.")

Workbook File Name

Worksheets Within the Workbook

Figure C9

	Date	Cash	Accounts Receivable	Supplies	Prepaid Insurance	Land	Building	Accounts Payable	Mortgage Payable	Contributed Capital	Retained Earnings	Explanation Retained Earning
1				ASSETS				LIABILITIES + OWNER'S EQUITY				
3	Beg.Bal. 6/1/00	$ 29,300	$ -	$ 1,000	$ -	$ 30,000	$100,000	$ 300	$ 110,000	$ 50,000	$ -	
4	6/1/00	(960)			960							
5	6/4/00	(300)						(300)				
6	6/15/00	2,000	1,000								3,000	Fees Revenu
7	6/16/00	(1,000)									(1,000)	Owner Withdrawal
8	6/30/00	1,100	1,100								2,200	Fees Revenu
9	6/30/00	(1,600)									(1,600)	Wage Expen
10	6/30/00						(200)				(200)	Depreciation Expense
11	6/30/00				(40)						(40)	Insurance Expense
12	6/30/00			(750)							(750)	Supplies Exp
13	6/30/00	(806)							(73)		(733)	Interest Expe
14	End.Bal. 6/30/00	$ 27,734	$ 2,100	$ 250	$ 920	$ 30,000	$ 99,800	$ -	$ 109,927	$ 50,000	$ 877	

Linking Worksheets

Having several different worksheets within the same workbook allows the spreadsheet preparer to easily link information from one spreadsheet to another. For example, as discussed in Module 2, the balance sheet is prepared from the ending balance row of the accounting transaction worksheet. When preparing the balance sheet, the worksheet preparer does not want to type in an amount for cash but rather wants to type in a cell reference. As shown in Appendix B, the formula entered for cash in cell D8 on the balance sheet is as shown:

	D
8	=[C3.xls]JWksht!B14

This signifies that the cash amount came from cell B14 on the worksheet named JWksht in the workbook file C3. The .xls extension shows that file C3 is an Excel file. The formulas for the Corliss financial statements for June presented in Module 2 are shown in Appendix B.

The main benefit of linking files together is that if you change the source file, any linked files will change automatically. For example, assume that the JWksht worksheet has been prepared as shown in Figure C9 above and that all the financial statements in this workbook have been properly linked to that worksheet. Row 7 of JWksht shows an owner withdrawal of $1,000. Suppose Devenie Corliss wants to see what effect a $1,200 withdrawal (instead of $1,000) would have had on her financial statements. If the amount of the withdrawal in row 7 is changed to $1,200, all the linked financial statements will change to reflect the revised amount.

EXCEL MENUS

Excel has a Menu Bar at the top of the screen. The menu bar shows that Excel has the following menus:

File menu	Edit menu	View menu
Insert menu	Format menu	Tools menu
Data menu	Window menu	Help menu

This appendix does not cover anything from the View or Data menus but covers various topics from the other menus. These menus and related topics are discussed below.

File Menu

This course will be using the File menu primarily to open, close, save, and print workbook files.

Saving Files

After completing part or all of a spreadsheet assignment, you will need to save the contents of your spreadsheet. You will use your formatted floppy disk (the one you inserted in the disk drive before you started Excel) for this purpose. While you are working, it is a good idea to save your work every 10 to 15 minutes to reduce the chance of accidentally losing your work. To save your spreadsheet on your floppy disk:

1. Click on "File." Click on "Save."

2. In the Save As dialog box, check that the "Save In:" listing is correct for your diskette location (A: or B:). If necessary, change the current drive by clicking on the down arrow to open the drop-down list box. Then click on the appropriate drive listing.

3. Click on the "File Name:" text box and type in the file name you want to give your spreadsheet, so it does not have the default name BOOK1.XLS. In Windows 95 and 97, file names can have up to 256 characters. However, it is best to limit them to 8 characters in case it becomes necessary to work on another computer. For example, if you are saving the "Laura's Law Practice" assignment, you might save it under LAURA. Microsoft Excel will automatically add a suffix at the end to identify the file as an Excel workbook. That is, it will appear as LAURA.XLS when the files on your floppy disk are listed when retrieving files. Depending on how the Open display is set up, Excel files are identified by an Excel icon, as shown in Figure C10, preceding the file name.

Figure C10

4. The "Save as type:" box contains a drop-down list of the file types Excel can save your file as. *When working with Windows 97 and Excel 97, remember that if you switch back to a computer with an older version of Excel, some of the information or*

formatting may be lost. Excel 97 does give you the option to save your work as an Excel 5.0/95 file. This is the best option if you are going to be switching computers often. The Excel 97 help files contain a section on what aspects may be lost if you open a filed saved in Excel 97 format with an older version of the software.

Ending Your Excel Session (Closing Files)

You may want to complete the entire assignment at one sitting or you may want to save your work and continue at some other time. Before concluding your work session, you must save the work you have done. Saving files is covered in the previous section. Do not exit your workbook until you have saved your work. To exit from Microsoft Excel, do the following:

1. Click on "File."

2. Click on "Exit," the screen will return to the Windows Desktop.

3. Click on the "Start" button on the bottom left of your windows desktop. Click on "Shut Down" and then click on "Yes".

4. Turn off the power to the computer. *Do not forget to take your floppy disk with you.*

Opening Files From Your Floppy Disk

When returning to the computer lab after saving your workbook file from a previous session, you will need to access Microsoft Excel in the way described at the beginning of this document. Once you have the blank Excel spreadsheet screen:

1. Click on "File" and then click on "Open."

2. In the Open dialog box, check that the drive listing (under "Look In:") is correct. (To change the drive, click on the drop-down menu box, and select the appropriate drive.)

3. The large window will contain a list of the Excel (.XLS) file(s) on your disk.

4. Click on the "LAURA.XLS" file. Click on "OK." Your spreadsheet will be retrieved onto the screen.

Printing The Spreadsheet

After completing your assignment, you will need to print the spreadsheet to turn in to your instructor. To print the spreadsheet once the file has been opened (see retrieving and saving files), follow these steps:

1. Click on "File."

2. Click on "Print Preview." This allows you to see what your spreadsheet will look like before printing it.

3. If your spreadsheet is more then one page, click on "Next" and "Previous" to see all of the pages.

4. Click on "Print" to print the document, or if you want to make any changes, click on "Close" to go back to your spreadsheet.

The amount that can be printed on one page depends on the capability of the printer and the size of the spreadsheet you wish to print. Following are some methods to change your page setup in order to get all or more of your spreadsheet on one page. Some of these methods will not be available to you, depending on your printer.

Printing Options. From the Print Preview window, you can do some or all of these options, depending on how much you need to get on a page:

1. Click on "Setup." In the Page Setup dialog box:

    a. On the Page tab under Orientation: click on "Landscape" (versus "Portrait"). This will allow more columns to be printed (but less rows.) Click on "OK" to see the changes in Print Preview.

    b. Also on the Page tab, under Scaling, you can click on "Fit to: 1 page wide by 1 tall." Click on "OK" to see the changes in Print Preview. Note: This method may reduce your spreadsheet to a type size too small to read.

    c. On the Margins tab, change the "Left:" and/or "Right:" to a smaller number. Click on "OK" to see the changes in Print Preview. Margin changes can also be made in the Print Preview window by clicking on "Margins."

Printing Gridlines. Printing gridlines can make it easier to see which information is in the same row or column. Under the "File," "Page Setup," "Sheet" tab, you have the option to print the spreadsheet with or without gridlines. The default is without. Click on the box next to the option to put an "x" in it, then press "OK."

Printing Row and Column Labels. Sometimes when printing a spreadsheet it is very helpful to have the spreadsheet printed with the row and column labels. This is especially helpful if you are also printing formulas because you can see the row and column designations that are mentioned in the formulas. Go to "File," then "Page Setup," then click on the "Sheet" tab. You have the option to print the spreadsheet with row and column labels or without them. The default is without. Click on the box next to the option to put an "x" in it, then press "OK." Your spreadsheet will now print with row and column labels. Figure C11 shows a partial spreadsheet with row and column labels.

Figure C11

	A	B	C	D	E
1	Date	Cash	Accounts receivable	Accounts Receivable	
2	1/1/00	1000	162		
3	1/1/00	500	300		
4	1/1/00	300	452		

Edit Menu

The Edit menu is used for copying a cell, deleting rows or columns, and cutting and pasting.

Copying a Cell—The Fill Command

One of the most powerful commands in an electronic spreadsheet is the Fill (Copy) command. This command allows you to duplicate one or more cells. As an example: In John Goodman's worksheet shown in Figure C8, if the layout was changed to represent six months of data, and column B represented January's revenue, then column C could be February's revenue, and so on, over to column G representing June. The appropriate data (if you wanted to do this example, you could just make up some numbers) for Business, Securities, Rent, and Total Exp. could then be entered in each column for the five months (February – June). New formulas would not have to be typed for Total Rev., Net Inc., etc.) for each month. The Fill Right command will duplicate the formulas in column B across to columns C through G and automatically change the addresses in the new formulas. Copy the Total Rev. formula in cell B7:

1. Put the mouse pointer in cell B7. To highlight the fill range, click and hold the mouse button down and drag the mouse pointer (to highlight) across to cell G7.

2. Now click on "Edit" (up in the Menu bar.)

3. Click on "Fill." Click on "Right."

4. Notice the new formulas add up the cells in their column. For example, the February column (column C) now has a formula in cell C7 that adds up C3, C4, and C5. The Fill Right command copied the original formula in B7, but changed the addresses to reflect the new locations.

5. Net Inc. in cell B12 and the relation of Net Inc. to Total Rev. in B13 can both be copied across in one step by highlighting from cell B12 down to B13 and across to column G. Then repeat steps 2 and 3 above.

The Fill Down command works the same way as the Fill Right except that it copies a cell down in a specified range.

Deleting Rows or Columns

Sometimes you may want to delete a row or a column. Perform the following:

1. Click on a cell(s) in the row(s) or column(s) you want to delete.

2. Now click on "Edit" (up in the Menu bar), then "Delete."

3. A dialog box will allow you to choose "Entire Row" or "Entire Column." Then click on "OK"

4. Row and column labels and formulas will adjust automatically.

Cut and Paste

If you want to move the contents of one cell to another cell, you can use the Cut and Paste commands. To cut and paste:

1. Click in the cell from which you want to cut the data.

2. Now click on "Edit" (up in the Menu bar), then "Cut." You will notice that the cell that you are cutting has been highlighted.

3. Move the mouse cursor to the cell in which you want to put the data.

4. Click on "Edit" (up in the Menu bar), then "Paste."

> There is a quicker way to move the contents of one cell to another. First, highlight the cell you want to move. There will be a highlighted box around the cell. Next, touch the mouse to an edge of the cell so that you can now see an arrow. Press the mouse button, holding down without releasing, and drag the cell to its new desired location.

Insert Menu

This course will be using the Insert menu to insert a blank row or column or to insert a function.

Inserting a Blank Row

Assume you want a blank row between rows 2 and 3:

1. Click on any cell in row 3 (the cell directly below where you want to insert the blank row).

   Note: To insert more than one blank row, click and drag down to highlight as many cells as you want blank rows.
2. Now click on "Insert" (up in the Menu bar), then "Rows."
3. You now have a new blank row between what used to be rows 2 and 3. What used to be row 3 is now row 4, etc. All formula and function addressing is automatically adjusted for the entire sheet.

Inserting a Blank Column

Assume you want a blank column between columns B and C:

1. Click on any cell in column C (the cell directly to the right of where you want to insert the blank column). Note: To insert more then one blank column, click and drag to the right to highlight as many cells as you want blank columns.
2. Now click on "Insert" (up in the Menu bar), then "Columns."
3. You now have a new blank column between what used to be columns B and C. What used to be column C is now column D, etc. All formula and function addressing is automatically adjusted for the entire sheet.

Inserting a Function

Microsoft Excel has many functions that you can use. A more thorough discussion of the functions used in the course is covered in the last portion of this appendix. To insert a function using the function wizard:

1. Click in the cell in which you want to put the function.
2. Click on "Insert" and then "Function." Select a function and then follow the steps in the function wizard.

Format Menu

The format menu is one that you will need to use often during this course to improve the quality of presentation.

Formatting for Currency

Each spreadsheet that you hand in should be properly formatted for currency where needed. To format for currency:

1. First, you need to highlight the range of cells that you want to format as currency (B3 to B12 in Figure C8). Put the mouse pointer at the beginning of the range on (cell B3). To highlight the range, click and drag (hold down the mouse button) to highlight down to cell B12. Release the mouse button.

2   Click "Format," "Cells." Select the "Number" tab. In the category box choose "Currency "and set the decimal place to "2." Click the "Use $" box so that there is a check or an "x" in it. Select the option for the negative numbers: "($1,234.00)" in black. Click "OK"

2. *Same as for 7.0, but in the "Symbol" box, select the "$" option without any words. You do not need to choose the "$ - English (United States)" option.*

3. If a number has more digits than will fit in a column (the currency format adds "$", "," and ".00") you will see pound signs (#) instead of values. To solve this problem, widen the column.

Changing the Column Width

For One Column

1. Make one of the cells in the column you want to enlarge the active cell.

2. Click on "Format." Click on "Column." Click on "Width."

3. In the Column Width window the present column width will already be highlighted, so you just need to type in a new width (e.g., 12,) and click on "OK." This column will now have the new width designated by you.

For More Than One Column

1. Put the mouse pointer in the first column, click and drag to highlight the desired columns.

2. Repeat steps 2 and 3 in the section for one column.

Or, if you do not wish to guess the appropriate column width, position the cursor on the right edge of the column header tab (A, B, C, etc.) of the column you wish to change. Your cursor should look like ✛. Drag the column edge until it is the desired width. (Double-clicking between two heading tabs will automatically adjust the column width of the left column to hold its cell contents.)

Hiding or Unhiding Rows or Columns

There are times you may want to "hide" specific rows or columns from appearing on the screen or on your printouts. Excel has the ability to hide and unhide columns or rows. You may want to do this if you have data or information that is not necessary for the viewer or would be confusing to the viewer. An example may be a situation in which you have adjustment figures, in column D, that you have referenced in formulas in column B. These adjustment figures are only important to you and would just be confusing to the viewer of your worksheet. If column D is hid, the adjustment figures are still there and calculate with column B, but they are not visible.

To Hide Rows or Columns. To hide rows or columns, perform the following steps:

1. Click on any cell in the row or column you wish to hide. You can also highlight multiple cells to hide multiple rows or columns.

2. Click on "Format" (up in the Menu bar).

3. To hide a column: click on "Column," then on the "Hide" option.

4. To hide a row: click on "Row," then on the "Hide" option.

5. You will notice that the column or row is no longer visible, nor is the column letter or row number. In our earlier example, column D would not show and the column letters would go from A, B, C to E. A printout of this worksheet would also be missing column D.

To Unhide Rows or Columns. To unhide rows or columns, do the following:

1. Click and highlight on any two cells in the rows directly below and above the hidden row, or to the columns directly to the left and right of a hidden column. In our example above, to unhide column D, you would click on any cell in column C (we'll use C3) and drag over to column E (E3.)

2. Repeat steps 2 and 3 (or 4) above, but click on the "Unhide" option.

Alignment

Aligning information in the cells helps organize it and makes it easier to view.

1. Select the cells you want to format by holding down the mouse button while dragging the cursor to the selection.

2. From the Menu bar, choose "Format," "Cells," then click on the "Alignment" tab.

3. You are given several options in Horizontal Alignment (Left, Center, Right), Vertical Alignment (Top, Center, Bottom), Text Orientation, and Text Wrap.

Word Wrap (Text Wrap)

Sometimes the text entered in a cell is too long for the cell. For an example, see the treatment of the word Accounts Receivable that was entered in cell D1 of Figure C11. If the text is too long to fit in the cell, the word will spill over into the next cell, in this case cell E1. It is possible to have Excel expand the cell vertically and put the text onto another line within the same cell. For example, the word "Accounts Receivable" was typed in cell C1 and then the cell was formatted with Text Wrap. Notice how the treatment of the word in cell C1 differs from the treatment of the same word in cell D1. To format a cell to Word Wrap:

1. Make the cell you want to format with Word Wrap the active cell by clicking in the cell.

2. From the Menu bar, choose "Format," "Cells," then click on the "Alignment" tab.

3. Click the box next to "Wrap Text" so that is has an "x" in it.

4. Click on "OK." The column width stays the same, but the row height adjusts so that all the words fit into the column and don't bleed over into the next column.

Automatic Cell Formatting

Cells start out with a general format. They have no specific format designation. As mentioned before, you can enter many types of data into cells—text, numbers, formulas, etc. When you begin typing into a cell, Excel makes a determination as to what type of data you are entering and formats the cell to what it thinks is the best match.

Text is aligned to the left margin of the cell and will bleed over into the next cell if it is too long and if there is no data in the adjacent cell.

Numbers align to the right edge of the cell and will not bleed over. Excel will convert them into scientific notation to make them fit into the cell, if possible, or display a cell full of pound signs (#) if it cannot. The Wrap Text command will not work with numerical data. To get rid of the pound signs, you need to widen the column.

You may find it necessary to correct Excel's formatting choices from time to time. The "Format," "Cells" option is the place to do this. A short cut to open the formatting dialog box is to press on the Ctrl and the 1 keys together.

Tools Menu

The main items you will need in the Tools menu are the spellcheck and the showing and printing formulas.

Spellcheck

Excel provides a spellcheck to check the spelling on the worksheet. To use the spellcheck, go to "Tools" and then to "Spelling."

Showing and Printing Formulas

There are times when you want to show or print your formulas in their cells. In order to do this:

1. Click on "Tools." Click on "Options." On the "View" tab, under Window Options, click on the box to the left of "Formulas." This will put an "x" in that box. Click on "OK."

2. This will automatically widen the columns, and you will see all your functions and formulas rather than their numerical results.

3. If you need a printout showing the formulas, use the normal printing procedures (see below).

4. To put your spreadsheet back to its original state, repeat step 1. By clicking on the box next to "Formulas," with the "x" in it, the "x" will be removed.

There is a useful short cut to this command. Pressing Ctrl and ~ at the same time will allow you to see formulas without having to go through the menu process., If you press those two keys together again when you are viewing the formulas, the spreadsheet will return to normal. You can toggle the formulas on and off by pressing the two keys at the same time repeatedly. The ~ key is generally located on the top left portion of your keyboard.

Window Menu

The Window menu will be used to freeze and unfreeze row and column headings and to arrange the worksheets in the workbook in a tiled fashion.

Freezing and Unfreezing Panes (Row and Column Headings)

On larger worksheets (i.e., there are more rows and/or columns than are visible on your monitor) when you scroll down or to the right (to see additional data) you can no longer see the column and/or row headings. To avoid this problem, Excel has the ability to freeze the row and/or the column headings portion of your worksheet. This feature keeps those rows and/or columns (containing headings) "frozen" on your screen, so you can always see them no matter how far you scroll down or to the right. Assume a large worksheet with row headings (Sales, Expenses, Income, etc.) in column A and column headings (i.e., January, February, etc. to December) in row 3 (there is also a title in row 1). If column A is frozen, you will always be able to see the row headings when scrolling out to the end months of the year. If rows 1, 2, and 3 are frozen, you will always be able to see the month column headings as you scroll down to the bottom of the worksheet (the last row is 60).

Freezing Panes. To freeze a window, perform the following:

1. Click on cell B4 (the cell to the right of the column to be frozen and below the rows you want to freeze).
2. Click on "Window" (up in the Menu bar), then "Freeze Panes."
3. Now as you scroll down or to the right your headings remain visible on the screen.

Unfreezing Panes. To unfreeze a window, just click on "Window" (up in the Menu bar), then "Unfreeze Panes."

Arranging Open Workbook Files

Oftentimes when you open a workbook, it is not easy to see the worksheet tabs that are within the workbook. There are several ways to arrange the open workbook files, tiled, horizontal, vertical, or cascade. The tiled option is the one used to ensure that all the worksheet tabs are visible. Go to "Window," "Arrange," and then click on "Tiled."

Spreadsheet Functions

Although there are many different functions that can be performed by Microsoft Excel, only a few functions are needed to complete introductory accounting spreadsheet assignments. Each function used in this course begins with an equal sign followed by the function name and parenthesis at the beginning and the ending of the function arguments. The various function arguments change depending on the function. Excel has a function wizard (go to the Insert menu and then "Function") that can help to explain the function arguments. Be sure there are no extra blank spaces in the formula. Each argument must be separated by a comma.

=Sum Function

If you want to add data contained in 10 cells you can physically type all cell addresses. Suppose you want to add data contained in cells C1 through C10, then you could type:

$$=C1+C2+C3+C4+C5+C6+C7+C8+C9+C10$$

This is a very tedious and inefficient approach. Instead there is an easier approach. Type:

$$=Sum(C1:C10)$$

Suppose the cells to add were not in the same row or column. For example, say we wanted to add the numbers in cell A1, B2, C4, and D5. We can still use the sum function but it will look like this:

$$=Sum(A1,B2,C4,D5)$$

The terms A1, B2, C4 and D5 are called the function arguments.

Loan Payment Function

It is often necessary to compute the payment required to amortize a loan over a specified period at a specified interest rate. You can do this using a calculator that allows you to perform that specific function. Excel can also compute the payment. For example, assume that a bank loans a home buyer $200,000 at 9 percent annual interest secured by a 30-year mortgage. The home buyer must make yearly payments of principal and interest. What yearly payment amount will amortize the loan over 30 years?

To compute the payment, the payment function is employed. The format of the function is:

$$=PMT(interest\ rate,total\ number\ of\ payment\ periods,present\ value\ of\ loan)$$

In the example, the following would be entered in the cell in which the payment was to be entered:

$$=PMT(.09,30,-200000)$$

The first number entered represents the interest rate for each payment period, 9 percent in our example. The second number entered in the parentheses is the number of periods over the life of the loan, 30 in this example. The third number entered in the parentheses represents the present value of the principal or loan amount of $200,000. The Excel PMT function requires a negative amount for the present value in order to have a positive payment result, so put a "minus" in front of this "present value" figure.

After typing "=PMT(.09,30,-200000)" in the cell and pressing the Enter key, the payment amount of $19,467.27 will be shown in the cell.

If the payments required were monthly payments, the interest rate and the number of payment periods would need to be adjusted accordingly. Instead of a 9 percent interest rate per period, the interest rate would now be 9 percent ÷ 12. Instead of 30 interest periods, there would now be 30 × 12 interest periods.

The equation to compute the monthly payment would therefore read:

$$=PMT(.09/12,30*12,-200000)$$

When Excel computes the payment, the software understands that .09/12 is one argument because each argument, as explained previously, is separated by a comma. For this reason calculations can be entered as arguments. Alternatively, the interest rate of .75 percent (instead of .09/12) and the interest periods of 360 (instead of 30*12) could be entered directly, but by entering the mathematical calculations themselves, rounding problems and errors are avoided. Notice that there are no blank spaces in the equation.

Linked Formulas and Absolute Cell References. What if you want to know what the payments will be if the mortgage is repaid over 25 years, or 35 years? Excel can be easily configured to compute the payment for various options, without making you edit the formula for each change in variable. We will use the PMT formula as an easy example. This example will demonstrate interlinking formulas and absolute cell references.

Enter the data as shown in Figure C12. Instead of typing the formula into every cell in row 3, you can copy them across. (For a shortcut to using the "Edit," "Fill," "Right" command, select the small box in the lower right corner of the active cell. Your cursor should change to a thinner ✚ shape and drag it across. You will notice that you get the same effect.)

Figure C12

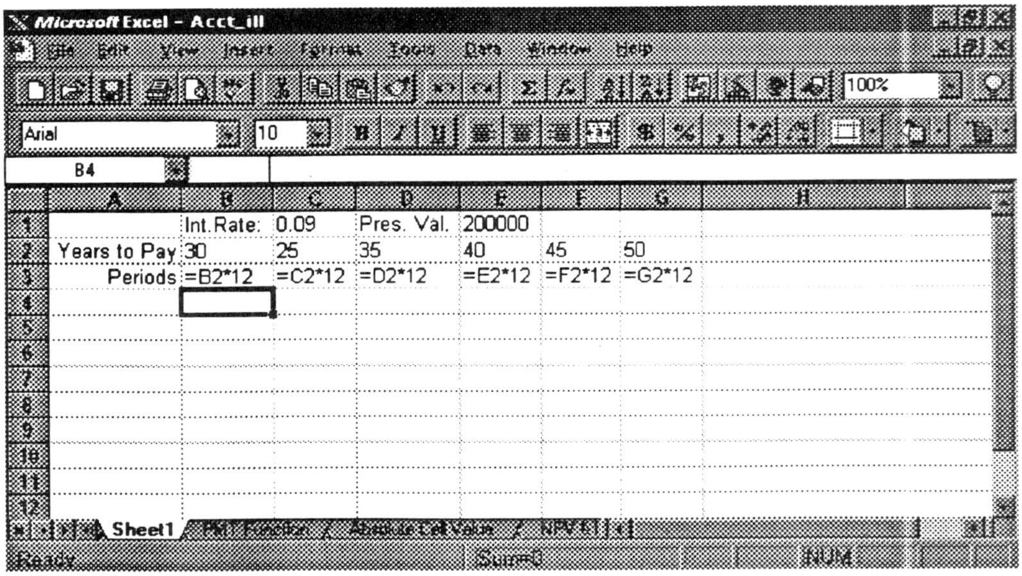

In cell B4, enter "=PMT(C1/12,B3,–E1)". The function arguments are as follows:

C1/12   The monthly interest rate (annual interest/12 months). Setting up the formula this way allows you to adjust the annual interest rate in cell C1 and see the changes, without having to edit every PMT formula. It also saves you the trouble of doing the math.

B3   The number of payment periods. For this cell it is 360. Entering the cell reference will pull in the appropriate number when we copy the formula across. Again, this will allow us to vary the number of periods without having to edit the PMT formula.

−E1   The principal amount, made negative so the end result will be positive.

You should have the answer of $1,609.25 showing in cell B4. If you copy cell B4 across to G4, you will notice that you don't get any useful information and that you get error messages of "VALUE!" and "#NUM!" in cells C4 and C5. Examine cell C4 to see why. You will notice that all the cell references in the formula shifted one cell to the right from the original. Unfortunately, cells D1 and F1 don't contain any information that is useful to us. There is a solution to this problem.

1. Go back to cell B4, and press F2 so you can edit it.

2. Position your cursor within the text "C1" and press F4. The text will change to "C1."

3. Do the same to "E1." Your formula should now read: "=PMT(C1/12,B3,-E1)".

4. Press Enter.

This procedure locks the cell references to C1 and E1. This is referred to as **an absolute cell reference**. Try copying the cells across again. You should have some coherent answers now. Examining the new formulas, you will notice that the only cell reference that has changed is the one we wanted, which referred to payment periods. The ones you locked have remained the same.

Figure C13 illustrates the results you get both with and without the cell references locked.

Net Present Value (NPV) Function

During the second half of this course, you will learn present value and net present value (NPV) concepts. This section of the instructions does not explain these concepts but tells you how to compute them using Microsoft Excel once you understand present value and net present value.

The NPV function of Microsoft Excel computes the present value of a series of future cash flows, discounted at a specified interest rate.

Figure C13

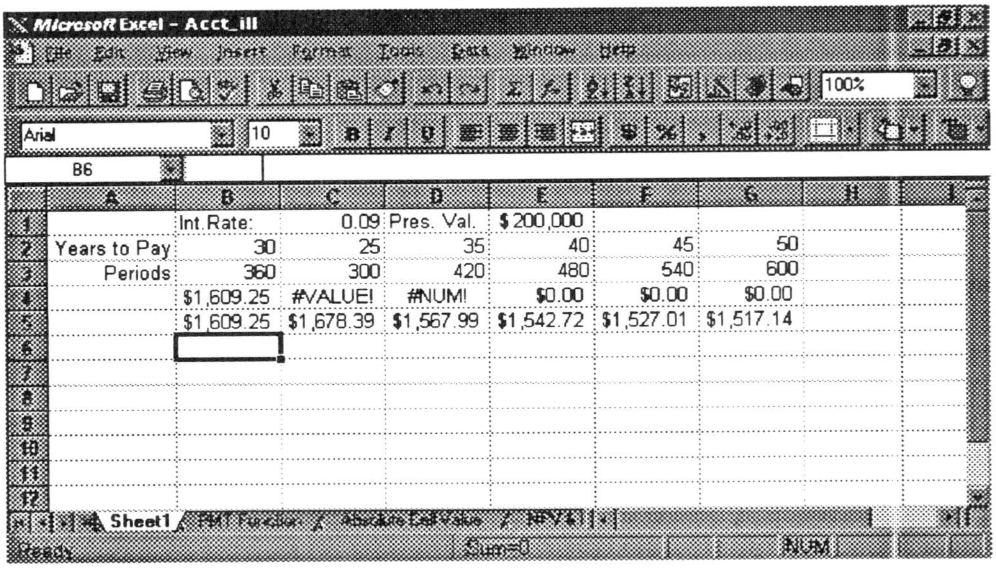

For example, assume it is now January 1, 2000, and a firm invests $3,000 to receive future cash flows of $800, $1,000, $1,400, $500, and $1,200 on December 31, 2000 through December 31, 2004, respectively. The appropriate interest (discount) rate is 10 percent. To compute the NPV of this investment in cell A1, do the following:

1. Enter the value -$3,000 in cell B1.

2. Enter the values $800, $1,000, $1,400, $500, and $1,200 in cells C1 through G1, respectively.

3. Move to cell A1 and type "=B1+NPV(.10,C1:G1)".

4. Press the Enter key.

The NPV of this stream of cash flows, discounted at 10 percent, will appear as $692.17 in cell A1. This indicates that the "true" interest rate, or the internal rate of return (see below), is higher than 10 percent.

In the function, "=B1+NPV(.10,C1:G1)," the investment is located in cell B1, the interest or discount rate is 10 percent, and the positive cash flows are located in cells C1 through G1. The interest rate may be entered as a percentage (10%) or a decimal (.1).

To compute a present value only (i.e., there is no original cash outflow in the present), simply enter a zero in the cell to which the initial investment part of the function refers. In the preceding example, if we wanted to find the present value of the five inflows with no initial investment in the present, a zero would have been entered in cell B1. The present value of $3,692.17 would appear in cell A1.

Internal Rate of Return (IRR) Function

During the second half of introductory accounting, you will learn the internal rate of return (IRR) concept. This section of the instructions does not explain this concept but tells you how to compute it using Microsoft Excel.

Briefly, the IRR is the interest or discount rate that equates the net present value to zero. Continuing the net present value example, we can compute what interest rate will give us a net present value of $0. Since the net present value at 10 percent was positive, we know that the internal rate of return is higher than 10 percent. To compute the internal rate of return, do the following:

1. Enter a guess of the IRR in cell B2. Ten percent (.10) will do. Your guess should be between 0 and 100 percent.

2. Make sure you have the value of -3000 in B1.

3. Move to cell A2 and type "=IRR(B1:G1,B2)."

4. Press the Enter key.

The IRR will appear as .1844 in cell A2. Your amount in cell A2 might differ depending on the number of decimal points you have specified in this spreadsheet session. For example, if only two decimal places are specified, you'll see .18, if three places, you'll see .184. The internal rate of return is 18.44 percent. This means that if the firm invests the $3,000 and receives the future cash inflows as specified, it will earn an 18.44 percent return on this investment.

Toolbars

Most Windows programs offer many shortcuts to common menu commands on the toolbars (Figure C14). Excel is no exception. If there are no toolbars showing when you start Excel, click on "View," "Toolbars," check the boxes next to "Standard" and "Formatting," then click "OK." You should get toolbars very similar to those shown in Figure C14. All of the buttons on the toolbars are shortcuts for commands you can access from the menus. You don't have to use them, but they can make things easier.

Figure C14

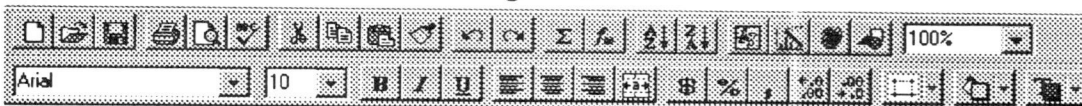

File Commands

New File: Opens a new workbook file without opening the template selection box.

Open File: Is a shortcut to the Open File dialog box for existing files.

Save File: Either opens the Save File dialog box (new files) or saves the changes you have made. (You cannot Save As with this icon.)

Print Commands

Print File: Prints using the options for that file set under Page Setup (File menu.)

Print Preview: Allows you to see how your spreadsheet will look when printed.

Spellchecker: Runs Excel's spellchecking utility on the spreadsheet.

Cut, Copy, Paste

Cut: Cuts the selection to allow you to move it to another location. The selection is surrounded by a marquee until a destination is selected. You can cut entire cells, or only part of the data from a cell. To cut the entire cell, make the cell active, then press the Cut button. To cut part of the cell, edit the cell (as described earlier in these instructions), highlight the part of the cell you wish to cut, then press the Cut button.

Copy: Copies the selection to allow you to use the information (or formulas, or formatting) elsewhere. The instructions are the same as for the Cut button.

Paste: Places the Cut or Copied material at the point of the active cell. Once you have cut or copied the material you want, select the destination for the information and select the Paste button.

Undo

The Undo button allows you to correct mistakes you have made in entering data. Be warned: Excel can only undo the last action and not all actions are undoable.

Function

Auto Sum: This button is a shortcut to the Sum function. It enters "=SUM()" into the cell, with the cursor between the parenthesis marks. You are then able to select the range of cells you desire to sum with the cursor, and then press Enter.

Function Wizard: This button brings up the Function Wizard dialog box and inputs the function selected into the active cell. Excel has many more functions available than have been detailed in these instructions. Most are explained in the Help documentation.

Zoom

The zoom box adjusts your view of the worksheet on the screen. You can either choose from the options in the drop-down box or highlight the number, type in a custom measurement, and press Enter.

Formatting

Font Style/Size: These drop-down boxes allow you to adjust the font displayed and the font size.

Bold: Makes the data in the selected cell(s) be displayed in **BOLD** print.

Italics: Makes the data in the selected cell(s) be displayed in *ITALIC* print.

Underline: Makes the data in the selected cell(s) be displayed in UNDERLINED print.

Left Justify: Aligns the data in the cell to the left edge of the cell.

Center Justify: Aligns the data in the cell to the center of the cell.

Right Justify: Aligns the data in the cell to the right edge of the cell.

Center Across Columns: Centers the data across the selected columns. (The data should be in the leftmost of the selected columns, otherwise it will only center itself with regard to the cells to the right of the data's location.)

Other Formatting

Note: There are buttons similar to these, only with quotation marks around the symbols ("$"). These are part of the Formula toolbar and enter the symbol into the formula bar for use in mathematical operations.

Currency: Inserts dollar signs, commas, and two decimal points.

Percent: Inserts percentage sign. Decimal location matters. (.13 = 13%; 13 = 1300%)

Comma: Inserts commas at the thousand breaks.

Decimal Point: Either adds (left arrow) or hides (right arrow) one decimal point.

Tapping the Full Potential of Microsoft Excel

Carefully reading these instructions should allow you to complete the spreadsheet assignments in this text. You are reminded that Microsoft Excel has much greater potential than outlined in these instructions. There is a complete overview of Excel under "Help" ("Microsoft Word Help Topics," then the "Contents" tab.)

Appendix D

THE ACCOUNTING PROCESS USING DEBITS/CREDITS

INTRODUCTION

In this appendix, the May and June transactions for the Corliss Accounting Firm are presented in the transaction worksheet format as shown in Case Reading 2-1 as well as in a traditional debit credit format. A chart of accounts is given; the transactions are recorded in the general journal and then posted to the general ledger. T accounts with balances are shown. The first part of the appendix deals with the May transactions (which include only balance sheet accounts), and the second part deals with June transactions (which include balance sheet, income statement, and owner's withdrawal accounts).

RECORDING TRANSACTIONS

In this text, students learn how to use spreadsheets to record transactions for various different types of business ventures. All accounting transactions of the firm are entered in the rows of the spreadsheet. The column headings are the account names. After all transactions have been entered for the period, the columns are summed, and the ending balances are used to prepare the balance sheet for the company. The retained earnings and the explanation of retained earnings columns are used to prepare the income statement and the statement of retained earnings. The benefits of using a spreadsheet are the following:

1. Students improve their spreadsheet skills.

2. Numerous transactions can be recorded in a very small space.

3. Spreadsheet formulas can be used to compute the ending balances and the adjustment amounts; this reduces human error.

4. Students can easily see the effect a transaction has on the balance sheet accounts and how each transaction must result in assets equaling liabilities and owner's equity (A = L + OE).

5. Financial statements can be easily and quickly prepared from cells on the spreadsheet using cell formulas.

6. Spreadsheets are more modern; students enjoy learning them and can see the benefit of the skill for future coursework.

7. "What if" analyses are easily prepared.

In practice, most companies use bookkeeping software to record transactions. This software analyzes transactions as increases or decreases to accounts just as we have been doing. Accountants, on the other hand, use specialized vocabulary that originated with manual accounting systems. Accountants use the terms **debit** and **credit** to reflect the effect of a transaction on an account and to ensure that transactions are recorded accurately in a manual accounting system. The terms come from the latin words *debitum* and *creditum* and were used by Luca Pacioli, who is known as the Father of Accounting.

Debits and Credits

The term debit identifies the left-hand side of the account, and the term credit identifies the right-hand side of the account.

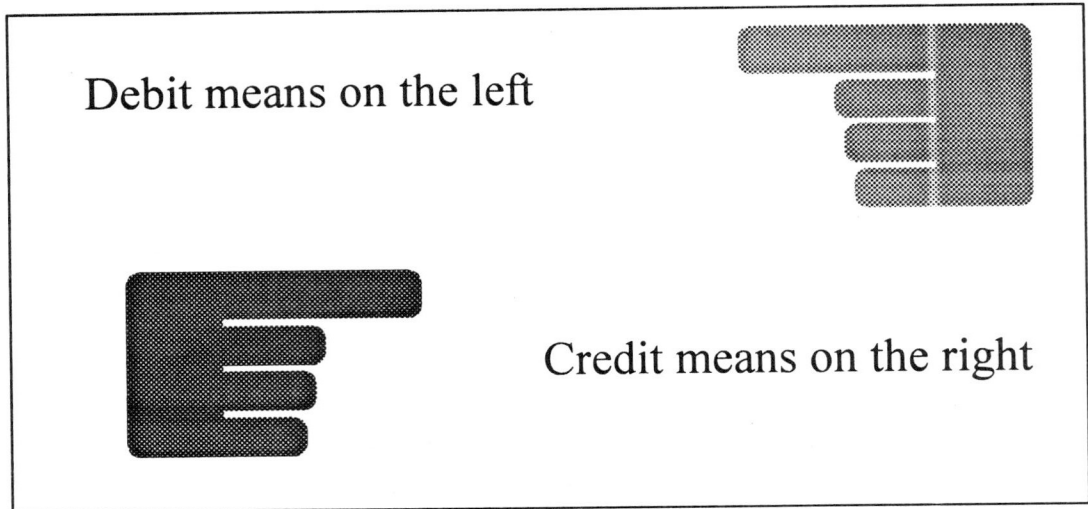

Debit means on the left

Credit means on the right

Debits are neither good nor bad; credits are neither good nor bad. The terms simply designate the side of the account on which to record the transaction.

The general rules of recording state the following:

- Increases in assets are recorded as debits (on the left side), thus decreases in assets are recorded as credits (on the right side).
- Increases in liabilities and owners' equity accounts are recorded as credits (on the right side), thus decreases in liabilities and owners' equity accounts are recorded as debits (on the left side).

The rules are summarized in Exhibit D1.

Exhibit D1

	Debit	Credit
Assets	Increase	Decrease
Liabilities & Owners' Equity	Decrease	Increase

Let's look at the transaction analysis for the May transactions for the Corliss Company that we recorded on a transaction spreadsheet in Case Reading 2-1. The May transactions were as follows:

May 25 Received a capital contribution of $50,000 cash from Devenie Corliss, the owner.

25 Purchased supplies for $1,000 from the Leslie Co.. amount to be paid in 30 days.

29 Paid $700 of the amount due to the Leslie Company.

31 Purchased land for $30,000 and a building for $100.000, making a cash down payment of $20,000 and giving a 30-year mortgage payable at 8 percent interest for the remainder. Monthly principal and interest payments are $806.

The transactions are recorded on an accounting transaction worksheet shown as Exhibit D2.

Exhibit D2
May Accounting Transaction Worksheet

Increases in Assets Are Debits | **Increases in Liabilities and Owner's Equity Accounts Are Credits**

	A	B	C	D	E	F	G	H	I
1				ASSETS			LIABILITIES + OWNER'S EQUITY		
2	Date	Cash	Supplies	Land	Building	Accounts Payable	Mortgage Payable	Contributed Capital	Retained Earnings
3	Beg.Bal. 5/25/00	$ -	$ -	$ -	$ -	$ -	$ -	$ -	$ -
4	5/25/00	50,000						50,000	
5	5/25/00		1,000			1,000			
6	5/29/00	(700)				(700)			
7	5/31/00	(20,000)		30,000	100,000		110,000		
8	End. Bal. 5/31/00	$ 29,300	$ 1,000	$ 30,000	$ 100,000	$ 300	$ 110,000	$ 50,000	$ -

As we learned in Case Reading 2-1, each transaction recorded on the accounting transaction worksheet must balance; that is, each row of assets must equal liabilities and owner's equity (A = L + OE). We can now add a second part to that rule that states for each transaction recorded:

| Total debits = Total credits |

Row 4 of the worksheet shown as Exhibit D2 shows that cash increased by $50,000 and contributed capital increased by $50,000. After recording that transaction, the balance sheet equation looks like this:

$$A = L + OE$$
$$\$50,000 = \$0 + \$50,000$$

The specific asset that increased is cash. If recording this entry in a debit/credit format, would cash be debited or credited?

Increases in assets are recorded by debits, so cash is debited for $50,000. What about the increase to contributed capital? Would the increase be a debit or a credit?

Increases in owner's equity accounts like contributed capital are recorded by credits, so contributed capital would be credited for $50,000.

After recording the transaction, total debits = $50,000 and total credits = $50,000 so the transaction balances.

Row 5 of the transaction worksheet shows an increase to supplies, an asset, of $1,000. Increases in assets are recorded as debits thus this would be a debit to supplies of $1,000.

The other portion of the transaction is an increase to accounts payable, a liability, for $1,000. Increases in liabilities are credits; this then would be a credit to accounts payable of $1,000. Total debits = $1,000 and total credits = $1,000. Our transaction is in balance.

Row 6 of Exhibit D2 shows cash decreased by $700 and accounts payable decreased by $700. How would this journal entry be recorded?

Decreases in assets, like cash, are recorded as credits so cash would be credited for $700.

Decreases in liabilities, like accounts payable, are debits, thus accounts payable is debited for $700.

In preparing a formal journal entry, *debits are always recorded first*. Does the entry balance? Yes, total debits = $700 and credits = $700

Row 7 of the worksheet shows a decrease in cash of $20,000, an increase in land of $30,000, an increase in building of $100,000, and an increase in mortgage payable, a liability, of $110,000. Would these items be recorded as debits or credits?

Decrease in assets are credits, thus the decrease in cash is recorded as a credit of $20,000. Land is increased, so this asset account would be debited for $10,000, building is increased so this asset would be debited for $100,000, and mortgage payable, a liability would be credited for $110,000 because increases in liabilities are recorded by credits.

General Journal

The **general journal** is called the book of original entry because this is the first place that a transaction is entered in the accounting records. Nowadays, the general journal is more likely to be the name of the printout generated by the computer system rather than a journal book. In either case, before recording transactions in the general journal, the bookkeeper needs to analyze the transaction in the same manner as performed before entering the transactions in the spreadsheet. The general journal is organized by date, and each entry on a given date is called a **journal entry**. A journal entry in the general journal is equivalent to an entry in a row of the transaction worksheet.

Below is the entry from row 4 of the transaction worksheet as it would be recorded in the general journal (this is page 1 of the general journal) shown as Exhibit D3.

Exhibit D3

General Journal - Page 1

GENERAL JOURNAL				Page No. 1
Date	Account Titles and Explanation	Ref.	Debit	Credit
2000 25-May (a)	Cash	101	$50,000	
	—Contributed Capital	301		$50,000
	To record owner investment			

Slightly indented

Date Column

A transaction is recorded on the date it occurs just like it is recorded in the date column on the spreadsheet. In this case, the transaction occurs on May 25, 2000. The (a) identifies the transaction further and will be discussed when the subject of T accounts is introduced.

Account Titles and Debit and Credit Columns

These columns are used to record the account names of the accounts that are affected by the transaction and the dollar amount of the transaction. The two accounts affected in Exhibit D3 are cash and contributed capital.

Look how the account titles are listed.

- Cash is shown first because it is the account that is debited, and all debits are *always* recorded before credits. The $50,000 amount that the cash account is debited is put in the debit column.

- The account title Contributed Capital is slightly indented. This indentation (notice the arrow) is to show that this account is credited. The $50,000 amount credited to contributed capital is shown in the credit column.

After recording any entry in the journal: total debits = total credits

Journal Entry Explanation

Each journal entry must also have a journal entry explanation. In this case the explanation states that the entry was made to record the owner investment.

Posting Reference Column

The posting reference column refers to the account number. When we recorded transactions in spreadsheets, we used the account titles as column headings. In reality, companies have hundreds of accounts. Each account is assigned an account number as well as a title, and this number is used internally by the computer to sort all activity into the proper accounts. The company maintains an index of all account titles and their corresponding numbers. This index is called a **chart of accounts**. The journal entry shows that the Cash account is account 101 and the Contributed Capital account is 301.

Chart of Accounts

A chart of accounts for the Corliss Company is shown as Exhibit D4. Notice the sequence of the accounts. A chart of accounts assigns the lowest numbers to assets, with the sequence of the accounts identical to the way the items are shown on a balance sheet. Notice how there are plenty of unused account numbers so that the company can add account numbers at a later time if needed. Liabilities are the next group of account numbers (200-299), and owner's equity types of accounts are last (300 and up).

Using a transaction worksheet, all revenues, expenses, and owner's withdrawals are recorded directly in the "retained earnings column" with additional descriptions of the specific account in the "explanations of retained earnings column." Companies, however, have separate specific account numbers and descriptions for accounts that we previously described in the "explanation of retained earnings column" on the worksheet. These accounts include revenues, expenses, and owner's withdrawals. In this case owner's withdrawal is account 303, revenues are assigned the 400 level of account numbers, and expenses are 500-level accounts. Setting up a chart of accounts is a relatively complex process, and professional help is advisable.

Recording May Transactions in the General Journal

The remaining transactions for May are recorded below in the general journal.

GENERAL JOURNAL				Page No. 1
Date	Account Titles and Explanation	Post Ref.	Debit	Credit
2000				
25-May	Cash	101	$50,000	
(a)	Contributed Capital	301		$50,000
	To record owner investment			
25-May	Supplies	121	$1,000	
(b)	Accounts Payable	201		$1,000
	To record purchase of supplies on account			
29-May	Accounts Payable	201	$700	
(c)	Cash	101		$700
	To record payment to Leslie Co.			
31-May	Land	131	$30,000	
(d)	Building	132	$100,000	
	Cash	101		$20,000
	Mortgage Payable	211		$110,000
	To record purchase of land & building			

Exhibit D4
Chart of Accounts

Chart of Accounts

100 - 199   ASSETS
100 -109   Cash
    101   Cash, Checking
    102   Cash, Change/Petty Cash Fund

110 - 119   Receivables
    111   Accounts Receivable

120 - 129   Prepaid Assets
    121   Supplies
    122   Prepaid Insurance

130 - 139   Property, Plant, and Equipment
    131   Land
    132   Building

200 - 299   LIABILITIES
200 - 209   Short-Term
    201   Accounts Payable

210 - 219   Long-Term
    211   Mortgage Payable

300 - 399   STOCKHOLDERS / OWNER'S EQUITY
    301   Contributed Capital
    302   Retained Earnings
    303   Dividends / Owner's Withdrawal

400 - 499   REVENUES
    401   Fees Revenue

500 - 599   EXPENSES
500 - 509   Wages & Salaries
    501   Wages - Hourly
    502   Salaries
510 - 519   Depreciation
    511   Building Depreciation
520 - 529   Office
    521   Supplies Expense
    522   Insurance Expense
530 - 539   Non-Operating
    531   Interest Expense

Look at the entry in the general journal on May 31. This entry is called a **compound journal entry**. A compound journal entry is an entry in which there is more than one debit and/or more than one credit; in other words at least three accounts are involved. In such cases, all the debits are shown first, before any credits are recorded. In describing this entry, one would say:

Debit Land $30,000; Debit Building $100,000; Credit Cash $20,000; Credit Mortgage Payable $110,000.

Notice how in each journal entry in the general journal, total debits = total credits.

The General Ledger

As mentioned previously, the general journal is organized by date. In other words, the lower the page number in the general journal, the older the date of the entry. The general ledger is another book used by companies, but this book is organized by account number. Most general ledgers, nowadays, are computer printouts. The general ledger is a very important accounting record because the ending account balances shown in the general ledger are the ones used to prepare the financial statements.

Transferring information from the general journal to the general ledger is called **posting**. Let's see how the first journal entry in the general journal is posted to the general ledger.

GENERAL JOURNAL					Page No. 1
Date	Account Titles and Explanation	Ref.	Debit		Credit
2000 25-May (a)	Cash	101	$50,000		
	Contributed Capital	301			$50,000
	To record owner investment				

GENERAL LEDGER						
Cash						Account No. 101
Date	Explanation	Post Ref.	Debit		Credit	Balance
2000 25-May	Owner contribution	GJ1	$50,000			$50,000
29-May	Payment to Leslie Co.	GJ1			$700	$49,300
31-May	Payment for land & building	GJ1			$20,000	$29,300

Contributed Capital						Account No. 301
Date	Explanation	Post Ref.	Debit		Credit	Balance
2000 25-May	Owner investment	GJ1			$50,000	$50,000

Before looking at the accounts involved and the actual amount of the entries, let's look at the cross-referencing.

- The account numbers from the general journal are cross-referenced to the account numbers in the general ledger. Notice that the general journal showed that the Cash account was 101, which agrees with the number of the cash account in the general ledger. The Contributed Capital account numbers agree as well.

- The pages that the transactions are recorded on are cross-referenced as well. The posting reference in the general ledger shows that the posting information came from page 1 in the general journal.

- The account names and the amounts are cross-referenced also as shown below:

GENERAL JOURNAL				Page No. 1
Date	Account Titles and Explanation	Ref.	Debit	Credit
2000 25-May (a)	Cash	101	$50,000	
	Contributed Capital	301		$50,000
	To record owner investment			

GENERAL LEDGER

Cash					Account No. 101
Date	Explanation	Post Ref.	Debit	Credit	Balance
2000 25-May	Owner contribution	GJ1	$50,000		$50,000
29-May	Payment to Leslie Co.	GJ1		$700	$49,300
31-May	Payment for land & building	GJ1		$20,000	$29,300

Contributed Capital					Account No. 301
Date	Explanation	Post Ref.	Debit	Credit	Balance
2000 25-May	Owner investment	GJ1		$50,000	$50,000

After each entry in a general ledger account, a new balance is computed for that account. For example, after recording the debit of $50,000 to the general ledger cash account, a new account balance shown in the balance column of $50,000 was computed. The balance column does not have to designate whether the account has a debit or a credit balance; the balance is assumed to be the "normal" type of balance that you would expect that account to have. If it is not a normal type of balance, the balance will be shown in brackets.

What types of balances would accounts normally have? The normal types of balances are identical to the type of transaction that causes the account to increase. In other words:

	Normal Balance
Assets	Debit
Liabilities & Owner's Equity	Credit

The general ledger asset accounts for the Corliss Company for May are shown below. Note how a new account balance is computed after each posting.

GENERAL LEDGER					
Cash					Account No. 101
Date	Explanation	Post Ref.	Debit	Credit	Balance
2000					
25-May	Owner contribution	GJ1	$50,000		$50,000
29-May	Payment to Leslie Co.	GJ1		$700	$49,300
31-May	Payment for land & building	GJ1		$20,000	$29,300

Supplies					Account No.121
Date	Explanation	Post Ref.	Debit	Credit	Balance
2000					
25-May	Purchase of office supplies	GJ1	$1,000		$1,000

Land					Account No.131
Date	Explanation	Post Ref.	Debit	Credit	Balance
2000					
31-May	Purchase of land	GJ1	$30,000		$30,000

Building					Account No.132
Date	Explanation	Post Ref.	Debit	Credit	Balance
2000					
31-May	Purchase of Building	GJ1	$100,000		$100,000

The liabilities and owner's equity account are shown on the next page.

GENERAL LEDGER						
Accounts Payable						Account No. 201
Date	Explanation	Post Ref.	Debit	Credit		Balance
2000 25-May	Purchase on account	GJ1		$1,000		$1,000
29-May	Payment to Leslie Co.	GJ1	$700			$300
Mortgage Payable						Account No. 211
Date	Explanation	Post Ref.	Debit	Credit		Balance
2000 31-May	Purchase of Building	GJ1		$110,000		$110,000
Contributed Capital						Account No. 301
Date	Explanation	Post Ref.	Debit	Credit		Balance
2000 25-May	Owner investment	GJ1		$50,000		$50,000

A balance sheet for the month of May can be prepared from the ending balance row in the transaction worksheet (row 8) from Exhibit D2 shown below or from the ending balances in the general ledger accounts. Both sources would result in the same balance sheet that is shown on the next page.

	A	B	C	D	E	F	G	H	I
1		ASSETS				LIABILITIES + OWNER'S EQUITY			
2	Date	Cash	Supplies	Land	Building	Accounts Payable	Mortgage Payable	Contributed Capital	Retained Earnings
8	End. Bal. 5/31/00	$ 29,300	$ 1,000	$ 30,000	$ 100,000	$ 300	$ 110,000	$ 50,000	$ -

Corliss Balance Sheet

Corliss Accounting Firm Balance Sheet May 31, 2000				
Assets			**Liabilities and Owner's Equity**	
Current Assets			Current Liabilities	
Cash		$ 29,300	Accounts Payable	$ 300
Supplies		1,000		
Total Current Assets		30,300		
			Long Term Liabilities	
Fixed Assets			Mortgage Payable	110,000
Land	$30,000			
Building	100,000		Total Liabilities	110,300
Total Fixed Assets		130,000		
			Owner's Equity	
			Contributed Capital	50,000
Total Assets		$160,300	Owner's Equity	$160,300

T Accounts

T accounts are very easy to use. The account title is placed on top of the T and any transactions to the account are entered on the appropriate debit or credit side of the account. After all transactions have been recorded, an ending balance is computed and placed on the appropriate debit/credit side of the T. Each entry to a T account also shows the date of the transaction and has an identifying letter that identifies the transaction.

Account Title

Debit	Credit

The T accounts for the May transactions for Corliss are shown on the following page. Each transaction is labeled with a transaction letter. This transaction letter was given to you in the general journal. (The general journal usually only shows the dates of the transactions versus transaction letters. The letters have been included here to make it easier to identify the transactions when preparing the T accounts. Although T accounts can be prepared using dates instead of transaction letters, oftentimes companies have numerous journal entries on any given date, and it can be difficult to identify which debits go with which credits if dates are used.)

T ACCOUNTS - MAY			
Cash		**Supplies**	
(a) $50,000		(b) $1,000	
	$700 (c)		
	$20,000 (d)		
Balance $29,300		Balance $1,000	
Land		**Building**	
(d) $30,000		(d) $100,000	
Balance $30,000		Balance $100,000	
Accounts Payable		**Contributed Capital**	
	$1,000 (b)		$50,000 (a)
(c) $700			
	$300 Balance		$50,000 Balance
Mortgage Payable			
	$110,000 (d)		
	$110,000 Balance		

For example, by looking at the T account, we can see that transaction (d) relates to the following journal entry in the general journal. A (d) is also shown under the date to show this relationship:

GENERAL JOURNAL				Page No. 1
31-May	Land	131	$30,000	
(d)	Building	132	$100,000	
	Cash	101		$20,000
	Mortgage Payable	211		$110,000
	To record purchase of land & building			

Once again, T accounts are not used to enter transactions in the accounting records. They are used for illustrative purposes only. Every economic event must first be recorded in the journal and then transferred to the ledger before it is reflected in the financial statements.

Where does the T come from? The T is merely a part of the general ledger page. Let's look at the cash general ledger account again.

GENERAL LEDGER					
Cash					Account No. 101
Date	Explanation	Post Ref.	Debit	Credit	Balance
2000					
25-May	Owner contribution	GJ1	$50,000		$50,000
29-May	Payment to Leslie Co.	GJ1		$700	$49,300
31-May	Payment for land & building	GJ1		$20,000	$29,300

Which is easier to use for demonstration purposes, a T account or the general ledger page?

PART 1 SUMMARY

In Part 1, we learned about debits, credits, the general journal, the general ledger, and T accounts. The primary emphasis was on recording transactions that affect the balance sheet only. Part 2 shows the June transactions for the Corliss Company, which includes both balance sheet and income statement activity.

Suggested Assignment

After completing and correcting the transaction worksheet for Case 2-1, perform the following:

1. For each transaction recorded in the spreadsheet, record that transaction as a journal entry in the general journal first and then post the information to the general ledger. A template for the general journal and the general ledger is available at the web site for this text.

2. For each transaction recorded in the spreadsheet, record that transaction in T accounts. A template for T accounts is available at the web site for this text.

If the assignment is completed correctly, the ending balances in the general ledger and T accounts should agree with the ending balances of the accounting transaction worksheet prepared in Case 2-1.

PART 2 INTRODUCTION

Part 2 addresses the June activity for the Corliss Company. The June activity is more complex than Part 1 in that it deals with balance sheet accounts and income statement accounts. Part 2 records the June activity in the general journal and posts it to the general ledger. T accounts are also given.

Temporary Vs. Permanent Accounts

As mentioned in Part 1, there is a separate general ledger page for each income statement account and also for the owner's withdrawal account. All income statement accounts and the owner's withdrawal account are called **temporary accounts**. This description originated because the ending balances in these accounts are transferred to the retained earnings account at the end of the accounting period. This results in all temporary accounts starting every period with a zero balance. Balance sheet accounts are called **permanent accounts** because their balances do not "close" or zero out at the end of the period. The ending balances for the permanent accounts become the beginning balance for the following period.

RECORDING JUNE TRANSACTIONS FOR CORLISS

On the June transaction worksheet in Case Reading 2-1, all revenues, expenses, and owner's withdrawals were recorded in the retained earnings account. The specific name for the revenue or expense account was found in the explanation of retained earnings column on the worksheet. Revenues were shown as increases in retained earnings, and expenses were shown as decreases in retained earnings. Owner's withdrawal was also a reduction to the retained earnings account. How would we apply the debit/credit rules to these temporary accounts?

An increase in retained earnings (an owner's equity account) is shown as a credit, thus revenues are credits.

A decrease in retained earnings (an owner's equity account) is shown as a debit, thus expenses are debits. Withdrawals by the owners is also a temporary account that reduces retained earnings; it will also be shown as a debit.

Even though a debit decreases retained earnings, at the same time the debit reflects an increase to the expense or withdrawal. It makes sense that when expenses go up, retained earnings goes down (less profit). The same would be true for owner's withdrawal.

	Increase	**Decrease**
Revenues	Credit	Debit
Expenses	Debit	Credit
Owner's withdrawal	Debit	Credit

The June transactions from Case Reading 2-1 are recreated below. The chart of accounts used to record the transactions was shown in Exhibit D4 in Part 1.

June	1	Purchased a two-year insurance policy for $960 cash.
	4	Paid off the remaining $300 liability due to the Leslie Company.
	15	The Corliss Company performed accounting services, billing its clients $3,000 for the first half of the month. A total of $2,000 was received in cash and the remainder will be received within 30 days.
	16	The owner, Corliss, withdrew $1,000 cash for personal use.
	30	Services were performed for clients for the last half of the month. Clients were billed $2,200, of which half had been received in cash.
	30	Paid employees' wages of $1,600 for the month.
	30	Recorded depreciation on the building for the month of June. The building has a 40-year life and a salvage value of $4,000.
	30	Recorded the expiration of insurance for the month of June.
	30	An inventory of supplies showed the supplies still on hand cost $250.
	30	Paid the first monthly principal and interest payment of $806 on the 8 percent mortgage loan.

The June transaction worksheet from Case Reading 2-1 is shown as Exhibit D5 on the next page.

Exhibit D5

Increases in Assets Are Debits   Increases in Liabilities/Equities Are Credits

	A	B	C	D	E	F	G	H	I	J	K	L
				ASSETS				**LIABILITIES + OWNER'S EQUITY**				
1												
2	Date	Cash	Accounts Receivable	Supplies	Prepaid Insurance	Land	Building	Accounts Payable	Mortgage Payable	Contributed Capital	Retained Earnings	Explanation of Retained Earnings
3	Beg.Bal. 6/1/00	$ 29,300	$ -	$ 1,000	$ -	$ 30,000	$ 100,000	$ 300	$ 110,000	$ 50,000	$ -	
4	6/1/00	(960)			960							
5	6/4/00	(300)						(300)				
6	6/15/00	2,000	1,000								3,000	Fees Revenue
7	6/16/00	(1,000)									(1,000)	Owner Withdrawal
8	6/30/00	1,100	1,100								2,200	Fees Revenue
9	6/30/00	(1,600)									(1,600)	Wage Expense
10	6/30/00						(200)				(200)	Depreciation Expense
11	6/30/00				(40)						(40)	Insurance Expense
12	6/30/00			(750)							(750)	Supplies Expense
13	6/30/00	(806)							(73)		(733)	Interest Expense
14	End.Bal. 6/30/00	$ 27,734	$ 2,100	$ 250	$ 920	$ 30,000	$ 99,800	$ -	$ 109,927	$ 50,000	$ 877	

The following page shows how these same entries would appear in a general journal.

GENERAL JOURNAL				Page No. 2
Date	Account Titles and Explanation	Post Ref.	Debit	Credit
2000				
1-Jun (a)	Prepaid Insurance Cash To purchase of 2 year insurance policy	122 101	$960	 $960
4-Jun (b)	Accounts Payable Cash To record payment to Leslie Co.	201 101	$300	 $300
15-Jun (c)	Cash Account Receivable Fees Revenue To record revenue from accounting services	101 111 401	$2,000 $1,000	 $3,000
16-Jun (d)	Owner's Withdrawal Cash To record owner withdrawal for personal use	303 101	$1,000	 $1,000
30-Jun (e)	Cash Account Receivable Fees Revenue To record revenue from accounting services	101 111 401	$1,100 $1,100	 $2,200
30-Jun (f)	Wage Expense Cash To record wages earned and paid this month	501 101	$1,600	 $1,600
30-Jun (g)	Depreciation Expense Building To record one month of depreciation	511 132	$200	 $200
30-Jun (h)	Insurance Expense Prepaid Insurance To record expiration of insurance	522 122	$40	 $40
30-Jun (i)	Supplies Expense Supplies To record supplies used	521 121	$750	 $750
30-Jun (j)	Mortgage Payable Interest Expense Cash To record first monthly mortgage payment	211 531 101	$73 $733	 $806

Note how each revenue and expense account has its own account number. As mentioned earlier, any increases in assets and decreases in liabilities and owner's equity accounts are debits; any decreases in assets and increases in liabilities and owner's equity accounts are credits.

Let's look at the last journal entry from the previous page. The debit to mortgage payable shows that mortgage payable decreased. The debit to interest expense shows that interest expense went up (remember, an increase to an expense is a decrease to retained earnings on the transaction worksheet). The credit to cash shows that cash decreased. This entry in the general journal shows the same information as row 14 on the June accounting transaction worksheet shown in Exhibit D5.

The general ledger accounts for June are shown on the next few pages. The permanent account balances from the previous period, May, become the beginning balances for this period. The income statement general ledger accounts still have balances until these account balances are "closed" or transferred to retained earnings. Note how the retained earnings account has *not* been updated for the month's activity. At this point, it still has the ending balance from the previous month, May, which was zero.

GENERAL LEDGER					
Cash					Account No. 101
Date	Explanation	Post Ref.	Debit	Credit	Balance
2000					
1-Jun	Beginning Balance				$29,300
1-Jun	Purchase of insurance	GJ2		$960	$28,340
4-Jun	Payment to Leslie Co.	GJ2		$300	$28,040
15-Jun	Sales	GJ2	$2,000		$30,040
16-Jun	Owner withdrawal	GJ2		$1,000	$29,040
30-Jun	Sales	GJ2	$1,100		$30,140
30-Jun	Wages paid - Hourly	GJ2		$1,600	$28,540
30-Jun	Mortgage payment	GJ2		$806	$27,734

Accounts Receivable					Account No. 111
Date	Explanation	Post Ref.	Debit	Credit	Balance
2000					
1-Jun	Beginning Balance				$0
15-Jun	Sales revenue	GJ2	$1,000		$1,000
30-Jun	Sales revenue	GJ2	$1,100		$2,100

Supplies					Account No. 121
Date	Explanation	Post Ref.	Debit	Credit	Balance
2000					
1-Jun	Beginning Balance				$1,000
30-Jun	Supplies used	GJ2		$750	$250

GENERAL LEDGER					
Prepaid Insurance					Account No. 122
Date	Explanation	Post Ref.	Debit	Credit	Balance
2000					
1-Jun	Beginning Balance				$0
1-Jun	Purchase of insurance policy	GJ2	$960		$960
30-Jun	Expiration of insurance	GJ2		$40	$920

Land					Account No. 131
Date	Explanation	Post Ref.	Debit	Credit	Balance
2000					
1-Jun	Beginning Balance				$30,000

Building					Account No. 132
Date	Explanation	Post Ref.	Debit	Credit	Balance
2000					
1-Jun	Beginning Balance				$100,000
30-Jun	Depreciation	GJ2		$200	$99,800

Accounts Payable					Account No. 201
Date	Explanation	Post Ref.	Debit	Credit	Balance
2000					
1-Jun	Beginning Balance				$300
4-Jun	Payment to Leslie Co.	GJ2	$300		$0

Mortgage Payable					Account No. 211
Date	Explanation	Post Ref.	Debit	Credit	Balance
2000					
1-Jun	Beginning Balance				$110,000
30-Jun	Payment	GJ2	$73		$109,927

The owner's equity accounts are shown on the next page. The retained earnings account does not reflect any entries to revenues, expenses, or withdrawals at this point. Entries to these items are still reflected in the temporary accounts.

GENERAL LEDGER					
Contributed Capital					Account No. 301
Date	Explanation	Post Ref.	Debit	Credit	Balance
2000 1-Jun	Beginning Balance				$50,000

Retained Earnings					Account No. 302
Date	Explanation	Post Ref.	Debit	Credit	Balance
2000 1-Jun	Beginning Balance				$0

Note how each revenue, expense, and owner's withdrawal has its own general ledger account as shown below.

GENERAL LEDGER					
Fees Revenue					Account No.401
Date	Explanation	Post Ref.	Debit	Credit	Balance
2000 15-Jun	Fees from Accounting service	GJ2		$3,000	$3,000
30-Jun	Fees from Accounting service			$2,200	$5,200

Wage Expense					Account No. 501
Date	Explanation	Post Ref.	Debit	Credit	Balance
2000 30-Jun	Wages Earned- Hourly	GJ2	$1,600		$1,600

Depreciation Expense					Account No.511
Date	Explanation	Post Ref.	Debit	Credit	Balance
2000 30-Jun	One month depreciation	GJ2	$200		$200

Supplies Expense					Account No.521
Date	Explanation	Post Ref.	Debit	Credit	Balance
2000 30-Jun	Supplies used	GJ2	$750		$750

GENERAL LEDGER					
Insurance Expense					Account No.522
Date	Explanation	Post Ref.	Debit	Credit	Balance
2000 30-Jun	Expiration of insurance	GJ2	$40		$40

Interest Expense					Account No.531
Date	Explanation	Post Ref.	Debit	Credit	Balance
2000 30-Jun	One month interest	GJ2	$733		$733

Owner's Withdrawal					Account No.303
Date	Explanation	Post Ref.	Debit	Credit	Balance
2000 16-Jun	Owner withdrawal	GJ2	$1,000		$1,000

The temporary accounts, with the exception of owner's withdrawal, are all income statement accounts. The income statement for the Corliss Company for June is prepared from the ending balances in these accounts.

Exhibit D6
Corliss Income Statement

Corliss Accounting Firm Income Statement Month Ended June 30, 2000		
Revenues		
Fees Revenue		$ 5,200
Expenses		
Wage Expense	$ 1,600	
Supplies Expense	750	
Interest Expense	733	
Depreciation Expens	200	
Insurance Expense	40	
Total Expenses		3,323
Net Income		$1,877

After the income statement is prepared, the account balances of each income statement account are transferred to retained earnings. Accountants refer to these entries as **closing entries**. Upon completion of this transfer, each income statement account will have a zero balance; the account will then be ready to start accumulating information for the next accounting period. The balance in the owner's withdrawal account is also transferred into retained earnings so that this temporary account will start the next period with a zero balance as well.

Exhibit D7 shows the retained earnings column from the June worksheet along with the explanation of retained earnings column. Exhibit D8 shows the retained earnings account after the balances from the income statement accounts and the owner's withdrawal account have been transferred. Note the similarities between the two representations of retained earnings.

Exhibit D7
Selected Columns from the Corliss June Worksheet

2	A	K	L
	Date	Retained Earnings	Explanation of Retained Earnings
3	6/1/00 Beg.Bal.	$ -	
4	6/1/00		
5	6/4/00		
6	6/15/00	3,000	Fees Revenue
7	6/16/00	(1,000)	Owner Withdrawal
8	6/30/00	2,200	Fees Revenue
9	6/30/00	(1,600)	Wage Expense
10	6/30/00	(200)	Depreciation Expense
11	6/30/00	(40)	Insurance Expense
12	6/30/00	(750)	Supplies Expense
13	6/30/00	(733)	Interest Expense
14	6/30/00 End.Bal.	$ 877	

Exhibit D8
The General Ledger Account for Retained Earnings
After Closing of Temporary Accounts

GENERAL LEDGER

Retained Earnings					Account No. 302
Date	Explanation	Post Ref.	Debit	Credit	Balance
2000					
1-Jun	Beginning Balance				$0
30-Jun	Transfer of Fees Revenue	401		$5,200	$5,200
30-Jun	Transfer of Owner's Withdrawal	303	$1,000		$4,200
30-Jun	Transfer of Wage Expense	501	$1,600		$2,600
30-Jun	Transfer of Depreciation Expense	511	$200		$2,400
30-Jun	Transfer of Insurance Expense	522	$40		$2,360
30-Jun	Transfer of Supplies Expense	521	$750		$1,610
30-Jun	Transfer of Interest Expense	531	$733		$877

Note how all the increases in retained earnings (revenues) on the worksheet are shown in the credit column of the general ledger; the decreases in the retained earnings account on the worksheet (expenses and owner's withdrawal) are debits in the general ledger. In both the transaction worksheet and the general ledger, ending retained earnings is $877.

T accounts for June (before closing) for the balance sheet accounts are shown below. Temporary account T accounts are on the following page.

T ACCOUNTS -JUNE			
Cash		**Building**	
Beg.Bal. $29,300	$960 (a)	Beg. Bal. $100,000	$200 (g)
	$300 (b)	Balance $99,800	
(c) $2,000			
	$1,000 (d)	**Accounts Payable**	
(e) $1,100			$300 Beg. Bal
	$1,600 (f)	(b) $300	
	$806 (j)		$0 Balance
Balance $27,734			
Accounts Receivable		**Mortgage Payable**	
(c) $1,000			$110,000 Beg. Bal.
(e) $1,100		(j) $73	
			$109,927 Balance
Balance $2,100			
Supplies		**Contributed Capital**	
Beg. Bal. $1,000			$50,000 (a)
	$750 (i)		
Balance $250			$50,000 Balance
Prepaid Insurance		**Retained Earnings**	
(a) $960			$0 Balance
	$40 (h)		
Balance $920			$0 Balance
Land			
(c) $30,000			
Balance $30,000			

As a reminder, T accounts are not entries in the accounting records. To enter transactions in the accounting records, journal entries are made in the journal and then posted to the general ledger. T accounts are used only for illustrative purposes.

Note on the previous page that no change has taken place in retained earnings during the period and won't until the temporary revenue, expense, and withdrawal accounts are transferred at the end of the month.

T ACCOUNTS -JUNE					
Fees Revenue			**Depreciation Expense**		
	$3,000	(c)	(g)	$200	
	$2,200	(e)			
	$5,200	Balance	Balance	$200	
Wage Expense			**Insurance Expense**		
(f)	$1,600		(h)	$40	
Balance	$1,600		Balance	$40	
Supplies Expense			**Owner's Withdrawal**		
(i)	$750		(d)	$1,000	
Balance	$750		Balance	$1,000	
Interest Expense					
(j)	$733				
Balance	$733				

After all activity for the month has been recorded, the temporary accounts are closed. To close a temporary account with a debit balance such as an expense account or the owner withdrawal account, credit that account for the amount of the existing balance. The debit and credit cancel each other out, leaving the account with a zero balance. If the temporary account has a credit balance such as a revenue account, the account will need to be debited to zero it out. All temporary accounts are zeroed out in one entry with their balances transferred to retained earnings. The T account balance on the following page shows the retained earnings account *after* all the temporary account balances have been transferred into retained earnings. After the transfer, all temporary accounts will have zero balances, and retained earnings will have a balance of $877. This is the amount that causes debits to equal credits. After the closing process, the temporary accounts are ready to begin accumulating transaction data for the new accounting period.

Retained Earnings			
		$5,200	Fees Revenue
Supplies Expense	$750		
Insurance Expense	$40		
Wage Expense	$1,600		
Interest Expense	$733		
Depreciation Expense	$200		
Owner's Withdrawal	1000		
		$877	Balance

The balance sheet for the Corliss Company at the end of June is prepared from the ending balances in the general ledger accounts after all transfers have been completed.

	A	B	C	D	E	F	G	H	I
1				**Corliss Accounting Firm**					
2				**Balance Sheet**					
3				**June 30, 2000**					
4									
5		Assets					Liabilities and Owner's Equity		
6									
7	Current Assets						Current Liabilities		
8		Cash		$ 27,734			Accounts Payable	$	-
9		Accounts Receivable		2,100					
10		Supplies		250			Long Term Liabilities		
11		Prepaid Insurance		920			Mortgage Payable		109,927
12	Total Current Assets			31,004					
13							Total Liabilities		109,927
14	Fixed Assets								
15		Land	$ 30,000				Owner's Equity		
16		Building	99,800				Contributed Capital	$ 50,000	
17	Total Fixed Assets			129,800			Retained Earnings	877	
18							Total Owner's Equity		50,877
19									
20	Total Assets			$ 160,804			Total Liabilities and Owner's Equity		$ 160,804
21									

Note how the balance sheet reflects the retained earnings balance after the closing process. The balance sheet is now in balance.

Suggested Assignment

For the accounting transaction worksheet given in Case 2-4 as Exhibit 2-4.1, perform the following:

1. For each transaction recorded in the spreadsheet, record that transaction as a journal entry in the general journal first and then post the information to the general ledger. A template for the general journal and the general ledger is available at the web site for this text.

2. For each transaction recorded in the spreadsheet, record that transaction in T accounts. A template for T accounts is available at the web site for this text.

GLOSSARY OF KEY TERMS

Accelerated depreciation: method for computing depreciation that measures depreciation expense at a larger portion of the cost of an asset in the early years and a smaller portion in the later years. Double declining balance and modified accelerated cost recovery system (MACRS) are examples.

Account balance: the net dollar amount in an account at a given point in time. Computed by adjusting the beginning account balance for transactions that increase or decrease the account during the period

Accountant: a professional who manages the collection of financial and nonfinancial data and is responsible for the analysis, reporting, interpreting of information to decision makers. Bookkeepers and accounting clerks, in contrast, are responsible for collecting and entering data into the accounting system.

Accounting: a system that collects and processes financial and nonfinancial information about economic activities and creates summarized reports for decision makers.

Accounting equation: See Balance sheet equation.

Accounting information: financial information about economic entities that is accumulated and communicated for decision-making purposes.

Accounting period: the time period covered by the financial statements. For most organizations, the primary accounting period is one year. Many organizations have secondary accounting periods of one month or one quarter.

Accounting principles: a set of concepts and procedures used to classify economic activities and to allocate costs for the purpose of creating financial statements. Multiple principles may exist for recording the same activity or making the same allocation. Also see the definition of Generally Accepted Accounting Principles (GAAP).

Accounting records: the books or computer files in which all transaction data and other information are recorded for the purpose of preparing financial statements and other reports. Journals and ledgers are examples in a manual accounting system.

Accounting reports: financial statements and other reports that are prepared from the accounting records and used by decision makers.

Accounting transaction worksheet: A structured form consisting of rows and columns. Columns are labeled with balance sheet elements. Each row is to record an accounting transaction, the entry appearing in the appropriate column depending upon the nature of the transaction. The row/column structure is generally found in all electronic spreadsheet software.

Accounts payable: amounts owed to suppliers for goods and services purchased that the company intends to use during the normal course of business operations.

Accounts receivable: open accounts owed to the business by customers.

Accounts receivable collection period: the time between a credit sale and collection of cash; found by dividing 365 by the accounts receivable turnover.

Accounts receivable turnover: an equation that computes the number of times the average receivable balance is collected during the year, computed by dividing net sales or net credit sales by average accounts receivable. This computation can then be used to compute the average collection period for accounts receivable. (See above for definition and computation of average collection period.)

Accrual basis accounting: under the accrual basis of accounting, revenues and expenses are recognized when earned or incurred without regard to when cash is received or paid.

Accrual income: income computed using the accrual basis of accounting whereby revenues are recognized when they are earned and expenses are matched with related revenues, not when cash changes hands. Accrual income is in contrast to cash basis income where both revenues and expenses are recognized only when cash is exchanged.

Accumulated depreciation: the sum of all depreciation expense recorded on an asset to date.

Additional paid-in capital: the difference between the total amount received for the issuance of stock and total par value of the issued stock.

Adjusted balance: the balance in an account after end-of-period adjusting entries have been made to bring the account to its proper amount. For example, the unadjusted balance in the accumulated depreciation account will not be correct until an entry is made at the end of the period to reflect the depreciation expense for the period.

Adjustments (adjusting entries): adjustments to the balances of the financial statement elements (assets, liabilities, revenues, and expenses) are needed at the end of the accounting period to bring these balances up-to-date before financial statements are prepared. Adjustments apportion transactions properly between the accounting periods affected as well as recognize any unrecorded transactions or events.

Adverse opinion: a report of a Certified Public Accountant that advises readers of financial statements that the accompanying statements do not present fairly the financial position, income and cash flow of the referenced company.

Agent: a legal concept referring to the authority of one person (the agent) to legally bind another person (the principal) to a contract.

Aging of accounts receivable: the process of categorizing each account receivable by the number of days it has been outstanding.

Allowance for doubtful accounts: See Allowance for uncollectible accounts.

Allowance for uncollectible accounts: a contra account deducted from accounts receivable that shows the amounts of accounts receivable that are expected to be uncollectible.

Allowance method: a method of estimating the expense of uncollectible accounts receivable that best matches the expense with revenues of the accounting period.

Amortization: allocation of the cost of an intangible asset over its useful life. This is the same concept as depreciation, but applies to intangible assets such as goodwill.

Annual report: a combination of financial statements, management discussion, and analysis, graphs and charts, and the annual external audit report that is provided by a company to investors.

Annuity: a series of equal cash payments or receipts occurring at regular time intervals.

Annuity due: a series of equal cash payments made at the beginning of each time interval.

Arms-length exchange: an expression referring to two independent parties in a transaction, each seeking an optimal outcome.

Assets: probable future economic benefits owned or controlled by the company that result from past transactions or events.

Audit: an examination of a company's financial records and statements to ensure that they conform with generally accepted accounting principles and fairly present the company's financial position, cash flow, and results of operation.

Audit committee: a group that reviews, recommends, and reports to the Board on (1) the independent auditors, (2) the quality and effectiveness of internal controls, (3) the engagement or discharge of the independent certified public accountants, (4) the professional services provided by the independent accountants, and (5) the review and approval of major changes in the accounting practices and principles used by the company in publishing its financial reports.

Audited financial statements: financial statements that have been examined/audited by an external accounting firm.

Auditor's opinion (report): a section of the annual report that describes the auditor's examination of accounting records and financial statements.

Authorized shares: the number of shares that a corporation is permitted to issue in accordance with its articles of incorporation.

Average collection period for accounts receivable: the average number of days it takes to collect an account receivable, which is computed by dividing 365 by the accounts receivable turnover.

Bad debt expense: an account that represents the portion of the current period's credit sales or ending accounts receivable balance that is estimated to become uncollectible.

Balance sheet: a financial statement that represents the equation Assets = Liabilities plus Owner's Equity. It is also called the Statement of Financial Position.

Balance sheet equation: Assets = Liabilities + Owners' (Shareholders') Equity. This equation explains the two sources of financing the entity has for its assets at a point in time.

Bankruptcy: a legal procedure used by companies and individuals to resolve a situation in which debts cannot be paid off. In some cases a company may be able to continue operations after bankruptcy, while in others the assets are sold and the firm goes out of business.

Basket purchase price (relative fair market value method): a way of allocating a lump sum or "basket" purchase price to individual assets acquired based on their respective market values.

Bill of lading: a document which is required to accompany goods shipped with a common carrier such as a trucking company that shows the name of the sender and destination, the type of goods being shipped, the weight, the freight rates, and other pertinent information.

Board of directors: a group of individuals elected by the stockholders to set policy for a corporation and to appoint its officers.

Bonds: a category of securities issued by corporations and governmental bodies to raise money for the organizations' financial needs. It is a legal document evidencing the indebtedness of the borrower and specifies the face value, maturity date, coupon rate, and other terms set at the time of issuance.

Bonds payable: the long-term liability on the balance sheet reporting the indebtedness of the issuer to its bondholders.

Book value (of fixed assets): historical cost of fixed assets less the accumulated depreciation of those assets. See Accumulated depreciation.

Book value per share ratio: the common stockholders' equity stated on a per-share basis. If a firm has no preferred stock, it is calculated by subtracting liabilities from assets and dividing the remainder by the number of outstanding shares of stock.

Bookkeeper: an individual who enters data into a company's accounting records and creates financial statements from the records. In many companies, much of the bookkeeping process has been computerized.

Bottom-up approach: a procedure that starts with a profit objective and then determines what level of sales is needed to attain your profit goal.

Breakeven analysis: a "what if" technique used to find the level of sales required for a company to report a zero net income.

Breakeven point: the level of sales at which total expenses equal total revenues; the point at which there is no profit or loss. See also Target sales.

Breakeven sales: see breakeven point

Budget: a quantitative plan of action that helps managers coordinate and implement their business strategy.

Budgeted variable rate: the percentage relationship of variable expenses to sales revenue.

Business investment: a transfer of personal funds to a separate entity which is expected to earn a return on that investment.

Capital: resources contributed to a company by its owners.

Capital account: an account whose balance is reflected in the shareholders' equity section of the balance sheet.

Capital lease: a leasing transaction that is recorded as a purchase by the lessee.

Capital stock: the portion of a corporation's equity contributed by investors (owners) in exchange for shares of stock.

Capital structure: the relative proportions of liabilities and shareholders' equity used to finance the assets of the business.

Capitalism: an economic system based upon private ownership of factors of production. Markets are uninhibited by government intervention allowing prices to float to their supply/demand equilibrium.

Cash: money or other instruments that financial institutions will accept for deposit or credit to a depositor's account.

Cash basis of accounting: a method contrary to GAAP which recognizes revenue when cash is collected and expenses when cash is disbursed.

Cash flow statement – direct method: see Statement of cash flows

Cash flow statement - indirect method: see Statement of cash flows

Cash flows: refers to the cash receipts and cash payments of the organization. Cash flows are classified as operating, investing, and financing events and reported in the statement of cash flows. Investing cash flows are cash transactions that involve: a) the purchase and sale of securities, property, plant, equipment, and other assets not generally held for resale; and b) the making and collecting of loans. Financing cash flows are cash transactions whereby resources are obtained from or paid to owners (equity financing) and creditors (debt financing). Operating cash flows are all cash flows not defined as investing or financing cash flows.

Certificate of deposit: interest earning funds on deposit at a bank not subject to withdrawal for a specified period of time without incurring a penalty.

Certified public accountant (CPA) an accountant who serves the general public rather than one particular business and is licensed to perform audits of financial statements.

Chart of accounts: a list of all the accounts used by the company and their corresponding account numbers. For example, cash may be account 100, accounts receivable 105 etc.

Classified balance sheet: the categorization of assets and liabilities into subgroups. Current assets, fixed assets, and intangible assets are typical categories for assets. Current liabilities and long-term liabilities are typical categories for liabilities.

Closing entry: a compound debit/credit entry into the general ledger accounts which has the effect of zeroing out all income statement and owner withdrawal accounts, placing the residual balance in the retained earnings account.

Collateral: assets put up (pledged) by a company to a creditor to secure a loan. If a company defaults on its loan, the creditor has a right to force the company to repay the loan by selling or forfeiting the collateral.

Common stock: representation of the "residual" ownership of a company. Holders of common stock are normally entitled to share the distribution of income (dividends) proportional to their percent ownership and to vote on important company matters. When a company is liquidated, common shareholders divide what assets are left after creditor, preferred stockholder and employee claims have been settled.

Comparability principle: requires that the financial statements must be comparable not only from year to year within the same company, but also between one company and another company.

Comparative financial statements: a presentation format of balance sheets, income statements and cash flow statements of a company for successive years, e.g. 1999, 2000.

Compound (journal) entry: an entry which changes three or more accounts in the company's accounting system.

Compound interest: a concept which explains the exponential growth in an income earning investment when the income for each period is not withdrawn but rather added to the investment for the next period.

Conservatism principle: when given a choice accountants will select the alternative that presents accounting information in the least optimistic way.

Consistency: a principle which favors the same accounting treatment of similar transactions in order for readers of financial statements to be able to make valid inferences about the trends inherent in the statements.

Consolidated: presentation of financial statements for an entire group of companies controlled by a parent corporation owning more than 50% of the voting stock.

Contra asset account: an account that is deducted from another account. An example of a contra asset account is accumulated depreciation. This account is shown as an offset to a fixed asset account.

Contributed capital: the portion of owners' equity contributed by owners.

Contributed capital in excess of par: See additional paid-in capital.

Contribution income statement: an income statement that separates expenses according to their behavior patterns; it shows revenue less variable expenses (= contribution margin) less fixed expenses.

Contribution margin: net sales minus variable expenses. It is the portion of sales revenue available to cover fixed expenses and to provide a profit.

Contribution margin ratio: the percentage of net sales revenue left after variable expenses are deducted; the contribution margin divided by net sales revenue.

Corporate charter: a statement of purpose approved in the formation of a corporation.

Corporate income tax: federal and state taxes that are computed based on the income a corporation earns. Sole proprietorships, partnerships, and certain special corporations do not pay this tax.

Corporation: a legal entity chartered by a state; ownership is represented by transferable shares of stock.

Cost-volume-profit (CVP) analysis: a set of techniques, including breakeven analysis, used to assess risk and project levels of profitability.

Cost behavior: a description of how costs change in response to any factor (most often sales volume) that affects costs.

Cost of goods available for sale: the sum obtained when beginning inventory is added to purchases for the period.

Cost of goods sold (COGS): in a retail company, this is defined as the purchase cost of the items sold. For a retail store, this is a variable expense.

Costs: cash or cash equivalent value sacrificed for goods and services that are expected to provide benefits to the organization.

Costs/benefits associated with a particular outcome: the various unfavorable/favorable (both quantitative and qualitative) effects on the decision-maker that result from the occurrence of a particular outcome.

Coupon interest rate: the stated interest rate to be paid on bonds issued by corporations and governments.

CPA (Certified Public Accountant): see Certified Public Accountant.

Credit: a procedure by which the right to borrow up to a stated limit is granted by a creditor to a borrower, who is often a customer of the creditor. The term is also used to mean that a vendor (seller) has reduced the amount a customer owes due to returns, damaged merchandise, or other reasons.

Credit entry: a posting to a ledger account which increases liabilities, shareholder account, and revenue balances and which decreases asset and expense accounts.

Credit policy: measures adopted by a company to evaluate the credit worthiness of each customer and to monitor credit sales to ensure that company policies are neither too restrictive nor too liberal.

Creditors: persons or entities to whom money is owed.

Cumulative preferred stock: preferred stock for which owners must receive all dividends in arrears before the corporation pays dividends to the common stockholders.

Current assets: cash and other assets that are expected to be converted to cash or consumed within one year or during the normal operating cycle, whichever is longer.

Current cash outlays: cash outflows that occur today.

Current liabilities: debts and other obligations that will be paid in cash or satisfied with other assets or services within one year.

Current ratio: the decimal number derived by dividing current assets by current liabilities.

Current value: the current value of an asset is the amount for which the asset could currently be sold.

Customer base: the group of individuals and companies that purchase a firm's goods and services.

Date of record: the announced date on which shareholders must be owners of the corporation stock to receive dividends or additional shares resulting from a stock split.

Days sales in inventory: the number of days a company theoretically could continue to make sales without replenishing inventory. It is found by dividing 365 by the inventory turnover ratio.

Debit entry: a posting into a ledger account which increases assets and expenses and which decreases liabilities, shareholders equity, and revenue.

Debt-to-equity ratio (DER): computed by dividing total liabilities by total stockholders' equity. This ratio is a measure of the financial risk faced by a company.

Debt financing: the financing of business needs through the use of creditors' funds rather than owners' funds.

Debts: money that is owed to creditors.

Decision making: a process of choosing among alternatives in to "solve a problem," i.e., in order to attain goals or objectives.

Decision making under uncertainty: a decision situation in which, at the time the decision must be made, a particular course of action may eventually lead to one of two or more mutually exclusive outcomes.

Declaration date: the date which the Board of Directors of a corporation decides that a dividend will be paid to shareholders.

Default: the breach of a provision in a loan agreement such as the failure to pay interest when due.

Deferred taxes: an estimated future tax liability that occurs because taxable income differs from net income.

Depreciable cost: the historical cost of a fixed asset minus the salvage value of the asset.

Depreciation expense: the amount of depreciation allocated for property, plant, and equipment (not land) for a given accounting period.

Direct write-off method: recognizing the expense of uncollectible accounts receivable at the time that information to that effect becomes known.

Dividend: distribution of money or other assets by a corporation to its stockholders.

Dividend yield: the cash dividend per year divided by the cost of the investment.

Dividends in arrears: a stated cumulative dividend on preferred stock that the board of directors omitted from the periodic declaration of dividends.

Dividends per share: the amount of cash dividends paid per share of common stock

Double-declining balance (DDB) depreciation: a depreciation method that is based on an annual depreciation rate that is twice the straight-line rate.

Double entry system: an accounting system in which every transaction is viewed as an exchange: something is given up and something of equal value is received.

Double taxation: refers to the taxation of corporation income and the taxation of individuals for the dividends received from corporations.

Duality: all transactions have a dual effect on the financial position of an organization. Equity is defined as the difference between assets and liabilities. Mathematically, this means that assets equals liabilities plus owners' equity. Duality is reflected in this accounting equation. It means that each transaction must have a dual impact on the financial position of a business entity. For Example, if an asset increases as a result of a transaction, either another asset must decrease or a liability or equity must increase. For each transaction, the effect on the organization's financial position can be explained in accordance with duality.

Earnings per share (EPS) ratio: net income for a period, divided by the average number of common shares and equivalents outstanding during that period.

Economic decision making: decisions that impact the cash flows and financial position of an organization.

Effective interest rate: the true rate found by dividing the interest payment by the principle; the effective rate is often slightly different than the nominal rate on bonds.

Employer identification number: a unique number that each employer must obtain from the Internal Revenue Service (IRS).

Entity concept: states that accounting information is accumulated and reported for a clearly defined economic entity regardless of its legal status. Accounting for the transactions of a sole proprietorship separately from the personal transactions of the owner of the business is one example of applying this concept.

Environmental accounting: a special branch of accounting which measures the costs and the benefits of policies designed to protect the environment.

Equality check: an electronic spreadsheet cell formula that tests whether the accounting equation is being observed for every transaction. An inequality means an error was made in a spreadsheet entry.

Equipment: an example of a fixed asset which has a useful life more than one year and is productive in generating revenue for the business.

Equity: the difference between total assets and total liabilities. For a sole proprietorship and a partnership, it is called owner's equity. For a corporation, it is called stockholders' equity.

Equity financing: the financing of business needs through the use of contributed capital or retained earnings.

Ethical behavior: making decisions that are consistent with the ethical norms of an organization and society.

Ethical dilemma: a situation involving a choice between two or more alternatives that has significant, often adverse, impacts on others.

Ethical failure: making decisions that are not consistent with the ethical norms of an organization or society.

Ethical principles: characteristics and values associated with ethical behavior such as honesty, fairness and loyalty.

Ethics: a set of values which cause a person to make difficult decisions in favor of one alternative over another.

Expense planning: projecting the level of expense expected for a given decision scenario.

Expenses: the cost of goods or services consumed in the process of generating revenue. Expenses represent gross decreases in owners' equity.

External (independent) audits: audits performed by an independent CPA firm. These are in contrast to internal audits performed by a company's own employees.

External decision maker: external decision makers consist of investors, creditors, the general public, and the government.

Face value: the denomination of a bond, such as $1,000.

Favorable (unfavorable) variance: a situation where actual expenses were lower (higher) than planned.

Feasible alternatives: courses of action that may be pursued in order to solve the identified problem.

Feedback: a concept of how a system adjusts its performance to reach a goal.

Federal Insurance Contributions Act (FICA): the Social Security tax that is withheld from an employee's paycheck and matched by the employer.

Fictitious business name statement: a legal requirement that all companies must disclose to the public information about the individuals operating a business.

FIFO: See First-in, First-out

Financial accounting: a branch of accounting that provides information to external decision makers such as stockholders, suppliers, banks, and government agencies.

Financial Accounting Standards Board (FASB): a private sector institution given the primary responsibility to decide the detailed rules that become generally accepted accounting principles.

Financial analysts: individuals who use primarily financial information to assess an organization's past performance and to estimate its future performance. External financial analysts prepare reports that help investors decide which stocks to buy. Internal financial analysts prepare reports to support management decisions.

Financial budget: see Budget.

Financial leverage: the relationship between the cost of borrowed funds and the rate of earnings from the assets acquired with those borrowed funds.

Financial obligations: commitments made by a company that create a future cash outflow.

Financial position (balance sheet): a summary of the assets, liabilities, and equity of an entity as of one moment in time. The financial position is reported in the balance sheet which, alternatively, is referred to as the statement of financial position.

Financial reporting period: the period of time for which the income and cash flow statements cover. All companies report annually, and most also report monthly or quarterly.

Financial risk: the risk of going bankrupt. The more a company borrows relative to its equity, the higher its financial risk.

Financial statements: the income statement, the statement of cash flows, and the balance sheet for a company.

Financing activities cash flows: those cash flows associated with the borrowing or the repaying of debt or owner investments or distributions.

First-in, first-out (FIFO): a method of valuing inventory and cost of goods sold that places the most recent purchase costs on the balance sheet and the previous purchase costs on the income statement. See Inventory profit.

Fiscal year: the year established by a business for accounting purposes. For example, the fiscal year for many retailers runs from February 1 through January 31 so that all Christmas activities can be easily included in the same accounting year.

Fixed assets: long-term operating assets acquired for use in the business rather than for resale. Examples include equipment, machinery, buildings etc.

Fixed expense: expenses that do not vary with changes in sales volume. Note that fixed expenses may vary from period to period, they just don't vary in proportion to changes in sales.

Flexible (performance) budget: see Performance budget.

FOB, shipping point: a term to describe sales terms when title to goods transfers at the shipping point or seller's place of business.

FOB, destination: a term to describe sales terms when title to goods transfers at the destination point or buyer's place of business.

Footnotes to the financial statements: supplemental information provided about the financial condition of a company in annual reports. Without this narrative and analytical information, financial statements cannot be fully understood.

Foreign Corrupt Practices Act (FCPA): a U.S. law that makes it a responsibility of management to report on the adequacy of internal control and to prevent bribes from being made to foreign organizations.

Form 10-K: an annual report that publicly traded companies must file with the Securities and Exchange Commission.

Form 10-Q: a quarterly report that publicly traded companies must file with the Securities and Exchange Commission .

Forensic accounting: a specialized branch of accounting used to investigate a fraud, embezzlement or other accounting irregularity after its discovery.

FUTA (Federal Unemployment Tax Act): the taxes an employer pays to fund the federal unemployment benefits program.

Future value: the value of an amount which is subject to compound interest. See Compound interest

Gain contingency: a future event which has a reasonable probability of occurring that will produce an economic benefit but which is still uncertain.

General journal: a chronological record of accounting transactions that indicates the changes to the accounts in accordance with a debit equaling credit rule.

General ledger: the record of all accounts contained in the chart of accounts for a company.

Generally accepted accounting principles (GAAP): a set of authoritative standards developed to define accounting practices for financial reporting purposes.

Goals/objectives: statements of what an organization wants to achieve.

Going concern concept: states that, for financial statement reporting purposes, it is assumed that the business will continue operating for the foreseeable future.

Gross margin on sales (also called gross profit on sales): the difference between net sales and cost of goods sold.

Gross margin (or gross profit) ratio: gross profit as a percentage of sales.

Gross profit margin: See gross margin.

Gross profit ratio: See gross margin percentage.

High-low method: a method of separating the fixed and variable components of a mixed expense by analyzing the total expenses at the high and the low activity levels within a relevant range.

Historical cost: the original amount that is paid to obtain an asset or service. Assets are generally reported on the balance sheet at the historical cost less accumulated depreciation or amortization.

Historical cost principle: states that assets should be recorded in the accounting records and reported in the financial statements at their historical (original) cost.

Horizontal analysis: uses percentage changes in financial statements over time for the same company to assess performance.

Income statement: the financial statement that summarizes revenues and expenses for a particular accounting period. It shows the net income or net loss for the period.

Income-to-sales ratio: see return on sales

Industry norms: ratios and other information that can be used for comparison purposes to assess a company's performance.

Intangible asset: an asset that does not have a physical form. Examples of intangible assets include trademarks, copyrights, goodwill, and patents.

Interest rate: the percentage rate that is multiplied by the principal amount of the loan to compute the amount of interest.

Internal controls: policies and procedures adopted to safeguard an entity's assets and to ensure that its financial records are accurate and reliable.

Internal decision makers: managers and other employees of a company who are responsible for making decisions.

Internal rate of return (IRR): the interest rate that will cause the net present value of an investment to equal zero.

Internal Revenue Service (IRS): a U.S. government agency that is responsible for implementing tax laws and collecting taxes.

Inventory: property (tangible) that is held for sale or will be used in the production of goods or services for sale.

Inventory "cost": the cost calculated for inventory that depends directly on which cost flow assumption is used; FIFO, LIFO etc.

Inventory profit: a phrase to describe the added income reported by a company which has used FIFO inventory cost rather than LIFO inventory cost to measure its cost of goods sold.

Inventory turnover ratio: a measure of the efficiency with which inventory is managed; computed by dividing costs of goods sold by average inventory for the period.

Investing: the act of placing personal funds into income producing assets and accepting risk of loss of income or loss of the original investment

Investing activities `(cash flows): cash flows that involve the buying or selling of assets (except inventory or prepaid items) and the making or collecting of loans.

Invoice: a document that states the amount the buyer is to pay the seller and the detailed explanation of the goods or services delivered for that amount.

Issued shares: the number of shares issued by a corporation.

Journal entry: a debit equaling credit description of an accounting transaction which is recorded in the general journal.

Last-in, first out: See LIFO.

Lease obligations (capital leases): the liability recognized for a capital lease calculated at the present value of the future lease payments at the given discount rate. This lease obligation will be reduced by future principal repayments.

Legal entity: a corporation or partnership which is recognized by the state in which it does business.

Lessee: a person who is leasing property from the owner (the lessor).

Lessor: the owner of property that is leased to another party (the lessee).

Level of activity: activities within an organization (e.g., sales activities, production activities, purchasing activities, etc.) may be measured in terms of output, input. or a combination of the two. Such measures express the "level" of activities. Examples of output measures are number of items produced in a manufacturing plant, sales volume for a merchandising firm, or hours billed in a service firm. Labor hours is an example of an input measure.

Liabilities: liabilities are obligations to transfer cash or other assets to other entities.

LIFO (last in, first out): an inventory cost flow method that transfers the cost of the last goods purchased to the cost of goods sold so that the ending inventory consists of the costs of the first goods purchased.

Limited liability partnership (LLP): a special legal form of partnership whereby the personal liability of the partners is restricted much as it is in a corporation. This type of entity is mostly used by professional partnerships such as are found in CPA and law firms.

Liquidity: refers to how quickly a company can convert its assets to cash and the length of time it takes for its liabilities to mature.

Liquidity ratios: a category of ratios which measure the relative ability of a company to pay its operating expenses and current obligations when they come due.

Loan covenant: a provision in a loan agreement between a lender and borrower which specifies conditions for maintaining the loan, such as current assets shall not fall below a certain amount.

Long-term assets: an asset whose life is expected to last longer than one year.

Long-term investment: the purchase of long term assets.

Long-term liabilities: debts or other obligations that will not be paid within one year, or the operating cycle, whichever is longer.

Loss contingency: a future event that will cause a loss of assets which had a reasonable probability of occurring but which is not yet high enough to recognize the loss.

Lower of cost or market (LCM): a method of valuing inventory by which the inventory is priced at either the cost to obtain the inventory, or its current replacement cost, whichever is lower.

MACRS (modified accelerated cost recovery system): depreciation method used for federal income tax purposes.

Manufacturing company: a company that produces products. This is in contrast to retail and service companies that do not produce goods. Accounting is more complex for manufacturing firms.

Margin requirements: the percentage of the purchase price of stock that must be paid in cash when stock is purchased. The remaining part of the purchase price can be borrowed. The purpose of this requirement is to reduce speculation in the stock market.

Market economy: an economy in which prices are free to find an equilibrium based upon private ownership of resources, supply, and demand.

Matching principle: the matching principle requires that all costs incurred in generating revenue be recognized in the same period as the related revenues.

Materiality principle: requires that only significant items be reflected in the financial statements.

Maturity date: the date a borrower must repay a debt.

Measurement: there are several ways to measure things. A very simple method is to count the quantity. For example, we might measure the wealth of a farmer by counting the number of chickens, the bushels of wheat, the acres of land, and so forth that he owns. However, a simple count cannot simultaneously measure the quality and quantity of items owned. For example, there are different grades of wheat and some land is more valuable than other land. By assigning dollar amounts to assets, this monetary measure conveys information about the quantity and quality in a single measure. That is, greater quantity and greater quality are both represented by a greater dollar amount being assigned.

Mixed expense: an expense item that is partially a fixed expense and partially a variable expense. An example is the electric utility bill which is based on a flat monthly amount plus a rate per kilowatt hour used.

Modified accelerated cost recovery system: See MACRS.

Mortgage amortization schedule: a schedule that shows the breakdown of interest and principal for each payment over the life of the mortgage.

Mortgage note payable: see mortgage payable

Mortgage payable: a written promise to pay a stated amount of money at one or more specified future dates; a mortgage is secured by the pledging of certain assets, usually real estate, as collateral.

Net assets: the amount that remains after subtracting liabilities from assets. This is the shareholders equity.

Net income: the increase in owner's equity from profitable operations. Net income is commonly referred to as profit.

Net present value of cash flows (NPV): defined as the difference between the sum of future cash flows discounted at the required rate of return (i) and the initial investment made at time zero.

Net realizable value of receivables: the net amount of cash expected to be received from all receivables; equal to total accounts receivable less the allowance for uncollectible accounts; also called the book value of accounts receivable.

Net sales: gross sales less sales discounts and sales returns and allowances.

Noncumulative preferred stock: preferred stock that does not accumulate dividends if a year goes by and a dividend is not issued.

Nonethical principles: ethically neutral goals such as safety, security and fame that are neither ethical nor unethical.

Note payable: can be either a short-term (current) liability or a long-term liability. Notes payable differ from accounts payable in that there is a written promise to pay and normally they are interest bearing.

Notes to the financial statements: see Footnotes to the financial statements.

Objectivity principle: states that measurements should be made as objectively as possible.

Operating activities (cash flows): cash flows that result from the income producing activities of a business and that are not investing or financing cash flows.

Operating cycle: the time in days it takes to acquire inventory, sell inventory, and collect the receivables generated by the sales.

Operating lease: a simple rental agreement.

Operating leverage: the relative sensitivity of a company's net income to changes in sales volume. The net income for a company with high operating leverage will both increase and decrease much faster than net income of a company with low operating leverage for the same percentage change in sales volume.

Operating performance ratio (OPR): see return on sales.

Operating plan: a detailed plan which specifies how a business will deploy its economic and human resources to attain financial goals.

Opportunity cost: the benefit that could have been obtained by following an alternative course of action. For example, if you go into business for yourself instead of taking a job at a salary of $30,000 per year, the $30,000 salary is an opportunity cost of having your own company. While accountants do not recognize opportunity costs in their measurement of profits, economists do.

Ordinary annuity: a time series of payments assumed to occur at the end of each period.

Organization costs: the costs incurred at the time a business is being established.

Organizational chart: a graphical depiction of the various administrative areas that exist in a company.

Outcomes: the particular event, consequence, or result that occurs in the future when the decision maker pursues a particular course of action (feasible alternative).

Outstanding shares: the number of shares of a corporation that are owned by shareholders; may be less than issued shares due to treasury stock.

Owner's or owners' equity: the difference between an entity's assets and liabilities. Equity represents that dollar amount of assets that has been supplied by the owner or owners of the business.

Owner's withdrawals: the distribution of cash or other assets from the business entity to the owner.

Paid-in-capital: refers to the amount of equity that is invested by the owners. For most companies, owners' equity minus paid-in-capital equals retained earnings.

Par value: Par value is an arbitrary valuation assigned to the stock at the time the stock is initially authorized (created).

Partnership: an association of two or more individuals or organizations to carry on economic activity.

Payroll taxes: taxes levied on an employer based on the amount of the employer's payroll. These include FICA and FUTA.

Percentage of sales method: a way to estimate bad debt expense that is based upon a fixed per cent of sales revenue.

Performance budget: a planning or static budget that has been revised by using actual instead of planned sales volumes. It is used as the standard against which actual performance is compared.

Performance variance: a difference between a performance budget amount and the corresponding amount shown for actual results at the end of the budget period.

Permanent accounts: refers to balance sheet accounts in contrast to income statement accounts which are closed at each fiscal year end.

Periodic inventory method: a system of accounting for inventory in which cost of goods sold is determined and inventory is adjusted at the end of the accounting period, not when merchandise is sold.

Perpetual inventory method: a system of accounting for inventory by which detailed records of the number of units and cost of each purchase and sales transaction are prepared throughout the accounting period as sales and purchases occur.

Personal investment: the transfer of savings into passive stock or bond investments to differentiate the type of investment into business assets which must be actively managed.

Physical count of inventory: the counting of each inventory item owned by the company.

Physical inventory: the inventory of goods held for resale.

Physical movement of merchandise versus "cost flow": physical movement of merchandise is the actual physical flow of the merchandise. For example the first goods purchased really are the first goods sold. The cost flow assumption is the assumed flow of goods for costing purposes. In accounting, the assumed flow of goods for costing purposes does not have to agree with the actual physical movement of the goods purchased and sold unless the company is using the specific identification method.

Planning budget: a budget prepared before the year (or other period) begins, used for planning, motivational, coordinating and communication purposes, but not for performance evaluation.

Planning variance: a difference between a planning (static) budget amount and the corresponding amount in the performance budget.

Posting: the procedure of placing the data contained in journal entries into the general ledger accounts by carefully observing the debit/credit direction of the entry.

Preemptive right: the right of existing shareholders to purchase more shares in the corporation so as to maintain their relative percentage ownership.

Preferred stock: stock that gives owners certain advantages over common stockholders, such as priority to receive dividends and priority to receive assets if a corporation liquidates. Preferred stockholders do not normally have voting privileges.

Prepaid expenses: miscellaneous assets that expire or get used up in the near future, e.g. prepaid rent, prepaid insurance, and supplies.

Present value of $1: the value today of $1 to be received or paid at some future date given a specified interest rate.

Present value factor: a decimal ratio less than one which when multiplied by the future value yields the present value at the assumed interest (discount) rate.

Price-earnings (PE) ratio: a ratio used by investors and analysts to compare stocks. The PE ratio is calculated by dividing the current market price by the annual earnings per share.

Principal: the amount borrowed (not including the interest amount).

Pro forma (projected) financial statements: financial statements that are projected for the future.

Profit: the excess of revenues over expenses. More correctly termed net income.

Profitability: an increase in owner's equity created by successfully operating the business. If owner's equity decreases as a result of operations, the business has suffered a loss.

Profitability ratios: ratios which measure net income in relation to assets, revenues and shareholders' equity.

Promissory note payable: a legal instrument which documents the debt of the borrower to the lender.

Proprietorship: a business owned by one person.

Publicly traded companies: corporations that issue stock for sale to the general public. These corporations have more extensive financial reporting requirements than other firms.

Purchase order: a written offer to buy goods or services from a vendor at a specified price for delivery by a specified date.

Purchase requisition: an internal document that expresses the need of a part of an organization to acquire certain materials or services to meet its goals.

Qualified opinion: a report by a CPA that the company's financial statements present fairly the financial position, income and cash flows in accordance with GAAP except for a certain aspect of the statements with which the CPA does not agree with the accounting treatment selected by the company. Generally the item in question is not so material as to render the financial statements misleading when taken as a whole.

Qualitative factors: items that cannot be easily expressed in numbers, but that are important is making a decision. Ethical issues are an example.

Quality of earnings: net income that is based on the use of more conservative accounting principles and more closely aligns with cash flow from operations is considered to be of higher quality.

Quantitative information: facts that can be expressed numerically. Financial information is an example.

Ratio analysis: a tool that measures proportional relationships between two financial statement amounts. Ratio analysis is used so that it is easier to compare performance of different companies or for one company over time.

Real-time: an attribute of modern computer systems that provide updated information instantaneous with the transactions which cause changes in the status of variables being measured.

Receiving report: an internal document which is created when goods are received from a vendor and is designed to verify purchase quantities and other specifications shown on the purchase order.

Recovery of bad debts: a rare occurrence in which an account receivable previously deemed uncollectible and accordingly written off is paid in full.

Recurring cost: a type of cost which is highly probable to occur period after period.

Relevance: information is relevant if it has the capacity to make a difference in decisions.

Relevant information: information which can influence a decision.

Relevant range: the range of volume over which fixed costs remain fixed. The relevant range may differ for each type of fixed cost.

Reliability: to be reliable, information about an item must be verifiable. A synonym of verifiability is objectivity. If data are verifiable they will demonstrate a high degree of consensus among different independent measures.

Reliable information: a measurement that accurately portrays the phenomenon it is meant to represent and is free from error and bias.

Remittance advice: an attachment to a check which gives details of the invoice numbers or other pertinent data to explain the intent of the payment.

Retail business: a business which sells to final consumers of goods.

Retained earnings: the cumulative amount of past earnings (net income) that has been retained in the business and not distributed to the owner or owners. Although this term is normally seen only in the balance sheet of corporations, the concept can apply just as readily to sole proprietorships or partnerships.

Retained earnings statement: a report that details all the changes that have affected the retained earnings account during the period.

Return on sales: net income divided by sales revenue.

Return on equity (ROE): a measure of operating performance; computed in its simplest form by dividing net income by average total equity.

Return on sales: This ratio computation is net income divided by sales. The ratio, also known as the return on sales or the net profit margin, is an overall measure of a company's relative profitability.

Revenue: an increase in the (net) resources of an entity from the sale of goods or services. Revenues represent gross increases in owner's equity.

Revenue recognition principle: revenue should be recorded when (1) the earning process has substantially been completed and (2) an exchange has taken place.

Risk: the probability (less than one and more than zero) that the economic objective of an investment will not be realized.

Risk ratios: a category of ratios which measure the relative ability of a business to avoid liquidity problems and possible insolvency.

Sales (cash)discount: a reduction in the selling price that is allowed if payment is received within a specified period.

Sales invoice: the document which bills customers for goods or services.

Sales mix: the combination of products that make up a company's total sales.

Sales order: an internal document which authorizes employees to ship goods to a customer.

Sales revenue: the total cash or other value received in return for goods or services delivered to customers.

Sales terms: the seller's policy on when payment is expected, who is responsible for shipping charges and insurance, and what discount is offered if an invoice is paid within a specified time period.

Salvage value: See scrap value.

Schedule C (Form 1040): an IRS form upon which business taxable income for a sole proprietorship is computed.

Scrap or salvage value: the amount received (or estimated to receive at a future date) when disposing of a long-lived asset at the end of its useful life.

Securities Act of 1933: a law that requires companies issuing new securities to the public to first file a registration statement (Form S-1) with the Securities and Exchange Commission.

Securities Exchange Act of 1934: the purpose of this law is to ensure that the public has access to current material information concerning publicly traded companies. The act also established the Securities Exchange Commission and its regulation of margin requirements.

Securities and Exchange Commission (SEC): the U.S. government regulatory agency that is charged with enforcing the Securities Acts of 1933 and 1934.

Selling price: the amount charged customers for goods or services.

Sensitivity analysis: a "what if" analysis that computes how much the end result will change if an underlying assumption changes. Managers use sensitivity analysis to assess decision risk.

Shareholders: see Stockholders.

Shareholders of record: the list of current shareholders of a corporation which is maintained by a transfer agent, often a bank clearing house which provides shareholders services to public corporations.

Shipping document: a packing slip and bill of lading that accompanies the shipment.

Sixteenth amendment: an amendment to the constitution creating the power of the federal government to levy a tax on income of individuals and corporations.

Short-term investment: an investment which is expected to be liquidated back to cash within a twelve month period.

Sole proprietorship: a business entity owned by only one individual.

Solvency: a company's long-run ability to meet all of its financial obligations.

Specific identification: a method of valuing inventory and determining cost of goods sold whereby the actual costs of specific inventory items are assigned to them.

Stable dollar concept: states that amounts in the financial statements are meaningful only when the dollar is a stable unit of measure. In other words, if inflation is significant, the historical cost principle will create distorted statements.

Stakeholders: all parties who may be affected by the alternative courses of action under consideration by the person faced with an ethical dilemma.

Standard industrial code (SIC) number: a unique number assigned to each industry. The SIC number is used when researching reference materials to find industry comparison data for a company.

Start-up costs: costs that will only occur once, at the time a company begins operation. These costs include personnel training, licenses/permits, and promotions for grand opening.

Statement of cash flows - direct method: a report presenting the activities which generate and use cash during the period. It is composed of three sections: cash flow from operations, cash flow from investing activities, and cash flow from financing activities.

Statement cash flows - indirect method: a report with the same purpose and same cash flow from operations as the direct method, but presented in a different manner. It is often called the reconciliation method because it starts with net income and shows the reconciliation from net income to operating cash flows.

Statement of income and retained earnings: an income statement which is appended with the beginning retained earnings amount, dividends declared during the income period, and the resulting retained earnings balance at the end of the income period being reported.

Statement of owner's equity: a statement showing the additional investments, withdrawals, income, and the total owner's equity at a specific date.

Statement of retained earnings: a statement showing the beginning retained earnings, net income, dividends, and ending retained earnings.

Static (planning) budget: see Planning budget.

Stock dividends: the pro rata distribution of additional shares of the corporation to shareholders of record on a specified date.

Stock market crash of 1929: a sudden, dramatic drop in the prices of stocks traded on the exchanges.

Stockholders: persons who owns stock in a corporation.

Stockholders' equity: the portion of a corporation's assets financed by the owners.

Straight-line depreciation: the depreciation method by which the depreciable cost of the asset is allocated equally over the periods of an asset's estimated useful life.

Subchapter S corporation: a special legal entity that has the limited legal liability of a corporation, but which is taxed as a partnership. It is a mechanism to avoid the double taxation faced by shareholders of a normal "C" corporation.

Supplies: incidental materials needed to carry out the operating plan. See Operating plan.

Supplies expense: represents the amount of supplies used during the period reported.

T accounts: refers to the debit/credit architecture of ledger accounts to record increases or decreases in accounts.

Tangible property: physical assets owned by a company. These include inventory, property, plant, and equipment.

Target income or profit: a profit level desired by management.

Target sales: the sales level needed to earn the target profit.

Taxable entities: individuals and corporations are tax-paying entities because they are required to prepare a tax return. Sole proprietorships and partnerships are not taxable entities.

Temporary accounts: income statement accounts that are closed at the end of each fiscal year. Also includes the owner's withdrawal account or, in the case of a corporation, the dividends account.

Time period assumption: states that financial statements are broken up into various time periods.

Time value of money: the concept that money has value over time because it earns interest; receiving money today is preferable to receiving the same amount of money at some later date.

Times interest earned: income before tax divided by the annual interest obligation.

Top-down approach: a procedure that starts with a total sales objective and then estimates what income will result from that level of sales.

Trade receivables: money due from customers for rendering services or selling merchandise on credit.

Traditional income statement: a categorized income statement which subtracts cost of goods sold from revenue resulting in gross profit, from which is subtracted operating expenses to determine net income before taxes.

Transactions: transactions are events that affect or change the amount or makeup of assets, liabilities, and/or equity of an entity. Most transactions affect more than one entity. Examples include the purchases and sales of assets or borrowing or lending activities between two organizations. However, not all transactions involve more than one organization. Changes in the value of assets related to fires, natural disasters and normal deterioration are also defined as transactions and reflected in the entity's financial position.

Treasury stock: common stock that has been repurchased by the company, but that has not been retired. Treasury stock receives no dividends and has no voting rights.

Uncollectible accounts: accounts receivable assets which will not be realized in cash.

Uncollectible accounts expense: the expense matched against revenue for the loss from accounts receivable expected to be uncollectible.

Unearned revenue: a liability arising from the receipt of cash in advance of the delivery of goods or services to customers

Unlimited liability: the lack of a ceiling on the amount of a liability a proprietor or a partner must assume, meaning that if business assets are not sufficient to settle creditor claims, the personal assets of the proprietor or the partner may be used to settle the claims.

Unqualified opinion: an opinion on financial statements by a CPA which states that they present fairly the financial position, income, and cash flow in accordance with GAAP.

Useful life: the term used to describe the life over which an asset is expected to be useful to a company; cost is assigned to the periods benefited from using the asset.

Users of accounting information: those decision-makers, both external and internal to an economic entity, who draw upon accounting information provided by the entity to make economic decisions.

Variable expense ratio: variable expenses as a per cent of sales.

Variable expenses: expenses that change in total in direct proportion to changes in the activity level.

Variance: any deviation from standard. It is most often the difference between the performance budget and actual amounts for a cost or revenue.

Vendor: a company from which goods or services are purchased.

Vendor's invoice: See invoice.

Vertical analysis: restatement of one company's financial statements to a percentage of sales basis for the income statement and percentage of assets basis for the balance sheet in order to better assess performance.

Weighted average: a periodic inventory cost flow alternative whereby the cost of goods sold and the cost of the ending inventory are determined by using a weighted average cost of all merchandise available for sale during the period.

"What if" analysis: a tool that asks what a result will be if a predicted amount is not realized or if an underlying assumption changes.

Withdrawals: distributions of assets to owners; in a corporate setting, most withdrawals are called dividends.

Working capital: Current assets less current liabilities.

Write-offs: the recording of actual losses from uncollectible accounts as a reduction in accounts receivable and a reduction in the allowance for uncollectible accounts.

INDEX

A

accelerated depreciation, *def.,* 443
account(s),
    allowance for doubtful, *def.,* 373;
    allowance for uncollectible, *def.,* 373;
    balance sheet, 69;
    chart of, *def.,* 71;
    contra, *def.,* 373;
    permanent, *def.,* D15;
    temporary, *def.,* D15;
    uncollectible, *def.,* 372
account balance, *def.,* 71
accountant, *def.,* 27
accounting, *def.,* 5;
    accrual basis of, 25, 176; *def.,* 112;
    and the environment, 22;
    careers in, 27;
    cash basis of, *def.,* 176;
    corporate, 30;
    employment outlook, 28;
    environmental, *def.,* 32;
    forensic, *def.,* 32;
    governmental, 31;
    tax, 30;
    types of, positions, 28
accounting documentation, and internal control, 355
accounting information, *def.,* 6;
    and society, 21;
    attributes of, 22;
    how, is used in business decisions, 5;
    in an economy, 21;
    introduction to uses of, 5;
    recording, 69;
    using, for economic decisions, 3;
    using, in business expansion, 223;
    using, to evaluate businesses, 351;
    using, to understand personal investments, 55
accounting period, *def.,* 114
accounting process using debits/credits, D1
accounting records, *def.,* 71;
    recording depreciation in the, 446;
    safeguarding of assets and, 361, 363
accounting regulations, evolution of, 23
accounting transaction worksheet, *def.,* 71;
    illus., 72, 73, 75, 79, 113, 114, 124, 128, 163, B2, D3;
    sorting activities in the cash column of the, 124
accounts payable, *def.,* 14, 70
accounts receivable collection period, *def.,* 380

accounts receivable turnover ratio, 511
accounts receivable turnover, *def.,* 380
accounts receivable, 420; *def.,* 69;
    aging of, report, *def.,* 377;
    decisions involving, 371;
    estimating the expense of uncollectible, 372;
    evaluation of, 380
accrual basis of accounting, 25, 176; *def.,* 112
accumulated depreciation, *def.,* 444, 447
additional paid-in capital, *def.,* 325
adverse opinion, *def.,* 190
agent, *def.,* 9
aging of accounts receivable report, *def.,* 377
allowance for doubtful accounts, *def.,* 373
allowance for uncollectible accounts, *def.,* 373
allowance method, *def.,* 373
amortization, *def.,* 144, 426
annual report, 382, *def.,* 188
annuity, ordinary, *def.,* 480;
    present value of an, 480
annuity due, def. ,480
arm's-length exchange, *def.,* 175
asset(s), 97, 173, 200; *def.,* 13, 69;
    current, *def.,* 69,77;
    fixed, 424; *def.,* 69, 77;
    identifying, and liabilities, 173;
    importance of inventory, 396;
    intangible, *def.,* 425;
    long-term, *def.,* 69;
    managing inventory, 395;
    net, 420;
    safeguarding of, and accounting records, 361, 363;
    valuation of business, 420;
    what is the cost of the, when acquired, 440;
    what is the estimated useful life, 441;
    which do not appear on balance sheets, 175
audit committee, *def.,* 362
auditor's opinion, *def.,* 189
auditor's report, *def.,* 189
authorized shares, *def.,* 326

B

bad debt(s), recovery of, *def.,* 373
bad debt expense, *def.,* 371
balance sheet, *def.,* 13, 76; *illus.,* 14, 77, 85, 98, 154;
    assets which do not appear on, 175;
    cell formulas for excel, *illus.,* B5;
    consolidated, 199; *illus.,* 201;
    excel, *illus.,* B4;